The SCARBERRYS (SCARBOROUGHS), DOUGHTYS, LEWISES and PAYNES of LAWRENCE COUNTY, OHIO

and

Their Virginia and West Virginia Connections

Mabel June Malan

HERITAGE BOOKS
2011

HERITAGE BOOKS
AN IMPRINT OF HERITAGE BOOKS, INC.

Books, CDs, and more—Worldwide

For our listing of thousands of titles see our website
at
www.HeritageBooks.com

Published 2011 by
HERITAGE BOOKS, INC.
Publishing Division
100 Railroad Ave. #104
Westminster, Maryland 21157

Copyright © 2011 Mabel June Malan

All rights reserved. No part of this book may be reproduced or transmitted in any form or by any means, electronic or mechanical, including photocopying, recording or by any information storage and retrieval system without written permission from the author, except for the inclusion of brief quotations in a review.

International Standard Book Numbers
Paperbound: 978-0-7884-5372-4
Clothbound: 978-0-7884-8967-9

The SCARBERRYS (SCARBOROUGHS), DOUGHTYS LEWISES and PAYNES

of
LAWRENCE COUNTY, OHIO

*Drawing on title page by Iris (Scarberry) Burd
(1934-2011)*

The SCARBERRYS (SCARBOROUGHS), DOUGHTYS LEWISES and PAYNES
of
Lawrence County, Ohio
and
Their Virginia and West Virginia Connections

By Mabel June Malan

In memory of Dad, who wanted to make the world a better place

and

Mom, who told us to do our best

Table of Contents

Preface   ix

Acknowledgements   xi

Section I.   The Scarberrys (Scarboroughs)   1
The Generations

Section II.   The Doughtys   91
The Generations

Section III.   The Lewises   103

Speculation on the father of James Lewis (d. 1720) of Middlesex County, Virginia, 103.
     Richard Lewis of Sunderland Creek, 103. James Lewis, likely son of Richard, 103. POSSIBLE RELATIVES OF JAMES LEWIS, WHO MAY HAVE BEEN A SON OF RICHARD LEWIS, 104. The Therriot-Wroughton (Wharton)-Heale connection, 104. The Kemp-Lawson-Kilby connection, 105.

The Lewises, the Generations, 106.
     James Lewis's court appearances, his precinct and community duties, 108. The will of James Lewis, 109. Chelton-Tignor-Bonner-Barbee-Beaumont connections, 110. James Lewis of Essex and Caroline Counties and the Long family, 114. William Lewis of Spotsylvania County and the Ellis family, 114. James Lewis of the 1780s, 115.
     John Bradley, Gabriel Tombs, Zebulon Lewis, Catherine Brockman, and the Rhodes family, 116. Captain Joshua Lewis and the Indian Wars, 117. Joshua Lewis's land sale and will, 118. The Kilby-Barnes-Morton connection, 120. Christopher and Katherine Kilby's move from Middlesex, 120.
     Leonard Ziglar and the Germans of Culpeper County, 121. Zebulon Lewis and the Pannell-Strother involvement, 122. John Asher and Joseph Jones, Esqr., 125. The O'Neal-Lewis lease and the Gores, 127. Alexander Fraizier's will, Isaac George, Robert Dawson, and Francis Hughes, 129. The Orange-Culpeper-Spotsylvania Lewis and Strother network and the Larues, 131. The Gartons, Durgans, Strothers, and Gores, 137. The Gartons, Hintons, and Maddys, 138. The administration of Samuel Lewis's estate, 138. The Estills, Bootons, Hills, and Kilbys, 139. August 1811, the estate sale of Samuel Lewis, 139. The Roaches, Goodalls, Maddys, and Stodgills of Orange County, 142.

Contents, continued

The Millers, Estills, Georges, Collins, Brockmans, O'Neals, and Larues, 143. The Muddy Creek Lewises, 143. The Singing Cave, 145. Indian Creek Primitive Baptist Church, 145. Samuel Lewis's heirs, 1814, 146. Monroe County and the Sweet Springs, 146.

Joshua Lewis and the Ballards and Halsteads,154. Joshua Lewis, soldier of 1812, 155. Joshua Lewis of the New Valley Church, 156. Catherine (Hill) Lewis in Ohio and her pension papers, 158. James J. Lewis of 1838, 165. The Bush-Roach-Madison connections in Orange and Albemarle Counties, 166.

Section IV.   The Paynes   237

Speculation on the ancestry of John Payne (b. ca 1760) of Bedford County, Virginia, 237.

Josiah Payne of Bedford County, 237. James Payne of Beaverdam Creek, 238. John and Sarah Payne who settled in Ohio, with attention to their close friends, the McCormacks, Wheelers, and Wrights, 239. John Payne, son of Joseph Payne, and the Barnett Paynes, 240. William Payne of Hanover County, Virginia, and the Shrewsburys, 241. Payne-McCormack-Wheeler associations, 244.

The Paynes, the Generations, 245.

The Rocky Creek group of Louisa County, Virginia, 250. The McCormack-Anderson-Payne-Pate-Ragland circle, 250. Ragland Castle and the Ragland immigrants, 251.

Index   283

Family Photography
    Scarberrys and Doughtys   74, 75
    Lewises and Paynes   205, 206

Maps of Pleasant Ridge, drawn by Iris (Scarberry) Burd   76, 77
Will of John Doughty   97-98
Estate Sale of Samuel Lewis   203-204

Preface

When we were growing up, my sister Rachel and I viewed Lawrence County, Ohio, as a kind of retreat, almost heaven. The Scottown-Rome area seemed a world away from Sciotoville, where we lived. Our relatives in Lawrence County drew drinking water from stone wells and after the sun went down, kerosene lamps lent soft lighting to the living rooms. Horses were used to plow fields. Biscuits were baked in stoves heated by wood. Our grandparents did not have electricity in their homes until after World War II. The dramatic change in lifestyle was fun for us, but it was the friendliness and warmth of our relatives that transformed a fairly poor farming region into a special place. In *History of Lawrence County, Ohio, 1990*, several of the writers tell of similar reactions. It is memories such as these, I'm certain, that inspire the writing of many family histories.

When Lawrence County was first settled, wolves were a major threat, and hogs and sheep had to be penned at night. Dogs could not walk in the woods alone. The howling of the wolves echoed from hill to hill, a few sounding like a thousand.

The Scarberrys who set foot on Lawrence County soil before 1820 had come a long way from their origins. Their story began in London, England. They were some of the earliest Quakers and were buried among the religious outcasts at Bunhill Fields. Members of my branch sailed to Philadelphia, made friends with the Indians, and later left their farms in Solebury Township for the spectacular Shenandoah Valley. When Indian attacks in Virginia were still a worry, they traveled south to the Virginia Piedmont and lived along the Little Otter River. The promise of a new life near Indian Creek, among the mountains of southern (West) Virginia beckoned. Then it was north to new land in the narrow valleys of the Coal River. They crossed the Ohio River and discovered the gentle hilly land drained by Indian Guyan and Paddy Creek, and they stayed.

During the War of 1812 John Doughty helped in the building of ships on Lake Erie for Commodore Oliver Perry. Afterwards he and his family found their way to the Symmes Valley of Lawrence and Gallia Counties, and they met the Scarberrys, apparently a family of like thinking, for there were several marriages between the two families.

My Lewis ancestors were lured away from the steamy Tidewater of Virginia, where the white caps of the Rappahannock River teased the shores, where "Hewitt," the stately home of Christopher Robinson, still sits with its little orchard and where the "mother church" of Christ Church Parish of Middlesex County continues to serve its community as it did in the beginning, amid the graves of the original settlers. These Lewises found their way to both sides of the Rapidan River in the Virginia Piedmont and made fast friends with the German colony that had cleared the way for other settlers. For some reason the Lewises moved on, choosing Indian Creek in Monroe County, (West) Virginia, as their new land. They lived there for close to 50 years before joining friends in Lawrence County, at the southern-most part of Ohio. Indian Guyan Creek was within easy walking distance of their homes, and the covered bridge that they crossed so many times is now a historic landmark.

The Paynes did not stop by West Virginia on their trek from the Virginia Piedmont to Lawrence County. Rather, they joined friends in Tennessee for a few years before migrating to Ohio. The Paynes may have been Quakers. Lawrence County was considered a refuge for slaves and people who did not believe in slavery. Proctorville, on the banks of the Ohio, was once called *Quaker Bottom*. The Paynes, however, settled a distance from the Ohio River, in Mason Township, and created their own community.

This is a story of men who volunteered to fight the Indians, of a man who succumbed to an epidemic while a soldier in the War of 1812; men who returned from the Civil War maimed for life; soldiers who endured grueling conditions in the trenches of World War I; a man who participated in the Normandy invasion of June 1944; two men who fought in the Pacific Theater during World War II, one in the Marshall Islands, and the other, a medic, serving in Australia.

And it's a story of people who did nothing that would catch the attention of historians but who labored on in the fields, sweated over hot stoves, and retained their dignity and their optimism. They were weathered by the sun and the wind and the cold, and they met at Pleasant Ridge and Wilgus and other churches on Sunday mornings and offered heart-felt praises to God.

My cousin Frank Lewis tells me that on the hill behind his house there are three old graves and that in the spring daffodils, planted there long ago, still bloom.

***

Note: The marriage dates taken from courthouse records usually reflect the license dates. There is no way of being certain that the lists of children born to a couple are complete. Children who died before their father wrote his will may not be known, nor children who moved far away. In early Virginia, the oldest son would automatically inherit his father's land, so he might not have been named in his father's will. Census records are a source of many of the children's names, and children who were born and died between census enumerations may have been left out. Census records after 1930 were not available to me. My intent was to locate the places my ancestors lived and to include the names of their principal associates. No family history is ever truly finished.

Acknowledgements

My intent with this history has been to locate my ancestors in time and place and to get a sense of what life was like for them. In the beginning it was my father, Clarence Young, who was the most helpful. He had grown up in the home of his grandparents, and they traded stories about their relatives and ancestors. And he remembered. His memory was always phenomenal. By the time I started this history, his eyesight was severely limited by macular degeneration, and his weak hearing made communication with him difficult. But he sat down with my sister Rachel Reinhard one day and helped her compose a chart of our ancestors, both the Scarberry and the Lewis branches. He dictated more of the history to my sister Rena Brown, who could take shorthand.

After discovering that the surnames *Scarberry* and *Scarborough* were one and the same, tracing the Scarberrys was relatively easy, especially with the help of Dwayne Scarberry, who is a diligent researcher. I am grateful to him for passing along to me the early history of the Scarboroughs. Jim Wood was generous with his research on the Harpers of Raleigh County, and his perspective and insights were most helpful. I cannot thank Jackie Lynch enough for so readily sharing with me Catherine (Hill) Lewis's War of 1812 pension papers. Without them I would not have discovered our ancestors in Monroe County, West Virginia. My gratitude goes belatedly to Lennie (Lewis) Bundy, who was a member of the Lawrence County History Book Committee. Sadly she is now deceased. Her article that appeared in *History of Lawrence County, Ohio, 1990* and that of many other contributors have indeed been helpful. Larry Shuck, who compiled several books on Monroe and Greenbrier Counties in West Virginia, kindly donated to me two of his works on Fayette County, West Virginia.

Many others have shared information for this book: Robert L. Lewis and his sister Patty (Lewis) Joyce have supplied material on the Scarboroughs, Lewises, and Burds. Ronnie Lee Scarbro furnished the history of some of John Ward Scarborough's descendants. Arnold Lewis charted recent Lewis families. Thanks goes to Iris (Scarberry) Burd for passing along some of the Scarberry lineages, to Janet Sailor for sending me her father's military record, to Betty (Lewis) Midkiff for information on her family. Frank Lewis enjoyed relating anecdotal information on our ancestors. And gratitude goes to my sister Edith Tews, who encouraged me. Life would not have been the same if my sister Rachel Reinhard had not been alert to everyone around her and found them colorful. This work could not have been produced without the aid of my husband, Greg, who steered me through computer software complications and went with me to visit sites where my ancestors once had lived in Virginia and in Monroe County, West Virginia.

Many thanks to the polite clerks at Campbell County Library and their patience with my frequent presence in the research room; to the staff of the Virginia Room at Roanoke Public Library for their kind assistance; to the staff of Jones Library in Lynchburg; to the friendly people at the Latter Day Saints Family History centers; to the Library of Virginia at Richmond; to the National Genealogical Society Library at Arlington, Virginia; to Briggs Lawrence County Public Library; to the Bossard Memorial Library at Gallipolis, Ohio; to the Ohio Historical Society in Columbus; and to the helpful clerks of courthouses in Virginia, West Virginia, and Ohio. The Bedford County Museum was a good source for information on the Paynes.

Iris (Scarberry) Burd produced the drawing for the title page and the maps of Pleasant Ridge for my father's 90th birthday party. Iris died, I am sorry to say, in July 2011. Her children, Della Lewis and Ricky Burd, have generously donated these works.

The SCARBERRYS (SCARBOROUGHS)

First Generation

1. **Isaac[1] SCARBOROUGH** was born about 1560.

Isaac was the progenitor of a long line of hardy people. Many of my ancestral Scarboroughs and their relatives lived into their eighties and nineties, including U.S. President Herbert Hoover, who descended from Sarah, daughter of John Scarborough (died 1727). My line survived the Great Plague of London. Isaac's son William was a Quaker, and Quakers were persecuted for their beliefs, some of them ending up in Newgate Prison, where overcrowding was conducive to spread of diseases. In 1665, when the Great Plague struck, London had half a million people, and about 4,000 of them were Quakers. It is estimated that about 100,000 residents of London died from the plague. Quaker records reveal that they lost 1,177.[1] It took strength of character to belong to the Society of Friends (the Quakers) when the Church of England was still the official religion. Much later, after being a Quaker became acceptable, several of Isaac's descendants on the Virginia frontier embraced the Methodist church, just taking hold in western Virginia. Doubtless it was in the blood of these Scarboroughs to be independent of the mainstream.

Isaac is said to have lived in London, England.[2] This Scarborough family's origins, to my knowledge, have not been traced beyond their appearance there. Naturally it would seem that they once had lived in Scarborough, England. I was told by a librarian in Scarborough that there is no evidence that any Scarboroughs lived there in the early days. But I discovered a Robert Scarborough who seems to have been a resident. He was a notorious pirate who, in 1577, took over the ship, "Le Bon Vouloir" of Quilbeuf, between Dover and Calais and sailed it to Scarborough. It contained 29 tons of wine and was owned by a Paris merchant. Apparently Scarborough was a pirate's haven, for 22 of its inhabitants were charged with piracy in 1578.[3]

Mention of this Isaac Scarborough is found in letters between John Scarborough (born about 1625) and John Scarborough (born 1646-49). These letters can be found at the Bucks County, Pennsylvania, Historical Society in the Archives of the Pennsylvania Genealogical Society in Philadelphia.[4]

The song "Scarborough Fair" is often the first thing that comes to mind when Scarborough is mentioned. In fact, Scarborough, England, was once an important trading center, attracting people from all over England, Denmark, Norway, the Baltic states, and points more distant. King Henry III of England (reigned 1216-1272) issued a charter stating that Scarborough could have a yearly fair between the Feast of the Assumption of the Blessed Virgin Mary and the Feast of St. Michael (that is, August 15 to September 29). Although the major trade fairs ended long ago, Scarborough celebrates its past with fairs in September.[5]

Scarborough sits on a bluff overlooking the North Sea, and there is an esplanade that is lined with bed and breakfast establishments. At one time seaside communities were resorts for people with tuberculosis. The poet and novelist Anne Bronte spent her last days in Scarborough, because she thought the sea air would be good for her tuberculosis. She is buried in the graveyard at St. Mary's Church, and her grave draws visits from her fans. Her whole family, including novelists Emily and Charlotte Bronte, were in the habit of going to this seaside resort every summer. The ruins of Scarborough castle sit on the promontory above Anne's grave.

He had the following child:

+ 2 i. **William[2] SCARBOROUGH** was born 1598 and died 28 February 1680.

Second Generation

2. **William² SCARBOROUGH** (Isaac¹) was born 1598 in London, England. He died 28 February 1680 and was buried in Checker Alley, Bunhill Fields, London, England.

William Scarborough belonged to the Society of Friends (Quakers), and members of my line of Scarboroughs stayed with their Quaker heritage into the mid 1700s. London has a burial ground called Bunhill Fields, and it was reserved for dissenters from the Church of England. This historic cemetery is well kept. Iron fences line the main walkway that runs through the ancient gravestones and large trees. An area was set aside for members of the Society of Friends (Quakers). Individual stones of Quakers were the victims of bombing during World War II, so a single monument was erected in their honor, but it does not have names of the deceased on it. My sister Rachel Reinhard and I visited the Quaker center and a staff member gave me a copy of records of the Scarborough family that were included in the London & Middlesex Quarterly Meeting. WilliamScarborough, 82, of Hosier Lane, Pulchres Parish, London, was said to have died of age, and he was buried at Checker Alley, Bunhill Fields. William was a member of the Peel Monthly Meeting of Quakers at St. John's Street, London, England.[6]

Below are some Scarboroughs named in the London & Middlesex Quarterly Meeting records who did not live on Hosier Lane:

> Richard Scarborough, a servant to Joane Holder of Shoreditch Parish, died in 1665 of the plague and was buried at Bunhill Fields in London.
>
> In 1682 Jonathan, two years old, son of John and Martha Scarborough of Magdalen Parish, Bermondsey, died of smallpox and was buried in Checker Alley. His parents were part of the Southwark Monthly Meeting. In 1683, Sarah, 14 weeks old, daughter of John and Martha Scarborough of Magdalen Parish, died. In 1683 John and Martha Scarborough's daughter Mary, 17 years old, died of consumption. She was buried at Southwark. In 1713 John Scarborough's wife, Martha, died at 75 of old age. She was buried at Long Lane. In 1719 Martha, age 60, daughter of John Scarborough of Long Walk, Magdalen Parish, Bermondsey, died of age and was buried at Long Lane. In 1724 John Scarborough, age 90, of Mary Magdalen Parish, died of age.
>
> In 1682 William, six months old, son of Roger and Margaret Scarborough, died of convulsions. His family was part of the Ratcliff Monthly meeting, and he was buried at Ratcliff. Roger and Margaret's daughter Abigail, two years old, died in 1682 of smallpox.[7]

Some people of note who are buried at Bunhill Fields: George Fox (1624-1691), who founded the Society of Friends (Quakers); Daniel Defoe (1661-1731), who wrote *Robinson Crusoe*; Susanna Wesley (1669-1742), mother of John Wesley, the founder of Methodism; Isaac Watts (1674-1748), hymn writer; John Bunyan (1628-1688), author of *The Pilgrim's Progress*.

William married **Agnes KING** on 22 July 1624 in London, England.[8]

William and Agnes had the following child:

+   3   i.   **John³ SCARBOROUGH** was born about 1625.

Third Generation

3. **John³ SCARBOROUGH** (William², Isaac¹) was born about 1625. He died in England.

Carrie Scarborough Thomas wrote a manuscript (dated 1956 and unpublished) in which she refers to letters sent between the John Scarborough who was born about 1625 and the John Scarborough born 1646-49. The John Scarborough who died in 1706 was the grandson of William Scarborough. Using information from the letters and other researchers, the following lineage emerges: Isaac Scarborough, born about 1560, was the father of William, born 1598, and he was the father of John, born 1625. All these Scarboroughs lived in London. The John Scarborough who bought land in America from William Penn was born about 1649 and the son of John, born about 1625.[9]

John, son of William, was a member of the Peel Monthly Meeting of Friends (Quakers) on St. John's Street. He was a blacksmith and coachman. He was thought to have had only one child, John.[10]

John married **Mary (?)**

John's wife may have been named *Mary*, for the Society of Friends records (London & Middlesex Quarterly Meeting) show Richard SCARBOROUGH, two weeks old, son of John and Mary Scarborough of Sepulchres Parish in Hosier Lane, dying in 1680 of convulsions.

There is also the possibility that Baldwin SCARBOROUGH, who was two weeks old when he died in 1679, was a son of the John Scarborough who was born about 1625. Baldwin, son of John Scarborough of Pulchers Parish, died of "wind & gripes," and was buried in Checker Alley. Hosier Lane was in Pulchers (or Sepulchres) Parish.[11]

They had the following child:

+   4   i.   **John[4] SCARBOROUGH** was born 1646-1649 and died 11 April 1706.

Fourth Generation

4.   **John SCARBOROUGH** (John[3], William[2], Isaac[1]) was born 1646-1649 in London, England. He was 60 years old and of Sepulchres Parish when he died of dropsy in April 1706. He belonged to the Peel Monthly Meeting (of Quakers).[12]

John and Sarah lived on Hosier Lane in London. John was one of the earliest members of the Friends' Meeting House (Quaker) in London, but Sarah did not join. John was a smith (black, white, and coach smith).[13]

King Charles the Second granted land in 1681 in North America to William Penn of London. This grant became the Province of Pennsylvania.[14] In 1682 John Scarborough bought from William Penn 250 acres on Neshaminy Creek in Middleton Township, Bucks County, Pennsylvania. John and son John arrived in America in October 1682. Two years later John, Sr., returned to London to get his wife, Sarah, but she refused to leave, so he stayed. His will of 1696 was witnessed by William Penn.[15]

On 15 October 1696 John Scarborough, blacksmith, of St. Sepulchres Parish, London, gave power of attorney to his son John, who was living in Solebury Township, Bucks County, Pennsylvania. The document, recorded in Bucks County (DB 2:251), gave his son permission to sell his lands.[16]

John married **Sarah ASHLEY** on 23 February 1663 in London, England. Sarah was born about 1648 in London, England. John and Sarah's marriage is recorded in the "Register of Marriages," St. Bride's Church, Fleet Street, London.[17]

John and Sarah had the children named below. (Roger S. Boone, the compiler of *Some Quaker Families*, questioned whether Sarah, born 1674, was really a part of this family. Data on the other children comes from his book)[18]:

     5   i.   **Ann[5] SCARBOROUGH** was christened 1 December 1664 in St. Sepulchre's, London, England.

+   6   ii.   **John SCARBOROUGH** was born 1667 and died 27 April 1727.

     7   iii.   **William SCARBOROUGH** was born 1669 in London, England.

     8   iv.   **Elizabeth SCARBOROUGH** was born about 1671 in London, England, and christened 17 October 1675.

     9   v.   **Susanna SCARBOROUGH** was christened 9 March 1672 in London, England.

    10   vi.   **Sarah SCARBOROUGH** was born in 1674 and died of fits when she was 12 days old. She was a daughter of John and Sarah Scarborough of Hosier Lane. She was buried at Checker Alley and belonged to the Peel Monthly Meeting.[19]

Fifth Generation

6. **John⁵ SCARBOROUGH** (John⁴, John³, William², Isaac¹) was born 1667 in London, England. He died 27 April 1727 in Bucks County, Pennsylvania.[20]

John's father returned to England, but John, Jr., stayed in Pennsylvania. He was apprenticed to a family but was said to have run away to live with Indians, staying with them five years. He served as an interpreter to William Penn.[21]

The book *Place Names in Bucks County, Pennsylvania,* first published in 1942, includes information on the early Scarboroughs as told by an 80-year old woman, Mrs. A. E. P. Darrow. She was living in Altadena, California. Her father was the late Wilson Pearson. Mrs. Darrow supplied background information on areas in Bucks County known as Burn Bridle Hill and Forest, in Solebury Township. The Forest was owned originally by the Scarboroughs, John Scarborough, having been persuaded by the Indians to sell his Langhorne farm and move there. Before leaving for England, John's father had instructed him to treat the Indians well, and they liked him. An old Indian trail went through the Forest, and it was on a branch of it that George Haworth and Samuel Pickering were said to have strolled among the chestnut trees and wild honeysuckle with their future wives. Wilson Pearson cut down the timber along this trail about the time his daughter was born. Mrs. Darrow reported that John Scarborough was known as a level-headed man, as were many of the early Scarboroughs. And she added that they had "an almost uncanny ability to help people to help themselves, and it is from them Hoover got his ability at relief work."[22] Following World War I, President Hoover was chief administrator for Relief Aid in Europe, and he was descended from Sarah, daughter of John Scarborough (d. 1727) and wife, Mary.

In 1700 John sold land in Middletown Township, Bucks County, Pennsylvania, and moved to Solebury Township, also in Bucks County. He may have been the first white settler in the Buckingham-Solebury Valley. Isaac Pearson Scarborough, a third great-grandson, lived on part of this farm.[23] Today Solebury Township is said to be peopled largely by descendants of English Friends (Quakers).[24]

John Scarborough was granted a patent for 510 acres by William Penn's Commissioners of Property on 22 October 1705. John sold it four years later to Jacob Holcombe in exchange for an 830-acre tract.[25]

In 1711 John began selling off parts of his farm. He sold 200 acres that year to Henry Paxon. This tract was on the east side and adjoined the Great Spring and Dawson tracts. On 8 February 1714 John sold 200 acres adjoining Paxon's land to Samuel Pickering, his son-in-law. On 17 December 1724 John sold to his son John 155 acres. This farm descended to Wilson Pearson of Solebury.[26]

John's will was proved 2 October 1727. He gave wife, Mary, the home plantation of 200 acres, including the lake meadow. It would revert to son William on her death. John divided building lots in Philadelpha among his children. Son Wm. was devised 60 acres whereon he was living, with the little meadow. Son Robert was given a 150-acre farm on the northeast corner of the Scarborough land. Son John had been sold 155 acres in 1724. The testator gave his Bible to son William, along with a brass mortar; son Robert was given a silver dram cup and pewter salt seller; daughter Sarah Haworth, the brass warming pan; daughter Mary Pickering, the great iron pottage pott; daughter Elizth. Fisher, the silver spoon and a pinquishin (pin cushion?) with a drawer for it and a pewter still; daughter Hannah was given a brass candle stick and a pair of iron snuffers and a joint stool. Execs: wife, Mary, sons William and John. Wits: Thomas Canby, Henry Paxson, Joseph Fell.[27]

John and Mary Scarburgh were charter members of the Buckingham Monthly Meeting of Bucks County, and by 10 February 1724 John was a minister. In his youth, it was said, he was thought of as "'somewhat airy...a man of remarkable self-denial and endowed with much mildness...with loving and kind deportment.'"[28]

John married **Mary PIERSON** (?) about 1690 in Bucks County, Pennsylvania. Mary was born about 1676 in Bucks County. She died 23 January 1751.[29]

Mary married (2) **Philip TORREY**.[30]

John and Mary had the following children:

+ 11   i.   **William⁶ SCARBOROUGH** was born 30 October 1691.

+ 12   ii.   **Sarah SCARBOROUGH** was born 2 March 1694.

   13   iii.   **Mary SCARBOROUGH** was born 8 August 1695 in Bucks County, Pennsylvania. She died in 1762 in Frederick County, Virginia.

Mary married (1) **Samuel PICKERING** in 1712 in Bucks County, Pennsylvania. Samuel was baptized 3 August 1684 in Salem, Massachusetts. He died 10 January 1727.[31]

Mary married (2) **Joseph LUPTON, Jr.** Joseph was a son of Joseph and Ann (HALL) LUPTON of Yorkshire, England.[32]

   14   iv.   **Susannah SCARBOROUGH** was born 31 August 1697 in Bucks County, Pennsylvania, and died about 1727. Susannah married **Richard BROCK** in 1718 Falls Monthly Meeting.[33]

   15   v.   **Elizabeth SCARBOROUGH** was born about 1699 and died in Bucks County, Pennsylvania, on 20 January 1792. Elizabeth married **John FISHER** in 1719. The marriage took place at the (Quaker) Meeting House in Buckingham Township.[34] John Fisher had been married previously. He was a son of John FISHER, Sr., and wife, Sarah HUTCHINSON.[35]

   16   vi.   **John SCARBOROUGH** was born about 1703 in Bucks County, Pennsylvania.

John's father sold him 155 acres on 17 December 1724.[36]

John married **Jane MARGERUM**. On 2 April 1731 it was reported to the Quakers that John and Jane had married. On 3 September 1731 Jane was granted a certificate to the Buckingham Monthly Meeting.[37]

   17   vii.   **Hannah SCARBOROUGH** was born 31 August 1704 in Bucks County, Pennsylvania.

Hannah married **Benjamin FELL** on 27 July 1728 in Bucks County, Pennsylvania.[38]

William Penn, Governor of Pennsylvania, had a granddaughter born in 1699 who married Charles Fell but I have been unable to discover the relationship between Charles and Benjamin.[39] The *Fell* name connects to the Quakers from their very beginnings. George Fox who got some dissenters organized into the Society of Friends in 1644, married Margaret Askew Fell, the widow of Judge Fell, in 1669.[40]

+ 18   viii.   **Robert SCARBOROUGH** was born 10 June 1708 and died 19 January 1805.

Sixth Generation

6.   **William⁶ SCARBOROUGH** (John⁵, John⁴, John³, William², Isaac¹) was born 30 October 1691 in Bucks County, Pennsylvania.[41]

In 1713 William was disowned by the Falls Monthly Meeting of Quakers.[42] William worked as a turner and a wheelwright.[43] After his mother's death, sometime before 1747, William Scarborough owned the homestead. He sold it to his son Euclides in 1762.[44]

William married (1) **Alice LONGSHORE** in 1712.

William married (2) **Mary.**[45]

William had the following child and four others:[46]

19   i.   **Euclides⁷ SCARBOROUGH**

12.   Sarah⁶ SCARBOROUGH (John⁵, John⁴, John³, William², Isaac¹) was born 2 March 1694 and died 4 February 1748 in Bucks County, Pennsylvania.[47]

Sarah married (1) **George HAYWORTH** in 1710 in Bucks County, Pennsylvania. They were married at the Falls Monthly Meeting in Buckingham Township.[48]

George and Sarah had the following children:

20   i.   **Stephanus⁷ HAYWORTH** was born 17 February 1713 in Bucks County, Pennsylvania, and died 1 September 1756 in what is now Guilford, North Carolina. Stephanus married **Rachel BEESON**, and they settled near Tenth Legion in what is now Rockingham County, Virginia.[49]

21   ii.   **Rachel HAYWORTH,** born in 1715, died young.[50]

22   iii.   **Absalom HAYWORTH** was born in 1716 in Solebury Township, Bucks County, Pennsylvania.

Absalom operated a mill in Back Creek Valley of Frederick County, Virginia. He owned land that abutted property of Robert Scarborough and Stephanus Haworth in what is now Rockingham County.[51]

He married **Elizabeth F. PAYNE**, daughter of Josiah and Martha (SHEPPARD) PAYNE, in 1738.[52]

23   iv.   **John HAYWORTH,** born November 1717, died November 1776, Delaware County, Pennsylvania.

In 1739 John and wife, Mary, moved to Back Creek Valley in Virginia to live with his brother Absalom. And in 1750 they returned to Bucks County, Pennsylvania.[53]

It is from this line that the ancestry of President Herbert Clark Hoover can be traced:

John and Mary Haworth had daughter Rachel, who married Aaron TOOLE. Aaron and Rachel Toole had daughter Ann, who married Henry WASLEY. Henry and Ann Wasley had daughter Mary, who married Theodore MINTHORN. Their daughter Huldah married Jesse Clark HOOVER and they were the parents of Herbert Clark HOOVER.[54]

President Herbert Clark Hoover was born 10 August 1874 in West Branch, Iowa. He died 20 October 1964 in New York, New York. Herbert Hoover served as president of the United States from 1929-1933. During World War I he had been Chief Allied Relief Administrator, and he served as Secretary of Commerce in 1921. In October 1929 the American stock market crashed and the Great Depression followed. His maneuvers to help the economy were not enough to alleviate the economic crisis, and Franklin D. Roosevelt, who was more of an activist, was elected in his place.

Hoover was a mining engineer, graduating from Stanford University in 1895. In many respects he was a great administrator, and after World War II he helped with famine relief in Europe.[55]

John married **Mary GARNER.**

24   v.   **James HAYWORTH**, born in 1719, died by September 1757 near Gainesboro in Frederick County, Virginia.[56]

On 4 August 1755 James Haworth, planter, and wife, Sarah, of Frederick County, Virginia, conveyed to Thomas Doster of same 227 acres granted to Haworth on 17 November 1752. The tract was on both sides of the Great Spring Branch of Back Creek by North Mountain.[57]

James married (1) **Sarah WOOD** in 1743 at Smith Creek Meeting, Virginia.
Sarah married (2) **Peter RUBLE** and in 1768 they settled in Newberry County, South Carolina.[58]

25   vi.   **Mary HAYWORTH**, born 1721, died 1771. She married **John MICHENER**.[59]

26   vii. **George HAYWORTH**, born 1724, died in 1747 in Bucks County, Pennsylvania. He married **Mary BROWN**.[60]

Sarah (Scarborough) HAYWORTH married (2) **Mathew HALL** in 1732.[61]

Sarah and Mathew moved to Chester County, Pennsylvania.[62]

18.   **Robert**[6] **SCARBOROUGH** (John[5], John[4], John[3], William[2], Isaac[1]) was born 10 June 1708 in Solebury Township, Bucks County, Pennsylvania. He died 19 January 1805.[63]

I have not found the source of Robert's given name, but a pirate by the name of Robert Scarborough was using the town of Scarborough, England, as his home port when he captured a French ship in 1577. That event, however, took place 131 years before Robert was born, and proof of a relationship between the London Scarboroughs and Robert Scarborough of Scarborough has not been established.

The Scarboroughs did tend to use the same given names over and over again. As we saw above, the progenitor of this family was named *Isaac*. My great-grandfather, born in 1853, was named *Isaac*. He and wife, Susan, named their first child *Nancy Rachel* and the name *Rachel* was given to a girl born around 1776 by her father, Isaac, son of Robert. My older sister is named *Rachel*.

When John Scarborough (d. 1727) made his will, he gave son Robert 150 acres, a silver dram cup, and a pewter salt seller.

In 1737 Robert sold 157 acres in Solebury Township, land devised to him by his father. He then moved to Virginia, settling in the Shenandoah Valley, five miles southwest of New Market. There he claimed 400 acres on Smith Creek, adjoining land of Absalom Haworth. A Quaker, Robert was a member of the Hopewell Meeting in Frederick County, Virginia.[64] The town of Tenth Legion, in present-day Rockingham County, sits on what was once Robert's farm. U.S. Route 11 passes through Tenth Legion, and Robert's farm would have included the path of U.S. 81.[65] The skyline to the east is dominated by the heavily forested Massanutten Mountain, about 50 miles long.

In 1738 Robert wrote a letter to his brother John and wife, Jane. It began, "This comes with kind love to you and yours, and to our dear mother, and to all brothers and sisters, and to all our relations." Robert said he intended to travel to Pennsylvania in the fall, health permitting. He thanked God for the health of his family and said he was pleased with his 300-acre farm. It had good meadows and water. A mill was being built about a mile away. And they were about a mile from a meeting (Quaker, implied). They had bought two cows. Elizabeth wanted to be remembered to her friends and asked for letters from old neighbors. Robert added that he had received John's letter just a few days before and a letter from Benjamin Fell. Robert's letter, yellowed with age, was found in a Bible belonging to Thomas Paxon. The Bible was printed in 1706.[66]

Somewhere around 1750 Robert moved south to Bedford County, Virginia.[67] Robert's survey for 44 acres was dated 28 March 1763, but settlers usually lived on their chosen land before the survey was done. The parcel was between the forks of the School House Branch of the South Fork of the Otter River. The point of beginning was Randolph's corner at the foot of Piney Mountain.[68] Today there is a Piney Mountain near Stewartsville in Bedford County. Both forks of the Otter River are considerably north of Stewartsville, so perhaps another mountain was called *Piney* in those days. Robert must have been fond of mountains, for the Peaks of Otter, near his chosen site in Bedford County, were as magnificent a presence as Massanutten up in the Shenandoah Valley. The most spectacular of Otter's peaks, Sharp Top, is 3,865 feet high.

About 12 years after Robert and his family moved to Bedford County, on 23 November 1762, Bedford Court ordered the church wardens of Russell Parish to bind out Rachel, William, James, Kiziah, and Isaac Scarbro, children of Robert Scarbro "according to law." No explanation was given in the order book.[69]

Robert Scarbrough was named among the accounts of William Boyd, deceased, of Bedford County. Boyd's executors were Stephen Goggin and Robert Russell. The report was signed by examiners Saml. Hairston, Chas. Lynch, and Christopher Irvine and returned on 23 September 1766.[70] The accounts for the estate of William Thomson of Bedford County were settled by examiners William Trigg and Isham Talbot and recorded on 22 September 1767. Rob.

Scarbrough was named among the numerous accounts.[71]

In 1767 the June court declared Robt. Scarborough exempted from paying levies.[72] Born in 1708, he would have been close to 60 at this time.

Robert Scarbrough sold 45 acres in Bedford County to Frederick Mayberry. The parcel was at the forks of Schoolhouse Creek. Wits: Robt. Ewing, Chas. Ewing, Geo. Dixon. (Recorded 23 May 1769.)[73]

William Irvine's accounts were submitted by Robert Cowan and returned on 28 November 1771. Examiners were John Phelps, W. Mead, and J. Talbot. Robert Scarburough was named among the accounts.[74]

As could be seen from the letter Robert wrote not long after settling in the Shenandoah Valley, he was literate and devoted to friends and relatives. He thanked God for the health of his family members. But something went wrong for him before or after his arrival in Bedford County. He had owned a 300-acre farm in Frederick County and had only 44 acres surveyed for him in Bedford County. Several of his children were put under the care of the Bedford County church wardens. In some way he was not an adequate father to them. This sudden drop in ability to provide for his own may have been due to illness—there was no social security in those days. The official church compensated its members for their care of the ailing. But when Robert and his family migrated to southern (West) Virginia, they thrived, his children eventually acquiring about 2,000 acres in Monroe County. Two of his sons became charter members of Rehobeth Methodist Church. I have not found a Scarborough named among the Quakers of Bedford County, so they may have had some disillusionment with the Society of Friends.

Robert and James Scarborough appeared together on the "Residents of 1782" enumeration (John Henderson's Company) for the part of Greenbrier that was later Monroe (compiled by Oren Morton for his *History of Monroe County, West Virginia*). William Scarborugh was also on the list in 1782 but in James Henderson's Company.[75] When taxes were recorded in 1783, Robert was shown as not tithable.[76]

In 1790 Robert patented 150 acres that had been surveyed for John Fisher on Lick Run, south of Swope's Knob, in what later would be Monroe County, (West) Virginia.[77] In 1790 Robert Scarborough had 100 acres surveyed at Swope's Knob.[78]

Robert's known children are named below. There was also a Seth SCARBOROUGH living in Monroe County during this time, but I have not discovered his origins. He and Joseph Hinchman witnessed the 1813 will of William Hinchman, Sr., of Monroe County.[79]

I have not found a record of Robert's death in Monroe County. Dwayne Scarberry, one of his descendants, states that Robert's grandson, Elijah Scarberry, son of James and Emily (Wood) Scarborough, was in possession of a Bible record showing his death in 1805.

Robert married (1) **Elizabeth FISHER**, daughter of John FISHER and Sarah HUTCHINSON.. Elizabeth was a sister of John Fisher, Jr., who married Robert Scarborough's sister Elizabeth.[80]

Robert and Elizabeth had the following children:

+   27   i.   **John⁷ SCARBOROUGH** was born 1734.

      28   ii.   **Elizabeth SCARBOROUGH** was born 1736 in Bucks County, Pennsylvania.[81]

Robert married (2) Miss **BAILEY**, daughter of William BAILEY.[82]

William Bailey was living in Bedford County, Virginia, by 28 September 1768, when he gave power of attorney to his son-in-law Robert Scarbrough, also of Bedford. William was moving and wanted Robert to collect debts for him from people in Frederick County, Virginia. Joseph Haskins owed him 2 lbs. 15 sh; Adam Leonard and Adam Rynard had forgotten their sums, but Evan Jones had a memorandum with the amounts on it; Thomas Hinton owed 5 lbs. 5 sh.; Conrad Mulvern(?) owed 2 lbs. 10 sh; Charles Stapleton owed 16 lbs. After signing (with an *X*) William noted that his son William Bailey, who was living in Frederick County, owed him 9 lbs. 11 sh, 6 p., but that debt was to be forgiven. This document was proved by the oaths of Michael Carnes and William Taylor in Bedford County Court on 25 October 1768.[83]

On 29 September 1768 William Bailey of Bedford County gave his son James Bailey a cow, two heifers, a calf marked with a crop in the left ear and an underkeel and slit in the right, one sorrel horse, a wagon and harness, a bed, a large iron pot, and all the pewter in his possession. Grandson William Scarbrough was given two cows, a heifer marked in the same way as the calf given to James, a bay mare branded WB, a bed, and a chest and all other movables belonging to him and not previously mentioned. Money due him from Frederick County was to be divided equally between son James Bailey and grandson William Scarbrough. Wits: Michael Carnes, WilliamTaylor.[84] William Bailey was prosperous, or he wouldn't have owned a wagon, but he was illiterate, for he signed with a mark.

They had the following children:

    29   iii. **Rachel SCARBOROUGH**

                  On 12 June 1788, 52 acres in Greenbrier County (later West Virginia) were surveyed for Rachel Scarborough. The parcel was on the waters of Indian Creek and adjoined lands of James Johnstone and David Scarborough. It was part of State Warrant No. 14,313 for 530 acres and had been assigned to her by James and David Scarborough, assignees of James McNutt.[85] When David and Elizabeth Scarbrow sold 35 acres to Bradley Dalton in 1798, it was recorded in the deed that Rachel Kenady had formerly lived on the property.[86]

                  Rachel married **James KENNEDY** on 9 September 1791.[87]

                  In April 1790 James Kannaday was given 39 lashes for stealing $4 from James Handley.[88]

+   30   iv. **William SCARBOROUGH** was born 1753 and died 1830.

+   31   v. **James SCARBOROUGH** was born 1755 and died 1809.

    32   vi. **Keziah SCARBOROUGH**.

+   33   vii. **Isaac SCARBOROUGH** was born about 1756.

+   34   viii. **Sarah SCARBOROUGH**

+   35   ix. **David SCARBOROUGH** was born about 1760.

    36   x. **Susannah SCARBOROUGH** married **John SMITH** on 22 March 1787 in Bedford County, Virginia. William Thornhill was surety, and Robert, father of Susanna, gave consent.[89]

    37   xi. **Elizabeth SCARBOROUGH** married **James JOHNSON** on 22 October 1785 in Bedford County, Virginia. Consent to marry was made by Elizabeth, herself. Francis Burks was surety.[90]

+   38   xii. **Robert SCARBOROUGH** died about 1840.

    39   xiii **Mary SCARBOROUGH** married **Joseph MCGUIRE** on 27 March 1786 in Bedford County, Virginia. Lawrence McGuire was surety for the marriage bond.[91]

Seventh Generation

27.   **John[7] SCARBOROUGH** (Robert[6], John[5], John[4], John[3], William[2], Isaac[1]) was born 1734.

      In 1757 John returned from Virginia to Solebury, Pennsylvania, with a certificate from the Hopewell Friends Monthly Meeting.[92]

John married (1) **Margaret KIRK** on 8 May 1760 at the Wrightstown meeting house in Pennsylvania.[93]

John and Margaret had the following children:[94]

    40   i. **John[8] SCARBOROUGH** was born 1761.

	41	ii.	**Robert SCARBOROUGH** was born 1763.
	42	iii.	**Rachel SCARBOROUGH** was born 1765.
	43	iv.	**Joseph SCARBOROUGH** was born 1767.
+	44	v.	**Isaac SCARBOROUGH** was born 1769 and died 1851.
	45	vi.	**Elizabeth SCARBOROUGH** was born 1772.
	46	vii.	**Charity SCARBOROUGH** was born 1774.

John married (2) **Johanna CAHOON** on 11 October 1779 in Germantown, Pennsylvania. Both John and Johanna were of Wrightstown, Pennsylvania, when they married. Johanna (?) had been married previously to a Mr. Cahoon.[95]

30. **William[7] SCARBOROUGH** (Robert[6], John[5], John[4], John[3,] William[2], Isaac[1]) was born 1753. He died in 1830 in Anderson County, Tennessee.[96]

On 29 September 1768, William's grandfather, William Bailey, deeded to him two cows and a heifer, a bay mare, a bed and its furniture, with a chest. William Bailey also divided money that was owed him in Frederick County equally between his son, James Bailey, and grandson William Scarborough.[97]

William Scarbro__r (damaged) was a witness to the 2 December 1777 will of Adam Beard of Bedford County, Virginia. Other witnesses: Robt. Ewing Wm. Armstrong, Alexr. Armstrong. David Beard was executor, and sureties were David Wright, James Buford, and James Patterson.[98]

Bedford County road orders of 26 June 1780 include William and James Scarborough. William Ewing was appointed surveyor of the road from the schoolhouse (opposite John Ewing's) up to the forks of the new road. People ordered to assist in the care of the road were Adam Sharp; Henry Fargeson; Sam'l Beard; Wm. & Jas. Scarborough; Adam Beard; Henry Grove, Frederick & Henry Mayberry; James Folden; Martha, Ro., Wm., & Jno. Ewing; and Absalom McClenahan.[99]

Bedford County, Virginia, Court Orders of 23 September 1782 show William Scarborough was reimbursed for letting his wagon and team remove military stores in July 1781 (this date was difficult to read).[100]

On 27 April 1784 William Scarborough claimed 300 acres on Turkey Creek in what was later Monroe County, (West) Virginia. The land was assigned to him by William Ewing.[101] In 1797 William and Mahala sold 300 acres on Turkey Creek to Thomas Johnston. William was living on the land, and he had acquired it as an assignee of Sam'l Ervin. It adjoined the lands of Jas. Scarborough and Thomas Kincaid. Milley [sic] signed with an X.[102]

Greenbrier County tithables for 1787 include William Scarborow. He had no white males between 16 and 21; 1 black above 16; 0 blacks under 16; 4 horses; 10 cattle.[103]

William owned a mill by November 1784, when an order was given for road care between William Scarborough's mill and John Kincaid's at the head of Indian (Creek).[104]

In December 1795 William Scarborough was given permission to free his Negro slave, York, on the condition that he be responsible for any illegal conduct of said York.[105] William seems to have been the first person in Monroe County to free a slave. The terrain of Monroe County did not lend itself to large plantations, so there were not many slaves in the county.[106] It is not certain how long before this time William and his brother James had ceased to be Quakers. The Quakers did not condone slavery, and early in the 1800s many of the Quakers in Bedford County headed to Ohio and other places where slavery was not allowed.

William and his brother James Scarborough were among the five trustees of the Rehobeth Methodist Church just east of Union, the county seat of Monroe County.[107]

William married **Emily (Milley) WOOD**.[108]

It has been suggested that Emily Wood's middle name was *Mahala*.

William and Milley had the following children and probably others.

	47	i.	**James[8] SCARBOROUGH** was born 5 November 1775.

James married **Jane SHANNON** on 24 September 1794 in Greenbrier County, West Virginia. Jacob Cook officiated.[109]

48   ii.   **William SCARBOROUGH** died in 1814. He married **Catherine** (?).

49   iii. **Jonathan Lupton SCARBOROUGH** died in 1867.

              He married (1) **Elizabeth NUNELY**; (2) **Frances E. DAVIS**.[110]

50   iv.   **John SCARBOROUGH**

              He married **Susannah SHANNON** and had daughter **Prudence,** who married a Mr. **GRUBB.** Susannah married (2) a Mr. **DORAN**.[111]

51   v.   **Agnes SCARBOROUGH** married a Mr. **HASSLER**.[112]

+ 52   vi.   **Edy SCARBOROUGH** was born 22 February 1771.

31.   **James⁷ SCARBOROUGH** (Robert⁶, John⁵, John⁴, John³, William², Isaac¹) was born 1755. He died in 1809 in Anderson County, Tennessee.[113]

Virginia colonial militia from Bedford County, Virginia, enlisted to fight in Lord Dunmore's War of 1774. Included was James Scarbara. He was in Capt. Buford's Company of Volunteers.[114] Dunmore's War was actually the beginning of the Revolution, as pointed out in an article in *The Ohio Archaelogical and Historical Quarterly* (July 1903), for Dunmore was suspected of double dealings.[115] Lord Dunmore, Governor of Virginia, asked Col. Andrew Lewis to meet him and his army at Point Pleasant, where the Kanawha River joins the Ohio, in hopes that a major attack against the Shawnees and their allies would prevent further raiding on the settlements. Col. Lewis gathered about 1,100 men at Camp Union at Lewisburg, and after arriving at the headwaters of the Kanawha, traveled downriver to Point Pleasant. When Lewis and his men arrived at Point Pleasant, he received word that Dunmore had decided to cross the Ohio on upstream and go directly to the Shawnee villages on the Scioto River.[116] The Shawnees, under the leadership of Chief Cornstalk, attacked at Point Pleasant, and Capt. Thomas Buford was fatally wounded.[117] The Indians lost fewer men than the colonists, but this battle was decisive, for the Shawnees signed a treaty agreeing not to raid on the east side of the Ohio.[118] Another list of Capt. Thomas Buford's men shows James Scarbara as James *Scarbaraugh*.[119]

In 1784 James Scarborough had surveyed 149 acres on Turkey Creek in what was then Greenbrier County.[120] In 1798 James and Rachel Scarbrough and others conveyed to Jno. McDugal 149 acres on Turkey Creek. Wits: James Handley, John Ruble, John Handley, Pattison Griffith. Scarbrough was entitled to the land by a patent of 8 November 1787, Christy giving up 3 ¼ acres he was living on and entitled to by patent. The total transferred was 152 acres.[121]

In 1786 James claimed 83 acres on Back and Laurel Creeks.[122] In 1787 he acquired 245 acres.[123] In 1793 he became the owner of 162 acres at the Little Mountain adjoining lands of James Henderson, Taylor, John Dougherty and William Scarbrough.[124]

Greenbrier County Personal Property Tax list for 1787, List A, includes James Scarborow. He was working for himself and had no white males in his household between 16 and 21. There was one black under 16. He owned four horses and eight cattle.[125]

On 26 April 1797 James Scarbrow bought 226 acres in Greenbrier County from Jeremiah Abell and wife, Hannah, of Fayette County, Kentucky. This tract was in the area known as the Sinks (later Monroe County) and adjacent Kounce, Keenan, McCart, Blanton, Henderson, and Johnston.[126] In 1797 James Scarbrough and wife, Rachel, sold 226 acres on Lick Run to Jno. Mahon. Rachel signed with an *X*.[127]

James and William Scarbrough were among the five trustees of the Rehobeth Methodist Church. It met about two miles east of Union in Monroe County. James Christy, who married Sarah Scarborough, sister of James and William, was one of the first pastors. Edward Keenan donated four acres for the church, but the actual deed was for five acres. The building, finished in June 1786, was placed in a circular depression so that Indians could not sneak up on it unseen. Edward Keenan signed bond to insure his commitment to the building, and it was addressed to William Scarborough, James Scarborough, Daniel McMullen, James Christy, and Alexander House (or any other trustees appointed). The building, 21 by 29 feet, was made of medium-size logs and had a gallery around the interior, except for the pulpit.[128]

That Methodism had reached the Greenbrier area by this time is remarkable, for the Methodists did not separate officially from the Church of England until 1784. People on the frontier felt a need to worship with more spontaneity than the Church of England allowed, however. Methodism was spread by circuit riders, who traveled over vast areas, preaching wherever they were welcome. Bishop Francis Asbury, the famous Methodist circuit rider, traveled on horseback, towing a second horse that carried his blanket and teapot (he remained close to his British roots). He held conferences at Rehobeth in 1792, 1793, and 1796. His notebooks show that he spoke well of his "friend Scarborough" on Turkey Creek.[129] (James's brother William also owned land on Turkey Creek.) The Rehobeth church building has been restored and is an historic landmark. Edward Keenan and his wife are among those buried in the churchyard.

On 30 August 1815, 64 acres, part of 147 acres that formerly belonged to James Scarborough, was returned delinquent for the year 1799. Michael Erskin, deputy, sold it to Frederick Baker.[130]

James married **Rachel WOOD**.[131]

James and Rachel had the following children (and possibly others):

53   i. **Agnes^8 SCARBOROUGH** married **Patterson GRIFFITH** on 14 August 1794 in Greenbrier County (West) Virginia. Jacob Cook performed the marriage ceremony.[132]

Patterson Griffith bought 21 acres on Turkey Creek (later Monroe County) from Thomas and Mary Johnson in 1798.[133] Patterson and Agnes moved to Anderson County, Tennessee.

54   ii. **Rachel SCARBOROUGH**

Given the date of her marriage, Rachel would have been a granddaughter of Robert Scarborough, but her parents are uncertain.

Rachel married **John NEAL** on 31 July 1794 in Greenbrier County, (West) Virginia. Jacob Cook performed the marriage ceremony.[134]

55   iii. **Eliza SCARBOROUGH** married **Tobyas PETERS** in 1797 in Greenbrier County (West) Virginia, J. Wiseman, the minister. The marriage record shows she was a daughter of James.[135]

Tobias Peters, age 61, presumably a son, appears on the U.S. 1880 census for Roane, Tennessee. Tobias's parents were born in Virginia, and his wife and children in Tennessee. Living next door was William Scarbrough, 34, and his family. Both men were mechanics.[136]

56   iv. **Elijah SCARBOROUGH**

Dwayne Scarberry reports that Elijah had a Bible record showing that his grandfather Robert Scarborough died in 1805.

33.   **Isaac^7 SCARBOROUGH** (Robert^6, John^5, John^4, John^3, William^2, Isaac^1) was born about 1756 in Bedford County, Virginia. He died in Lawrence County, Ohio, before 1820.

Bedford County, Virginia, Court Orders of 1782-1783 include what apparently are road orders for Isaac Scarbrough and others. The people from Mobley's Ford on Otter to Will. Moon's and Tho. Lumpkin's lands at Otter River, Henry Brown, Jr., John Thompson & Isaac Scarbrough, were ordered to (incomplete).[137] In Bedford County as well as elsewhere in Virginia the roads were cared for (stumps cleared and bridges repaired) by people who lived near them.

Isaac Scarborough was living in Bedford County when the names of Virginia Tax Payers were polled between 1782 and 1787. He was charged for 1 tithable.[138]

On 27 January 1783 Isaac Scarborough, as executor of the will of John Ward, deceased, made oath and gave bond with security. He was given a certificate of administration.[139]

Isaac Scarborough and wife, Mary, of Bedford County, Virginia, on 24 January 1785, sold 150 acres for 150 lbs. current money to William Candler of same. The land was part of a patent made to Obadiah Perry in 1749. The point of beginning for the tract was a white oak on Lick Run and the tract abutted land of John Phelps. Wits: James Guthry, Sr., James Guthry, Jr., John Robards.[140]

In 1786 Isaac patented 170 acres on Cooper's Run, a branch of Indian Creek, in what later would be Monroe County, (West) Virginia. Isaac was entitled to the land by a state warrant for 797 acres assigned to him by James McNutt (assignee of Jean Cunningham).[141]

Tax List A of the 1787 personal property taxes for Greenbrier County, (West) Virginia, include Isaac Scarborough. He was working for himself and had no white males in his household between the ages of 16 and 21. There was one black person above 16, none under 16. He owned two horses and four cattle.[142]

Isaac Scarbrough was granted 200 acres in Greenbrier County (later Monroe) on 19 November 1788. This tract was on the headwaters of Back Creek and the head of Cooper's Run, a branch of Indian Creek. He used State Warrant No. 11,951 for 797 acres, assigned to him by James McNutt.[143] Note: I have not discovered that Isaac sold any of the 170-acre patent of 1786. The two tracts of 77.5 acres, one to James Folding and one to Robert Scarber, that he sold in 1819 and the 45-acre tract to John Scarbrow add up to 200 acres (more details on these deeds below). It is likely that the 1788 patent for 200 acres included the 1786 patent for 170 acres.

When an election was held on 3 November 1800, Isaac Scarbrough was among the voters. He voted again in November 1804.[144]

On 18 August 1807 Isaac Scarbrow and wife, Mary, conveyed 45 acres to John Scarbrow, part of a 200-acre survey made for Isaac. The tract was described as beginning at a white oak and locust, crossing a spring branch, and extending to three chestnut oaks and a maple ... to the "Beginning Course of the old line from the white oak and Locust on top of the Mountain...." Wits: Thos. Wiatt, George Bailey, Henry Maddy. Only Maddy and Wiatt did not sign with an *X*.[145]

Isaac moved northwest. On 1 January 1812 he had surveyed 56 acres on the White Oak Branch of the Clear Fork of the Coal River.[146] The Coal River is a tributary of the Kanawha River, which flows through Charleston, West Virginia. The coal found along its banks was valuable for heating and lighting.

The mountains in this part of West Virginia are high, and the valleys are crowded by the mountains, so the main draw to this region almost had to have been good hunting and trapping rather than farming. When the English first started exploring the land west of the Alleghanies, in what is now West Virginia, they found few Indian villages. Oren Morton (*A History of Monroe County, West Virginia*) estimates there were less than a half dozen.[147] During the time of English settlement Indians had a salt-making camp at the salt spring at Campbell's Creek, and they visited Ansted, near present-day Hawk's Nest State Park, to obtain flint for their arrowheads.[148]

Evidence of much earlier settlement (believed to have been Indian) is found below Mount Carbon, beside the Kanawha River near Montgomery. There is a burial ground there, thought by some to have belonged to the Adena Indians, who thrived from 1,000 to 200 B.C. The Adenas were famous for their burial mounds, the largest, 69 feet high, being the Grave Creek Mound found at Moundsville, West Virginia.[149] But the graves below Mount Carbon and also at the mouth of Paint Creek were not found in mounds,[150] so these people may have been buried at a later or earlier period.

The Scarboroughs who settled on the Clear Fork of Coal would have been aware of the extensive ancient walls, constructed to the north of them near the top of Mount Carbon on the south side of the Kanawha. The walls, probably about seven or eight feet high, were made of loosely stacked rocks, some of them culminating in tower-like structures. The walls were at least three miles long and may at one time have gone on for ten miles. There was a similar wall on Paint Mountain, this one about ten feet high, but only about a half-mile long. The walls were placed near the top of the mountains, and people in their vicinity would have had a good view of the sunrise. At one time these walls were thought to have been built as game runs, because so many bones of bear, elk, deer, and other wild animals are found at the gaps in the walls.[151] Recent studies, however, suggest the walls were created as centers for flint gathering and shaping, and that they were used for many generations. The Indians believed in a Flint Spirit, and the springs near the walls would have been a blessing from the spirit of the underworld.[152] Sadly, rocks from the walls were carted away. Coal mining has destroyed some remnants of the walls, and scarcely any evidence of their existence remains.

The Scarboroughs and Harpers were among the first settlers along the Coal River in what later would become Raleigh County. Isaac Scarborough and John Scarborugh (m. Eleanor Harper) owned land on Back Creek in Monroe

County, and my ancestor Samuel Lewis (d. 1811) owned land on Back and Indian Creeks. Isaac Estill's home on Indian Creek was just east of Samuel Lewis's. Estill was instrumental in getting roads built into the wilderness areas of southern West Virginia. He and John Byrnside and James Alexander of Monroe County were fur traders, and they wanted a trail created for people who hunted and trapped in southwestern West Virginia. In 1797 they hired Francis Farley, an excellent woodsman, to clear a trail six-feet wide between the New River, near its confluence with the Bluestone, to Louisa, Kentucky, on the Big Sandy River, a tributary of the Ohio. The trail went to Beckley before turning west. The contract between Farley and his sponsors called for a path that could be developed into a wagon road. But Farley was never paid, because his trail, Farley's Trace, was said to be inadequate. In the end, however, the discovery of salt sources brought with it a wagon road that went north to the Kanawha. Elisha Brooks discovered shallow brine wells in the Kanawha Valley and constructed a furnace in 1797 to produce the salt. Prior to his discovery people in western Virginia primarily got their salt from ports along the coast. In 1785 George Washington had requested a wagon road between Lewisburg and the lower falls of the Kanawha, near Montgomery. This road followed the path of what today is U.S. Route 60. By 1800 the road had been continued to the Ohio River. Still, the distance between Monroe County and the salt supply needed to be shortened. In 1811 Isaac Estill, Samuel Clarke, Andrew Johnston, Claudius Buster, John Reynolds, and Isaac Hutcheson were appointed commissioners to supervise the building of a road between the mouth of the Bluestone and Lower Loop Creek (at Montgomery) on the Kanawha. This road became known as the Bluestone Road. (See Jim Wood's, *Raleigh County, West Virginia*, for a more complete account of the building of these roads.)[153]

Readers of the story of Mary Draper Ingles and her capture by the Shawnees in 1755 would find the Coal River banks familiar. After Mary and her older companion, Mrs. Bingamin, escaped the Shawnees in Kentucky, they trekked the south bank of the Ohio River to the Big Sandy, which separates Kentucky and West Virginia. Unable to swim, they stuck to its west bank until it narrowed at the confluence of the Tug River, crossed it, and backtracked to the Ohio, following it to the Kanawha. Keeping to its south bank, which was level and easy underfoot, they reached the Coal River and followed it until they found a place to cross. Then it was back up the other side to the Kanawha. Ravaged by hunger, Mrs. Bingamin became increasingly mad, and Mary separated from her. On down the New River, Mary came upon a settler who helped her return home to what is now Blacksburg, Virginia.[154]

Within seven years of his Coal River survey, Isaac was a resident of Ohio. On 15 September 1819 Isaac Scarborough of Lawrence County, Ohio, sold 77.5 acres to James Folding, part of 200 acres granted to Scarborough on 19 November 1788. The parcel was on Indian Creek in Monroe County and adjoined lands of Richard Neel, John Brown, and others.[155] On 14 September 1819 Isaac Scarber of Ohio conveyed 77.5 acres to Robert Scarber of Monroe County, part of a 200-acre tract. On 17 March 1822 the deed was delivered to Robert Scarbrough.[156]

Although Isaac's father was literate, Isaac signed with an *X*. His father was a devout Quaker at one time, but Monroe County records reveal Isaac owned a slave. He may have embraced Methodism as had brothers William and James. His brother William was the first man in Monroe County to set a slave free, and perhaps Isaac followed his example.

The Lawrence County, Ohio, tax list of 1818 includes Isace Scarber. He was not on the 1820 Federal census.[157]

Isaac married **Mary WARD** daughter of John WARD and wife, Catherine, in Virginia.

Researcher Dwayne Scarberry has found that Mary Ward was born 2 June 1754 in Munslow, England. She had a brother, Zachariah, who was deceased by 6 August 1782 when her father, by then of Bedford County, Virginia, made his will. Zachariah Ward had daughter Elizabeth, for John Ward named her in his will. He also named daughter Betty Phinny and her son Joshua, devising to Betty the tract of land whereon she and her husband were living. Daughter Mary Scarborough had son John Ward. The testator favored daughter Mary, for legacies given wife, Catherine, would revert to Mary upon Catherine's death, including the home place. Legacies not doled out in his will went to daughter Mary. John signed his will with a vertical line crossed in the middle by a short horizontal line, a symbol so often used in those days in place of a *J*. Isaac Scarborough was the executor, and his bond was secured by Thomas Lumpkin and William Hudnall. Witnesses were Henry Brown, Sr., Henry Brown, Jr., and Samuel Adams. Henry Brown and Samuel Adams proved the will on 23 December 1782.[158]

They had the following children:

+   57   i. **John Ward**[8] **SCARBOROUGH** died 1863.

+   58   ii. **Robert "Robin" SCARBOROUGH** was born 1782.

+   59   iii. **Zachariah SCARBERRY** was born 1785 and died 1856.

+   60   iv. **Mary SCARBOROUGH**, "Polly," died 21 June 1843.

       61   v. **Elizabeth SCARBOROUGH** married **Jim CANTER** on 11 September 1817 in Lawrence County, Ohio. Information on this marriage was supplied by Dwayne J. Scarberry.

+   62   vi. **Rachel SCARBOROUGH** was born 1776 and died 7 February 1872.

34.   **Sarah**[7] **SCARBOROUGH** (Robert[6], John[5], John[4], John[3], William[2], Isaac[1]).

Sarah married **James CHRISTY** on 5 July 1780 in Greenbrier County, (West) Virginia.[159]

     In 1787 James Christy had 296 acres surveyed in what would later be Monroe County. The tract was on Indian Creek, adjacent John Handley.[160]

     On 27 September 1791 James McNutt of Madison County deeded 195 acres to James Christie. The tract was adjacent John Robinson, John Handley, and James Christy, and the deed was recorded in Greenbrier County.[161]

     James Christy and Wineford Neel, widow of Walter Neel, were the administrators of the estate of Walter Neel of Monroe County. The appraisal was returned on 20 October 1801 by Samuel Clerk, John Hanly, Sr., John Hanly, Jr.[162] Walter and Wineford's daughter Agnes married John Wiseman in 1812.[163] The Wiseman family had moved to Monroe from Bucks County, Pennsylvania.[164]

     John Nicholas and wife, Margaret, on 16 November 1802, sold to James Christy 123 acres on Swope's Knobs. The tract adjoined lands of Michal Beckett, Elisha Riston, and William Gartin. Wit: John Hutchison.[165] On 15 August 1815 James and Catharine Christy, Sr., sold this tract to George Bailey.[166]

     On 17 December 1805 James Christy, Sr., conveyed 195 acres to Robert Christy. The land was on Turkey and Indian Creeks, adjacent John Handly and lands once belonging to Edward Wyatt, James Scarbrough, and James McNutt.[167] The same day James Christy, Sr., conveyed 195 acres to James Christy, this tract adjacent John Handly and John Robinson.[168]

     By 3 February 1806 Sarah Scarborough must have died, for on that date, James Christy, Sr., married Katey DeBOY (DuBois). James Christy was surety.[169]

Sarah and James had the following children:

       63   i. **Isabel**[8] **CHRISTY** married **George BAILEY** on 10 January 1797.[170]

       64   ii. **James CHRISTY** married **Elizabeth GARTON** on 11 October 1804 in Monroe County (West) Virginia.[171]

       65   iii. **Robert CHRISTY** married **Margaret CROZIER**, daughter of Andrew CROZIER and Elizabeth MAXWELL, in 1804 in Monroe County, (West) Virginia. John Wiseman was the minister.[172]

           On 5 May 1813 Hugh and Jane Caperton deeded 116 acres on Indian Creek to James and Robert Christy.[173]

       66   iv. **Elizabeth CHRISTY** was born 1785. .Betsy married **Andrew ALLEN** on 10 December 1802. Josiah Phillips was the minister.[174]

35.   **David**[7] **SCARBOROUGH** (Robert[6], John[5], John[4], John[3], William[2], Isaac[1]) was born about 1760.

     In 1784 David Scarborough acquired 140 acres on Indian Creek, adjacent Philip Cooper. Part of the certificate for this land was assigned to David Scarborough and Philip Cooper by Robert Scarborough.[175] In 1787 David claimed

190 acres on the head waters of Burgan's and Humphries' Run, both branches of Indian Creek. He was using Warrant No. 14,313 for 530 acres.[176] In 1791 he claimed 27 acres on Indian Creek, adjacent his own land.[177] And in 1797 he claimed 318 acres on Indian Creek.[178]

The 1787 Personal Property Tax lists for Greenbrier County (List A) show David working for himself and having no white males between 16 and 21 living with him. He owned no slaves, had two horses and three cattle.[179]

On 19 December 1795 Jacob Pope of Rockingham County sold 80 acres to David Scarbough of Greenbrier. The parcel was by land of Hugh Gallaspie, deceased, and had been sold by Wm. Varner to Pope. It was known as Warran's Place in the Big Levels. Wits: Charles Arbuckle, George Hoover, Henry Leaps, Michael Rader.[180] David bought 10 acres at Weaver's Knobs from Henry and Elizabeth Pope in 1798.[181]

In 1798 David and Elizabeth sold 94 acres on the waters of Indian Creek to William Fletcher of Botetourt County, Virginia.[182] Also in 1798 they sold 4 1/2 acres on the waters of Indian Creek to William Campbell. The parcel adjoined lands of George Spickard, William Garviss, and Campbell's land.[183] In 1798 David and Elizabeth sold 186 acres to George Spickard (also written Shepheard). The tract was part of a larger one of 335 acres, and Scarbrow and Spickard were living on it.[184]

David and Elizabeth, on 11 October 1798, sold 190 acres on the waters of Burgan's and Humphry's Branches of Indian Creek to Joseph Wiseman. Wits: William Campbell, Isaac Scarbrow, Ralph Clark.[185]

On 26 June 1798 David and Elizabeth sold 35 acres on Indian Creek to Bradley Dalton. Rachel Kanady had formerly lived on this parcel. It was part of David's survey of 335 acres that adjoined lands of William Campbell and John McNutt. On 15 April 1800 Bradley Dolton and wife, Dorothy sold the 35 acres to George and Phillip Wykle. Wits: George Spikerd, William Fletcher, John Maddox.[186]

David married **Elizabeth ANDERSON** on 3 May 1786 in Greenbrier County, (West) Virginia.[187]

38. Robert[7] SCARBOROUGH (Robert[6], John[5], John[4], John[3], William[2], Isaac[1]) died about 1840 in Missouri.[188]

Bedford County, Virginia, Court Orders of February 1785 show Robert Scarborough, son of Robert Scarborough, being bound by the church wardens as an apprentice to Thomas Overstreet, hatter, according to law.[189] Note that Robert Scarborough married Mary McGuire in November 1785. Court Orders show that Thomas Overstreet was indexed as apprenticing a child in February 1785. At that time Robert may have been officially a child because he was under 21.

On 7 December 1795, John Bates of Franklin County, Virginia, sold to Robert Scarborough (Scarberry) of same 100 acres on the branches of Story Creek. The tract was adjacent lands of McLary and Dert Fuson and Michael Coats.[190] On 6 February 1798 Robert sold this land to Swinfield Hill, Walter Barnard, and William Armstrong.[191]

Robert married **Mary MCGUIRE** on 21 November 1785 in Bedford County, Virginia. Lawrence McGuire was surety.[192]

They had the following child and probably others.

    67   i. **Samuel[8] SCARBOROUGH**

Eighth Generation

44. Isaac[8] SCARBOROUGH (John[7], Robert[6], John[5], John[4], John[3], William[2], Isaac[1]) was born 1769. He died 1851 and was buried in Bucks County, Pennsylvania.[193]

Isaac married **Amy PEARSON** on 24 Dec 1794. Amy was born in 1769 and died in 1835[194].

They had the following children:[195]

    68   i. **Crispin[9] SCARBOROUGH** was born 31 October 1795..

    69   ii. **John SCARBOROUGH** was born 1797.

70	iii.	**William SCARBOROUGH** was born 1799.
71	iv.	**Asa SCARBOROUGH** was born 12 September 1800 and died 24 November 1800.
72	v.	**Cynthia SCARBOROUGH** was born 17 November 1801.
73	vi.	**Isaac SCARBOROUGH** was born 1804.
74	vii.	**Charles SCARBOROUGH** was born 6 October 1806. He died 26 January 1839.

        Charles took part in the battle between Texas and Mexico, serving under General Sam Houston.[196] In April of 1836 Gen. Houston and his army defeated the Mexicans at San Jacinto.

75	viii.	**Amy SCARBOROUGH** was born 16 October 1809.
76	ix.	**Pearson SCARBOROUGH** was born 7 April 1813.
77	x.	**Elijah Wilson SCARBOROUGH** was born 4 October 1817.

52.   **Edy**[8] **SCARBOROUGH** (William[7], Robert[6], John[5], John[4], John[3], William[2], Isaac[1]) was born 22 February 1771.[197]

    Her parents are assumed.

Edy married **John LEONARD** on 17 June 1796 in Greenbrier County, West Virginia. John was born 7 April 1754 in Germany. He died 7 October 1841 in Hawkins County, Tennessee.[198]

    John Leonard was reared in Germany and sold into the British service when the British and Americans were fighting. John deserted at first opportunity and enlisted with the Americans in 1781 in Shenandoah County, Virginia. Right to his pension (Pn 1850. F-W1625 R1550) was applied for in 1823 in Hawkins County, Tennessee, where he died. Hawkins County shares its northern border with Virginia. Kingsport, Tennessee, is partly in Hawkins County. Note that James Scarborough moved to Anderson County, also in northeastern Tennessee, and Tobias Peters, doubtless a descendant of James and Rachel Scarborough, was found in Roane County, Tennessee, when the 1880 U.S. census was taken.

John and Edy had the following children:[199]

78	i.	**David**[9] **LEONARD** was born 30 March 1797.
79	ii.	**Elizabeth LEONARD** was born 14 February 1799.
80	iii.	**John LEONARD** was born 19 February 1801.
81	iv.	**William LEONARD** was born 5 February 1803.
82	v.	**Agnes LEONARD** was born 11 July 1805.
83	vi.	**Jacob LEONARD** was born 12 November 1807.
84	vii.	**Edy LEONARD** was born 11 March 1811.

57.   **John Ward**[8] **SCARBOROUGH** (Isaac[7], Robert[6], John[5], John[4], John[3], William[2], Isaac[1]) died 1863 at Rock Creek, West Virginia. The year and place of John's death are supplied by Ronnie Scarbro of Rock Creek, West Virginia.

    Monroe County, (West) Virginia, records of 1803 show John claiming 116 acres on Back Creek.[200] On 21 January 1806 he bought 150 acres on Back Creek from John Canterbury and wife, Nancy. The land had been granted to John Maddy and was adjacent Andrew Beirne, Isaac Scarbrow, George Wykle, and William Campbell.[201] John and Elender [*sic*] Scarborough conveyed 150 acres to Richard Williams of Greenbrier County on 17 June 1806. This tract was on Back Creek, adjoining lands of Bradley Dalton, Isaac Scarborough, Bradley Meredith, and William Campbell.[202] On 18 August 1807 Isaac Scarborough and wife, Mary, conveyed 45 acres to John Scarborough. The tract was part of Isaac's 200-acre survey.[203]

On 16 February 1808 John and Eleanor Scarborough conveyed 45 acres to Richard Neele. This parcel was part of a survey for 200 acres made to Isaac Scarborough. Ellinor and John also deeded 60 acres to Richard, part of a 116-acre survey for John Scarborough. Only Eleanor signed with a mark.[204]

In 1811 John W. Scarbrough had surveyed 170 acres on Toney's Fork of the Coal River in what was then Giles County, Virginia.[205] In 1850 this area would become part of Raleigh County, (West) Virginia. On 8 May 1815 John W. Scarborough had surveyed 60 acres on Horse Creek and the Coal River.[206]

On 26 May 1836 John W. Scarbrough and wife, Nelly, sold land on Toney's Fork of the Coal River to Robert Scarbrough, Jr.[207]

John W. Scarbrough was considered to be of Logan County on 6 September 1836 when he bought 1,700 acres on Buffalo Ridge. It was bordered by land of Joseph Harper.[208] Some of the land in Logan County was later incorporated into Raleigh County.

On 18 July 1839 John Scarborough of Fayette County, (West) Virginia, conveyed 20 acres to Henry N. Payne of Monroe County. This parcel was on the waters of Back Creek and adjoined lands of Henry Payne and said John Scarborough. It was part of the 116-acre patent he acquired in 1805 in Monroe. No wife signed with him.[209]

In 1845 there were three election precincts in what is now Raleigh County, (West) Virginia, one of them at Daniel Lacy's on the Coal River. The commissioners were Joseph Harper, Lemuel Jarrell, John W. Scarbrough, John Stover, and Lewis Williams.[210]

In 1850 Wilson Abbott, the Raleigh County assessor, entered in his records that John W. Scarbrough owned 2,100 acres of land.[211]

As noted above, several members of Robert Scarborough's family had become Methodists. Jim Wood, a descendant of John W. Scarbrough, notes in his book, *Raleigh County, West Virginia*, that in 1854 John W. Scarbrough donated two acres in Raleigh County for the building of a Methodist Episcopal Church, North. The lot was at the mouth of Horse Creek in the Clear Fork District. The trustees were William Johnson, James Kincaid, John Kincaid, Robin Scarbrough, and John Wriston. The building was also to be used as a day school. Because of the slavery issue the Methodist Church in Raleigh County split into a northern and southern faction in 1858.[212]

John married **Eleanor HARPER**, daughter of John HARPER and Elizabeth, on 20 May 1805 in Monroe County, (West) Virginia. Sureties for the marriage bond of John and Eleanor were John Harper and Hamilton Harper.[213] Eleanor was a sister of Joseph Harper.[214]

John and Eleanor had the following children:

+   85   i.   **John Bryant[9] SCARBOROUGH** was born May 1807 and died 1 March 1886.

+   86   ii.   **Robert Webb SCARBOROUGH**

58.   **Robert[8] SCARBOROUGH**, "Robin," (Isaac[7], Robert[6], John[5], John[4], John[3], William[2], Isaac[1]) was born 1782.[215]

On 14 September 1819 Isaac Scarber of Ohio deeded 77 1/2 acres to Robert Scarber of Monroe County. The deed was delivered to Robert Scarborough on 17 March 1822.[216] On 18 March 1822 Robert and Polly signed a deed of trust to Wm. Vols, John Clarke, and George Beirne. A debt was owed on the land, and Robert was living on it. By 18 March 1833 he had to pay George Beirne $90 plus interest.[217] On 23 November 1824 Hugh Caperton and Henry Alexander, Justices of the Peace, and Robert Scarbro and wife, Mary, made a deed to Joseph Baker.[218]

In 1850 Robert Scarbrough was named among owners of land on Toney's Fork in Raleigh County, (West) Virginia, formed from Fayette County in 1850.[219] On 20 June 1863 West Virginia separated from Virginia and became a part of the Union (the American Civil War was between 1861 and 1865).

The federal census of 1850 for Fayette County, Virginia, includes Robert Scarber, 68. He was a farmer, and Mary was 61. Living in their home (household no. 476) were two females, MacEnda, 21; and Salina, 18. Household no. 475 was John W. Scarber, 25, and wife, Lucy, 24; Isabinda, 4, Deresa, 2., and Jas. D. Scarber, 4 mos.[220]

Robert married **Mary FOLDEN**, "Polly," daughter of James FOLDEN, in 1808 in Bedford County, Virginia. Mary was born 1789. James Foldin was surety for the marriage bond.[221]

Robert and Mary had the following children:

+ 87 i. **Isaac[9] SCARBOROUGH** was born 1813.
+ 88 ii. **James SCARBOROUGH** was born 1816.
+ 89 iii. **Appa SCARBOROUGH** was born 1822.
+ 90 iv. **John Wesley SCARBOROUGH** was born 1825.
    91 v. **MacEnda SCARBOROUGH** was born 1829.
    92 vi. **Salina SCARBOROUGH** was born 1832.
+ 93 vii. **Mary SCARBOROUGH**

59. **Zachariah[8] SCARBERRY** (Isaac[7], Robert[6], John[5], John[4], John[3], William[2], Isaac[1]) was born 1785 in Virginia. He died 1856 in Ohio.

Much of the information on Zachariah and Celia's descendants that is not documented was passed on by Clarence H. Young, whose mother was Nancy Rachel Scarberry. Clarence was reared in the home of Isaac and Susan (Doughty) Scarberry, and they and other relatives enjoyed telling stories about their ancestors.

In 1815 Wilson Cary Nicholas, Esq., Governor of the Commonwealth of Virginia, granted Zachariah Scarbrough 26 acres on the Clear Fork of the Coal River (Giles County, Virginia, at the time, later Raleigh County, West Virginia). The survey had been made 2 January 1812, using Treasury Warrant No. 4,599, dated 8 December 1809. One of the pointers was the bank of the river.[222]

Zacheriah Scarberry (written *Scarbriee*) was present in Lawrence County, Ohio, in 1818 when the tax lists were made. He was also present for the 1820 federal census and the tax lists of 1821.[223]

Tax duplicates for Windsor Township, Lawrence County, Ohio, show Zachariah Scarborough living there in 1826. He owned 1 horse and 2 neat cattle.[224]

The Zephaniah Scarbery who appears on the 1830 census for Windsor Township is surely Zachariah. At that time his household had 1 male child under 5, 1 male 10-15, 3 males 15-20, and one male 40-50 (probably Zachariah). Females included one 30-40 (probably Celia), 1 under 5, 1 age 5-10, 1 age 10-15. Zachariah Scarbery's immediate neighbors were Daniel Nance and Isaac Sowards.[225]

In April 1835 Seymore Brunson and wife, Harriet, of Windsor Township, Lawrence County, Ohio, sold 10 acres to Zachariah Scarburry of same. The parcel began at the northeast corner of the northeast half of the south half of Section 11, Township 2 (Windsor), Range 16. The parcel abutted lands of James McMakhan and John T. Henderson and the land on which sat Zachariah's home. Wits: Thos. and Francis Machin(?).[226]

Zachariah and Sealey Scarbury (spelled *Scarborough* within the document) sold 10 acres of a larger tract to John Burcham, Jr., on 16 February 1836. This tract was in Section 11, Township 2 (Windsor), Range 16. Wits: Isaac Scarbury and Joseph Scarbury. All these people signed with an *X*.[227] During that time period often only one child in a family was sent to school, and Zachariah and Celia sent son Noah.

The U.S. census of 1850 shows Zachariah Scarber [sic] living in Guyan Township, Gallia County, Ohio. He was a 65-year-old farmer, and his wife, Celia, was 50, both born in Virginia. Living with them were John Scarber 24, born in Ohio; and George, age 4, and James 2.[228] Celia was married in 1805, so she was certainly older than 50.

Zachariah's daughter Rachel reported to census takers in 1900 that she was born in Ohio, her father in West Virginia, and her mother in Virginia. At the time she was living with daughter Phebe and her husband, Elijah Williams, in Jackson County, West Virginia. Living next to Zachariah Scarber in 1850 were John and Lucinda Williams and children Elijah, 30; Elizabeth, John L., Sarah, Ellen, William, Letha, James, and Ann Williams. The father, John, 54, was born in Pennsylvania.[229]

Zachariah married **Celia HARPER**, on 28 December 1805 in Kanawha County, (West) Virginia.[230]

In 1811 John Harper claimed 32 acres on the Coal River in what is now West Virginia; it was Giles County, Virginia, at the time. The parcel abutted lands of Isaac Chapman and Joseph Harper.[231] In 1815 Joseph Harper patented 54 acres on the Dry Fork of the Clear Fork of the Coal River.[232]

Celia's parents are unproven, but she was obviously one of the Harpers who moved to the Coal River and lived near the Scarboroughs. The Coal River joins the Kanawha River at St. Albans, west of Charleston.

Nancy Harper and John Stover signed marriage bond on 25 February 1816. Jacob Stover and John Harper signed as surety/witness.[233]

Joseph Harper born 16 September 1791, married Fanny Stover, daughter of Jacob Stover.[234] Jacob Stover and Sallie McGhee had married on 16 March 1788 in Franklin County, Virginia. Holdin McGhee was surety.[235]

Between 1848 and 1850 Joseph Harper was sheriff of Fayette County (Raleigh County was taken from Fayette in 1850). Joseph and Fanny's son Henry Harrison Harper (1851-1923) founded the Harper Land Company. He owned a 500-acre farm, sawmills at Paint Creek and Harper, and a grist mill. He owned five stores. The location of four of them are known: at Harper, at Beckley, at Sand Lick, and Clear Creek. Henry loved to read. His favorite books were the *Bible*, *The West Virginia Code*, and *Dr. Pierce's Medical Discovery*. He was an adept public speaker and acted as his own attorney in the Raleigh County courts. He constructed the Methodist Church at Harper and maintained it at his own expense. Henry had 10 children, one born to his first wife, Jane Kincaid, who died four years after their marriage, and the others to his second wife, Ella Davis.[236]

Nancy Harper, daughter of John, was born in 1800. She was the great-great-grandmother of James Lee Wood Jr., author of *Raleigh County, West Virginia*. Jim's mother, Ressie Snuffer Wood, descended from the Harpers, Stovers, and Scarbroughs of early Raleigh County. Jim served as the managing editor of the *Beckley Post-Herald* and was the editor of *The Raleigh Register*.

While scanning the names of the children of Zachariah and Celia, listed below, note that two of the names, *Nancy* and *Joseph*, were used by the Harpers.

They had the following children:

	94	i.	**Elizabeth**[9] **SCARBERRY** married **Samuel MANNON** on 17 December 1826 in Lawrence County, Ohio.[237]
	95	ii.	**Mary "Polly" SCARBERRY** died when a child.
+	96	iii.	**Isaac SCARBERRY** was born 1808 and died 1879.
+	97	iv.	**John SCARBERRY** was born 1810 and died 15 July 1891.
+	98	v.	**Joseph SCARBERRY** was born 1815.
+	99	vi.	**Rachel SCARBERRY** was born April 1816 and died 1902.
+	100	vii.	**Noah Harper SCARBERRY** was born 13 February 1818 and died 1898.
+	101	viii.	**Nancy SCARBERRY** was born 1817 and died 1879.
+	102	ix.	**Celia SCARBERRY** was born 1827.
	103	x.	**Zachariah SCARBERRY** married **Julia HASKINS**.
	104	xi.	**Lucinda SCARBERRY** married **Joel Salem SARTEN** on 4 February 1848 in Gallia County, Ohio.[238]
	105	xii.	**Sally SCARBERRY** married **Joel BABCOCK** in 1849 in Gallia County, Ohio.[239]

60. **Mary**[8] **"Polly" SCARBOROUGH** (Isaac[7], Robert[6], John[5], John[4], John[3], William[2], Isaac[1]) died 21 June 1843. Mary married **Elijah STOVER**. Elijah died 8 October 1824.[240]

A list for tax purposes was taken on the Sycamore Fork and Clear Fork of the Coal River on 8 April 1815. Following Reason Riston were Thomas Riggin, John Scarbrough, Zachariah Scarbrough, Elijah Stover, Jacob Stover, and David Shumate.[241]

They had the following child:

106   i. **Jubel⁹ STOVER** was born 11 October 1817 in Lawrence County, Ohio. Jubel married **Mary J. DOUGHTY**, daughter of John DOUGHTY and Phoebe COMPTON, on 22 March 1842 in Gallia County, Ohio. Mary was born 22 July 1826 in Elizabeth, Pennsylvania.[242]

Descendants can be found in the DOUGHTY Section.

62. **Rachel⁸ SCARBOROUGH** (Isaac⁷, Robert⁶, John⁵, John⁴, John³, William², Isaac¹) was born 1776. She died 7 February 1872.

Rachel's husband must have died by 1850, for the census for that year shows Rachel Wriston living on White Oak Fork., the implication being that she was head of household. Also on White Oak Fork was Isaac Wriston. When Personal Property Taxes were taken for 1861, Rachael Wriston, 85, was named as a midwife.[243]

Rachel married **Reason RISTON** on 21 May 1805 in Monroe County, West Virginia. The Rev. John Wiseman married Reason and Rachel, and Michael Bickett secured the bond.[244]

According to an article by Ralph Honaker in *History of Fayette County, West Virginia 1993*, Reason Wriston, Sr., was responsible for the naming of Skitters Creek (also called Skeeters Creek). Reason wore moccasins as he hunted for ginseng, and while searching along this creek, he fell several times on the slick rocks in its bed. He thought that Skeeters Creek would be a good name for it. U.S. Interstate 64/77 passes over this creek.

Reason and Rachel had the following children:

107   i. **Rebecca⁹ RISTON**.

+ 108   ii. **Robert RISTON** was born 1812.

109   iii. **Isaac RISTON** was born 1807.

Isaac was living on the White Oak Fork (of the Coal River) by 1850. The 1880 U.S. census for Clear Fork, Raleigh County, West Virginia, shows Isaac Wriston as a 73-year-old farmer, born in West Virginia. His father was born in Maryland, and his mother in Virginia. His wife, Elizabeth, was 71. Paulina Stover was a 30-year old woman working for them. Isaac Armstrong, a grandson, 12 years old, was living with them.[245]

Isaac married **Elizabeth**, born 1809.

+ 110   iv. **Zachariah RISTON** was born 1813.

111   v. **Reason RISTON**.

Ninth Generation

85. **John Bryant⁹ SCARBOROUGH** (John Ward⁸, Isaac⁷, Robert⁶, John⁵, John⁴, John³, William², Isaac¹) was born May 1807 in Monroe County, West Virginia. He died 1 March 1886 in Rock Creek, West Virginia.

The 1850 census for Fayette County, (West) Virginia, includes John B. Scarber [*sic*], 41, and wife, Lucy, 35. Also in their household were Elizabeth, 16; Doras, 14; John M., 12; Elam, 10; Emezella, 7; Jane, 6; Ellen, 3; and Rhoda, 1 month. John's household was no. 478; no. 477 was that of Isaac Williams; 476 was Robert Scarber; 475, John W.

Scarber; 474, James Scarber; 473, Robert Riston; 472, Isaac Scarber.[246]

Information on John Bryant Scarborough and family was supplied by Ronnie Scarbro of Rock Creek, West Virginia. Ronnie, born in 1948, at Dry Creek, West Virginia, is a son of Speed SCARBRO, born 1 October 1910, and Evelyn ASH, born 26 September 1923. Speed was a son of Thomas Byron SCARBRO, born 27 July 1883 and Florence Belle CANTLEY born 12 August 1884. Thomas was a son of Elam SCARBRO, born 24 May 1840, Fayette County, West Virginia, and Martha MASSEY, born 10 February 1847. Elam was a son of John Bryant SCARBROUGH and Lucrezia "Lucy" DICKENS, born January 1814.

John married **Lucy DICKENS,** who was born January 1814.

They had the following children:

    112   i.   **Elizabeth**[10] **SCARBOROUGH** was born 1834.

    113   ii.   **Doras SCARBOROUGH** was born 1836.

    114   iii.   **John M. SCARBOROUGH** was born 1838 in Fayette County, (West) Virginia. John married **Sarah ALIFF** on 19 June 1869 in Raleigh County, West Virginia. Sarah was born 1848 in Roanoke County, Virginia. At the time of the marriage, John was 25 and Sarah, 21.

    115   iv.   **Elam SCARBOROUGH**, born 1840, married **Martha MASSEY**.

    116   v.   **Emezella SCARBOROUGH** was born 1843.

    117   vi.   **Jane SCARBOROUGH** was born 1844.

    118   vii.   **Ellen SCARBOROUGH** was born 1847.

    119   viii.   **Rhoda SCARBOROUGH** was born 1850.

86.   **Robert Webb**[9] **SCARBOROUGH** (John Ward[8], Isaac[7], Robert[6], John[5], John[4], John[3], William[2], Isaac[1]).

Robert married **Mary SCARBOROUGH,** daughter of Robert "Robin" SCARBOROUGH and Mary "Polly" FOLDEN. This information is furnished by Dwayne Scarberry.

Robert and Mary had the following children:

+   120   i.   **Morrison S.**[10] **SCARBOROUGH** was born May 1841.

+   121   ii.   **Gilbert SCARBOROUGH** was born 1845.

87.   **Isaac**[9] **SCARBOROUGH** (Robert "Robin,"[8] Isaac[7], Robert[6], John[5], John[4], John[3], William[2], Isaac[1]) was born 1813.

The 1850 U.S. census for Fayette County, (West) Virginia, shows Isaac, 37, to have been a farmer. Wife, Rebecca, was 35. Also in the household (no. 472) were Mary, 13; Noah, 11; Rachel, 9; Silas, 7; Nancy, 5; and Martha, 11 months.[247]

Isaac married **Rebecca RISTON** on 29 September 1835 in Fayette County, West Virginia.[248] Rebecca was born 1815.

They had the following children:

    122   i.   **Mary**[10] **SCARBOROUGH** was born 1837.

    123   ii.   **Noah SCARBOROUGH** was born 1839.

    124   iii.   **Rachel SCARBOROUGH** was born 1841.

    125   iv.   **Silas SCARBOROUGH** was born 1843.

    126   v.   **Nancy SCARBOROUGH** was born 1845.

127 vi. **Martha SCARBOROUGH** was born about 1850.

88. **James[9] SCARBOROUGH** (Robert "Robin"[8], Isaac[7], Robert[6], John[5], John[4], John[3], William[2], Isaac[1]) was born 1816.

The 1850 U.S. census for Fayette County, (West) Virginia, shows James Scarber [sic] as a 34-year-old farmer. In his household (no. 474) were Jane, 30; E.E., 12; Jno. W., 10; Miram, 8; Malinda, 8.[249]

James married **Jane SCARBOROUGH** on 3 April 1835. Jane was born 1820.[250]

The marriage record shows Jane's last name as *Scarbrough*, but according to an article entitled "The Scarbrough Settlement," by Ralph Honaker (*History of Fayette County, West Virginia, 1993*), her name was Sarah "Jane" **BALL**. She and James lived on Paint Creek opposite Bishop Fork.[251]

James and Jane had the following children:

128 i. **E. E.[10] SCARBOROUGH** was born 1838.

129 ii. **John W. SCARBOROUGH** was born 1840.

130 iii. **Miram SCARBOROUGH** was born 1842.

131 iv. **Malinda SCARBOROUGH** was born 1842.

89. **Appa[9] SCARBOROUGH** (Robert "Robin"[8], Isaac[7], Robert[6], John[5], John[4], John[3], William[2], Isaac[1]) was born 1822.

Appa married **Isaac WILLIAMS**. Isaac was born 1814.

The 1850 census for Fayette County, (West) Virginia, reveals that Isaac Williams was a 36-year-old farmer at that time. Appa was 28. Also in their household (no. 477) were P., 7; Loyd, 4; and Letha, 1.[252]

They had the following children and probably others:

132 i. **P.[10] WILLIAMS** was born 1843.

133 ii. **Loyd WILLIAMS** was born 1846.

134 iii. **Letha WILLIAMS** was born 1849.

90. **John Wesley[9] SCARBOROUGH** (Robert "Robin"[8], Isaac[7], Robert[6], John[5], John[4], John[3], William[2], Isaac[1]) was born 1825.

When the 1850 census was taken for Fayette County, (West) Virginia, John W. Scarber [sic], was 25, a farmer. In his household (no. 475) were Lucy, 24; Isabinda, 4; Deresa, 2., and Jas. D., 4 months.[253]

John married (1) **Lucy,** born 1826.

They had the following children:

135 i. **Isabinda[10] SCARBOROUGH** was born 1846.

136 ii. **Deresa SCARBOROUGH** was born 1848.

137 iii. **James D. SCARBOROUGH** was born about 1850.

John married (2) **Betsey KINCAID** on 6 December 1874. He was 50 and she was 40. He was a son of Robt. and Polly.[254]

93. **Mary[9] SCARBOROUGH** (Robert "Robin"[8], Isaac[7], Robert[6], John[5], John[4], John[3], William[2], Isaac[1]).

Mary married **Robert Webb SCARBOROUGH**, on 19 February 1835.[255] He was a son of John Ward SCARBOROUGH and

The Scarberrys (Scarboroughs), Doughtys, Lewises, and Paynes of Lawrence County, Ohio

Eleanor HARPER. *See above.*

96. **Isaac[9] SCARBERRY** (Zachariah[8] SCARBERRY, Isaac[7], Robert[6], John[5], John[4], John[3], William[2], Isaac[1]) was born 1808 in West Virginia. He died 28 December 1895.

When Isaac wanted to claim title for land he had bought in Ohio, he had to walk the 80 miles to Chillicothe to get it. On 3 August 1840, David and Rebecca Robertson sold 40 acres in Section 27, Range 15, Township 2 to Isaac. Wits: Nathaniel Burcham and Hudson Brice Robertson.[256] On 31 August 1853, George W. and Susan Bowen sold to Isaac Scarbury 80 acres in Section 33, Township 2, Range 15. Wits: S. M. Cown and D. Reese.[257]

Isaac and his family lived near the Pleasant Ridge Church in Lawrence County, Ohio. The 1850 Rome Township census shows Isaac as 42. Polly was 38, both of them born in Virginia. In their household were Francis M., 12; Joseph, 9; and James, 5, were all born in Ohio.[258]

When the 1860 census was taken for Rome Township, Isaac was 50, and Mary (Polly) 47. Living with them were Joseph, 17; James, 15; George, 8; Elizabeth, 5; and Chas., 3.[259]

The 1870 census for Rome Township includes Isaac's family; his wife, Mary, was 65 and born in Kentucky; the rest of the household were George, 16; Mary, 15; and Charles, 13.[260]

Isaac married (1) **Polly MCKINSEY** on 18 June 1832 in Lawrence County, Ohio.[261] Polly was born 1805 in Kentucky.

They had the following children:

+ 138 i. **Elizabeth[10] SCARBERRY**, "Betsy," was born 2 November 1832 and died 2 December 1914.

+ 139 ii. **Francis Marion SCARBERRY** was born 6 June 1837 and died 17 February 1916.

+ 140 iii. **Joseph SCARBERRY** was born 1841 and died 30 July 1921.

+ 141 iv. **James SCARBERRY** was born April 1845 and died 3 October 1905.

  142 v. **George SCARBERRY** was born 1852.

  143 vi. **Elizabeth SCARBERRY**, "Mary," was born 1855.

  One of Isaac and Polly's daughters was known to have married a Henderson. The 1860 census lists her as Eliz. M. The 1930 census for Rome Township, Lawrence County, Ohio, includes James Henderson, age 77. He had wife, Mary, 73 years old.[262]

  Elizabeth married **James HENDERSON**.

+ 144 vii. **Charles SCARBERRY** was born July 1856 and died 1932.

Isaac also married (2) **Zilda**, born 1840. This marriage is revealed by the 1880 census for Rome Township. It includes Isaac Scarberry, 65, and wife, Zilda, 40, both born in Virginia.[263]

97. **John[9] SCARBERRY** (Zachariah[8] SCARBERRY, Isaac[7], Robert[6], John[5], John[4], John[3], William[2], Isaac[1]) was born 1810 in Virginia. He died 15 July 1891 in Corn, West Virginia.

The 1850 census for Guyan Township, Gallia County, Ohio, shows John and Malinda Scarbery living in dwelling no. 161. John's parents, Zachariah and Celia Scarber [*sic*] were in dwelling 155. John was 40 and Malinda was 36. In their household were Gordon Scarbery, 18; Joseph, 14; Noah, 11; Oscar, 10; Alexander, 8; William, 6; Malinda, 4; Catherine, 2, and John, 1. (Some of the handwriting was hard to decipher.)[264]

Information on the date and place of death of John and Malinda came from Dwayne J. Scarberry, one of their descendants. Dwayne has also supplied the birth dates of John and Malinda's children and marriage information for Rosanna. He is compiling an extensive history of the Scarberrys.

The 1880 U.S. census for Hannon District, Mason County, West Virginia, includes John Scarberry, 68, and wife, Malinda, 67, both her parents having been born in North Carolina. John and Malinda were on page 284D and

Elemonder Scarberry, 38, born in Ohio, and his family were listed just before them.[265]

John married **Malinda HIX** on 21 August 1834 in Lawrence County, Ohio. They were married by John Pinkerman, J. P.[266] Malinda died 11 April 1887 in Corn, West Virginia.

They had the following children:

    145   i.   **Gordon[10] SCARBERRY** was born about 1832 in Ohio.

    146   ii.   **Joseph SCARBERRY** was born about 1833 in Ohio. Joseph married **Easter SCARBERRY** on 20 August 1857 in Lawrence County, Ohio. Nathaniel Burcham, J.P. married this couple.[267]

    147   iii.   **Noah SCARBERRY** was born 1838 in Ohio. He died 22 July 1899 in Cabell County, West Virginia. The death record says that he was 61 years old at his death.[268]

    148   iv.   **Oscar SCARBERRY** was born 1840 in Guyan Township, Gallia County, Ohio. He died 24 August 1864 in Andersonville Prison in Georgia during the Civil War.

+   149   v.   **Elemender SCARBERRY** was born 5 November 1841 and died 1 September 1921.

    150   vi.   **William SCARBERRY** was born 1844.

    151   vii.   **Malinda SCARBERRY** was born 1846.

    152   viii.   **California SCARBERRY** was born about 1848.

    153   ix.   **John R. SCARBERRY** was born 1849.

    154   x.   **George SCARBERRY** was born about 1851.

    155   xi.   **Mary F. SCARBERRY** was born about 1851.

    156   xii.   **Alexander SCARBERRY** was born 1852.

    157   xiii.   **Albert SCARBERRY** was born about 1855.

    158   xiv.   **James F. SCARBERRY** was born about 1858.

    159   xv.   **Rosanna SCARBERRY** was born about 1860 in Guyan Township, Gallia County, Ohio. Rosanna married **Augustus GALLOWAY** on 28 November 1877 in Gallia County, Ohio.

98.   **Joseph[9] SCARBERRY** (Zachariah[8] SCARBERRY, Isaac[7], Robert[6], John[5], John[4], John[3], William[2], Isaac[1]) was born 1817 in Virginia.

    The 1850 census shows Joseph living in Rome Township, 35 years old, born in Virginia. His wife, Elizabeth, was 33 and born in Kentucky. Living in the household were Zachariah, 12; Sarah C., 11; Isaac, 8; John 7; Rachel A., 5; Joseph M., 4; Elizabeth, 2; and Noah W., 3 months.[269]

    Living with Joseph and Elizabeth, both 68, in 1880 in Rome Township were sons Columbus, 20; and William, 18. Next door was Joseph's brother Noah Scarberry, 37, and wife Hannah 31, and children.[270] Elizabeth was said to have been 33 in 1850. If that was the case, she would have been born in 1817 and 45 when son William was born, so he was probably her last child. George and the last four children named below died young, and dates of birth are not available. Their names are included thanks to an article by Dan and Ruth Scarberry in *Gallia County, Ohio: People in History to 1980*. They also gave the name of John J. Scarberry's wife and the wife of Christopher Columbus Scarberry.[271]

Joseph married **Elizabeth SOWARDS** on 12 May 1836 in Lawrence County, Ohio.[272] Elizabeth was born 1817 in Kentucky.

They had the following children:

    160   i.   **George V.[10] SCARBERRY** died at the age of 10.

    161   ii.   **Zachariah SCARBERRY** was born 1838 in Ohio. He died October 1864 at Cedar Creek, Virginia.

According to Clarence H. Young, Zachariah was killed at the Battle of Cedar Creek in the Shenandoah Valley of Virginia. It was a critical battle. General Sheridan of the Union Army repulsed General Jubal Early's army to the extent that it never again could threaten Washington, D.C. [273]

A pension claim was made on 5 August 1879 on behalf of Elizabeth, mother of Zachariah Scarbury. He had served in K2 Ohio Infantry.[274]

    162   iii.   **Sarah C. SCARBERRY** was born 1839. Sarah married **Christopher C. BERRIDGE** on 15 June 1862.[275]

    163   iv.   **Isaac SCARBERRY** was born 1842 and died 1852.

    164   v.   **John J. SCARBERRY** was born 1843. John married **Mary Ann ENOCH**.

The auditor's military roll for 1865 for Rome Township, Lawrence County, Ohio, includes John Scarbury, age 22. In 1863-1864 he was listed as John H. Scarberry, K2-Ohio Cav.[276]

John J. Scarberry applied for a pension on 2 July 1888 for serving in the Ohio Cavalry during the Civil War.[277]

    165   vi.   **Rachel A. SCARBERRY** was born 1845. Rachel married **Joshua LEWIS** on 5 January 1867.[278]

    166   vii.   **Joseph M. SCARBERRY** was born 1846. Joseph died from measles as a Civil War soldier.

    167   viii.   **Elizabeth SCARBERRY** was born 1848. Elizabeth married **William SITES** on 18 November 1869 in Lawrence County, Ohio.[279]

+   168   ix.   **Noah Webster SCARBERRY** was born 1843.

    169   x.   **Christopher Columbus SCARBERRY** was born 1860. He married **Emma BLAKE**.

    170   xi.   **William Preston SCARBERRY** was born 1862. William married **Maggie DILLON** on 14 September 1883.[280]

    171   xii.   **Margaret SCARBERRY died** when one year old.

    172   xiii.   **Archie SCARBERRY** died at 12 years old.

    173   xiv.   **Sylvester SCARBERRY** died at 6 months.

    174   xv.   **Ellen SCARBERRY** died at the age of 3.

99.   **Rachel^9 SCARBERRY** (Zachariah^8 SCARBERRY, Isaac^7, Robert^6, John^5, John^4, John^3, William^2, Isaac^1) was born April 1816 in Lawrence County, Ohio. She died 1902.

Rachel's husband, Wesley Doughty, had served in the Civil War, and her widow's pension was dropped 16 October 1902 because of death.[281] At the time of the 1900 census for Washington District, Jackson County, West Virginia, Rachel was living with daughter Phebe and her husband, Elijah Williams.[282] Rachel and Isaac are buried at Cleek-Poling Cemetery, Kentuck, Jackson County, West Virginia (burial information furnished by Dwayne Scarberry).

Rachel married **Isaac Wesley DOUGHTY,** "Wesley," on 19 January 1853 in Gallia County, Ohio. Wesley was born 1828 in Mercer, Pennsylvania. He died 17 July 1886 in Jackson County, West Virginia.[283] He was a son of John DOUGHTY and Phoebe COMPTON.[284]

Isaac grew up at Platform in Lawrence County, Ohio. His mother died in 1836, and his father remarried. When Isaac's father married Mary WOOD in 1837,[285] most of the children moved out, but Isaac stayed, for he could get along with his step-mother.

Several members of the Doughty family moved to West Virginia around 1870, to live in Jackson and Roane Counties. The 1880 census for the Washington District of Jackson County, West Virginia, includes Isaac W. Doughty, 54, born in Pennsylvania, both parents born in Pennsylvania. Wife, Rachel, was 53, both her parents born in West Virginia. They had four daughters: Hester A. was 25; Celia J., 21; Elizabeth S., 18; Phoebe A., 15.[286]

Rachel Scarberry, Isaac's second wife, was at least 12 years his senior, so the age entered for her in the 1880 census records is wrong. She and Isaac moved around a lot, spending a year in Pike County, Ohio, and going on to Texas for a time. But they did not buy land in Texas. While there, Isaac was a medicine man to the Indians.

Before marrying Rachel, Isaac had married **Mary BENNER** (on 14 March 1850 in Gallia County, Ohio).[287] According to their divorce papers of 5 November 1852, he had abandoned her by 20 November 1851 and moved in with Rachel Scarberry. Mary got full custody of their son, **William DOUGHTY**.

Isaac volunteered for the Civil War on 19 August 1864. One out of three in the Union Army died, but hopes of surviving and getting a pension were a big draw. His enlistment papers show that he was born in Mercer, Pennsylvania, and that he was a 36-year-old farmer from Guyan, Ohio. His term was for one year, "unless sooner discharged." He was described as five foot six inches, with a fair complexion, blue eyes, and light hair. He was officially mustered on 16 September 1864, at Gallipolis, Ohio, and placed in Company B, 183rd (later papers say 173rd) Regiment of Ohio Infantry Volunteers.

His service did not last long, for it was noted in his records that he had been sick in the U.S.H., Nashville, Tennessee, since 10 December 1864. He was discharged on 31 May 1865 at Johnsonville, Tennessee, with a certificate of disability, and his home address was Mercerville, Gallia County, Ohio.[288] Part of his trek home was by boat on the Ohio River, and he landed at Crown City, Ohio, and began walking home. To relieve the burden of carrying his bag up hills, he tossed it forward and caught it. A neighbor noticed how sick he was and loaned him a horse. Rachel saw him coming and in her hurry to meet him, made a daring and successful leap over Sugar Creek.

During that time Isaac and Rachel lived over a hill near Crown City, and when President Lincoln was assassinated, Rachel could hear boats on the Ohio River blowing their whistles in his honor.

Although Isaac lived 20 years after his discharge, life was not easy for him. The severe case of measles he had contracted in the army left him with chronic diarrhea and chronic bronchitis and unable to do hard physical labor. His declaration for an invalid pension was dated 20 September 1865 and witnessed by James M. Garlick and David F. Hoover, both of Gallia County, the latter having been his captain. Isaac's mark for this document was an *O*, but he signed an affidavit made when he was 58 years old with an *X*. In the latter claim, asking for further compensation, he was complaining of piles and kidney trouble. At that time his address was Kentuck, Jackson County, West Virginia. Witnesses were M. E. Scarbery and John W. Doughty. (Kentuck is south of Ripley and just east of U.S. 77, an interstate that connects Charleston with Parkersburg.) In a document written on 22 June 1875 Noah Hanes and H. H. Sanders testified that Isaac had not prolonged his condition through intemperance or other bad habits[289].

Susan, daughter of Rachel and Isaac Doughty, had been born in 1862, and she had been married about five years before her father died. She and her husband, Isaac Scarberry, lived on the Ohio side of the Ohio River. They had a visit from Susan's father early in the summer before he died. Isaac had taken a ferry across the Ohio River and rented a horse at one of the stables found at river crossings. The visit must have been sad, for his bad health was obvious. After he left the Scarberry farm, Susan began milking a cow, and her sister Hester noticed that she was crying. When Hester asked her what was the matter, Susan replied that she wasn't going to see her daddy anymore. And she was right, for he died not long afterward.

Rachel applied for a widow's pension on 18 September 1886. To support her claim, Dr. J. C. Casto of Jackson, West Virginia, had to sign an affidavit describing Isaac's illnesses over the years. He said he had been treating him for kidney trouble and tended him about 48 hours before he died. The cause of death was chronic bronchitis.[290]

A certified copy of Isaac and Rachel's marriage record was included in her widow's pension file.

Wesley and Rachel had the following children:

    175   i. **George[10] SCARBERRY** was born 1841. He died 1869. His father is uncertain.

        George died at age 28 from tuberculosis. In 1857 he was plowing and suffered a pain in his ribs and had to continue using only one hand. He weighed less than a 100 pounds by the time he died.

+   176   ii. **Zachariah DOUGHTY** was born October 1850 and died 24 December 1934.

+   177   iii. **Hester A. DOUGHTY** was born January 1854 and died 1938.

+   178   iv. **John Wesley DOUGHTY** was born 28 February 1856 and died November 1934.

+	179	v.	**Celia Jane DOUGHTY** was born 1858 and died 1930.
+	180	vi.	**Elizabeth Susan DOUGHTY**-was born 20 May 1862 and died 17 February 1950.
+	181	vii.	**Phoebe A. DOUGHTY** was born June 1864 and died 1944.

100. Noah Harper^9 SCARBERRY (Zachariah^8 SCARBERRY, Isaac^7, Robert^6, John^5, John^4, John^3, William^2, Isaac^1) was born 13 February 1818 and died 1898.

The trend during Noah's childhood was for one child in each family to be sent to school, and Noah was chosen, so he was literate.

The family-group worksheet of Kathy and Bob Lewis states that Noah's middle name was Harper, and they give his birth date and that of his wives and children. Kathy and Bob obtained these dates from Joseph Scarberry of Doylestown, Ohio, who sourced a Bible record.

Noah married (1) **Elizabeth SOWARDS** on 15 January 1837 in Lawrence County, Ohio.^{291}

Noah and Elizabeth had the following children:

182	i.	**Amanda Ann^{10} SCARBERRY** was born 11 June 1837 and died 1862.

Noah married (2) **Esther Ann Bates JOHNSON** on 4 August 1842 in Gallia County, Ohio.^{292} Esther was born 17 February 1818 and died 1897.

Noah and Esther had the following children:

183	ii.	**John SCARBERRY** was born 23 October 1842 and died 1887.
184	iii.	**Zachariah SCARBERRY** was born 25 November 1844 and died 12 December 1844.
185	iv.	**Mary SCARBERRY** was born 11 October 1845 and died 18 May 1924.
186	v.	**Catharine SCARBERRY** was born 18 June 1848 and died 23 March 1853. The West Virginia Death Register shows Catherine Scarberry, age 4, dying on 28 March 1853 in Braxton County, West Virginia, the county of her birth. Her mother was Ester and her father Noah E. Scarberry.^{293}
187	vi.	**Eliza Jane SCARBERRY** was born 1 January 1851 and died 18 June 1938.
188	vii.	**Albert E. SCARBERRY** was born 5 January 1854 died 8 August 1899.
189	viii.	**Charles Owen SCARBERRY** was born 28 March 1855 and died 27 December 1929.
190	ix.	**Virginia C. SCARBERRY** was born 31 December 1857 and died 18 November 1858.
191	x.	**Noah J. SCARBERRY** was born 25 September 1859 and died 22 January 1944.
192	xi.	**William P. SCARBERRY** was born 6 March 1862 and died 31 January 1929.

101. Nancy^9 SCARBERRY (Zachariah^8 SCARBERRY, Isaac^7, Robert^6, John^5, John^4, John^3, William^2, Isaac^1) was born about 1817 in Ohio. She died 1879.

Nancy Scarbery's age on the 1850 Mason Township census was 27, and she was born in Ohio. Living with her were Rachel Scarbery, 9; Polly, 7; James 2; and John, 2.^{294} The latter two must have been the twins known later as Tom and Bill, who were born in 1847. Their father was a Clark, and Bill referred to himself as a Clark most of the time.

The 1860 census for Rome Township shows Nancy with her married name, Brooks. Her age here is 44, making her born in 1816. Children living with Nancy in 1860 were Polly, 16; twins William and Thomas, 11; Isaac, 7; Luis, 5; and Milley, 1.^{295}

The Scarberrys (Scarboroughs), Doughtys, Lewises, and Paynes of Lawrence County, Ohio

Nancy lived a disreputable life style, having a series of children by different fathers, but her brothers helped her rear her children. According to family tradition, the fathers of Rachel and Polly were unknown, and they may not have been the same man; the father of the twins was a Clark, and Bill used the Clark name; Isaac's father was said to have been a Pinkerman; Milly's father was said to have been a Dornen; and Lewis was the son of his official father, Lewis Brooks. But it should be emphasized that other than fathers Clark and Brooks, the paternity rumors, to my knowledge, are unproven.

By 1870 Nancy had reverted to her maiden name. The 1870 Rome census shows her as a 53-year-old weaver. The names of her children and their professions were taken from this list: Rachel, 20, a spinner; Mary, 25, a house domestic; William, 22, a sawmill hand; Isaac 17, a farm laborer; Lewis 16, made staves; Melissa, 14, did house work. Also in the household were Nancy, 7, and Eliza, 5..[296] The two younger children must have been grandchildren. Tom, the twin of William, had died by this time in a sawmill accident. Nancy died of cancer of the jaw.

Nancy married **Lewis C. BROOKS** on 19 December 1855 in Gallia County, Ohio.[297]

By 1860 Lewis and Nancy had separated, or he had died, because she was head of household for the U.S. Census.

Nancy had the following children:

193   i.   **Rachel**[10] **SCARBERRY** was born 1841. She died 1913.

Rachel appeared on the 1870 census as 30 years old, living with her mother, and working at spinning. Rachel died of cancer.

Rachel married **George H. HOFFMAN** on 23 November 1876 in Lawrence County, Ohio.[298]

+   194   ii.   **Mary SCARBERRY,** "Polly," was born 1843.

195   iii.   **Tom CLARK** was born Apr 1847. He died 18 August 1872.

The twins, Tom and Bill, both fought in the Civil War, and their father was a Clark. Tom worked at a sawmill and died a few years after the war in a sawmill accident. Joseph Miller reported Tom's death as due to an explosion at a mill. In this instance his last name was recorded as "Scarberry," and it was stated that he was born and died in Rome Township.[299]

Tom must have been close to his brother Isaac, for Isaac called out Tom's name as he was dying.

196   iv.   **William CLARK** was born April 1847 in Ohio and died 1933.

The obituary for William Clark (from an unidentified newspaper) states that he was born in 1847 and enlisted to fight in the Civil War at age 16 and served through the end of the war. He was 85 at the time of his death, and he left a widow and a daughter. He was buried in the family cemetery (in reality a plot on his land at Proctorville).

On the 1870 Rome Township census, William's age was 22 and he was working as a sawmill hand.

The U.S. census for 1900, Rome Township, LaBelle Precinct, includes William Scarberry, born in April 1847, and wife, **Debby**, born in March 1842 in Tennessee.[300] Tradition says that the twins were the only out-of-wedlock children of Nancy Scarbery who used their father's last name. Apparently Bill wavered.

Debbie died in the 1900s. After preaching her funeral, the minister took her up to the forks of the road and just left her.

Bill then married **Ellie**, and she died in 1919.

+   197   v.   **Isaac Edward SCARBERRY** was born 9 August 1853 and died 4 September 1927.

198 vi. **Lewis BROOKS-** was born 1855. .

The Nancy Brooks household, as shown on the 1860 U.S. census for Rome Township, Lawrence County, Ohio, shows Lewis as 5 years old. In 1870 Lewis was 16 and his profession was making staves.

+ 199 vii. **Melissa SCARBERRY** was born 1860 and died 1932.

102. **Celia**[9] **SCARBERRY** (Zachariah[8] SCARBERRY, Isaac[7], Robert[6], John[5], John[4], John[3], William[2], Isaac[1]) was born 1827 in Ohio.

Celia never married, but a Sealy Scarbery appeared on the 1850 Mason Township census, 25 years old. Living with her were Jackson Scarbery and Mason(?) Scarbery, both 2. She was part of the household of William Haskins, 76, and wife Nancy, 70, both born in Virginia.[301] According to researcher Dwayne J. Scarberry, Andrew Jackson Scarberry was Celia's son, and his twin was Edwin Maxium. They had brother Thomas Jefferson.

She had the following children:

200 i. **Andrew Jackson**[10] **SCARBERRY** was born 2 Jul 1848.

201 ii. **Edward Maxium SCARBERRY** was born 2 Jul 1848.

202 iii. **Thomas Jefferson SCARBERRY** was born 26 May 1854.

108. **Robert**[9] **RISTON** (Rachel[8] SCARBOROUGH, Isaac[7], Robert[6], John[5], John[4], John[3], William[2], Isaac[1]) was born 1812.

Robert and family are found on the 1850 census for Fayette County, (West) Virginia. He was a 38-year-old farmer; Keziah was 30. In their household were James, 14; Isaac 11; Rachel, 9; Mary, 7; Virginia, 5; Malinda, 3; and Anderson, 1.[302]

Robert married **Keziah,** born 1820.

They had the following children:

203 i. **James**[10] **RISTON** was born 1836.

204 ii. **Isaac RISTON** was born 1839.

205 iii. **Rachel RISTON** was born 1841.

206 iv. **Mary RISTON** was born 1843.

207 v. **Virginia RISTON** was born 1845.

208 vi. **Malinda RISTON** was born 1847.

209 vii. **Anderson RISTON** was born 1849.

110. **Zachariah**[9] **RISTON** (Rachel[8] SCARBOROUGH, Isaac[7], Robert[6], John[5], John[4], John[3], William[2], Isaac[1]) was born 1813.

The 1850 census taken for Raleigh County (annotated) shows Rachel (Scarbrough) Wriston, 70, living in the home of Zachariah Wriston, 37, a farmer on the Clear Fork. Amanda, 35, apparently his wife, was part of the household. Children: William A, 14; Floyd, 12; James, 10, Robert, 7; Nancy, 2.[303] Note the name is spelled *Wriston*.

Zachariah married **Amanda,** born 1815.

They had the following children:

210 i. **William A.**[10] **RISTON** was born 1836.

211 ii. **Floyd RISTON** was born 1838.

212 iii. **James RISTON** was born 1840.

213 iv. **Robert RISTON** was born 1843.

214 v. **Nancy RISTON** was born 1848.

Tenth Generation

120. **Morrison S.**[10] **SCARBOROUGH** (Robert Webb[9], John Ward[8], Isaac[7], Robert[6], John[5], John[4], John[3], William[2], Isaac[1]) was born May 1841 in West Virginia.

The 1880 U.S. census for Washington District, Jackson County, West Virginia, shows M.S. Scarbrough as a 40-year-old farmer, both his parents born in Virginia. His wife, Minerva M., was 36, and both her parents were born in Virginia. Son Geo. W. was 15 and born in West Virginia, as was his brother Wm. L., 13.[304] Morrison and Minerva were listed near Uriah Hatcher, 40, and wife, Mary F., 40, and their children. Listed nearby was Isaac W. Doughty as head of household. Isaac' daughter Hester was 25 at the time, and Morrison would marry her in 1884.[305]

Morrison's last name was pronounced *Scarbro*.

Morrison married (1) **Minerva M. HATCHER**, daughter of Uriah HATCHER, on 15 April 1861 in Jackson County, West Virginia. Minerva was born 1844 in Kanawha County, West Virginia. The marriage record shows the name of parent/person attending as Uriah Hatcher.[306]

Morrison and Minerva had the following children:

215 i. **George W.**[11] **SCARBOROUGH** was born 1865 in West Virginia.

216 ii. **William L. SCARBOROUGH** was born 1867 in West Virginia.

Morrison married (2) **Hester A. DOUGHTY**, daughter of Isaac "Wesley" DOUGHTY and Rachel SCARBERRY, on 20 November 1884 in Jackson County, West Virginia. Hester was born January 1854 in Ohio and died 1938.

The 1900 census for Jackson County, West Virginia, includes Morrison S. Scarbrough as head of household. He was born May 1841; wife, Hester A., was born January 1854. They had three sons, Darris D., born February 1886; Dellis M., born March 1888; Samuel F., born December 1890; daughter Mary J., born January 1893.[307]

Morrison and Hester had the following children:

217 iii. **Darris D. SCARBROUGH** was born February 1886 in West Virginia.

+ 218 iv. **Dellis M. SCARBROUGH** was born March 1888.

219 v. **Samuel F. SCARBROUGH** was born December 1890 in West Virginia.

220 vi. **Mary J. SCARBROUGH** was born January 1893 in Ohio.

121. **Gilbert**[10] **SCARBOROUGH** (Robert Webb[9], John Ward[8], Isaac[7], Robert[6], John[5], John[4], John[3], William[2], Isaac[1]) was born 1845 in West Virginia.

It is assumed that Gilbert was a brother of Morrison, for he lived near him and Gilbert lived next to Jessee Hatcher, 33. Morrison married first Minerva Hatcher.

The 1880 census for Jackson County, West Virginia, shows Gilbert as a 35-year-old farmer, born in West Virginia, and both his parents were born there also. His wife, Lucinda, was 34, and born in West Virginia. Children: Mary F., 11; Robert C., 9; Lorenzo D., 7; Geo. L., 5; Leah J., 2; James D., 6 months.[308]

The Scarberrys (Scarboroughs), Doughtys, Lewises, and Paynes of Lawrence County, Ohio

Gilbert married **Lucinda**, born 1846 in West Virginia.

They had the following children:

    221   i.   **Mary F.**[11] **SCARBOROUGH** was born 1869 in West Virginia.

    222   ii.   **Robert C. SCARBOROUGH** was born 1871 in West Virginia.

    223   iii.   **Lorenzo D. SCARBOROUGH** was born 1873 in West Virginia.

    224   iv.   **George L. SCARBOROUGH** was born 1875 in West Virginia.

    225   v.   **Leah J. SCARBOROUGH** was born 1878 in West Virginia.

    226   vi.   **James D. SCARBOROUGH** was born about 1880 in West Virginia.

138.   **Elizabeth**[10] **SCARBERRY**, "Betsy," (Isaac[9] SCARBERRY, Zachariah[8] SCARBERRY, Isaac[7], Robert[6], John[5], John[4], John[3], William[2], Isaac[1]) was born 2 November 1832 in Ohio. She died 2 December 1914.

Betsy married (1) **George A. BURD**, on 11 January 1849 in Lawrence County, Ohio.[309] He was a son of David BURD and Susannah GREAVER.. George was born 1828 in Virginia. He died 24 June 1863.[310]

    The 1850 census for Rome Township shows that George and Betsy Bird, ages 23 and 16, respectively, were living in the household of Horatio Murphy, age 27, born in Ohio, and Elizabeth McBride, 56, born in Virginia. Also living there was Mary Burd, 13, born in Virginia. Next door lived Isaac and Polly Scarbery, Betsy's parents.[311]

    By the taking of the 1860 census, George and Betsy were on their own. He was a 32-year-old farmer, and she was 26. Children: Oliver P., 9; Mary A., 7; Emily R., 5; Susan A., 3; Harriet E., 6 months.[312]

    George served in the Civil War in the 117th Ohio Volunteer Infantry in Kentucky and died of smallpox in Cincinnati. He is buried there in Spring Grove Cemetery.[313] Clarence Young tells the tale of Betsy's visit to Cincinnati to see her ailing husband. She complained that every time she went to the outhouse she heard laughter. Finally someone revealed that a parrot had been installed along the way and trained to belt out a laugh when people walked by.

    The Rome Township census of 1870 includes Rebecca Arthur, 35, as head of household. Living with her were members of the Burd family: Perry, 20; Mary, 15; Emily, 14; Susan, 13; Harriet, 9; James, 7; and Isaac, 2. This family was living next to Isaac and Mary Scarberry, 60 and 65 respectively.[314]

    In 1880 Betsy Bird, 48; sons James Bird, 17; and Isaac, 10, were living next to Perry Bird, 30, and wife, Rebecca, 19.[315]

They had the following children:

+   227   i.   **Oliver Perry**[11] **BURD** was born 7 December 1849 and died 20 May 1915.

+   228   ii.   **Mary Ann BURD** was born 15 September 1852 and died 1922.

+   229   iii.   **Emily R. (?) BURD** was born 1855 and died 1928.

    230   iv.   **Susan A. BURD** was born 1857. Susan married **Thomas BLAIR**.[316]

+   231   v.   **Harriet E. BURD** was born 1860 and died 1886.

    232   vi.   **James Francis BURD** was born 1862. He died 1926. James married **Clara WORKMAN**. Clara was born 1873 and 25 June 1928.[317]

Betsy married (2) **James ARTHUR** on 7 April 1867. James died 29 November 1892.[318] Betsy and James separated.

James and Betsy had the following children:

    233   vii.   **Isaac ARTHUR** was born 1868.

        On the 1870 Rome Township census, Isaac is listed as Isaac Burd. He obviously was a son of James

Arthur, however.

Isaac married **Laura FULLER**.

139. **Francis Marion[10] SCARBERRY**, "Marion," (Isaac[9] SCARBERRY, Zachariah[8] SCARBERRY, Isaac[7], Robert[6] John[5], John[4], John[3], William[2], Isaac[1]) was born 6 June 1837 in Lawrence County, Ohio. He died 17 February 1916 and was buried in Pleasant Ridge graveyard, Lawrence County. Marion's birth date and death date were supplied by Clifford Scarberry.[319]

Marian Scarbury, 22, a farm laborer, was on the 1860 census for Rome Township. Wife, Margaret, was 23, daughter Sophronia, 2.[320]

The 1870 census for Rome Township, shows Marion Scarbery as a farmer, 30 years old, wife Margaret, 30; daughter Sofronia, 12; Mary, 10; William, 8; daughter Missouri, 1.[321]

In 1880 Marion, 42, was head of household, with wife, Margaret, 43; son Wm., 18; daughter Missouri, 12; son Marion, 7; and daughter Margaret, 5.[322]

Marion's household appears on the 1900 census for Millers Precinct. He was 65 years old, born in June 1834. Wife, Margaret, was 66, born in February 1834. A granddaughter, Maggie McKinley, 11 years old, born in September 1888, was living with them, as well as a grandson, Harrison McKinley, 8 years old, born in September 1891. Next door was the household of George Scarbery, born in June 1875, and his wife, Henrietta, born in May 1874. They had daughter Goldie, born May 1895 and son McKinley, born June 1896.[323]

Marion served in the infantry during the Civil War, and was allowed to come home because of "necessity." Many soldiers are listed in the Lawrence County records as being called home because they were needed on their farms.[324] Francis M. Scarberry filed for a pension on 29 October 1879.[325]

Marion married (1) **Margaret J. WALLS** on 22 September 1856 in Lawrence County, Ohio.[326] Margaret was born February 1834 in Ohio.

They had the following children:

234	i.	**Sophronia[11] SCARBERRY** was born 1858.
235	ii.	**Mary SCARBERRY** was born 1860.
236	iii.	**William SCARBERRY** was born 1862.
237	iv.	**Missouri SCARBERRY** was born 1869.
238	v.	**Marion SCARBERRY** was born 1873.
239	vi.	**Margaret SCARBERRY** was born 1875.

Francis M. married (2) **Ella SHOENLEY(?)** in 1912 in Lawrence County, Ohio. Francis M. Scarbery was 76, a widower, and Ella was 39. Francis was a farmer from Platform and the son of Isaac and Margaret J. (Watts) Scarbery. Ella's father was Joseph PICNEUS and her mother, Sarah J. MOORE. Ella had been married once before.[327] It looks as if Francis M. Scarberry, or the person who recorded the information, was confused. Francis's mother was Polly, and his deceased wife was Margaret Walls.

140. **Joseph[10] SCARBERRY** (Isaac[9] SCARBERRY, Zachariah[8] SCARBERRY, Isaac[7], Robert[6], John[5], John[4], John[3], William[2], Isaac[1]) was born 1841 in Lawrence County, Ohio. He was buried in Pleasant Ridge graveyard, Lawrence County.

On 1 January 1864 Joseph enlisted at Barboursville, West Virginia, to fight in the Civil War. He was 21 years old, a farmer, had hazel eyes, black hair, a dark complexion, and was six-feet tall. Muster took place at Charleston, West Virginia. He was placed in the 3rd Regiment of the West Virginia Cavalry Volunteers, and Jos. C. Wheeler was his captain.

On 14 July 1864 Joseph Scarbury was promoted from private to sergeant. By winter something had gone wrong, for he was included on a list of deserters dated 31 January 1865. Information was given on the engagements he participated in. They were Lynchburg, Va,, 18 June 1864; Liberty, Va,, 20 June 1864; Salem, Va,, 21 June 1864; Masons Gap, 21 June 1864; Winchester, 19 July 1864. Battles included Winchester, Virginia, Sept. 19th and Oct. 19th; Cedar Creek, Fisher's Hill, Rood's Hill, Minerah, 1864. Also mentioned were battles of Martinsburg, Va,, 25 July 1864; McConnelsburg, Pa., 30 July 1864; Moorfield, Va., 7 Aug. 1864; Martinsburg, Va., 31 Aug. 1864; Bunker Hill, Va., 2 Sept.1864, Buckletown, Va., 3 Sept. 1864.[328]

Not long before a leave was scheduled, Joseph had got into a fight with his captain. A friend told him the captain would make it very rough for him and advised him not to return. Joseph took his advice. Officials searching for men who had gone AWOL showed up at his father's house, and Isaac met them at the door with a shotgun and told them not to come back. They did not.

Notations regarding Joseph's desertion read: "Absent without leave Jan 18 Hagerstown. Feb 1865 Absent Jan. 25: Winchester to Hosp. Loss: Jan 26/65 On furlough. Failed to return." Another place on the record notes that he deserted 26 Jan. 1865, Camp Averell, Va.[329] Camp Averell was named for Union Cavalry Gen. William Woods Averell. The camp was dug in after the Third Battle of Winchester and was used as a base for raiding parties. The winter huts were built over shallow pits, and some of them can still be seen.[330]

Charges of desertion were removed for Joseph by order of the president on 21 November 1866. A note followed: "No statement to be made from records without calling up SCE 377-68 & getting an order from officer in charge...SCE 377-68 453-P-76." [331]

Known as the strongest man around, Joseph proved his running ability at a young age by saving the life of Isaac Edward Scarbery (b. 1853), his cousin. Baby Isaac was airing outside his home in a cradle, and a boar broke through a fence on the hill above. Joseph spotted the danger and leaped over the fence, racing the boar down the hill, scooping up Isaac and saving his life. Isaac's descendants may owe their very existence to Joseph. The story of Joseph's heroic deed was told by Iris (Scarberry) Burd, a grandchild of Isaac Edward.

Joseph Scarbery appeared on the 1870 U.S. census for Rome Township as 28 years old, wife, Amanda, also 28. Daughter Amanda was 8; son Joseph, 6; son Herman, 2, and Sayres was 6 mos.[332]

When the census was taken in 1880, Jos. was described as a 38-year-old farmer, whose father and mother were born in Virginia. Wife, Amanda, was also 38, both parents born in Virginia. Children: Amanda, 18; Jos., 14; Herman, 11; Sayres, 9; Mary, 7; Banks, 5; and Eve, 3.[333]

Joseph married **Amanda WALLS**.

Amanda's last name and the birthdates for their children were supplied by Iris (Scarberry) Burd.

Joseph and Amanda had the following children:

- 240   i.   **Amanda[11] SCARBERRY** was born 17 April 1862..
- + 241   ii.   **Joseph SCARBERRY** was born September 1863.
- 242   iii.   **Isaac SCARBERRY** was born 22 January 1866 in Lawrence County,
- 243   iv.   **Herman SCARBERRY** was born 30 January 1868.

    The 1930 census for Rome Township, Lawrence County, Ohio, includes Herman Scarbery, age 62, a widowed farmer.[334]

- 244   v.   **Sayres SCARBERRY** was born 15 May 1870.
- 245   vi.   **Mary SCARBERRY** was born 6 September 1862.
- + 246   vii.   **Banks SCARBERRY** was born 1875 and died 5 February 1941.
- 247   viii.   **Mona Eve SCARBERRY** was born 2 January 1878.
- 248   ix.   **Unknown SCARBERRY** was born 11 May 1880.
- 249   x.   **Laura SCARBERRY** was born 30 November 1882 in Lawrence County, Ohio.

The Scarberrys (Scarboroughs), Doughtys, Lewises, and Paynes of Lawrence County, Ohio

141. **James[10] SCARBERRY** (Isaac[9] SCARBERRY, Zachariah[8] SCARBERRY, Isaac[7], Robert[6], John[5], John[4], John[3] William[2], Isaac[1]) was born April 1845 in Lawrence County, Ohio. He died 13 October 1905.

When still a teen James Scarberry volunteered to fight in the Civil War. He enlisted on 1 August 1862 at Millersport, Ohio, in Co. D, 91st Infantry Regiment of Ohio Volunteers. He was mustered as a private at Camp Ironton, Ohio. His enlistment papers show he was 18 years old, 5 feet 9 inches tall, had a fair complexion, blue eyes, light hair, and was a farmer by profession. On 20 May 1864, he was sent to General Hospital at Gallipolis, Ohio, for a gun-shot wound suffered at Cloyd's Mountain on May 9th. On July 31st he was discharged for disability, having lost his left leg during action at Cloyd's Mountain. He received an invalid's pension for his service.[335] He had lost his left leg below the knee and got about afterwards with a peg leg.

James must have been proud of his part in the Cloyd's Mountain engagement, for the battle was declared a Union victory, despite the greater number of casualties on their side (688 to 538 for the Confederacy). General George Crook commanded the Union Army of West Virginia, Division of the Kanawha, and his goal was to destroy the Virginia & Tennessee Railroad at Dublin, Virginia, where General Albert Jenkins was headquartered. General Jenkins had decided to take a stand at Cloyd's Mountain. Jenkins was captured by Union Soldiers, and General John McCausland took over and withdrew. General Crook destroyed the Virginia and Tennessee railroad at Dublin. Union Cavalry General William Averell destroyed several Confederate railroad bridges. The Confederacy's only rail connection to East Tennessee was no more.[336] James Scarberry certainly had his heart in the war, for he named one son *Averell* and another *Sherman*, doubtless after Generals Averell and Sherman.

As seen above James Scarberry served in the 91st Infantry Regiment, and it was part of Col. Carr B. White's 2nd Brigade. They were green, but they led the charge that followed the artillery barrage. There were heavy casualties. The other two brigades were led by Horatio G. Sickel and Rutherford B. Hayes, the latter becoming president of the United States in 1877. William McKinley also fought at Cloyd's Mountain, and he became president in 1897.[337] James lived to see both of them take office.

James Scarberry appeared on the 1870 census for Rome Township, a 25-year-old farm laborer, born in Ohio. Lucy, his wife, was 27, and born in Virginia. Son Sherman was 3.[338]

In 1880 James and his family were still living in Rome Township. He was 35, a farm hand. Wife, Lucy, was 37; son Wm. S. was 13; son Jas. P. was 11; George F., 7; Chas., 5; Ada, 2; Perry, 3 months.[339]

On 15 January 1898, the Department of the Interior, Bureau of Pensions, sent James a questionnaire asking for the maiden names of his wives, names of his children, and when his first wife died. Information supplied is shown below.[340]

In 1900 James and his wife, Julia, were on the Union Township census for Lawrence County, James 55, and Julia 38. Sons Benjamin, 10, and William G., 8, were part of the household. Also living with them was Dollie Hamlin, 28, son-in-law.[341]

James married (1) **Lucy SUTHARDS**. Lucy was born 1844 in West Virginia. She died on 24 March 1884 in Millersport, Ohio. The Civil War pension papers state that she was 40 years and 4 months old at the time of her death, as recorded in the Record of Deaths, No. 1, page 286.

They had the following children:

    250   i.   **William Sherman[11] SCARBERRY** was born 1867.

    251   ii.   **James Preston SCARBERRY** was born 1869.

    252   iii.   **George Fred SCARBERRY** was born 1873.

    253   iv.   **Charlie SCARBERRY** was born 1875.

    254   v.   **Ada SCARBERRY** was born 1878

    255   vi.   **Perry SCARBERRY** was born 1880.

James married (2) **Mary Ann TRAINER**. She was born in 1845 and died 14 March 1889.

James did not mention Mary Ann in the form he filled out for the Department of the Interior in 1898, so it is not certain whether she was the mother of any of his children. Julia named her as his second wife when she applied for her widow's pension. The application was stamped Oct. 31, 1905. The drop order from the Department of the Interior, Bureau of Pensions, dated 11 November 1905, stated that James had been paid $40 a month until 4 September 1905. Mary was referred to as M. E. Scarbery in her death record (No. 2:422). She died at 44 of consumption.

James married (3) **Julia HAMLIN** on 28 August 1889 in Millersport, Ohio. Rev. Daniel Nance officiated. Julia was born February 1862. This date comes from the marriage certificate. Julia's widow's application for accrued pension dates the marriage as 29 August 1888 at Athalia.

Julia was 43 when she applied for her widow's pension (form stamped Oct. 31, 1905). Her address was Getaway, Lawrence County (Union Township). G. W. Hamilton and Albert Hamilton of Getaway signed sworn statements saying that Julia was the widow of James Scarberry. She signed a statement describing her assets. She owned 12 acres of land, but it was worth only $200 because it was hill land. She was paying eight percent interest on the $75 mortgage against her real estate. She had about $40 worth of personal property and did not own any stocks and bonds. The only property she had disposed of since 30 October 1905 was two head of cattle. Her husband had not left any life insurance. She declared that she had not been married before.

They had the following children:

- 256   vii.   **Benjamin Harrison SCARBERRY,** "Harrison," was born 10 June 1890, Union Township (Record of Births, 4:235).
- 257   viii.   **William Gilbert SCARBERRY,** "Gilbert," was born 10 November 1891, Union Township (Record of Births 4:237). Julia declared in her pension statement that Gilbert was born on 8th November.
- 258   ix.   **Albert SCARBERRY** was born 15 November 1900, Union Township (Record of Births 4:254).
- 259   x.   **Averill SCARBERRY** was born 15 November 1900, Union Township (Record of Births, 4:254).

144.   **Charles^{10} SCARBERRY** (Isaac^9 SCARBERRY, Zachariah^8 SCARBERRY, Isaac^7, Robert^6, John^5, John^4, John^3, William^2, Isaac^1) was born July 1856 in Ohio. He died 1932.

The 1880 census for Rome Township includes Chas. Scarberry, a 24-year-old farm worker. Wife, Mary, was 27; daughter Fidelia, 9.[342]

The Millers Precinct census for 1900 shows Charles Scarberry as 43 and born July 1857. Wife, Martha E., was 40, born August 1859. Children: Charles, born June 1883; Isaac, born May 1887; Marion, born June 1891; Pearlie, born October 1892; Richard, born May 1896; Louis G., born October 1899.[343]

A Charles Scarberry is found on the 1930 U.S. census for Rome Township, Lawrence County, Ohio. He was 78 years old and living with James and Mary Henderson, ages 77 and 73 respectively.[344]

Charles married **Martha E.,** born August 1859 in Ohio.

They had the following children:

- 260   i.   **Fidelia^{11} SCARBERRY** was born 1871.
- 261   ii.   **Charles SCARBERRY** was born June 1883.
- 262   iii.   **Isaac SCARBERRY** was born May 1887.
- 263   iv.   **Marion SCARBERRY** was born June 1891.
- 264   v.   **Pearlie(?) SCARBERRY** was born October 1892.
- 265   vi.   **Richard SCARBERRY** was born May 1896.
- 266   vii.   **Louis G. SCARBERRY** was born October 1899.

149. **Elemender**[10] **SCARBERRY** (John[9] SCARBERRY, Zachariah[8] SCARBERRY, Isaac[7], Robert[6], John[5], John[4], John[3], William[2], Isaac[1]) was born 5 November 1841 in Guyan Township, Gallia County, Ohio. He died 1 September 1921 in Cabell County, West Virginia. The West Virginia death register names his parents: mother Malinda Hicks and father John Scarberry.[345]

The date and place of Elemender's birth and the birth dates of his children are furnished by Dwayne J. Scarberry, a descendant of Elemender and Elizabeth Jane Kitterman.

Elemander Scarberry served in the Ohio Infantry during the Civil War and applied for a pension on 14 June 1880.[346]

The 1880 U.S. census for Hannan District, Mason County, West Virginia, includes the household of Elemonder Scarberry, age 38. His wife, Elisabeth J., was 37; children named were Elemonder J., 16; Martha J., 14; Eliza, 9; Mary E., 6, and Isaac, 4.[347]

Elemender married **Elizabeth Jane KITTERMAN** on 27 July 1862 in Gallia County, Ohio.[348] Elizabeth was born 1843 in Virginia and died 12 December 1907. The death record states that Elizabeth was 64 years old and of Bryan Creek, Cabell County, West Virginia. Her spouse was E. Scarberry.[349]

They had the following children:

+ 267 i. **Elemender**[11] **SCARBERRY** was born 13 March 1864 in Guyan Township, Gallia County, Ohio.
  268 ii. **Martha Jane SCARBERRY** was born 1866 in Gallia County, Ohio.
  269 iii. **Eliza SCARBERRY** was born 3 September 1870 in Gallia County, Ohio.
  270 iv. **Mary Elizabeth SCARBERRY** was born 7 June 1873 in Gallia County, Ohio.
  271 v. **Isaac SCARBERRY** was born 1876 in Ohio. He died 12 April 1896 in West Virginia. Isaac died at the age of 19 of consumption. He had been born in Ohio and was single, had lived 18 years in West Virginia.[350]
  272 vi. **John SCARBERRY** was born 13 January 1884. He died 24 April 1909 in Cabell County, West Virginia. John Scarberry of Glenwood died of consumption on 25 April 1908. He was 25 years old. He was single and the son of E. Scarberry.[351]
  273 vii. **Austella SCARBERRY** was born 15 February 1886 in Cabell County, West Virginia.

168. **Noah Webster**[10] **SCARBERRY** (Joseph[9] SCARBERRY, Zachariah[8] SCARBERRY, Isaac[7], Robert[6], John[5], John[4], John[3], William[2], Isaac[1]) was born 1843 and died in Logan County, West Virginia.

On 21 July 1879 Noah applied for a pension for serving in D87 of the Ohio Infantry during the Civil War. Noah's widow, Harriet B.(?) Scarberry, applied for her pension in 1899 (Certificate No. 487,434, WVA).[352]

The 1880 census for Rome Township, Lawrence County, Ohio, shows Noah as a 37-year-old farmer; wife, Hannah, was 30; son Judson was 4, and son Wilbert was 1.[353]

Noah married **Henrietta (Hattie) LEWIS**.[354] She was a daughter of Samuel F. Lewis and Rachel Dillon. Henrietta was born 1848 and died in 1928 in Logan County, West Virginia.

Hattie kept boarders for many years.

Noah and Henrietta had the following children:

  274 i. **Cecil Judson**[11] **SCARBERRY** According to the LDS IGI v5.0 records, Judson's first name was *Cecil*, and he was born 13 June 1877 in Gallia County, Ohio, and died 17 June 1953. He married **Cora Mae HENSLEY**.
  275 ii. **Wilburt SCARBERRY** was born about 1879.
  276 iii. **Lewis Brille SCARBERRY** was born 7 March 1879. He died 13 October 1965. He married **Helen GROVE**.
  277 iv. **Leona SCARBERRY** was born 26 August 1882. She died 1966. She married **James LANNING**.

278   v. **Betsy SCARBERRY** was born 1885. She married **William MUSIC**.

279   vi. **Roy Dallas SCARBERRY** was born 5 February 1892 in Gallia County, Ohio. He was a casualty of the flood at Buffalo Creek in Logan County, West Virginia. He married **Marvell MARKS**.

280   vii. **Nellie R. SCARBERRY** was born 10 July 1895. She married **Louie ARTHUR**.

176.   **Zachariah[10] DOUGHTY** (Rachel[9] SCARBERRY, Zachariah[8] SCARBERRY, Isaac[7], Robert[6], John[5], John[4], John[3], William[2], Isaac[1]) was born October 1850. He died 24 December 1934.

The 1880 census for Washington District, Jackson County, West Virginia, includes Zachariah Doughty, 30, as head of household. Wife, Mary, was 34. They had four daughters: Missouri A., 17; Arminta S., 8; Manda E., 3; Eliza Jane, 1.[355]

Zachariah married **Mary Elizabeth SCARBERRY** on 5 July 1871 in Jackson County, West Virginia. Mary was born 1845 in West Virginia. The marriage record states that Mary was 26 at the time of her marriage; Z. was 20.[356]

Zachariah and Mary had the following children:

281   i. **Missouri A.[11] DOUGHTY** was born 1863 in West Virginia.

    According to the 1880 U.S. census, Missouri was 17 when it was taken, and her mother, 34, making her mother 17 at her birth. If Missouri's age was correct, then her mother had had a previous marriage.

282   ii. **Arminta S. DOUGHTY** was born 1872 in West Virginia.

283   iii. **Manda E. DOUGHTY** was born 1877 in West Virginia.

284   iv. **Eliza Jane DOUGHTY** was born 1879 in West Virginia.

285   v. **Orville Fleet DOUGHTY** was born 28 August 1884.

286   vi. **Ina DOUGHTY**.

177.   **Hester A.[10] DOUGHTY** (Rachel[9] SCARBERRY, Zachariah[8] SCARBERRY, Isaac[7], Robert[6], John[5], John[4], John[3], William[2], Isaac[1]) was born January 1854 in Ohio. She died in 1938.

Hester's age of 25, as shown on the 1880 U.S. census, would place her birth year at around 1855. She was living with her parents at that time, and her last name was *Doughty*. Tradition says she married at least three times. I have no record of the name of her third husband.

Hester married (1) **Morrison S. SCARBOROUGH**, son of Robert Webb SCARBOROUGH and wife, Mary, on 20 November 1884 in Jackson County, West Virginia. Morrison was born May 1841 in West Virginia.

Hester married (2) **MR. COLLIER**

See Morrison S. Scarborough above.

178.   **John Wesley[10] DOUGHTY** "Wesley" (Rachel[9] SCARBERRY, Zachariah[8] SCARBERRY, Isaac[7], Robert[6], John[5], John[4], John[3], William[2], Isaac[1]) was born 28 February 1856 in Cabell County, West Virginia. He died November 1934 in Charleston, West Virginia.

According to Clarence Young, Wesley died on Thanksgiving Day, 1934, at age 78. He was born in West Virginia, because the Ohio River was frozen over, and his parents could not get back across. It was the same year that his grandfather Zachariah Scarberry died.

Wesley claimed he had 17 children. His first wife, Lucinda, died of tuberculosis and she had a young baby at the time. His second wife left him in 1920.

The 1900 census for Washington District, Jackson County, West Virginia, shows John, born in February 1856, and head of household. Wife, Mary C., was born March 1878. Children: James W., 21; Albert L., 17; William A., 15; Rachel C., 13; Nora N., 7; Ivy M., 5; Ennis L., 3; and Arstella B., 1.[357]

When the 1910 census was taken for Jackson County, John W. Doughty was 52; wife, Mary, was 32. Children: Rachel, 21; Nora N., 17; Iva M., 15; Enus L., 13; Austella B., 10; John A., 8; Henry C., 6; Obra C., 4; and Milford O., 1 1/12.[358]

Wesley married (1) **Lucinda MOORE**, who was born in Roane County, West Virginia. The name of John's first wife was reported by Clarence Young. The death certificate of son James Wesley Doughty confirms this marriage and supplies Lucinda's birth place.

Wesley and Lucinda had the following children:

287   i.   **James W.**[11] **DOUGHTY** was born 17 February 1877 in Jackson County, West Virginia. He died 15 October 1944 in Kanawha County, West Virginia, and was buried in Bodkins Cemetery at Cooper's Creek, West Virginia.

James Wesley Doughty died from drowning in the Kanawha River due to a fracture of left temple. He had been struck on the head by a blunt instrument, and it was not certain whether the blow was accidental. The death certificate shows his parents as John W. Doughty and Lucinda Moore. The informant for the death certificate was his wife, Dovie Hester Doughty, age 52.[359]

James married **Dovie HESTER**. Dovie was born 1892.

288   ii.   **Albert L. DOUGHTY** was born January 1883 in West Virginia. He died of tuberculosis.

289   iii.   **William A. DOUGHTY** was born June 1884 in West Virginia.

290   iv.   **Rachel C. DOUGHTY** was born March 1888 in West Virginia. She married **Louis CASTO**, an excellent checker player.

Wesley married (2) **Mary Cordelia CARPENTER** on 4 February 1892 in Jackson County, West Virginia. Mary was born in Roane County, West Virginia. See her son Obra's death certificate for proof of this marriage.

Mary was about half the age of Wesley. A man named McIntyre became a widower, and in 1920 he took Mary and her children to Charleston, West Virginia, with him, leaving Wesley alone. He filed for divorce in Huntington, accusing Mary of adultery. He got the divorce easily. John then lived with daughter Rachel and her husband, Louis Casto, but the situation did not work out, so he came over to Ohio and lived in an old house down in a hollow. It wasn't winter proof, so he stayed for a while at Isaac and Susan Scarberry's home. When he got word that son Albert was dying, he went to Jackson County, West Virginia, to be with him until he died. Wesley died while staying with his daughter Rachel in Charleston.

Wesley and Mary had the following children:

291   v.   **Nora N. DOUGHTY** was born March 1893 in West Virginia.

292   vi.   **Ivy M. DOUGHTY** was born October 1894 in West Virginia.

293   vii.   **Ennis L. DOUGHTY** was born January 1897 in West Virginia.

He was a very good shot with a gun, could aim from the hip and kill a rabbit. Ennis moved to Akron, Ohio, to work at the rubber plant.

294   viii.   **Arstella B. DOUGHTY** was born May 1899 in West Virginia.

295   ix.   **John A. DOUGHTY** was born 1902 in West Virginia.

296   x.   **Henry C. DOUGHTY** was born 1904 in West Virginia.

297   xi.   **Obra C. DOUGHTY** was born 7 March 1906 in Jackson County, West Virginia. He died 6 March 1917 and was buried in Fletcher, West Virginia.

Obra's death certificate shows him living at Fletcher in Washington District, Jackson County, West Virginia. He died of the measles, and bronch. pneumonia was a contributing factor. The death certificate shows his father, John Doughty, born in Cabell County, West Virginia, and his mother, Mary Carpenter, born in Roane County, West Virginia.[360]

298   xii. **Milford DOUGHTY** was born about 1909 in West Virginia.

179. **Celia Jane**[10] **DOUGHTY** (Rachel[9] SCARBERRY, Zachariah[8] SCARBERRY, Isaac[7], Robert[6], John[5], John[4], John[3], William[2], Isaac[1]) was born 1858 in Gallia County, Ohio. She died 1930 in Cabell County, West Virginia.

Celia married **James ANDERSON**.[361]

James and Celia lived in Union Ridge, West Virginia, where he was a minister for a church.

James and Celia had the following child and three others.

+   299   i. **Rachel Minerva**[11] **ANDERSON** died 25 April 1973.

180. **Elizabeth Susan**[10] **DOUGHTY** (Rachel[9] SCARBERRY, Zachariah[8] SCARBERRY, Isaac[7], Robert[6], John[5], John[4], John[3], William[2], Isaac[1]) was born 20 May 1862 in Gallia County, Ohio. She died 17 February 1950 and was buried in Pleasant Ridge graveyard in Lawrence County, Ohio.

    For several years Susan and her husband, Isaac, took care of their grandson Clarence Young. The 1920 census for Rome Township, Lawrence County, Ohio, shows both Clarence and his mother living with her parents. Three of her brothers were there, also, at that time, and Clarence remembered good times with them. His mother, Nancy, worked in Huntington part of the time when he was growing up, and when the 1930 U.S. census was taken for Rome Township, Nancy was not living at the old home place. Clarence H. Young, 16, and Susan E. Scarbery, 68, were the only people left there. Isaac had died in 1927. Susan's household followed that of her son, Manuel (written Emanuel), and wife Mary. Following Susan's household was that of Mark and Mary Hayes.[362]

    When Susan was young, she lived near Crown City, Ohio, but about 1870 her family moved to Jackson County, West Virginia. She and Isaac Scarberry were married at Ripley, West Virginia, and he was the son of Nancy Scarberry, sister to her mother, Rachel. In other words, Susan and Isaac were first cousins. Fortunately, there was no sign of birth defects in their children. They all turned out to be healthy and intelligent.

    Susan was about six-feet tall and known as a meek and kind person and was well liked. She was an expert in folk medicine, and neighbors came to her for advice. She suffered from a heart condition many years before she died, but she refused to go to a doctor. She was afraid of being put in a hospital and not being allowed to stand up and stomp to keep her heart going. She kept a bottle of whiskey handy to slow down her heart whenever necessary. And she kept a spittoon by her rocking chair, for she chewed tobacco. She warned me never to start the habit.

    While growing up in the 1940s, I remember seeing Granny's supply of homemade lye soap that was stored in an outbuilding behind the house. There were several other other constructions: a coal house, a chicken house and pen, a pig house and pen, a corn crib; there was a cellar and a cow shed. The cistern was directly behind the house, for it caught rain water from the roof. Wash day was interesting to me, for clothes were washed outside in a large tub, the water heated nearby in a pot over a fire. A washboard was used for scrubbing.

    Susan's rocking chair was in her living room by the radio and she sat there and braided rugs. Her view out the window included the barn, and between the house and the barn was a large vegetable garden with berry vines growing along side. The windows in the old farmhouse were divided into panes, and the glass distorted the view somewhat as old glass would. The house had been built before the turn of the century and was constructed of logs. Later the logs were covered by wood siding. The smell of paint made Granny sick, so the wood weathered. A large kitchen was added to the back of the house, producing an inset porch on the barn side. A broad covered porch was on the other. A porch extended across the front of the house, and I remember sitting there in the summertime, next to a vine with creamy white flowers that climbed up the trellis.

Behind the living room was the dining room, housing a heavy oak table standing on clawed feet. A door to the rear of the dining room opened onto the large country kitchen, its walls covered in oil cloth of a light-blue pattern. A pantry was on the left and a door to the partially enclosed porch to the right.

A large fieldstone fireplace dominated the inside wall of the living room and behind it was a bedroom. My first memories of visiting the old home place were of sitting around the blazing fire on a cold fall evening, a kerosene lamp flickering in the corner. Homes in that part of Lawrence County were not wired for electricity until after World War II. By World War I telephone service had been installed, but when automobiles became common, people no longer felt they needed phones, for their most important use had been for calls to the doctor. When I was growing up, I knew of no household in that part of Lawrence County that had telephone service, but it was restored sometime after World War II. In the first floor bedroom was the wind-up Victrola phonograph. Clarence Young said that when a Carter family record was brought in, people would come from miles around to hear it.

The upstairs was one large room, and it had a curtain to divide it into two sections. A door at the back of the living room opened on the stairwell. It was lined in the same wood planks as the living room and painted with the same light-gray enamel. There was a window on either side of the upstairs, and the view in the summer was of the tops of tree-covered hills as far as the eye could see. No other houses were visible.

Granny's front yard seemed large to me as a child. A fence enclosed it, and roses and pink sweet peas climbed the fence, and dahlias and other flowers lined it. I remember pulling my sister Rena around the yard in a wagon one summer on a Sunday morning before church. My cousin Iris Scarberry and her little brother, Danny, and their parents, Della and Orval, lived in a house built across the back yard from the main house, and Della's sister Dessie Gilfilen and her family were visiting. Dessie had made Iris a Sunday dress of dimity, flocked with delicate yellow flowers, and Iris was going to wear it to church. Dessie was a talented seamstress and could cut fabric to the right dimensions without a pattern, and I stood in awe of her ability. I could hear the bustle inside the house as everyone prepared for church, and there was dew on the roses. It was a beautiful morning.

Orval took his mother to the outhouse on a cold day in February of 1950, and he had a funny feeling in his stomach as he helped her walk. Not long after he returned her to the house, she died quietly in her rocking chair. A large crowd attended her funeral at "Tick Ridge" church, where she was a member, for many people thought well of her. Evangelist C. M. Cleveland officiated.

Elizabeth married **Isaac Edward SCARBERRY**, son of Nancy SCARBERRY, on 18 December 1881 in Ripley, West Virginia. Isaac was born 9 August 1853 in Lawrence County, Ohio. He died 4 September 1927 and was buried in Pleasant Ridge graveyard, Lawrence County.

When the 1870 U.S. census for Rome Township was taken, Isaac was a 17-year-old farm laborer. It looks as if he was running the farm, for his brother William, 22, was working in a sawmill; his brother Lewis, 16, was making staves; his sister Rachel, 30, was a spinner; his mother was a weaver. Isaac's sister Mary was a house domestic, and his sister Melissa, 14, did housework.[363]

Following are the names and ages of Isaac and Susan's household as recorded when the 1900 U.S. census was taken for Miller's Precinct. Isaac was shown as 47; Elizabeth, 38; Rachel N., 17; Manuel N., 15; Alve E., 11; Chloe M., 9; Grover C., 7; Jasper L., 4; and Orville F., 8/12.[364]

Isaac's son Alva married in 1909, so he had left home by the taking of the 1910 census. People remaining were Isaac E., 57; Elizabeth S., 48; Rachel N., 25; Manuel N., 23; Chloe M., 19; Grover C., 17; Jasper L., 14; Orville F., 11; and William A., 7.[365]

Isaac and Susan's farm was about 88 acres. I have a record of only two of the land purchases: On 5 March 1898, I. E. Scarberry bought 2 acres from T. R. Thomas. The parcel was in Township 2, Range 15.[366] Both Rome and Windsor Townships were numbered *Township 2*, but Windsor was in Range 16 and Rome was in Range 15, the ranges being east-west divisions. On 13 March 1914 Isaac Scarbery paid $10 to Thos. Dalton for Lots 1309 and 1310 in Section 34, Township 2, Range 15.[367]

Households nearby at the time of the 1920 Rome Township census were that of John and Mary Galloway, Mark and Mary Hayes, James and Sarah Burd, and William H. and Rachel Lewis. At home at the time, besides Isaac and Susan, were sons Grover, Orval, and Arthur (entered as William A. in the 1910 census); daughter Nancy Young and her son, Clarence.[368]

Isaac Scarberry and John Galloway built the schoolhouse on the main road just off the Scarberry land. But Isaac had mixed feelings about education. He felt his children should not attend school beyond a certain level, and one of his sons deliberately failed a grade so he could continue to go to school. His daughter Nancy never went beyond the lower grades (because she was needed at home, it was said), but she could read and write well and kept up with the news and was knowledgeable. Isaac became quite angry with grandson Clarence Young when he found him reading *The Surprising Adventures of Baron Munchausen*. The tales were fantasy, of course, but Isaac considered them simply untrue

The old home place where Isaac and his family lived was within walking distance of Tick Ridge (Pleasant Ridge) Church, but when the ground was covered with snow, the family found the best transportation was a horse-drawn sled. By the 1920s most people owned cars, and radios as well.

Both Isaac and Susan were well coordinated. They sometimes challenged their children to hoeing contests, and Isaac and Susan usually won. In the winter when snow was on the ground, their sons would race each other around the outside of the house barefoot.

Bright's Disease was considered the cause of Isaac's death. And he had had a stroke a few years before he died. Grandson Clarence Young said that not long before Isaac died, he stood up, which was not easy for him, because his legs were weak, and with the aid of his cane walked outside, picked up an ax, and chopped down a small tree. Clarence was watching and was impressed because Isaac never missed his mark.

Notes for Isaac's obituary, in the handwriting of daughter Nancy Young, show that two of the songs requested for his funeral were "We'll Know Our Loved Ones, There," and "When the Roll is Called up Yonder." The obituary states that he served as a deacon at Pleasant Ridge Church, that he "was spoken of highly as a good neighbor and citizen...." It also states he was survived by his two daughters, Mrs. Young of Proctorville and Mrs. T. H. Galloway of Huntington. The six sons were named, "Manuel and Alva of Proctorville, Grover of Athalia, Jasper, Arthur, and Averiel [Orval] of Columbus, Ohio." Isaac was survived by one brother, William Scarbery of Five-Mile, and one sister, Mrs. John Smith, of Coryville.

They had the following children:

+   300   i.   **Nancy Rachel**[11] **SCARBERRY** was born 13 November 1882 and died 19 November 1967.

         301   ii.   **Manuel Newton SCARBERRY** was born 25 January 1884 in Lawrence County, Ohio. He died May 1980 in Lawrence County. He was buried at Pleasant Ridge graveyard in Lawrence County.

Manuel and Mary had no children of their own, but they loved children, and Mary baked favorite cookies and cakes for my father and other children in their neighborhood. A niece, Virginia Fitch, about 5 years old, was living with them at the time of the 1930 census for Rome Township. Manuel's name was written *Emanuel*, and he was 45 years old; wife, Mary, was 42. This census shows Manuel's household between that of Girard R. Fuller and Susan E. Scarbery.[369]

Bob Jones, the son of friends, was reared by Manuel and Mary. Manuel's obituary in the *Ironton Tribune* states that he was 96 at the time of his death, dying at the home of his stepson, Bob Jones. Wife, Mary Ada, had died in 1969. Manuel had retired from ACF Industries in Huntington.

Manuel and Mary spent much of their lives in their home on Pleasant Ridge Road, not far from the house where Manuel had grown up. He had once owned property in Huntington, West Virginia, selling it in 1909.[370]

Manuel married **Mary Ada ADAMS** in 1908. Mary was born 1888 in West Virginia. She died in 1969.

An obituary appeared in *The Huntington Advertiser* (no date visible on the clipping) for Mrs. Emmer ADAMS, 89 years old. It reveals that she was the mother of Mrs. Manuel Scarberry and also of Mrs. John Fitch and Mrs. J. W. Wray.

+   302   iii.   **Alva E. SCARBERRY** was born 7 July 1887 and died 1960.

The Scarberrys (Scarboroughs), Doughtys, Lewises, and Paynes of Lawrence County, Ohio

303   iv.   **Chloe M. SCARBERRY** was born 30 June 1890 in Lawrence County, Ohio. She died April 1977 in Lawrence County, Ohio.

Chloe appeared on the 1900 U.S. census for Millers Precinct, and her birth date was shown as June 1891. She was 9 years old.

Chloe and her husband, Tom, were childless, and they kept my father, Clarence Young, in their home while his mother, Nancy, worked in Huntington, West Virginia. The time came when Chloe told Nancy she wanted either to adopt Clarence or return him to her. Nancy took him to live with her parents.

Tom and Chloe owned a home on a rise at Rome. It had an expansive view of the Ohio River and a large willow in the front yard with a table encircling its trunk. Chloe donated some of the land she and Tom owned for the Church of Christ building at Rome, constructed in 1951.

Chloe enjoyed books and poetry, still attending book club meetings in her eighties. One of her poems was published in a Huntington newspaper in "The Poet's Corner." Chloe introduced her poem in this way: "While making a trip to my old homestead in Lawrence County, Ohio, and musing over the scenes and changes that had taken place, this poem formed in my mind. I am sure there are many things more that I have failed to mention." Two verses especially demonstrate her fond recollections:

> So I fell to thinking tenderly
> Of the folks I used to know;
> Where the Wild Sumac and Sassafrass
> And May Apple used to grow.
>
> It brings me soothing memories
> Of a school house on a hill
> And the voices of many children
> And the school bell loud and shrill.

In addition, Chloe won a letter-writing contest. A newspaper in Huntington invited people to write letters that showed the need for a new bridge across the Ohio. Chloe's was chosen as the best.

Chloe married (1) **Thomas Hastings GALLOWAY**, son of John GALLOWAY and Harriet BURD, on 20 June 1910. Thomas was 29 and Chloe, 20.[371] Thomas was born 16 November 1881. He died 15 May 1944 and was buried in Pleasant Ridge graveyard in Lawrence County, Ohio. Tom's birth and death dates are taken from his funeral announcement.

Tom's mother, Harriet BURD, was a daughter of George BURD and Betsy SCARBERRY. Harriet died in 1886, and John Galloway married (2) Mary LEWIS, daughter of James J. LEWIS and Rebecca BURD.

Tom had been a postal worker. In 1918 Chloe's brother Grover wrote from France asking if Chloe was still in Columbus and if Tom was still working at the post office. Tom died of a bad heart condition in his home by the Ohio River.

Chloe married (2) **Wilbur RECKARD**.

Chloe married Wilbur late in life. They had been neighbors for years. He was a retired businessman, one of his enterprises having been a hardware store. He willed a large amount of money to a hospital in Huntington.

+   304   v.   **Grover C. SCARBERRY** was born 8 February 1893 and died 5 July 1976.

+   305   vi.   **Jasper Lewis SCARBERRY**, "Jay," was born November 1895 and died October 1949.

	306	vii.	**Orval Franklin SCARBERRY** was born 13 November 1898 and died November 1974.
+	307	viii.	**Arthur William SCARBERRY** was born 1 January 1903 and died October 1979.

181. Phoebe A.[10] **DOUGHTY** (Rachel[9] SCARBERRY, Zachariah[8] SCARBERRY, Isaac[7], Robert[6], John[5], John[4], John[3], William[2], Isaac[1]) was born June 1864 in Ohio. She died 1944.

Phoebe married **Elijah WILLIAMS**, son of Elihu WILLIAMS and Malissa J. COTTRELL. Elijah was born 24 November 1862 in West Virginia. He died 7 May 1925 of chronic Bright's Disease. His last address was Kenna, Ripley District, Jackson County, West Virginia. His father was born in Harrison County, West Virginia.[372]

Clarence Young remembered Elijah as a big strong man. He was a blacksmith and a farmer.

Rachel (Scarberry) Doughty was living with her daughter, Phoebe, and her husband, Elijah Williams, when the 1900 U.S. census was taken for Jackson County, West Virginia. Rachel, mother-in-law, was 84, born April 1816. Elijah, head of household, was born November 1862. Wife, Phoebe A., was born June 1864. Children: Icy B., born August 1883; Mary J., born October 1881; Annie G., born March 1893; Elijah G., born September 1897.[373]

Elijah and Phoebe had the following children:

	308	i.	**Mary J.**[11] **WILLIAMS** was born October 1881 in West Virginia.
	309	ii.	**Icy B. WILLIAMS** was born August 1883 in West Virginia.
	310	iii.	**Annie G. WILLIAMS** was born March 1893 in West Virginia.
	311	iv.	**Elijah G. WILLIAMS** was born September 1897 in West Virginia.

194. Mary[10] **SCARBERRY**, "Polly," (Nancy[9] SCARBERRY, Zachariah[8] SCARBERRY, Isaac[7], Robert[6], John[5], John[4], John[3], William[2], Isaac[1]) was born 1843 in Ohio.

Polly married **David FULLER** on 21 September 1872.[374] David was born 1850 and died 1920.

Living with David and Mary and their daughters when the U.S. census was taken in 1880 for Rome Township, Lawrence County, Ohio, was Arminta Scarberry, age 4, her relationship unstated. David was 30 and wife, Mary, 37. Daughter Jennette was 6; daughter Tina was 4.[375]

David loved to entertain people with stories and his grand nephew Clarence Young always enjoyed his company. In 1919 David gave Clarence a pearl-handled knife.

They had the following children:

	312	i.	**Jeanette**[11] **FULLER** was born 1874.
	313	ii.	**Tina FULLER** was born 1876.
	314	iii.	**Henry FULLER** was born 1884. He married **Bessie PRITCHARD** on 8 July 1909. The marriage certificate states that Henry was born in Lawrence County, Ohio, to David FULLER and Polly SCARBERRY. Bessie was the daughter of George PRITCHARD and Maggie WHITE.[376]

Henry Fuller, 25, and wife, Bessie, 17, appear on the 1910 Census for Rome Township.[377]

197. Isaac Edward[10] **SCARBERRY** (Nancy[9] SCARBERRY, Zachariah[8] SCARBERRY, Isaac[7], Rober[t6], John[5], John[4], John[3], William[2], Isaac[1]) was born 9 August 1853 in Lawrence County, Ohio. He died 4 September 1927 in Lawrence County and was buried in Pleasant Ridge graveyard, Lawrence County.

Isaac married **Elizabeth Susan DOUGHTY**, daughter of Isaac Wesley DOUGHTY and Rachel SCARBERRY, on 18 December 1881 in Ripley, West Virginia. Elizabeth was born 20 May 1862 in Gallia County, Ohio. She died 17 February 1950 and was buried in Pleasant Ridge graveyard.

See above

199. Melissa[10] SCARBERRY "Milly" (Nancy[9] SCARBERRY, Zachariah[8] SCARBERRY, Isaac[7], Robert[6], John[5], John[4], John[3], William[2], Isaac[1]) was born 1860. She died February 1932 in Ironton, Ohio, and was buried in Pleasant Ridge graveyard, Lawrence County.

Milly, one year old, was part of the 1860 U.S. census for Rome Township, Lawrence County, Ohio. Her mother at that time was referred to as Nancy Brooks. On the 1870 Rome Township Census she was 14 and listed as Melissa. Her mother had reverted to her maiden name.

Melissa's obituary, appearing in an unidentified newspaper, states Mrs. Millie Smith was 71 years old and that she died at the home of her daughter, Mrs. Charles Feil, of 705(?) North Sixth Street, Ironton, Ohio. Surviving her were her husband, John H. Smith, daughters Mrs. Charles Feil of Ironton, Mrs. Burl Wilks, and Mrs. John Foster of Bradrick, Ohio. Four sons who survived her were Lewis Smith of Cebee, Ohio, John W. and Preston of Proctorville, Ohio, and J. A. Smith of Ironton, Ohio. Someone wrote on the obituary what is presumably its date, 7 February 1932.

Milly married **John H. SMITH** on 18 September 1879 in Lawrence County, Ohio.[378]

They had the following children:

315   i.   **Girl[11] SMITH** married **Charles FEIL**.

           Son **Clarence FEIL** held a good position with Ohio Power Company. He was married to a psychiatrist who had an office in Huntington, West Virginia. In the 1950s my sister Rachel and I heard her give a lecture at our high school in Sciotoville, Ohio.

316   ii.   **Rebecca Ella SMITH** was born 28 August 1892. Rebecca married **Burl WILKS** on 20 April 1912 in Lawrence County, Ohio.[379]

317   iii.   **Girl SMITH** married **John FOSTER**..

318   iv.   **Lewis SMITH**..

319   v.   **John W. SMITH**.

320   vi.   **Preston SMITH**.

321   vii.   **J. A. SMITH**.

Eleventh Generation

218. Dellis M.[11] SCARBROUGH (Morrison S.[10], Robert Webb[9], John Ward[8], Isaac[7], Robert[6], John[5], John[4], John[3], William[2], Isaac[1]) was born March 1888 in West Virginia.

Dellis married **Bertha BELL** on 20 August 1913. Bertha was born 10 March 1890. She died 29 June 1923.

An obituary from an unknown newspaper gives Bertha Bell Scarbrough's date of birth and death and the date of her marriage. The birth years of her five children were deduced from their ages. The last, Avie Basil, was 30 days old. The obituary states she was a devoted Christian.

They had the following children:

322   i.   **John Winfred[12] SCARBROUGH** was born about 1914.

323   ii.   **Mildred May SCARBROUGH** was born about 1917.

The Scarberrys (Scarboroughs), Doughtys, Lewises, and Paynes of Lawrence County, Ohio

    324   iii. **Teddy Roosevelt SCARBROUGH** was born about 1918.

    325   iv. **Raymond Ray SCARBROUGH** was born about 1921.

    326   v. **Avie Basil SCARBROUGH** was born 1923.

227.   **Oliver Perry**[11] **BURD** (Elizabeth[10] SCARBERRY, Isaac[9] SCARBERRY, Zachariah[8] SCARBERRY, Isaac[7], Robert[6], John[5], John[4], John[3], William[2], Isaac[1]) was born 7 December 1849. He died 20 May 1915.

    The 1860 U. S. census for Rome Township lists Oliver as Oliver P. The 1900 Millers Precinct census includes Perry Burd, 49, and wife, Rebecca, 38. Children: Delia, 16; Martha, 15; Raymond, 11; Otis, 9; William, 6; and Charles, 11 months. The month and year of birth were included in this census,[380] and they are revealed below.

Oliver married **Rebecca PETRY**. Rebecca was born October 1861. (For proof of Rebecca's last name, see marriage certificate of daughter Delia.)

They had the following children:

    327   i. **Delia**[12] **BURD** was born December 1883. She married **Benjamin F. BRICKER** on 19 September 1906. Delia was 22, the daughter of O. P. BYRD and Rebecca PETRY of Proctorville. Benj. F. Bricker was the 25-year-old son of John BRICKER and Ruhama TULL.[381]

    328   ii. **Martha BURD** was born June 1886.

    329   iii. **Raymond BURD** was born February 1889.

    330   iv. **Otis BURD** was born December 1890.

    331   v. **William BURD** was born 1894.

    332   vi. **Charles BURD** was born January 1900.

228.   **Mary Ann**[11] **BURD** (Elizabeth[10] SCARBERRY, Isaac[9] SCARBERRY, Zachariah[8] SCARBERRY, Isaac[7], Robert[6], John[5], John[4], John[3], William[2], Isaac[1]) was born 15 September 1852. She died 1922 and was buried in Pleasant Ridge Cemetery, Lawrence County.[382]

Mary married **Richard Clark LEWIS**,[383] son of Richard Burton LEWIS and Mary Ann WHITE, on 18 September 1870. Richard was born 30 November 1843. He died 25 October 1916 and was buried in Pleasant Ridge graveyard.

See the LEWIS Section for more on the Richard Clark Lewis family.

229.   **Emily Catherine**[11] **BURD** (Elizabeth[10] SCARBERRY, Isaac[9] SCARBERRY, Zachariah[8] SCARBERRY, Isaac[7], Robert[6], John[5], John[4], John[3], William[2], Isaac[1]) was born 1855 and died 1928.[384]

Emily married **George HARBOUR** on 11 February 1872 in Gallia County, Ohio. George was born 5 August 1850 and died 5 June 1931.[385]

George and Emily had the following child:

    333   i. **Elizabeth Jane**[12] **HARBOUR** was born 8 December 1872 in Guyan Township, Gallia County, Ohio. She died 10 January 1949 in Lincoln County, West Virginia.

               Elizabeth married **Francis Marion LEWIS**,[386] son of Wallace LEWIS and Elvira NASH, on 12 March 1891 in Lincoln County, West Virginia. Francis was born 25 February 1863 in Rome Township, Lawrence County, Ohio. He died 25 January 1933 in Lincoln County, West Virginia.

               See the LEWIS Section for more on the Francis Marion Lewis family.

231.   **Harriet E.**[11] **BURD** (Elizabeth[10] SCARBERRY, Isaac[9] SCARBERRY, Zachariah[8] SCARBERRY, Isaac[7], Robert[6], John[5],

The Scarberrys (Scarboroughs), Doughtys, Lewises, and Paynes of Lawrence County, Ohio

John[4], John[3], William[2], Isaac[1]) was born 1860 and died 1886.

Harriet married **John Thomas Morton GALLOWAY**,[387] son of Henry GALLOWAY and Susannah, in 1877. John was born May 1856 in Ohio and died 1946.

The 1880 census for Rome Township includes John Galloway, 25, and head of household. Wife, Harriet E., was 20. They had son Wm. H. Galloway, 10 months.[388]

They had the following children:

- 334 i. **William H.**[12] **GALLOWAY** was born 1879.

- 335 ii. **Thomas Hastings GALLOWAY** was born 16 November 1881. He died 15 May 1944 in Lawrence County, Ohio, and was buried Pleasant Ridge graveyard in Lawrence County, Ohio.

    Thomas married **Chloe M. SCARBERRY**, daughter of Isaac Edward SCARBERRY and Elizabeth Susan DOUGHTY. Chloe was born 30 June 1890 in Lawrence County. She died April 1977.

    See above.

+ 336 iii. **Delia Clara GALLOWAY** was born 1884.

John Galloway married (2) **Mary LEWIS**, daughter of James J. LEWIS and Rebecca BURD.

See LEWIS Section.

241. **Joseph**[11] **SCARBERRY** (Joseph[10] SCARBERRY, Isaac[9] SCARBERRY, Zachariah[8] SCARBERRY, Isaac[7], Robert[6], John[5], John[4], John[3], William[2], Isaac[1]) was born September 1863 and died 29 November 1915.[389]

The 1900 census for Millers Precinct, Lawrence County, shows Joseph Scarberry as 36 years old, born September 1863. Wife, Susan, was 33. Children: Phoebe, 8; Adam, 6; Lawrence H., 3 months. Also in the household was nephew George R. Rigney. The year and month of birth of each of the children is shown below.[390]

When the census was taken in 1910, Joseph and Susan were enumerated with the Athalia Village Precinct of Rome Township. Joseph was 46 and Susan 45. Daughter Eva was 18; son Herbert, 9; daughter Lucy, 7.[391]

Joseph died in 1915, and when the 1920 census was taken, Susan, 53, was head of household. Son Herbert, 19, was at home, as was Lucy, 16.[392]

Joseph married **Susan RIGNEY**. Susan was born 24 September 1863 and died 26 December 1936. She was the daughter of George W. RIGNEY and Sarah Jane BURD.[393] Marriage is proven by marriage record of daughter Eva.

They had the following children:

- 337 i. **Phoebe (Eva)**[12] **SCARBERRY** was born December 1891. She married **George MANNON**, 41, of Athalia, on 18 May 1912. Eva, 20, was also of Athalia, the daughter of Jos. Scarberry and Susan Rigney. George was a son of Jno. MANNON and Mary J. McCONNELL.[394]

- 338 ii. **Adam SCARBERRY** was born August 1893.

- 339 iii. **Lawrence H. SCARBERRY** was born March 1900.

+ 340 iv. **Herbert SCARBERRY** was born 1901.

- 341 v. **Lucy SCARBERRY** was born 1903.

246. **Banks**[11] **SCARBERRY** (Joseph[10] SCARBERRY, Isaac[9] SCARBERRY, Zachariah[8] SCARBERRY, Isaac[7], Robert[6], John[5], John[4], John[3], William[2], Isaac[1]) was born 1875. He died 5 February 1941.

When the census for Rome Township, Lawrence County, Ohio, was taken in 1930, Banks was 54; his wife,

Mary, was 46. Children were son Hollie, 20; Thomas W., 16; Maggie, 13; Mary, 10; and Irene, 7.[395]

Iris (Scarberry) Burd supplied much of the information on this family.

Banks married **Mary Susan BROOKS**, daughter of Lewis Edward BROOKS, on 21 November 1900. Mary was born 10 January 1885. She died 16 May 1968.

Banks and Mary had the following children:

    342   i.   **Goldie Marie**[12] **SCARBERRY** was born 21 April 1902.

    343   ii.   **Sylvia Banks SCARBERRY** was born 27 March 1904.

    344   iii.   **Lewis Edward SCARBERRY** was born 29 June 1906.

    345   iv.   **Girl SCARBERRY** was stillborn 29 September 1908.

    346   v.   **Hollie SCARBERRY** was born 31 October 1909.

    347   vi.   **Joseph Lee SCARBERRY** was born 19 June 1912.

    348   vii.   **Thomas William SCARBERRY** was born 29 August 1914.

    349   viii.   **Maggie Virginia SCARBERRY** was born 27 November 1916.

    350   ix.   **Roy Odell SCARBERRY** was born 23 March 1919.

    351   x.   **Mary SCARBERRY** was born 1920.

    352   xi.   **Cloie Irene SCARBERRY** was born 8 February 1923.

    353   xii.   **Boy SCARBERRY**.

267. **Elemender**[11] **SCARBERRY** (Elemender[10] SCARBERRY, John[9] SCARBERRY, Zachariah[8] SCARBERRY, Isaac[7], Robert[6], John[5], John[4], John[3], William[2], Isaac[1]) was born 13 March 1864 in Guyan Township, Gallia County, Ohio. He died 27 April 1954.

Most of the information on this family was furnished by Dwayne J. Scarberry of Ona, West Virginia.

Elemender married (1) **Agness Setty AMOS**.

Elemender married (2) **Nancy Ann LYKINS** on 24 February 1889 in Mason County, West Virginia. Nancy was born 9 September 1864. She died 16 December 1931.

Elemender and Nancy had the following children:

    354   i.   **Ernest E.**[12] **SCARBERRY** was born 21 October 1889 and died 6 September 1943.

    355   ii.   **Gilbert "Bert" SCARBERRY** was born 7 September 1891 and died 25 August 1936.

    356   iii.   **Elmer C. SCARBERRY** was born 9 August 1893 and died 23 January 1979.

    357   iv.   **Icy Harriet "Hattie" SCARBERRY** was born 1895

    358   v.   **Charles E. SCARBERRY** was born 29 May 1897 and died 1 September 1961.

    359   vi.   **William SCARBERRY** was born 1897. He died 10 September 1899 in Cabell County, West Virginia. The death register shows him as two years old, having parents Nancy and E. J. Scarberry.[396]

+   360   vii.   **Ira SCARBERRY** was born 28 September 1900 and died 11 August 1971.

    361   viii.   **Laura Elizabeth SCARBERRY** was born 28 September 1900 and died July 1991

299. **Rachel Minerva**[11] **ANDERSON** (Celia Jane[10] DOUGHTY, Rachel[9] SCARBERRY, Zachariah[8] SCARBERRY, Isaac[7],

Robert[6], John[5], John[4], John[3], William[2], Isaac[1]) died 25 April 1973.

Rachel married **William Henry Harrison LEWIS**, "Willie," son of Richard Clark LEWIS and Mary Ann BURD, on 15 November 1913. Willie was born 1891 in Ohio. He died 27 May 1940.

See the LEWIS Section for more on this family.

300. Nancy Rachel[11] SCARBERRY "Nanny" (Elizabeth Susan[10] DOUGHTY, Rachel[9] SCARBERRY, Zachariah[8] SCARBERRY, Isaac[7], Robert[6], John[5], John[4], John[3], William[2], Isaac[1]) was born 13 November 1882 in Lawrence County, Ohio. She died 19 November 1967 in Portsmouth, Ohio.[397]

Nancy's son, Clarence, was born on 23 February 1914, and his birth certificate shows his mother to have been 30 at her last birthday, and her residence was Proctorville, Ohio. Her husband, Louis Young, was said to have been 31 at his last birthday, and his place of residence was 2583 ½ N. High Street, Columbus, Ohio. His occupation was laborer; hers was housework.

Clarence was born in Lawrence County, Ohio, for Nancy had returned from Columbus to the comfort of her own home. Louis had not treated her the way she had expected. She must have had serious complaints about him, but she never voiced them to her grandchildren. She and Louis were officially divorced on 5 December 1918.[398]

Her stoicism about life with Louis did not extend to a boy who shoved her out of her chair one day when she was in elementary school. She was humiliated and mentioned this incident more than once. She said he had never asked her to forgive him and she never did.

Nancy was reserved and kept her feelings to herself. She attended school for only a few years, but she read the newspapers, was knowledgeable, and always dignified. She kept her back straight and looked neat at all times. Whenever she went to church, she wore floral patterned rayon dresses, as did most women of her age, and the standard low black pump that laced. And she usually wore a hat, often decorated with artificial flowers. She was proud of her right to vote, and she always dressed up for the occasion.

When I knew Grandma, she was plump in a grandmotherly sort of way. But once she showed me a dress she had worn as a young woman. It had a waist of 18 inches or less—she was proud of her small waist, but I cannot remember exactly how small it was. The dress required a corset, but still I was impressed. She had been pretty and had had several suitors.

What prompted Nancy to go to Columbus to work as a maid, I have never heard. Perhaps she knew of no one in her immediate vicinity that she wanted to marry and decided to explore new ground.

Nancy took comfort in the lyrics to favorite hymns, and she left copies of them in her trunk. She was close to her brother, Jasper, and she saved some of the letters he sent her. He joined the army at 16 and wrote her regularly. A letter dated 18 June 1913 begins, "Dear Sister I thought I would answer your most kind and welcome letter that came to hand several days ago and certainly was pleased to hear from you… " He signed it, "good by from your loving brother, Jasper." There are others sent to her while he was still in service. Nancy also saved a letter dated 13 February 1921 from Columbus, and another dated 8 July 1924 from Jackson Center, Ohio. And Nancy's brother Grover sent her a letter from France (dated 15 September 1918) and one from Germany (dated 15 January 1919). When the war was over, Susan Scarberry got a call from someone at a village on the Ohio River. She was told that one of her soldiers (I am not sure which one) had found his way there. It was suggested someone come and get him. He was suffering from shell shock. Both Jasper and Grover had successful careers after the war, so the shock and terror of war must have healed fairly quickly.

On 30 August 1926 the superintendent of the Ohio Hospital for Epileptics in Gallipolis, Ohio, sent a letter to Mrs. Nancy Young of Proctorville, Ohio, offering her a job as an attendant. To my knowledge, she never accepted. She did participate in a cooking school and then worked as a cook for the State Hospital in Huntington, West Virginia.

I have a clipping entitled "Pleasant Ridge" from an unidentified newspaper. It tells of a February meeting of the Ladies Sewing Circle of Pleasant Ridge (the year not given). The women were quilting at the home of Mr. and Mrs. W. B. Moser, and a dinner followed. The event honored a minister, a Mr. E. P. Watson, and his wife and son Paul, who were leaving for Bowling Green, Kentucky. The Watsons were from Huntington, as were Mr. and Mrs. W. D. Pine. People present included Mrs. Nannie Young. Others were Mr. and Mrs. Lew Callicoat and son Billy; Mr. and Mrs. Earl

Edwards; Mr. and Mrs. Willie Hesson and son Charles; Mrs. Mary Galloway; Mrs. Mary Scarberry, Mrs. Chester Bradley and son Robt.; Mr. and Mrs. Dillie Edwards; Lizzie Peredo, Mrs. Nannie Bricker; Mrs. May Johnson.

Nanny married **Louis YOUNG**, son of Maria "Elizabeth" YOUNG, on 12 March 1913 in Columbus, Ohio. For the marriage application Louis declared that he was 30 years old, said his father was Frank Young, and that his mother's name was unknown. Nancy's age was said to have been 23, but she was 30.[399] Louis was born 1877 in Truro Township, Franklin County, Ohio. He died 9 August 1941 in Columbus, Ohio.

Louis was a tall, unusually strong man with a receding chin. Before he met Nancy Scarberry, he traveled to Germany and worked in a shipyard. Louis's mother, Maria Elizabeth Young (Jung), was a German immigrant. She had come to the United States with her uncle and aunt, Edward and Elizabeth Achenbach, in 1866 or 1867. Elizabeth (Jung) was 13 at the time of the 1870 U.S. census for Truro Township, Franklin County, Ohio, and she was helping in the Achenbach house. Her last name was considered *Achenbach*, but that was an error. Edward was 48, a saloonkeeper, and his wife was 46. Also in the household was Amalie Achenbach, age 7, relationship unstated. All were born in Prussia. Two households away lived John and Elizabeth Huffman, ages 57 and 43, respectively. A two-year-old female, Miner (?), lived with them. John Huffman was born in Saxony and Elizabeth in Bayerne (?) (Germany).[400] Thirty years later, in 1900, Elizabeth Huffman would be living in Elizabeth Achenbach's home.

Family tradition says that Elizabeth Young came to Columbus with relatives, that one of them had a brewer's license, and that the established brewers in the area would not let him compete. Edward Achenbach would seem to have been that person, for he made his living as a saloonkeeper. The 1880 United States census for Truro Township shows Ed Archenbach [*sic*], 56, born in Nasau; wife, Elizabeth, 58, born in Nasau; and Elizabeth Young, niece, 24, born in Nasau, employed as a servant. The mother and father of each of them had been born in Nasau. John Kentsler, 39, born in Baden, was living with them, and both his parents were born in Baden.[401] The German state of Nassau became Hesse-Nassau in 1866.

On 6 October 1890 Charles Brecht, widower, of Franklin County, sold to Maria Elizabeth Young one acre of land in half section 30, Section 18, Township 12, Range 21. Witnesses to the deed were Arthur Hayde (Notary Public) and Irving Seleger (?).[402] The 1880 U.S. Census for Columbus, Ohio, includes Chas. Brecht, age 55, born in Baden, Germany. His wife, Catharine, was 52, and from Wuertemberg. Children were George, 20; David 14; Mary 17, all born in Ohio.[403]

The 1900 census for Franklin County, Ohio, shows Elizabeth Young as head of family, born June 1856. She and both her parents were born in Germany. Elizabeth had a boarder, George Ruppenburg, 50, born in Germany. Elizabeth was in Dwelling 34. Dwelling 27 housed Elizabeth Achenbach, born May 1822 in Germany. Living with her was Elizabeth Huffman, born May 1820 in Germany, and a servant, Charles Souvene, 53, born in Holland.[404]

On 7 July 1906 James W. Evenden, trustee of property belonging to Edward Wolf, sold Lot No. 542 to Marie E. Young. It was in Wicklow Extension, an addition to the city of Columbus. The lot had been recorded in Plat Book 7, pages 65-66. Witnesses were Willis Heid and Hannah Freidenberg.[405] This property was on the west side of High Street.

The 1920 census for Truro Township puts Elizabeth Young on the National Road (Main Street), immigrating in 1867. She was a washerwoman, and she owned her own home. George Ruppenberg, named as a boarder in 1900, was still part of Elizabeth's household. He was 71 and also had immigrated in 1867. He and both his parents were born in Germany.[406]

The 1930 census, City of Columbus, shows Elizabeth Young as owner of her home. She was 72 and born in Prussia, immigrating in 1866. Her father and mother both were born in Rhine, Germany. Language spoken in the home was German. She was living alone and working as a laundress in private homes. Her address was 2839 Main Street.[407] Elizabeth Young had been in America for 64 years and her primary language still was German. Her daughter-in-law, my grandmother, said that when she spoke English, her accent was thick, and she sometimes spoke an English word so that it sounded like foul language, an embarrassment to my grandmother when she was with her in public.

Elizabeth (Jung) Young died in St. Anthony Hospital in Columbus on 8 August 1940. Her doctor said he had attended her from 1 January 1940 to 7 August 1940. The principal cause of her death was arteriosclerosis. Contributing factors were hernia and senility. She was 84 and single. Her profession was housekeeper. The informant for her death certificate was Mrs. Wm. Will of Columbus. She stated that Elizabeth had been born in Baden, Germany, and she did not know the names of her parents.[408] Elizabeth was buried in Greenlawn Cemetery in Columbus, and her only child, Louis, never placed a marker on her grave. In his defense, he may have been ill, for he died almost exactly a year later, and his cancer had spread from its origins. On the other hand, when Louis filled out his marriage certificate, he claimed he did not know who his mother was and that his father's name was Frank. Louis may have resented her for having him out of wedlock.

Family tradition says that Louis met Nancy Scarbery (she did not double the last *r*) while she was working as a maid in his home. His marriage certificate states that he was a dairyman. He may have been managing a farm that was not his own, however. Louis willed his estate to John H. Wolf. The U.S. census of 1920 shows John H. Wolf, 46, head of household. His wife was Margaret M., 43. Children were Rozellia, 22, a clerk in a drygoods store; John P., 17, Mary E., 13, Tressa, 11, Henry, 9; and Lorelene (?) 5. They were living on Granville Road (State Route 161). It runs across the north end of Columbus, between Granville on the east and Dublin on the west, but the Wolf family was still in Truro Township, which is east of central Columbus and includes Whitehall. John H. Wolf was a dairy farmer. He had been born in Ohio, his parents in Germany.[409] By 1930 this family was living on Yearling Road in Truro Township. John's profession was still dairy farming.[410]

Why Louis quit the dairy farm work is not known by my family. But he did enjoy giving milk that was left over from the day's deliveries to hospitals, and thus he was said to have an interest in charities. Correspondence between him and Nancy shows that, in an effort to satisfy her ideas on his employment, he took a job in Montpelier, Ohio, near the Michigan and Indiana lines. On 6 January 1915 he wrote a letter from Montpelier on The Smith Hotel letterhead.

> *Dearie, Dearie,*
> *I have received my clothes from you and your letter...I am very much surprised by your statement that you are sorry that I was not liking my position as well as I might. It is a poor time now to be sorry when there is nothing to be sorry for. When I lost ever thing that I myself worked for you did not feel sorry for that. As I have nothing left and lost every thing on account of my married life and not once did you feel sorry for me. I have come to the conclusion to make the best of what is left in life.*
> *Do what ever you see fit and send my truck and all of my books home to me mother...*
> *.Yours, L. Young.*

Louis was a curious man and was said to read everything he could get his hands on; therefore his collection of books.

Grandma saved another of his letters. It was written 15 January 1916 and again on The Smith Hotel letterhead. His handwriting was well-formed, forward leaning, and full of flourishes.

> *Mrs. L. Young*
> *825 N. Summit Street*
> *Columbus, Ohio.*
>
> *As you wanted to see me as soon as possible, I will be home some time the latter part of January.*
> *Your last letter is just what I expected from you, and as I have broad shoulders I can stand for all of it.*
> *Respectfully yours,*
> *Louis Young*

These letters, of course, reveal only Louis's side to their differences. One reason Nancy went home to her mother to have her baby was that Louis had proclaimed that she did not need any special care during delivery—after all, cows didn't. Son Clarence was born in 1914, and his mother was living in Columbus in 1915 and 1916, so she may have had second thoughts about leaving Louis. She may have spent some time with her sister, Chloe, and her husband. Their brother Grover sent a letter to Nancy during his service in France. It was dated 15 September 1918. In it he asked if

The Scarberrys (Scarboroughs), Doughtys, Lewises, and Paynes of Lawrence County, Ohio

Chloe was still in Columbus, her husband, Tom, still working at the post office. When Clarence was a small child, Louis traveled to Lawrence County to visit him. Louis was Catholic and was concerned that his son had not been baptized. He wanted Nancy to go back to him, but she said that too much had passed between them. When she found out later that Louis and his second wife, Eleanor, had divorced, she felt redeemed, that for sure he was a difficult person to live with.

A certificate of divorce was granted to Louis and Nancy in Lawrence County on 3 December 1918, the agreement having been signed on 27 June 1918. Nancy was given full custody and Louis was to pay the court costs of $149.76, plus some other notes amounting to $172.57. After 1 September 1918 he was responsible only for $10 a month until Clarence became 16. Louis signed the document in his usual beautiful hand, but Nancy's signature was shaky.[411] A letter to Nancy from her attorneys (dated 27 June 1918) revealed that Louis's mother had signed the two $50 notes that were due. The attorneys assured Nancy that if Louis failed to meet his obligations, he would be arrested by the sheriff and sent to the penitentiary.[412] Louis made the monthly payments until Clarence turned 15. Nancy and Clarence were resentful, because they knew Louis had calculated that they wouldn't bother with prosecuting him at that late date. But considering that Louis rarely saw his son during his growing years, his record of payment was actually quite good.

Robert Reinhard, who married Louis's granddaughter, Rachel Young, taught music at a high school in Dublin, now a suburb of Columbus, and the elderly janitor there said he had known Louis, having worked for him when he owned a gas station. Louis would refuse the use of his restrooms to customers who did not buy gas, stating his position coarsely on what was to be accepted in return for what. Louis's home in Dublin, at 37 Bridge Street, was at a good location, overlooking the Scioto River.

Clarence and wife, Faye, lived in Columbus the first five years of their marriage. And one day, when Faye was home alone, a man came to the door under some pretense. While Faye tried to answer his questions, he kept peering over her shoulder at Rachel, who was a toddler at the time. Faye described the man to Clarence, and he fit his father's description.

Clarence and Faye were living in Portsmouth, Ohio, when his father died. Henry W. Wolf sent a telegram to Clarence Young on 9 August 1941, stating that his father had died that day. He asked Clarence to call him. Louis died of a carcinoma that had metastasized, primary in the penis. His doctor had begun attending him on 28 July 1941. Henry Wolf, of 840 Erickson Avenue, was the informant for the death certificate, and also executor of the will.

Louis's death certificate said he was a self-employed trucker who hauled ice and that he was divorced from Eleanor Young. His first wife was not mentioned. Louis was buried at St. Joseph's Cemetery.[413]

Clarence sent a letter to his mother after his father's funeral:

> *My father was buried today about 10 A.M. Faye, I, & Mrs. Wright & her girl were there at the funeral & graveyard. There were 3 old men (who knew him) were there & his lawyer. I don't think there was any unnecessary delay in getting in touch with me. He willed me $50.00 (To make it legal) and the rest to the lawyers father which was an old friend of his. He died in St. Francis hospital. His home was in Dublin. Dublin is a few miles beyond Columbus. He was 64. His mother died about 37 or 38. They were not sure of the exact date.*
>
> *We have to go back to Columbus a Thursday to get that place sold. That lawyer I had has been on a vacation.*
>
> *I guess we will be up Saturday evening.*

The Wrights had been good friends of Mom and Dad when they lived in Columbus. The "place" that Dad said must be sold would have been the home that he and Mom had owned on the north side of Columbus.

Henry W. Wolf told Dad that Louis felt like he did not owe him anything, for he had not treated him like a father. Dad did side with his mother. After she died, he bought a stone marker for his father's grave.

Henry W. Wolf was executor of Louis's estate, and Louis had been named administrator of his mother's estate but had not acted on his responsibilities. A document was recorded in Probate Court of Franklin County, Ohio, on 2

November 1943. It stated that Mr. Wolf should keep the case of Louis Young (No. 94,675) open another six months, until the estate of Maria E. Young (Case No. 90,333) was administered. Henry Wolfe had wanted to sell Maria's real estate to pay debts, but no buyer had been found.

The assets that Henry had to administer were the house in Dublin, at 37 Bridge Street, valued at $850.00; the one-acre lot at 3928 East Main Street, in Truro Township, Columbus, valued at $2,000. (Maria Elizabeth's death certificate places her at 2937 East Main Street. The 1930 Census places her at 2839. The description of the one-acre lot—1/2 section 30, Section 18, Township 12, Range 21--matches the lot sold to Maria Elizabeth Young in 1890 by Charles Brecht.) Louis had cash on hand of $117.06, and personal chattels amounting to $135.00. Included were a 1926 Dodge truck, a 1930 Ford truck, a 1926 Ford truck, an ice machine, scrap iron, and a platform scale (the rest indecipherable). Incidentally, Louis's death certificate gives his address as 137 Bridge Street, Dublin, Ohio.

As to expenses, what is bothersome is a $103-charge for tombstones as per will, recorded as an expense for 10 January 1944. Maria Elizabeth Young has no marker on her grave, and, as stated above, it was Dad who eventually had a stone laid at the head of his father's grave. Margaret Wolfe, widow, was sole heir of John P. Wolf, and she received $182.82. (See the census records above. Margaret's husband and Henry's father was John *H.* Wolf.) Expenses summarized: $294.73 for McNamara Funeral Home, Columbus; $24.70 to R. H. Carpenter, Dublin; $42.38 to St. Francis Hospital; $125, estimated cost of 2 grave markers requested by will; $5.00 to Rev. Robert Harwick; $55 to Henry Wolf as administrator of estate of Maria E. Young. Total assets were $3,102.06; total liabilities were $546.81; net value was $2,555.25. Clarence Young, son, of Sciotoville, Ohio, received $50; John Wolf of 388 Yearling Road, Columbus, no relationship to the deceased, received the rest. The estate was officially settled on 23 July 1945.[414]

Louis and Nanny had the following child:

+ 362 i. **Clarence Hasten[12] YOUNG** was born 23 February 1914 and died 8 December 2005.

302. **Alva E.[11] SCARBERRY** (Elizabeth Susan[10] DOUGHTY, Rachel[9] SCARBERRY, Zachariah[8] SCARBERRY, Isaac[7], Robert[6], John[5], John[4], John[3], William[2], Isaac[1]) was born 7 July 1887 in Lawrence County, Ohio. He died in 1960 in Lawrence County and was buried in New Rome Cemetery, Lawrence County.

Clarence H. Young, Iris Burd, and Alva's grandson Floyd Scarberry, have furnished information on this family.

When the 1920 Rome Township census was taken, Alva and Lennie were both 32; daughter Hazel was 10; Marie, 8; and Forrest, 7.[415] By the time the 1930 census was taken, only Marie and Forrest were still at home with their parents.[416]

Alva and Lennie had a farm on down the hill below the old Scarberry home place. Their house was secluded and cozy and had a well-tended yard with a large willow. The long narrow road, about the width of a driveway, now called Scarberry Road, edged past the old Scarberry home place and on down past Alva's to Pleasant Ridge Road. Recently it has been paved, but when I was growing up, cars could not travel down below Granny's place. The large sandstones made it too bumpy. But when we were walking, it was a shortcut between Susan Scarberry's home at the top of the ridge and the home of the Ezra Lewis family on the valley part of Pleasant Ridge Road.

Alva married **Lennie WORKMAN** on 23 January 1909 in Lawrence County, Ohio. The marriage record reveals that Lennie was a daughter of David WORKMAN and Myrtle ELLIOTT. Both she and Alvah were 21 years old at the time of their marriage. Alva signed his name *Alvie*.[417] Lennie was buried in New Rome Cemetery, Lawrence County.

They had the following children:

+ 363 i. **Hazel[12] SCARBERRY** was born about 1910.

+ 364 ii. **Marie SCARBERRY** was born 22 February 1911 in Lawrence County, Ohio. She died 11 February 2000. Marie's exact birth date and date of death was taken from the U. S. Social Security Death Index.

+ 365 iii. **Forrest B. SCARBERRY** was born 14 January 1913 and died November 1985.

304. **Grover C.[11] SCARBERRY** (Elizabeth Susan[10] DOUGHTY, Rachel[9] SCARBERRY, Zachariah[8] SCARBERRY, Isaac[7], Robert[6], John[5], John[4], John[3], William[2], Isaac[1]) was born 8 February 1893 in Lawrence County, Ohio. He died 5 July 1976 in Proctorville, Ohio, and was buried in Miller Cemetery, Millersport, Ohio.[418]

Grover served in France during World War I, enlisting 29 April 1918 at Ironton, Ohio, at the age of 25. He was a private and participated in the battles of Meuse, Argonne, and Verdun. His records declare him to have been of excellent character, six-feet tall, with brown eyes, red hair, and a light complexion. He was honorably discharged on 4 June 1919. Reason given, ETS (expiration of term of service).[419]

Grover had joined when American divisions were still used mostly in support of French and British units. But after the Americans had a victory at Cantigny in May 1918, the American Expeditionary Force commanders were increasingly in charge. The Battle of Argonne lasted from 27 September to 6 October 1918, General John J. Pershing leading more than one million American and French soldiers. More than 200 square miles of French territory was recovered from the Germans.[420] And Grover was part of that force.

On 15 September 1918, Grover sent a letter from France to his sister Mrs. Nannie Young. He told her to tell Clarence, "I think we will soon Get the Kiser an come home." Grover signed with the number of his battery, D. 324 FA Heavy, American Expeditionary Forces. Nannie (Nancy) saved another letter of his, this one dated 15 January 1919 and from Kansen, Germany. He mentions that the 84th Division already had gone home. He requested three books of postage stamps so he could send home some souvenirs and added, "tell Clarence Ill send him German post cards so he can Get some Idea of Germany tell Clarence to send me a cake of chewing gum when he rites." There are some punctuation, capitalization, and spelling errors in Grover's letters, but he was doing well considering his father had limited the number of years his children could spend in school.

When the census was taken in 1930 for Rome Township, there was a boarder, Homer Patton, 18, in his household. Grover was 37, a farmer; wife, Georgia, was 33; son Clifford was 9; Russell was 7; and Leo was 2 years 1 month.[421]

One of Grover's jobs after the war was managing the locks on the Ohio River.

Grover married **Georgia FAULKENER** about 1919. Georgia was born 1897 in Ohio.

They had the following children:

    366   i.   **Clifford[12] SCARBERRY** was born 1921.

    367   ii.   **Russell SCARBERRY** was born 1923.

                      Russell owned a store in Rome, Ohio, and later moved to Ripley, West Virginia. He married a woman named Catherine and had several children.

    368   iii.   **Leo SCARBERRY** was born 1927. Leo married a **Miss FORTNER.**.

305. **Jasper Lewis[11] SCARBERRY**, "Jay," (Elizabeth Susan[10] DOUGHTY, Rachel[9] SCARBERRY, Zachariah[8] SCARBERRY, Isaac[7], Robert[6], John[5], John[4], John[3], William[2], Isaac[1]) was born November 1895 in Lawrence County, Ohio. He died October 1949 in Columbus, Ohio, and was buried at Port Jefferson, Ohio.

At the age of 16 Jasper was eager to join the army, and being under age, he got his brother Alva to sign for him. Jasper was with Company F, 18th Infantry. He was at Fort MacKenzie, Wyoming, in 1912. His assignments took him on to Texas, to Arizona, and to France, where he was wounded twice and hospitalized. He had shrapnel in his back, and a bullet went through the calf of his leg.

Jasper wrote a letter to his sister Nancy from Texas City, Texas, on 18 June 1913. He expressed how pleased he had been to hear from her and learn she was having a good time. He asked how everything was in Columbus and mentioned a letter he had received from home. He complained about the heat and the blowing sand. Another letter, dated 2 March 1915, came from Douglas, Arizona. Again he complained about the sand. But he was glad the state was "dry," for that eliminated the problems of dealing with drunks.

Douglas, Arizona, was on the border with Mexico. The Mexican government became unstable when the

Mexican dictator Porfirio Diaz was ousted. In March 1911, in response to the unrest, President Taft ordered 30,000 troops sent to the Mexican border. Most of the troops were sent home by August. In 1912, however, the 9th Cavalry was ordered to Douglas, Arizona, and the 13th Cavalry to El Paso, Texas. Soon there were nearly 7,000 troops along the border. General Pancho Villa, formerly known as a bandit, gained the upper hand in Mexico, but on 1 November 1915 was defeated at Agua Prieta, across the border from Douglas, Arizona. As a result, Villa resorted to his old bandit ways, and he attacked Columbus, New Mexico, on 9 March 1916. Brig. Gen. John J. Pershing of the U S. then made a punitive raid into Mexico.[422] When the U.S. declared war on Germany in April 1917, President Wilson put General Pershing in charge of the American Expeditionary Force.

On 22 April 1917 Jasper's address was still Douglas, Arizona. He told his sister that he was stuck drilling recruits for the next two months. The schedule was from 8:00 in the morning to 5:00 in the evening, and it was making him very tired.

Jasper's 30 December 1917 letter to Nancy was from France. He said, "We are having a hard winter hear with plenty of snow. I got a letter from Chloa, and they are thinking of going to the country where they can raise their own eats. The worse trouble hear is getting magazines to read and tobacco. It was almost impossible to get tobacco when we first came hear. How is all the Family....from your Loving Brother, J.S." The censor, Lt. Pollard marked *O K* at the end of the letter. On 23 February 1918 Jasper wrote, "Dear Sister, Recieved your most kind and welcome letter and certainly was glad to hear from you and to know that you was all ok." Recently he had received a letter from Chloe. There was more rain than snow, but the rain could hinder his work as much as the snow. He signed, "With Love and best wishes to all from your loving Brother. J.L.S." Nancy was the oldest child in her family and had helped rear her younger brothers and sister. She and Jasper were good friends.

Jasper's daughter Janet Sailor has in her possession a document signed by J. L. Topham, Jr., Lieut. Colonel of Infantry. The letterhead is "United States Disciplinary Barracks, Fort Leavenworth, Kansas." It is dated 24 July1919, and the subject is *Services of Sergeant Jasper L. Scarberry, 2nd Co., U.S.D.B. Guard*. In the body of the document Lt. Topham, Jr., describes an incident that took place on 21 May 1919. Jasper was called to the prison yard to control some mutinous prisoners. A prisoner was attempting to go into a restricted area, and when Jasper tried to stop him, the prisoner picked up a "missle" to throw at him. Jasper struck the prisoner on the head and arms. At that, many other prisoners rushed him. Jasper retreated, but knowing he must report the incident to his superior officer, he armed himself with a gun so he could walk to his destination with some protection. On entering the prison yard, he again was rushed, this time by several hundred prisoners, who were throwing things at him. Jasper drew his weapon, but it malfunctioned. He fixed it and fired high, but by then all the guards were being assaulted by the prisoners. The guards were armed only with clubs, so Jasper shot a prisoner in the leg. A thorough investigation of the incident was completed and no charges were brought against Jasper. The lieutenant declared him to have "proven himself to be an excellent soldier, brave and fearless in the performance of his duty."

After Jasper was discharged, he studied agriculture at Purdue University in Indiana. He began his career as the manager of a creamery in Jackson Center, Ohio, but the damp coldness of his work gave him sinus trouble. Most of his career was spent as a welding foreman at Jeffrey's Manufacturing Company in Columbus, Ohio. Clarence Young, his nephew, graduated from Bliss Electrical College during the Great Depression, and Jasper found him employment at Jeffrey's.

Janet Sailor said her father was a skilled craftsman, designing bookends to be made out of lead and making the molds for them. He had a heart attack and died in a hospital while listening to an Ohio State football game on the radio. He was buried at Port Jefferson, Ohio. His mother could not attend his funeral, so his widow, Thelma, sent her a photograph of him in his casket and swatch of the fabric used for his burial suit. In her accompanying letter Thelma praised Susan for having produced such a fine son.

Jasper married **Thelma RUNYAN** on 8 January 1927. The marriage announcement by Mr. and Mr. J. C. RUNYAN is the source of the date. Thelma was born 18 July 1902 and died August 1985 in Phoenix, Arizona.[423]

Thelma was a school teacher, born to J. C. and Nell (Littlejohn) RUNYAN.

Jasper and Thelma had the following children:

The Scarberrys (Scarboroughs), Doughtys, Lewises, and Paynes of Lawrence County, Ohio

  369 i. **Jean Emily**[12] **SCARBERRY** was born 13 July 1929 in Columbus, Ohio. She died 9 October 1991 in Ohio.[424]

    Jean's second husband was **Louis DeORTO**, and they had a happy life together. He preceded her in death, but he taped messages that would give her comfort after his demise. She had worked for the state of Ohio as a civil servant.

+ 370 ii. **Janet Marian SCARBERRY** was born in 1931.

306. **Orval Franklin**[11] **SCARBERRY** (Elizabeth Susan[10] DOUGHTY, Rachel[9] SCARBERRY, Zachariah[8] SCARBERRY, Isaac[7], Robert[6], John[5], John[4], John[3], William[2], Isaac[1]) was born 13 November 1898 in Lawrence County, Ohio. He died November 1974 in Lawrence County and was buried in Pleasant Ridge graveyard.

  My first memory of Orval goes back to a time when he and his family were living in a cabin down in the little valley below his mother's farmhouse. He had tuberculosis and was quarantined, but his wife, Della, opened the door to his room briefly so we could say hello. He smiled broadly, glad to see us.

  Orval and his family lived for a short time in Springfield, Ohio. He was talented in many ways: He was a farmer, an insurance salesman, and a surveyor. He drove a streetcar in Columbus, Ohio, and taught beginning tap dancing at Arthur Murray Studios.

  Orval had a jolly disposition and was fun to be around. He built a home behind the farmhouse where he had grown up and ran the farm for his mother. After she died, he and his family moved into the old home place, and it was there he passed away. The circumstances were not to be regretted. His wife, Della, said he had been reading the Bible and then stood up and did a little dance shuffle. And he died.

Orval married **Della Mae GALLOWAY**, daughter of James Nicholas GALLOWAY and Mary Elizabeth ROBINSON. Della was born 28 August 1908 in Lincoln County West Virginia. She died September 1985 in West Virginia and was buried in Pleasant Ridge graveyard, Lawrence County.

  Elizabeth, Della's mother, died when Della was three years old, and her father, James, died when she was a teenager. Della lived for a while with her brother Walter Galloway and later worked in Huntington, West Virginia, living at that time with her sister Dessie and her husband, Louis Gilfilen.

  Della was a pretty woman, with black hair and intense blue eyes. She was known for her musical talent. She could sing a tune, calling the notes by name. She played the banjo, and when my sister Rachel and I visited, she would gather us all around her in the evening, and we sang folk songs such as "Whipporwill" and "Juanita." An oil lamp glowed softly in the shadows. They were the best of times.

They had the following children:

+ 371 i. **Iris Mae**[12] **SCARBERRY** was born in 21 May 1934 and died 28 June 2011.

+ 372 ii. **Danny Douglas SCARBERRY** was born in 1947.

307. **Arthur William**[11] **SCARBERRY**, "Red," (Elizabeth Susan[10] DOUGHTY, Rachel[9] SCARBERRY, Zachariah[8] SCARBERRY, Isaac[7], Robert[6], John[5], John[4], John[3], William[2], Isaac[1]) was born 1 January 1903 in Lawrence County, Ohio. He died October 1979 in Columbus, Ohio.[425]

  Arthur was entered as William A. Scarberry, age 7, on the 1910 U.S. census for Rome Township, Lawrence County, Ohio.[426]

  Arthur worked for Columbus Transit Company for over 40 years. He began as a conductor on trolley cars. When he retired, he was driving a bus for the Bexley crosstown section of Columbus. Arthur liked meeting people, and he liked his job, joking that he had the privilege of telling women "where to get off." He received an award for his safety record, at the time the oldest bus driver in the system.

  People called Arthur "Red" because of his red hair. He belonged to the Masonic Lodge. Bowling was one of his hobbies, and he bowled with the Columbus Transit Bowling League, averaging 157.

Arthur married **Hazel SCHAUB** in 1922. Hazel was born 26 October 1903. She died March 1991[427]. Hazel was the daughter of William SCHAUB, born in Switzerland, and his wife, Barbara.

They had the following children:

+ 373 i. **Ruth Lucille**[12] **SCARBERRY** was born in 27 November 1922 and died July 2011.

    374 ii. **Paul Arthur SCARBERRY** was born 12 June 1929. He died December 2007.

        Paul was in the army about three years, serving in Korea as a tank driver. He retired from a plumbing factory and lived in the home of his deceased parents on Frank Road in Columbus.

        Paul married **Virginia HEAPPS**. Virginia died in the1980s.

+ 375 iii. **Marian Eileen SCARBERRY** was born in 20 August 1932 and died December 2010.

Twelfth Generation

336. **Delia Clara**[12] **GALLOWAY** (Harriet E.[11] BURD, Elizabeth[10] SCARBERRY, Isaac[9] SCARBERRY, Zachariah[8] SCARBERRY, Isaac[7], Robert[6], John[5], John[4], John[3], William[2], Isaac[1]) was born 1884.

Delia married Mr. **DANIELS**.

They had the following children:

    376 i. **Ira**[13] **DANIELS**

    377 ii. **Myrtle DANIELS**

340. **Herbert**[12] **SCARBERRY** (Joseph[11] SCARBERRY, Joseph[10] SCARBERRY, Isaac[9] SCARBERRY, Zachariah[8] SCARBERRY, Isaac[7], Robert[6], John[5], John[4], John[3], William[2], Isaac[1]) was born 1901.

The U.S. census reveals that by 1920 Herbert's mother, Susan, was head of household. (Herbert's father, Joseph, was only 46 when the 1910 census was taken.) In 1920 Herbert was 19, and his sister Lucy was 16. They were living next door to John Rigney, 56. In his household were his mother, Sarah J., 76, and Arch Rigney, 57, a cousin.[428] Herbert's mother was Susan Rigney.

The 1930 census for Cabell County, West Virginia, includes the family of Herbert Scarberry, 30, and wife, Ona, 36. Son Homer was two years old and some months.[429] They lived in Huntington.

Herbert married **Ona PAYNE**, daughter of John Shannon PAYNE and Emily J HIGGINS. Ona was born March 1894 in Lawrence County, Ohio. She died 15 September 1966 in Huntington, West Virginia. Ona was 71 years and 6 months old at the time of her death, caused by a vascular accident.[430]

They had the following children:

    378 i. **Homer E.**[13] **SCARBERRY** was born 29 July 1927. He died November 1971.[431]

        Homer appeared on the 1930 U.S. census as over two years old. He married a woman named **Pauline** and had several children.

    379 ii. **Mary SCARBERRY**

        Mary had recently married when I last saw her. Her husband was in the service and making $80

The Scarberrys (Scarboroughs), Doughtys, Lewises, and Paynes of Lawrence County, Ohio

telephone calls to her from Alaska. She seemed to be a very happy person.

360. **Ira^{12} SCARBERRY** (Elemender^{11} SCARBERRY, Elemender^{10} SCARBERRY, John^9 SCARBERRY, Zachariah^8 SCARBERRY, Isaac^7, Robert^6, John^5, John^4, John^3, William^2, Isaac^1) was born 28 September 1900 in Huntington, West Virginia. He died 11 August 1971 in Ona, West Virginia.

Ira married **Bertha Ann BLAKE** on 28 March 1920 in Huntington, West Virginia. Bertha was born 14 July 1902 in Ona, West Virginia. She died 3 February 1972 in Huntington, West Virginia.

Marriage information and dates are provided by Dwayne J. Scarberry.

Ira and Bertha had the following child:

    380   i. **David Merle^{13} SCARBERRY** was born 3 April 1942.

                 David married **Marilyn Kay CHAPMAN**. Their son **Dwayne J. SCARBERRY** is an excellent genealogical researcher.

362. **Clarence Hasten^{12} YOUNG** (Nancy Rachel^{11} SCARBERRY, Elizabeth Susan^{10} DOUGHTY, Rachel^9 SCARBERRY, Zachariah^8 SCARBERRY, Isaac^7, Robert^6, John^5, John^4, John^3, William^2, Isaac^1) was born 23 February 1914 in Lawrence County, Ohio.^{432} He died 8 December 2005 in Columbus, Ohio.

Clarence was born in Lawrence County, Ohio, because his mother had separated from his father and gone back to her parents' home. After Clarence's birth, she temporarily rejoined his father in Columbus, but finally gave up on the relationship and returned to the farm in Lawrence County. Nanny, as she was called, found employment in Huntington, West Virginia, and for a time Clarence lived with Chloe Galloway, Nanny's sister, and her husband, Tom, at their house with its view of the broad Ohio River and all its barges and other river traffic. Eventually Clarence was placed in the home of his grandparents, and there he was reared.

Clarence read widely and easily absorbed new concepts and information. His aunt Chloe offered to pay his way through medical college, but that idea was abandoned. Once, he had discovered a cow with her throat bleeding from a barbed wire puncture, and he quickly packed the wound with mud and led her back to the barn, so he had a reputation for saving one kind of life.

When the 1930 census was taken for Rome Township, Clarence Young, 16, was living with his grandmother, Susan Scarbery, 68.

Clarence was a good student and in 1931 graduated salutatorian of his class at Rome High School. He attended Bliss Electrical School in Washington, D.C., where he graduated on 1 June 1932. He and Faye Lewis married in 1934. It was not easy to find employment during the Great Depression, but Clarence's uncle Jasper Scarbery was a foreman at Jeffrey Manufacturing Company in Columbus, Ohio, and he was able to get him hired as a welder. After five years in Columbus, Clarence and Faye moved to Portsmouth, Ohio, Clarence having found a position at Ohio Power Company, Ninth Street Station. In 1941 Clarence and family were living at 1414 McConnell Avenue in Portsmouth. They moved from there to the Portsmouth suburb of Sciotoville, living first on Auburn Avenue and then buying a home on Wilson Avenue, where they remained until neither one could drive. About the time Faye turned 80, they moved into a duplex on Northwest Avenue in Upper Arlington, a suburb of Columbus. Dad said he liked living there more than anywhere else he had ever lived, although during the last two years of his life, when he was senile, he let his imagination run to the farm where he had grown up and remembered his uncles, especially Orval.

For entertainment, while his daughters chattered and argued around him, Clarence read. Favorites were *Josephus* and Gideon's *Decline and Fall of the Roman Empire*. When I was 14 we joined the growing number of owners of television sets. We girls and Mom enjoyed dramas and comedies, but Dad sought out specials on historic events or went into the back room to read.

During the 1940s Clarence invented a continuously variable transmission and sent his idea to the magazine *Popular Science* (or it may have been *Popular Mechanics*). Or he tried to. His idea seems to have been intercepted, for the reply he received from the magazine had nothing to do with his idea. Later one of the major rubber companies advertised their small engine with a continuously variable transmission, using much of the exact terminology he had used in his description. His invention had been stolen. Naively, he had made no attempt at getting it patented. After he retired, he constructed a continuously variable transmission for a bicycle and considered getting a patent for it, but a friend who was an engineer said it needed refining, for the mechanism was large and clumsy.

Dad did get to enjoy one of his own inventions. He liked canoeing, but wanted his rowing efforts to move him forward instead of backward. He designed a gear system for his oars that would do just that He kept his canoe at Lake Vesuvius in Lawrence County. One time he arrived at the lake to find his canoe had been borrowed by someone. The culprit must have been surprised when he started rowing!

Dad said more than once that he wanted to make the world a better place. He would smile as if to admit he knew his goal was perhaps unreal, but that was his desire. He instilled a love of learning in us girls, and good has come from that and his other areas of influence. He believed in honesty to the extent that he added an explanation to one of his tax deductions, and, as might be expected, the Internal Revenue Service investigated him. Still, a high standard of adherence to truth (and Mom shared it) was good for all of us.

Not long before Dad retired, he presented an idea to his boss at Ohio Power Company. When there was a power failure in an area, the information came into the system a few seconds too late to make the source obvious. He figured out how to get the information earlier. Dad's boss asked him to present his idea on a chalkboard for an engineer. He did so, and the engineer just watched, said nothing, and left the room. He made some modification to Dad's idea and it was put to use throughout American Electric Power. .

Dad had the courage to be different. He was fascinated by famous eccentrics, especially Thomas Edison. Independent thinking, however, is not always appreciated during church discussions. While still in Lawrence County, he and Mom had become members of the Church of Christ, and we all made serious effort to be at services on Sunday morning, Sunday evening, and Wednesday evening. Dad brought to discussion facts from his study of history, and they were not necessarily well received. He was often frustrated, for he had no associates who read as much as he, and at work he was, for the most part, under employed. A few years after he moved to Portsmouth to work for Ohio Power, he was invited by a fellow employee to move to Elyria, Ohio, and design motors with him. Dad, however, felt he should stay close to his mother, who lived in neighboring Lawrence County.

Several years before he retired Dad's hearing began to fail, and his ability to hear music that he enjoyed became limited. He used ear phones when he watched television, for normal volume would not do. In the meantime, he developed macular degeneration, and his eye sight became drastically impaired. His son-in-law, Tom Brown, who was always kind and helpful to him, marked the controls on his TV set and videos so he could continue with some entertainment. He was provided with a closed-circuit TV and then he could put books on a tray and magnify them greatly. He continued to read until just a few years before his death. His inability to connect with the world around him, however, caused confusion to take over, and he began hearing music that wasn't there and visiting with people who weren't there. Yet he retained his knowledge, spatial ability, and sense of humor. He spent his last couple of years at the Columbus Alzheimer's Care Center (although he had a different form of dementia) and was much appreciated by the staff, for he could communicate. Several of them came to his funeral.

Clarence married **Ernestine Faye LEWIS**, daughter of Ezra Clare LEWIS and Edna Mae PAYNE, on 22 December 1934 in Ironton, Ohio. Ernestine was born 24 December 1911 in Lawrence County, Ohio. She died 10 April 2001 in Columbus, Ohio.

Mom went by her middle name, Faye, and her brother Ernest Ray used his middle name. Mom had thick, coarse red hair that lay in gentle waves. Her hair was much like her father's. By the time she was 40 her hair had turned auburn, and it seemed more brown than red until the rays of the evening sun made it gleam. Ray's hair was black, like his mother's, and a neighbor commented on the beauty of seeing Mom and Ray picking strawberries side by side, one with red hair and one with black. But Mom did not work outside much, because she had fainted once when working in the fields.

Mom's parents were living at Polkadotte, Ohio, when she was born. They built the house where she grew up, around the bend from her grandfather Lewis, at a later date. Windsor High School, at Willowood, was about five miles from Mom's home. Sometimes she had a horse to ride, but if one was not available, she walked the distance. She was hardier than she looked. During the Great Depression, people used the general store at Scottown for trading, and once she walked the mile or so to the store with two chickens to barter, each hand grasping the legs of a chicken.

Faye graduated from Windsor High School in May 1930, and she delivered the class will at commencement exercises on 22 May 1930. She reported that Mabel Wall was leaving "her slow careful articulation and well modulated voice to Sadie McMahan and Margaret Pinkerman. Her calm disposition and mild temper she leaves to Pauline Zimmerman." Faye left "her secret for reducing to Beulah Donley and Rose May Lafore." The class presented the play, "The Old Oaken Bucket," and Faye played the part of Lizzy Lawrence.

Faye's graduation certificate reveals that she was a student who scored mostly in the mid to upper 80s. Twice she earned a 90 in English.

A newspaper clipping in my possession, probably from the Ironton paper, included an article on graduation ceremonies at Windsor High. In a column adjoining was an article urging parents to protect their children from tuberculosis (TB). Parents were urged to have their children tested for it. And parents were warned about the chronic form present in older people. "In many and many a home, there is a loving old grandfather, a sweet aunt or an affectionate relative who has without knowing the disease in its chronic form, calling it, perhaps, bronchitis, heart disease or asthma." I know of at least three of my relatives in Lawrence County who contracted tuberculosis. When my mother was a senior citizen, living in Portsmouth, she would have a yearly chest x-ray, and a scar would show on her lungs. She had had a mild case of TB at one time and conquered it, but a scar had been left.

Faye was always involved with friends and neighbors in Sciotoville and Portsmouth, Ohio, and missed them a lot when she moved to Columbus at the age of 80. She had worked on projects with women at the Portsmouth Church of Christ and served as treasurer of the band boosters at East High School when her daughters attended. She was a social person and enjoyed contributing to her community, but she was truly in a state of bliss when holding a baby in her lap.

Clarence and Faye had the following children:

+ 381 i. **Rachel May**[13] **YOUNG** was born 1936.

+ 382 ii. **Mabel June YOUNG** was born 1938.

+ 383 iii. **Rena Sue YOUNG** was born 1943.

+ 384 iv. **Edith Marie YOUNG** was born 1949.

363. **Hazel**[12] **SCARBERRY** (Alva E.[11] SCARBERRY, Elizabeth Susan[10] DOUGHTY, Rachel[9] SCARBERRY, Zachariah[8] SCARBERRY, Isaac[7], Robert[6], John[5], John[4], John[3], William[2], Isaac[1]) was born about 1910.

Hazel married **Clifton DUNCAN**.

They had the following children and possibly others:

385 i. **Mary Lou**[13] **DUNCAN.**

386 ii. **Opal DUNCAN**.

364. **Marie**[12] **SCARBERRY** (Alva E.[11] SCARBERRY, Elizabeth Susan[10] DOUGHTY, Rachel[9] SCARBERRY, Zachariah[8] SCARBERRY, Isaac[7], Robert[6], John[5], John[4], John[3], William[2], Isaac[1]) was born 22 February 1911 in Lawrence County, Ohio. She died 11 February 2000.[433]

Marie married **Chester EDWARDS** and they divorced.

They had the following child:

387 i. **Ernestine**[13] **EDWARDS**

She lived in California and had a daughter who was an outstanding runner. She was a candidate for the summer Olympics of 1984, but she didn't make the final cut.

365.   Forrest B.[12] SCARBERRY (Alva E.[11] SCARBERRY, Elizabeth Susan[10] DOUGHTY, Rachel[9] SCARBERRY, Zachariah[8] SCARBERRY, Isaac[7], Robert[6], John[5], John[4], John[3], William[2], Isaac[1]) was born 14 January 1913 in Lawrence County, Ohio. He died November 1985 in Grand Rapids, Ohio.[434]

Forrest appears as Forest B. Scarberry on the 1920 Rome Township census. He married Thelma Harrison, and they divorced. He and his second wife lived in Indiana and had several children. Thelma married secondly Clinton BAILEY.

Forrest married **Thelma HARRISON**.

They had the following children:

+   388   i.   **Thelma Marylene[13] SCARBERRY** was born in 1937.

+   389   ii. **Galen Forrest SCARBERRY** was born in 1944.

+   390   iii. **Floyd Garland SCARBERRY** was born in 1946.

370.   Janet Marian[12] SCARBERRY (Jasper Lewis[11] SCARBERRY, Elizabeth Susan[10] DOUGHTY, Rachel[9] SCARBERRY, Zachariah[8] SCARBERRY, Isaac[7], Robert[6], John[5], John[4], John[3], William[2], Isaac[1]) was born in 1931 in Ohio.

Janet worked as a radio announcer and sales manager of a radio station. She and her husband were divorced in 1967. She was transferred to Ogden, Utah, and worked there for several years. She enjoys talking about her family history and supplied information on her father.

Janet married **John SAILOR** on 28 August 1953.

They had the following children:

     391   i.   .**Rhea Lynette[13] SAILOR** was born 7 September 1954. She died 1990.

             Rhea lived in Ogden, Utah. She had an interest in interior decorating and attended Weaver State College. She married **Michael OBERT** There were no children. She died in 1990 in a car accident.

+   392   ii. **Robert Lewis SAILOR**, "Bobby," was born in 1956.

371.   Iris Mae[12] SCARBERRY (Orval Franklin[11] SCARBERRY, Elizabeth Susan[10] DOUGHTY, Rachel[9] SCARBERRY, Zachariah[8] SCARBERRY, Isaac[7], Robert[6], John[5], John[4], John[3], William[2], Isaac[1]) was born 21 May 1934 and died 28 June 2011.

When Iris was young, she lived in a home in the small valley off what is now Scarberry Road. I remember her sitting on the bed in her room, and there were shelves above it full of books. She introduced the joy of reading to my sister Rachel and me. I remember *A Girl of the Limberlost* and some Zane Grey books in particular. She missed a lot of school while living there, for her mother feared she would get pneumonia during the long walk to the school bus stop. Iris graduated from Fairland High School, formed from Rome High and Proctorville High in 1949. Iris was talented in drawing, painting, and photography, having won awards for the latter. Sadly, she died of a stroke about a month after her 77th birthday.

Iris married **Okey Gene BURD** on 27 March 1953. Okey was born 18 July 1930. He died 7 January 1998.

Gene was the son of Charles Oliver BURD and wife, Myrtle Marie BOWMAN. Charles's parents were Perry and Becky BURD. He enlisted in the U.S. Navy and later worked at Appalachian Power Company.

They had the following children:

+ 393 i. **Della Marie**[13] **BURD** was born in 1954.

+ 394 ii. **Rickey Ryan BURD** was born in 1958.

372. Danny Douglas[12] **SCARBERRY** (Orval Franklin[11] SCARBERRY, Elizabeth Susan[10] DOUGHTY, Rachel[9] SCARBERRY, Zachariah[8] SCARBERRY, Isaac[7], Robert[6], John[5], John[4], John[3], William[2], Isaac[1]) was born in 1947.

With the encouragement of his aunt Chloe Galloway, Danny took art lessons at a museum in Huntington, West Virginia, where he was praised for his extraordinary drawing ability. When he was a baby, his grandmother Susan Scarberry would hang a bright red cloth near his bed, and he would be content just staring at it. He also has musical talent, learning to play a violin at a young age.

Danny joined the navy and served on the USS Howard W. Gilmore as an electrician. Danny was the head electrician at American Car when he retired. He owns his own heating and air conditioning business.

Danny married **Janet Diana NULL**.

Janet has been employed by Food Fair. She and Danny love to travel, having made trips to Myrtle Beach, the Grand Tetons, and Hawaii.

They had the following children:

+ 395 i. **Gretchen Elizabeth**[13] **SCARBERRY** was born in 1973.

  396 ii. **Stacie Danielle SCARBERRY** was born in 1976.

  Stacie qualifies in medical massage therapy and is in demand for her Rolfe therapy skills. She lives in Denver and has enjoyed visiting Australia, England, and Costa Rica.

  397 iii. **Christopher Ashly SCARBERRY** was born in 1980.

  Christopher is a skilled gun smith. He has been working for Bayer Aspirin and soon will be entering the Police Academy.

373. Ruth Lucille[12] **SCARBERRY** (Arthur William[11] SCARBERRY, Elizabeth Susan[10] DOUGHTY, Rachel[9] SCARBERRY, Zachariah[8] SCARBERRY, Isaac[7], Robert[6], John[5], John[4], John[3], William[2], Isaac[1]) was born 27 November 1922 and died 29 July 2011.

Ruth met her future husband, Elza "Woody" Wood, son of George and Marietta WOOD, in Columbus, Ohio. During World War II, Woody served in the Marine Corps. He was among the Seabees who landed on the Solomon Islands and on Okinawa. His hand was injured, and he was discharged before the war was over.

In 1959 Ruth and Woody's 150-acre farm produced the top dairy herd in Delaware County, Ohio. Later they sold the herd and moved to Licking County. Woody then went to work at Lockbourne Air Force Base (now known as Rickenbacker AFB). By the time he retired, he was Chief of Planning for Civil Engineering. Ruth also worked at the base. She was a bookkeeper for the Non-appropriated Fund. Previously she had worked at a bank as cashier and bookkeeper.

Ruth spent the last couple of years of her life in a nursing home, for she had become blind from glaucoma. Two children, belonging to Woody and his first wife, preceded her in death. They were Fred E. WOOD and Wilma R. HARTFORD.

Ruth married **Elza F. WOOD**, "Woody," on 5 August 1945. Elza was born 21 August 1918 and died 20 September 1998.[435]

There was a large turnout at Woody's funeral, for he had been active in his community and was held in high esteem.

They had the following children:

+ 398   i. **David Lynn**[13] **WOOD** was born in 1946.

+ 399   ii. **William Francis WOOD** was born in 1948.

375. Marian Eileen[12] **SCARBERRY** (Arthur William[11] SCARBERRY, Elizabeth Susan[10] DOUGHTY, Rachel[9] SCARBERRY, Zachariah[8] SCARBERRY, Isaac[7], Robert[6], John[5], John[4], John[3], William[2], Isaac[1]) was born 20 August 1932 and died December 2010.

Marian lived in Butler, in Seneca County, in the northern part of Ohio. She was once employed by Nationwide Insurance in Columbus, did cafeteria work at Heidelberg University, and worked as a nurses' aide at Ruffing Family Care Center. Preceding Marian in death were her husband, son Mark Derr, and a great-grandson, Roan Mackay.

Marian belonged to the Zion Lutheran Church in Republic, Ohio, and to the Republic Senior Citizens. (Information taken from her obituary of 26 December 2010, appearing in the *Sandusky Register*.)

Marian married **Raymond A. DERR** on 12 June 1955 in Columbus, Ohio.

Raymond was a manufacturing representative for Allis Chalmers in Seneca County, Ohio. He preceded Marian in death.

They had the following children:

+ 400   i. **Timothy**[13] **DERR**

+ 401   ii. **Diane DERR**

+ 402   iii. **Mark R. DERR** was born 6 July 1959 and died 5 July 2010.

Thirteenth Generation

381. Rachel May[13] **YOUNG** (Clarence Hasten[12] YOUNG, Nancy Rachel[11] SCARBERRY, Elizabeth Susan[10] DOUGHTY, Rachel[9] SCARBERRY, Zachariah[8] SCARBERRY, Isaac[7], Robert[6], John[5], John[4], John[3], William[2], Isaac[1]) was born in 1936 in Columbus, Ohio.

From the very beginning, Rachel enjoyed being part of the world around her. Mom said that not long after Rachel was born, she was lying on her stomach and raised up her head and looked around with big wide eyes.

While still attending Portsmouth East High School, Rachel worked part time at a small grocery store in Sciotoville, Ohio. After graduation she took courses at the Portsmouth Branch of Ohio University in the evenings, working part time in a book store during the day. After two years and a summer, she qualified to teach and began teaching at Minford, Ohio, near Portsmouth. She moved to Cleveland, teaching in one of its suburbs a couple of years, before settling in Columbus. A wide range of students in Columbus and neighboring Upper Arlington benefitted from her superior teaching skills: She taught first and fourth grades in Columbus; taught English at Jones Junior High in Arlington, and moved on to teach high-school English at Arlington High. She was enthusiastic about teaching and creative in her approaches. A member of the Ohio Writing Project, she conducted seminars for other teachers.

She obtained her undergraduate degree in education from Ohio State University in 1967 and later her master's degree. She contributed a chapter to the textbook *Religion in Ohio: Profiles of Faith Communities*.[436] Her chapter gives background on the Church of Christ, its beliefs, and its Ohio history. The book is used throughout the schools in the state of Ohio.

Rachel married **Robert Vernon REINHARD**, son of Charles Vernon REINHARD and Hazel Lucille AMSTUTZ, on 20 August 1960 at the Seventh Avenue Church of Christ, Columbus, Ohio. Robert was born 13 June 1929 in Fostoria, Ohio. He died 7 August 2007 in Columbus, Ohio.

Bob's mother died two years after his birth, and he was reared by his grandparents, Charles and Lilly (Hakes) Reinhard. Charles and Lily owned a large farm outside Fostoria, Ohio, and that is where Bob grew up. They moved into town when Charles retired.

Bob graduated from the Ohio State School of Music and was a member of the marching band. He joined the National Guard, training at Fort Hayes in Columbus in 1956. He served as band master with the 37th Division of the Ohio National Guard Infantry Band. He taught band for a couple of years at Richwood, Ohio.

He worked on his master's degree in music education at Ohio State and had a reputation for being an outstanding music director for Dublin, Ohio, schools. He was song leader at Fishinger & Kenny Church of Christ in Columbus and served there as deacon. He painted landscapes as a pastime. Rachel and Bob divorced late in life.

Robert and Rachel had the following child:

+ 403 i. **Rawn Howard**[14] **REINHARD** was born in 1963.

382. **Mabel June**[13] **YOUNG** (Clarence Hasten[12] YOUNG, Nancy Rachel[11] SCARBERRY, Elizabeth Susan[10] DOUGHTY, Rachel[9] SCARBERRY, Zachariah[8] SCARBERRY, Isaac[7], Robert[6], John[5], John[4], John[3], William[2], Isaac[1]) was born in 1938 in Columbus, Ohio.

After graduating from Harding College in Searcy, Arkansas, I became a fifth-grade teacher for Bakersfield, California, schools. The school system was excellent, but I became homesick and returned east, doing post-graduate work in English at Tulane University during the summer. The academic atmosphere at Tulane was exciting.

Having been impressed with Austin, Texas, when I visited there with friends from Harding, I moved to Austin to teach sixth grade and stayed for five years. During the summer I studied fine arts at the University of Texas and received a degree in 1971.

It was at a graduate-student party for engineers at Barton Springs in Austin that I met my future husband, Greg Malan. He obtained a position at Babcock & Wilcox in Lynchburg, Virginia. There we remained, rearing our children.

In 1990 I graduated from Lynchburg College with a master of arts in education, having completed the 48-hour program in school counseling. Part of the program was a course in adult education. It included an exercise in family history, and genealogy immediately became my favorite pastime.

Mabel married **Gregory Franklin MALAN**, son of Paul Franklin MALAN, "Jack," and Geraldine COSTON, on 30 August 1969 in Corpus Christi, Texas. Gregory was born in 1943 in Corpus Christi.

Greg Malan was the only child born to Paul and Geraldine Malan. Paul served in the Army Air Corps during World War II as a flight engineer for B-17s and B-24s. He was born in Muskogee, Oklahoma, and Geraldine in Sand Springs, Oklahoma, and they both grew up in Beggs, Oklahoma. Paul and Geraldine married 10 June 1939. At that time Paul was a roustabout for Phillips Oil, and in 1941 he and Geraldine joined her sister Lesterine and husband, H.C. Jones, in Corpus Christi, Texas. Paul's army duties took him to Michigan, but he and Geraldine settled in Corpus Christi after the war. Paul began working at the Naval Base, eventually becoming a management analyst. During the VietnamWar one of his main responsibilities was emergency preparedness. He had to see that helicopters were protected from tropical storms. Geraldine's sister Gloria Darlene and her husband, Bill Bullard, settled in Corpus Christi, also. Their brother J. R. Coston and wife, Juanita, remained in the Tulsa area of Oklahoma. J.R. was president of the machinists' union at American Airlines in Tulsa. He served during the Korean War. Geraldine's brother Chester settled in Wyoming.

Paul Malan's brother Bill rose to the rank of colonel in the U.S. Air Force, and he was a member of the Strategic Air Force Command. His group advised President Kennedy on one occasion. Eventually Bill and wife, Eileen, and children found themselves in Washington, D.C., stationed at the Pentagon. Both Bill Malan and Chester Coston served in World War II and became prisoners of war. Bill escaped twice.

Paul Malan's sister Lucille Jarboe married and divorced. She worked for a newspaper while rearing her two children in Oklahoma. Paul's half-sister, Ruby Shull, also remained in Oklahoma, marrying D.J. Laurie late in life.

Greg grew up in Corpus Christi, Texas, but his parents moved to Chula Vista, California, when the Naval base at Corpus was shut down for a few years. Greg graduated in 1961 from Hill Top High School in Chula Vista. Returning to Corpus Christi with his family when the base reopened, Greg attended Del Mar Junior College, graduating in 1963.

He received his master of science degree in mechanical engineering in 1967 from the University of Texas and studied toward his doctorate of philosophy, concentrating on nuclear engineering. He finished his course work and accepted a position in the Nuclear Power Division at Babcock & Wilcox in Lynchburg, Virginia, where he remained until he retired in 2000, the name of his firm having undergone several transformations. After retirement he enjoyed working part-time for nHance Technologies in Lynchburg.

Greg's favorite pastimes are investment analysis and racquetball.

They had the following children:

+ 404 i. **Tamara Michelle**[14] **MALAN** was born 1972 in Lynchburg, Virginia.

405 ii. **Eric Paul MALAN** was born in 1975 in Lynchburg, Virginia.

Eric graduated from Holy Cross Regional School in Lynchburg, Virginia, in June 1993. He very much appreciated his circle of friends there and played on the basketball team. He entered Central Virginia Community College, majoring in business. Statistics was his forte. Between 1996 and 1998 he was enrolled at Radford University, Radford, Virginia, where he majored in mathematics, the degree in statistics having been removed from the curriculum. He has an associate degree in business from Central Virginia Community College.

Eric moved to Atlanta, Georgia, to join his sister, Tamara, who was working as a real estate appraiser. She introduced him to the profession, and he worked as a residential appraiser in Atlanta for six years before returning to Lynchburg, Virginia, where he continued his career as an appraiser and became certified.

Between semesters at college Eric did some trading on the stock market and found the process fascinating.

383. **Rena Sue**[13] **YOUNG** (Clarence Hasten[12] YOUNG, Nancy Rachel[11] SCARBERRY, Elizabeth Susan[10] DOUGHTY, Rachel[9] SCARBERRY, Zachariah[8] SCARBERRY, Isaac[7], Robert[6], John[5], John[4], John[3], William[2], Isaac[1]) was born in 1943 in Portsmouth, Ohio.

When Rena was born, her father declared her the prettiest baby he had ever seen. She was a high-school cheerleader and a homecoming attendant. She graduated with honors from Ohio State University, Columbus, Ohio, in 1976 and taught high-school business and English courses in Upper Arlington, a suburb of Columbus. Obtaining a master's degree from Ohio State in 1985 in school counseling, she worked as a high-school counselor for 16 years.

Rena is a natural-born athlete and has enjoyed playing volleyball. She takes on walking challenges. She also has musical talent and sang with the Sweet Adelines in Columbus. She was often in demand to sing as part of a quartet.

She is highly involved with her church and plans monthly birthday parties for women members.

Rena married **Thomas Garfield BROWN**, son of Lloyd BROWN and Edna BEARDMORE, on 25 July 1962 at the Sciotoville Church Of Christ, Portsmouth, Ohio. Thomas was born in 1939 in Woodsfield, Ohio.

After graduating from high school in Woodsfield, Ohio, Tom joined the marines. He trained at Camp Lejeune, North Carolina, and served in Puerto Rico. He became a fireman for the city of Columbus and was devoted to his work, his photograph once appearing in the newspaper because he had located the source of a fire. During his last years as a fireman, he repaired self-contained breathing apparatus. After retiring he worked as a barber.

Tom enjoys golfing and is clever at finding practical solutions to household maintenance problems. He has artistic talent. He is known for his polite manner and drives elderly members of his church to doctor appointments.

They had the following children:

+ 406 i. **Clay Vaughn**[14] **BROWN** was born in 1967.

+ 407 ii. **Rebecca Faye BROWN** was born in 1969.

384. **Edith Marie[13] YOUNG** (Clarence Hasten[12] YOUNG, Nancy Rachel[11] SCARBERRY, Elizabeth Susan[10] DOUGHTY, Rachel[9] SCARBERRY, Zachariah[8] SCARBERRY, Isaac[7], Robert[6], John[5], John[4], John[3], William[2], Isaac[1]) was born in 1949 in Portsmouth, Ohio.

When Edith was born, I was nearly 11 years old, and she made life fun for all of us. She was a happy baby and displayed her sense of humor from the beginning. When she was still small enough that I could cradle her in my arms, she would deliberately go limp, and then giggle at my alarm.

Edith and Rena both were born with red hair, and Edith's hair hung in strawberry-blond ringlets. In high school Edith was elected a homecoming attendant. In 1972 the *Portsmouth Times* issued a segment on June brides, and it featured photographs of Edith in her wedding gown.

Edith graduated from the Agricultural College of Ohio State University and worked as a health inspector for the state of Ohio. She and her husband, Paul, moved to Madison, Wisconsin, after their marriage and then to Houston, Texas. There she became certified to teach elementary school and taught kindergarten and first grade for the Cy Fair school system. After qualifying as a high-school English teacher, she began teaching English as a second language and found it highly rewarding.

Edith took in the sights of Paris, the Netherlands, Russia, and Germany when Paul was transferred to Paris. She especially enjoyed the museums.

Edith married **Paul Arthur TEWS**, son of Arthur TEWS and Margaret Norma DOERR, on 17 June 1972 at the Sunshine Church of Christ, Scioto County, Ohio. Paul was born in 1950.

Paul's father, Arthur Tews, was born in November 1915 in a box car in Russia. His last name was actually *Kletke*. He was reared by his aunt and uncle in Sheboygan, Wisconsin.

Paul did his undergraduate work at Ohio State University, where he also received his master's degree in welding engineering. He earned a doctorate in mechanical engineering from the University of Wisconsin at Milwaukee. He is a man of much initiative and has designed equipment that is used by an oil company at Hudson Bay. He has taught at Texas Agricultural and Mechanical College. For several years he worked for Subsea 7 in Paris, France.

They had the following children:

+ 408 i. **Erin Patricia[14] TEWS** was born 1977 in Columbus, Ohio.

    409 ii. **Zachary Paul TEWS** was born 1979 in Milwaukee, Wisconsin.

        Zachary Tews graduated from the United States Air Force Academy on 29 May 2007 with a bachelor of science degree in mechanical engineering. He was commissioned as a second lieutenant and worked as an engineer at Vandenberg Air Force Base. He has flown refueling tankers for the U.S.A.F. and served in the Middle East.

        While stationed in North Dakota, Zachary was able to pursue his love of flying on a different level: He sailed over the farms and cows in his paramotor. He is now a captain.

+ 410 iii. **Julia Marie TEWS** was born 1984 in Houston, Texas.

388. **Thelma Marylene[13] SCARBERRY**, "Marylene," (Forrest B.[12] SCARBERRY, Alva E.[11] SCARBERRY, Elizabeth Susan[10] DOUGHTY, Rachel[9] SCARBERRY, Zachariah[8] SCARBERRY, Isaac[7], Robert[6], John[5], John[4], John[3], William[2], Isaac[1]) was born 1937.

Marylene has worked in a day-care center.

Marylene married (1) **George HOLLINGWORTH** on 5 June 1953. They divorced after three years.

Marylene married (2) **Mervil STENCER**.

They had the following child:

    411   i. **Karen Renee[14] STENCER** was born 1960.

Marylene married (3) **Daniel SCOTT**.

389.   **Galen Forrest[13] SCARBERRY** (Forrest B.[12] SCARBERRY, Alva E.[11] SCARBERRY, Elizabeth Susan[10] DOUGHTY, Rachel[9] SCARBERRY, Zachariah[8] SCARBERRY, Isaac[7], Robert[6], John[5], John[4], John[3], William[2], Isaac[1]) was born 1944.

    Galen is retired from Orbit Construction Company.

Galen married (1) **Lola JONES**.

They had the following child:

    412   i. **Michael[14] SCARBERRY**

Galen married (2) **Nan GREEN**.

They had the following child:

    413   ii. **Marriah SCARBERRY**.

390.   **Floyd Garland[13] SCARBERRY** (Forrest B.[12] SCARBERRY, Alva E.[11] SCARBERRY, Elizabeth Susan[10] DOUGHTY, Rachel[9] SCARBERRY, Zachariah[8] SCARBERRY, Isaac[7], Robert[6], John[5], John[4], John[3], William[2], Isaac[1]) was born in 1946.

    Floyd worked as an electronics technician, specializing in computer manufacturing and robotics. He is retired from International Harvester. He and wife, Linda, own a farm near Urbanna, Ohio. It offers trail riding.

Floyd married **Linda COLLINS** on 4 August 1967. Linda was born in 1947, the daughter of Cass and Marie COLLINS.

They had the following children:

+   414   i. **Shane Anthony[14] SCARBERRY** was born in 1968.

    415   ii. **Kimberly Paige SCARBERRY** was born in 1972. Kimberly married **Andrew CONNELL**.

392.   **Robert Lewis[13] SAILOR** (Janet Marian[12] SAILOR, Jasper Lewis[11] SCARBERRY, Elizabeth Susan[10] DOUGHTY, Rachel[9] SCARBERRY, Zachariah[8] SCARBERRY, Isaac[7], Robert[6], John[5], John[4], John[3], William[2], Isaac[1]) was born in 1956.

Robert married (1) **Sheila NICHOLS**.

They had the following children:

    416   i. **Sarah Rae[14] SAILOR** was born in 1986.

    417   ii. **Nichole Lynn SAILOR** was born in 1988.

Robert married (2) **Laural JOHNSON**.

393.   **Della Marie[13] BURD** (Iris Mae[12] SCARBERRY, Orval Franklin[11] SCARBERRY, Elizabeth Susan[10] DOUGHTY, Rachel[9] SCARBERRY, Zachariah[8] SCARBERRY, Isaac[7], Robert[6], John[5], John[4], John[3], William[2], Isaac[1]) was born in 1954 in Columbus, Ohio.

    Della worked as a paralegal in Huntington, West Virginia. She enjoys photography and has won awards. She has worked part time for the *Herald-Dispatch* of Huntington as a photographer-reporter. Della publishes electronic novels under a pen name, and she has three in print.

Della married **Ernest Robert LEWIS**, son of Ernest. Ray LEWIS and Molly BAILEY, on 17 March 1973. Robert was born in 1952 in Lawrence County, Ohio.

Robert was a good student. After graduating from high school, he and Della Burd married, and they moved to Los Angeles, California, where he was a promising corporate employee. Robert and Della divorced, and he moved to Marietta, Georgia.

They had the following child:

418   i. **Evan Robert[14] LEWIS** was born in 1978 in Orange County, California.

Evan majored in education at Marshall University in Huntington, West Virginia. He is now certified to teach in the state of Ohio. He has always enjoyed science, astronomy, and bicycling.

Evan married (1) **Meridith Brooke DISHMAN** on 27 July 2002 in Athalia, Ohio. They divorced.

He married (2) **Nicole KENDALL** in June 2009.

Nichole majored in sports medicine at Marshall University and is employed as Athletic Director by a Christian College in Circleville, Ohio.

394.   **Rickey Ryan[13] BURD** (Iris Mae[12] SCARBERRY, Orval Franklin[11] SCARBERRY, Elizabeth Susan[10] DOUGHTY, Rachel[9] SCARBERRY, Zachariah[8] SCARBERRY, Isaac[7], Robert[6], John[5], John[4], John[3], William[2], Isaac[1]) was born in 1958 in Ironton, Ohio.

Rickey enjoys construction work, especially when he can make use of his skills as a carpenter.

Rickey married (1) **Loretta Kay EDWARDS**.

They had the following children:

419   i. **Tiffany Renae[14] BURD** was born in 1980 in Huntington, West Virginia.

420   ii. **Brandie Nickole BURD** was born in 1985 in Huntington, West Virginia.

Rickey married (2) **Sarah EDWARDS**.

Rickey married (3) **Terrie BIAS**.

395.   **Gretchen Elizabeth[13] SCARBERRY** (Danny Douglas[12] SCARBERRY, Orval Franklin[11] SCARBERRY, Elizabeth Susan[10] DOUGHTY, Rachel[9] SCARBERRY, Zachariah[8] SCARBERRY, Isaac[7], Robert[6], John[5], John[4], John[3], William[2], Isaac[1]) was born in 1973.

Gretchen was a student at Marshall University in Huntington, West Virginia, when she met the man she would marry. They are now divorced and she has entered nurses' training.

Gretchen married **Samih JAMMAL**. Samih was born in 1969.

They had the following children:

421   i. **Muhammad Samih[14] JAMMAL** was born in 1994.

422   ii. **Zackariya Samih JAMMAL** was born in 1996.

423   iii. **Yousef Fadel JAMMAL** was born in 1999.

424   iv. **Issa Samih JAMMAL** was born in 2001.

425   v. **Ayah Samih JAMMAL** was born in 2002.

398. **David Lynn[13] WOOD** (Ruth Lucille[12] SCARBERRY, Arthur William[11] SCARBERRY, Elizabeth Susan[10] DOUGHTY, Rachel[9] SCARBERRY, Zachariah[8] SCARBERRY, Isaac[7], Robert[6], John[5], John[4], John[3], William[2], Isaac[1]) was born in 1946.

David studied engineering drafting at Mata College in Columbus. He worked for 25 years for Columbia Gas and currently works for Chase Manhattan Mortgage.

David married (1) **Deborah MOORE**.

David married (2) **Bonnie WRIGHT**.

They had the following children:

    426   i. **Nancy April[14] WRIGHT**. (After her parents' divorce, she reverted to her mother's maiden name.)

    427   ii. **Megan Amanda WOOD**. She married **John HALL**.

David married (3) **Clair Elizabeth ELLINGER**, "Betsy," in July 2003.

399. **William Francis[13] WOOD** (Ruth Lucille[12] SCARBERRY, Arthur William[11] SCARBERRY, Elizabeth Susan[10] DOUGHTY, Rachel[9] SCARBERRY, Zachariah[8] SCARBERRY, Isaac[7], Robert[6], John[5], John[4], John[3], William[2], Isaac[1]) was born in 1948.

William and Wilma Wood sold their home in Licking County, Ohio, after his retirement and moved to Primeville, Oregon. They live up in the mountains and enjoy their view and hiking. Their daughter Zea Renee lives in Klamath Falls, Oregon, where she is a student adviser at a college. William and Wilma's son, Zachary Norman, lives in Hilliard, Ohio, where he works for an underground gas company.

William married **Wilma**.

They had the following children:

    428   i. **Zea Renee[14] WOOD**. She married **Paul MILLET**.

    429   ii. **Zachary Norman WOOD**. He married **Elizabeth**.

400. **Timothy[13] DERR** (Marian Eileen[12] SCARBERRY, Arthur William[11] SCARBERRY, Elizabeth Susan[10] DOUGHTY, Rachel[9] SCARBERRY, Zachariah[8] SCARBERRY, Isaac[7], Rober[6], John[5], John[4], John[3], William[2], Isaac[1]) is a son of Raymond DERR.

Timothy was living in Bellevue, Ohio, in 2010.

Timothy married **Marge**.

They had the following children:

    430   i. **Erica[14] DERR** was living in Huron, Ohio, at the time of her grandmother Marian's death.

    431   ii. **Timmy DERR**.

401. **Diane[13] DERR** (Marian Eileen[12] SCARBERRY, Arthur William[11] SCARBERRY, Elizabeth Susan[10] DOUGHTY, Rachel[9] SCARBERRY, Zachariah[8] SCARBERRY, Isaac[7], Roberrt[6], John[5], John[4], John[3], William[2], Isaac[1]) is a daughter of Raymond DERR.

Diane was living in Sandusky, Ohio, in 2010, when her mother died, as were sons John and Kevin Bye. Son Tony was living in Toledo.

Diane married **Albert BYE**.

They had the following children:

The Scarberrys (Scarboroughs), Doughtys, Lewises, and Paynes of Lawrence County, Ohio

432   i.   **Tony^{14} BYE**.

433   ii.   **John BYE**.

434   iii.   **Kevin BYE**.

402. **Mark R.^{13} DERR** (Marian Eileen^{12} SCARBERRY, Arthur William^{11} SCARBERRY, Elizabeth Susan^{10} DOUGHTY, Rachel^9 SCARBERRY, Zachariah^8 SCARBERRY, Isaac^7, Robert^6, John^5, John^4, John^3, William^2, Isaac^1) was a son of Raymond DERR. Mark died 5 July 2010.

Mark graduated from Terra Community College in Fremont, Ohio. He was a U.S. Army veteran and worked for the Seneca County Sheriff's Office as the warrant and transportation supervisor. He belonged to the Buckeye Sheriffs' Association and was a member of Zion Lutheran Church in Republic, Ohio. His father had preceded him in death. (Information from the *Sandusky Register*.)

Mark married **Lea Ann OHLER** on 17 October 1992 in Republic, Ohio. They divorced.

They had the following child:

435   i.   **Katelyn^{14} DERR**. She was living in Sycamore, Ohio, at the time of her father's death.

Fourteenth Generation

403. **Rawn Howard^{14} REINHARD** (Rachel May^{13} YOUNG, Clarence Hasten^{12} YOUNG, Nancy Rachel^{11} SCARBERRY, Elizabeth Susan^{10} DOUGHTY, Rachel^9 SCARBERRY, Zachariah^8 SCARBERRY, Isaac^7, Robert^6, John^5, John^4, John^3, William^2, Isaac^1) was born in 1963 in Columbus, Ohio.

Rawn displayed superior verbal skills from the time he was a toddler. And he loved reading. He graduated from Upper Arlington High School in Columbus, Ohio. He spent a year at Ohio State University, but found the familiar setting dull, so he transferred to David Lipscomb University in Nashville, Tennessee, a college affiliated with the Church of Christ. There he put his skills to use on the debate team. After graduation he entered law school at Duke University in Durham, North Carolina, and was appointed to the *Law Review*. Upon graduation he clerked for a judge in Jacksonville, Florida, and obtained a position as a corporate lawyer in Chicago.

Rawn and his family enjoy living in Chicago and take advantage of its many cultural events. He leads the singing at a Church of Christ congregation.

Rawn married **Christy Dyan GARRISON** on 28 June 1991 in Greenville, North Carolina. Christy was born in 1969 in Lexington, Kentucky, to Charles and Maureen (WALL) GARRISON.

Christy grew up in Greenville, North Carolina, and graduated from the North Carolina School of Sciences and Mathematics in Durham. After earning a degree from Duke University, she completed medical school at Rush University in Chicago, Illinois. Christy finds her work as a pediatrician fulfilling. She grew up taking dancing and gymnastic lessons and still enjoys dancing and attending cultural events.

They had the following children:

436   i.   **Robert Garrison^{15} REINHARD** was born in 1998 in Chicago, Illinois.

437   ii.   **Dorothy Maureen REINHARD** was born in 2000 in Chicago, Illinois.

438   iii.   **Charles McCormick REINHARD** was born in 2002 in Chicago, Illinois.

404. **Tamara Michelle^{14} MALAN** (Mabel June^{13} YOUNG, Clarence Hasten^{12} YOUNG, Nancy Rachel^{11} SCARBERRY, Elizabeth Susan^{10} DOUGHTY, Rachel^9 SCARBERRY, Zachariah^8 SCARBERRY, Isaac^7, Robert^6, John^5, John^4, John^3, William^2,

Isaac[1]) was born 1972 in Lynchburg, Virginia.

Tamara graduated from Rustburg High School, Rustburg, Virginia, in 1990. She was a cheer leader and was usually in the top ten in her class academically. She entered Virginia Institute of Technology at Blacksburg, Virginia, as a student of architecture but changed her major to psychology and graduated in 1994. Shortly thereafter she joined a friend in Atlanta and held a variety of jobs until she settled into real estate appraising. She is well suited to real estate work and in 2004 started her own company, Malan Real Estate Services. Tamara Cottle enjoys skiing and cooking.

Tamara married **Marc Elliott COTTLE**, son of E. Joe COTTLE and Diana CONNER, on 3 April 2004 in New Orleans, Louisiana. Marc was born in 1971.

Marc grew up near Beckley, West Virginia. His father, Joe Cottle, was a pilot for one of the coal companies based in the area, and his mother, Diana (Conner) taught high-school business courses. Marc and his older brother, Joe, both graduated from the United States Military Academy at West Point. Joe has a master's degree in business administration from the University of Michigan. Their sister, Jennifer, has a master's degree in computer science from Wake Forest. She loves horses and has worked as a horse trainer.

Marc served in the First Armored Division in Germany and Yugoslavia. After his discharge from the army, he obtained a master's degree in business administration from Carnegie Mellon in Pittsburgh. His career has centered around financial advising, and he currently works for General Electric in Salt Lake City, Utah. He enjoys skiing and fishing.

They had the following children:

439   i. **Finnegan[15] Michael COTTLE** was born 2011 in Salt Lake City, Utah.

440   ii. **Rowan Summer COTTLE** was born 2011 in Salt Lake City, Utah.

406.   **Clay Vaughn[14] BROWN** (Rena Sue[13] YOUNG, Clarence Hasten[12] YOUNG, Nancy Rachel[11] SCARBERRY, Elizabeth Susan[10] DOUGHTY, Rachel[9] SCARBERRY, Zachariah[8] SCARBERRY, Isaac[7], Robert[6], John[5], John[4], John[3], William[2], Isaac[1]) was born in 1967 in Columbus, Ohio.

Clay graduated from David Lipscomb University, Nashville, Tennessee, in 1990, majoring in religion. He served as youth minister at Fishinger & Kenny Church of Christ in Columbus before becoming the youth minister at a Church of Christ in Henderson, Tennessee. In 2003 he returned to the Columbus area to serve as pulpit minister at the Westerville Church of Christ. Clay is good natured and has always enjoyed working with people. He was a dormitory counselor at David Lipscomb.

Clay married **Jennifer Lynn HORNE**, daughter of Eldon HORNE and Lorene SPERRY, on 19 May 1990 in Fishinger & Kenny Church Of Christ, Columbus, Ohio. Jennifer was born in 1964 in Scioto County, Ohio.

Jennifer was a good student and enjoys sports. She graduated from David Lipscomb University in Nashville, Tennessee, in 1986. She is an exceptionally good teacher, and teaches elementary school at a church-affiliated school in Westerville, Ohio.

They had the following children:

441   i. **Jared Eldon[15] BROWN** was born in 1993 in .Columbus, Ohio.

      In the fall of 2011 Jared enrolled at Pepperdine University in Malibu, California, on scholarship.

442   ii. **Kathryn Lorena BROWN** was born in 1996 in Tennessee.

443   iii. **Joshua Thomas BROWN** was born in 1999 in Tennessee.

407. Rebecca Faye[14] BROWN (Rena Sue[13] YOUNG, Clarence Hasten[12] YOUNG, Nancy Rachel[11] SCARBERRY, Elizabeth Susan[10] DOUGHTY, Rachel[9] SCARBERRY, Zachariah[8] SCARBERRY, Isaac[7], Robert[6], John[5], John[4], John[3], William[2], Isaac[1]) was born in 1969 in Columbus, Ohio.

Becky graduated from Ohio State University, having majored in violin performance and music education. She played violin in the Richmond, Indiana, Symphony. At the University of Cincinnati she received her master's degree in violin performance.

At Ohio State University she met her future husband, Mark Fulton, who also took music classes. After Becky and Mark married, he joined the Navy and was assigned to Hawaii. While there, Becky gave violin lessons to children and played for the Honolulu Symphony Orchestra. She played for the Fairfax, Virginia, Women's Symphony when Mark was stationed in the D.C. area. She has always been dedicated to music, playing the piano by ear before starting first grade.

Rebecca married **Marcus FULTON**, son of Michael and Mary FULTON, on 28 December 1996 in Columbus, Ohio. Marcus was born in 1969 in Marysville, Ohio.

Mark studied comparative literature and music at Ohio State University. He and his future wife, Becky, played violin in ensembles. He graduated from the University of Cincinnati College of Law, joined the U.S. Navy, and became a Judge Advocate General's Corps (JAG) lawyer. He enjoys sailing.

They had the following children:

    444   i.   **Claire Elaine[15] FULTON** was born in 2003 in Maryland.

    445   ii. **Nathaniel Thomas FULTON** was born in 2006 in Oak Harbor, Washington.

408. Erin Patricia[14] TEWS (Edith Marie[13] YOUNG, Clarence Hasten[12] YOUNG, Nancy Rachel[11] SCARBERRY, Elizabeth Susan[10] DOUGHTY, Rachel[9] SCARBERRY, Zachariah[8] SCARBERRY, Isaac[7], Robert[6], John[5], John[4], John[3], William[2], Isaac[1]) was born in 1977 in Columbus, Ohio.

Erin graduated from David Lipscomb University, Nashville, Tennessee, in 1999. A National Merit Scholar, she entered on a music scholarship and majored in biology. She obtained a degree from the North Texas School of Osteopathic Medicine in 2004. Erin is now an obstetrician and a fellow of the American College of Obstetricians and Gynecologists. She likes to run in her spare time.

She married **Mathew Hunsaker STEIDL** on 17 June 2000 in Nashville, Tennessee. Mathew was born in 1977, the son of Peter and Susan STEIDL.

Mathew graduated from David Lipscomb University in Nashville, Tennessee, in 2000 with a major in computer science. After he and Erin married, they moved to the Dallas-Fort Worth area, and he began designing software at Lockheed Martin Aeronautics in Fort Worth. He took an interest in health care and now qualifies as a physician's assistant. He enjoys running and competing in races.

They had the following children:

    446   i.   **Evie Marie[15] STEIDL** was born in 2008 in Texas.

    447   ii. **Amelia Celice STEIDL** was born in 2011 in Texas.

410. Julia Marie[14] TEWS (Edith Marie[13] YOUNG, Clarence Hasten[12] YOUNG, Nancy Rachel[11] SCARBERRY, Elizabeth Susan[10] DOUGHTY, Rachel[9] SCARBERRY, Zachariah[8] SCARBERRY, Isaac[7], Robert[6], John[5], John[4], John[3], William[2], Isaac[1]) was born 1984 in Houston, Texas.

Julia graduated from Cypress Creek High School in Texas in 2002 and entered Harding College, Searcy, Arkansas, graduating in the spring of 2006. She majored in marketing and completed a course of study in Florence, Italy, as part of the program. Julia married and began working for the Wood Group in Houston. Julia Sammons is now in marketing at Haliburton.

Julia married **Justin Mark SAMMONS** on 3 June 2006 in Houston, Texas.

A son of Don and Susan SAMMONS, Justin majored in Business at Lubbock Christian College in Lubbock, Texas, graduating in 2006. He writes a sports column for a local newspaper and sells insurance.

They had the following child:

    448   i. **Troy^{15} SAMMONS** was born in 2011 in Texas.

414.   **Shane Anthony^{14} SCARBERRY** (Floyd Garland^{13} SCARBERRY, Forrest B.^{12} SCARBERRY, Alva E.^{11} SCARBERRY, Elizabeth Susan^{10} DOUGHTY, Rachel^9 SCARBERRY, Zachariah^8 SCARBERRY, Isaac^7, Robert^6 John^5, John^4, John^3, William^2, Isaac^1) was born in 1968.

Shane married **Melissa GRIMM**.

They had the following children:

    449   i. **Logan Alexander^{15} SCARBERRY** was born in 1994.

    450   ii. **Trevor Anthony SCARBERRY** was born in 1997.

    451   iii. **Hannah Renee SCARBERRY** was born in 2001.

The Scarberry brothers: *Seated*, Grover, Alva, Manuel; *Standing*, Orval, Arthur, Jasper

The Scarberry sisters: Nanny and Chloe

Clarence Young, reading with an aid while nearly blind

Susan (Doughty) Scarberry (1862-1950)

Clarence Young (1914-2005)

Phoebe Doughty and Elijah Williams

Iris (Scarberry) Burd (1934-2011) and Ruth (Scarberry) Wood (1922-2011)

Calling cards: Hester Doughty (1854-1938) and husband Morrison S. Scarbrough (b. 1841)

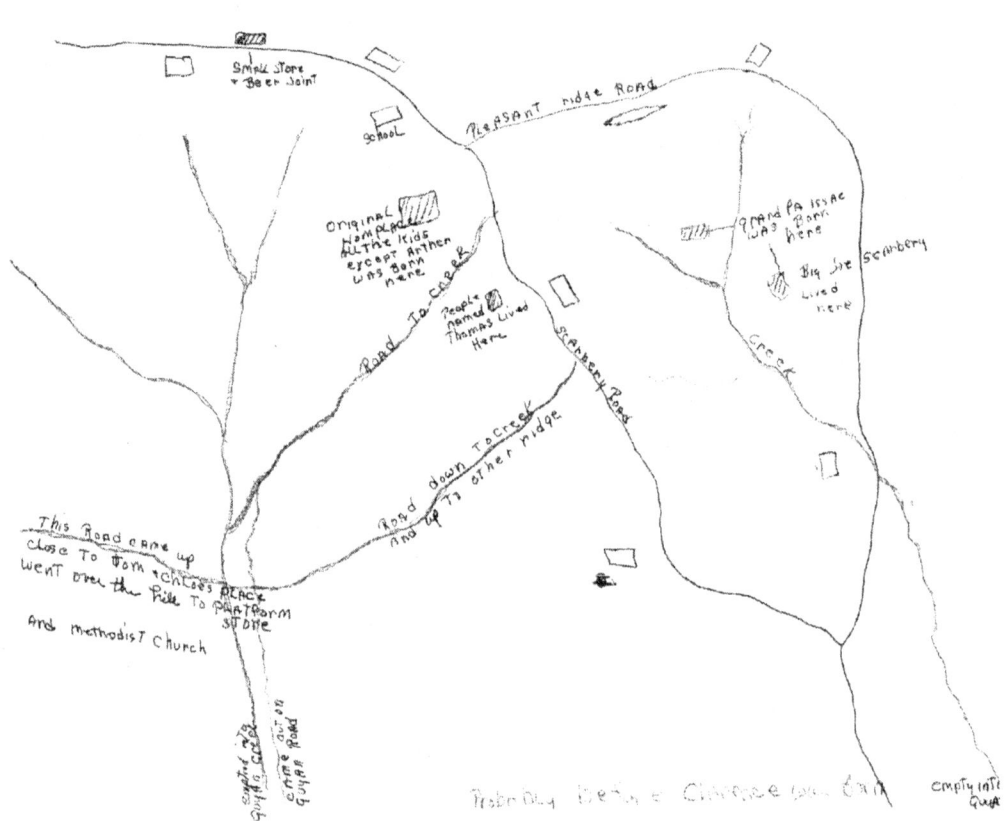

Pleasant Ridge map by Iris (Scarberry) Burd: Includes first Scarberry home place.

The Scarberrys (Scarboroughs), Doughtys, Lewises, and Paynes of Lawrence County, Ohio

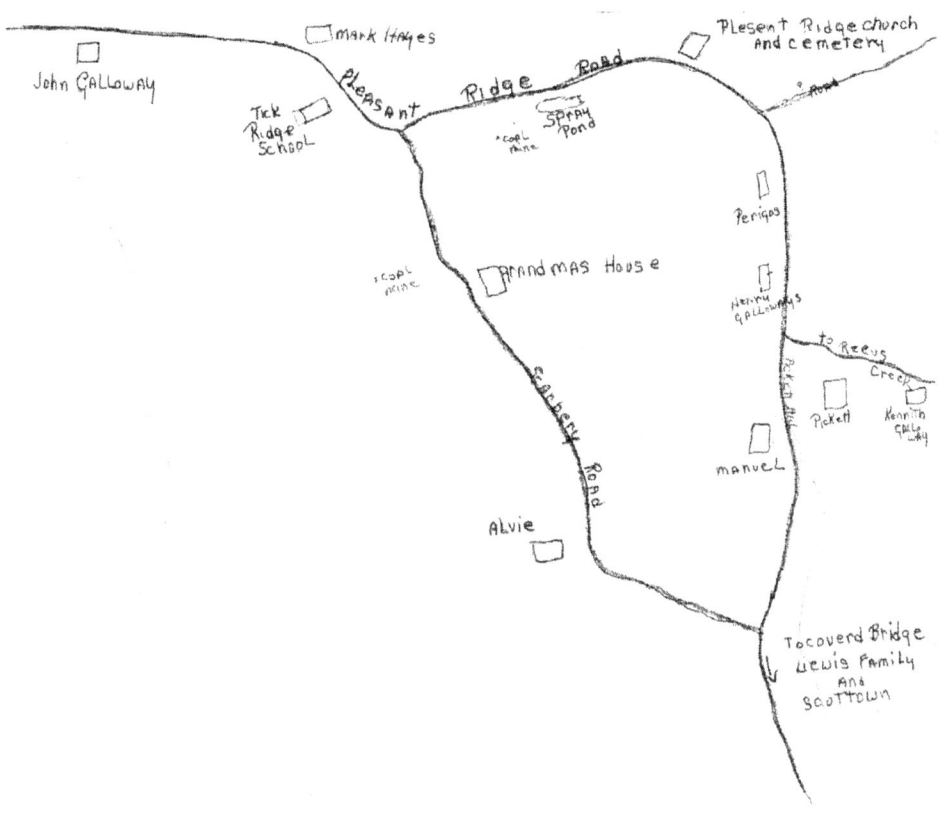

Pleasant Ridge map by Iris (Scarberry) Burd: Includes "Grandma's House," where Susan and Isaac Scarberry's children grew up.

Sources

[1] Walter George Bell, *The Great Plague of London* (1924; reprinted London: Bracken Books, 1994), 190, 118, vi-vii, 181.
[2] Roger S. Boone, comp., *Some Quaker Families, Scarborough/Haworth* (Wichita, Kansas: M. Morgan, 1991-1994), 1:1.
[3] Arthur Rowntree, ed., *The History of Scarborough* (Letchworth, Herts: Temple Press, 1931), 218-219.
[4] RootsWeb: ASHBY-L John Scarborough md Sarah Ashby. (http://archiver.rootsweb.com/th/read/ASHBY/2004-01/1074236712. - accessed 2-4-2008).
[5] "Scarborough Fair," from *Wikipedia, the Free Encyclopedia* (http://en.wikipedia.org/wiki/Scarborough_Fair - accessed 12-19-2010).
[6] "The Scarborough Family, London & Middlesex Quarterly Meeting," printout from Quaker Center at Bunhill Fields, London.
[7] Ibid.
[8] "J. Huber Haworth, Generation No. 9. http://www.haworthassociation.org/Bios/Huber/Generation9.htm.
[9] RootsWeb: ASHBY-L John Scarboroughand Sarah Ashby.
[10] Boone, *Some Quaker Families, Scarborough/Haworth*, 1:1.
[11] "The Scarborough Family, London & Middlesex Quarterly Meeting."
[12] Ibid.
[13] Boone, *Some Quaker Families, Scarborough/Haworth*, 1:1.
[14] Bucks County Historical Society, *The Bucks County Historical Society Papers, Read Before the Society and Other Historical Papers* (Allen, PA: Berkemeyer-Keck Co. Press, 1937), 8:137.
[15] Boone, *Some Quaker Families, Scarborough/Haworth*, 1:1-2.
[16] Eastburn Reeder, *Early Settlers of Solebury Township, Bucks County, Pa., Compiled from Deeds, Wills and the Records of Friends' Meetings*, 2nd edition (Doylestown, Pa.: Bucks County Historical Society, 1971), 20.
[17] Boone, *Some Quaker Families, Scarborough/Haworth*, 1:1.
[18] Ibid., 1:2.
[19] "The Scarborough Family, London & Middlesex Quarterly Meeting."
[20] Boone, *Some Quaker Families, Scarborough/Haworth*, 1:2.
[21] Ibid.
[22] George MacReynolds, *Place Names in Bucks County, Pennsylvania, Alphabetically Arranged in an Historical Narrative*, 2nd edition (1942; Doylestown, Pa.: Bucks County Historical Society, 1955), 59-60.
[23] Boone, *Some Quaker Families, Scarborough/Haworth*, 1:2.
[24] "Solebury.. (http://www.freepages.genealogy.rootsweb.com/-buckscounty/solebury.html)//
[25] Reeder, *Early Settlers of Solebury Township, Bucks County, Pa.*, 30-31. The deed was recorded in Philadeophia, Deed Book A, v. 3, p. 170.
[26] Ibid., 21.
[27] Ibid., 21-22.
[28] Boone, *Some Quaker Families, Scarborough/Haworth*, 1:2.
[29] Ibid.
[30] Ibid.
[31] Ibid.
[32] Ibid.
[33] Ibid., 199.
[34] William Wade Hinshaw, *Encyclopedia of American Quaker Genealogy* (Ann Arbor, Michigan: Edwards Brothers, Inc., 1936-1950), v. 2 (New Jersey and Pennsylvania Monthly Meetings), 1025.
[35] Kerns, *Frederick County, Virginia: Settlement and Some First Families of Back Creek Valley*, 199.
[36] Reeder, *Early Settlers of Solebury Township, Bucks County, Pa.*, 21.
[37] Hinshaw, *Encyclopedia of American Quaker Genealogy*, 2:1025.
[38] Reeder, *Early Settlers of Solebury Township, Bucks County, Pa.*, 21.
[39] MacReynolds, *Place Names in Bucks County, Pennsylvania, Alphabetically Arranged in an Historical Narrative*. See chart.
[40] "English Dissenters, Quakers," (http://www.exlibris.org/nonconform/engdis/quakers.html - accessed 12-19-2010).
[41] Kerns, *Frederick County, Virginia: Settlement and Some First Families of Back Creek Valley, 1730-1830*, 198.

[42] Hinshaw, *Encyclopedia of American Quaker Genealogy*, 2:1025.
[43] Kerns, *Frederick County, Virginia: Settlement and Some First Families of Back Creek Valley*, 198.
[44] Reeder, *Early Settlers of Solebury Township, Bucks County, Pa.*, 22.
[45] Kerns, *Frederick County, Virginia: Settlement and Some First Families of Back Creek Valley*, 198 (citation for both marriages).
[46] Ibid.
[47] Ibid.
[48] Hinshaw, *Encyclopedia of American Quaker Genealogy*, 2:1025.
[49] Kerns, *Frederick County, Virginia: Settlement and Some First Families of Back Creek Valley*, 192.
[50] Ibid.
[51] Ibid.
[52] Ibid.
[53] Ibid., 193.
[54] Joint Committee of Hopewell Friends, Society of Friends, Hopewell, *Hopewell Friends History 1734-1934* (Strasburg, Va.: Shenandoah Pub. Co., 1936), 191.
[55] *The New Encyclopaedia Britannica in 30 Volumes*, 15th edition (International Copyright Union, 1980), Micropaedia, 5:123-124.
[56] Kerns, *Frederick County, Virginia: Settlement and Some First Families of Back Creek Valley*, 193.
[57] Amelia C. Gilreath, *Frederick County, Virginia, Deed Books 1, 2, 3, 4, 1743-1758*, Deed Book series (Nokesville, Va.: the author, 1989), 1:139.
[58] Kerns, *Frederick County, Virginia: Settlement and Some First Families of Back Creek Valley*, 193.
[59] Ibid., 194.
[60] Ibid.
[61] Reeder, *Early Settlers of Solebury Township, Bucks County, Pa.*, 21.
[62] Ibid.
[63] Kerns, *Frederick County, Virginia: Settlement and Some First Families of Back Creek Valley*, 199.
[64] Boone, *Some Quaker Families, Scarborough/Haworth*, 1:9.
[65] Kerns, *Frederick County, Virginia: Settlement and Some First Families of Back Creek Valley*, 199.
[66] Reeder, *Early Settlers of Solebury Township, Bucks County, Pa.*, 22-23.
[67] Boone, *Some Quaker Families, Scarborough/Haworth*, 1:9.
[68] Bedford County, Virginia, Survey Book 1:57.
[69] Bedford County, Virginia, Order Book 2:86.
[70] Joida Whitten, *Abstracts of Bedford County, Virginia, Wills, Inventories and Accounts, 1754-1787* (Dallas, Texas: the author, 1968), 6.
[71] Ibid., 14-15.
[72] Bedford County, Virginia, Order Book 3:364.
[73] Ann Chilton, *Bedford County, Virginia, Deed Book, C-3* (Signal Mountain, TN.: Mountain Press, 1992), 30.
[74] Whitten, *Abstracts of Bedford County, Virginia, Wills, Inventories and Accounts, 1754-1787*, 28-29.
[75] Oren F. Morton, *A History of Monroe County, West Virginia* (1915; reprint, Baltimore: Regional Pub. Co., 1988), 478, 477.
[76] Ibid., 400.
[77] Greenbrier County, West Virginia, Deed Book 2:190.
[78] Greenbrier County, West Virginia, Survey Book 3:33.
[79] Larry G. Shuck, *Monroe County, [W] Virginia, Abstracts, Deeds (1799-1817), Wills (1799-1829), Sim's Land Grant Index (1780-1862)* (Apollo, Pa.: Closson Press, 1996), 85.
[80] Kerns, *Frederick County, Virginia: Settlement and Some First Families of Back Creek Valley*, 199.
[81] Boone, *Some Quaker Families, Scarborough/Haworth*, 1:9.
[82] Bedford County, Virginia, Deed Book C-3: 229-230.
[83] Ibid.
[84] Bedford County, Virginia, Deed Book C-3:228-229.
[85] Monroe County, West Virginia, Old Surveys 3:26-27.
[86] Greenbrier County, West Virginia, Deed Book 2:166.
[87] Boone, *Some Quaker Families, Scarborough/Haworth*, 1:9.
[88] Morton, *A History of Monroe County, West Virginia*, 74.

[89] Earle S. Dennis, Jane E. Smith, *Marriage Bonds of Bedford County, Virginia, 1755-1800* (Baltimore: Genealogical Pub. Co., 1975), 62.
[90] Ibid., 37.
[91] Ibid., 47.
[92] Joint Committee of Hopewell Friends, *Hopewell Friends History, 1734-1934*, 190.
[93] Reeder, *Early Settlers of Solebury Township, Bucks County, Pa.*, 31.
[94] Ibid.
[95] Ibid.
[96] Boone, *Some Quaker Families, Scarborough/Haworth*, 1:25.
[97] Bedford County, Virginia, Deed Book C-3:228-229.
[98] Whitten, *Abstracts of Bedford County, Virginia, Wills, Inventories and Accounts, 1754-1787*, 76-77.
[99] Bedford County, Virginia, Order Book 6:286.
[100] Bedford County, Virginia, Order Book 7:2.
[101] Monroe County, West Virginia, Deed Book 3:146.
[102] Greenbrier County, West Virginia, Deed Book 1:683.
[103] Netti Schreiner-Yantis and Florene Speakman Love, *The 1787 Census of Virginia: An Accounting of the Name of Every White Male Tithable Over 21 Years*....3 vols. (Springfield, Va.: Genealogical Books in Print, 1987), 1:158.
[104] Morton, *A History of Monroe County, West Virginia*, 73.
[105] Ibid., 75.
[106] Ibid., 185-186.
[107] Ibid., 231.
[108] Boone, *Some Quaker Families, Scarborough/Haworth*, 1:9.
[109] Greenbrier County, West Virginia, Index to Marriages, 1-A:136.
[110] Boone, *Some Quaker Families, Scarborough/Haworth*, 1:25.
[111] Ibid.
[112] Ibid.
[113] Ibid. 1:25.
[114] William Armstrong Crozier, *Virginia Colonial Militia, 1651-1776* (1905; reissued, Baltimore: Genealogical Pub. Co., 1982), 86.
[115] Mrs. Livia Simpson-Poffenbarger, "Battle of Point Pleasant," in *Battle of Point Pleasant, First Battle of the American Revolution, October 10, 1774* (Pt. Pleasant, W.Va.: Mattox Printing Service, 1984), 16.
[116] "Dunmore's War" from Wikipedia, the free encyclopedia (http://en.wikipedia.org/wiki/Dunmore's_War - accessed 11-17-2010).
[117] Marcus Bainbridge Buford, *History and Genealogy of the Buford Family in America, with Records of a Number of Allied Families*, rev. edition (LaBelle, Mo.: Mildred Buford Minter, 1924), 40.
[118] Morton, *A History of Monroe County, West Virginia*, 38-40.
[119] Warren Skidmore and Donna Kaminsky, *Lord Dunmore's Little War of 1774: His Captains and Their Men Who Opened up Kentucky & the West to American Settlement* (Bowie, Md: Heritage Books, 2002), 125.
[120] Greenbrier County, West Virginia, Survey 3:156.
[121] Greenbrier County, West Virginia, Deed Book 2:97.
[122] Greenbrier County, West Virginia, Survey Book 3:10.
[123] Greenbrier County, West Virginia, Survey Book 3:223.
[124] Greenbrier County, West Virginia, Survey Book 3:250.
[125] Schreiner-Yantis and Love, *The 1787 Census of Virginia*, 1:158.
[126] Larry G. Shuck, *Greenbrier County (West) Virginia Records* (Athens, Ga.: Iberian Pub. Co., 1988-1995), 5:43.
[127] Greenbrier County, West Virginia, Deed Book 1:678.
[128] Morton, *A History of Monroe County, West Virginia*, 230-231, 233.
[129] Ibid. 229-232.
[130] Monroe County, West Virginia, Deed Book E:123.
[131] Boone, *Some Quaker Families, Scarborough/Haworth*, 1:9.
[132] Greenbrier County, West Virginia, Index to Marriages 1-A:47.
[133] Morton, *A History of Monroe County, West Virginia*, 94.
[134] Greenbrier County, West Virginia, Index to Marriages 1-A:47.

[135] Ibid., 1-A:113.
[136] 1880 U.S. Census, pop. sch., Roane, Tennessee, p.436A. FHL microfilm 1,255,275; NA microfilm T9-1275.
[137] Bedford County, Virginia, Order Book 7:9.
[138] Augusta B. Fothergill and John Mark Naugle, *Virginia Tax Payers, 1782-1787; Other Than Those Published by the United States Census Bureau* (1940; reprint, Baltimore: Genealogical Pub. Co., 1978), 110.
[139] Bedford County, Virginia, Order Book 7:21.
[140] Bedford County, Virginia, Deed Book 7:572-573.
[141] Greenbrier County, West Virginia, Survey Book 1:411.
[142] Schreiner-Yantis and Love, *The 1787 Census of Virginia*, 1:158.
[143] Monroe County, West Virginia, Old Survey Book 3:23.
[144] Monroe County, West Virginia, Deed Book A:105-106; Deed Book B:616-617.
[145] Monroe County, West Virginia, Deed Book B:395-396.
[146] Giles County, Virginia, Survey Book 1:142.
[147] Morton, *A History of Monroe County, West Virginia*, 17.
[148] J. T. Peters and H. B. Carden, *History of Fayette County, West Virginia* (1926; reprint, Parsons, W.Va.: McClain Pr. Co., 1972), 13.
[149] "Adena Culture," *Wikipedia, the Free Encyclopedia* (http://en.wikipedia.org/wiki/Adena_culture, accessed 11-27-2010).
[150] Peters, *History of Fayette County, West Virginia*, 25.
[151] "Prehistory of West Virginia," from *Wikipedia, the Free Encyclopedia*, main article: "History of West Virginia" (http://en.wikipedia.org/wiki/Prehistory_of_West_Virginia, accessed 11-25-2010).
[152] Mary Gage and James Gage, "Analysis of the Mount Carbon Stone Walls Site (46-Fa-1), Fayette County, West Virginia," *Stone Structures of Northeastern United States* (http://www.stonestructures.org/html/mount-carbon.html, accessed 11-25-2010).
[153] Jim Wood, *Raleigh County, West Virginia* (Beckley, W. Va.: J. Wood, 1994), 33-39.
[154] Gary Jennings, "An Indian Captivity," *American Heritage Magazine*. (http://www.americanheritage.com/articles/magazine/ah/1968/5/1968_...- accessed 11/23/2010).
[155] Monroe County, West Virginia, Deed Book G:119.
[156] Monroe County, West Virginia, Deed Book G:130.
[157] John L. E. Jones, Name List of Lawrence County, Ohio Residents from 1820 Federal Census and 1818 and 1821 Tax Lists (Ironton, Ohio: Lawrence County Genealogical Society, 1984), 12 (?).
[158] Bedford County, Virginia, Will Book 1:430-431.
[159] John Walter Wayland, *Virginia Valley Records: Genealogical and Historical Materials of Rockingham County, Virginia, and Related Regions (With Map)* (Baltimore: Genealogical Pub. Co., 1965), 155.
[160] Morton, *A History of Monroe County (West) Virginia*, 83.
[161] Shuck, *Greenbrier County, (West) Virginia, Records*, 5:17.
[162] Shuck, *Monroe County, [W] Virginia, Abstracts, Deeds (1799 1817), Wills (1799-1829)*, 75.
[163] Morton, *A History of Monroe County, West Virginia*, 384.
[164] Ibid., 418.
[165] Monroe County, West Virginia, Deed Book A:219.
[166] Monroe County, West Virginia, Deed Book D:439-440.
[167] Shuck, *Monroe County, [W] Virginia, Abstracts, Deeds (1799-1817), Wills (1799-1829)*, 21.
[168] Ibid.
[169] Norma Pontiff Evans, *Monroe County, (West) Virginia, Marriages, A Compiled List, 1799-1850* (Beaumont, Texas: N.P. Evans, 1985), 10.
[170] Boone, *Some Quaker Families, Scarborough/Haworth*, suppl., 19.
[171] Evans, *Monroe County, (West) Virginia, Marriages*, 7.
[172] Ibid.; Morton, *A History of Monroe County, West Virginia*, 332.
[173] Monroe County, West Virginia, Deed Book D:160-161.
[174] Evans, *Monroe County, (West) Virginia Marriages*, 4.
[175] Greenbrier County, West Virginia, Survey Book 1:76.
[176] Monroe County, West Virginia, Survey Book 3:14.
[177] Monroe County, West Virginia, Survey Book 3:44.

[178] Monroe County, West Virginia, Survey Book 3:307.
[179] Schreiner-Yantis and Love, *The 1787 Census of Virginia*, 1:158.
[180] Shuck, *Greenbrier County, (West) Virginia, Records*, 5:34.
[181] Morton, *A History of Monroe County, West Virginia*, 100.
[182] Greenbrier County, West Virginia, Deed Book 2:167.
[183] Greenbrier County, West Virginia, Deed Book 2:172.
[184] Greenbrier County, West Virginia, Deed Book 2:169.
[185] Monroe County, West Virginia, Deed Book A:9.
[186] Monroe County, West Virginia, Deed Book A:223-224.
[187] Greenbrier County, West Virginia, Index to Marriages, 1:135.
[188] Boone, *Some Quaker Families, Scarborough/Haworth*, 1:9.
[189] Bedford County, Virginia, Court Orders 8:100.
[190] Sara Motisher Beck, *Abstracts of the Eighteenth Century Deed Books, Franklin County, Virginia* (Rocky Mount, Va.: Franklin County History Project, 1978), 2:70.
[191] Ibid., 2:139.
[192] Dennis and Smith, *Marriage Bonds of Bedford County, Virginia, 1755-1800*, 62.
[193] Boone, *Some Quaker Families, Scarborough/Haworth*, 1:81.
[194] Ibid.
[195] Ibid.
[196] Ibid.
[197] Patrick G. Wardell, *Virginia/West Virginia Genealogical Data from Revolutionary War Pension and Bounty Land Warrant Records* (Bowie, MD.: Heritage Books, 1988), 3:117.
[198] Ibid.
[199] Ibid.
[200] Monroe County, West Virginia, Survey Book 1:157.
[201] Shuck, *Monroe County, [W] Virginia, Abstracts, Deeds (1799-1817), Wills (1799-1829)*, 21.
[202] Monroe County, West Virginia, Deed Book B:184-187.
[203] Shuck, *Monroe County, [W] Virginia, Abstracts, Deeds (1799-1817), Wills (1799-1829)*, 27.
[204] Monroe County, West Virginia, Deed Book B:466-468.
[205] Giles County, Virginia, Survey Book 1:141.
[206] Ibid., Survey Book 1:230.
[207] Fayette County, West Virginia, Deed Book B:110.
[208] Fayette County, West Virginia, Deed Book B:77.
[209] Monroe County, West Virginia, Deed Book M:196.
[210] Wood, *Raleigh County, West Virginia*, 43.
[211] Ibid., 113, 117.
[212] Ibid., 575.
[213] Scarborough-Harper marriage, 20 May 1805, in Marriage Registry, Monroe County, (West) Virginia, courthouse; File 1, Jacket 504.
[214] Wood, *Raleigh County, West Virginia*, 503.
[215] Larry G. Shuck, *Fayette County, (West) Virginia, Records, The Federal Census of 1850 for Fayette County*, Virginia (Athens, Ga.: Iberian Pub. Co. ; John Vogt, 1991), 1:84.
[216] Monroe County, West Virginia, Deed Book G:130.
[217] Monroe County, West Virginia, Deed Book G:601-602.
[218] Monroe County, West Virginia, Deed Book H:168.
[219] Wood, *Raleigh County, West Virginia*, 113, 117.
[220] Shuck, *Fayette County, (West) Virginia, Records, The Federal Census of 1850 for Fayette County, Virginia*, 1:84.
[221] Hinshaw, *Encyclopedia of American Quaker Genealogy*, 6:990.
[222] Giles County, Virginia, Deed Book 1:373-374.
[223] Jones, *Name List of Lawrence County, Ohio Residents from 1820 Federal Census and 1818 and 1821 Tax Lists*, 12 (?).
[224] Tax Records, Lawrence County, Ohio, 1820-1829, 1-2095, GR2533, Microfilm by Genealogical Society, Salt Lake City, Utah, filmed at The Ohio Historical Society, Columbus, Ohio, June 8, 1967, v. 742.

[225] 1830 U.S. Census, Lawrence County, Ohio, Windsor Township, p. 334.
[226] Lawrence County, Ohio, Deed Book 7:28-29.
[227] Ibid., 20:342.
[228] 1850 U.S. Census, pop. sch., Gallia County, Ohio, Guyan Township, dwelling/family 155/155.
[229] Ibid., dwelling/family 156/156.
[230] Julia Wintz, *Kanawha County Marriages, January 1, 1792, to December 31, 1869* (Parsons, W.Va.: McClain Printing Co., 1975), 7.
[231] Giles County, Virginia, Survey Book 1:140.
[232] Giles County, Virginia, Survey Book 1:139.
[233] *Giles County, Virginia, History—Families*, 98.
[234] Wood, *Raleigh County, West Virginia*, 503.
[235] Marshall Wingfield, *Marriage Bonds of Franklin County, Virginia, 1786-1858* (Baltimore: Genealogical Pub. Co., 1973), 218.
[236] "Joseph Harper, Fayette Sheriff in 1848; Son Farmed 500 Acres, Owned Five Stores," from *Beckley Post Herald*, August 26, 1950.
[237] International Genealogical Index v5.0. (http://www.familysearch.org/eng/search/frameset_search.asp).
[238] General Index to Marriages, 1803-1890, Gallia County, Ohio, Courthouse, 2-88.
[239] Ibid., 2-142.
[240] "Personal History Department—Gallia County," *History of Gallia County, Containing a Condensed History of the County; Biographical Sketches; General Statistics; Miscellaneous Matters, &c* (1882; reprint, Chicago and Toledo: H. H. Hardesty & Co., Publishers, 1976), 23.
[241] Wood, *Raleigh County, West Virginia*, 40.
[242] "Personal History Department—Gallia County," *History of Gallia County*, 23.
[243] Wood, *Raleigh County, West Virginia*, 117, 122.
[244] Riston-Scarborough marriage 21 May 1805 in Marriage Register, Monroe County, West Virginia courthouse, File 1, Jacket 555.
[245] 1880 U.S. Census, pop. sch., Raleigh County, West Virginia, Clear Fork, p. 132D. FHL microfilm1255412; NA microfilm T9-1412.
[246] Shuck, *Fayette County, (West) Virginia, Records, The Federal Census of 1850 for Fayette County, Virginia*, 1:83-84.
[247] Ibid., 1:83.
[248] Larry G. Shuck, *Fayette County, [W] Virginia, Marriages, 1832-1853 and 1865-1903* (Apollo, PA: Closson Press, 1995), 19.
[249] Shuck, *Fayette County, (West) Virginia, Records, The Federal Census of 1850 for Fayette County, Virginia*, 1:84.
[250] Shuck, *Fayette County, [W] Virginia, Marriages, 1832-1853 and 1865-1903*, 19.
[251] Fayette County Chamber of Commerce, *History of Fayette County, West Virginia, 1993* (Marceline, MO: Heritage House Publishing).
[252] Shuck, *Fayette County, (West) Virginia, Records, The Federal Census of 1850 for Fayette County, Virginia*, 1:84.
[253] Ibid.
[254] Shuck, *Fayette County, [W] Virginia, Marriages, 1832-1853 and 1865-1903*, 19.
[255] Ibid.
[256] Lawrence County, Ohio, Deed Book 8:417.
[257] Lawrence County, Ohio, Deed Book 15:179-180.
[258] 1850 U.S. Census, pop. sch., Lawrence County, Ohio, Rome Township, dwelling/family 161/163.
[259] 1860 U.S. Census, pop. sch., Lawrence County, Ohio, Rome Township, p. 163, dwelling/family 1095/1085.
[260] 1870 U.S. Census, pop. sch., Lawrence County, Ohio, Rome Township, p. 43, dwelling/family 323/313.
[261] Billee Hammond Schlaudt, *Marriage Records of Lawrence County, Ohio* (Houston: B. H. Schlaudt, 1987), books 1-6 (1817-1863), 147.
[262] 1930 U.S. Census, pop. sch., Lawrence County, Ohio, Rome Township, dwelling/family 75/74.
[263] 1880 U.S. Census, pop. sch., Lawrence County, Ohio, Rome Township, p. 295A, FHL microfilm 1,255,039; NA microfilm T9-1039.
[264] 1860 U.S. Census, pop. sch., Gallia County, Ohio, Guyan Township, dwelling/family 161/161.
[265] 1880 U.S. Census, pop. sch., Mason, West Virginia, Hannan, p. 284D, FHL microfilm 1,255,408; NA microfilm T9-1408.
[266] Schlaudt, *Marriage Records of Lawrence County, Ohio*, Books 1-6, 147.
[267] Ibid.

[268] Noah Scarbery, death July 22, 1899, Cabell County, West Virginia, West Virginia death register, (http://www.wvculture.org/vrr/va).
[269] 1850 U.S. Census, pop. sch., Lawrence County, Ohio, Rome Township, dwelling/family 131/122.
[270] 1880 U.S. Census, pop. sch., Lawrence County, Ohio, Rome Township, p. 288C, FHL microfilm 1,255,039; NA microfilm T9-1039.
[271] Dan and Ruth Scarberry, "Scarberry," *Gallia County, Ohio: People in History to 1980* (Gallipolis? Ohio: Gallia County Historical Society, Taylor Pub. Co., 1980), 304.
[272] Schlaudt, *Marriage Records, Lawrence County, Ohio*, Books 1-6, 147.
[273] "Battle of Cedar Creek," Wikipedia, the Free Encyclopedia (http://en.wikipedia.org/wiki/Battle_of_Cedar_Creek - accessed 11-29-2010).
[274] Zachariah Scarbury file 749.3781; certificate 215,395. United States Veterans Administration, General Index to Pension Files, 1861-1934; NARA T0288; United States-Military Records-Civil War, 1861-1865-Pensions-Indexes, FHL microfilm 540883.//
[275] General Index to Marriages, 1803-1890, Gallia County, Ohio, Courthouse.
[276] John Scarberry, Lawrence County(Ohio) Auditor, Military Records, Civil War, 1861-1865, Militia Roll 1863-1864, a List of Volunteers, Rome Township, John H. Scarberry, K2-Ohio Cav.; 1864, 1865, Rome Township, John Scarberry, 22 (Columbus, Ohio: Ohio Historical Society, 1981), FHL microfilm 476171, Item 2.
[277] John J. Scarberry, file 662,666, certificate 954,408, B8 Ohio Cavalry, K2 Ohio Cavalry, July 2, 1888, United States Veterans Administration, General Index to Pension Files, 1861-1934, NARA T0288, FHL microfilm 540883, Civil War.
[278] General Index to Marriages,1803-1890, Gallia County, Ohio, Courthouse, 3:173..
[279] Sites-Scarberry marriage, Pedigree Resource File, Compact Disc #7, Family History Library (http://www.familysearch.org/eng/search/frameset_search.asp).
[280] General Index to Marriages, 1803-1890, Gallia County, Ohio, Courthouse, 5:514.
[281] CW Pension File 107,895, Isaac W. Doughty, Co. B. 173 Regt.; widow's pension 236,913, Rachel Doughty (National Archives Administration, Washington).
[282] 1900 U.S. Census, pop. sch., Jackson County, West Virginia, Washington District, dwelling/family 91-91.
[283] Certified copy of Marriage Record in CW Pension File 107,895, Isaac W. Doughty.
[284] "Personal History Department—Gallia County," *History of Gallia County, Ohio*, 23.
[285] Doughty-Wood marriage, May 16, 1837, in Marriage Registry, Gallia County Courthouse, Gallia County, Ohio, 1:283, FHL microfilm 317,652, roll 299.
[286] 1880 U.S. Census, pop. sch., Jackson County, West Virginia, Washington, p. 413D, FHL microfilm 1,255,404; NA microfilm T9-1404.
[287] Doughty-Benner marriage, March 14, 1850, in Marriage Registry, Gallia County Courthouse, 2:143, FHL microfilm 317,652, roll 299.
[288] CW Pension File 107,895, Isaac W. Doughty.
[289] Ibid.
[290] Ibid.
[291] Schlaudt, *Marriage Records, Lawrence County, Ohio*, Books 1-6, 147.
[292] General Index to Marriages, 1803-1890, Gallia County, Ohio, Courthouse, 1:391.
[293] Catharine Scarberry, death March 23, 1853, Braxton County, West Virginia, West Virginia Death Register http://www.wvculture.org/vrr/va).
[294] 1850 U.S. Census, pop. sch., Lawrence County, Ohio, Mason Township, pp. 716-717, dwelling/family 54/54.
[295] 1860 U.S. Census, pop. sch., Lawrence County, Ohio, Rome Township, p. 163, dwelling/family 1097/1087.
[296] 1870 U.S. Census, pop. sch., Lawrence County, Ohio, Rome Township, p. 44, dwelling/family 331/321.
[297] Brooks-Scarberry marriage certificate no. 306, Gallia County, Ohio, Probate Records, 1803-1862, FHL microfilm 317,652.
[298] Hoffman-Scarberry marriage, 23 November 1876, Lawrence County, Ohio, International Genealogical Index, FHL Batch M514,524, extracted marriage records, Lawrence County, Ohio.
[299] Thomas Scarberry death, August 18, 1872, Death Records, 1867-1938, Ohio Probate Court (Lawrence County), v. 1 (1867-1888), FHL microfilm 317,746.
[300] 1900 U.S. Census, pop. sch., Lawrence County, Ohio, Rome Township, LaBelle Precinct, p. 9A, dwelling/family 164/164.
[301] 1850 U.S. Census, pop. sch., Lawrence County, Ohio, Mason Township, p. 726, dwelling/family 114/116.
[302] Shuck, *Fayette County, (West) Virginia, Records*, 1:83-84.
[303] Wood, *Raleigh County, West Virginia*, 523.

[304] 1880 U.S. Census, pop. sch., Jackson County, West Virginia, Washington District, p. 413C. FHL microfilm 1,255,404; NA microfilm T9-1404.

[305] Ibid., p. 413D.

[306] Scarbrough-Hatcher marriage, April 15, 1861, in Marriage Registry (1832-1875), Jackson County, West Virginia, FHL microfilm 250,023.

[307] 1900 U.S. Census, pop. sch., Jackson County, West Virginia, Washington District, dwelling/family 91/91.

[308] 1880 U.S. Census, pop. sch., Jackson County, West Virginia, Washington, p. 412A, FHL microfilm 1,255,404; NA microfilm T9-1404.

[309] Schlaudt, *Marriage Records, Lawrence County, Ohio,* Books 1-6, 12.

[310] Patricia Lewis Joyce, "David and Susannah Bird," in *History of Lawrence County, Ohio, 1990,* Lawrence County Historical Book Committee, eds. (Walsworth Publishing, 1990), 80-81.

[311] 1850 U.S. Census, pop. sch., Lawrence County, Ohio, Rome Township, p. 837, dwelling/family 162/164 (the Murphy household), dwelling/family 161/163 (the Isaac Scarberry household).

[312] 1860 U.S. Census, pop. sch., Lawrence County, Ohio, Rome Township, p. 163, dwelling/family 1098 1088.

[313] Joyce, "David and Susannah Bird," in *History of Lawrence County, Ohio, 1990,* 80-81.

[314] 1870 U.S. Census, pop. sch., Lawrence County, Ohio, Rome Township, p.43, dwelling/family 324/314 (Arthur household), dwelling/family 323/313 (Isaac Scarberry household).

[315] 1880 U.S. Census, pop. sch., Lawrence County, Ohio, Rome Township, p. 295A, FHL microfilm 1,255,039; NA microfilm T9-1039.

[316] Joyce, "David and Susannah Bird," in *History of Lawrence County, Ohio, 1990,* 81.

[317] Ibid.

[318] Ibid.

[319] Clifford Scarberry, "Lawrence County Death Records." (http://www.scioto.org/Lawrence/deaths/deathrecords/S.html - accessed 11-11-03).

[320] 1860 U.S. Census, pop. sch., Lawrence County, Ohio, Rome Township, p. 163, dwelling/family 1096/1086.

[321] 1870 U.S. Census, pop. sch., Lawrence County, Ohio, Rome Township, p. 41, dwelling/family 310/301.

[322] 1880 U.S. Census, pop. sch., Lawrence County, Ohio, Rome Township, p. 289B, FHL microfilm 1,255,039; NA microfilm T9-1039.

[323] 1900 U.S. Census, pop. sch., Lawrence County, Ohio, Millers Precinct, p. 42, dwelling/family 378/379 (Marian Scarberry household), dwelling/family 378/380 (George Scarberry household).

[324] Marion Scarberry, Lawrence County (Ohio) Auditor, Military Records, Civil War, 1861-1865, Militia Roll, 1863-1864, A List of Volunteers, Rome Township, F117 0 Infantry, FHL microfilm 476,171.

[325] Francis M. Scarberry, File 318,856, Certificate 361,031, Ohio (indecipherable), United States Veterans Administration, General Index to Pension Files, 1861-1934, FHL microfilm 540, 883, NARA T0288, Civil War.

[326] Schlaudt, *Marriage Records, Lawrence County, Ohio,* Books 1-6, 147.

[327] Lawrence County, Ohio, Marriages, v. 23-25 (p. 1-300), 1910-1916, certificate 7329, FHL microfilm 1,574,145.

[328] CW Veteran Record 1688, Joseph Scarbury, priv., Co. M, 3 Reg't W. Va. Cavalry (National Archives Administration, Washington).

[329] Ibid.

[330] The third Battle of Winchester Marker, HMdb.org, The Historical marker Database (http://www.hmdb.org/marker.asp?/marker=3196 – accessed 2-18-2010).

[331] CW Veteran Record 1688, Joseph Scarbury.

[332] 1870 U.S. Census, pop. sch., Lawrence County, Ohio, Rome Township, dwelling/family 191/183.

[333] 1880 U.S. Census, pop. sch., Lawrence County, Ohio, Rome Township, p. 286D, FHL microfilm 1,255,039; NA microfilm T9-1039.

[334] 1930 U.S. Census, pop. sch., Lawrence County, Ohio, Rome Township, dwelling/family 69/68.

[335] CW Pension File 37,781, James Scarberry, D-91 Ohio Inf. National Archives and Records Administration, Washington.

[336] "Battle of Cloyd's Mountain," from Wikipedia, the free encyclopedia (http://en.wikipedia.org/wiki/Battle_of_Cloyd's_Mountain - accessed 12-1-2010).

[337] Ibid.

[338] 1870 U.S. Census, pop. sch., Lawrence County, Ohio, Rome Township, dwelling/family 65/62.

[339] 1880 U.S. Census, pop. sch., Lawrence County, Ohio, Rome Township, p. 288D, FHL microfilm 1,255,039; NA microfilm T9-1039.

[340] CW Pension File 37,781, James Scarberry.

[341] 1900 U.S. Census, pop. sch., Lawrence County, Ohio, Union Township, p. 21B, dwelling/family 328/435.

[342] 1880 U.S. Census, pop. sch., Lawrence County, Ohio, Rome Township, p. 295A, FHL microfilm 1,255,039; NA microfilm T9-1039.

[343] 1990 U.S. Census, pop. sch., Lawrence County, Ohio, Millers Precinct, p.14A, dwelling/family 257/258.

[344] 1930 U.S. Census, pop. sch., Lawrence County, Ohio, Rome Township, dwelling/family 75/74.

[345] Elemender Scarberry, death September 1, 1921, Cabell County, West Virginia, West Virginia Death Register (http://www.wvculture.org/vrr/va).

[346] CW Pension File 308,511, Elemander Scarberry, Ohio Infantry, General Index to Pension Files, 1861-1934, NARA T0288, FHL microfilm 540,883, Civil War.

[347] 1880 U.S. Census, pop. sch., Mason County, West Virginia, Hannan District, p. 284D, FHL microfilm 1,255,408, NA T9-1408.

[348] Scarberry-Kitterman marriage, 27 July 1862, General Index to Marriages, 1803-1890, Gallia County, Ohio, Courthouse, 3:7.

[349] Elizabeth Scarberry, death December 12, 1907, Cabell County, West Virginia, West Virginia Death Register (http://www.wvculture.org/vrr/va).

[350] Isaac Scarberry, death April 12, 1896, in Death Register, West Virginia (http://www.wvculture.org/vrr/va).

[351] John Scarberry, death April 25, 1908, in Death Register, West Virginia (http://www.wvculture.org/vrr/va).

[352] CW Pension File 295,238, Noah Scarberry, D87 Ohio Infantry, General Index to Pension Files, 1861-1934, NARA T0288, FHL microfilm 540,883, Civil War.

[353] 1880 U.S. Census, pop. sch., Lawrence County, Ohio, Rome Township, p. 288C, FHL microfilm 1,255,039; NA microfilm T9-1039.

[354] Scarberry, "Scarberry," *Gallia County, Ohio: People in History to 1980*, 304.

[355] 1880 U.S. Census, pop. sch., Jackson County, West Virginia, Washington, p. 420A, FHL microfilm 1,255,404; NA microfilm T9-1404.

[356] Doughty-Scarbery marriage, July 5, 1871, in Marriage Registry, Jackson County, West Virginia, Marriages, Jackson County, 1832-1875, FHL microfilm 250,023.

[357] 1900 U.S. Census, pop. sch., Jackson County, West Virginia, Washington District, dwelling/family 239/247.

[358] 1910 U.S. Census, pop. sch., Jackson County, West Virginia, Washington District, dwelling/family 130/130.

[359] John Wesley Doughty, death certificate no. 12,046 (1944), West Virginia State Department of Health (http://www.wvculture.org/vrr/va - accessed 4-6-2008).

[360] Obra Doughty, death certificate no. 6895 (1917), West Virginia State Department of Health (http://www.wvculture.org/vrr/va - accessed 4-6-2008).

[361] Lennie Lewis Bundy, "Virginia Helen Lewis," *History of Lawrence County, Ohio, 1990*, 218.

[362] 1930 U.S. Census, pop. sch., Lawrence County, Ohio, Rome Township, pp. 6A-6B, dwelling/family 118/116 (Susan E. Scarbery household); dwelling/family 117/115 (Emanuel Scarbury household); dwelling/family 119/117 Mark Hayes household)..

[363] 1870 U.S. Census, pop. sch., Lawrence County, Ohio, Rome Township, p. 44, dwelling/family 331/321.

[364] 1900 U.S. Census, pop. sch., Lawrence County, Ohio, Millers Precinct, p. 12B, dwelling/family 230/231.

[365] 1910 U.S. Census, pop. sch., Lawrence County, Ohio, Rome Township, pp.8A-8B, dwelling/family 134/134.

[366] Lawrence County, Ohio, Deed Book 62:489.

[367367] Lawrence County, Ohio, Deed Book 98:94.

[368] 1920 U.S. Census, pop. sch., Lawrence County, Ohio, Rome Township, p. 2B, dwelling/family 38/38 (Isaac Scarbery household); dwelling/family 36/36 (John Galloway household); dwelling/family 37/37 (Mark H. Hayes household); dwelling/family 39/39 (James O. Burd household); dwelling/family 40/40 (William H. Lewis household).

[369] 1930 U.S. Census, pop. sch., Lawrence County, Ohio, Rome Township, p. 6A, dwelling/family 117/115 (Emanuel Scarbury household); dwelling/family 116/114 (Girard R. Fuller household); dwelling/family 118/116 (Susan E. Scarbery household).

[370] Cabell County, West Virginia, Deed Books 79:18; 100:78.

[371] Lawrence County, Ohio, Marriages, v. 23-25 (p. 1-300), 1910-1916, certificate no. 6411, FHL microfilm 1,574,145.

[372] Elijah Williams, death certificate no. 6025 (1925), West Virginia State Department of Health (http://www.wvculture.org/vrr/va - accessed 4-6-2008).

[373] 1900 U.S. Census, pop. sch., Jackson County, West Virginia, Washington District, dwelling/family 91-91.

[374] Fuller-Scarberry marriage, September 21, 1872, Extracted Marriage Records, Lawrence County, Ohio, 1866-1874, FHL microfilm 317,718, Batch M514,523.
[375] 1880 U.S. Census, pop. sch., Lawrence County, Ohio, Rome Township, p. 295A, FHL microfilm 1,255,039; NA microfilm T9-1039.
[376] Lawrence County, Ohio, Marriages, v. 21-22, 1905-1910, certificate no. 5647, FHL microfilm 317,724.
[377] 1910 U.S. Census, pop. sch., Lawrence County, Ohio, Rome Township, p. 8B, dwelling/family 140/140.
[378] Smith-Scarberry marriage, September 18, 1879, Lawrence County, Ohio, International Genealogical Index, v.5, FHL.
[379] Wilks-Smith marriage, April 20, 1912, Lawrence County, Ohio, International Genealogical Index, v.5, FHL.
[380] 1900 U.S. Census, pop. sch., Lawrence County, Ohio, Millers Precinct, p. 13A, dwelling/family 237/238.
[381] Lawrence County, Ohio, Marriages, v.21-22, 1905-1910, certificate no. 4158, FHL microfilm 317,724.
[382] Joyce, "David and Susannah Bird," in *History of Lawrence County, Ohio, 1990*, 80.
[383] Ibid.
[384] Ibid., 80-81.
[385] Ibid.
[386] Ibid.
[387] Ibid., 81.
[388] 1880 U.S. Census, pop. sch., Lawrence County, Ohio, Rome Township, p. 289B, FHL microfilm 1,255,039; NA microfilm T9-1039.
[389] Clifford Scarberry, Lawrence County Death Records.
[390] 1900 U.S. Census, pop. sch., Lawrence County, Ohio, Millers Precinct, pp. 9A-9B, dwelling/family 166/167.
[391] 1910 U.S. Census, pop. sch., Lawrence County, Ohio, Athalia Village Precinct of Rome Township, p. 4B, dwelling/family 76/81.
[392] 1920 U.S. Census, pop. sch., Lawrence County, Ohio, Rome Township, p. 1B, dwelling/family 12/12.
[393] Clifford Scarberry, Lawrence County Death Records.
[394] Lawrence County, Ohio, Marriages, v. 23-25 (p. 1-300), 1910-1916, certificate no. 7144, FHL microfilm 1,574,145.
[395] 1930 U.S. Census, pop. sch., Lawrence County, Ohio, Rome Township, p. 4A, dwelling/family 72/71.
[396] William Scarberry death September 10, 1899, Cabell County, West Virginia, West Virginia Death Register (http://www.wvculture.org/vrr/va).
[397] Nancy Young, death certificate, registrar's no. 660 (1967), State of Ohio, Division of Vital Statistics.
[398] Nancy Young vs. Louis Young, Common Pleas Court, Lawrence County, Ohio, certificate no. 13,042, 3 December 1918, witnessed by A.L. Corn, Clerk, on 5 December 1918, 42:543.
[399] Young-Scarberry marriage, March 13, 1913, by Rev. Sparks, Columbus, Ohio, certificate no. 31,331, Probate Court, Franklin County, Ohio.
[400] 1870 U.S. Census, pop. sch., Franklin County, Ohio, Truro Township, p. 20, dwelling/family 137/140 (Achenbach household), dwelling/family 140/143 (Hoffman household).
[401] 1880 U.S. Census, pop. sch., Franklin County, Ohio, Truro Township, p. 308A, FHL microfilm 1,255,015; NA microfilm T9-1015.
[402] Franklin County, Ohio, Deed Book 217:555-556.
[403] 1880 U.S. Census, pop. sch., Columbus, Franklin County, Ohio, p.35A, FHL microfilm 1,255,016; NA microfilm T9-1016.
[404] 1900 U.S. Census, pop. sch., Franklin County, Ohio, Truro Township, p. 2B, dwelling/family 34/34 (Elizabeth Young household), p. 2A, dwelling/family 27/27 (Elizabeth Achenbach household).
[405] Franklin County, Ohio, Deed Book 352:625.//
[406] 1920 U.S. Census, pop. sch., Franklin County, Ohio, Truro Township, p. 4B, dwelling/family 97/98.
[407] 1930 U.S. Census, pop. sch., Franklin County, Ohio, Truro Township, p. 3B, dwelling/family 60/61.
[408] Elizabeth (Jung) Young, death certificate no. 49,478, State of Ohio, Department of Health.
[409] 1920 U.S. Census, pop. sch., Franklin County, Ohio, Truro Township, p. 11A, dwelling/family 253/262.
[410] 1930 U.S. Census, pop. sch., Franklin County, Ohio, Truro Township, p. 6A, dwelling/family 148/151.
[411] Young vs. Young, certificate of divorce no. 13,042, 5 December 1918, Common Pleas Court, Lawrence County, Ohio, 42:543.
[412] Letter of June 27, 1918, from A. R. Johnson of Johnson & Jones, Attorneys & Counselors at Law, Ironton, Ohio.
[413] Louis Young, death certificate no. 48,471 (1941), State of Ohio, Department of Health.

[414] Henry W. Wolf, executor's account of estate of Louis Young, case no. 94,675, Probate Court of Franklin County, Ohio, Record of Accounts 253:49.
[415] 1920 U.S. Census, pop. sch., Lawrence County, Ohio, Rome Township, p. 12B, dwelling/family 246/246.
[416] 1930 U.S. Census, pop. sch., Lawrence County, Ohio, Rome Township, p. 6B, dwelling/family 124/122.
[417] Lawrence County, Ohio, Marriages, v. 21-22, 1905-1910, certificate no. 5431, FHL microfilm 317,724.
[418] Grover C. Scarberry, Graves Registration Card, Army, Lawrence County Courthouse, Ironton, Ohio.
[419] Grover C. Scarberry, Honorable Discharge from the Army of the United States, WWI File No. C2759.
[420] The Stars and Stripes, 1918-1919, The American Expeditionary Forces, A Closer Look at *The Stars and Stripes* (http://memory.loc.gov/ammem/sgphtml/sashtml/aefhtml - accessed 2-27-2010).
[421] 1930 U.S. Census, pop. sch., Lawrence County, Ohio, Rome Township, p. 9A, dwelling/family 186/182.
[422] "The Situation in Mexico," *Huachuca Illustrated*, vol. 1, 1993 (http://net.lib.byu.edu/estu/wwi/comment/huachuca/HI1-08.htm - accessed 12-11-2010).
[423] Thelma Scarberry, no. 290-28-0843, U.S. Social Security Death Index, *FamilySearch*.
[424] Jean DeOrto, no. 286-26-6478, U.S. Social Security Death Index, *FamilySearch*.
[425] Arthur Scarberry, no. 275-01-7397, U.S. Social Security Death Index, *FamilySearch*.
[426] 1910 U.S. Census, pop. sch., Lawrence County, Ohio, Rome Township, pp. 8A-8B, dwelling/family 134/134.
[427] Hazel Scarbery, no. 297-20-4563, U.S. Social Security Death Index, *FamilySearch*.
[428] 1920 U.S. Census, pop. sch., Lawrence County, Ohio, Rome Township, p. 1B, dwelling/family 12/12 (Susan Scarberry household); dwelling/family 11/11 (John Rigney household).
[429] 1930 U.S. Census, pop. sch., Cabell County, West Virginia, Huntington, p. 13B, dwelling/family 334/273.
[430] Ona Scarberry, death September 15, 1966, in Death Registry, West Virginia Vital Records (http://www.wvculture.org/vrr/va).
[431] Homer Scarberry, no. 236-32-8598, U.S. Social Security Death Index, *FamilySearch*.
[432] Clarence Hasting Young, certificate of birth, file no. 15,267, registration district no. 703, State of Ohio, Bureau of Vital Statistics. An affidavit was filed on 18 June 1942 by Nancy Young to correct the misspelling of Clarence Young's middle name so that it would be spelled *Hasten*.
[433] Marie Scarberry, no 232-42-1775, U.S. Social Security Death Index, *FamilySearch*.
[434] Forrest Scarberry, no. 280-05-7809, U.S. Social Security Death Index, *FamilySearch*.
[435] Elza Wood, no. 301-03-3987, U.S. Social Security Death Index, *FamilySearch*.
[436] Tarunjit Singh Butalia and Dianne P. Small, eds., *Religion in Ohio: Profiles in Faith Communities* (Columbus: Ohio University Press, 2004).

The DOUGHTYS

First Generation

1. **John¹ DOUGHTY** was born about 1785 in Pennsylvania. He died June 1852 in Symmes Township, Lawrence County, Ohio.

We have met the enemy and they are ours! is a famous line by Oliver Perry. It is associated with the defeat of the British on Lake Erie in September 1813. Two ships, the USS Niagara, and the flagship, USS. Lawrence, had been built at Erie, Pennsylvania, for Oliver Perry who was commander of the American fleet. The British had taken control of Lake Erie in 1812, and thanks to this battle, control was returned to the U.S.[437] John Doughty, who died in Lawrence County, Ohio, in 1852, was a boat builder, and he helped in the building of Perry's ships.[438]

An article on John Doughty's son-in-law, Jubel Stover, that appears in *History of Gallia County* states that both John Doughty and his wife, Phoebe, were born in Pennsylvania. Jubel Stover's father, Elijah (d. 8 October 1824), was living in Gallia County in 1819. Elijah's wife was Mary Scarberry (d. 21 June 1843).[439] The Scarberrys of Gallia and Lawrence Counties had lived previously in what is now Raleigh County, West Virginia, along the Clear Fork of the Coal River. There is a town called Stover on Coal River Road (State Route 3). The mountains in that part of West Virginia create scant valleys, sometimes hardly wide enough for a good road, but a valley widens around Stover, creating a beautiful farming area. On 8 April 1815 the Giles County tax officer, who was enumerating people on the Sycamore Fork and Clear Fork of the Coal River in what is now Raleigh County, found Elijah and Jacob Stover, as well as John and Zachariah Scarbrough, living there.[440]

Jubal Stover married Mary Jane Doughty, and Jubal's mother was a Scarborough. This is the first marriage that I am aware of between the Scarberry (the usual spelling on the north side of the Ohio River) and Doughty families. Other Doughty-Scarberry marriages figure in my direct line, Rachel Scarbery to Isaac Wesley Doughty in 1853, and Elizabeth Susan Doughty to Isaac Edward Scarbery in 1881. Indirectly there was another Stover-Scarborough connection: Joseph Harper married Fanny Stover, daughter of Jacob Stover.[441] And Zachariah Scarborough married Celia Harper in Kanawha County, West Virginia, in 1805.[442]

Muster Rolls of the Pennsylvania Volunteers in the War of 1812-1814 include a Corporal John Doty, but I have been unable to determine if he is my ancestor.[443] Wayne B. Ingles has written and compiled a delightful book entitled *Symmes Creek*. It tells of life along this broad tree-lined stream. The book includes many stories passed along by the generations. A chapter in the book, "Early Days in Symmes," is actually an article written by John T. Irwin and originally published in the *Ironton Register* on 26 January 1889. Irwin says that his father had the second wagon in the region. "It was made by the late Lewis Doughty, who owned the ship axe spoken of by the Register some time ago, and which A. N. Stewart donated to the relic room. I saw it many a time, as Uncle John Doughty lived on father's land when he first came to Ohio."[444]

Silas Spurlock built the first cabin in Symmes Township in 1820. John C. Stewart, George Pine, and William G. Robinson were named among the very first settlers. George Erwin and John Doughty were named among the group that followed soon afterwards. A grist-mill was built in 1824 and school was being taught by 1834.[445]

John Doughty was on the 1840 U.S. census for Symmes Township. His household consisted of one male 10-15 years old, one 16-20, one 50-60; there was one female 10-15, one 15-20, one 50-60.[446] John Doughty bought 19 acres from Philip R. Cooper on 29 August 1840.[447] On 18 December 1848 John Doughty and wife, Mary, sold the land back to Cooper.[448]

On 3 June 1852 John Doughty wrote his will. He identified himself first as being of Decatur Township, but crossed it out and wrote *Symes*. He left the farm, with all the household goods, furniture, and chattels, to his wife, "in lieu of her Dower." He owned 43 acres and 36 hundredths in the northeast quarter of the northeast quarter of Section 31, Township 5 (Symmes), Range 17, and land in the northwest quarter of the northwest quarter of Section 32, Township 5, Range 17, containing 43 acres and 76 hundredths. After the death of his wife, the real estate and personal property were to go to his beloved children: Lewis M., Jessy D., Robert, John A., James L., Hester M., Charles M., Mary J., and Isaac W. Doughty, "and their heirs except the household furniture which shall be equally divided between all of my own heirs and wife's heirs respectfully." He authorized his heirs to exchange 10 or 12 acres with Wm. Blagg. Wits: Thomas M. Lain, George W. Stewart. John Doughty's signature matches the handwriting of the will. His sentence structure and spelling were good. George W. Stewart presented John's will to the probate judge on 25 June 1852.[449]

George W. Stewart was born in 1821, and he married Cynthia A. Griffith (1821-1875). Both were said to be natives of Lawrence County.[450] George Stewart was the son of John C. and Sarah Lavisa (McCartney) Stewart.[451] John C. Stewart lived at the mouth of John's Creek. George Irwin, father of John T. Irwin, who referred to John Doughty as *uncle* in his article in *Symmes Creek*, moved into a log house in Symmes Township in 1827. The log cabin was still standing in 1899 (on R. M. Wickline's property at that time). John T. Irwin once owned the land on which the town of Waterloo is built. He built the first mill, first blacksmith shop, and first brick store.[452]

An interesting aside: In the winter of 1933-34 and the winter following, Waterloo produced a basketball team that became famous as the Waterloo Wonders. They won the Ohio State Class B Championship both years and had learned to play on a dirt surface. They were used to playing barefoot, and during the period of the tournament were seen strolling the streets of Columbus with their shoes slung over their shoulders. Wayne Ingles, in his book, *Symmes Creek*, includes a photograph of the team. It includes their names: Orlyn Roberts, Wyman Roberts, Berl Drummond, Curtis McMahon, Stewart Wiseman, Edgar Griffith, and Owen (Nubby) Knox..[453]

There has been some speculation that Major John Doughty, who designed Fort Harmar, constructed on the north side of the Ohio River at the mouth of the Muskingum River (present-day Marietta), was the father of the John Doughty who married Phoebe Compton. Evidence does not support this idea. Major John Doughty was born on 25 July 1754 in New York City. In 1776 he became captain-lieutenant of the Eastern Artillery Company of New Jersey. He helped direct the construction of Fort Harmar in 1785. He spent his last years on his estate at Morristown, New Jersey, dying there in 1826. A short biographical piece mentions only one child, James Doughty, who became an ensign in the New Jersey Militia.[454]

Fort Harmar was not built to protect settlers from the Indians. Rather, it was built to discourage squatters (people without government-issued land titles) from settling on the north side of the Ohio. But it was also built to protect federal surveyors from the Indians. The Northwest Ordinance was passed by Congress under the Articles of Confederation in 1785, the final version in 1787. It required that land north of the Ohio was to be surveyed in a grid, townships being six by six miles and containing 36 sections. Each section was a square mile (640 acres).[455] The major north-south boundaries of the sections were called ranges. Lawrence County's Rome Township, home to my Scarberry ancestors, was in Range 15, and it had the Ohio River for its eastern border. Range 16 included Mason Township, where my Payne ancestors settled. And Windsor Township, where my Lewis ancestors settled, sits on the south side of Mason. Just to the west of Mason is Aid Township, with Symmes Township on its northern border. These two are in Range 17. Symmes, Mason, and Rome all border Gallia County, Ohio.

John married (1) **Phoebe COMPTON** in Elizabeth, Pennsylvania. Phoebe was born in Pennsylvania and she died in 1836 in Ohio.[456]

They had the following children (year of birth for most of them approximated):

+   2   i. **Lewis M.² DOUGHTY** was born about 1813.

     3   ii. **Robert DOUGHTY** was born about 1814.

> On 22 April 1844 Robert Doughty and wife, Lucinda, sold 22 acres to Adam Coulter and Charles Neal, Sr., of Gallia County. The tract was in Section 1, Township 4 (Aid), Range 17. Wits: Joab Powell, Permelia Ann Powell.[457]
>
> In 1846 R. Doughty and wife, Lucinda, and J. McMahan, and wife, Marion, sold land to R. Davisson and J. Burgess.[458]

The Scarberrys (Scarboroughs), Doughtys, Lewises, and Paynes of Lawrence County, Ohio

Robert married **Lucinda POWELL** on 30 September 1834 in Lawrence County, Ohio.[459]

+ 4 iii. **James L. DOUGHTY** was born about 1819.

5 iv. **John A. DOUGHTY** was born about 1825.

This may be the John Doughty who was on the 1850 U.S. census for Symmes Township, Lawrence County, Ohio. He was 23 years old, and wife, **Mary**, was 20. He was a farmer, born in Ohio. No children were named. Living nearby were Calvin Stewart and Geo. Stewart and their families, all born in Ohio, except George's wife, Cynthia, who was born in Virginia. John Stewart's household was listed just before George's. John was 50 and born in Pennsylvania; his wife, Sarah was 48, born in Ohio.[460] George W. Stewart would present the will of John Doughty Sr. in court.

+ 6 v. **Mary J. DOUGHTY** was born 22 July 1826 in Elizabeth, Pennsylvania.

+ 7 vi. **Charles M. DOUGHTY** was born about 1827 in Pennsylvania.

+ 8 vii. **Isaac Wesley DOUGHTY** was born 1828 in Pennsylvania and died 17 July 1886.

John married (2) **Mary WOOD** on 16 May 1837 in Gallia County, Ohio. James P. Wood, J.P., officiated.[461]

The children below appear to have been born to Mary and John. In his will John did not seem to name his children in order of birth, so assumptions are being made about which children were Mary's as opposed to Phoebe's. The names of Mary's children by her previous marriage do not appear here. She is rumored to have been born a Wiseman.

9 viii. **Hester M. DOUGHTY** was born 1844 in Ohio. Hester married **George W. DOLTON** on 8 February 1866 in Lawrence County, Ohio.[462]

10 ix. **Jesse D. DOUGHTY**

Second Generation

2. **Lewis M.² DOUGHTY** (John¹) was born about 1810 in Pennsylvania.

The birth years of Lewis and his family (1850 minus age) and the birth places of him and his wife were taken from the 1850 census for Aid Township, Lawrence County, Ohio.[463]

Lewis M. Doughty purchased 45 acres in 1858 (?) from James Dinnen.[464]

The 1880 U.S. census for Aid Township includes Lewis M. Doughty, 74, and his family. He was born in Pennsylvania. His wife, Elizabeth, was 50, and born in Ohio. Still at home were children Robert Doughty, 46; Sarah E. Doughty, 24; James M. Doughty, 22; and Laura Susan Doughty, 18. All these children and Elizabeth, as well, were listed as "other" instead of as children, but the father of all of them was said to have been born in Pennsylvania, so "other" was probably an error.[465]

Lewis married (1) **Millie M. DAWSON** on 8 August 1833 in Gallia County, Ohio.[466]

Lewis and Millie had the following children:

11 i. **Robert³ DOUGHTY** was born 1835 in Ohio.

This is likely the Robert E. Doughty who was 31 in 1864 and unfit for duty in the military. He was living in Aid Township. Lawrence County, Ohio.[467]

12   ii.   **John DOUGHTY** was born 1837 in Ohio.

A map of early Lawrence County that shows the townships and land owners reveals that J.M. Doughty owned 45 acres in Aid Township. The parcel was sandwiched between lands of Walter Neal, Jr., and A. Tipton. Land of Walter Neal, Jr., crossed John's Creek, near Vermillion Fork. South of Doughty's land was 168 acres owned by Etna Iron Works. Lawrence Furnace Company owned 195 acres southwest of Doughty's land. Both Etna Iron Works and Lawrence Furnace Company owned other tracts in Aid Township.[468] To get a glimpse of the time frame, we note that Walter Neal, Jr., was born in 1786 and died in 1873.[469] Lawrence County had some of the highest quality iron ore in the world, and pig iron from the Hanging Rock region was shipped upstream to Pittsburgh for manufacturing.[470] The stack from the Oakridge iron furnace in Aid Township is still standing.[471] This 45-acre parcel in Aid Township may have belonged to James M. Doughty, born 1858.

13   iii.   **Nancy DOUGHTY** was born 1842 in Ohio.

Lewis married (2) **Elizabeth ROACH** on 24 December 1843 in Lawrence County, Ohio. Elizabeth was born in 1824 in Virginia. Jesse Corn officiated at this marriage.[472]

Lewis and Elizabeth had the following children:

14   iv.   **Hester A. DOUGHTY** was born 1844 in Ohio.

+   15   v.   **Phebe E. DOUGHTY** was born 1846 in Ohio.

16   vi.   **Alvira(?) DOUGHTY** was born 1848 in Ohio.

17   vii.   **Sarah E. DOUGHTY** was born in 1856 in Ohio.

18   viii.   **James M. DOUGHTY** was born in 1858 in Ohio.

See John Doughty, above, born 1837, regarding 45 acres in Aid Township that belonged to J. M. Doughty. James M. Doughty would have been only 15 when Walter Neal, Jr., died, and thus would not have been old enough to own land, but the particular owner of the land is uncertain.

19   ix.   **Laura Susan DOUGHTY** was born in 1862 in Ohio.

4.   **James L.[2] DOUGHTY** (John[1]) was born about 1819 in Pennsylvania.

James married **Alvira PORTER** on 26 December 1839 in Gallia County, Ohio.[473]

They had the following children:[474]

20   i.   **Phoebe[3] DOUGHTY** was born about 1841 in Gallia County, Ohio.

21   ii.   **Clarissa DOUGHTY** was born about 1844 in Jackson, Illinois.

22   iii.   **Francis DOUGHTY** was born about 1847 in Jackson, Illinois.

23   iv.   **Marion Lafayette DOUGHTY** was born about 1849 in Jackson, Illinois.

6.   **Mary J.[2] DOUGHTY** (John[1]) was born in 22 July 1826 in Elizabeth, Pennsylvania.

She married **Jubel STOVER**, son of Elijah STOVER and Mary SCARBOROUGH, on 22 March 1842 in Gallia County, Ohio. Jubel was born 11 October 1817 in Lawrence County, Ohio.[475]

Mary and her husband lived in Guyan Township, Gallia County, Ohio.

Mary and Jubel had the following children:[476]

 24 i. **Mary M.³ STOVER** was born 11 October 1843.

 25 ii. **Phebe J. STOVER** was born 14 July 1845 and died 11 August 1847.

 26 iii. **Marinda STOVER** was born 26 November 1847.

 27 iv. **Charles STOVER** was born 11 August 1849 and died 22 August 1852.

 28 v. **Elijah STOVER** was born 31 March 1851 and died 20 August 1852.

 29 vi. **Rachel E. STOVER** was born 18 July 1853.

 30 vii. **Lewis M. STOVER** was born 8 October 1855.

 31 viii. **Malinda A. STOVER** was born 1 December 1857.

 32 ix. **Clarinda C. STOVER** was born 2 March 1860.

 33 x. **Sarilda C. STOVER** was born 19 February 1862.

 34 xi. **Jubel M. STOVER** was born 26 November 1864.

 35 xii. **Cynthia STOVER** was born 1 January 1867.

 36 xiii. **Elza STOVER** was born 12 August 1870.

7. **Charles M.² DOUGHTY** (John¹) was born about 1827 in Pennsylvania.

The U.S. census for 1880 for Precinct 1, Wellston, Ohio, includes the family of Charles Doughty, age 53, born in Pennsylvania. His parents were both born in Pennsylvania. His wife, Catharine, 51, was born in Ohio, her parents in Virginia. They had sons George, 26; Thomas, 22; Henry, 19; Percy, 16; daughter Bertha, 16; son Franklin, 12. Also living in this household were Robert Burden, 30, born in Ireland, a coal miner, and William Jones, 30, born in Wales. He worked at the blast furnace.[477]

Charles married **Catherine COLIER** (Collier?) on 10 May 1846 in Lawrence County, Ohio. John Vermillioan, J.P., officiated.[478]

Charles and Catherine had the following children

 37 i. **George³ DOUGHTY** was born 1854 in Ohio.

 38 ii. **Thomas DOUGHTY** was born 1858 in Ohio.

 39 iii. **Henry DOUGHTY** was born 1861 in Ohio.

 40 iv. **Percy DOUGHTY** was born 1864 in Ohio.

 41 v. **Bertha DOUGHTY** was born 1864 in Ohio.

 42 vi. **Franklin DOUGHTY** was born 1868 in Ohio.

8. **Isaac Wesley² DOUGHTY** "Wesley" (John¹) was born in 1828 in Mercer, Pennsylvania. He died 17 July 1886 in Jackson County, West Virginia.

Isaac Wesley married (1) **Mary BENNER** on 14 March 1850 in Gallia County, Ohio.[479]

Isaac and Mary had the following child:

 43 i. **William³ DOUGHTY**

Isaac Wesley married (2) **Rachel SCARBERRY**, daughter of Zachariah SCARBERRY and Celia HARPER, on 10 January 1853 in Gallia County, Ohio.

Descendants of Isaac Wesley and Rachel Doughty can be found in the SCARBERRY (SCARBOROUGH) Section.

Third Generation

15. **Phebe E.³ DOUGHTY** (Lewis M.², John¹) was born about 1846 in Ohio.

Phebe married **Alfred BROWN** on 5 October 1865 in Lawrence County, Ohio.[480]

The 1880 U.S. census for Windsor Township, Lawrence County, Ohio, shows Alfred Brown, 42, both parents born in Ohio, and head of household. His wife, Phebe, 36, was born in Ohio, her father in Pennsylvania, and her mother in Ohio. They had children Arminta, 14; Ann, 12; Lizetta, 10; Philena, 8, Nervella, 6; son Eltie T., 2; and daughter Olie, 1 month.[481]

Alfred and Phebe had the following children:

- 44   i. **Arminta⁴ BROWN** was born 1866.
- 45   ii. **Ann BROWN** was born 1868.
- 46   iii. **Lizetta BROWN** was born 1870.
- 47   iv. **Philena BROWN** was born 1872.
- 48   v. **Nervella BROWN** was born 1874.
- 49   vi. **Eltie T. BROWN** was born 1878.
- 50   vii. **Olie BROWN** was born 1880.

Will of John Doughty (d. 1852), Loose Wills, Lawrence County, Ohio, Courthouse

In the name of the Benevolent Father of all.

I John Doughty of Symmes Township Lawrence County and State of Ohio do make and publish this my last will and testament

I do let [give] unto [my dearly] beloved wife in lieu of her Dower the farm on which we now reside situate in Lawrence County and State of Ohio to wit the North east quarter of the North east quarter of section No Thirty one, Township No Five of range No seventeen, containing forty three acres and Thirty six hundredths. And also the North west quarter of the North west quarter of section No Thirty two Township No five of range No seventeen containing Thirty three acres and seventy six hundredths, during her natural life and all the stock household goods, furniture, provisions, and other goods and chattels which may be thereon, at the time of my decease, during her natural life as aforesaid, she however selling so much thereof as may be sufficient to pay my just debts, At the death of my said wife the real estate aforesaid and such part of the personal property or the proceeds thereof as may then remain unconsumed and unexpended, I give to and devise to my beloved children Lewis M. Doughty, Jessy D. Doughty, Robert Doughty, John A. Doughty, James S. Doughty, Lester M. Doughty, Charles M. Doughty, Mary J. Doughty

Isaac W. Doughty, and their heirs except the household furniture which shall be equally divided between all of my own heirs and wife's heirs respectfully. I do also authorize and empower them to exchange about ten or twelve acres of land with W. Blagg, according to my former calculation but not otherwise, nor to diminish the value of my farm by such exchange. I do hereby revoke all former wills by me made.

In testimony whereof I have hereunto set my hand and seal this 3rd day of June in the year AD 1854.

Signed sealed & published John Doughty (seal) by said John Doughty as his last will and testament in our presence and signed by us in his presence.

Thomas McK——
George M. Stewart

Sources

[437] Kennedy Hickman, "War of 1812: Battle of Lake Erie," About.com. Military History (http://militaryhistory.about.com/od/navalbattles1800s/p/lakeerie.htm - accessed 12-13-2010).

[438] "Personal History Department – Gallia County," *History of Gallia County, Containing a Condensed History of the County; Biographical Sketches; General Statistics; Miscellaneous Matters, &C.* (1882; reprint ,Chicago and Toledo: H.H. Hardesty, 1976), 23.

[439] Ibid.

[440] Jim Wood, *Raleigh County, West Virginia* (Beckley, West Virginia: Raleigh County Historical Society, 1994), 40.

[441] Ibid., 503.

[442] Julia Wintz, *Kanawha County Marriages, January 1, 1792 – December 31, 1869* (Parsons, WV: McClain Printing Co., 1975), 7.

[443] "Muster Rolls of the Pennsylvania Volunteers in the War of 1812-1814: With Contemporary Papers and Documents," Item 1, Pennsylvania Archives (series); Pennsylvania, General Assembly, Items 1-2. Family History Library, Salt Lake City, Utah, 541.

[444] Wayne B. Ingles, *Symmes Creek, Historical Events and Stories of "The Symmes Valley," including Jackson, Gallia, and Lawrence Counties, Ohio* (Franklin Printing Co., Zanesville, Ohio: Wayne B. Ingles, 1976), 98-99.

[445] "Symmes Township," in *Atlas of Lawrence County, Ohio; Hardesty – 1882, Lake – 1887* (1882; parts of D.J. Lake, *An Atlas of Lawrence County, Ohio, from Actual Surveys*; reprint Lawrence County Historical Society, 1985), 216.

[446] 1840 U.S. Census, Lawrence County, Ohio, Symmes Township, 41.

[447] Lawrence County, Ohio, Deed Book 10:3.

[448] Lawrence County, Ohio, Deed Book 13:104.

[449] John Doughty will, filed June 25, 1852, Lawrence County, Ohio, Loose Wills, No. 6, Journal 14, 42, Record fol. 100, Courthouse, Ironton, Ohio.

[450] Kevin C. Cade, "Richard B. Little," in *History of Lawrence County, Ohio, 1990*, Lawrence County Historical Book Committee, eds. (Waynesville, N.C., Don Mills, Inc.: Walsworth Publishing Co., 1990), 219.

[451] Lois Lawson, "Calvin and Rebecca Stewart," in *History of Lawrence County, Ohio*, 314.

[452] Ingles, *Symmes Creek*, 94, 123.

[453] Ibid., 106.

[454] Francis B. Heitman, *Historical Register of Officers of the Continental Army, During the War of the Revolution, April, 1775, to December, 1783* (1932; reprint, Baltimore: Genealogical Pub.Co.,1982), 202; "Fort Harmar, Military Field Headquarters on the Ohio," *Marietta, Ohio Chapter, Sons of the American Revolution* (http://mariettasar.com/FortHarmar3.htm - accessed 3-2-2010); "John Doughty," from *Wikipedia, the Free Encyclopedia* (http://en.wikipedia.org/wiki/John_Doughty - accessed 12-16-2010); "Descendants of John Doughty (FamilyTreeMaker.com, User Home Pages.

[455] George W. Knepper, *Ohio and Its People* (Kent, Ohio, and London, England: Kent State University Press, 1989), 55-59.

[456] "Personal History Department—Gallia County," *History of Gallia County*, 23.

[457] Lawrence County, Ohio, Deed Book 9:534-535.

[458] Lawrence County, Ohio, Deed Book 11:230.

[459] Billee Hammond Schlaudt, *Marriage Records, Lawrence County, Ohio* (Houston: B.H. Schlaudt, 1987), books 1-6 (1817-1863), 49.

[460] 1850 U.S. Census, pop. sch., Lawrence County, Ohio, Symmes Township, dwelling/family 80/82 (John Doughty household); dwelling/family 79/81 (Absolem Stewart household); dwelling/family 78/80 (Calvin Stewart household); dwelling/family 77/79 (Geo. Stewart household); dwelling/family 76/78 (John Stewart household).

[461] Gallia County, Ohio, Marriages, vol. 1, 1803-1843, p. 283, FHL microfilm 317,652, roll 299.

[462] Dalton-Doughty marriage, International Genealogical Index (IGI) (Salt Lake City, Family History Library), microfilm 317,717, v. 6-8, batch M514,522.

[463] 1850 U.S. Census, pop. sch., Lawrence County, Ohio, Aid Township, p. 693, dwelling/family 45/48.

[464] Lawrence County, Ohio, Deed Book 16:380.

[465] 1880 U.S. Census, pop. sch., Lawrence County, Ohio, Aid Township, p. 14C, FHL microfilm 1,255,039; National Archives microfilm T9-1039.

[466] Gallia County, Ohio, Marriages, vol. 1, 1803-1843, p. 214, FHL microfilm 317,652, roll 299.

[467] Robert E. Doughty, Auditor, Lawrence County (Ohio), Militia Rolls, 1863-1865, A List of Volunteers, Aid Township, FHL microfilm 476,171, item 2.

[468] *Atlas of Lawrence County, Ohio, 1887*, found at Lawrence County Courthouse, Ironton, Ohio.

[469] Rev. Chester I. Miller, "Miller-Neal," *History of Lawrence County, Ohio, 1990*, 241-242.
[470] "History of Lawrence County," *Atlas of Lawrence County, Ohio: Hardesty—1882-1887.*
[471] Garland E. Shafer, "Aid Township," *History of Lawrence County, Ohio, 1990*, 2-3.
[472] Schlaudt, *Marriage Records, Lawrence County, Ohio*, books 1-6, 49.
[473] Gallia County, Ohio, Marriages, vol. 1, 1803-1843, FHL microfilm 317,652, roll 299.
[474] James Doughty children from International Genealogical Index (IGI), *FamilySearch,* v5.0
[475] "Personal History Department—Gallia County," *History of Gallia County*, 23.
[476] Ibid.
[477] 1880 U.S. Census, pop. sch., Jackson County, Ohio, precinct 1, Wellston, p. 173D, FHL microfilm 1,255,036; NA T9-1036.
[478] Schlaudt, *Marriage Records, Lawrence County, Ohio*, books 1-6, 42.
[479] Gallia County, Ohio, Marriages, vol. 2, FHL microfilm 317,652, roll 299, p. 143.
[480] Brown-Doughty marriage, Individual Record, *FamilySearch*, Ancestral File v4. 19.
[481] 1880 U.S. Census, pop. sch., Lawrence County, Ohio, Windsor Township, p. 403B, FHL microfilm 1,255,039; NA T9-1039.

The LEWISES

Speculation on the father of James Lewis (d. 1720) of Middlesex County, Virginia.

On the eastern edge of the North American continent, at Urbanna, in Middlesex County, Virginia, recreational boats are docked in the shimmering waters of Rappahannock River and Urbanna Creek. Although Urbanna is not the county seat these days, it still is a center of activity for Middlesex County. The Old Tobacco Warehouse, once used for trading, is now the visitors'center. Urbanna Creek was called *Nimcock* by the Indians, and *Rosegill* by Ralph Wormeley, who acquired a plantation there that originally had 3,200 acres and later doubled its acreage.[482] North of Rosegill was Robinson's Creek, and Sunderland Creek enters the Rappahannock just a short distance on up river. Middlesex was created from Lancaster County in 1669. Middlesex could then hold its own court sessions on the south (or west) side of the Rappahannock River. The lower part of Middlesex is a peninsula, with the Rappahannock forming its northern boundary and the Piankatank River its southern. The Rappahannock and Piankatank Rivers follow the banks of Stingray Point and then their waters flow into Chesapeake Bay. A gentle surf brushes the shores. The Piankatank is formed from the Dragon Swamp that separates Middlesex from King and Queen County. Across the Piankatank is Gloucester County. Its lower part, Kingston Parish, became Mathews County in 1791. North of the narrow middle of Middlesex County, at Sunderland Creek, is the land where Richard Lewis, the progenitor of many of the Lewises of Middlesex County, settled.

Richard Lewis of Sunderland Creek:
Richard Lewis, thought to have been born in 1609 in Wales, was named as a headright of Capt. Christopher Wormeley on 17 January 1638, when he patented 1,420 acres in what is now Middlesex County.[483] And Richard Lewis was a headright for Capt. Ralph Wormeley's 3,200-acre grant received in 1649 for land on Rosegill Creek.[484] England wanted to encourage migration to the New World, so she worked out a system whereby would-be land owners could pay the passage across the Atlantic of an immigrant (a "head') and receive 50 acres in return. The headright was then supposed to work the land.[485] As in the case of Richard Lewis, names of headrights were used more than once, but this fraud obviously was not taken very seriously, for it happened again and again.

Richard is on record as acquiring 300 acres on Sunderland Creek in 1653[486] and 500 on a branch of Sunderland Creek on 16 January 1658. On the same day he was granted another 200 acres, this tract at the head of Sunderland Creek. The 500-acre tract abutted lands of Robert Kemp and Minor Minson.[487]

James Lewis, likely son of Richard:
People seemed to sue each other a lot during the colonization of Virginia. Perhaps they needed some assurance of law and order. Often the parties to the suits were relatives or neighbors. Lancaster County Court Orders of 11 April 1666 reveal that Edward Boswell was ordered to pay his debt of 1,654 lbs. of tobacco and cask to James Lewys, who had sold him some goods.[488]

That this James Lewis was a son of Richard is implied by his having a dispute with a close neighbor of Richard's. The tax collectors went door to door, so their lists are evidence of who lived next to whom. The lists of 6 February 1655 show Richd. Lewis (3 tithables, that is, males 16 or over) between Evan Davies (3), and Mr. Boswell (4).[489] We can assume that Richard's 3 tithables were sons. By 1663 Richd. Lewys had 7 tithables, and he was listed between Tho. Willys (6) and Tho. Willyams (2). Edward Boswell followed, with 7; Mr. Cuth. Potter, 19; and Hen. Nichols, 20.[490] The tithables of large land owners included servants.

Henry Nichols' presence on Sunderland Creek is significant to our story, for his family intermarried with the George family[491] (see Zebulon Lewis of Orange County, Virginia, for more on them), and Mary Lewis, daughter of Richard, married John Nichols in 1684.[492] It is believed that John Lewis, son of Richard, married Sarah, daughter of

Henry Nichols, and moved to New Kent County, Virginia.[493] John's son John, of New Kent County, settled on Sunderland Creek and married Elizabeth O'Brissell in 1681.[494] Eusebias O'Bressell was buried 17 March 1680/90,[495] and the name *Eusebias* was carried on in the Lewis lineage. Thomas Obrisell and Jno. Burke were securities when Elizabeth Lewis was granted administration of the estate of Richard Lewis (Jr.) in 1698.[496] And in 1691 Thomas O'Bristle, Tobias Mickleburrough, Maxwell Mosely, and John Nash took an inventory of the Middlesex County part of the estate of Mr. William Therriot of Lancaster County.[497] See Edmund Lewis for more on the Therriots.

In 1684 Jane Lewis, possibly the daughter (or maybe the widow) of the James Lewis who sued Boswell, was servant to Capt. Walter Whitaker of Middlesex County.[498] Whitaker lived near Richard Robinson and was guardian to Joseph Goare for a time.[499] Zebulon Lewis of Orange County, seemingly a grandson of James Lewis (d. 1720), knew the Goare (Gore) family—more on them later. When John Robinson patented 300 acres on the north side of the Rappahannock River, abutting land of Col. Burbage, two of his headrights were James Lewis and Jane Lewis. The patent has no date but is inserted between one made in 1654 and one in 1652.[500] John Robinson married Edward Dudley's widow, who then resided in Lancaster County. Her descendants lived in Middlesex and Gloucester Counties.[501]

A James Lewis was a headright of Arthur Nash when he patented 950 acres in New Kent County on 6 December 1654. This grant was at the head of Poropotank Creek by the swamp and land surveyed for Tho. Cox.[502] Poropotank Creek divides King and Queen County (formed from New Kent County in 1691) from Gloucester County, and the Lewises later referred to as the Warner Hall Lewises, laid claim to considerable acreage along this creek.[503] The Nashes settled in Middlesex, and William Lewis, a descendant of Richard Lewis, witnessed the 1718 will of Arthur Nash, son of John Nash.[504]

POSSIBLE RELATIVES OF JAMES LEWIS, WHO MAY HAVE BEEN A SON OF RICHARD LEWIS:

In the absence of direct proof of parentage, I look for relatives among neighbors and associates of the person I'm researching. It is my assumption that the James Lewis who won a lawsuit against Edward Boswell in 1666 was a son of Richard Lewis of Sunderland Creek.

+   **James LEWIS** was born by 1668 and died 10 May 1720.

         Edmond LEWIS died 1662 in Lancaster County, Virginia.

Edmund Lewis is thought by genealogists John Bennett Boddie and R.J.C.K. Lewis to have been the father of James Lewis (d.1720) of Middlesex, and it may be true.[505] Edward Dale, however, became administrator of Edmund's estate, "according to act," which meant he was either the nearest relative or his greatest creditor.[506] Edward Dale was Clerk of Lancaster County and he recorded that he gave security (for the administration bond) according to law, but the name of his surety was not given. Curiously, the entry in Lancaster County Court Orders of 9 July 1662 reveals that Dale had first written that he was administrator of the estate of Richard Lewis and written *Edmund* over *Richard*. The appointed appraisers of Edmund's estate were Mr. John Edwards, Mr. Will. Neesham, and Dnc. Therryott.[507] No person was designated as guardian of any children. James Lewis (d. 1720) would have been born by 1668, for in 1689 he was involved in a lawsuit. Edmund Lewis, son of James (d. 1720), named "the little boy" Richard Lewis in his will. If the little boy was his son, the choice of his given name becomes even more interesting, considering Edward Dale's entry in the court records.

The Therriot-Wroughton (Wharton)-Heale connection:

We recall that a James Lewis sued Edward Boswell in 1666. Boswell had patented 150 acres on Sunderland Creek adjacent Denis Coniers and Evan Davies, and land of Bartram Hobert (Obert), on 5 March 1651. He sold the land to Jno. Pedro and Evan Davies.[508] A debt due from the estate of Epa. Lawson, assigned from Major Jno. Carter to Wm. Neesam and Jno. Merriman, was paid to Edw. Boswell and recorded 6 June 1654.[509] Lancaster County Orders of 14 November 1666 include the notice that Joseph Bayley had married the mother of Eliz. Davys, who had lived for a long time with

Edward Boswell, deceased.[510] Joseph Bailey of Lancaster County made his will in 1672, naming Jos. Ball and Wm. Therriott as executors.[511]

William Wroughton (Wharton?) may have been the person who secured Dale's administration bond for the estate of Edmund Lewis, for Lancaster County Court of 10 September 1662 ordered that Wroughton be paid for funeral charges and other disbursements of the estate of Edmund Lewis, deceased.[512]

William Wroughton sold Robert Swan one half of a parcel on the northernmost side of the Corotoman River on 21 May 1662, and Edmond Lewys and Tho. Daniell witnessed the deed.[513]

On 6 December 1670 Will. Wroughton deeded all lands in his occupation and that of Mary Hale, widow, and Henry Clerke, to Dne. Therryott. Mary Hale's lease was reserved as well as a lease to said Wroughton. Wits: Robt. Bray and Hen. Bradley. Will Wroughton gave power of attorney to Mr. Tho. Marshall to acknowledge the lease.[514] Mary Hale's last name may actually have been *Heale*, for the Heales (or Hailes) had a long history of association with the Wroughtons and their friends. Mary had died by 13 March 1672, when the administration of her estate went to George Hale, her son.[515] George Heale died by 2 February 1698. William Ball was his son-in-law.[516] William Lewis of Lancaster County made his will on 13 December 1733, and he devised his 48-acre farm in Harfordshire, Great Britain, to Capt. Geo. Heale. The farm was called Webstershall and had been given to him by his great grandfather, Charles Lewis. Capt. Geo. Heale was named as executor, and Jas. Wharton, Jno. Norris, and Timothy Thornton were witnesses. William Ball, Gent., was referred to as administrator when he returned the appraisement in 1743.[517] Ellen Heale, in her will of 1710, named her daughter Mrs. Hannah Ball, wife of Capt. Wm. Ball.[518]

If Edmund Lewis was descended from Charles Lewis, then he would not have been closely related to Richard Lewis (b. 1609) in Wales. Charles was a descendant of the Thorndon Hall Lewises (through Edward Lewis of Richmond County, Virginia). Sir John, progenitor of the Thorndon Hall Lewises of Essex County and neighboring Hertfordshire, England, had been forced to prove he was free-born in Wales. Sir Lewis John, who died in 1443, had been knighted by King Henry VI. John had sons Lewis, Edmond, Philip, John, and Henry. The Kilbys of the same area knew a Philip Lewys, for in 1627 Nicholas Kilby and his wife and children entered the home of Philip Lewys and attacked his wife with a hatchet.[519]

Vincent Stanford, in his will of 1658, devised 800 acres to Mary, daughter of Edward Dale.[520] And Robert Pollard, who married the widow of Vincent Stanford,[521] was involved with the Heales. An entry was made in Lancaster County records on 8 January 1668, stating that before Robert Pollard (by then deceased) had gone to England, he had committed his son Robert Pollard to the tuition of Nich. Hale.[522]

Dominie [*sic*] Theriott was given administration of the estate of Hen. Lee, for Dominic had married Joan, the relict of Hen. Lee.[523] Joan Lee was a witness to the 1652 will of Epaphroditus Lawson.[524]

The Kemp-Lawson-Kilby connection:

Mathew Kemp, Jr., was close to the Lewis-Kilby family of Middlesex, and the reason is not obvious. James Lewis (d.1720) became guardian of Catherine Kilbee, daughter of William Kilbee.[525] Both the Kemps and the Kilbys were related to the Lawsons, however. In 1680 Mary Kilbey married John Lanson [Lawson], and after the death of James Lewis, Catherine Kilbee chose Mrs. Jane Lawson of Lancaster County as her guardian.[526] Matthew Kempe, Sr., was living in Gloucester County, Virginia, on 8 November 1677, when he and wife, Dorothy, sold 1,000 acres in Lancaster County to George Heale. Matthew's wife, Dorothy, was referred to as his "now wife," a sign of a previous marriage.[527] Dorothy had rights to land that had belonged to Thomas Madestard, whose sister, Elizabeth, married Epaphroditus Lawson. Thomas made over land to Robert Griggs on 2 June 1668, and Dorothy Kempe gave power of attorney to Thomas Madestard to acknowledge her rights to the land. The deed was witnessed by Richard Kentish and Edward Carter and recorded 15 February 1668.[528] After Epaphroditus Lawson died, his widow married William Clapham, Jr.[529]

Edward Dale married Diana Skipwith, whose mother was a Kemp.[530] Matthew Kemp, a cousin of Diana's, had an interest in the welfare of William Kilby's children, taking their mother to court when she and her new husband, John Degge, were misusing their inheritance.[531] William Frissell, who married Christopher Kilby's widowed mother-in-law, gave security for John Upshur who inherited 75 acres from Joseph Pye. This land had formerly belonged to Edward Lunsford, who had bought it from Robert Swan.[532] Remember that Edmund Lewis had witnessed a deed from William Wroughton to Robert Swan. So Edmund Lewis would likely have been acquainted with the Kilbys. Edward Dale, Edmund's administrator, bought land in Lancaster County from Edward Lunsford on 2 February 1664,[533] and Christopher Kilby and wife, Catherine (Hill), were living along the Corotoman River in Lancaster County when Christopher went on record as having received his wife's inheritance from his father-in-law, William Frizle. Geo. Flower and Dme. Therryott witnessed the document.[534] When Robert Kempe sold 300 acres along Sunderland Creek to Joseph Smith and Humphry Jones in 1663, Joseph Pye (note the Pye-Kilby involvement with Lunsford) was a witness, along with Will. Michell.[535]

Edward Dale's daughter Mary married Humphrey Jones and had son Humphrey, born in Lancaster County, and baptized 11 March 1682/3 in Middlesex, where Humphrey lived.[536] Humphrey Jones (Sr.) died 16 October 1684.[537] William Killbee, James Webb, and John Smith, were sureties when Thomas Hipkins became administrator of the estate of Humphrey Jones (Jr.) in 1699.[538]

The mother of Edward Dale's wife, Diana Skipwith, was a Kemp. Matthew Kemp was an heir of Edmund Kemp, so *Edmund* was a Kemp name.[539]

William LEWIS.

When Thomas Allomaine patented 52 acres in Kingston Parish, Gloucester County, on 20 April 1684, his land was described as adjacent Mr. William Elliott, William Lewis, and Lt. Col. Jno. Armistead.[540] In 1686 Thomas Alloman bought 300 acres, part of a larger tract, at Stingray Point in Middlesex County, In 1690 Thomas Hill, Patrick Miller, Richard Farrell, and John Ashburn bought parts of the same tract. It belonged to William Dudley, whose wife, Mary Bawdes, had inherited it from her father. By 1703 William Churchill had bought out Alloman, Miller, and Farrell. Churchill hired William Kilbee, who lived in the lower precinct, to collect debts for him.[541] Actually the fate of Thomas Alliman's land was more complicated. On 5 November 1697 Thomas Allamann and wife, Sarah sold the 50 acres he had bought from Richard Farrell to William Churchill. Wits: Othniell (?) Barker, John Sandiford, and Simon Adcock.[542] A deed was recorded on 3 August 1696 from Thomas and Contiten Alliman of Kingston Parish, Gloucester County, to daughter Judith, wife of Phillip Parr, of Middlesex. The Allimans were transferring land bought on 6 September 1686 from William Dudley. After daughter Judith's decease, the land was to go to her daughter Judith Parr, with reversion to her sister Mary Parr.[543]

Thomas Allaman's daughter Judith married first Phillip Parr and secondly James Edmondson.[544] His son, James Edmondson, Jr., secured the bond when Joshua Lewis, son of James Lewis (d. 1720) became administrator of the estate of his brother Edmund Lewis in 1732.[545] Because both William Lewis and James Lewis (d.1720) had a connection to Thomas Alliman, we are encouraged to assume they were related.

First Generation

1. **James¹ LEWIS** was born by 1667. He died 10 May 1720 in Middlesex County, Virginia.

Documents show that James Lewis associated with several people who lived near Richard Lewis on Sunderland Creek. In 1689 James Lewis won a lawsuit against Willm. Attley's estate, which was "in ye hands of Mr. Willm. Daniell

Senior for three hundred pounds of good tobacco."[546] In 1695 William Daniell, Jr., and wife, Constance, assigned land to Andrew Wilson of King and Queen County. The tract bordered on lands of Mr. Robert Price, Henry Nicholls, John Beauford, Mr. Randolph Seager, Nicholas West, and Humphrey Jones.[547] Henry Nicholls was a neighbor of Richard Lewis on Sunderland Creek.

William Southern sued James Lewis, and on 1 February 1697 the court ruled in Southern's favor.[548] In 1703 William Mountague of Jamaco became constable in place of John Southerne.[549] Jamaco was in the same part of Middlesex County as Richard Lewis's land at the head of Sunderland Creek. In his will of 1726 John Southern referred to 200 acres of land granted to Matthew Kemp.[550]

George Wortham witnessed James Lewis's will,[551] and he also witnessed the will of John Stamper, dated 9 November 1688. William Valliert (Vallot) was the other witness to Stamper's will. John Stamper's executors were wife, Carew (Cary?) and son John Stamper, underage.[552] Powell Stamper, Henry Tugel, and John Lewis were witnesses to the 1726 will of Benjamin Williamson. Benjamin was a son of Robert Williamson and Katherine, daughter of Richard Lewis.[553]

A non-suit was granted to James Lewis and his wife in their case against Tho. Williamson and wife on 5 July 1697. On the same day James Lewis was granted a non-suit against James Williamson, with damages.[554] The reason for these lawsuits is not explained, but since husbands and wives were both involved, it sounds as if it was a dispute over land. Not all deeds were recorded. I have not found a deed made out to James Lewis nor record of his selling land.

On 9 November 1696 Thomas Williamson became guardian of the orphans of William Dudley. Thomas had married William's widow, Mary (Bawd). Edward Clarke and James Williamson secured the guardian bond, and Tho. Gregson and Edwin Thacker witnessed it. On 19 October 1696 Thomas Williamson and wife, Mary, bound over to Edward Clarke and James Williamson two Negroes (Jack and Bess). Wits: William Downing, Jane Mitchell.[555] William Downing's daughter Ruth had married Edward Clark.[556] An Edward Clark, seemingly the father of this man, married Ann Allison in 1681.[557] Ann's sister Mary married Joseph Goare,[558] whose granddaughter Sarah Gore and her husband, John O'Neal, would rent land in Culpeper County, Virginia, to Zebulon Lewis and his son, Samuel. (See Zebulon, supposed grandson of the James Lewis who died in 1720.) Richard Robinson was an administrator of the estate of David Allison, Mary's father. Robinson signed bond with Edward Clark on 30 January 1682.[559] After the death of John Goare, his widow, Margritt, married George Ransome, and moved to Kingston Parish, Gloucester County. She and George had daughter Elizabeth, who married Robert Dudley.[560]

Robert Williamson, who married Katherine, daughter of Richard Lewis (of Sunderland Creek), was a witness, with his brother James Williamson, to the assignment of land by William Johnson to John Sumers in 1695. Augustine Williamson, planter, of Middlesex had sold the 50-acre parcel to William Johnson. It was on the upper side of the Ferry Road and extended to lands of Esquire Wormeley. Witnesses to this deed were William Valliott, John Vivion, and James Williamson. On 7 March 1698 Margrett Sumers, widow, assigned the land to Ann Dunkinton. Richard Shelford and Simon Adcock witnessed.[561] The ferry across the Piankatank was less than five miles south of the "Mother Church" of Christ Church Parish.[562] This church is still active today, and in its graveyard rest some of the first members of the parish.

Both Robert Williamson and James Lewis were associated with Richard Robinson. He was a justice of Middlesex County and allowed court to meet at his home in the middle precinct.[563] Richard Robinson witnessed the 1681 will of Robert's father, Andrew Williamson. Andrew mentioned sons Augustine and Andrew and referred to the rest of his children without naming them. He did not name his wife. Other witnesses besides Richard Robinson were Thomas Wharton and Thomas Hurblesrett.[564] *Hurblesrett* would have been Thomas Hucklescot, Robinson's bookkeeper, and Wharton was an attorney.[565] Andrew Williamson had land abutting Richard Robinson's.[566]

A relative of Richard Robinson devised land to Robert Williamson. Frances Robinson, a sister of Christopher Robinson, married Mr. John Sheppard.[567] John made his will in 1682, naming his wife, Frances, and son and daughter John and Frances Sheppard, both underage. John also named daughter Clara Sheppard and his brother Mr. Alexander Sheppard of Suffolk County, England. Some godchildren were named: goddaughters Frances Mackrory and Ann Robinson; godsons Richard Robinson and Robert Williamson. Brother Mr. Christopher Robinson, kinsman Mr. Richard Robinson, and Mr. Alexander Smith were mentioned.[568] In 1691 Frances Macrory married William Scarbrough,[569] and on 8 November 1697 Frances, goddaughter of John Sheppard, deceased, and Robert Williamson, godson, were in court.[570] A deed and bond signed by Robert Williamson and recorded on 9 May 1698 reveals that the land matter had been settled.[571] The Reverend John Sheppard began serving the parish as minister in 1668.[572] In 1673 Richard and Ann Robinson sold land to the parish, and it was to be used as glebe land. The 400-acre tract ran southwest from Nimcock (or Rosegill) Creek. It included the plantation of John Sheppard, minister, and one of the boundaries was 70 poles from Andrew Williams' fence side.[573]

James Lewis, George Anderson, and Robert Boodle were witnesses to the will of Richard Robinson (dated 16 August 1689). Richard's legatees were his two sisters, Ann [Robinson] and Margritt [Robinson]; grandsons John and George Haselwood, their mother, Ann Haselwood, having already been given her share of the estate. Exec: son Richard Robinson; overseers: Ralph Wormeley, Esq., Dr. Walter Whitaker, Mr. Edward Thomas, and kinsman Christopher Robinson.[574] Christopher Robinson's home, Hewitt, is now a historical landmark in Middlesex County. John Vause, who died 26 February 1679, asked to be buried in Mr. Christopher Robinson's orchard.[575] When I visited Hewitt not long ago, it still had an orchard.

James Lewis's court appearances, precinct and community duties:
Robert Boodle won a case against James Lewis for 430 pounds of tobacco in April of 1693.[576] On 3 May 1703, Samuell Low's case against James Lewis and others was dismissed.[577]

James Lewis, John Davis, Sr., John Vivion, Sr., and John Smith were in court on 5 July 1703, accused of swearing on the Sabbath Day. All were found not guilty, for no proof was presented against them.[578]

On 5 March 1705 James Lewis, John Smith, and Charles Williams (or any two) were ordered to appraise the estate of John Whitehead, deceased. Administration was granted to Charles Haines because he was the greatest creditor.[579] A John Whitehead was among the headrights when Richard Longest received his patent for 680 acres in Kingston Parish, Gloucester County, in 1678. This land abutted that of Jacob Johnson, Wm. Beard, Col. Dudley, John Waters, Wm. Elliott, and Capt. Armestead.[580] When appraisers were appointed, at least one of them was supposed to be familiar enough to the deceased to have some knowledge of his belongings.

John Dudley, "the younger," was a friend of James Lewis, for Dudley loaned him money for his doctor bill. A man by the name of Thornton had set his leg, and Dudley paid the bill for him. James delayed paying him back, however, and John took him to court on 2 January 1717.[581]

On 16 March 1703 John Dudley sold 60 acres to George Curtis of Northumberland County (Virginia). The land was near the lower chapel and adjoined the land of Mr. Edwin Thacker. Wits: Thomas and John Marston. Jno. Dudley bought the land back from George Curtis of Northumberland County on 4 March 1706. Curtis signed an accompanying bond. Witnesses for deed and bond were Joseph Goare and Geo. Berrick.[582] As explained earlier, Joseph Goare, through his step-sister, was an in-law of Robert Dudley. John Marston and George Berrick lived near the lower chapel. John Marston's father, Thomas, was of Kingston Parish, Gloucester County, when he bought 100 acres from James and Elizabeth Dudley of Middlesex on 23 March 1681. The tract was next to the road with the Beaver Dam and was bordered by lands of Davey Barrick and Wid. Hackney.[583] The Barricks seem to have been related to the Kilbys, for Christopher Kilby's wife, Catherine, was the daughter of Charles Hill and wife Audrey (Barrick?).[584] An Ardry *Barratt* was among the headrights recorded for Mr. Robert Chowning on 30 March 1659.[585] *Audrey* was a rare name in those days, so the likelihood is strong that it was Audrey Barrick who married Charles Hill. On 3 February 1712, a few years after the death of William Kilby, his son, Christopher, became the ward of George Barrick. Witnesses to the bond: William Gray, Wil. Stanard.[586]

James Lewis, Thomas Smith, and James Smith returned their inventory of the estate of John Watts on 5 April 1715.[587] Eliza Watts was administrator of John's estate. Her bond was secured by John Gibbs. Wits: John Thacker, Jno. Curtis.[588]

James Lewis was appointed constable for the middle precinct in April of 1705, replacing John Gibbs, and on 1 April 1706, he petitioned to be relieved of the duty. Mr. John Vivion took his place.[589] Based on their associations we could say that James and Johanna Lewis lived near children of Andrew Williamson and near Mr. Richard Robinson. The Kilby seat of residence was in the lower precinct,[590] so it is doubtful James and Johanna were living on Kilby land.

Robert Logan sued James Lewis, and a special imparlance was granted James Lewis at Middlesex Court on 1 August 1709.[591]

In 1718 the Vestry paid James Lewis for keeping William Anderson three months and two weeks.[592] It was the church that provided social welfare, and people in the community were paid for caring for the ill. William Anderson and George Wortham were witnesses on 2 March 1696, when William Downing of Middlesex County gave power of attorney to Mr. Henry Goare of Essex County. Downing referred to Mr. Henry Goare as his "well and truly beloved friend."[593] Henry Goare was a brother to Joseph Goare of Middlesex County, and Henry married Elizabeth Allison, sister to Joseph's wife. Their sister Ann married Edward Clark, and their sister Catherine married Benjamin Marsh.[594]

James Lewis signed bond to become guardian of Kathi. Kilbey, daughter of Will. Kilbey, deceased, on 30 (December?) 1718. Christopher Kilbey secured the bond. Thos. Edwards and H. Thacker were witnesses. It was recorded on 3 January 1718.[595] (The old-style calendar was usually used in these records, and the date of recording would have been 3 January 1719 by the new calendar.) In 1721, following the death of James, Catherine requested that Jane Lawson of Lancaster County be her guardian.[596]

The will of James Lewis:

James wrote his will on 13 September 1715, and it was probated 7 July 1720. He asked that his two younger children, Joshua and Zebulon, who were under 21 at the time, be under the care of their mother. Other children were James, Edmund, and Katherine. Exec: wife, Joana. Wits: George Wortham, John Sanders.[597] The inventory showed payments made by John Jones, Mr. Vicarus, Mr. Thomas Read, and Capt. Digges.[598]

Capt. John Degge married Johanna, widow of William Kilby, on 21 January 1706/7.[599] They had son John in 1707; daughter Johanna in 1711; son Anthony in 1714; and son James in 1718.[600] John Degge and Joseph Goar were sureties for James Dudley when he became guardian of Acquilla Snelling, orphan of Alexander Snelling Wits: Thomas Kidd, William Elliott (recorded August 1, 1709).[601] John Degge's father, John Degge, patented 1,800 acres in Kingston Parish, Gloucester County, Virginia, in 1678.[602] In 1683 John Deggs was granted 1,425 acres on the south side of Garden Creek (in Kingston Parish) in Gloucester County.[603] With that kind of background, we wonder why John Degge and wife, Johanna, were misusing the Kilby children's inheritance. John and Johanna were asked to give an accounting of the estate of William Kilbee, deceased, because the terms were not being complied with.[604] Francis Hooper, in his will of 14 February 1703 (probated 8 July 1713), asked William Killbee to be his executor. Hooper's heirs were William Kilbee's children, Katherine and William Killbee.[605] When Johanna became administrator of the estate of her deceased husband, William Kilbee, on 2 December 1706, Matthew Kemp and William Barbee secured her bond.[606] Matthew Kemp and William Barbee had John Degge and wife, Johanna, in court on 7 August 1713.[607] Before the official probate date of Hooper's will, on 7 April 1713, Joan MacDaniell, wife of Randolph MacDaniell of Lancaster County, was slated to give evidence regarding Hooper's will. When she testified on 5 May 1713, she was said to be the wife of *Daniell* MacDaniell of Fleet's Bay.[608]

I have not been able to identify the John Jones who made a payment to the Lewis estate. Parson Vicaris, however, appeared in Christ Church Parish records. He and Mr. John Grimes were godfathers of Benjamin Gray, born to Mr. Samuel Gray, minister, and Madam Ann Gray, and baptized in 1696. Madam Elizabeth Wormeley was godmother.[609] Thomas Reade was a witness to the 1726 will of Joseph Goare of Middlesex.[610]

Mary Vicaris, born about 1675 in Petsworth Parish, Gloucester County, to the Rev. Thomas Vicaris and Dorothy (Pritchett), married Robert Nettles Sr., of Gloucester County, who also married Mary Brookings.[611] About ninety years later, William Brookings, who had roots in Gloucester County, bought several items at the 1811 estate sale of Samuel Lewis of Monroe County (WV). (Monroe County was part of Virginia until 1863, when West Virginia was formed from the western regions of Virginia.) William's sister Rhoda Brooking married Henry Miller, and their daughter Rhoda married Samuel D. Lewis, grandson of Samuel Lewis (d. 1811). More on them later. And Robert Brooking, also with Gloucester County roots, must have been close to George Wortham, one of the witnesses to the will of James Lewis, for Brooking stepped forward to sign bond for him.

In September 1711 Capt. George Wortham was charged with the murder of Benjamin Davis. The two were outside the courthouse, and Wortham mentioned a mare that had been stolen by William Matthews and Davis took his side. An argument followed, and Davis drew his sword. Wortham defended himself with his cane. When Davis knocked the cane out of his hand, Wortham drew his sword, and Davis fell into the sword, suffering a fatal stab. Several people testified on Wortham's behalf. Wortham signed a bond on 22 September 1711, and it was recorded. John

Grymes, Wm. Roan, William Callanone, Ralph Baker, and Robert Brooking were sureties.[612] Wortham was acquitted.[613]

George Wortham, who lived in the middle precinct, was the son of John and Mary Wortham.[614] One of John's wives (he married several times), Prudence (Needham), witnessed a deed for Richard Robinson, whose will James Lewis witnessed. In 1688 Richard Robinson and wife, Ann Moone Curtis,[615] sold to Walter Whittaker 150 acres that lay between the Ferry Road and the Church Road. Geo. Haslewood, Paul Thilman and Prudence Wortham witnessed.[616] John Wortham, in his will of 1692, named wife, Jane, sons George and Oswald, and daughter Elizabeth Wortham. He referred to the rest of his children, but didn't name them. He mentioned a Negro boy belonging to the children of Roger Shackelford. John appointed son George executor, but named Capt. William Daniell and Mr. Richard Robinson as overseers. Wits: William Downing, Sr., William Downing, Jr., and Robert Humphery.[617] John's last wife, Jane, had been married previously to Roger Shackelford of Gloucester County.[618]

John Sanders, the other witness to James Lewis's will, was added to Mr. Wormeley's list of tithables in 1713, along with Gabriell Ray and James Lewis, Jr.[619] John and Elizabeth Sanders had son Edmund on 2 December 1718.[620]

James married **Joanna KILBY**, possibly a daughter of Christopher KILBY and Catherine HILL, about 1689. Joanna was born about 1673.

Joanna Lewis, wife of James Lewis, is thought to have been a daughter of William Kilby, but if she were, her mother would have born children over a 45-year period. James's wife, Joanna, bore her first child in 1690, so we could presume she was about 17 at the time, and therefore born around 1673. Joanna, widow of William Kilby, married John Degge in 1707 and bore her last child in 1718. James's wife, Joanna, may have been a daughter of Christopher Kilby, William's father. James and Joanna named their only daughter Katherine, probably after Catherine Hill, the wife of Christopher Kilby and daughter of Charles Hill. William Kilby's daughter Catherine chose James Lewis as guardian, so it would seem that Joanna, wife of James, was a Kilby, or at least a relative of one.

In 1704 Johannah Lewis took William Downing to court for "beating wounding and violently strikeing" her, but she agreed to dismiss the case.[621] Will. Downing, taylor, bought 300 acres from Jo. and Ann Curtys on 28 July 1664. The land he purchased adjoined that of Davyd Allyson and was near the path that went to the great swamp. Wits: Peter Cyavanne, William Haighe.[622] William Downing, Sr., in his will of 1694, allowed only one shilling to son William Downing, "for his disrespect to me."[623]

Since we have no primary evidence that Joanna Lewis was born a Kilby, we should take a second look at her relatives and acquaintances who were named *Joanna*. Note that William Downing owned land next to Davyd Allyson, and his wife was a *Joan*.[624]

Joan was a name favored by the Lawsons. Rowland Lawson of Lancaster County made his will in 1716, naming daughter Joanna. Rowland's wife was Jane, and she would have been the woman who became guardian of Catherine Kilby in 1721.[625] Johanna Lawson married John Steptoe, Jr., in 1727. Her mother was said to be *Joan* Lawson, but that kind of error was common in old records.[626] Mary Kilby married John Lanson (Lawson) in 1680, and they had son Efferydytus born in 1684.[627] In 1701 Epaphraditus Lawson's case against John Hadley was dismissed for want of prosecution. It was taken to court by Lawson's "nearest Friend," William Killby.[628]

Rowland Lawson, brother of the immigrant Epaphroditus,[629] died by 12 May 1665, when the division of his land was recorded. His widow was to have a third of his estate plus 500 acres, and the rest was to be divided into five parts, with Lancelott Sockwell receiving a fifth in right of his wife.[630] Lancelott had married Rowland's daughter Johannah.[631] Rowland Lawson had son Epaphroditus, born about 1644,[632] and he could possibly be the Epaphratitus Lawson who called William Kilby his nearest friend.

Epaphroditus Lawson (d. by 12 January 1653) possessed large land grants. By 15 February 1642/3 he owned 1,400 acres on Mount Lawson's Bay in Upper Norfolk County, Virginia. On 22 May 1650 he patented two grants, totalling 3,000 acres, along the Rappahannock River.[633]

Chelton-Tignor-Bonner-Barbee-Beaumont connections:

James and Joanna Lewis had son Zebulun baptized on 22 October 1699.[634] Peter Chelton and wife, Abigall, had son Zebulun baptized on 4 August 1700.[635] I have run my finger down many indexes of early Virginia records and rarely have I discovered anyone called *Zebulon,* so the question arises as to whether Zebulun Lewis was related to Zebulun Chelton. Zebulon Lewis was related to Charles Hill, and Peter Chelton had some connection to the Tignors, who intermarried with the Hill family of Middlesex. William Tignor, Jr., of Northumberland County, Virginia, married Dorothy Hill of Middlesex on 18 July 1682.[636] William had died by 11 November 1695 when his widow, Dorothy, was on record as administering his estate. Land belonging to the estate of William Tignor, deceased, was in the possession of Peter Chilton by 6 January 1695.[637]

William Tignor owned land once belonging to James Bonner. On 4 November 1656 William Tigner was granted 750 acres on the south side of the Rappahannock River. The tract was adjacent his own land at Troublesome Point and Tigner's Creek. He bought 550 acres of this land from Richard Axome and Thomas Goodwin. The rest was assigned to him by James Bonner, who had acquired the land on 15 September 1651.[638]

William Blackburn and William Bristow were executors of the 1718 will of Peter Chilton, and Blackburn was also an executor of the 1721 will of William Barbee,[639] who went to court to protect the interests of the orphans of William Kilby (d. 1706). Tignor had land by Bonner's Creek, as did Christopher Kilby. In 1689 Christopher Kellbee patented 590 acres in Middlesex County. The land had been granted to Charles Hill on 6 March 1655 and was bordered by land of John Niccols *(als.* Tigner's), line of Deal's, land of Wm. Churchill, Gent., by a branch of Beners Creek.[640] James Bonner and George Wadding were assigned administration of the estate of Mr. Wm. Bowdes, deceased (recorded in Lancaster County records on 20 January 1662/3).[641] In 1663 Matthew Kemp became the administrator of the estate of James Bonner, deceased. Matthew Kemp's daughter, Elizabeth, had married James Bonner. Apparently they had no children.[642]

John Niccols lived near Christopher Kilby, and a John Nicholls and Mary Lewis married on 30 November 1684.[643] Genealogist Robert J.C.K. Lewis believed that this Mary Lewis was a daughter of Richard Lewis of Sunderland Creek.[644] Ezechias Rhodes and Elizabeth Nicholls married on 22 October 1684.[645] John Nicholls, in his will of 1705, named grandson John Roads, son of Hezekiah Roads, and grandson Thomas Bristow, son of John Bristow. Wits: William Kilbee, George Benick (Barrick), Richard Ransted and Thomas Howell.[646] Mary Lewis must have been the second wife of John Nicholls or perhaps he had son John who married Mary Lewis. In 1693 Hezekiah Rhodes patented 410 acres by Killbee's on a branch of Bonner's Creek in Middlesex County. The tract abutted lands of William Hackny, Sir William Skipwith, and Capt. Mathew Kemp. Included in this tract were 60 acres overplus. The rest had been granted Wm. Frissall on 20 December 1667.[647]

William Barbee, who was committed to the welfare of William Kilby's children, acquired land that had belonged to Perregrine Bland. In 1656 Edmond Kempe, Gent., was granted 1,100 acres parallel to the land of Peregrin Bland, deceased. The tract crossed branches of Bonner's Creek.[648] On 6 June 1699 William Barby was granted 200 acres along the Piankatank River in Middlesex County. William Beamount had given 100 acres of this tract to William Barby, son of William Barby, on 1 January 1690. The 200 acres was part of 1,000 acres that had been granted Perregrine Bland in 1642 and transferred to Hope Bland, his daughter, on 19 January 1650. She devised it to her son William Beaumont.[649]

Hope Branmount (Beaumont), apparently the daughter of William Beaumont and Hope Bland, married Christopher Sutton in 1703.[650] Mrs. Hope Sutton is mentioned in the 1762 will of William Morgan of Middlesex. Morgan had bought land from Mrs. Hope Sutton, Mrs. Marston, and John Dudley, and Morgan devised it to son John, who also received 400 acres in Fauquier County [Virginia]. William Morgan gave to son Josiah 222 acres in Fauquier County and land purchased from William Barby, John Ingrom, and Samuel Ingrom, his son, and William Crutchfield Other legatees: daughters Ann Sutton, Johannah Lee, Letitia Hill, Rose Jones; Mary Stevens. Execs: sons John and Josias Morgan, Rowland Sutton, and Needles Hill. Wits: John Dudley, Lindsay Jarvis, Edward Wilson, and James Deagle.[651]

William Barbee's daughter Ann married John Morgan. In his will of 5 January 1720 William Barbee named sons William and John Barbee and daughter Ann Morgan. Executors were Matthew Kemp, George Harden, and William Blackburn. Wits: Hugh Goath, Edward Blackborne, and Robert Umphries.[652] John Morgan of Essex County named wife, Ann, in his will of 1731. He gave son John Morgin only a shilling. Other legatees were daughter Rosamond and sons William, Edward, Mark, James, Barbee, Nathan, and Joseph. Wits: John Davis, Robert Wimpey, Thomas Newton and Mark Weekes. Wife, Ann, was executor, and Wm. Goulding, John Watkins, and Edmond

Connolly secured her bond.[653]

Vincent Stanford, we saw above, devised land to Mary, daughter of Edward Dale. Stanford obtained a land grant of 700 acres on the north side of the Rappahannock River in 1656. Among his headrights were Richard Robinson, Giles Robison, and Jone Barby.[654] So *Joan* was also a Barbee name.

Johanna Lewis, whatever her maiden name, certainly belonged to the Kilby group and the Hill, Kemp, Barbee, and Lawson cluster.

James and Joanna had the following children:

+   2   i. **James² LEWIS** was christened on 30 November 1690.

        3   ii. **Edmund LEWIS** died in 1732 in Essex County, Virginia.

> Edmund was accused of "firing in the woods" on the Sabbath and brought before a grand jury on 7 December 1714. He was found not guilty, but ordered to pay costs. His father, James Lewis, Sr., paid his fine.[655]
>
> In 1717 Edmond Lewis went to court to get satisfaction from a bill to Thomas Elliott, deceased, and was awarded 170 lbs. of tobacco and costs. Others holding accounts against the estate of Elliott included William Hill, Sarah Hadley, Joseph Goar, John Dudley, Edmond Ryan, John Anderson.[656]
>
> Edmund Lewis took Zebulon Chilton to court on 3 May 1720, for debt.[657] On 20 February 1721 Zebulum Chelton and Mary Goar were wed.[658]
>
> On 7 June 1720 John Dudley was ordered to pay Edmund Lewis for two days' attendance in his suit against Thomas Dudley. John was also ordered to pay Diana Bromell and Joseph Goar for same.[659] On 7 November 1721 Edmund Lewis was in court suing Samuel Low over a debt.[660] On 4 August 1724 Edmund Lewis sued George Chowning, administrator of William Davis.[661]
>
> Edmund's will was probated in Essex County, Virginia. It reveals he was a kind and caring man. Here follows a transcription:
>
>> In the name of God Amen I Edmon Lewes being sick and weak and of perfect memory doth commend my self to the Almighty...I bequeath my wareing aparol with my mare & sadoll which I hath here to John Cargin in order for my Christtian buriall and of trouble of his home. I give and bequeath to my two brothers one in Midelsex and of other in the Ile a waite Joshua Lewes & Zebalon Lewes I bequath to Joshua his chrn. of the negros I give my three crops to poor widos and other pore people who has no land after the charges is defrayd to be dispos'd as [viz.] my brother Joshua and some honest man shall think fit from Midelsex Court house....I give of rest of my estate to my brother Joshua for bringin up of little boy named Richard Lewes and to defray my other debts. This being my last will and testament in witness I set my hand and seale
>>
>>   Sined and Seald
>> in presans of us
>> This 6th of September 1732   Edmund
>>   his   Lewis
>> Jon ( ) Cargin
>>   mark
>>   his
>> James ( ) Mark Danil
>>   mark
>> Michael Wharton
>
> In Essex County court on 21 March 1732 [1733] Edmund's will was proved by John Cargin

and Joshua Lewis, the latter being granted administration. James Edmundson, Jr., and John Caragan secured the administration bond.[662] I have no further information on John Cargin.

James Edmundson married Christian Gregory in Middlesex County on 17 April 1732.[663] The death of a James Edmundson who died 24 March 1727 was recorded in Middlesex County.[664] (The date entered in the parish records was 1726, but these records consistently follow the old calendar, the new year beginning on 25 March, so the date was converted to the new calendar.)

Joshua was asked to be responsible for bringing up the "little boy named Richard Lewes," but Joshua did not refer to him in his will of 1757, so it is not clear what happened to him, and it is not certain he was a son of Edmund.

The Michael Wharton who witnessed Edmund's will was likely the Dr. Whorton who was named in the accounts of John Morgan, deceased, as per Essex County records of 17 March 1742.[665]

4   iii. **Thomas LEWIS** was christened 5 November 1693 in Christ Church Parish, Middlesex County.[666]

He was not named in his father's will. No further record.

+   5   iv. **Zebulon LEWIS** was christened 22 October 1699 and died October 1738.

+   6   v. **Joshua LEWIS** was born 27 December 1702 and died about 1760.

+   7   vi. **Katharine LEWIS**.

Second Generation

2.   **James² LEWIS** (James¹) was christened 30 November 1690 in Christ Church Parish, Middlesex County.[667]

In the summer of 1712 James Lewis, Jr., John Sanders, George Rhodes, Daniel Hughes, and John Street were living as tenants on 3,100 acres of land leased to Robert Faldoe by William Stanard and wife, Anne, when an eviction notice was delivered to them (to John Street by way of a Negro woman at the Hill Quarter). Faldoe's lease had not expired.[668] On 3 February 1713 Ralph Wormeley was in court offering a plea in abatement in Faldoe's ejection suit against him, and Faldoe asked for time to consider the proposal.[669] Faldoe appeared rather suddenly on the scene in Middlesex County, and Middlesex records reveal little about him. There may have been no connection between the two ejectment suits.

In May of 1712 William Stanard and wife, Anne, were sued by Wm Daingerfield and wife, Elizabeth, administrator of William Tomlin. William Stanard had married Ann, daughter of George and Anne Haslewood, George having married the daughter of Richard and Anne Robinson. After George died, Anne married William Tomlin. Their daughter Elizabeth married William Daingerfield. The quarrel was over the possession of some Negro slaves and had cloak and dagger overtones. At midnight in October 1710 William Daingerfield arrived by boat at Perrott's landing and asked the Negroes and Mulattos that had belonged to William Tomlin to come away with him. All came except one named *Robin*. Essex County court had awarded to Elizabeth Tomlin the administration of the estate of her deceased husband. The administration of the estate of George Haslewood of Middlesex County was granted to William Stanard and wife, Anne, the only surviving child of George Haslewood.[670]

On 7 January 1713 James Lewis, Jr., and Gabriel Ray were added to Mr. Wormeley's tithables.[671] On 22 November 1713 Gabriel married Elizabeth Gibbs.[672]

On 7 April 1719 the sheriff ordered James Lewis to be put in stocks for an hour for misbehaving in court. He was taken into custody until he could give security for his good behavior.[673] At the next court James confessed to misbehaving and was fined only five shillings.[674]

James had a child by Rebecca Jameson, and on 1 May 1722 he was ordered to give bond to the church wardens in the amount of 4,000 lbs. of tobacco for the care of the child.[675] Unfortunately, whether the child of James and Rebecca was male or female was not divulged.

This may be the James Lewis, who, with Christopher Robinson, served as surety for Mary Greecion and Wm Row when they became administrators of the estate of James Greecion of King George County, Virginia, in 1740. On 1 December 1721 Mary Clark and James Gressain had been cited for living together in formication.[676] On 5 January 1722, the case was dismissed, for they had married.[677] What raises the possibility that this James Lewis was the son of James and Joanna, is 1) the association with the Robinson family, and 2) the association with a Greecion. Daniel Hughes, who was a tenant on the same tract as James Lewis, Jr., in 1712, married Frances Gresham on 19 December 1711.[678] *Greecion* and *Gresham*, of course, may not have been the varied spellings of the same name, but they probably were, as *Gresham*, *Grasham*, and *Gressom* are cross-referenced in *Christ Church Parish Register*.[679] James Lewis's brother Joshua married Martha Marston, daughter of John and Ann.[680] Martha's brother Thomas Marston married Elizabeth Roach and had son William born in 1732.[681] On 7 April 1761 William Marston went on record as administrator of the estate of Ann Gressum. John Buckner witnessed.[682]

James Lewis of Essex and Caroline Counties and the Long family:

There was a James Lewis living in Essex County, Virginia, during this period, however. He was married by 21 February 1720 when Richard Long and wife, Ann, of Essex County deeded land to their daughter Elizabeth and her husband James Lewis. At about the same time Richard and Ann conveyed land to John Lawrence, to Ann and Sherwood James, and to Anthony Head.[683] James Lewis died in 1761, a resident of Caroline County, and his estate was left in the hands of a series of administrators: Robert Lowry, David Herndon, John Collins, and Samuel Wortham.[684] Jeremiah Long had been married to a Judith, and after his death, James Lewis married his widow, and became administrator of his estate. Nicholas and James Ware secured his bond. People ordered to appraise Jeremiah's estate were John Munday, Robt. Taliaferro, Thomas Samuel, and William Row.[685]

When proof of family ties are lacking, we must rely on circumstantial evidence to figure out who was related to whom. Despite having Samuel Wortham (George Wortham witnessed the will of James Lewis, Sr.) as an administrator of his estate, James Lewis of Essex and Caroline Counties does not seem to have been the son of James Lewis (d. 1720) of Middlesex County. James Lewis of Essex and Caroline Counties may have been related to William Lewis (d. 1763) of Spotsylvania County, for both had Herndon and Long connections. William Lewis and wife, Sarah, had sons James, John, William, and George. William's will of 1763 was witnessed by Wm. Knox, William Hartwell, and Hugh Mercer. The executors were wife, Sarah, Charles Yates, Joseph Brock, and Edward Herndon.[686] Sarah's will of 1771 names daughters Elizabeth Richards and Winifred Richards; grandson James Lewis; granddaughter Sarah, daughter of Elizabeth Richards; William and Sarah Richards, son and daughter of Winifred Richards.[687] In 1756 William Lewis became guardian to Elizabeth Long, orphan of Samuel Long. Thomas Haydon was surety.[688]

William Lewis of Spotsylvania County and the Ellis family:

In 1752 William Lewis and Thomas Blossingham were sureties for William Ellis when he became guardian of Alexander Davidson, orphan of Alexander Davidson.[689] Hezekiah Ellis, father of William Ellis, was of Middlesex County when he made his will in 1726. Hezekiah had wife, Mary; children John, Elizabeth, Mary, Anne, William, Hezekiah, Robert, and Sarah Ellis. And daughter Ellis Faulkner was named. Exec: wife. Trustees: Thomas Meacham John Fearn. Wits: George Sanders, Savanah Curtis, and Thomas Falkner.[690]

John Lewis, brother of William Lewis, died by 8 November 1749, when his widow, Elizabeth, became administrator of his estate. Larkin Johnston and James Parks secured her bond. The appointed appraisers of John's estate were William Miller, Thomas Estis, William Ellis, and Robert Dudley (or any three).[691] The latter two had Middlesex County roots. On 6 March 1750 John Lewis's brother William was granted administration of the rest of his estate. Benjamin Davis secured his bond.[692]

William's son James Lewis was prominent in Spotsylvania County affairs. He was serving as steward for Alexander Spotswood, Esq., in 1777 when Spotswood gave him power of attorney.[693] James' home was called Laurel Hill, and he was a colonel during the Revolutionary War. He married first Elizabeth (1752-1786), daughter of John and Sarah (Carr) Minor.[694] His second wife was a daughter of Edward Herndon.[695] Elizabeth Maury of Albemarle County, Virginia, was his third wife.[696] The Minors were among the earliest settlers of Middlesex County. Remember that David Herndon was one of the administrators of the estate of James Lewis of Caroline County. On the other hand, the

Herndons were a large group, so this connection may not be significant.

Hugh Mercer, who witnessed the will of William Lewis, was a physician and was soon to become a Revolutionary War hero. He died 12 January 1777 from wounds suffered at the Battle of Princeton. Confederate General Hugh Weedon Mercer, General George S. Patton, Jr., and songwriter Johnny Herndon Mercer were direct descendants of Dr. Mercer.[697]

Genealogist Michael Lewis Cook suspected that Samuel Lewis (d. 1811) of Monroe County (WV) was related to William Lewis of Spotsylvania County. Cook believed that William Lewis was descended from Richard Lewis of Sunderland Creek, Middlesex.[698] Samuel had son Zebulon; and Zebulon Lewis of Orange County, Virginia. and son Samuel rented land in Culpeper County, Virginia, from John O'Neal and wife, Mary (Gore) in 1770.

James Lewis of the 1780s:

In the late 1700s a James Lewis owned land in Middlesex County. Land of James Lewis was used as a pointer for a 129-acre lot being sold in Middlesex in 1788 by Thomas and Catherine Turner to William George. The lot was "bounded by the land of Richard Corbin, Harry B. Yates, Williamson Davis, Agrippa Dunn, Ann Gardner, James Lewis, and Benjamin Williams." Witnesses were James Lee, Jno. Healy and Overton Daniel. This was a deed of trust, and William George assigned it to Francis Corbin, and the witnesses were John George, Edward Ware.[699]

Note that Ann Gardner lived next to James Lewis. Frances Gresham (spelled *Francis* in this case), daughter of Thomas and Mary Gresham, married Daniel Hughes, who was a tenant on the same property as James Lewis. Frances had brothers Charles (b. 10 March 1687), Thomas, and John Gresham They had a half-sister named Amey born on 12 July 1700 to Mary's "first husband Gardner...."[700] If Amey had been born to Mary's first husband, she would have been born before Charles Gresham was born. There is an error in the reporting here, but the fact is that the Greshams and the Gardners were related in some way. Matthew Kemp, in his will of 1715, included Martha Gardner as one of his legatees. Others were son Matthew and daughter Ann Kemp; Gray Skipwith, son of Sir William Skipwith; "well beloved brother Sr. William Skipwith and friend Maj. Edmund Berkeley"; Martha Hilliard and her son Thomas.[701]

I have found no record of a marriage of James Lewis, Jr., nor have I found a record of his death.

James Lewis, Jr., and **Rebecca (HACKNEY) JAMESON** never married, but she and James had a child. William and Mary HACKNEY, had Rebecca baptized on 3 February 1695.[702]

On 13 September 1716 Rebecca Hackney had an illegitimate son that she named *John*.[703] She married James Janison on 5 September 1717, and he died 17 January 1721.[704] The entry reads 17 January 1720. Most of the time, entries in the register are in the style of the old calendar, the new year beginning on 25 March. By 1 May 1722 James Lewis was paying the church wardens for the upkeep of a child he had sired by Rebecca Jameson.

Rebecca married John Bradley on 24 August 1728, and they had son James on 6 December 1729 and daughter Mary on 11 September 1732.[705]

John Bradley bought 100 acres from William and Francis Sandiford on 9 February 1713. This land was in the lower part of Middlesex and included a cove. The tract was by Allaman's line, Sr. Henr. Chicheley's corner tree, lines of Richard Steevens, Madm. Churchill, and Henr. Armistead. Wits: Rebecca Hewes, William Chancelor, John Johnson.[706]

In April 1722 John Bradley was sued by John Lewis and Mary Lewis, executors of Zachary Lewis, deceased. The case was dismissed.[707] Zachary is believed to have been a son of John Lewis and Sarah Nichols, John having been the son of Richard Lewis of Sunderland Creek. Zachary's sister Sarah married Francis Shackleford, son of Roger Shackleford.[708] Roger Shackleford's widow married John Wortham. His son George witnessed the will of James Lewis (d. 1720).

Rebecca and John Bradley seemed to have moved to Caroline County, Virginia. A Rebecca Bradley died there in 1780, and Peyton Stern was the administrator of her estate.[709] The Sterns of Caroline County were prominent land owners and businessmen.[710] David Stern's daughter Frances married William Pannell, father of the William Pannell who settled in Orange County, Virginia.[711] Zebulon Lewis of Orange County (supposed son of James Lewis, Jr.) and his friends were involved with the Pannell-Strother group of Orange County. John Bradley was an appraiser of the estate of William Pannell of Caroline County who died in 1750, leaving wife, Priscilla.[712]

John Bradley, Gabriel Tombs, Zebulon Lewis, Catherine Brockman, and the Rhodes family:

When Gabriel Toombs of Caroline County wanted someone to secure his license to own an ordinary in 1748, he obtained John Bradley.[713] Zebulon Lewis first appeared on the Orange County tithables lists in 1747. He was absent for about 15 years, reappearing in 1762, and at that time, Gabriel Toombs was listed next to him.[714] Robert Dawson of Orange County, formerly of Caroline, was named, along with Zebulon Lewis, in the will of Alexander Fraizier. There seems to have been a marriage between the Dawson and Toombs families (to be elaborated on later). The trail of James Lewis and Rebecca Bradley goes from Middlesex to Caroline to Orange County.

John Bradley and Mary Rhodes had married on 2 November 1711.[715] They had twin sons, Ezekiah and William Bradley, baptized on 21 September 1712; daughter Elizabeth was born 18 May 1715; son John was born 28 October 1718; son Robert was born 21 January 1721; daughter Ann was born 5 July 1725.[716] On 15 March 1728 Mary Bradley died.[717] In August John Bradley married Rebecca Jameson.

Mary Rhodes was the daughter of Hezekiah Rhodes and Elizabeth Nichols. Elizabeth was the daughter of the John Nicholls who made his will on 27 November 1705, with William Killbee and George Benick (Barrick) as two of the witnesses.[718] Mary Rhodes had brother Hezekiah Rhodes, who married Anne Hill in 1720.[719] Hezekiah was living in Orange County, Virginia, in 1762, when he made his will. He named grandchild Epaphroditus Rhodes.[720] *Epaphroditus* was a Lawson name, but I am not certain which side of the family was its source.

Epaphroditus had son Thomas Rhodes who married Mary Brockman, sister to the Catherine Brockman who married John F. Lewis, grandson of Samuel Lewis (d. 1811) of Monroe County (WV), son of Zebulon Lewis of Orange County. More on them later.

Whether the child of James Lewis and Rebecca Jameson was named *Zebulon*, or whether James married someone else and had child Zebulon, the circumstantial evidence is strong that Zebulon Lewis of Orange County was a grandson of James Lewis (d.1720) of Middlesex.

James and (?) had the following child:

+   8   i.   **Zebulon³ LEWIS** was born about 1720 and died about 1775. (He may have been the child of James Lewis and Rebecca Jameson. Circumstantial evidence places him in the family of James Lewis, who died 1720.)

5.   **Zebulon² LEWIS** (James¹) was christened 22 October 1699 in Christ Church Parish, Middlesex County.[721] He died 1738 in Isle of Wight County, Virginia.

Zebulon Lewis sued Henry Gilpin over a debt, and on 3 November 1724, the case was dismissed.[722]

On 16 August 1732 Christopher and Katherine Killbee conveyed 100 acres in Isle of Wight County to Zebulon Lewis. The tract began at a corner of William Kinchen's line and extended to the mouth of the Beaver Dam Branch and the Nottaway Indian Line. Wits: Robert Nicholson, John Pittman.[723]

Zebulon's will was dated 6 August 1738, and it was recorded 23 October 1738. He named loving wife; sons Benjamin, Nathan, and Zebulon, daughter Patience. Wits: Christopher Kilbee, John Harris, Benjamin Cooper. The appraisal of Zebulon's estate was done by John Brassell, John Fort and Christopher Foster. Zebulon's widow, Jane, was administrator.[724] By 22 February 1741, Jane had married John Brassell, for John and Jane Brassell signed the statement of accounts for Zebulon's estate. The accounts were examined by J. Simmons, Timothy Thorpe, James Ridley.[725]

Zebulon married **Jane COOPER (?)**

Benjamin Cooper witnessed Zebulon's will, so it is assumed that Zebulon had married a Cooper. A Benjamin Cooper was named as a son in the will of William Cooper, recorded 12 August 1762, Southampton County, Virginia. He also had sons James, Demsey, John, and Jessee. Wife, Mary, was executor. Wits: John Hatfield, Mathew Wills, Francis Wills.[726]

They had the following children:

+ 9 i. **Benjamin³ LEWIS** was born about 1725 and died 1789.

10 ii. **Nathan LEWIS**.

In 1748 Nathan Lewis of Albemarle Parish apprenticed himself to George Long to learn the blacksmith trade. Wits: Edward Shaton(?), John Paynter. Nathan signed with an X.[727] George Long bought 117 acres on 16 June 1719 from Joseph Wall, Jr., and his wife, Mary, of Lawnes Creek Parish. The tract was on the west side of the Great Branch near the Nottoway Indians' land and was part in Isle of Wight County and part in Surry. The tract was part of 217 acres Wall had been granted in 1711, the other 100 acres having been sold to William Bailey. Wits: William Gray, Jr., William Ruffin.[728]

When Joseph and Hannah Petway had son Sterling baptized on 3 October 1749, Nathanial Lewis, John Bradley, and Patience Harris were sponsors.[729] When John White, son of Benjamin and Lucy, was baptized on 2 April 1752, Nath'l. Lewis, Joseph Bell, and Susanna Bane were sponsors.[730]

On 13 March 1754 a Nathan Lewis enlisted to fight in the French and Indian War.[731] Just after the battle of Great Meadows, on 9 July 1754, a report was made of companies of the Virginia Regiment under the command of Col. Washington at Will's Creek. It shows Nathaniel Lewis as one of the men still fit for duty.[732] A list of Capt. Stobo's Company who received pay included a Nathan Lewis, Corp.[733] On 8 May 1756 Gov. Robert Dinwiddie signed a death warrant for Nathan Lewis and sent it to Col. Washington.[734]

It would seem that Nathan married and had son **Zebulon**, for the 1787 personal property taxes (List A) for Surry County shows the following: Dolly Browne, Archd. Campbell, Robt. Campbell, Campbell & Hinson, John H. Cocke, John Cocke...Zebulon Lewis, Saml., Magot, Wm. Magot, Jno. Petteway. This list was made according to the date the people were interviewed.[735] The alphabetized list shows Zebulon Lewis sandwiched between Archd. Campbell and Robt. Campbell, all working for Campbell & Hinson, Robert being in the age group 16-21.[736]

+ 11 iii. **Zebulon LEWIS** was born about 1730 and died 1799.

+ 12 iv. **Patience LEWIS**.

6. **Joshua² LEWIS** (James¹) was born 27 December 1702 in Middlesex County, Virginia.[737] He died about 1760 in Southampton County, Virginia.

Joshua Lewis was a buyer at the estate sale for John Hackney Dodson of Middlesex County on 3 July 1727. He bought at the estate sale of Jacob Rice on 5 November 1728.[738]

Joshua was still living in Middlesex County in 1732 when his brother Edmund Lewis of Essex County asked him to be executor of his estate. Yet Christ Church Parish records of Middlesex show no children born to Joshua and wife, Martha, after 1729. It must have been soon after Edmund's death that Joshua joined his brother Zebulon in Isle of Wight County.

Joshua bought 200 acres in Isle of Wight County on 14 July 1740 from William Page, Page having bought the land in 1710 from William Carver and wife, Jane. Jane had inherited it from her father, John Moor. Wits: Thomas English, Sr., Thomas English, Jr.[739]

When Christopher Kilbee and wife, Catherine, sold 300 acres to Benjamin Simmons in 1745, the land was described as being on the Nottoway River, the Three Creeks, the Nottoway Indians' Line, and adjoining Joshua Lewis.[740]

William Spivey gave 30 acres to his son Aron Spivey on 11 May 1749, and this parcel, on the Reedy Branch, adjoined lands of Col. Bridger, Heiond, Joshua Lewis, and Thomas Inglish.[741]

Captain Joshua Lewis and the Indian Wars:

Captain Joshua Lewis, believed to be the same man that was born to James and Joanna Lewis of Middlesex,[742] proved himself courageous during the struggles between the colonists and the French and Indians. British General

Braddock led British regulars, along with American soldiers, in an attack on the French and Indians at Fort Duquesne (the site of present-day Pittsburgh). His troops were soundly defeated, and the Indians, finding the frontier settlers vulnerable, unleashed their fury against them. In the spring of 1756 the Indians conducted a raid in what was then northern Virginia, and they took prisoners, a girl of about 13 and Mrs. Horner (a mother of seven or eight children). Capt. Joshua Lewis and his men went after them. He led 18 men in pursuit of the Indians down the north branch of the Capon River, near the Maryland border. Joshua and his men managed to kill one Indian before the others ran off. Indian plans for a raid on Fort Frederick in Maryland were spoiled.[743]

General Braddock died in July 1755 following the attempt on Fort Duquesne.[744] In September 1755 a list was made of the return of Virginia Regiment Officers. Joshua Lewis was named among the captains, as were George Mercer, Thomas Waggener, William Bronaugh, John Mercer, and Charles Lewis. There were 17 altogether. Major Andrew Lewis was named. The late General Braddock and Colonel George Washington were mentioned.[745] Capt. Charles Lewis would have been the brother of Major Andrew. Charles was promoted to major in 1757 and later to colonel. He left a journal, now stored in the Library of Congress. In it he mentioned Capt. Joshua Lewis.[746] Major Andrew Lewis was a colonel by the time he and his troops pushed back the Indians at the Battle of Point Pleasant in October 1774.[747] Andrew was later promoted to brigadier general.[748]

A Council of War was held at Fort Cumberland on 16 April 1757, and present were Col. George Washington (president), Lt. Col. Adam Stephens, Capt. Tho. Waggener, Capt. Willm. Bronaugh, Capt. Chas. Lewis, Capt. David Bell, Capt. Henry Harrison, Capt. Joshua Lewis, Capt. Lt. John McNeill.[749]

On 16 May 1757 Governor Robert Dinwiddie instructed Col. George Washington, Commander in Chief of the Virginia Regiment, to reduce the Virginia Regiment to ten companies of one hundred men each. Captains that were to be retained were "Mercer, Waggener, Stewart, Joshua Lewis, Woodward, Spotswood, and McKenzie."[750]

George Mercer and William Bronaugh were named above as captains in 1755, along with Joshua Lewis. Wm. Peyroune was recorded as ensign on 20 April 1754, and John Carlyle was commissary on 25 January 1754.[751] An accounting of the estate of William Perouney was returned on 20 February 1756 by George Mercer, William Bronaugh, John Dalton, Joshua Lewis, and "Mr. Carlyle of Mr. Speaker." John Dalton was the administrator, and the accounting was recorded in Fairfax County, Virginia.[752] Mercer, Bronaugh, Lewis, Peyroune, and a John Carlyle were all officers in the French and Indian War, and so we can assume that this Joshua Lewis was Capt. Joshua Lewis.

Joshua Lewis's land sale and will:

On 5 November 1759 Joshua Lewis of Southampton County sold 200 acres to William Watkins, son of John, of Isle of Wight. The land was on Blackwater and adjoined that of William Raiford, William Gay, Charles Norsworthy, Thomas Inglish, Nathan Inglish, Aaron Spivey, and Col. Bridger. Wits: John Watkins, Thomas Inglish, Jr., Thomas Inglish, Sr. Joshua signed with an X.[753]

Joshua's will was dated 9 April 1757. He made legacies to wife, daughters Joanna, Catherine, Sarah, Martha, Mille, and sons James and Edmond. Execs: wife and son James. Wits: Charles Travers, Joseph Holden, Thomas Westbrook, Jr. The date of recording is missing, but his will precedes one recorded on 8 May 1760. Martha Lewis returned the appraisal of Joshua's estate on 9 October 1760. Appraisers were Thomas Westbrook, Joshua Fort, William Taylor.[754]

Joshua married **Martha MARSTON** on 7 October 1725 in Middlesex County, Virginia.[755] Martha was born 7 December 1702 in Middlesex to John and Ann Marston.[756] She died about 1788 in Northampton County, North Carolina.

Joshua and Martha Lewis must have had a grandson named Joshua Lewis, and probably one named Henry, as would be deduced from a deed of 8 January 1778 from Matthew Buffoon and wife, Ann, of Northampton County to Henry Lewis of same. The 200-acre tract being sold adjoined lands of Hermon Hill and Henry Hill. Wits: James Lewis, Joshua Lewis.[757]

And grandson Joshua Lewis must have died about the same time as his grandmother Martha, for the estate sales of Joshua and Martha Lewis were put on record at the same time. Buyers at Martha's estate sale of 1788 were James Lewis, Charles Gregory, Selby Taylor, Swan Prichard, James Warr, Elisha Hays, Abraham Artis, Thos. Barrett Jr., Wm. Eaves, Hill Webb, Jonas Hail, Thomas Lowe, Jechonias Parks, Martin Vaughan, Hermon Hill, Jessee Webb, Batt

Jordan, Elijah Hays, and Henry Hill. The accounts paid by James Lewis as executor of Joshua Lewis and administrator of Martha included money paid to William Lewis, Blake Baker, Mathew Buffoon, James Warr, Swan Prichard (dec'd.), Patience Griggs, Charles Thompson, Michael Fulgham, Will Peete (dec'd.), Sheriff Thomas Parker, John Winburne, Lawrence Smith, Hermon Hill, Jessee Webb. People paid for expense, labor, and trouble, were Jno. Peterson, David Short, Frederick Stanton.[758]

People who bought at Joshua's estate sale but not at Martha's were Dorcas Lewis, Elisha Hays, Hill Webb, Jonas Hall, Thomas Lowe, Hermon Hill, Jesse Webb, Batt Jordan, Elijah Hays.[759]

They had the following children:

+ 13 i. **James³ LEWIS** was born 5 September 1726 and died 1815.

14 ii. **Anne LEWIS** was born 8 November 1727 in Middlesex County, Virginia. She died 22 January 1728.[760]

15 iii. **Edmund LEWIS** was born 20 January 1729 in Middlesex County, Virginia (recorded as 1728).[761]

On 26 February 1753 Edmund and **Tene** Lewis of Northampton County sold 20 acres of land adjoining their own to Humphrey Revell of same. Wits: James Lewis, Priscilla Benson.[762]

Edmond Lewis of Northampton County sold 165 acres on 26 May 1757 to Charles Gregory, Jr. The tract adjoined lands of Hardy Hart and Arthur Wall. Wits: Sampson Wall, Nathan Pease.[763]

On 23 February 1758 Edmond Lewis of Northampton County, North Carolina, sold 205 acres to James Lewis of same. The land adjoined Hardy Hart, Francis Boykins and George Jordan. Wits: Flood Smith, Benjamin Sauls.[764]

16 iv. **Joanna LEWIS**

17 v. **Catherine LEWIS.**

18 vi. **Sarah LEWIS.**

19 vii. **Martha LEWIS.**

20 viii. **Mille LEWIS.**

7. **Katharine² LEWIS** (James¹). Although her birth was not recorded in Christ Church Parish Register, she likely was born in Middlesex County. She must have preceded her husband in death.

Katharine married **Christopher KILBY**, son of William KILBY and Johanna, on 1 January 1719 in Middlesex County, Virginia. Christopher was christened 9 February 1696 in Christ Church Parish, Middlesex County.[765] He died 1752 in Northampton County, North Carolina.

On 3 February 1713 Christopher Kilbee became the ward of George Barrick. Thomas Machen and Jacob Stiffe secured the guardianship bond. Wits: William Gray, Wil. Stanard.[766] In 1708 Geo. Barrick married Elizabeth Bristow.[767] Thomas Machen married Mary Chelton in 1711.[768] And Jacob Stiffe married Elizabeth Clarke in 1708.[769]

Christopher Kilby had a brother named *William*, who was baptized 13 March 1698, and sister Katherine was baptized 9 September 1702.[770] Elizabeth was born on 13 January 1705 to Mr. William Killbee and wife, Hannah.[771] (*Hannah* and *Johanna* were sometimes substituted for each other.)

William Kilby appears in the records of Richmond County, Virginia. On 4 February 1724 Frances Ingo and Mary Killbee became executors of the will of James Ingo of Richmond County. Their bond was secured by William Killbee and Richard Barnes.[772] James Ingo had married Frances Moss,[773] and the estate accounts of William Moss were recorded in Essex County as per order of 19 August 1725. Ja. Alderson and Thos. Cooper Dickenson were the auditors. Payments had been made to "Butler'orphans, Mr. Robert Jones, Mr. Rob. Parker, Capt. Muscoe Wm. Fraisier's part of the crop." Wm. Kilby, executor, sued Wm. James and his wife, Agnes, who was administrator of Wm. Moss.[774] On 4 February 1729 Mary Killbee, Joseph Patterson, and Edward Tomlinson signed the administration bond for the estate of

William Killbee, deceased.[775]

The Kilby-Barnes-Morton connection:
Captain Richard Barnes married Frances Ingo, sister of Mary Ingo, who married William Kilby. Richard and Frances Barnes had one child, Thomas, who married (1) Winifred Brockenbrough, and (2) Mary Beckwith Morton, daughter of Joseph and Margaret Beckwith Morton. After Frances Barnes died, Richard married Penelope Manly, and their daughter Eleanor married John Morton Jordan, Esq.[776]

The Mortons figure in the relationships of many of the friends of Zebulon Lewis and his son Samuel of Orange County. George Morton married Margaret, daughter of Major William Strother and Margaret Watts.[777] George Morton was a godson of Alvin Mothershead of Richmond County, who made his will on 3 January 1735. George's brothers Jeremiah, John, and Elijah Morton were legatees, as well as their sisters Sarah, Elizabeth, and Jane.[778] Jeremiah Morton married Sarah Street, and their daughter Ann married William Pannell of Orange County.[779] Zebulon Lewis of Orange County was close to this Pannell-Strother family.

Margaret Strother (m. George Morton) had sister, Jane, who married Thomas Lewis, brother of Gen. Andrew Lewis. Margaret and Jane had sister, Elizabeth, who married John Frogg.[780] Their son Capt. John Frogg married Agatha Lewis, daughter of Thomas and Jane (Strother) Lewis. Their daughter Elizabeth Strother Frogg, in 1788, married Isaac Estill,[781] who was administrator of the estate of Samuel Lewis (d. 1811) of Monroe County (WV).

Christopher and Katherine Kilby's move from Middlesex:
On 1 December 1724 Christopher and Catherine Kilby made a deed to Armistead Churchill.[782] A deed recorded in 1751 in King George County, Virginia, reveals that Christopher Kilby's land was by the Piankatank River, for it was included in Armistead Churchill's tract of 2,685 acres along the Piankatank. When the large tract was described, it showed Kilby's land following that of John Robinson, Esqr. Following Kilby were William Bolter, William Hill, William Hackney, and John Bradley. William Churchill, son of Armistead Churchill of Middlesex, was engaged to Betty Carter, daughter of Charles Carter, Esq., of King George County. Armistead was showing his support for the marriage by declaring that his son William would inherit the land. Another tract was added to the above, one for 410 acres, bought from John Rhodes of Middlesex. Armistead also said he was going to have built there a "Mansion house of Brick to contain 45 foot in length and 20 in Breadth at the least...." He would also give the couple 42 Negro slaves. Carter pledged 1,000 lbs. upon their marriage.[783]

By 1727 Christopher Kilby had established himself well enough in Isle of Wight County, Virginia, that he could serve as a processioner for Newport Parish.[784] (Land boundaries had to be confirmed every four years, and men were selected to check property lines.) In 1728 the Newport Parish Vestry appointed Christopher Kilby and Thomas Newsom tellers of tobacco.[785]

On 16 August 1732 Catherine and her husband, Christopher Killbee, sold 100 acres in Isle of Wight County to Zebulon Lewis. The tract began at the corner of William Kinchen's property and extended to the mouth of the Beaver Dam Branch and the Nottaway Indians' line. Wits: Robert Nicholson and John Pittman.[786]

In 1744 Christopher and Catherine Lewis sold 300 acres in Isle of Wight County to Benjamin Simmons. The tract, along the Nottoway River, had on its borders the Three Creeks, the Nottoway Indians' Line, and Joshua Lewis. It was part of a patent for 1,750 acres granted to Nathaniel Harrison, Esq., on 16 June 1714. Wits: John Eley, Thomas Inglish, Joseph Atkinson.[787]

On 27 November 1751 Christopher Killbe of Northampton County, North Carolina, conveyed 362 1/2 acres to Edward Lewis of same. This land adjoined the Mill Swamp and Root Branch and a Granville grant to said Killbee, made in 1749. Wits: Wm. Baker, John Gulley.[788] Most likely this was *Edmund* Lewis, Christopher's nephew.

Christopher wrote his will on 9 February 1742, and it was probated in 1752 in Northampton County, North Carolina. None of the children born in Middlesex County was named in his will. He named "two sons," Epaphroditus and Christopher; daughters Sarah, Elizabeth, and Frances; "friend" Joshua Lewis and John Fort. Execs: Major Joseph Gray and Thomas Jarrell. Wits: John Brassell, Thomas Westbrook.[789] Epaphroditus was no doubt named for Epaphroditus Lawson. See above.

Christopher and Katherine had the following children:

	21	i.	**Joanna³ KILBY** was born 27 October 1719 in Middlesex County, Virginia.⁷⁹⁰
	22	ii.	**Catherine KILBY** was born 5 July 1721 in Middlesex County, Virginia.⁷⁹¹
	23	iii.	**William KILBY** was born 19 December 1723 in Middlesex County, Virginia.⁷⁹²
+	24	iv.	**Epaphroditus KILBY**.
	25	v.	**Christopher KILBY**.
	26	vi.	**Sarah KILBY**.
	27	vii.	**Elizabeth KILBY**.
	28	viii.	**Frances KILBY**.

Third Generation

8. **Zebulon³ LEWIS** (James², James¹) was born about 1722 in Middlesex County, Virginia.

There is no primary proof that Zebulon Lewis of Orange County, Virginia, descended from James Lewis (d. 1720) of Middlesex County. Genealogist Michael Lewis Cook thought perhaps he was Zebulon Lewis, Jr., son of Zebulon Lewis (b. 1699 to James),⁷⁹³ but there is evidence that Zebulon, Jr., stayed in southside Virginia. Another possibility is that Zebulon of Orange County was a son of Thomas Lewis, born in 1693, to James and Jone Lewis James never mentioned son Thomas in his will, and there is no record of his death in the parish register. The name *Thomas*, however, was not carried forward in the children of Zebulon's son Samuel, his only child of record.

It is the rarity of the name *Zebulon* that drives me to think of him as part of the family of James Lewis (d.1720) and an accumulation of circumstantial evidence. Zebulon had some link to the Pannell-Strother family, and that connection extended into Monroe County (WV), where the estate of Samuel Lewis, undoubtedly son of Zebulon (d. about 1775), was administered by Isaac Estill, who married into the Strother family. After the death of William Pannell of Orange County, his widow, Sarah (Bailey) Pannell, married William Strother. Sarah was said to have been from Urbanna, Middlesex County.⁷⁹⁴ (I have failed to come up with any Bailey connections to Zebulon, however.) Rebecca (Hackney) Jamison Bradley, the mother of a child by James Lewis, Jr., of Middlesex, was associated with the Sterns, who intermarried with the Pannells. And John Bradley, Rebecca's husband, was close to Gabriel Toombs, who was related to Robert Dawson, who was an heir, along with Zebulon Lewis, of Alexander Fraizier of Orange County. A further connection to James Lewis (d. 1720) stems from the Middlesex County Gore family. Joseph Goare of Middlesex was surety, along with John Degge, for a bond signed by James Dudley. John Degge had married Joanna Kilby, and her son Christopher married Catherine, the daughter of James Lewis (d.1720). Joseph Goare's son John married Mary Madras in 1725, and their daughter Sarah married John O'Neal. Sarah and John were living in Culpeper County when they leased land to Zebulon Lewis and his son Samuel Lewis. See below.

Leonard Ziglar and the Germans of Culpeper County:

Zebulon first appeared on the Orange County tithables lists in 1747. He was named on the county court judgments, having been charged with 1 tithable, but not found. He was sandwiched between John Dowdy (1 tithable and no effects) and Wm. Tanner (1 tithable and not found).⁷⁹⁵ Tithable lists that were not alphabetized give clues as to who an individual's neighbors were, but the judgment lists may not. The Tanners were part of the German community,⁷⁹⁶ originally a colony on the south side of the Rapidan River in Orange County, however, and Zebulon was close to the German Ziglar family of Culpeper County. In 1749 land on the north side of the Rapidan was taken from Orange to form Culpeper County, and it looks as if Zebulon didn't live on the south side of the Rapidan until 1762.⁷⁹⁷

On 3 December 1757 Zebulon witnessed the will of Leonard Ziglar of Culpeper County. Leonard devised his home plantation to sons Christopher and Leonard; daughter Elizabeth Ziglar received land on Stoney Run, adjoining Fredrick Zimmerman; daughters Ann and Susana Ziglar were to share 262 acres adjoining Col. Spotswood and

Gutridge Lightfoot. Barbery Ziglar (his wife) and Frederick Zimmerman were to be executors. Wits: James Conner, Samuel Sirket, Zeblun Lewess. Zeblun signed with a circle.[798] Ziglar had married Barbara Zimmerman,[799] also a German. Zebulon was a smith by trade[800] and Leonard a potter,[801] so they may have had shops that served the German colony.

In 1717 Governor Spotswood had established a fort about 10 miles west of the Rapidan's juncture with the Rappahannock River. In the fort he installed 29 German families, and he used their skilled labor to run his iron mines. As the area, then Spotsylvania County, became more populated, the threat of Indians diminished, and the Germans moved out of the fort. Spotswood had erected a furnace about a mile from the mine and built himself a fine home, referred to as a castle, and his wife kept pet deer inside. The grounds included cherry trees and a marble fountain. The slopes were terraced as they descended toward the Rapidan. The settlement was referred to as Germanna, but eventually the Germans moved further up river.[802] The road (now State Route 3) between the town of Culpeper and Fredericksburg was called the German Road and still is today.

In his will of 30 November 1748, Christopher Zimmerman, Leonard Ziglar's father-in-law, gave daughter Barbara Zeigler his second best horse. Son Frederick was devised 200 acres on Stony Run. Son Christopher was to receive 200 acres of the home plantation, after the decease or remarriage of his mother; his sister Elizabeth was to get the remainder of this 440-acre tract. Daughter Katherine Zimmerman was devised 400 acres on the west side of the Blue Ridge, in Augusta County. Son John was given 5 lbs. current money, and he and his brother Frederick and their mother, Elizabeth, were to be executors. Wits: Francis Tyler, Francis Strother, Frederick Cobler, Christopher Zimmerman, Jr.[803]

On 24 June 1726 Christopher Cimberman [Zimmerman] patented 400 acres in the fork of the Rappahannock River on the east side of Potato Run.[804] Potato Run begins on the south side of Mount Pony and flows southeasterly to the Rapidan. Mount Pony is not high, but it can be seen from places along Black Walnut Run on the Orange County side of the Rapidan, where Zebulon's friend William Strother owned land. In 1773 William Strother of Culpeper County leased 626 acres on Black Walnut Run to John Morton of Orange County. The lease was for the lives of John Morton and his then wife, Sarah, and their son John Morton, Jr. Wits: Francis Bourn, Uriah Mallory, William Morton.[805] Today the Black Walnut Run area is sparsely populated and heavily wooded.

James Conner, who also witnessed the will of Leonard Zigler, owned land at Mount Pony. On 20 November 1740 Chs. Carter leased for life land on Mountain Run known as his Mount Pony tract, and the list of his renters included James Conner. Others were Samuel Ball, Gent., John Buttler, William Johnson, John Rennols, Francis Strother, James Strother, John Weetherall, Wm. Wood, and John Wright.[806] James Conner was a son of Margaret Conner, who made her will on 4 March 1744/5. She devised the home plantation, of 400 acres, to son James. Other heirs were son William Conner; daughters Margaret Winn, Ann Kelly, Hannah Wood, Elizabeth Lynch, and Sarah Balynger.[807] Margaret had moved in 1736 from St. Margaret's Parish, Caroline County, Virginia, into what would later become Culpeper County. In November of that year William Conner of Spotsylvania County sold her 200 acres by the property of the Widow Stamps in the fork of the Rappahannock River. The land had been granted to Alexr. McQueen in 1728.[808]

The third witness to Ziglar's will, Samuel Sirket, I have been unable to trace.

<u>Zebulon Lewis and his Pannell-Strother involvement:</u>

If Zebulon Lewis was not related to the Pannell-Strother family of Orange and Culpeper Counties, he certainly belonged to their circle of friends, and when the guardian accounts for William Pannell's orphans were reported on 16 November 1753 by Wm. Strother, who had married Pannell's widow, Zebulon Lewis was shown to have been paid for smith's work. The accounts also included Sarah (Bailey) Pannell Strother's part of 50 lbs. received from Joseph George; money given to Richard Morton for his crop; a hilling hoe bought from John Long; an account of James Stewart; payment to William Cornelius for a week's work; ferriage for John Pannil at Falmouth; shoes for Samuel Pannel; William Pannil's board with John Marks; cash to Mr. John Taylor; payment to Mr. Sands for goods bought for the estate; payment for goods bought from William Hunter. An old account of Lewis Fune [Tune?] was mentioned. Payment was made to Jeremiah Morton, sheriff of Orange County, for quit rents for 400 acres of land in Orange that had been left to William and David Pannell. John Williams paid for one year's rent of this land.[809]

When accounts for the estate of Mr. William Pannill were entered in the records on 12 October 1757, among them was one from Dr. Wallis. This time Mr. George Roberts was paid for smith work. Mr. George Buckner was paid for mending the well chain; John McQueen for covering a 40 by 20-foot house; Wm. Pound for making shoes; Col. Thos. Slaughter for wagoning and shoemaking. Also mentioned were rents due from Lewis Toon for land in Orange County during 1754 and 1755.[810] Dr. Wallis is of especial interest, for he would have been Dr. Michael Wallace, who jointly patented land in 1749 with John Frogg, who married Elizabeth Strother.[811] John and Elizabeth Frogg's granddaughter Elizabeth Frogg would marry Isaac Estill, the administrator of the estate of Samuel Lewis (d.1811) of Monroe County (WV).

When William Pannill made his will on 25 February 1749, he described himself as "being very sick and in a languishing condition but in perfect Sence and memory." He named sons Samuel, William, David, John, and Joseph, and daughter Frances Pannill. Wife, Sarah, and son Samuel were to be executors. Wits: John Lowen, Hannah Larney. The will was proved on 16 August 1750, and Sarah refused the executorship. Edward Spencer was granted administration.[812]

After an absence of 15 years from the Orange County tithables lists, Zebulon Lewis appeared on the 1762 list taken by John Williams for Orange County. He was responsible for 2 tithables and appeared between Gaberel Tooms (1 tithable) and Thomas Welch (2). Welch was followed by Wm. Strother (10), Wm Bell (7), Fendeley Moris (7). Before Gabriel Tombs was Benemun [Berryman?] Davis (5), and prior to him was James Killy. Four households on up the list was Robert Dosun (4).[813] See Rebecca (Hackney) Jamison Bradley for more on Gabriel Tombs.

John Williams, Thomas Welch, and Wm. Strother lived on land once belonging to William Pannell, deceased, by permission of sons William and David Pannell. On 28 April 1763 the land was divided between the two sons, William receiving a lot of 204 acres on the north side of Southwest Mountain Run; and the other lot, containing 196 acres, on both sides of the run went to David.[814] Since the list of tithables shows Zebulon Lewis living near William Strother in 1762, we can assume he lived near Southwest Mountain Run when he was a resident of Orange County. Henry Nixon of Middlesex County, who married Sarah Daniel of same,[815] received a grant for 425 acres on big Mountain Run in 1735, and in 1783 Thomas Morrison and wife, Hannah, sold 61 acres of it to William Pannell. Wits: Wm. Morton, J. Pannell, John Morrison, Zachariah Cogswell.[816]

On 31 December 1735 (1734?) Alexander Spotswood, Esq., had leased 172 acres on the south side of the Rapidan to William Pannell and wife, Sarah. Wits: John Lightfoot, Elliott Benger, Abraham Chambers. The deed was recorded 2 September 1735. On the same day a deed was recorded between Spotswood and John Ingram. This deed, also for 172 acres, included John's wife, Hannah, and their son John Ingram, Jr. Wits: And. Landale, James Gibbs, Luke Thornton. The deed was dated 30 November 1734.[817] The Ingrams of Middlesex County were referred to earlier when William Morgan of Middlesex County wrote his will in 1762. John Ingrom and son Samuel's land and lands of William Barbee, and William Crutchfield had been bought by Morgan and devised by him to son Josiah. On 4 November 1740 John Ingram and his son Samuel of Orange County had conveyed to Wm. Morgan the 136-acre plantation whereon Patrick Knight was living. Wits: Caleb Holder, Wm. Moore, Christopher Sutton.[818] On 19 June 1752 Elizabeth Marston and son John conveyed 136 acres by the Piankatank to Wm. Morgan. Wits: John Berry, Edward Wilson, John Dudley.[819] Obviously, friends and relatives of James and Johanna Lewis would have known John and Samuel Ingram (Martha Marston married Joshua Lewis, James and Johanna's son). Since both the Ingrams and Pannells purchased lots of the same size at about the same time in Orange County, the lands may have been side by side. A John Pinnell married Elizabeth Ingram of Middlesex in 1710,[820] but I have been unable to connect him to the William Pannell who married Sarah Bailey.

An Elizabeth Pannil married Daniel Carter of Lancaster County, Virginia, around 1720. Daniel was a descendant of Edward Dale.[821]

Land referred to as the Potato Neck had been granted to John and Francis Taliaferro in 1728, and some of it had been bought by the Pannells. In 1774 William Pannell leased 67 acres, part of the the Potato Neck tract, to Zachariah Coghill. The parcel extended to the fences of Hughes and Mothershead and the peach orchard fence of Mrs. Hughes.[822] In 1765 the Orange County tithables show Nathl. Motherhead, followed by Robert Dawson, Sen., John Hughes, Zebulon Lewis (2 tithables), Jno. Angil, Jermannah (Germanna) Quartor, River Quarter.[823]

Orange County Order Book 1763-1769 includes the suit of John Gore, Jr., vs. William Strother. Berryman Davis was Strother's security.[824] Berryman Davis, John Mallory, and William Lewis were sureties in 1758 for Uriel

Mallory when he became guardian of Mary and Roger Mallory, orphans of Roger Mallory.[825] The identity of this William Lewis is uncertain. Orange County tithable lists during that period do not reveal a William Lewis. Yet, a William Lewis served on an Orange County jury on 23 July 1761. On that date Berryman Davis made a motion that he be paid for appearing as a witness for James Stepp in his suit against John Bramham, Jr.[826] Benjamin Davis of Spotsylvania County was security for William Lewis when he became administrator of his brother John's estate on 6 March 1750, but I have not found proof that Benjamin and Berryman Davis were related. Here are some other facts to consider: William Lewis of Spotsylvania County at one time lived on land belonging to William Waller, as was revealed in Waller's will of 1756.[827] In 1793 land of Berryman Waller was a pointer when Elisha Dismukes sold land in Spotsylvania County to John Shirley, Jr. Other pointers: lands of Thos. Dillard, Sarah Morris, Jas. Gimbo, Ambrose Shackleford, and Jno. Shirley, Jr.[828] Benjamin Davis became guardian of Thomas, orphan of Thomas Morris, in 1751.[829] In his will of 1741, Thomas Morris of Spotsylvania County named wife, Margaret; Thomas Morris, son William Morris; daughters Mary and Sarah Morris; daughters Elizabeth and Margaret. His wife was an executor, along with Zachary Garton.[830] Members of this Garton family moved on to Monroe County (WV),[831] and Isaac and Elizabeth H. Estill were witnesses in 1797 when Elijah Garton and wife, Sarah, sold land on Swope's Knob to Nathaniel Gartin.[832] Elijah Garton was on the Orange County Court Judgments list for November 1767. He was followed by William Richards. On up the list a short ways was Uriah Garton, placed between Jas. Shirley and John Dare.[833] (This Elijah Garton was probably father or uncle of the one who moved to Monroe County.) William Lewis of Spotsylvania County referred to son William in his will of 1763, and either William Lewis, Jr., or Sr. could have been the surety in 1758 for Uriel Mallory.

The family of Henry Lewis of Spotsylvania and Culpeper Counties also was involved with the Strothers. On 28 January 1739/40 both Henry Lewis and Berry Lewis of Spotsylvania County registered their cattle marks. Henry's was an underkeel in the right ear and a crop in the left. Berry's was a crop under and an overkeel in each ear.[834] Cattle roamed the woods, and the gardens were fenced in, so the cattle had to be marked. In 1741 John Wiglesworth and wife, Mary, of Spotsylvania sold 50 acres to Benjamin Waller of Williamsburg. Wits: Edmund Waller, Thos. Cowper, Henry Pendleton, and Beery Lewis. Genealogist Michael Lewis Cook believed that Henry Lewis of Spotsylvania County was descended from Richard Lewis of Sunderland Creek, Middlesex.[835] Henry Lewis's son Henry married Anna, daughter of John and Judith (Early) Beauford, of Bromfield Parish, Culpeper County. (Bromfield Parish became Madison County in 1793.) Anna had a brother, John "Thomas" Buford, who was captain of a company from Bedford County, and he was killed at the Battle of Point Pleasant. In 1781 General Andrew Lewis, trying to make it home to Botetourt County because of failing health, stopped at Buford's home on Goose Creek, and there he died.[836]

Orange County Order Book 1763-1769 includes Zebelon Lewis's making a motion that Wm. Strother pay him 50 lbs. of tobacco for attending two days as a witness in his suit against Josephus Philips.[837]

On 21 June 1761 William Strother and wife, Sarah, of Orange County sold 282 acres below Mountain Run to Benjamin Bohan (Bohannan). The land was bounded by that of John Bewford. Wits: John Williams, John Williams, Jr., Jacob Williams.[838] The association of Jacob Williams with John Williams would indicate that he was from the same family that had been living on the Pannell land in 1753. Jacob was surety for Isaac George when he administered the estate of Alexander Fraizier, as shown below. Henry Lewis, discussed above in conjunction with the Bufords, had a granddaughter named Frances Dicken who married Thomas Bohannan in 1789.[839] The Bufords had Middlesex County roots, John Buford's father, Thomas, dying there in 1761,[840] and John Bohannan married Agnes Newberry in 1729 in Middlesex County.[841]

Some of Henry Lewis's associates moved on to Monroe County (WV). Henry's son John bought 388 acres in Culpeper County in 1782 from John Buford. The tract was next to Gibbs on Beautiful Run in Bromfield Parish. Wits: Simeon Buford, Samuel Brooking, Robert Brooking.[842] Charles Brooking of Bromfield Parish made his will in 1792. He named his four sons, William, Samuel, Robert, and John, and niece Rhoda Brooking. Execs: sons William and Robert, and James Coleman. Wits: William Twyman, Jr., William Presledge, Samuel Yager.[843] Rhoda Brooking of Monroe County married Henry Miller in 1799. Rhoda's father, Charles, and wife, Ann, were said to have migrated to Monroe from Albemarle, Virginia.[844] Henry and Rhoda Miller's daughter Rhoda married Samuel D. Lewis, grandson of Samuel Lewis (d. 1811).

Madison County court records of 24 October 1811 include a list of bonds, notes, and accounts due the estate of

Henry Lewis, deceased. Advances had been made to Henry's heirs: Martha Dicken; Erasmus Chapman; Frances Harrison; John and Thomas Kirtley; Abraham, Henry, James, John, Simeon, Thomas, and William Lewis. Cash had been paid to Mrs. Caty Lewis. People in charge of the accounting were Robert Thomas, Leo'd Barnes, and William Strother.[845] Nancy Lewis had married Erasmus Chapman in 1785.[846] Henry Lewis's second wife was Katie Twyman. They were married in 1794, and she was a daughter of Wm. Twyman.[847] George Twyman and Agatha Buford married in Middlesex County in 1724, and they had son William in 1727.[848] The William Strother who did the accounting was probably the son of Joseph Strother, son of John Dabney Strother, brother to the William Strother of Orange County who so often catches our interest. The William Strother whose father was Joseph had daughter Harriet, who, according to one author, married Rev. Horace Stringfellow.[849] Madison County marriages show Louisa G. Strother marrying Horace Stringfellow in 1823 and Harriet Strother marrying Charles R. Gibbs in 1808.[850]

John Asher and Joseph Jones, Esqr.

On 25 June 1766 Zebulon Lewis signed a deed of mortgage to John Asher, Sr. It was for 790 lbs. of crop tobacco, with interest. Zebulon's security was "Three cows marked with an underkeel in the left Ear and a Swallowfork in the right and their Calves also one Bed and Furniture one other bed & Furniture not in Goodness." Zebulon was also responsible for interest and the cost of the suit. Jos. Jones was the witness.[851] On Thursday, 27 November 1766, the deed of mortgage was proved by the witness, Joseph Jones, Esqr., and ordered to be recorded. The gentlemen justices who were sitting in Orange County court that day were James Madison, Francis Moore, Richard Thomas, Reuben Daniel, and William Bell.[852]

The witness to the mortgage, Joseph Jones, Esq., was married to Mary Taliaferro at that time, and one of his brothers-in-law was Charles Lewis, a member of the Warner Lewis family. Mary Taliaferro was a daughter of Col. John Taliaferro and wife, Mary.[853] The Strothers enter the picture: William Strother, son of Jeremiah, married Mildred Taliaferro, daughter of Charles Taliaferro, a brother of John Taliaferro.[854] William and Mildred Strother of Culpeper County sold 392 acres to William Pannell in 1749. The tract was on the north fork of Mountain Run and had belonged previously to Richard Buckner and Col. John Catlett.[855]

There is no obvious reason why such a high-powered witness as Joseph Jones, Esq., was used for a small mortgage. I have found no evidence that Joseph Jones was related to either John Asher or Zebulon Lewis. But the Taliaferro-Waugh-Johnston connection might be a source of ties.

Some background: the Hon. Joseph Jones had a sister, Elizabeth, who in 1752 married Spence Monroe, Gent., of Westmoreland County. President James Monroe (1758-1831) was their son. Joseph's father, James Jones (d. 1744), came from Wales to King George County, Virginia, and was by profession a bricklayer, undertaker, and ordinary (inn) keeper. He used his talents well, for he managed to own land in Orange, Prince William, Culpeper, and Fauquier Counties, as well as in King George.[856]

Joseph's wife, Mary, died in 1777 and he then married Mary (Waugh), the widow of Rev. Musgrove Dawson of Caroline County, who had died in 1764.[857] Robert Dawson, who belonged to Zebulon Lewis's circle of friends, lived in Caroline County before moving to Orange, but I do not know whether the two Dawsons were related. R. Dawson, however, was working for Wm. Taliaferro when the Orange County tithables were assessed in 1765. Robert Dawson, Sr., was on the same list, followed by John Hughes and Zebulon Lewis.[858]

Mary, the widow of Musgrove Dawson, was a daughter of Alexander Waugh of Orange County. Alexander, in his will of 1787, named wife, Sarah; sons Edward, Richard, Alexander, John, Abner, and George; daughter Elizabeth (married to Joseph Thomas); grandchildren John Dawson and Mary Thomas; daughter Mary and her son Joseph Jones. Wits: Joseph Thomas, Catlett Conway, Edward Spencer.[859] (Edward Spencer was granted administration of the estate of the William Pannell who married Sarah Bailey.[860])

Edward Spencer and Alex. Waugh signed bond with John Christopher in 1747. The bond was to Mary Taliaferro and Laurence Taliaferro and William Hunter, Esqr., executors of John Taliaferro, son and heir of Francis Conway, deceased, and Benjamin Porter. John Taliaferro and Francis Conway, the father, and Benjamin Porter became bound as securities for Ann James in her administration of the estate of Edward Southall in 1728. Witnesses to the 1747 bond were T. Lewis and George Wythe.[861]. Francis Conway (d. 1732) married Rebecca Catlett, and their son Francis married, around 1744, Sarah Taliaferro, daughter of Charles.[862] Mr. George Wythe married Mrs. Anne Lewis in 1747,

125

and William Hunter and Martha Taliaferro married in 1744.[863] Martha was a sister to Joseph Jones's first wife. John Taliaferro made his will in 1744, naming wife, Mary; sons Lawrence and William Taliaferro; William Hunter; daughters Lucy and Molly (Mary). Land in Orange County was mentioned.[864] T. Lewis appeared as a witness, along with George Wythe, to Orange County deeds, but I have not placed him.

Mary Taliaferro, Lawrence Taliaferro, and William Hunter, the executors of John Taliaferro, Gent., were in Spotsylvania County court on 1 July 1746 suing Peter Johnston. The jury ruled against Johnston, his nonperformance (not elaborated on) being a factor. Alexander Waugh made a motion that he be paid for his court attendance on behalf of the executors.[865]

On 24 March 1742/3 Peter Johnson of Orange County had purchased 800 acres in the Great Fork of the Rappahannock River from John Gorden of Spotsylvania County. The tract was in St. Mark's Parish (later Culpeper County) on the branches of Blue Cowslip Run by land of John Asher, at the foot of Mount Pony.[866]

The trail of Alexander Waugh's associates goes on to Gallia County, Ohio. Above we saw that Benjamin Porter was close to Alexander Waugh. Benjamin Porter of Orange County died in 1761, naming son Ambrose as his oldest. Other children were Nicholas, Thomas, Charles, Abner, Benjamin, Joseph, Jane, Betty, Mary, and Frances. Children of daughter Ann were to be educated. Alexander Waugh, Benja. Hawkins, and Frans. Moore appraised his estate.[867] Benjamin Porter's son Ambrose died in 1773 in Pittsylvania County, Virginia. Ambrose's son Benjamin Porter and Henry McDaniel were executors of the estate.[868] Henry McDaniel had married Ambrose's daughter Mary. Henry died in 1819 in Monroe County (WV),[869] and his son Henry was of Gallia County, Ohio, when he died in 1838. He is believed to have been the first settler of Walnut Township. It's been reported that he lived in the hollow of a tree while he built his log cabin near Symmes Creek.[870] Symmes Creek is 70 miles long, and it flows through Jackson, Gallia, and Lawrence Counties, releasing its waters to the Ohio River near the village of Chesapeake.

Back to Henry McDaniel, Sr. Henry's first wife, Mary Ann Porter, died, and in 1793 he married Anna Catherine Keller, whose father, Conrad Keller, enlisted from Shenandoah County to fight in the militia.[871] Anna had been married previously to Henry Gore, but he had been killed along the New River in 1791 by Indians.[872] Henry Goar appeared on the 1787 personal property tax list for Shenandoah County.[873] He was a witness, with Joseph Gore and Patrick Grymes, to a 1762 deed from John Oneal of Culpeper County to Robert Oneal of Frederick County. Oneal was selling 502 acres on the Shenandoah River that he had bought in 1750.[874]

Henry and Anna McDaniel had daughter Peggy, who married Wilson Lewis,[875] son of the Wilson Lewis who married Rachel Griffith of Botetourt County, Virginia, in 1774.[876] And here comes the intrigue: Rowland Madison was a witness to this marriage. He was a son of John Madison and Agatha Strother, daughter of Maj. William Strother,[877] and sister to the Elizabeth Strother who married John Frogg. Samuel Lewis (d. 1811) had son John, and he had a son named *Wilson*. Madison Lewis, born about 1823, to Catherine, widow of Joshua Lewis, son of Samuel, also named a son *Wilson*. *Wilson* was not a common first name, and the Wilson Lewis who married Rachel Griffith is thought to have been a brother of Samuel. DNA testing of Samuel and Wilson Lewis's descendants, however, denies a connection.[878]

Peter Johnston, who was involved with relatives of Joseph Jones, owned land next to John Asher. No hint is given as to why Zebulon owed Asher, but some background on him is in order: On 26 June 1731 John Asher was granted 400 acres on the Blew Cowslip Run adjacent Col. Alexander Spotswood and John Lightfoot. Another patent for 400 acres on the Blew Cowslip was granted to Asher on the same day, this tract next to lands of William Coursey and David Mitchel.[879] Note that the Blue Cowslip area was where the Gore family from Middlesex County lived and it may have been Gore land that was leased to Zebulon and Samuel Lewis in 1770. Sarah Gore had married John O'Neal.

On 7 April 1740 Alexander Spotswood, Esq., leased 150 acres to John Asher, planter, and his son, Charles Asher. They were to plant 300 fruit trees, one third of them apple trees, and the orchard was to be enclosed with a fence. No more than six laborers were to be employed. Robert Lines and John Asher, Jr., were witnesses. On 22 October 1740 Wm. Pannell made a motion that the deed be admitted to record. This land was on the north side of the Rapidan and therefore in Culpeper County when it was formed from Orange in 1749. And the deed was also recorded there, for on 27 September 1750 John and Charles Asher made over the lease to Michael Whatley. Wits: John Read, Thomas Wooten, Moley Asher. On 9 September 1752 Michael Whatley assigned the land to Roger Dixon. Wits: J. Lewis, Jno. Battaley, G. Hume.[880]

My best guess is that J. Lewis was the son of Zachary Lewis, Jr., who married Mary Waller, sister to the

William Waller who rented land to William Lewis of Spotsylvania County. Both John and Zachary Lewis sometimes signed with their first initial and full last name. It was Zachary's daughter Ann who married George Wythe, mentioned above. John Lewis was known as the honest lawyer, for he would not defend anyone he thought was guilty. He married Ann Lewis, daughter of Robert Lewis and Jane Meriwether. Robert was a brother of Col. Fielding Lewis, and their mother was Elizabeth Warner. Fielding's brother Charles was mentioned earlier as the husband of Lucy Taliaferro.[881] The lawyer John Lewis made his will in 1766, giving land in Culpeper and Orange Counties to son Robert. John asked friends Fielding Lewis and Joseph Jones to be trustees.[882]

John Asher petitioned in 1738 for release from bearing arms and doing road work because he was past 60 years of age.[883] He then would have been born before 1678 and could easily have been the John Asher who appeared in Middlesex County records early in the 1700s. On 2 March 1707 John and Susanna Ashur had daughter Diana baptized.[884] On 18 September 1709 they had son William baptized.[885] On 4 July 1710 Middlesex court ordered John Grymes to pay John Ashur for going to court on his behalf in his suit with John Comer.[886] It is not certain where Ashur was living, but John Grymes bought land from Joseph Gore,[887] so Ashur may have lived in the middle precinct of Middlesex County. Years later Leonard Ziglar, who was living in what was then Orange County, sued William Asher.[888]

Henry Nixon, who had migrated from Middlesex County, owned land next to William Bohannon in Orange County by 1740. On 27 February 1750 Henry Nixon, planter, sold 200 acres to Charles Askew of St. Mark's Parish, Culpeper County. The land was in Orange County, on the south side of Taliaferro's mill.[889] John Asher had son Charles. There were Askews in Orange County during this time period, and Ashers and Askews were sometimes confused.

On June 23 1748 Orange County court put four-year-old Sarah Asher, daughter of Sarah Asher, in the care of Margaret Conner, who was to teach her to read and write, knit and sew, and provide for her needs until she turned 18.[890]

The O'Neal-Lewis lease and the Gores:
On 14 March 1770 John Oneal and wife, Sarah, of Culpeper County leased land to Zebulon Lewis and his son Samuel of Orange County. The lease was for 21 years. Zebulon was to pay rent of 6 lbs. currency for the first two years, and 5 lbs. a year afterwards, "yearly if lawfully demanded." The Lewises were to plant 100 apple trees and care for the orchard. They were to work no more than three tithables. Wits: John Johnston, John Corbly. The deed was delivered to William Strother, no date given.[891]

John Oneal married Sarah Gore, whose parents, John Goar and Mary Madras, were married in 1725 in Middlesex County.[892] John Gore was the son of Joseph Goare, who married first Mary Allison and secondly Lucretia Tuggle.[893] The lives of the Tuggles and the Richard Lewis family of Middlesex were entwined. In 1662 Richard Lewys and wife, Fran., sold 100 acres at the head of Sunderland Creek to Thomas Trickwell.[894] (The name *Tuggle* had various spellings. *Trickwell* was an attempt at *Tugwell*.) Joseph Goare lived in the Middle Precinct of Middlesex County, and James Lewis, seemingly grandfather of Zebulon, served as constable for the Middle Precinct in 1705.

The John Gore who married Mary Madras lived for a while in the same area in Spotsylvania County as William Lewis, for on 4 December 1750 William Lewis was asked to take his place as constable. The area he served was from Chiswell's Mine Road to the upper line of the county and from the Rappahannock River to the River Ny.[895]

Mary Gore was called to task by Spotsylvania County Church wardens and on 4 March 1745/6 an agreement was reached, and the case was dismissed.[896] John and Mary Gore had daughter Mary Gore, and she may have been the one making the agreement. John was of Culpeper County when he made his will on 3 September 1766, and he named grandson Reuben Gore, son of daughter Mary. He lumped four of his children and two grandchildren together, so we must deduce who was who: "Henry Gore, Joseph Gore, Mary Breedlove, Sarah Oneal, Reuben Gore & Rachel Parks." Son John was to get one shilling and no more. Son Joseph was to get the home plantation after the decease of his mother. And the servant Daniel Welsh, a mulatto, was to be freed after John's wife, Mary, died. Execs: wife, Mary, and son Henry. Wits: Ephraim Hubbard, Mary Hubbard. When the will was proved, on 21 December 1769, Henry Gore refused the executorship.[897]

A deed made in 1767 from the executors of John Spotswood, Esqr. to Lynn Banks reveals that the Gores owned land on the Cowslip. Banks was being leased 90 acres on the Rapidan River, and pointers were the corner of John

Gore's property near Cowslip Run and John Wharton's line.[898]

John Corbly, one of the witnesses to Zebulon's lease, was a neighbor of John Wharton and Richard Waugh, as is shown in the deed made on 19 October 1769 from William Strother of Orange County to Sarah Strother of Orange County. William was granting Sarah 68 acres adjoining lands of John Wharton and Richard Waugh on the Cowslip Run, extending to line of John Corbly. The deed was delivered to John Wharton on 17 December 1770.[899]

Corbly owned property at one time on the Orange County side of the Rapidan. On 16 September 1774 William Pannill leased 67 acres to Zachariah Cogwell. This parcel was part of the land that William Strother and John Corbly had owned, part of the Potato Neck Tract, granted to John and Francis Taliaferro in 1728. The parcel was bounded by Hughes's fence, Mothershead's fence, and Mrs. Hughes' peach orchard.[900]

The Baptist denomination was earning a foothold in Orange County during this time, and John Corbley, Allan Wiley, Elijah Craig, and Thomas Chambers were taken to court on 28 July 1768, charged with assembling themselves unlawfully and preaching "schismatick doctrines." They were all found guilty and each ordered to enter into bond for 50 lbs. and have it signed by two sureties. If any failed to post bond by October 25th, he would go to jail and stay there until the bond was signed.[901] Semple's book on the Baptists in Virginia notes that John Corbley was born in Ireland and lived in Pennsylvania before moving on to Virginia. Corbly was put in jail in Culpeper County for his preaching. He returned to Pennsylvania and was imprisoned there for being involved in the Whiskey Insurrection (a protest over taxes leveled on whiskey producers to pay for the Revolutionary War). He died in 1805, his wife and some of his children having been murdered by Indians.[902]

John Johnston was another witness to the lease from the O'Neals to Zebulon and Samuel Lewis. He was likely the son of Peter Johnston of Culpeper County, whose will was witnessed by Isaac George and Alexander and John Frazier. Peter's will of 1755 was proved 21 October 1756 by the two Fraziers. Peter wanted the land whereon he was living to go to son William Johnston. Peter ordered 400 acres of his Mount Pony land sold to pay debts. He devised 100 acres of his Mount Pony land to daughter Elizabeth; son Peter was given 147 acres at Mount Pony; the rest of the Mount Pony land was to be divided between sons John and Andrew Johnston. Other children named were Catherine Morrison and Anne, Sarah, and Prescilla Johnston. Execs: wife, Margaret, and Francis Moore, John Lowen.[903] Harbin Moore, William Ball, and John Gray were ordered to divide the slaves belonging to Peter's estate in 1769. By this time Ann Johnston had married John Threlkeld.[904]

Peter's daughter Catherine married Findley Morrison of Orange County, and John Johnston and William Threlkeld witnessed Findley's will of 1768. Findley named wife, Catherine, and his six children, Hugh, William, John, Margaret, Sarah, and Lucy Morrison. Execs: wife, Catherine, and Taliaferro Craig, Jr., and Charles Bruce. Thomas Porter, Wm. Pannill, and Wm. Strother secured the executors' bond.[905] Charles Bruce's father, Charles, had married Elizabeth Pannell, sister of the William Pannell who married Sarah Bayley.[906] Elizabeth would have been a daughter of William Pannell and Frances Sterne.

Harbin Moore, who helped with the division of Peter's estate, had married into the Marks family, as had Isaac George. On 27 April 1753 Sarah Marks and others sued Berryman Davis for slander. On 28 June 1753 Isaac George and wife, Sarah, sued Berryman Davis for slander.[907] John Marks's will was probated in Culpeper County on 17 May 1759. He named daughters Anne Moore, Mary Bramham, and Sarah George. He gave his cooper's tools to Harbin Moore and his carpenter's tools and gun to Isaac George. He left furniture to William (no last name given). Execs: wife (Elizabeth) and Ignatius West. Wits: John Lowen, William Garrett, Lucy Knight. Andrew Bourn, John Bourn, and James Stewart inventoried the estate. Furniture went to Wm. Pinion.[908] Orange County court orders of 26 April 1759 include a motion by John Marks. He was requesting that William Lewis pay him for coming 14 miles out of Culpeper to testify on his behalf. Walter Shropshire had sued William Lewis over debt.[909]

Berryman Davis died in 1764, leaving wife, Susannah. In his will he mentioned oldest daughter, Sarah, but did not name the other children. Wits: John Morton, John Hughes, William Beckham. Uriel Mallory was the executor, and Edward Thomas secured his bond. In 1774 the accounts show Lewis Conner as guardian to Mary and Susannah Davis. Payment was made to Thomas Lowen.[910] The Orange County tithe lists of 1765 include the following: Widow Davis's Quarter, Widow Davis (Join on Mothers), John Williams, Joseph Cragg, Nathl. Motherhead, Robert Dawson, Sr., John Hughes, Zebulon Lewis, all near Germanna.[911] I'm assuming that Widow Davis was to be included with Nathaniel Mothershead's tithables. Or perhaps her mother was still living. In 1766 the list shows James Thornton,

Daniel Thornton, Henry Brown, Zeblon Lewis, Mrs. Susannah Davis, Henry Bourn, Henry Beckham, Jacob Williams, Wm. Pannill, Uriel Malory, John Williams. Thirteen households on down we see James Jameson, Robt. Dawson, Isaac George, Mrs. Davis, Mrs. Hugh, Robt. Dawson, Jr.[912] The Bourns and the Mortons had intermarried, and the Mortons and Mothersheads and Pannells had intermarried. On 28 August 1746 Henry Bourn ordered recorded in Orange County that he had received a Negro due him because of his rights to the estate of Alvin Mothershead or George Morton, deceased. The Negro was due in the right of Ann, daughter of William Morton. Wits: Elijah Morton, Lewis Toone.[913] William Pannell, son of William and Sarah (Bailey) Pannell, married Ann Morton, daughter of Jeremiah Morton and Sarah Mallory.[914] (Some researchers believe his wife was Sarah Street.) Jeremiah Morton's guardian's account for Berryman Davis was recorded in 1748.[915]

Zebulon and Samuel Lewis were already living on the Oneal land in Culpeper County when the formal lease was drawn up, but Orange County road orders for 28 November 1771 reveal who Zebulon's neighbors had been in Orange County. Note that he had appeared on the tithables lists next to Thomas Welch in 1762 and 1764. In 1771 Benjamin Martin was appointed overseer of the road that led from the Wilderness to the Old Trap and up the Neck Road. The people along the road who were to assist in keeping the road in good condition were "Robert Dawsons, Mrs. Hughes, Hunter's Qr., Thomas Welsh, Francis Hughs, Charles Bruce, Wm. Underwood's Qtr. Nathl. Mothershead, Moses Burt, Richard Reynolds, Joseph Reynolds, John Nicholas, Wm. Chisam, Thomas Chambers, James Roach, Eli Griffen, Isaac Johnson Thomas Morrison, James Beckham, John Kelley, John Morton, Wm. Collings, Thomas Clerk, Wm. Sisson, Wm. Hawkins, Wm. Beckham, and Joseph Parish...." This area was close to Raccoon Ford, for on 23 March 1775 Uriel Mallory, Isaac George, and Robt. Dawson were ordered to study Henry Bourn's proposition for a new road from the Raccoon Ford towards and Old Trap.[916]

Alexander Fraizier's will, Isaac George, Robert Dawson, and Francis Hughes:
Zebulon Lewis was remembered by Alexander Fraizier of Orange County, when he made his will on 27 April 1771. He gave 32 lb. cash to friend John Frazier, should he ever appear in person. If not, the money would go to John's oldest son, William Frazier, when he came of age. He gave to Zebulon Lewis a plough hoe, hilling hoe, and weeding hoe, a pair of haimes and traces, two blue jackets, a duffel and a chamblet, his old saddle and bridle. John Frazier would receive all the rest of his clothing. Alexander willed his mare and ax to Isaac George. Execs: Isaac George and Robert Dawson. Wits: Francis Hughs, Daniel Lamburt, Nelly Bramham. On 23 May 1771 Isaac George and Robert Dawson presented Frazier's will in court, and Daniel Lamburt and Nelly Bramham proved it. Jacob Williams provided security for the executor's bond.[917] The inventory of Alexander's estate was returned on 9 September 1771, by Isaac George, the executor. The inventory had been taken by Chs. Bruce, Wm. Morton, and Joseph Spencer.[918]

When the accounting was reported in 1763 for the estate of Leonard Ziglar of Culpeper County, Alexander Fraizier's name was included next to that of Chr. Ziglar. Frederick Zimmerman was the administrator.[919] Of course, it's very possible that names were filled in where it was convenient and that showing Alexander's name next to Christopher Ziglar's was of no significance. Both men were being paid from the estate.

Robert Dawson must have been a very good friend of Alexander Fraizier, or possibly a relative. Or maybe he was closer to Isaac George. In his will of 1770 Robert Dawson bequeathed all his estate to his wife, Mary, and after her decease, it was to be divided equally among all his children. He named his wife and son Robert Dawson, Jr., as executors. Witnesses were Isaac George, Lewis Conner, and Betsy Newport. Isaac George and Caleb Sisson secured the executors' bond.[920] John Dawson was a witness to the 1781 will of Isaac George.

The possibility that Robert Dawson was related to Musgrove Dawson of Caroline County was mentioned above. Musgrove had married Mary, daughter of Alexander Waugh. In 1756 Robert Dawson bought 350 acres in Orange County from Mumford Stevens of Culpeper County. Pointers were Harden's line and Thornton's line. Wits: Alexr. Waugh, Joseph Thomas, Richd. Waugh, and Lucy Clark.[921] In 1749 William Lewis served as security for Mumford Stevens when he was sued in Spotsylvania County court by Robert Richards.[922]

There must have been a marriage between the Dawsons and Tombs, for in 1790 Ann Dawson Tombs married John Spearman.[923] Caroline County court orders of March 1749 show Robert Dawson, Wm. Pannell, and Richard Hill as securities for the administration bond of Thomas Fox, heir of John Fox.[924] Essex County wills of 1728 include the will of Henry Hill of St. Mary's Parish (later Caroline County). Henry named wife, Ann; son Richd. and daughter

Elizabeth Hill. Neither child was 20 years old. Wits: Robt. Thomas, Gabrill Tombs, Francis Milkin. Wife, Ann, was executor, and Fran. Conway and Robt. Thomas secured her bond.[925]

About the witnesses to Fraizier's will: Francis Hughes was part of the Strother family. Thomas Hughes and Frances Stern had daughter Ann who married Francis Strother.[926] They also had sons Thomas and John Hughes. Thomas Hughes and his second wife, Elizabeth, had son Francis. Their other children were Anthony, Matthew, William, and Thomas Hughs, the younger. In his will of 1765, Thomas Hughes, Sr., asked his wife, Elizabeth, and John and Christopher Threlkeald to be executors. Wits: John Lowen, Wm. Strother, Robt. Dawson. Robert Dawson, Lyn Banks, and Thomas Morrison were sureties for the executors' bond.[927]

See below for another reference to Daniel Lamburt, witness to Fraizier's will.. Lamburt also appeared in Spotsylvania County deeds.

The witness Nelly Bramham I have not placed. *Milly* Branham, daughter of John Branham and wife, Rachel, married Caleb Sisson on 20 July 1771.[928] John Branham, in his will of 1761, named wife, Rachel. He named only his youngest sons, Daniel, Richard, Gaydon, Taverner, and James Webb Branham. John Lowen was given 10 shillings. Wits: Harbin Moore, William Games, Margaret Johnson. John's widow, Rachel, served as executor, and Wm. Strother, John Morton, and John Harvey were her sureties.[929] Margaret Johnson may have been the widow of Peter Johnston.

Alexander Fraizier and John Fraizier were witnesses to the 1755 will of Peter Johnston, as was Isaac George. Both Peter Johnston and Isaac George had ties to the Harbin Moore family. And William Strother and John Morton were part of the group. Note that William Games (Gaines?) was a witness to John Branham's will. John Harvie and Martha Gaines had son John, born in 1742. He was a colonel in the Revolutionary War and married Margaret Morton Jones, daughter of Gabriel and Margaret (Strother) Jones.[930] This is the Margaret Strother who had married first George Morton. She was sister to Elizabeth (Strother) Frogg. Gabriel and Margaret Jones had two other daughters, one of them marrying John Hawkins, and the other marrying John Lewis, son of Fielding Lewis and Catherine Washington. (She was John Lewis's third wife.) Gabriel and Margaret's son, Strother Jones, born in 1756, was a captain in the Revolutionary War.[931]

There seems to have been another John Harvey in Orange County during this time period, however. On 3 November 1756 William Anderson and wife, Sarah, and John Harvey and wife, Mary, sold 564 acres in Orange County to William Strother. Pointers were lands of John Taliaferro, William Connocoe, and Richd. Sharp. John Smith had claimed 164 acres in 1735, and William Anderson 400 acres in 1736. Wits: Lewis Toome, John Williams, Jacob Williams, Frans. Strother.[932]

When Isaac George of Orange County made his will on 25 April 1781, he named as executors Joseph Spencer, Uriel Mallory, and William Pannill. Isaac named children William, Edward, Joseph, and Winiford. Wits: Sarah Spencer, Lewis Perry, John Dawson. Isaac's wife was Catherine. Around 1771 he had married Catherine Spencer.[933]

Information is lacking that would explain why Jacob Williams was so close to Isaac George that he would secure his executor's bond.

A deed made on 28 May 1767 from John Long and Isabella, his wife, to John Gutrich was delivered to Jacob Williams. The land being transferred was a 200-acre tract on the White Oak Branch and part of a patent granted to Richard Mauldin. It bordered on lands of Beale, William Howard, and Thomas Hill, deceased. Wits: J. Lewis, Vivion Daniel, James Daniel.[934]

William Leak and wife, Elizabeth, granted William Pollock 325 acres adjoining lands of John Embree, Sr., Jacob Williams, and John Lewis. The deed was recorded in Orange County in 1774.[935] The Daniels and Lewises of Middlesex County intermarried: Grace Lewis, daughter of Richard Lewis, married William Nicholson, and their daughter Grace married Thomas Mountague in 1716.[936] Their son Thomas married Jane Daniel, daughter of Charles Daniel and Jane Micklburrough.[937] So this John Lewis may have belonged to that group. Charles Daniel was a brother of Vivion Daniel. An assumption is being made that there was only one Jacob Williams in Orange County at this time. A Jacob Williams married Mary Delaney of Orange County in 1786. John Atkins secured the bond. Leeza Delaney married Robert Rhodes of Albemarle County in 1782. Andrew Shepherd secured the bond.[938]

Thanks to military records we know something of Alexander Fraizier's appearance. Militia records show that while residing in Culpeper County he had enlisted at Winchester; he had been born in Scotland. He was swarthy, with pock marks, and he squinted both eyes. At the time of his enlistment, he was 26 and a planter. His height was five-foot six and one-half inches.[939] The Culpeper Militia without arms for 1757 included Alex:r Frazier, French Strother, Sam:l Panhill, Oliver Fowles (Towles), Chris:r Ziglar, Allen Wiley, and John Bradley as men who had signed up to fight in the Indian Wars. There were 46 in all. Those who had guns and were ready to take on the frontier were fewer, only 26. They included Fran:s Strother, Jacob Broil, Peter Fleshman, John and Anthony Strother. W. Lightfoot presented the lists.[940] Members of the Fleshman-Broil family would move to Monroe County (WV).

The Orange-Culpeper-Spotsylvania Lewis and Strother network and the Larues:

A Culpeper County deed made on 4 February 1776 from Alexander Spotswood, Esq., to Richard Hackley, his wife, Elizabeth, and John Hackley brings together several members of Zebulon's far-reaching network. The deed was for 210 acres on the north side of the Rapidan River, part of the 40,000 acres left to Alexander Spotswood by his grandfather. It was witnessed by John Craig, Benja. Burbege, Allen Wiley, Anthony Huges, James Lewis, Wm. Strother, and Robt. Dawson. On 15 November 1779 Richard and Elizabeth Hackley assigned their rights to most of the lease to Robert Pollard. Wits: John Johnston, Richd. Gaines, Absalem Bradley, Thomas Brown, W. Bradley. Twelve acres had been sold to William Pannell on 21 October 1776. This parcel lay between Potato Run and the Rapidan River. Pannell, in turn, assigned it to Robert Pollard.[941] When John and Sarah O'Neal leased land to Zebulon Lewis and son Samuel, they allowed for three tithables, so Zebulon may have had another son, perhaps one named *James*, but Allen Wiley appeared in Spotsylvania County records with members of the William Lewis family of same, and William had son and grandson named *James*.

Benjamin Burbridge was a witness to the will of Sarah Lewis of Spotsylvania County, widow of William Lewis. It is therefore possible that the James Lewis who witnessed the above deed was son of William and Sarah. Another point to consider, however: William Lewis, son of Henry Lewis of Double Top Mountain (later Madison County) had land abutting that of the Fields.[942] When Henry Field and wife, Jean, sold land in 1784, it was said to abut that of Henry Taliaferro and Hackley. John Lewis (presumably a son of Henry) was one of the witnesses, and he had a brother named *James*. Other witnesses: Richard Waugh, Robt.Slaughter, Jr., and Leonard Barnes.[943]

John Craig, Anthony Hughes, James Lewis, Wm. Strother, and Robt. Dawson were witnesses to the 4 February 1776 lease of land to Joshua Stap (usually spelled *Step* or *Stepp*) and Eve Salmon, Antherd Salmon, and Edmund Garnet. The deed was delivered to James Garnet.[944] James Garnet owned land abutting that of William Lewis, as shown when he bought 250 acres on Mountain Run from Richard Parker and wife, Grissell, of Culpeper County in 1783. The tract abutted John Smith, James Yowill, James Garnet, and Elijah Sims. Wits: John Hume, Jas. Yowell, Henry Lewis 33 (presumably his age).[945] William Ballard married Elizabeth Stepp, and they moved from Orange County to Monroe County, (West) Virginia.[946]

The witness Anthony Hughes was a son of Thomas Hughes and his second wife, Elizabeth. His first wife was Frances Sterne. She had been married previously to William Pannell, father of the William Pannell who married Sarah Bailey of Urbanna. Sarah later married William Strother.[947] Anthony's brother, Francis, witnessed the will of Alexander Fraizier.

There were numerous witnesses for a 210-acre deed, but most can be proved to have been connected to someone else in the group. John Craig was of the same family as Taliaferro Craig, who married Elizabeth Johnston, daughter of Peter. Allen Wiley appears in Culpeper and Spotsylvania County records, but I have not discovered his connection to the others. Thomas Brown may have been part of the Brown family of Culpeper that intermarried with the Colemans and Lightfoots. A Richard Gaines married Jemima Pendleton.[948] As for witnesses W. Bradley and Absalem Bradley, it would seem they were part of the John Bradley family of Middlesex, for his wife, Rebecca, was part of the Hackney family who used the name *Absolom*,[949] a name not common in these early records.

The Hackleys had Taliaferro connections, as revealed in the 1799 will of John Hackley of Culpeper County. He referred to his sister, Ann Taliaferro. He mentioned his uncle and Aunt Barrow, his brother Jas. Hackley, Fanny Ball Long (daughter of Gabriel Long), Fanny Ball Thomas (daughter of Edw. Ball Thomas, of Kentucky). John named his uncle Wm. Ball; brothers-in-law Thos. Jameson (m. Lucy Hackley), Sam'l Reed (m. Sarah Hackley), Richard Hackley (m. Elizabeth Hackley).[950]

Several of the same witnesses lent their signatures to another deed. On 15 February 1776 Alexander

Spotswood, Esqr., leased 268 acres in St. Marks Parish, Culpeper County, to Philip Drake. The lease was to last the lives of Philip Drake, his wife, Ann, and Peter Lerue, or the person who lived the longest. Wits: John Craig, James Lewis, Ben. Burbridge, Wm. Strother, Allen Wiley, Robt. Dawson.[951] According to Oren Morton, in his *History of Monroe County, West Virginia,* Ann, daughter of Abraham Larew, married a Drake.[952] Peter Larue acquired land in Monroe County (WV). The tract had been previously owned by a legatee of John Estill. The Larew family was associated both with the friends of Zebulon Lewis and the Estill-Strother family.

The Larews (Larues) who migrated to Monroe County (WV) also spent some time in Orange County. On 28 July 1770 Reuben Larew of the Jersies bought 400 acres in Orange County from John Hill of Fairfax and Betty Hill, his mother. The tract was on a branch of the Mattapony. Wits: John Sanders, John Faulconer, Daniel Lambert, Jno. Craig, William Pannill, and Uriel Mallory.[953] John Sanders married Jane Craig, daughter of Toliver Craig and wife, Mary Hawkins.[954] Taliaferro Craig, Jr., married Elizabeth Johnston.[955] She was a daughter of Peter and Margaret. Joyce Craig married John Faulkener.[956] Priscilla, daughter of Peter Johnston, married William Faulkener. William was of Orange County when he made his will in 1777. He named wife, Pricilla; children Lucy, Nicholas, John, and Johnston Faulkner. Execs: William Johnston and Taliaferro Craig, Jr.. Wits: James Jameson, John Brown, Mary Bourn.[957]

Zebulon was relieved of paying Orange County tithes in August 1767 because he was "an Anticent poor man."[958] The term *ancient* was used broadly in early Virginia records, sometimes being applied to roads that couldn't have been all that old. Normally men were relieved of levies after turning sixty. If that were the case, Zebulon would have been born in 1707. It is interesting that an exact age is not mentioned. James Lewis, son of James and Jone, was christened in 1690 and would have been old enough to have fathered a child by 1707. And James, Jr., was living on his own in 1712, when he was leasing land that belonged to William Stanard and wife, Ann. Whatever age Zebulon was in 1767, he still could have been a son of James Lewis, Jr.

Although he was obviously not a prosperous man, Zebulon was considered honest and reliable or William Strother would not have asked him to testify in court and Leonard Ziglar would not have asked him to witness his will. Zebulon was well liked by Alexander Fraizier, who gave him farm tools, clothing, and a saddle. Zebulon must have owned a horse. Surprisingly, not everyone did. It is not certain when Zebulon died, but there is no mention of him in Monroe County records, so he may have died before his son Samuel moved there.

Zebulon married (?).

They had the following child and probably another (Zebulon was allowed to work three tithes on his leased land):

+ 29 i. **Samuel**[4] **LEWIS** was born about 1740-50 and died 1811.

9. **Benjamin**[3] **LEWIS** (Zebulon[2], James[1]) was born about 1725. He died 1789 in Southampton County, Virginia.

Benjamin was a witness on 28 April 1746 when Peter Butts deeded 130 acres in Isle of Wight County to Benjamin Clements. The land adjoined Benjamin Clements, Jr., Richard Parker, Jr., and the Nottoway Indians. Other witnesses: Charles Simmons, Richard Kerby, Jr.[959] On 13 April 1749 Benjamin Lewis, John Kirby, and Michael Blow were witnesses when Thomas Day and wife, Jane, conveyed 355 acres to Richard Kirby, Sr., Thomas Day had bought 45 acres of the tract from Benjamin Simmons in 1742.[960]

Benjamin Lewis, Benjamin Simmons, and Charles Barham audited the estate accounts of Turner John Smith, recorded 11 May 1758, Southampton County.[961]

By 8 October 1761 Benjamin Lewis was serving as guardian of Sarah and Elizabeth Crocker, orphans of Benjamin Crocker.[962]

On 13 January 1763 Benjamin Lewis and Gregory Rawlings, administrators of the estate of Priscilla Newsum of Southampton County, returned the accounts. Auditors: Miles Cary, Henry Taylor, Benjamin Simmons.[963]

On 9 August 1765 Benjamin Lewis, Benjamin Simmons, and John Simmons returned their appraisal of the estate of Arthur Fort.[964]

Benjamin Lewis and John Simmons audited the estate accounts of Jesse Holt, recorded 14 August 1766, Southampton County.[965] Benjamin Lewis, Joshua Fort, and Charles Taylor appraised the estate of Benjamin Simmons, and it was recorded 11 June 1772, Southampton County.[966]

In June of 1776 Benjamin Lewis became a member of the Southampton County Committee of Public Safety.[967]

Thomas Westbrook of Southampton County made his will on 8 May 1777, and John Simmons, Sr., Susannah Simmons, and Benjamin Lewis were witnesses.[968] Joshua Fort's will of 15 March 1781 was witnessed by John Simmons, Spratley Simmons, and Benjamin Lewis.[969]

Benjamin's will of 13 August 1788 was recorded 14 October 1790. He was of St. Luke's Parish. He named wife, Mary, and devised land adjoining Joshua Thorp to son Zebulon; son Benjamin received land bought from Mial Harris; also named were daughters Elizabeth Butts, Fanny Butts, Nanny Turner (with reversion to her children Edwin and Elizabeth), Sally Rochelle (with reversion to her children), Becky, and Jenny Lewis. Execs: wife, son Zebulon, son-in-law Benjamin Butts. Wits: Etheldred Taylor, James McNiel, Henry Westbrook, John Simmons, Sr.[970]

Benjamin married **Mary HARRIS**, daughter of Edward HARRIS and Mary THORP, on 10 November 1752 in Southampton County, Virginia. Mary Thorp married secondly Owen Myrick.[971]

Mary Myrick of St. Luke's Parish made her will in 1775 (probated 1781). Legatees included sons Edward, Lewis, Hardy, and Amos Harris; daughters Mary Lewis, Anne Applewhite; granddaughter Olive Harris (wife of Joseph) and granddaughter Priscilla Harris. Wits: William Moore, Mary Nicholson, and Joshua Nicholson.[972]

Benjamin and Mary had the following children:

30   i.   **Zebulon⁴ LEWIS**.

   Zebulon Lewis, Lewis Fort, Archibald Parker, and Jno. Dyer were witnesses on 9 July 1793, when Philip Felts of Southampton County and Kinchen Felts of Sussex sold 145 acres to Joseph Fort of Southampton. The tract was adjacent Thos. Adams and had been devised to Philip Felts by John Morgan, deceased.[973]

31   ii. **Benjamin LEWIS**.

+ 32 iii. **Elizabeth LEWIS** died 1798.

33   iv. **Frances LEWIS** married **James BUTTS** on 10 April 1783 in Southampton County, Virginia, Thomas Butts surety for the marriage.[974]

34   v.   **Nancy LEWIS** married **Arthur TURNER** on 26 April 1781 in Southampton County, Virginia. Thomas Turner gave his consent to the marriage, and Littleton Turner was surety. Wit: Richard Kello.[975]

35   vi. **Sarah LEWIS** married **Levi ROCHELLE** on 9 August 1787 in Southampton County. Moses Foster was surety for this marriage.[976]

36   vii. **Rebecca LEWIS**.

37   viii. **Jane (Jenny) LEWIS** married **William SIMMONS** on 9 September 1790 in Southampton County. The surety for her marriage was Francis Young, Jr. And the bond was witnessed by Joseph Ruffin and Levi Rochelle.[977]

38   ix.. **Mary LEWIS** married **Thomas TURNER** on 15 January 1773 in Southampton County. Her marriage bond referred to her as the daughter of Benjamin Lewis. Benjamin Turner was surety, and William Turner and Richard Kello were witnesses.[978]

11.   **Zebulon³ LEWIS** (Zebulon², James¹) was born about 1730. He died 1799 in Brunswick County, Virginia.

Zebulon served in the militia in 1758 during the French and Indian War. In 1777 he became an ensign, and on 10 March 1780 he was promoted to first lieutenant.[979] Lt. Lewis served under General Marquis de LaFayette during the Revolution. Lt. Lewis was in General Peter Muhlenburg's Brigade, and they marched into Dinwiddie County and on to

Portsmouth and Suffolk.[980]

A list of St. Andrews Parish Parishoners between 1762 and 1773 was compiled, and the list includes Eleaner, Peter, and Zebulon Lewis. They were all grouped under the name *Lewis*, but they may not necessarily have belonged to the same household.[981]

Vestry records of St. Andrews Parish (Brunswick County) for 22 December 1766 show Zebulon Lewis being paid to keep Tabitha Jackson for one year.[982] The Vestry at the Middle Church met on 18 August 1784, and their records show that Zebulon Lewis, Robert Baley, and Ephraim Parham were to procession lands between Ingram's Road, Mize's Road, the county line, and the Meherrin River.[983]

A patent made to Matthew Hubard in Brunswick County on 12 July 1762 was included in one made to Zebulon Lewis on 6 April 1769. Hubard's patent for 310 acres was adjacent lands of Powell and Morris, near Loyd's Run of Sturgeon Creek. On 25 August 1762 the land was conveyed to Gronow Owen, a poet and famous Welsh minister. Zebulon included this 310 acres when he obtained a new patent for 714 aces in Brunswick County on Loyd's Run adjacent Morris, Simmons, and Edwards.[984]

Zebulon Lewis, Frederick Burgess, Buckner Stith, Jr., and Benjamin Blick appraised the estate of Robt. Nicolson of Brunswick County on 1 July 1773. Thomas Stith and Rebecca Nicolson were executors.[985]

On 24 May 1779 Zebulon Lewis and wife, Sandal, John Mitchell and wife, Dianna, of Brunswick County sold 200 acres to William Mitchell.[986]

Zebulon Lewis, Robert Harris, Lewis Dunn, Richard and William Boulden, Wm. Clark, and John Tram were witnesses on 1 June 1788, when Lewis Deupree of Mecklenburg County sold 110 acres in Charlotte County, Virginia, to Edmund Dunn. This tract was on the south fork of the Meherrin River.[987]

On 27 August 1792 the appraisal of the estate of Eliza Anderton was returned to Brunswick Court by Thomas Edmunds and Edward Birchett, administrators. The appraisers were Robert Morris and Zebulon Lewis.[988]

Accounting between 1789 and 1792 for the estate of John Ingram of Brunswick was returned by Jemima Ingram, the administrator. Named among other accounts were Charles Edmunds, S. Edmunds, Matthew Laffoon, Fredk. Lucas, Nathl. Lucas, Wilson More, William Williams, and Zebulon Lewis. The accounts were audited by Sterling Edmunds and Thomas Edmunds.[989]

Although Benjamin was the only child mentioned in Zebulon's will (see below), a William Lewis appeared among Zebulon's associates. William purchased items from the sale of the estate of John Turner, deceased, on 8 February 1794. John Turner's executors were John C. Short and William Short. William D. Orgain was among the buyers, and he was a business associate of Zebulon. The King family was represented: John, and Nathaniel King, and they may have been related to Zebulon, for Zebulon King, Benjamin Lewis, and Ishmael Dunn were appraisers of the estate of William Williams in 1792. Members of the Short family were buyers at the Turner estate sale. They were Anderson Short, John Short, Sr., and William Short, Jr., as well as the executor John C. Short.[990] This William Lewis may have been the son of Sophia Lewis, daughter of Dr. Peter Lewis of Barbadoes. Sophia apparently had a "natural child" named *William* by William Ponsonby, and the Lewis name was retained. William Ponsonby, merchant, made his will on 18 September 1760. Legatees: "my natural son, William Ponsonby, alias Lewis; my natural daughter Mary Ponsonby, alias Lewis; to Sophia Lewis." Execs: Mrs. Sophia Lewis, Joseph Scott. Wits: William Ponsonby, Jr., Mary Ponsonby, Joseph Fulgham.[991] William Ponsonby, Ann Ponsonby, Ann Hunt, and Elizabeth Daniel were witness to the 1746 will of Ann Applewhaite.[992] Mary Myrick (d. 1781), mother-in-law of Benjamin Lewis, had daughter Anne Applewhite. Peter Lewis was listed with Zebulon in St. Andrews Parish registry.

Isle of Wight County, Virginia, deeds includes one dated 3 June 1761. Sophia Lewis said that William Ponsonby had in his possession some slaves that belonged to her late father, Dr. Peter Lewis, of Barbados. She was releasing them to William Ponsonby (alias Lewis). Wits: Robert Tynes, John Joyner, Arthur Applewhaite.[993]

On 3 December 1797 Joel Moore and wife, Sarah, of Lunenburg County sold 145 acres to Zebulon Lewis of Brunswick County. The tract abutted lands of John Elliott and William Moore and Stony Creek. Wits: Edward Birchill, Mordecai Howard, John Orgaine, Benjamin Lewis.[994]

Zebulon's will was written 10 April 1799 and probated 24 June 1799, in Brunswick County. The only child named in his will was Benjamin Lewis.[995]

Zebulon married **Sandal JACKSON**, daughter of Henry JACKSON and his first wife.[996]

Henry Jackson of Brunswick County made his will in 1789. He named wife, Ann; sons David and Stephen. He gave Negroes to his first five children (born to his first wife), and daughter Rebecca was to have an equal share with them. Henry wanted two tracts sold (one in Brunswick and one in Orange County). Execs: wife, Ann; friend Wm. Edwards Brodnax, Isham Smith, William Brodnax (lawyer). Wits: William Bennett, Sterling Peebles, and Mark Jackson. Administration was granted to Edmund Cooper. Securities: William E. Brodnax, Thomas Hardiway, Henry Bailey, and David Jackson.[997]

Zebulon and Sandal had the following child:

+ 39 i. **Benjamin⁴ LEWIS** was born November 1763 and died 24 September 1824.

12. **Patience³ LEWIS** (Zebulon², James¹).

Patience and husband, John, lived in Albemarle Parish, which served Surry and Sussex Counties. On 15 April 1749 John and Patience Harris had daughter Mary baptized, and Mich'l Blow and Mary Porter were godparents. The twins, John and Lewis, were baptized that year, and godparents were Richard Field, Beuford Pleasant, Anne Field, Joseph Petway, Nathan Lewis, and Hannah Petway.[998]

In attendance on 3 October 1749 when Joseph and Hannah Petway had child Sterling baptized, were Nathaniel Lewis, John Bradley, and Patience Harris. On 5 January 1752 Joseph and Hannah had daughter Lucy baptized, and attending were John Harris, Eliz. Bradley, and Jane Adkinson.[999]

Patience married **John HARRIS.**.[1000]

They had the following children::

40 i. **Mary⁴ HARRIS** was born about 1748. She was christened at the same time as her brothers John and Lewis.. Mich'l. Blow and Mary Porter attended.

41 ii. **John HARRIS** was christened 15 April 1749 in Albemarle Parish, Surry County, Virginia.

John and Lewis were twins, and the date given in the parish records appears to have been date of baptism. Sponsors were Richard Field, Beuford Pleasant, Anne Field, Joseph Petway, Nathan Lewis, Hannah Petway.

42 iii. **Lewis HARRIS** was christened 15 April 1749.

43 iv. **Benjamin HARRIS** was born 1761. Benjamin married **Bethany ODOM**.

44 v. **Edward HARRIS**.

45 vi. **Jesse HARRIS**.

46 vii. **Frances HARRIS**.

47 viii. **Mollie (Mary?) HARRIS**.

48 ix. **Rebecca HARRIS**.

49 x. **Nancy HARRIS**.

50 xi. **Lydia HARRIS**.

13. **James³ LEWIS** (Joshua², James¹) was born 5 September 1726 in Middlesex County, Virginia.[1001] He died 1815 in Northampton County, North Carolina.

Joshua Lewis of Isle of Wight County, Virginia, sold to James Lewis of Northampton County, North Carolina, 400 acres on the north side of the Mill Swamp on 21 May 1748. This land was at the mouth of the Grassy Branch and the swamp and had been patented to Gabriel Parker on 4 August 1741. Wits: Chris. Kilbee, Cattarine Kilbee, Epar. Kilbee.[1002]

On 5 August 1761 Harmon Hill sold to James Lewis, heir of Joshua Lewis, deceased, 160 acres adjoining the Mill Swamp. Wits: Green Hill, Jr., Thos. Pace, Francis Deloach.[1003]

On January 1778 Matthew Buffoon and wife, Ann, of Northampton County sold 200 acres to Henry Lewis of same. The land adjoined Hermon Hill and Henry Hill. Wits: James Lewis, Joshua Lewis.[1004] It is likely Joshua and Henry were sons of James Lewis.

James Lewis qualified as executor of the will of Jane (Jean) Lewis in September 1794. Jeremiah Warwick proved the will.[1005]

The will of James Lewis was proved by the oath of John R. Moore. At the June court of 1815, Henry Hill qualified as executor.[1006]

24.   **Epaphroditus**[3] **KILBY** (Katharine[2] LEWIS, James[1]) was born around 1725.

Epaphridites Kilbee and John Brasell were witnesses on 23 February 1758 to a deed from James Massinghall of Northampton County (North Carolina) to William Wills of Southampton County, Virginia. The 175-acre tract was on the north side of Corriroy Swamp.[1007]

A deed was recorded in May 1763 in Northampton County, North Carolina, to Epaphroditus Killbee and children of Anthony Armistead for 1,364 acres on the west side of Whelers Mill Swamp. The deed included 36 slaves, livestock, and personal property in addition. It was a deed of gift from Anthony Armistead, Sr., and wife, Mary, of Northampton County, to their children Anthony Armistead, Jr., Robert and Elizabeth Armistead, with Epaphroditus Killbee "of the third part." Wits: Ephr. Killbee, Mary King.[1008]

Epaphroditus married **ARMISTEAD (?)**.

Anthony Armistead had married Mary, daughter of Anthony Tucker and wife, Rosea, and widow of Joshua Curle. Joshua and Mary (Tucker) had daughters Judith (m. John Herbert) and Mary (m. Wm. King).[1009]

They had the following child:

+   51   i.   **James**[4] **KILBY** was born about 1755 and died 1830. His parents are assumed.

Fourth Generation

29.   **Samuel**[4] **LEWIS** (Zebulon[3], James[2], James[1]).   Samuel was born probably between 1740 and 1750 and died 1811 in Monroe County, (West) Virginia.

When moving into a new area, a settler selected the land he wanted and placed his request for it in a land entry book. The survey was made later, often with the settler already living on the land. Sometime later he would receive his patent. Samuel Lewis's surveys were made in 1793 in what was then Greenbrier County.

Samuel appeared on the 1787 census for Greenbrier County. He was on List A, made by Commissioner John Hutchison. Unfortunately the list was alphabetized, so it is difficult to determine neighbors, but people in the same district included Francis Best, whose daughter Jane would marry Samuel's son Zebulon. People whose relatives would move to Lawrence County, Ohio, where my Lewis and Scarborough ancestors migrated, included Thomas Sowards, Isaac Sowards, Sr., and Jephtha Massey. Also on the list was Henry McDaniel, Sr., whose son Henry would move to neighboring Gallia County, Ohio. Doubtless there were others. My Scarborough ancestor, Robert Scarboro, and sons David, James, and William were on this list. A Benjamin Lewis was also in this district.[1010] Benjamin was the only Lewis on the list of residents in this Monroe area in 1782, and he seems to have been a member of the Muddy Creek group. He was in the militia company of James Henderson. (These lists were used for tax purposes.) The company of John Henderson had no Lewises named, but it did include associates of Samuel Lewis and his family: Wallace and

Boud Estill, Mathew Creed, Joseph Ellison, James Ellison, Sr., and Jr., Mathew Kessinger, Adam and Jacob Mann and another Jacob Mann, and Jacob Miller.[1011]

Samuel had two surveys made in Greenbrier County, one for 300 acres on 3 January 1793 (Survey Book 2:197), and the other for 200 acres on 4 January 1793 (SB 2:198). The latter survey bordered land of Paul Long, and the pointers included the top of a ridge. Samuel used Treasury Warrant No. 11,948 for 686 acres as an assignee of James McNutt in order to claim the 200 acres. Both parcels were east of Greenville in what is now Monroe County and were on Back Creek, a branch of Indian Creek. The survey for 300 acres shows Samuel's line briefly crossing over a curve in Indian Creek by the mouth of Back Creek. About 127 acres of this tract had originally belonged to Mathias Kissinger, who acquired it in 1781. The rest was assigned to Samuel by James McNutt, who had Treasury Warrant No. 11,948.[1012] In 1799 Samuel's son Zebulon Lewis claimed 100 acres adjoining lands of Samuel Lewis, James Miller, and Richard Gartin. The land was said to be on Indian and Laurel Creeks.[1013] A small covered bridge, built in 1911, crosses Laurel Creek. There are few homes in this valley and it is enclosed by tree-covered mountains. It seems a place unto itself.

On 18 January 1803 Samuel and Mary Lewis sold their 200-acre survey to John Plimon of Monroe County. This tract was the one that abutted the land of Paul Long. The only witness was John Hutchison, Clerk of Court. The clerk of court made no indication that Samuel had not signed his own name. Mary signed with a wavy line, similar to an S.[1014] Sometime between this date and the summer of 1811 Mary must have died, for she was not mentioned in the records following Samuel's death. Botetourt County records of 31 October 1791 show John Plymale (Plyman?) marrying Jane Tweley. Anthony Plymale was surety.[1015] Monroe County deeds of 20 December 1803 include one for 75 acres from John Plyman and wife, Jane, to Richard Johnson. The parcel was adjacent Matthias McGlennery.[1016] Isaac Estill was one of the executors of the 1817 will of Mathew McClamary. Mathew had wife, Lydia, and children Bathshaba and Sarah McClamary; son-in-law John Ray and wife, Sarah. Execs: wife, Lydia, John Wray, and Isaac Estill. Wits: Thomas Wray, James Murphy.[1017] Isaac Estill's half-brother, John Estill, had daughter Priscilla who married Thomas Ray. In 1809 Thomas Ray and wife, Pricilla, formerly Pricilla Gold, legatee of John Estill, sold 150 acres on Hands Creek/Indian Creek to William Young.[1018] Peter Larew owned this land by 18 February 1806.[1019] We met Peter Larue earlier, in Orange County, Virginia.

The Gartons, Durgans, Strothers, and Gores:

Richard Garten was a neighbor of Samuel Lewis, Richard's land also on Indian and Laurel Creeks. The Gartens had lived in Orange County, Virginia, and knew the Brockmans of that county, Saml. Brockman witnessing a 1763 deed from Uriah Garton and wife, Mary, to James Shirley.[1020] Samuel Lewis's grandson John F. Lewis married Catherine Brockman, great-granddaughter of Samuel Brockman of Orange County.

Elijah Garten entered 200 acres in the Greenbrier Land Entry Book on 21 March 1786. This land was on a south branch of Laurel Creek, and he used the state warrant of Wm. Boyd. Elijah entered an additonal 200 acres between his own land on Swope's Knob and land of William Middy (Maddy?) on Indian Creek.[1021] Elijah had married Barbara Bold (Boyd?) on 16 March 1782, in Rockingham County, Virginia.[1022] In 1768 Nathaniel Garten, born in 1759 in Orange County, had moved from there to Rockingham County with his father.[1023] William Garten claimed 107 acres on Swope's Knobs in 1783 and Griffy Garton, 380 acres in 1786.[1024] Nathaniel Garten married Peggy Durgan on 16 April 1811 in Monroe County, and Barnabas Durgan secured Garten's bond.[1025]

Reuben Hill married Samuel's daughter Polly (Mary), and they sold land to Barnabas Durgan. A dispute followed, and the deed wound up in chancery. But Barnabas was close to Samuel Lewis before he was deeded the land, for he bought several items at Samuel's estate sale. On 17 April 1816 Barnabas Digan [sic] and wife, Nancy, sold 53 acres to Andrew and George Beirne. The parcel was on Back Creek, a branch of Indian Creek, and was part of the 300-acre patent granted Samuel Lewis on 18 March 1796.[1026]

Barnabas Durgan lived over the mountains in Botetourt County, Virginia, before moving to Monroe. Barney Dirgin and Nancy Knox, daughter of Elixha (Elisha) Knox, Sr., married in Botetourt County, Virginia, on 26 August 1799. And on 2 November 1790 John Dirgin married Elizabeth Hewit, daughter of Patrick Hewit.[1027] On 27 March 1802 Patrick Hewitt and wife, Mary, of Montgomery County, Virginia, sold 50 acres in Botetourt County to Patrick Lockhart. The parcel was adjacent land of said Lockhart, James Trener, and John McCreary. Witnesses were Jas. Trenor, Isaac Taylor, (?), Jno. Smyth, B. Dirgan.[1028] Patrick Lockhart served as sheriff of Botetourt County and lived at its county seat, Fincastle. As a delegate from Botetourt, Lockhart took part in the first General Assembly of the Commonwealth of Virginia. In 1770 he married Mary McDonald.[1029] Apparently he married more than once. An Augusta County, Virginia, lawsuit, Calvert vs. Kennerley, noted that James Kennerley's daughter Mary had married Patrick Lockhart.[1030] Mary Kennerly had been married previously to George Strother (d. 1767) of Culpeper County. George was a son of Francis Strother and Susannah Dabney and brother of the William Strother who married Sarah (Bailey) Pannell.[1031] This Strother-Pannell family was close to Zebulon Lewis of Orange County.

George Strother and wife, Mary (Kennerly), had daughter Margaret, who, in 1781, married Col. George Hancock.[1032] Fotheringay was the name of Hancock's home near Shawsville in Montgomery County, Virginia. His grave is famous, because he wanted to be buried sitting up. George and Margaret Hancock's daughter Julia married General William Clark, part of the Lewis and Clark expedition to the northwest.[1033] Mary Kennerly was a daughter of James Kennerly, whose father, Samuel, was of Culpeper County when he wrote his will in 1749. One of his heirs was daughter Margaret Ruddell.[1034] Margaret and her husband, George Ruddell, had son George, who, in 1786, married Mary, widow of Joseph Gore.[1035]

The Gartons, Hintons, and Maddys:

Names of buyers at the 1815 estate sale of Zachariah Garten included Richard MacNeer, who would be mentioned many years later in a letter from Evan Hinton to Richard Burton Lewis, Samuel's grandson. Even Hinton (seemingly the uncle of the friend of Richard Lewis) and James Maddy also were buyers.[1036] Evan Henton had married Peggy, daughter of Wm. Burnsides, in Rockingham County in 1811.[1037] The Maddys were neighbors of Samuel Lewis, and Eleanor Maddy married John Hinton in 1813.[1038] John and Eleanor Hinton's son Evan is considered the father of Summers County, West Virginia.[1039] In 1887 he would write to Richard Burton Lewis of Ohio.

On 19 January 1795 Wm. Maddy and wife, Elizabeth, conveyed 4 acres on Indian Draft of Indian Creek to Samuel Allen. Wits: Eliza Gerton, Isaac Estill, Jacob Miller.[1040] Isaac Estill and Elizabeth H. (S?) Estill, Coonrad Deboy, and Samuel Allen were witnesses on 11 October 1797, when Elijah and Sarah Gartin deeded 156 acres on Swope's Knob to Nathaniel Gartin. The land was adjacent Nathaniel Gartin and John Deboy.[1041] Isaac Estill's interest in the Gartons may have stemmed from Griffith Garton's marriage to Hanna Miller in 1787.[1042] Jacob Miller married an Estill.[1043]

James Gore, Bartly Pack, and Isaac Milburn appraised the estate of Charles Gartin in 1828. Administrators were John H. Vawter and Charles Gartin. Buyers at Gartin's estate sale were Jerry Bush; Jos. Ellison; Elizabeth Goodall; Isaac, and Thompson Gartin; James Gore, James Graham, Thomas Green, John Hinton, Samuel Maggart; Elijah and Jerry Meadows; Isaac Milburn; Bartlett and William Pack; Lanty Roach, M. Roles, Samuel Smith, and Mary West.[1044]

The administration of Samuel Lewis's estate:

Samuel Lewis died without a will and on 16 July 1811 Isaac Estill signed as administrator of his estate. Samuel Lewis was surety, J. Hutchison the witness. The bond was for $1,000.[1045] Jacob Cook, William Shanklin, and Michael Miller appraised Samuel's estate on 27 July 1811.[1046] By 20 May 1817 there was a need to settle Samuel's estate accounts, and Wm Shanklin, George Walker, and Jacob Cook were appointed to settle it with Isaac Estill. On 7 September 1818, Shanklin, Walker, and Cook met at the home of Jacob Cook to go over the accounts. The amount of money collected was $131.65; money paid out was $120.89; $20 was allowed the executor, leaving a balance of $40.76.[1047] During this time period, 1817-1818, Isaac Estill and Conrad Peters were delegates to the General Assembly of Virginia.[1048]

It is curious that Isaac Estill was appointed administrator of the estate of Samuel Lewis, for sons Zebulon, Samuel, and Joshua Lewis were still in the area. Isaac's home, just east of the Lewis property, had been built by his father. It has 18-inch walls, for it was used as a blockhouse (a type of fort) for protection from the Indians. The house was extended and sits on a well-run farm on the southside of Indian Creek. Owners Arnold and Adonna Dowdy hosted the dedication of the house as an historic landmark on 10 July 1999. Isaac Estill had married Elizabeth Strother Frogg in 1788,[1049] and was thus a relative of the Strother family of Orange County, who were friends of Samuel's father.

Wallace Estill, Isaac's father, died in 1792.[1050] It was he or Wallace, Jr., who entered 20 acres adjoining his own

The Scarberrys (Scarboroughs), Doughtys, Lewises, and Paynes of Lawrence County, Ohio

land in the Greenbrier *Land Entry Book* on 17 May 1785. He was using part of the Treasury Warrant for 2,025 acres belonging to James Kelly. James Kelly's land was on the waters of Rich Creek and on the south side of the property of Widow Gotliff (Gatliff).[1051]

Martha Gatliff made her will on 11 June 1798, naming children Charles Gatliff, Hannah Neely, Leah Toney, Mary Pine, Happy Willey, Abby Tremble, and Grandson James Willey. Wits: Alexander Stuart, Isaac Clendinen, and Joseph Gore. The appraisers of her estate were Alex Stuart, James and William Henderson. Henry McDaniels was named in the accounts.[1052] Ann Catherine Kellar married first Henry Goar and secondly, in 1793, Henry McDaniel. She was Henry McDaniel's second wife, for he had married first Mary Ann Porter, whose family had lived in Orange County, Virginia.

The Estills, Bootons, Hills, and Kilbys:

In 1786 Wallace Estill claimed two tracts, one for 220 acres on Dropping Lick adjacent John Miller; the other for 280 acres on Indian Creek, adjacent Lewis Booton. Ruth Estill, Wallace's daughter, married first Travis Booton and second William Kavanaugh.[1053]

Travis Booton was a son of Lewis Booton, who moved from Culpeper County to Indian Creek, buying land there in 1788.[1054] In 1772 Lewis Booton had bought land on Beautiful Run in Culpeper County.[1055] His land on Indian Creek was near lands of James Ellison and John Halstead on the Quaking Asp.[1056] Lewis was a son of William Booton and wife, Judith Hill, who married on 22 January 1737/8 in Middlesex County. Judith was a daughter of William Hill and Frances Needles.[1057] Judith's brother, Needles Hill, had married into the Morgan-Barbee family of Middlesex. William Hill was surely related to Charles Hill, ancestor to the Kilbys of Middlesex, for Christopher Kilby owned land near William Hill, who owned land next to William Hackley and John Bradley. See Christopher Kilby (m. Catherine Lewis).

August 1811, the estate sale of Samuel Lewis:

The estate sale of Samuel Lewis, deceased, took place on 16 August 1811. Estate sales attracted mostly relatives and neighbors. One or more members of Samuel's family was literate, for several books were sold. Isaac FISHER bought 5; Thos BUCKETT, 1; Barnabas DIRGAN, 4; Abraham MARS, 4. Samuel LEWIS bought a large Bible, a log chain, 2 augers, a handsaw, a mattock, wool, 3 hogs, and other items (hard to decipher). Reuben HILL purchased a bed, stockings, and 1 bag(?). Other buyers were Henry MILLER, John LARENCE, William BROOKENS, Adam MAN, Jr., John MAN, James MADDY, John MADDY, James CHAMBERS, Stephen BUCKLAND, William ROACH, Agustine COMER, Joseph BUSH, Richard McNEER, John BYRNSIDE, Thomas CHAPMAN, and Jacob MAN. John MADDY bought several items, including a basket and vices, a shot gun, a frow, a bed, a hat, coat, jacket, loom, steers, a reel, shovel, and a "sang hoe," a tool used for digging ginseng. Samuel's family seems to have made their own linen, for a small quantity of unwatered flax was part of his inventory, along with 11 casks of wool and check[sic], a large spinning wheel and 16 spools. James MADDY bought linen.[1058] The buyers are discussed below, their surnames written in all capitals.

The Brooking family was associated with the Henry Lewis and Buford families of Madison County, Virginia. See Zebulon Lewis of Orange County (his Pannell-Strother involvement). The Brookings moved from Albemarle County, Virginia, to Humphrey's Run. In 1804 Charles Brookin and wife, Ann, sold 100 acres on Humphreys Run/Indian Creek to Bartholemew Ramsey.[1059] In 1772 Bartholomew Ramsay of Amherst County sold 400 acres on Micham's River in Albemarle County to Robert Boyd of Albemarle. It was by land of Col. John Chiswell. Wits: John Wood, Wm. Wood, Jr., Bradley Berry, Josias Dodd.[1060] Rhoda Brooking, daughter of Charles and Ann Brooking, married Henry Miller of Monroe in 1799; her sister Mary married James Curry in 1803; sister Susanna married John LAWRENCE in 1803, and sister Nancy married William Lawrence in 1803.[1061] Henry and Rhoda Miller's daughter Rhoda, in 1836, would marry Samuel D. Lewis, grandson of Samuel (d. 1811). William BROOKENS, the buyer at Samuel's estate sale, was probably a son of Charles and Ann, for he married Sarah Ruble of Monroe in 1804,[1062] and he would seemingly have been of the same generation as Rhoda and her sisters.

Oren Morton, in his *History of Monroe County*, however, did not name William Brooking as a brother to Rhoda and her sisters.[1063] So we should consider other possibilities. The Charles Brooking of Madison County, Virginia, who died in 1795, left son William, who was an executor of his will. In 1796 William and Robert Brooking and James Coleman, heirs of Charles Brooking, used a power of attorney from Samuel and John Brooking of Kentucky to sell 40 acres in Madison County to Ambrose Medley. Wits: Wharton Canaday, Jacob Redman, Joseph Redman.[1064] The witness Wharton Canaday is of especial interest, for he was a nephew of Leroy Canaday.[1065] In 1793 John Wayt and wife, Keziah, of Madison County; James Wayt of Orange County; George Wayt and wife, Elizabeth, of Albemarle; and Elizabeth Lobb and Leeroy Canaday and wife, Salley, of Madison County sold land to Churchill Gibbs.[1066] Leroy Canaday shared land ownership with Elizabeth Lobb. The name *Lobb* was not common, and William and Catherine Lobb of Louisa County sold 50 acres in Culpeper County to Richard Lewis of Orange County in 1755. The parcel was by land of Edward Dillard and Vivian Daniel.[1067] Richard Lewis appeared among the Orange County tithables in 1754 and 1755, in both instances shown as living near the Daniels from Middlesex and the Brockmans. In 1756 he was between Wm. Watson and Edwd. Poe. Margt. Tilley followed, and John Brockman was seven households away.[1068] (Samuel Lewis's grandson, John F. Lewis, would marry Catherine Brockman of Albemarle County, whose grandfather had lived near Richard Lewis.) Richard Lewis and wife, Elizabeth, sold 100 acres in 1757 to John Wright. Richard had bought the land from Henry Tilly.[1069] In 1769 David Lewis, Jr., of St. Anne's Parish, Albemarle County, and brother to Joel Lewis discussed below, sold 129 acres to Henry Tilley of same. The tract was along Meachum's River.[1070]

A descendant of Zebulon Lewis of Orange County would marry into the Brockman family of Albemarle and Orange Counties, but Zebulon and Richard Lewis did not seem to share the same circle of friends. Jacob Williams (he secured the executor's bond for Alexander Fraizier, who bequeathed items to Zebulon Lewis) did live by a John Lewis and John Embry, however, as was revealed in the deed from William and Elizabeth Leak to William Pollock. John Embree (Embry) of Orange County made his will in 1786, naming Thomas Woolfolk and Samuel Brockman, Sr., as executors. Wits: Jacob Williams, Mallory Williams, and John Noel. The testator named son Richard, and Richard Embree and Jacob Williams secured the executors' bond.[1071] In 1767 J. Lewis, Vivion Daniel, and James Daniel witnessed a deed that was eventually delivered to Jacob Williams (see Zebulon Lewis above). Of course, we have only proven that Wharton Canaday knew the Brookings and the Lobbs, and that the Lobbs were involved with Richard Lewis of Orange County, who lived near the Daniels, who also lived near a John Lewis and Jacob Williams.

The Brookings, we saw above, were close to George Wortham of Middlesex, who witnessed the 1715 will of James Lewis. After George accidentally killed Benjamin Davis, he was tried for murder and acquitted. A bond was signed by George Wortham in 1711 and recorded in Middlesex County, Virginia. Robert Brooking was one of the securities for the bond. Charles Wortham was a witness to the will of Thomas Hipkins of Essex County. Thomas Hipkins married Cordelia Upshaw, daughter of Captain William Upshaw (d. 1720) of Gloucester County, Virginia. Cordelia's sister Susanna married William Brooking. Robert Brooking of King and Queen County, Virginia, bought land in Essex County in 1750. John Upshaw was a witness. Thomas Hipkins was a son of John Hipkins of Middlesex County.[1072] John Hipkins had married Sarah Williamson,[1073] a sister to Robert Williamson, who married Katherine, daughter of Richard Lewis, in 1682.

Although I have not found the direct line between the Charles Brooking family of Monroe and the Brookings of Gloucester, there is more reason to believe that they were related than to believe that they were not. The Brookings of Monroe were unquestionably related to the ones living in Madison and Orange Counties. The Brookings were said to have moved to Monroe from Albemarle, and Albemarle bordered on Orange County, where we find Charles Brooking and Saml. Brooking living in 1787. They were on Tax List B, which included Zachy. Burnley.[1074] The town of Burnley is by Preddy's Creek in Albemarle County, not far from the Orange County line. In 1792 Charles Brooking of Madison County willed to niece Rhoda Brooking (Rhoda Brooking of Monroe married Henry Miller in 1799), and Rhoda was not a common name. In 1761 Charles Brooking was paid from the estate of George Turmon of Culpeper County, along with Mrs. Ann Turmon. William Kirtley, executor of Francis Kirtley, deceased, was reporting on the accounts.[1075] Ignatius Tureman married Mary Pace of Middlesex in 1731, and Hannah Booton married William Pace in 1733.[1076] Ignatius appears to have been a son of George. Ignatius died in 1784, naming Tureman Lewis in his will.[1077] Ignatius and Mary's daughter Mary married Joel Lewis, son of David Lewis and Miss Terrell. David, born about 1685 in Hanover County, was a son of John Lewis.[1078] David Lewis may have been a son of John Lewis and Sarah Nichols of Middlesex, for on 6 January 1712/13 a David Lewis, along with William Gardner, was paid by Middlesex County court for work on the Dragon Bridge.[1079]

Thos. BUCKETT may have been a Bickett. Bickett's Knob, the highest of Swope's Knobs, was named for the Bicketts who settled there. One of them was Thomas. Bickett's Knob is 3,327 feet high, but it sits on a plateau north of Union, so it doesn't seem enormously high. Greenville is about 1,700 feet above sea level.

Stephen BUCKLAND, who bought at Samuel's estate sale, also bought at the 1815 estate sale for Mickleberry Roach.[1080] Richard Garton was surety when Thomas Buckland married Margaret Wickline in 1806. Stephenson Buckland married Milly Meadows in 1811.[1081]

Joseph BUSH married Polly Cartwright in Monroe County on 13 November 1808.[1082] Because a member of the Roach family was also a buyer at Samuel Lewis's estate sale, I am assuming that Joseph Bush was a member of the Bush family that had intermarried previously with the Roaches and Meadows, both in Monroe County and Rockingham. In 1800 Elijah Meadows married Milly Gartan of Monroe County. Jeremiah Meadow and Esther Roach married in 1803. Jeremiah Meadows and Nancy Roach married in 1804. William Meadows married Esther Roach in 1817.[1083] In Rockingham County in 1804 Archibald Bush and Mary Meadows married. Francis Meadows and Frances Bush married in 1797.[1084]

John BYRNSIDE lived just south of Union on a large plantation.[1085] John's father, James Byrnside, was of Montgomery County when he made his will in 1806. It was probated in 1812 and recorded in Monroe County. He referred to seven children he had had by wife Ezebeler [sic]: Kathern, John, James, Rachele, Sarah, Martha, and Mary Byrnside. And then he mentioned three children he had had with Suanner [sic] Meadows: Joseph, Joshua, and Benjamin Byrnside. He asked Isaac Estill and Suanner Meadows to be his executors. Wits: Matt Farley, Hugh Caperton, James Byrnside, Ester Farley, Wm Clark, Alexander Dunlap, and Samuel Clark.[1086]

James CHAMBERS owned land in the area called the Sinks (Sinks Grove is north of Union). When Robert Wiley bought 218 acres from Samuel and Mary Black in 1792, the land was said to be at the Sinks adjacent James Chambers, John King, William Blanton, and Isaac Poleton.[1087]

Thomas CHAPMAN, named above as a buyer at the estate sale, was likely the one who married Ankey Harvey, daughter of Benjamin Harvey.[1088] Benjamin had married Susan Ballard, daughter of William.[1089]

Augustine COMER was born near the Rapidan River to German parents. His children were Elizabeth (m. Daniel Miller, 1801), Frederick (m. Polly Mitchell in 1814), Jacob (m. Anna Meadows), Michael (m. Lucy Willis), John (m. Mary J. Mitchell), Catharine (m. Joseph Ball), Barbara, Augustus (m. Sarah Fore), Sarah (m. John Peters).[1090] Mary Comer married William Roach in 1804.[1091] In 1802 Solomon Sowards and wife, Sophia, sold 78 ares on Indian Creek to John Comer and Thomas Stuart.[1092] Solomon Sowards was surely related to Isaac Sowards of Monroe, who died in 1803.[1093]

Barnabas DIRGAN had married Nancy Knox in 1799 in Botetourt County, and his daughter Peggy married Nathaniel Gartin on 17 April 1811, a few months before Samuel's death. Somehow I get the sense that Barnabas was a blood relative of Samuel Lewis or an in-law, but the proof eludes me.

Isaac FISHER was deeded 147 acres on Indian Draft by Daniel Shepherd and wife, Cloe, in 1797. The tract was adjacent lands of Thomas Henton, Valentine Cook, and Samuel Daley.[1094]

Reuben HILL had married Samuel Lewis's daughter Mary in 1810, and it isn't certain what other Hills he was related to, although we would naturally suspect he was part of the family of Catherine Hill, who married Samuel's son Joshua.

John LARENCE was part of the Brooking family, having married Susanna Brooking in 1803. See the Brooking family above.

The buyer Samuel LEWIS would have been the son of Samuel, deceased.

Buyers James and John MADDY belonged to the Maddy family that came to Monroe from Rockingham and Orange Counties. Samuel's survey for 200 acres bordered land of Paul Long, who married Elisabeth Maddy on 8 February 1785. They were married by John Alderson, who had preached in Rockingham County before settling along the Greenbrier River. Alderson's records also show Anny Maddy marrying George Parker on the same day. On 8 August 1785 John Maddy married Barbara Miller. Adam Man married Mary Maddy on 9 December 1783, and William Maddy and Elisabeth Man married on 25 February 1783.[1095]

In 1808 James Maddy and wife, Anne; Richard Gartin and wife, Anne, sold 194 acres to Andrew Allen. The tract was a mile northeast of the Singing Cave.[1096] James Maddy had married Anne Kessinger.[1097]

The Jacob MANN who moved to Indian Creek after 1770 and helped build Cook's Fort married Mary Kessinger. Jacob's brother Adam MANN married 1) Polly (Mary) Maddy and 2) Polly Flinn. Jacob Mann, son of Jacob, married Millie Ballard in 1804. Other children of Jacob, Jr. were Isaac, who married Lucy Stephenson in 1825; John (b. 1770) married Millie Harvey in 1801; Adam MANN (b. 1771) married Elizabeth Young in 1808 and Nancy Harvey in 1812; James (b. 1785) married Lucy Keaton in 1808; Parthena; Moses Mann married secondly Sarah Swinney; Michael (b. 1793) married Cynthia Walker; Susan married John C. Maddy in 1828.[1098]

Information on Abraham MARS (Mares) is scant. An Abram MARRS and wife lived on Indian Creek. He was a hackle maker. He was named, along with the Bucklands, when a list of free Negros and Mulattoes was made for 1810.[1099]

In 1810 Richard McNEER married Elizabeth Maddy, sister to Eleanor, wife of John Hinton, and sister to James Maddy who married Elizabeth Lowry in 1812.[1100] Richard lived on Hans and Indian Creeks.[1101]

Henry MILLER and Rhoda Brooking married in 1799. John Halstead was surety for the bond, and Jacob Cook was the minister.[1102] Henry and Rhoda's daughter, Rhoda, would marry Samuel Lewis, son of Joshua; and her sister, Elizabeth, would marry Jacob Halstead,[1103] who bought the remaining Lewis land in 1840. The Millers, Manns, and Maddys intermarried: Barbara Miller married Jacob Mann; Anna B. Miller married Rev. John MADDY. Oren Morton, in his *History of Monroe County*, made this comment about the Miller family: "The descendants of Jacob, Sr., are an industrious, law-abiding people and have intermarried with the best families around them." [1104]

William ROACH was likely a son of the Jonathan Roach who was born in Rockingham County in 1761 and was in Orange County, Virginia, when he enlisted to fight in the Revolutionary War in 1779. In 1781 he substituted for John Craig of Rockingham. Jonathan migrated to Monroe County in 1785.[1105]

The Roaches, Goodalls, Maddys, and Stodgills of Orange County.

David Roach of Orange County, Virginia, who died in 1742, was devised land by Ambrose Madison. In 1762 Reuben Roach, son of David, deeded this land over to James Madison.[1106] When David Roach of Orange County mortgaged a mare, two pregnant cows, and some household items to George Taylor, in 1741, the witnesses were John Rucker, Wm. Bonton (Booton?), James Barnett, and John Goodall.[1107] On 24 October 1765 Moses Harris and wife, Sarah, sold 175 acres in Orange County to John Goodall. The tract was on Taylor's Run at the foot of the Great Mountains (the Blue Ridge). Wits: John Golding, John Harris. A companion to this deed was one from Moses and Sarah Harris to Reuben Roach for 175 acres. The tract was also on Taylor's Run, and it was bordered by lands of John Goodall, John Harris, and Colonel Taylor. Wits: John Goodall, John Golding.[1108]

James and Ann Mady of Orange County, Virginia, sold 76 acres to James Stodhill on 28 March 1770. The parcel was part of a greater tract bought by Silvester Murphey from Moses Harris, and it was on Swift Run at the foot of the Great Mountains. Madey's deed was recorded on 28 March 1771, the same day that John Goodall granted Charles Goodall, his oldest son, 300 acres on Swift Run by the race ground. John Goodall was moving.[1109] Swift Run is in present-day Greene County, and it shares a border with Rockingham County. James C. Maddy of Rockingham County had died by 20 June 1785, when Ann Maddy became administrator of his estate. Ann's bond was secured by Col. Wm. Null and Henry Armentrout.[1110]

John, Isaac, and Jonathan Roach, along with Garrison Gibbons, witnessed the 1824 will of Michael Fleshman of Monroe County. Wm. Stodghill and Delaney Livisay were his executors.[1111] Peter Fleshman of Culpeper County, Virginia, died a resident of Monroe County, and Samuel Lewis (Jr.) bought at his estate sale in 1814.

Thomas Buckland bought 87 acres on Indian Creek from Solomon Sowards in 1809 and another tract of 180 acres the same day. The latter tract was between Hans and Indian Creek, adjacent John Rosebrough, Bruten Smith, and Mathew Creed.[1112] A Mathew Creed lived in Orange County at the same time that Zebulon Lewis and son Samuel were living there. A deed Mathew Creed and wife, Margaret, made in 1760 for land on Swift Run was witnessed by James Stodghill,[1113] whose family intermarried with the Ballards and moved to Monroe. In 1766 Matthew and Margaret Creed sold 86 acres to Will Grant. This parcel was on the west side of Roach's River, in the Shanando Pass.[1114] Roach's River originates in the Blue Ridge near Powell's Gap. Swift Run Gap is northeast of Roach's River, and today's U.S. 33 runs through the gap. Matthew Creed owned property approximately 50 miles from the area where Zebulon seems to have lived. But Matthew Creed and the Maddys, Goodalls, Roaches, Stodghills, and Zebulon Lewis would have gone to the same court house and the men may have met at muster, for the militia had to meet regularly.

The Millers, Estills, Georges, Collins, Brockmans, O'Neals, and Larues:

Jacob Miller's son Jacob married a Miss Estill. In his will of 13 October 1808 Jacob Miller, Sr., appointed his sons John and George Miller, Isaac Estile, and William Vawter, Jr., his executors. Children Jacob named in his will were Joseph Miller, Jacob Miller of Kentucky, John, George, and Peter Miller, Elisabeth Caperton (alias Smith), Mary Price, Catharine Walker, Barbara Maddy, Margaret, Sally, and Rhoda Miller. Wits: John Hutchison, John Harvey, and Reuben George.[1115]

Reuben George deserves special attention, for his lineage goes back to Middlesex County, and his family connects with Richard Lewis of Sunderland Creek, and the Gore-O'Neal family. Robert George of Middlesex County, Virginia, had daughter Elizabeth, who married Robert, son of Robert Williamson and Katherine Lewis, daughter of Richard. Elizabeth George had a sister named Catherine, who married Hugh McTyre on 5 January 1708. Hugh had brother James who married Hannah Boseley of Middlesex on the same day.[1116] James and Hannah's daughter Jane married John Oneal in 1733.[1117] Indications are that it was their son John O'Neal who married Sarah Gore. Jane McTyre had sister Elizabeth who married William Collins,[1118] son of Joseph Collins and Catherine Robinson. Joseph and Catherine Collins had son Capt. Joseph Collins, who married Susanna Lewis, supposed daughter of Zachary or his brother John. Joseph and Susannah's daughter Mary Collins is thought to have married John Brockman (d. 1756 Orange County).[1119]

Reuben George of Caroline County, Virginia, died in 1799. Sons Reuben, Bird, and William George were executors.[1120] Reuben George, Sr., was born to John George of Caroline County, son of Robert George of Middlesex County. John George married first Mary Jordan, and, secondly, Ursula Dudley, daughter of John Dudley and Ursula Beverley.[1121] Richard Dudley George and William Francis George of Monroe seem to have been sons of John Dudley George, who married Lucy Dickinson of Caroline County.[1122]

On 31 July 1792 Richard Dudley George and his wife, Sarah, and William Francis George sold to James Wylie 103 acres on the "South Line of Green Brier River it being part of the Survey William F. & Richard D. George now lives on joining the Lands of William F. George and Augus. Connell[?]...." This tract joined Fleatherer's line.[1123] William George married Jane Johnson by 8 April 1805, for on that date, as heirs of Barnabas Johnson, deceased, they joined with Barnabas Johnson and Jane Johnson to give power of attorney to Robert Johnson of Monroe Coounty to handle their inheritance for them. William and Jane George and Barnabas Johnson had moved to Madison County, Kentucky.[1124]

Boud Estill also moved to Madison County, Kentucky, and on 18 February 1806 Bond (Boud) Estill and his wife, Jane, heir of John Estill, by way of a power of attorney given to Isaac Estill, sold to Thomas Kilpatrick and James Kilpatrick (devisees of Roger Kilpatrick) "400 acres on Hands Creek/Indian Creek adj. William Young now dec'd and Pricilla Gold (now land of Peter Larew)." [1125] In 1798 Peter Larew had bought 200 acres on Hans Creek (a branch of Indian Creek that runs northward towards Greenville) from Thomas and Priscilla Ray of Augusta County, the deal considered a swap.[1126] Peter Larew (1774-1840) had children Margaret, Jacob, Polly F., Nancy, Sarah, Wilson, Elizabeth, Rebecca, Ann, John M., Martha J. This Peter Larew had married Ann Sheilds and was the son of Abraham Larew of Augusta County. Peter's sister Anna married a Mr. Drake.[1127] The Larews had owned land in Spotsylania and Orange Counties, and associated with friends of Zebulon Lewis of Orange.

The Muddy Creek Lewises:

Michael Lewis Cook, in his *Pioneer Lewis Families*, speculated that Samuel Lewis was in some way related to the William Lewis family of Spotsylvania County, Virginia.[1128] Cook theorized it was the sons of William's son George who settled on Muddy Creek, on the north side of the Greenbrier River in Greenbrier County. Yet, to my knowledge, that family was not represented at the estate sale of Samuel Lewis. Isaac Estill, however, became administrator of Samuel's estate, and Isaac's sister, Susanna, married Capt. John McCreery. Their daughter, Susanna, married Benjamin Lewis, and his brother John (d. 1787) married Mary McCreery, sister of Susanna.[1129] John and Benjamin Lewis lived near Muddy Creek in Greenbrier County (WV).

In his will of 1787 John Lewis of Muddy Creek named wife, Mary; sons John, George, Robert, Wm., and Benjamin Lewis; daughters Sarah and Phebe Lewis, Agnes Howard (m. Charles Howard), and Catherine Keeny.

Execs: wife and Mosias Jones and W. H. Cavendish. Wits: Jas. Huston, John Rodgers, and Wm. Jones.[1130] In 1807 Wilson Lewis of Knox County, Kentucky, sold 300 acres on Muddy Creek to David Keeny. The tract abutted lands of Thomas Caraway, Martin Coyser (Kaysor, Kizer), and John Shoemaker. Wits: John Welch, John Humphreys, Thomas Frazer, Moses Keeney.[1131] Wilson Lewis has been assumed to have been a brother of Samuel Lewis (d.1811), but DNA tests do not confirm a relationship. It seems more likely Wilson belonged to the Muddy Creek Lewises, for he settled near them. Yet they did not mention him or his children in their wills. The situation is puzzling: Samuel Lewis's son John named a son *Wilson*, as did a son of Joshua's widow.

John Lewis (d.1787) was of Albemarle County in 1770, when he sold 164 acres in Augusta County to William Graves. This tract, which John patented in 1762, was on the South River of the Shenandoah and abutted lands of Joseph Hannah and Robert Frazier. Wits: Thomas Rodgers, James Kennerley, Jr., and Thomas Turk.[1132]

Mosias Jones, who was an executor of John Lewis's will, sold two tracts in Albemarle County in 1780 to David Mills. The tracts were on the south fork of Rocky Creek and would total about 350 acres. Jones had received two patents on 24 October 1752, one for 400 acres and one for 134. Some land had been set aside for sons Mosias (83 acres) and John (100 acres). Wits: William Jones, Robert Harris, George Webb Jones. On 9 November 1780 David Mills sold the land to Thomas Ballard. The deed was delivered to Js. Ballard, executor of Thos. Ballard, in 1824.[1133] In 1796 Moses [*sic*] Jones of Madison County, Kentucky, appointed his son Thomas Jones of Greenbrier his attorney in order to sell 130 acres to James Kincaid. Wits: Foster Jones, Robt. Jones. In 1797 Moses Jones and wife, Elizabeth, conveyed 130 acres in Greenbrier County to James Kincaid. The tract was near the courthouse and adjacent Gallaspie.[1134] One Mosias Jones, probably the father of the one who married Elizabeth, married Lucy Foster. She married secondly George Webb.[1135]

Land of Mosias Jones was a pointer in 1752 when John Eubank of Fredericksville Parish, Louisa County, sold 290 acres to John Goodall. This tract was on the south fork of Rocky Creek at the foot of the Ragged Mountains and met lands of John Goodall, Mosias Jones, ___Jones, Henry Bunch, and Capt. Joseph Martin's corner.[1136] The David Lewis family owned land at the Ragged Mountains. In 1750 David Lewis gave William Terrell Lewis 200 acres on Moor's Creek. Pointers were the main county road and Joel Terrell's line. Wits: John Lewis, David Lewis, Joel Lewis. In June 1749 David Rees, William Terrell Lewis, and Jno. Harris reported on the improvements on the land of John Grills, located on the Long Branch of Moore's Creek at the Ragged Mountains.[1137] Part of Fredericksville Parish was absorbed by Albemarle County, and the Ragged Mountains are southeast of Charlottesville.

Note that one of the witnesses to the Power of Attorney of Moses (Mosias) Jones was Foster Jones. The Jones family of Orange County had intermarried with the Fosters. Joseph Jones of Orange County, Virginia, made his will in 1781. He referred to his father, Hugh, and his mother, Elizabeth; his sisters Elizabeth and Frances Foster; brother Morton. Exec: William Morton. Wits: Robert B. Morton, Anthony Foster, and George Jones.[1138] In 1766 Henry Foster of Albemarle County sold to Anthony Foster of same 210 acres in Orange County. The tract was bounded by lands of Anthony Foster and John Haskew. Wits: Spencer Bobo, James Walker, Jude Bobo, Andrew Shepherd, John Foster, John Ogg, Manoah Claxton.[1139] In 1770 Lawrence Taliaferro leased 100 acres in Orange County to Hugh Jones and his wife, Elizabeth. The tract abutted lands of Fitzhugh and Wm.Morton. Wits: Joseph Thomas, Jr., George Jones, William Minor. A memorandum followed the deed, cautioning that Hugh Jones did not have the power to sell. Wits: O. Towles, Ephraim Rucker, John Walker.[1140] In 1788 Hugh Jones of Orange County made his will. Legatees were wife, Catey; sons George, Hugh, Morton, Benjamin, Catlett; daughters Frances Foster and Elizabeth Jones; grandson Joseph Jones, son of Elizabeth Jones. Execs: son Catlett Jones and friend William Morton. Wits: Urial Mallory, Jere. Morton, William Mallory.[1141]

Anthony Foster had roots in Spotsylvania County, where his father, Anthony, died in 1763. In his will he referred to his wife, Sarah, and her daughter Sarah Sparks. Legatees: sons Thomas, Anthony, and John Foster; son-in-law James Frasher; granddaughter Mary Foster, daughter of Edmund Foster; grandson Henry Foster, son of John Foster; grandson Robert Foster, son of Thomas Foster; grandsons Anthony and Edmund Bartlett, and their father, Thomas, and his wife, Mary; grandson Anthony Crutcher and his father, Thomas, and wife, Martha. Execs: son Anthony and son-in-law James Frasher. Wits: Isaac Darnett, Thomas Crutcher, Edward Herndon.[1142] William Lewis of Spotsylvania County teamed up with Anthony Foster and John Holloday to secure the bond of Susannah Carr in 1760. Susannah was guardian to orphans of Wm. Carr, Gent. The orphans were Charles Brooks Carr, Agnes Brooks

Carr, Walter Chiles Carr, Phebe Carr, and Thomas Carr.[1143] This Foster connection between John Lewis and Mosias Jones of Albemarle and Greenbrier and William Lewis of Spotsylvania County lends support to Michael Lewis Cook's suspicion that John and William were related. Anthony Foster had married Sarah, the widow of Zachary Sparks.[1144]

Further support for a connection between the William Lewis family of Spotsylvania County and the Muddy Creek Lewises of Greenbrier: The John Lewis of Spotsylvania who married Mary Ann was involved with the Fosters. In 1795 Jno. and Mary Ann Lewis of Spotsylvania County sold 4 ½ acres to John Ferneyhough of Fredericksburg. This parcel was at Sligo, below Fredericksburg, and Jas. Frazer and Jno. Minor had sold it to Gen. Thos. Posey, who had sold it to said Lewis. Wits: Thos. Foster, R. Wellford, Jas. Frazer, Jas. Lewis, Jr., and Wm. Herndon.[1145] In 1795 Jno. Lewis and Mary, his wife, of Spotsylvania County sold 15 acres in Spotsylvania County to Wm. Richards of Culpeper County.[1146] Winifred Lewis, daughter of William and Sarah Lewis of Spotsylvania County, had children William and Sarah Richards. In 1791 John Lewis and wife, Mary Ann, of Spotsylvania County sold 380 acres on Big Clear Creek in Greenbrier County. The tract was adjacent George Clendinen and Wm. McClung. John Lewis appointed Thomas Edgar his attorney to complete the transaction.[1147]

George Jones, who was part of the Hugh Jones family (see will of Joseph Jones), owned land next to William Pannell of Orange County. In 1789 George Jones and wife, Pheeby, sold 200 acres to James Beckham. The tract abutted lines of William Hawkins, William Pannell, Nixon's old road, land of James Beckham, James Robb, and Joseph Hillman. Wits: Seth Spencer, William Herring, William Twisdill.[1148] The Orange County Tithables for 1766 show George Jones following Joseph Dawson, who followed Henry Martin, James Reins, James Roach, Robt. Dawson, Jr., Mrs. Hugh, Mrs. Davis, Isaac George, Robt. Dawson. On this list Zeblon Lewis was several households away from the Dawsons. Zeblon Lewis was followed by Mrs. Susannah Davis, Henry Bourn, Henry Beckham, Jacob Williams, and Wm. Pannill.[1149] Unquestionably, Zebulon Lewis would have known the Jones-Foster family.

Isaac Estill married Elizabeth Frogg, who was part of the General Andrew Lewis group, but also part of the Strother family of Orange and Culpeper Counties. You could say the Andrew Lewis family was represented in Samuel's estate matters, but it seems more likely that Samuel was related to the Strothers than to Andrew Lewis.

In 1797 John and Nancy Walton sold to George Lewis 400 acres that included the saltpetre cave. The land was in Monroe County on Indian and Roaring Creeks adjacent John Williams.[1150] Apparently no representative of that Lewis family (seemingly the Muddy Lewis group) bought at Samuel Lewis's estate sale.

The Singing Cave:
In 1804 William Maddy and wife, Elizabeth, through power of attorney to James Henderson, conveyed to James Maddy 128 acres on the southwest end of Maddy's 1787 survey for 421 acres on Laurel Creek/Indian Creek. The tract was adjacent James Miller, near the Singing Cave.[1151] People enjoyed singing in this cave, because the music would echo repeatedly. It is about a mile from Greenville.[1152]

Indian Creek Primitive Baptist Church:
Samuel Lewis's funeral may well have been held at the Indian Creek Primitive Baptist Church, for it was built on a knoll above Indian Creek and the mouth of Back Creek, and Samuel's land abutted. Today the church still sits, proudly overlooking Highway 122, which follows Indian Creek from south of Union towards the New River. According to Oren Morton's *History of Monroe County, West Virginia*, the church was founded in 1792, and the original building was made of logs and without a fireplace. In the winter, bark fires were constructed on the earth floor. When Indians threatened, sentries were placed on duty outside. The church met once a month, and communion was served on the first Sunday in June. Thousands of people then gathered at the church, many of them traveling long distances and bringing food, which most of them must have eaten under the trees.[1153] Beautiful Indian Creek, racing over its rocky bed, would have been a source of water.

Unfortunately the church records go back only to 1876. The absence of earlier records is blamed on the second wife of Elder Lewis Mann, who is said to have got mad at him and burned the records. Elder Mann was the great uncle of Elder Norvel P. Mann, the author of *The History of Indian Creek Primitve Baptist Church, Greenville, West Virginia*. Elder John Alderson, Jr., became pastor in 1797,[1154] and he officiated when Samuel's son Joshua married Catherine Hill.

Samuel Lewis's heirs, 1814:

The result of the chancery suit over Samuel's land was recorded on 19 August 1814 in Monroe County Court. Members of Samuel's family who were ordered to deed 65 acres to Barnabas Dirgan were John and Zebulen Lewis; Samuel Lewis and wife, Lucy; Joshua Lewis and wife, Catharine; Reuben Hill and wife, Mary, late Mary Lewis; Joseph Scaggs, the late husband of Ann Lewis (who was daughter of Samuel Lewis, Sr., deceased); Samuel, Mary, James, John, and Zebulin Scaggs, children and heirs of said Ann Scaggs. Isaac Hutchison was appointed to convey to Barnabas Dirgan the deed to the parcel, which lay on Back and Indian Creeks.[1155]

The estate settlement of Samuel Lewis was returned on 7 September 1818, by Wm. Shanklin, George Walker, and Jacob Cook.[1156]

Monroe County and the Sweet Springs:

As the crow flies, Samuel's land was eight miles from the New River, but Indian Creek flows northwest from Greenville and then makes a major dip down to Red Sulphur Springs before finding its way to the New River, and the road probably followed the stream. Samuel would have had occasion to fish in its waters, or perhaps to canoe. The New River came into my view on a sunny day, and its sparkling waters played over rocks, tree branches dangling over its banks.

Sweet Springs is about 25 miles to the east of Greenville, and all the activity at the spa would surely have attracted visitors from miles around. William Lewis, brother of General Andrew, settled there in 1783. The stately home, Lynnside, sits on William's property. He married Ann Montgomery, and their daughter Agatha married Oliver Towles of Spotsylvania County in 1793.[1157] Oliver Towles had roots in Middlesex County. His father, Oliver, was born to John Towles and wife, Margaret Daniel, in 1736.[1158] Oliver married Mary Chew, widow of John Smith. Their children were Oliver, Henry Beverley, Ann, and Mary (m. Archibald Dick).[1159] Oliver and Agatha Towles and Archibald Dick, Jr., transferred land in Spotsylvania County in 1796.[1160] Socially it was a surprisingly small world.

The Indians claimed that the Sweet Springs had health benefits, and people from all over the country visited. President George Washington was there in 1797.[1161]

Today water from the springs is bottled and sold. I first saw Sweet Springs on a bright September afternoon as I descended the curvy road down Peters Mountain. Looking to the right and to the left I saw mostly hill sides and the valley road. Buildings and homes were few, and cattle grazed in the meadows. The peaceful beauty of the valley was overwhelming. Surely Samuel Lewis and his family had some occasion to visit the resort.

Samuel married **Mary**. Mary died about 1810 in Monroe County, (West) Virginia.

They had the following children:

+ 52 i. **John^5 LEWIS** was born about 1770.

+ 53 ii. **Zebulon LEWIS** was born Feb 1773.

   54 iii. **Samuel LEWIS** was born about 1775.

> It may have been this Samuel Lewis who was a witness with George Stevenson, Samuel Stevenson, and Samuel Snyder to a deed made on 30 September 1803 between Peter Fleshman and wife, Hannah, and Robert Thomas. The Fleshmans were selling 13 acres in Madison County, Virginia, to Robert Thomas, and the land was bounded by Andrew Glassell's road from his store to Frederick Tanners...."[1162] Oren Morton, in *History of Monroe County, West Virginia*, states that Peter and Michael Fleshman went to Monroe from Madison County, Virginia.[1163] Samuel Snyder appears to have been a son of Adam Snyder and Ann Towles, daughter of Joseph Towles and Sarah Terrill.[1164] Samuel Snyder and Elizabeth, daughter of Barbary Cook, married on 5 September 1796 in Madison County. Daniel Cook was bondsman and he and Tobias Briels (Broyles) were witnesses.[1165] Daniel Cook moved to Monroe County and acquired land on Hans Creek.[1166]
>
> George Stephenson of Monroe married Mary Canterbury. He was born in eastern Virginia

in 1781.[1167] George Stephenson was a buyer at the 1815 estate sale of Jacob Mann, as were Barnabes Durgen and John Halsted.[1168] Jacob Halsted bought 24 ½ acres of the Lewis land on 6 April 1840,[1169] and Chancery awarded a claim on the Lewis land to Durgen. George Stephenson owned part of Samuel Lewis's 300-acre grant by 30 October 1811 when Zebulon Lewis, on behalf of himself and his brother John Lewis of Ohio, sold their part to Reuben Hill, Samuel Lewis, Jr., and Joshua Lewis. George Stepenson's [sic] part was referenced.[1170] And Richard K. (B) Lewis and wife, Mary Ann, of Lawrence County, Ohio; James J. Lewis; Zebedee B. Lewis and wife, Elizabeth, of Monroe County, Virginia, conveyed an additional 39 acres of the Lewis land on 6 April 1840 to George Stephens [sic]. This parcel was described as bordering on lands of Jacob Halstead, Jacob Maddy, and land of the said George Stephens. This deed was delivered to Geo. A. Mann for G. Stevenson on 17 June 1850.[1171]

When Zebulon Lewis first appeared on the Orange County tithables (judgments), he was next to John Tanner, so finding a Tanner named on the same deed as Samuel Lewis sparks our interest. John Tanner, Sr., Abraham Tanner, and John Tanner, Jr., were witnesses on 5 November 1801, when Mary Zimmerman sold 150 acres in Madison County to Paschal Early, land granted to Mary by John Zimmerman in 1776. The land abutted land of Christopher Zimmerman and Andrew Glassell.[1172] The Early family had their roots in Middlesex County, intermarrying with the Bufords who moved to Madison County. Zebulon Lewis, grandfather of this Samuel Lewis, witnessed the will of Leonard Ziglar, who had married Barbara Zimmerman, daughter of Christopher Zimmerman (the immigrant).

The Snyders and Tanners shared a long history: Henry Sneider of Orange County made his will on 30 November 1742, making legacies to wife, Dorothea, and to his daughter Ann Magdalena Aler, who was a widow. He devised to his grandson Henry Aler a tract of 77 acres and half a tract of 400 acres in Shannondore (Shannandoah?). The other half the land he gave to his granddaughter Elisabeth Tanner. Execs: friends Michael Smith and Andrew Gare. Wits: Michael Smith, Andrew Gare, Michael Kafer. George Utz and Michael Kafer were securities for the administration bond.[1173] Benjamin Gaar and William Zachary were sureties for the executors' bond for the estate of Charles Brooking (d. 1795) of Madison County.[1174] *Gaar, Garr, Gare* were varied spellings of the same name.

The 1810 Census for Monroe County included Samuel Lewis: 1 male, age 25-45; 1 female, 26-45; 2 females, age 10-16. He was on page 4. Samuel Lewis, Sr., age 45 years or older, was living alone (page 15); Joshua Lewis's household had 1 male, age 25-45; 1 female, age 26-45; 3 males under 10 years. On the original handwritten page Reuben Hill preceded Saml. Lewis, Sr., and he was followed by Joshua Lewis, and Wm. Tillet followed him. On another handwritten page (page 4?) was Peter Fleshman, followed by Saml. Lewis, two female children in the household, with the two adults.[1175]

On 17 May 1819 William and Hannah Tillett gave permission for their daughter, Lucy Tillett, to marry Jesse Kelly, and Samuel and Lucy Lewis were witnesses. The minister was Mr. David French.[1176] This marriage took place in Giles County, Virginia. Giles had taken some of Monroe's territory in 1806, and at that time it included counties now in south-central West Virginia and western Virginia.

Samuel Lewis was a buyer at the 20 August 1824 sale of Isaac Fisher's estate. Other buyers were John Cook, Thomas Crawford, Robert Cummins; Polly, William, and Rachel Fisher; Charles Gartin, John Gill, Thomas Harvey, Jacob Larew, Wm. Maddy, Isaac Paul, John Peters, Absolam Shanklin, William Smith, Jesse Stodghill, John H. Vawter; George and Harper Walker.[1177]

Samuel and Lucy Lewis sold 46 acres to Elizabeth Halstead on 18 January 1825. This tract was part of the land on Back Creek that Samuel had inherited from his father, and it was the land they were then living on. Some of their land was fenced in, for "Lewises fense" was used as a boundary. Some other markers were a steep hillside, a small branch at the corner of the fence, and Henry Miller's field. The trees marking boundaries included a buckeye, a dogwood, a sugar tree, a hickory, beeches, willows, and a white oak. The deed was delivered in 1826 to William Halstead.[1178]

Samuel married (1) **Elizabeth ELLISON**, "Betsy," daughter of Asa ELLISON and Elizabeth KILPATRICK, on 8 December 1799 in Monroe County, (West) Virginia. Jes Ellison gave permission for his daughter to marry Samuel Luis, and Amos Halsted was surety for Samuel's bond.[1179]

The Ellisons had intermarried with the Kilpatricks, who were part of Isaac Estill's extended family. Ase Ellison and Elisabeth Kilpatrick married on 17 December 1782.[1180] Hugh Paul and Ann Kilpatrick married in 1787.[1181]

John Ellison and Isaac Paul were executors of the will of Roger Kilpatrick, and accounts were settled on 24 August 1801 and recorded in Greenbrier records. The account administrators were Isaac Estill, John Cook, and Thomas Hinton. Buyers and debtors included John Byrnsides, Thomas Hinton, Adam Keller, Thomas Kilpatrick, James McDaniels, Geo Miller, John Paul, Christian Peters, John Reaburn, Richard Shanklin, Robert Steele.[1182]

The progenitors of the Monroe Ellisons were James (d. 1791), and wife, Ann, and they settled on the New River. Their son John (d. 1845) married Frances Paul; and James and Ann Ellison's daughter Mary married Isaac Paul.[1183] Isaac Paul was a son of Hugh Paul and Jane Lynn, sister of Margaret Lynn, who was the mother of Gen. Andrew Lewis.[1184]

Samuel married (2) **Lucy STEPHENSON** on 19 November 1800 in Monroe County, (West) Virginia. Thomas Oliver was surety for Samuel's marriage bond, John Hutchison the witness.[1185]

+ 55 iv. **Anna LEWIS** was born about 1776 and died about 1807.

+ 56 v. **Joshua LEWIS** was born about 1780 and died 22 March 1814.

    57 vi. **Mary LEWIS**, "Polly," was born about 1790.

Polly married **Reuben HILL** on 8 February 1810 in Monroe County, (West) Virginia. Samuel Lewis secured the marriage bond.[1186]

On 30 October 1811 John Lewis (using Zebulin Lewis as his attorney) and Zebulin Lewis, heirs of Samuel Lewis, Sr., conveyed to Reuben Hill, Samuel Lewis, and Joshua Lewis 206 3/4 acres near the mouth of Back Creek, what was left of the 300 acres patented on 10 March 1796 by Samuel Lewis, deceased. The boundaries would be more fully detailed after the land of Barnabas Durgan and George Stepenson's part of the grant were determined.[1187]

Reuben and Mary "Polly" Hill were probably not in Monroe County in May of 1812, for at that time Adam Miller of Albemarle County, acting as attorney on their behalf, sold for $100 their share of the land they inherited from Samuel Lewis, Sr., to Barnabas Durgin. No particular day in May was entered on the deed, but it was recorded on 19 May 1812, no witnesses.[1188] This sale was disputed and wound up in Chancery. See notes involving Joseph and Ann Skaggs.

On 22 June 1815 Jacob Cook, George Walker, and William Shanklin, commissioners, were appointed by Chancery Court, to lay out the lands of Samuel Lewis, deceased, considering both quantity and quality. Reuben and Mary's deed had simply designated their part of the inheritance. Barnabas Dirgan had been allotted 65 1/4 acres along Back Creek. George Stephenson had been deeded 28 acres. In the end Dirgan received 53 acres.[1189]

32. **Elizabeth⁴ LEWIS** (Benjamin³, Zebulon², James¹) died 1798 in Southampton County, Virginia.

Elizabeth was of St. Luke's Parish when she made her will on 2 July 1798. Legatees: four children, Benjamin, Robert, and Jenny Butts, and Polly Nicholson. Execs: friends Zeblon Lewis, Benjamin Lewis. Wits: Zebulon Lewis, Richard P. Clements, James Simmons.[1190]

Elizabeth married **Benjamin BUTTS** on 4 January 1775 in Southampton County, Virginia. Benjamin Lewis was surety for their marriage license, and it was witnessed by Richard Kello and Hardy Harris.[1191]

They had the following children:

    58   i.   **Benjamin[5] BUTTS**

    59   ii.   **Robert BUTTS**

    60   iii. **Jenny BUTTS**

    61   iv. **Polly BUTTS**

39.   **Benjamin[4] LEWIS** (Zebulon[3], Zebulon[2], James[1]) was born November 1763 in Brunswick County, Virginia. He died 24 September 1824 in Brunswick County.[1192]

St. Andrews Parish (Brunswick County) records of 1788 show Benjamin Lewis, Ephraim Parker, and William Mitchell processioning properties between Ingram's and Mize's Road.[1193]

On 27 March 1792 Zebulon King, Benja Lewis, and Ishmael Dunn returned to Brunswick County Court an appraisal of the estate of William Williams. The administrators were John R. Williams, Amy Williams.[1194]

Benjamin's home was called *Woodstock*. He was a merchant and operated wagon trains that went to Petersburg, Virginia. By the time he died, he had acquired large land holdings. Here follows most of the legacies from his will of 1817: He bequeathed the plantation where he was then living (the Gresham Hagood's tract) to wife, Elizabeth; she also was devised the Freeman's tract, land adjoining that sold to Edwin G. Lewis, and land bought from Andrew Ramsey. Son Nicholas E. Lewis received 465 4/10 acres bought from Benjamin E. Brown; son Henry Lewis land bought from Elisha Charles and other parcels, some purchased with money from the settlement of his grandfather Zebulon Lewis's estate; son Zebulon was devised two 130-acre tracts, one of them adjoining the mill; son John F. Lewis received land; son Benjamin all the land in Lunenburg County; son Warner the land whereon Peter Birthright was living, 102 acres bought from Ramsey and John Gee, and 108 acres purchased from Edwin G. Lewis; son James was devised land adjoining land of Nicholas E. Lewis; three sons (Warner, James, and Norborne) received 100 lbs. each. When son John F. Lewis became 21, he was to receive $1,000 left to him by John Clarkson (?). Children John F., Benj., James, Warner, Norborne W., Amanda, and Sally Lewis were each to draw 800 lbs. in Negroes and bonds. Son-in-law Thomas Hicks was willed all the property advanced to him, 30 of the 100 shares of bank stock, the remaining 70 shares to be divided among his (the testator's) six youngest children. Execs: sons Nicholas E. and Henry Lewis, friends Mailease (?) and Thomas Hicks. Wits: James Edmunds, Peter Birthright, Benjamin Seward, Julia Marlin.[1195]

Purchasers at the estate sale included Henry, Benjamin, John F..E. Lewis; Mrs. Lewis; Reuben Hicks; Robert Jackson; Freeman, William, and Edward Walker; Reuben and Thomas Hicks; John Booth; Capt. Mitchell; W.H. Edwards; John B. and Hartwell Rawlings; Capt. M. Davis; Littleberry Baugh; Littleberry Orgam; and Dr. Lewis.[1196]

Benjamin married **Elizabeth Gray EDMUNDS**, daughter of John Flood EDMUNDS and Lucy GRAY, on 13 September 1787 in Brunswick County. . Elizabeth was born 27 January 1771. She died 26 May 1834 in Brunswick County.[1197]

Elizabeth's will was probated 23 June 1834, and legatees included sons Norborne W., Nicholas E., James W., Henry, and John F. E. Lewis; Miss Betsy McKenney (?); grandchildren Benjamin Lewis, Louisa Hicks, Ann E. Hicks, Sally E. Hicks, John H. Lewis, Edwin Hicks. The Methodist Missionary Society was given $150. In a codicil of 23 May 1834, she gave granddaughter Harriet Hicks a Negro boy, daughter Sally E. Hicks, $600. The will was witnessed by Eaton J. Mosely and Sarah T. Moseley.[1198]

Benjamin and Elizabeth had the following children:

    62   i.   **Nicholas Edmunds[5] LEWIS** was born 8 August 1788. He died 28 March 1821. Nicholas married **Martha Ann CLAIBORNE**.[1199]

    63   ii.   **Edwin Gray LEWIS** was born 10 January 1791. He died 10 April 1816.

    64   iii. **Henry LEWIS** was born 12 September 1792. He died 24 August 1879.

                  Henry Lewis graduated from the University of North Carolina and earned his medical degree from the

University of Pennsylvania. Henry had son **James Edmunds LEWIS**, born 1834, who married **Elizabeth ESTILL**.[1200] But I do not know whether she was connected to the Estills of Monroe County.

In 1836, after the end of the Mexican War, the Brunswick Land Company was formed. Each of the directors purchased 20 shares of stock in it, at $1,000 a share, and Dr. Henry Lewis was one of them. The mission of the land company was to speculate in lands in the United States and Texas, and an agent acquired the area now known as Freeport, Texas.[1201]

Henry married **Frances Gibbons STUART**, daughter of Charles Edward STUART and Sarah Blair ASHTON, on 27 March 1817. Frances was born 25 September 1801 in King George County, Virginia.[1202]

65   iv.   **Zebulon LEWIS** was born 6 October 1794. He died 20 March 1816.

66   v.   **Lucy Gray LEWIS** was born 20 October 1796. She died 5 March 1816. Lucy married **Thomas HICKS**.[1203]

67   vi.   **Elizabeth Sandal LEWIS** was born 7 August 1798. She died 11 November 1829. Elizabeth married **Reuben HICKS**.[1204]

68   vii.   **John Flood Edmunds LEWIS** was born 5 April 1800 and died 30 March 1883.

69   viii.   **Benjamin LEWIS** was born 5 January 1803. He died 14 January 1828. Benjamin married **Harriet BOOTH**.[1205]

70   ix.   **Amanda Melvina LEWIS** was born 13 January 1805. She died 28 March 1822. Amanda married **Nicholas Edmunds DAVIS**.[1206]

71   x.   **Sally Edmunds LEWIS** was born 24 February 1807. She died 1 August 1878. Sally married **Thomas HICKS**.[1207]

72   xi.   **Joseph Warner LEWIS** was born 24 February 1809. He died 17 August 1823.

73   xii.   **James William LEWIS** was born 1 October 1810. He died 11 July 1835.

74   xiii.   **Norborne Wesley LEWIS** was born 9 November 1813. He died 6 March 1842.[1208]

51.   **James[4] KILBY** (Epaphroditus[3] KILBY, Katharine[2] LEWIS, James[1]) was born about 1755.

The parentage of James Kilby is unproven, but Christopher Kilby and wife, Catherine Lewis, sold land to Armistead Churchill in 1724, and we would assume that the Armistead Kilby who married in Culpeper County in 1794 was part of this family. Epaphroditus Kilby had brothers William and Christopher, and James could have descended from one of them. Christopher Kilby (d. 1752 in North Carolina) had brother William who lived in Richmond County, Virginia. I have found no mention of his having children, but there is always that possibility. The lawsuit below reveals the children of James and Lucy Kilby. Armistead is not mentioned, so he could have come from a different line than James.

On the other hand, James Kilby may have been the son of the John Kilby whose name appeared among the accounts of Christopher Yowell's estate recorded in Culpeper County in 1763. Some other names in the accounting that are of interest to our story are John Timmerman (Zimmerman?), and John Fleshman. Joseph King was Yowell's administrator.[1209]

The John Kilby who, with wife, Agathy, sold 72 acres to Thomas Gaines of Culpeper County in 1777 may have been the same man. The tract lay between lands of John and Thomas Kilby.[1210] Or this John Kilby may have been the son of James and Lucy.

James married **Lucy SPARKS**, daughter of Thomas SPARKS and Mary TOWLES.[1211]

In his will of 1784 Thomas Sparks named wife, Mary. The children he named: Humphry, Thomas, John, Henry, Ann, Lucy, Mary, and Franky (female). He devised land to James Kilby, Richard Vawter, and Jacob Aylor. Execs: wife, Col. Henry Hill, and Adam Snyder. The lawsuit *Clark v. Towles* provides further information: there was another daughter, Mildred, not named in the will; daughter Mary married 1) Russell Vawter, 2) James Smith; Ann married Jacob Aylor; and Lucy married James Kilby. The children of James and Lucy Kilby were revealed: Thomas, Joseph, LeRoy, John, Henry, and Fannie (married John Creel).[1212] See Samuel Lewis, son of the Samuel Lewis of Monroe County who died in 1811, for more on the Snyders and Aylors.

They had the following children:

75   i.   **Thomas[5] KILBY** married **Matilda HAWKINS** in 1817 in Culpeper County, Virginia.[1213]

76   ii. **Joseph KILBY** married **Celia JENKINS** in 1801 in Culpeper County.[1214]

77   iii. **LeRoy KILBY** married **Eleanor MARY** in 1820 in Culpepr County.[1215] A LeRoy Kilby married **Sarah HILL** in Culpeper County on 13 January 1825.[1216]

78   iv. **John KILBY**

79   v.   **Henry KILBY**.

80   vi. **Fanny KILBY** married **John CREEL** in 1811.[1217]

81   vii. **Armistead KILBY**. Parents unproven. Armistead married **Sarah HAWKINS** in 1794 in Culpeper County Virginia.[1218]

Note that Thomas Kilby also married into the Hawkins family.

The name *Armistead* was also used by the Hill family. Russell and Needles Hill of Culpeper County had migrated there from Middlesex County. And William Hill, son of Russell, married a Miss Wood and had son *Armistead* Hill. Russell Hill and wife, Ann Towles, had son Henry Hill, who married Ann Powell. Their son Thomas Hill married Frances Baptist and had son Ambrose P. Hill, who died on 2 April 1865 during the Union siege of Petersburg during the Civil War. He was a lieutenant general. Fort A.P. Hill in Caroline County is named in his honor.

The Kilbys and Armisteads were involved with each other in North Carolina. See Epaphroditus Kilby, above.

Fifth Generation

52.   **John[5] LEWIS** (Samuel[4], Zebulon[3], James[2], James[1]) was born about 1770.

Information on the ages of the children of John and Rebecca Lewis comes from Michael Lewis Cook's book, *Pioneer Lewis Families*. John died sometime after 1845 in Gallia County, Ohio.[1219]

John Lewis ordered a survey for 250 acres on Laurel Creek in Monroe County in 1805.[1220]

John and Rebecca Lewis moved from Monroe County to Champaign County, Ohio, and after his father, Samuel, died, a power of attorney from him to his brother Zebulon was recorded in Monroe County. The date of the power of attorney was 2 October 1811, and witnesses were Joel Walker and Jonathan Donnel. Zebulon was asked to manage his part of the inheritance.[1221]

Zebulon followed through on 30 October 1811, selling his own and John's part of Samuel's 300-acre patent to Reuben Hill, Samuel Lewis, Jr., and Joshua Lewis. Zebulon and John were assuming that what was left was 206 ¾ acres. Land of Barnabas Durgan and George Stephenson's part of the grant were referred to. Witnessing were Isaac Hutchison, R. Shanklin, John Hutchison, and H. Alexander.[1222]

John Lewis did not find Champaign County to his liking and soon moved to Gallia County, Ohio, where he is named among the early settlers in Walnut Township, along with Henry and Alexander McDaniel, also from Monroe County.[1223]

John married **Rebecca SOWARDS** on 29 April 1791 in Greenbrier County, (West) Virginia.[1224]

Isaac SOWARDS, father of Rebecca, made his will on 21 January 1803. He was a religious man, thanking God for blessing him with his worldly estate. He gave wife, Mileston, the home plantation, including all the buildings and orchards; 1 horse, 2 cows, and their increase, 4 sheep and their increase; 22 hogs, all the fowl; all the furniture. After her death, Isaac Sowards, Jr., was to inherit her estate. The other children were each given 5 shillings sterling. They were Thomas, Griffin, Ruth, Mileston, Rebeka, and Nelly. Execs: wife, Mileston, and son Isaac. Wits: Elijah Ballard, Richard Ramsay, William Brown, and Phillip Ballard.[1225]

They had the following children:

      82   i.   **Eleanor**[6] **LEWIS** was born 1795 in Greenbrier County, (West) Virginia. Eleanor married **Henry EAGLE** on 18 November 1817 in Gallia County, Ohio.[1226]

+   83   ii. **Samuel LEWIS** was born 1797.

+   84   iii. **Jesse LEWIS** was born 1800.

+   85   iv. **Wilson LEWIS** was born 1803 and died 11 December 1883.

+   86   v.   **Joshua LEWIS** was born 1806. He died 1859.

      87   vi. **Mary LEWIS** was born 1808. Mary married **Joseph HASKINS** on 1 June 1826.[1227]

      88   vii. **Anna LEWIS** was born 1811. Ann married **Thomas CLARK** on 25 December 1831 in Gallia County, Ohio.[1228]

53.   **Zebulon**[5] **LEWIS** (Samuel[4], Zebulon[3], James[2], James[1]) was born February 1773. He died in Ohio.

The names and birth and death dates of the children of Zebulon and Jean were taken from *Pioneer Lewis Families*, by Michael Lewis Cook. Cook also supplied information on their marriages, birthdates, Zebulon's date of birth, and Jean's birth and death date. Zebulon and Jane were systematic in the naming of their children, the first two named for her parents and the second two for his.[1229]

A survey for 100 acres of land was recorded for Zebulon Lewis on 16 March 1799. The tract was "on the Waters of Indian Creek & Laurel Creek joining the lands of Samuel Lewis, James Miller & Richard Gartin...." Zebulon had been assigned the use of Treasury Warrant No. 1,962, belonging to Robert Cumming.[1230]

Clark County, Ohio, Newspaper Abstracts 1829-1832, include a notice of a farm sale in Springfield Township by James L. Torbert, agent for the heirs of John O. Farrell, deceased. Zebulon Lewis was living on the land.[1231]

Zebulon married **Jean BEST**, daughter of Francis BEST and Isabella COALTER, on 1 March 1800 in Monroe County, (West) Virginia. Francis Best secured the marriage bond for Zebulon Lewis.[1232] Jean was born 13 May 1784 and died 3 March 1841.

Zebulon and Jean had the following children:

      89   i.   **Francis**[6] **LEWIS** was born 11 December 1800.

      90   ii. **Isabella LEWIS** was born 3 June 1802.

      91   iii. **Samuel LEWIS** was born 7 February 1804 in Virginia and died 8 December 1845.

      92   iv. **Mary LEWIS** was born 7 August 1806 in Virginia and died 5 February 1891. She did not marry.

      93   v.   **Elizabeth LEWIS** was born 11 May 1808 in Virginia and died 16 January 1881. She did not marry.

      94   vi. **John LEWIS** was born 6 March 1810 and died 23 January 1858.

      95   vii. **Jane LEWIS**.

      96   viii. **Zebulon LEWIS** was born 13 November 1813 in Virginia. Zebulon married **Mary COON** on 15 February 1838.

      97   ix. **Eliza Ann LEWIS** was born 1 January 1816 in Virginia and died 10 May 1895. Eliza Ann married a MR. **PERKINS** (Isaac or James) on 23 May 1861 in Montgomery County, Indiana.

      98   x.   **James G. LEWIS** was born 18 November 1817 and died 6 November 1899. He did not marry.

99	xi.	**Joseph LEWIS** was born 24 September 1819.
100	xii.	**Nancy Best LEWIS** was born 5 December 1822 in Springfield, Ohio, and died 15 March 1897 in Crawfordsville, Indiana. On 11 October 1840 she married **WARREN ROWAN POOLE** (1819-1861).

55. **Anna**[5] **LEWIS** (Samuel[4], Zebulon[3], James[2], James[1]) was born about 1776. She died about 1807.

On 19 August 1814 a decision was made in Chancery Court to award Barnabus Durgan 65 1/4 acres of land from Samuel Lewis's 300-acre survey. The heirs of Samuel Lewis, deceased, were named in the deed: John Lewis, Zebulon Lewis, Samuel Lewis and wife, Lucy; Joshua Lewis and wife, Catharine; Reuben Hill and wife, Mary; Joseph Scaggs, "the late husband of Ann Lewis who was the daughter of Samuel Lewis, Senr., Dec'd," and Samuel, Mary, James, John, and Zebulin Scaggs, heirs of Ann Scaggs.[1233]

Anna married **Joseph SKAGGS** on 24 November 1796 in Greenbrier County, (West) Virginia.[1234]

Anna's marriage to Joseph Skaggs appears in the Greenbrier County records, because Monroe County was not separated from Greenbrier until 1799. John Alderson was the minister. Alderson preached at different locations and could very well have performed the marriage at the Primitive Baptist Church on Indian Creek.

It is assumed that Joseph was a son of John and Catherine Scaggs, for on 19 October 1802 they conveyed 125 acres on Wolf Creek to Joseph Scaggs. On the same day John and Catherine conveyed 125 acres to Richard Scaggs. On 19 November 1802 they conveyed 125 acres to James Scaggs.[1235]

In 1774 Thomas Skaggs had 270 acres surveyed along Wolf Creek. At that time the area was still part of Botetourt County, Virginia.[1236] John Skaggs claimed 668 acres along the Wolf, adjacent John Hall, in 1795. Thomas Alfred bought part of the 668-acre survey in 1787, and in 1795 John Skaggs was claiming part of it. Between 1802 and 1809 it was conveyed to Joseph Skaggs.[1237]

In 1808 Joseph Skaggs married Margaret Swope, and her sister Jane married Samuel Stephenson in 1802.[1238]

This Skaggs family were among the charter members of the Greenbrier Baptist Church, established by Elder John Alderson, Jr., in 1781. The original members were John, Mary, and Thomas Alderson; John Kippers; John, Katherine, Lucy, and Joseph Scaggs; John Sheppard; Bailey, Ann, and James Wood. Alderson served as pastor for two years at Linville Baptist Church in Rockingham County, Virginia. (Under colonial rule he could not be called *Reverend* because he was not part of the established church.) He made his first home in the Greenbrier area at Jarrett's Fort on Wolf Creek (now in Monroe County). Later he claimed 1,750 acres on the south side of the Greenbrier River just west of the Alderson Hotel (Alderson, WV).[1239]

They had the following children:

101	i.	**Samuel**[6] **SKAGGS** was born about 1797.
		On 19 October 1816 Joseph and Anne (Lewis) Scaggs's children, Samuel, Polly, James, John, and Zebulen, of Greenbrier County sold 50 acres to John and Jacob Mann of Monroe County. It was the land Anne had inherited from her father, Samuel Lewis, Sr. Samuel Skaggs had married by this time, and he and his wife, **Icy**, signed the deed. Their dividend was on the north side of Indian Creek, at the mouth of Back Creek.[1240]
102	ii.	**Mary (POLLY) SKAGGS**.
103	iii.	**James SKAGGS**.
104	iv.	**John SKAGGS**.
105	v.	**Zebulon SKAGGS**.

56. **Joshua⁵ LEWIS** (Samuel⁴, Zebulon³, James², James¹) was born about 1780 in Virginia. He died 22 March 1814 in Norfolk, Virginia.[1241]

Christopher and Margaret Hand gave permission on 23 October 1802 for Joshua Lewis to marry their daughter Margert. Joshua's marriage bond was signed on the same day, Wm. Hutchinson, security. John Hutchison was the witness.[1242] Yet, on 21 April 1806 Christopher Hand wrote this note, "This is to sertyfy that I give My Douter Margret Hand Unto John Shirs in Marage as witness My Hand. Test. George Hand." On 28 April 1806 John Shires signed his marriage bond, with George Hand his security.[1243] Oren F. Morton, in his book, *History of Monroe County, West Virginia*, states that Margaret Hand, daughter of Christopher and Margaret Hand, married John Shires in 1806, no mention of its being Margaret's second marriage.[1244] So it looks as if the marriage planned between Joshua and Margaret Hand never took place. Divorce was uncommon in those days.

On 29 October 1804 Joshua Lewis signed the bond for his marriage to Catharine Hill "of this county." Samuel Lewis was surety. The witness was Isaac Hutchison, DC.MC. (Deputy Clerk, Monroe County). No record was in the file showing that anyone gave permission for Catherine to marry, so she must have been 21 or older. Joshua and Catherine were married by Elder John Alderson.[1245]

The birth years of Joshua and Catherine's sons James J. Lewis, Richard Burton Lewis, and Samuel Lewis were derived from ages given by their mother, Catherine, when she applied for her widow's pension on 10 March 1853 in Lawrence County, Ohio. James was 47, Richard 44, and Samuel 42.[1246] On the Monroe County Census of 1810, Joshua was in the 25-45 age group, Catherine in the 26-45 age group, and they had 3 sons under 10.[1247]

Joshua Lewis was selected to become a constable in 1799, when Monroe County was separated from Greenbrier County. Other constables chosen were Isaac Cole, John Cottell, William Dickson, Robert Dunbar, George Foster, Enos Halstead, Thomas Lowe. Joshua was told to serve in the militia company of Estill.[1248]

Greenbrier County records of 1801 include the appraisal of the estate of William Feamster. Joshea Lewis and a John Lewis were named among the numerous bonds and notes.[1249]

Joshua Lewis and the Ballards and Halsteads:

Margaret Ballard wrote a book on the Ballards of Monroe County, and in it she noted that Philip Ballard dug for salt near the mouth of Indian Draft in Monroe County. She mentioned a note that was found among the Young papers at the homestead on Indian Creek. It was dated 4 November 1800 and was from Joshua Lewis and John Halstead to Philip Ballard for 1 pound, 10 shillings, 6 pence.[1250]

John Halstead and Elisabeth Mann married on 27 May 1799, Adam Mann, witness, and Henry Miller, surety.[1251] Adam Mann had married Polly Maddy in 1783.

This Ballard family had lived in Spotsylvania, Orange, and Albemarle Counties in Virginia. In 1756 Phillip Ballard and wife, Ann, of Orange County sold 200 acres in Spotsylvania County to John Penn. Wits: Peter Gatewood, Alexr. Spence Head, and John Tureman.[1252] On 5 July 1791 John Craig of Albemarle County sold 400 acres on Doyle's River to Johnston Ballard of Orange County.[1253] Doyle's River begins up in the Blue Ridge near Albemarle's border with Rockingham County and flows south.

Johnson Ballard was a son of William Ballard (1732-1799) who married Elizabeth Step (d. 1830) of Orange County, Virginia. William and Elizabeth had other children: Jeremiah, who married Jaley Thompson; Millie, who married Jacob Mann in 1804; William, who married Mollie Snow; Nancy, who married William Farrell; Mollie, who married Mathias Kessinger in 1803; Willis, who married Isabel Thompson in 1813; James, who married Jennie Keaton in 1804; Lucy, who married, first, John Stodghill.[1254] Lucy's second husband was John Goodall, whom she married in 1808 in Monroe County.[1255] This John Goodall may have been the one who was surety when Parks Dare married Susannah Harvey of Monroe in 1810.[1256] Parks Deer would be a witness for Joshua Lewis's widow in Lawrence County, Ohio. See below.

The Harvey family of Orange County is at the center of a lot of Monroe County ties. About the time the Revolutionary War ended (the British surrendered in 1781), children of John Harvey and wife, Margaret, of Orange moved to Monroe. Benjamin (b. 1751) married Susan, daughter of William Ballard; Nicholas married Sarah; John married Elizabeth; Elizabeth (b. 1768) married John Stodghill. A James and a Joseph Harvey may have been other children.[1257]

The Harvey-Stodghill connection would seem to place the Harveys in the western part of Orange County, but in 1764 a John Harvey was a witness to a deed from Robert Dawson and wife, Mary, to Arjalon Price. The tract abutted lands of Ware, Conway, and Thornton. Other witnesses: J. Cr. Webb, William Beckham, Wm. Pitcher.[1258] Robert Dawson lived in the northern part of Orange County, near Germanna. There may have been two separate Harvey families in Orange County during this period. See Zebulon Lewis of Orange County.

We find John Goodall and John Stodghill involved with the same people in Orange County. A John Goodall was surety for Edward Williams in 1766 when he became executor for the will of his father, Francis Williams, of Orange County. Francis named his wife, Elizabeth, in his will and sons Edward and Francis. Wits: Wm Morris, John Stodghill, and Samuel Bullis. Other sureties were John Ogg and John Shackleford.[1259]

James Step, son of Joshua (d. 1783) of Orange County, married Elizabeth Lucas, daughter of John.[1260] It may have been their daughter who married William Ballard.

In 1776 William Strother, Robert Dawson, James Lewis, Anthony Hughes, and John Craig were witnesses to a deed to Joshua Step, Eve and Antherd Salmon, and Edmond Garnet. See Zebulon Lewis of Orange County for more on this deed. Anestar Step married Capt. William Sims, and their daughter Nancy married Ambrose Brockman, uncle of the Catherine Brockman who married John F. Lewis, son of Joshua.[1261]

Joshua Lewis of Monroe County knew John Halstead well enough to sign a note jointly with him. When Joshua's brother Samuel married Elizabeth Ellison in 1799, Amos Halsted was surety for Samuel's bond. How did this Lewis family become so close to the Halsteads? There is no evidence of a marriage between the two families at that time. Yet, we remember that Joshua's father, Samuel, had a survey made that abutted land of Paul Long. In 1743 Philip Long of Orange County sold 205 acres to Henry Heastand (Halstead?) of same. The tract was on the Sharendo (Shenandoah) River side. Wits: John Newport, Christopher Zimmerman, Abraham Strigler, Joseph Bloodworth.[1262] This deed was recorded in Orange County, Virginia, because Augusta County was not formed until 1745, when land west of the Blue Ridge was separated. Christopher Zimmerman's daughter Barbara married Leonard Ziglar, and Zebulon Lewis, father of Samuel, witnessed his will, recorded in Culpeper County. Joseph Bloodworth's road is referred to in Culpeper County records. The first settler in the area that is now Rockingham County was Jacob Stover, who claimed 5,000 acres in 1733. In 1738 Adam Miller bought some of Stover's Massanutten land, and Joseph Bloodsworth bought 820 acres from Stover. In 1742 Bloodsworth sold it to Adam Miller.[1263] Philip Long and Paul Long had also bought some of Stover's Massanutten land.[1264] Zebulon Lewis and son Samuel may have made the acquaintance of Paul Long before moving to Monroe.

In Monroe County the Halsteads lived beside the Bootens, descendants of the Hill family of Middlesex County, relatives of this Lewis family. On 28 June 1790 Joseph Lawyers and wife, Elizabeth, sold 74 acres to James Holstead. The tract was on Indian Creek, adjacent Wm. Booten and Ellison. On 28 June 1791 Joseph and Elizabeth Lawyers (or Liars) sold 95 acres to Wm. Booten on Indian Creek, adjacent James Holstead and Nicholas Null.[1265]

Travis Booton, son of Lewis Booton, married Ruth Estill in 1786 in Greenbrier County. Lewis Booton was a son of William Booton and Judith Hill, who married in Middlesex County, Virginia, in 1738. See the section on Samuel Lewis, father of Joshua.

Joshua Lewis, soldier of 1812:

In Ohio in 1853 Catherine applied for her pension as a widow of Joshua Lewis, who died in service to his country during the War of 1812. Joshua served under Capts. Henry Hill and Thos. Bibb from 29 January 1814 to 14 May 1814. Parks Deer, about 59 years old, on 8 July 1853 signed a statement on behalf of Catherine Lewis, saying that he had served with Joshua and that Joshua died of a disease contracted during service. Deer had been issued Land Warrant No. 9,053 for his service.[1266] Oren Morton, in *History of Monroe County*, states that soldiers from Monroe defended Norfolk and suffered from the change of climate.[1267] In 1836 the Common Council of Norfolk, grateful for the service of the soldiers from the upper country who had defended their town, arranged to have a brick wall built around their graves. Many were victims of a terrible plague that swept through their area in the winter of 1814-1815. The plan was to put the bodies in a common grave and erect a monument to them.[1268] I talked with a librarian in Norfolk a few years ago. He was of the opinion that a parking lot had been built over the graves of these soldiers.

At the beginning of the War of 1812 the newly enlisted men wore "unbleached, tow-linen hunting shirts and trousers." They wore low-crown hats. The soldier could carry a tomahawk, knife, cartridge box, bayonet and tin canteen thanks to the leather girdle he strapped around his waist. He had a musket and a linen knapsack with a blanket. These were covered with oilcloth to keep out the rain. The arms and pack weighed 35 pounds, and the soldiers often marched 25 miles a day. In January of 1812, due to complaints, Governor James Barbour changed the uniform requirements, the main body of the militia being assigned blue hunting shirts with a red fringe. Yet many soldiers wore the same clothing in which they had enlisted.[1269]

Joshua Lewis of the New Valley Church:

A curious coincidence: When John Alderson, Jr., was still serving as minister in Rockingham County, Virginia, a Joshua Lewis presented himself to Alderson's congregation with recommendation from the New Valley Church. He had an interest in becoming a preacher in Greenbrier County, and on 11 July 1772 he was to try out his gifts. There was no mention that anyone else from New Valley, a wife, for instance, had accompanied him. Mary Henton, wife of Evan Hinton, was baptized in 1772 at Alderson's church.[1270] A relative of this Evan Hinton was in touch with Richard Burton Lewis, son of Joshua Lewis of Monroe County, over a hundred years later.

The New Valley Church of Loudoun County, Virginia, met north of Leesburg in the Lucketts area. It was officially established as a Baptist Church in 1767 by people from the Great Valley in Pennsylvania, with some Virginians in addition.[1271] William Jones of Loudoun County, in his will of 26 March 1771, donated one and one-half acres adjoining his own plantation to the Baptists, who already had built a meeting house on it. Joseph Thomas was the minister, and William Lewis and Thomas George were elders. William Jones named his wife, Mary, daughter Mary Griffith, sons Joshua and James Jones. Son James was the executor, and William asked him to make deeds to William Lewis and John Griffith after they paid what was due. Wits: J. Clapham, William Lewis, Sarah Griffith.[1272] The Claphams settled in Lancaster County in the middle 1600s and intermarried with the Lawsons and the Thatchers, who intermarried with the Pannells of King George County. The William Pannell who married Sarah Bailey had sister Catherine, who married Thomas Thatcher. Catherine and Thomas had children Frances, Elizabeth, William, Thomas, Samuel, Joshua, James, and John. Thomas Thatcher's father was Sylvester Thatcher, and his sister Mary married William Clapham.[1273] William Clapham's father, William, married Elizabeth Madestard, widow of Epaphroditus Lawson of Lancaster County (d. 1652).[1274] I was at the Loudoun Museum in Leesburg a few years ago and was told that there had been a migration of Lancaster County families to Loudoun County.

A "Jahua" Lewis was charged with one tithable, that is, 5 (squirrel) scalps, in 1770 in Loudoun County, Virginia. "Jahua" Lewis was preceded by Henry Daniel and John Daniel, who were preceded by Joseph Growa (Gore?). William Brown, David Carson, Jno. Nipton were grouped together following Jahua Lewis.[1275] If this was the same Joshua Lewis who showed up at John Alderson's church in Rockingham County in 1772, he would have been 16 years old or more and, given his proximity to some Daniels and a man who seems to have been a Gore, he had Middlesex County connections. Presumably it was this Joshua Lewis who showed up at Alderson's church. If this man had been born in 1750, he would have been 64 in 1814 and too old to join the fight against the British in Norfolk. He may have been related somehow to the Joshua Lewis who married Catherine Hill, but he wasn't the same man.

Joshua married **Catherine HILL** of Monroe County, (West) Virginia, on 29 October 1804. Samuel Lewis was surety.[1276]

Catherine and Joshua's marriage license declared her to be of Monroe County, so we look for her parents among the Hill families that were living in Monroe at the time. There was a family of Hills that resided in Sinks Grove, about half-way between Union and the Greenbrier River. Spencer and William Hill, sons of Martin, built the first houses there. Martin married Margaret Boyd. Son Spencer married Margaret Patton; son William married Barabara Nickell; daughter Nancy married James Curry, and daughter Malvina, William Nickell.[1277]

The Literary School records for Monroe County (WV) for 1836 show Catherine Lewis's name entered as the parent or guardian of Madison Lewis, age 14.[1278] Madison is rumored to have been a son of Catherine's son James J. Lewis by a marriage to an unknown person, but proof has yet to be revealed. Catherine would not likely have been thought of as guardian or parent if James were the father and living in the area at the time.

The question arises as to why Catherine called her son *Madison*. There may have been a Madison Hill living in the Greenbrier area at about the same time that Catherine Hill was born. Greenbrier court records of 1787 include this entry: "John Dyer, Hugh Miller & Samuel Price ordered to locate a road from John Dyers to Madison Hill, where the Great Road leads up to the court." [1279] But Madison Hill may have been a hill that happened to be called *Madison*. And Dyer owned land in the Muddy Creek area, on the north side of the Greenbrier River.[1280]

There was a Madison Hill found in Amherst County, Virginia, where a Hill family from the Goochland-Louisa-Albemarle region of Virginia had settled. On 14 August 1790 Maddison Hill married Polley Day; Mary Ann Day was named as parent. Wits: Samuel Day, Wm. Loving, Sukey Loving, Thos. Day.[1281] In 1791 Mark Lively married Mary Hill, daughter of John Hill of Amherst. Sureties and witnesses included Joseph Lively, Jr., Will Loving, Jr., S. Brown, Lawrence Long.[1282]

Madison and Polly Hill were of Russell County, Virginia, in 1809 when they conveyed 104 acres on Buffalo Ridge in Amherst County to Francis Hill. The land was adjacent that of Reuben Norvell and Jas. Dillard. Wits: Ricd.Thurmond, Abner Padget, Archibald Crews, Wm. Lyon.[1283] The *Douglas Register* of Goochland County, Virginia, includes the marriage of Spencer Norvil and Frances Hill on 22 February 1770.[1284] Spencer Norvell appears in Amherst County records. In 1821 Wm. D. Hill and wife, Nancy, of Amherst County made a deed of trust to Reuben Norvell and Prosser Powell for 89 acres on the Lynch Road. They owed to Spencer Norvell and Nelson C. Dawson.[1285]

. Madison Hill was the son of Susannah Gilliland of Amherst County, who made her will on 15 October 1807. (She had been married previously to William Hill.) Reuben Norvel qualified as administrator, and bondsmen were Anthony Rucker and Nich. Harrison. Her will named her daughters Eliz. Thurmond and Judith Lyon (wife of Alex. Lyon), granddaughter Susanna Lyon; and granddaughter Susannah Hill, daughter of son Maderson. Execs: Reuben Norvell and Js. Marr. Wits: Stephen Rees, Pasey Rees, Betsey Rees, Rebecca Rucker.[1286] Judith Hill had married Alexander Lyon of Culpeper County on 7 October 1786 in Amherst. He was a son of Wm. Lyon of Culpeper and she, the daughter of Wm. and Susannah Hill. Wits: Francis Woods, George Loving, John Taliaferro, Orson Knight, Jessay Wood, Thos. Johnson, Reuben Penny, Thos. Grimes.[1287] Peter Lyon of Albemarle County marred Bettie Norvil of Goochland County in 1771.[1288]

With the close association of Reuben Norvell with this Hill family, we would expect to find a Reuben Hill. In 1822 Eliz. Thurman of Amherst County conveyed to her only son, Wm. D. Hill, slaves, stock, furniture. The stock was to be delivered to Polly Ricketts. Wits: Jno. London, Sally Ricketts, Reuben D. Hill.[1289] Note: Catherine Hill and Joshua Lewis married in 1804 and Joshua's sister Mary (Polly) Lewis and Reuben Hill married in 1810. It would be surprising if Catherine and Reuben were not related. I have not discovered the identity of the wife of Reuben D. Hill.

Catherine Hill named a son *Madison,* and Madison Hill had connections to the Lively family. Catherine may have been related to James Hill and wife, Elizabeth Lively, for by 1826 they had moved from Amherst County to Monroe County. On 19 February 1826 Jas. Hill, Jr., and Eliz. of Monroe County conveyed to Jas. Hill, Sr., 41 ½ acres on the Lunch (Lynch) Road. This deed, recorded in Amherst County, was witnessed by Wm. Graham and Jno. Henchman, justices of the peace of Monroe County.[1290] In 1833 Philip Lively of Monroe County gave to Jas. Hill of Monroe County $425 (a seventh part of interest in the estate of Jas. Lively). Wits: Jos. R. Hill, Levi Skaggs, Lanty Graham.[1291]

Mark Lifely (Lively) of Albemarle County made his will in 1750. He named wife, Mary; sons William, Bethel, John, Joseph, and Benjn. Lifely. Execs: wife and Thomas Cawthorn. Wits: Thomas Cawthorn, William Woodson. Wife, Mary, obtained probate, and Samuel Talliaferro, Thomas Jopling, and Henry Burrus were securities for her bond.[1292] We can see below that Cottrell Lively had son Mark, and above we saw that Mark Lively married Ann Hill in Amherst. I have not found the exact connection between Cottrell Lively of Monroe and the Livelys of Amherst, but they obviously were related.

Before the Revolution, Cottrell Lively, Sr., had moved from Albemarle County to Monroe. His homestead was near Brush Creek, in a village called *Cashmere*, south of Ballard in Monroe County. Cottrell had son Cottrell born in 1773, who married Sarah Maddy. Other children born to Cottrell, Sr., were Benjamin, who married Sarah Bostick in 1803; Joseph, Mark, and Judith; and Martha, who married a Burris. Cottrell, Jr., and Sarah (Maddy) had the following children: Jane, who married Loammi Pack in 1811; William (O.); Judith, who married Peter McGhee; John, who married Polly Parker; Thomas, who married Polly Riner in 1828; Madison, who drowned; Mary, who married John Smith in 1840; Sarah, who married Anderson Smith in 1833; and Wilson (1815-1865), who married successively Rebecca Swinney, Jane Coalter, and Eliza Gwinn. Wilson Lively served as sheriff for Monroe County and was a member of the Virginia Assembly.[1293]

Catherine (Hill) Lewis's son Madison named a son *Wilson*. And the given names *Madison* and *Wilson* appeared among descendants of Cottrell Lively and Sarah Maddy. The name *Wilson* appeared in more than one line of the Maddy family of Monroe.[1294] The Ballards of Albemarle named a son *Wilson*: Wilson Ballard and Fanny Austin married in 1812 in Albemarle County. Eli Austin signed the bond, and Nancy Austin, guardian of Fanny, gave consent. Wits: David O. Ballard, Eli Austin. In 1816 Parks Goodall of Orange County married Elizabeth Austin, Eli and Nancy Austin giving consent for their ward to marry him. Garrett and David Austin witnessed the consent. Garrett Austin signed the bond, and William Wertenbaker was the witness.[1295]

In 1815 Monroe County Commissioner Isaac Hutchison had 161 acres conveyed to James Maddy. The tract was on Laurel Creek, adjacent Joseph Lively.[1296] So Catherine Hill for sure would have known the Lively-Hill family that had connections to Madison Hill.

Catherine Hill's name appeared among notes due to or from John Maddy's estate. The appraisal was returned on 25 November 1824 by Robert Shanklin, John H. Vawter, and John Thomas. There were also notes on John McNeally, Thomas Dunn, John Ferrell, Henry Maddy, Jesse Minter, and Nancy Barnes.[1297]

Catherine (Hill) Lewis in Ohio and her pension papers:

By sometime in 1840 Catherine Lewis had migrated to Lawrence County, Ohio. Most likely she traveled with her son James and his wife, Elizabeth Asbury. The route they took is unknown to me. Farley's Trace (see Isaac Scarborough, who m. Mary Ward) would have taken them to Louisa, Kentucky, where Tug Fork joins Levisa Fork to form the Big Sandy River. The Big Sandy separates Kentucky and West Virginia and becomes part of the Ohio River opposite Lawrence County, Ohio.

It is more likely Catherine and her family took the Old State Road (now U. S. 60) from Lewisburg to Charleston and on to the Ohio. The road had been completed to the Big Sandy by 1832.[1298] Stage coaches pulled by horses traveled daily between Richmond, Virginia, and the Ohio River, carrying mail and passengers. Families trekked westward in their Conestoga wagons. Herds of cattle and hogs were driven along this road, and road-side taverns sprung up.[1299] It wouldn't have been a lonely route.

Roads often followed the rivers and streams, and much of Route 60 follows the banks of the Kanawaha. The New River, on the edge of Monroe County, flows north and joins the Gauley (famous for its white-water rapids), and the two become the Kanawha River. Not long after its waters pass through Charleston, the mountains end. The Kanawha continues in a northwest course towards Point Pleasant to its confluence with the Ohio River opposite Gallia County, but Route 60 goes west to Kenova, where the Big Sandy and the Ohio meet. Whatever route that Catherine and her family took, it must have been good to leave the mountains and have only hills to contend with. It seems strange that in this day and age I should get a sense of relief after making it through the mountains of central West Virginia. They are beautiful, by the way. But after driving through Charleston, I turn off U.S. 64 to follow the Kanawaha toward Point Pleasant, and I relax. Moisture from the river fills the air and breathing seems easier. The fields that line the river are filled with corn and other crops and there are silos, barns, and large frame farm houses. Cattle graze in lush meadows. Villages have sprung up. The Kanawha and Ohio River valleys must have given people a sense that life would be easier.

Catherine seems to have been in Lawrence County about 10 years before she got the paper work started on the pension due her as a war widow. According to a document of 1853 signed by James E. Stewart, Examining Clerk, the Act of 16 April 1816 allowed Catherine, as the widow of an 1812 soldier, half pay as a pensioner. It indicated her marriage had been proved by a former document (a letter from John Hutchinson, Clerk of Monroe County, dated 23 November 1850) and that she was due five years half pay at the rate of $3.50 per month, beginning 3 February 1853. Her lack of a remarriage and the authenticity of her claim were supported by the testimony of Nathaniel Burcham, a Justice of the Peace and an acquaintance of hers for 11 years. S. McCown, also a J.P., took a similar statement from James J. and Richard B. Lewis. On 30 May 1851, Lewis Anderson, Clerk of the Court of Common Pleas for Lawrence County, verified the qualifications of Burcham and McCowan. In 1853 Parks Deer of Lawrence County, Ohio, who had served with Joshua in Capt. Thomas Bibb's company, signed a statement that declared he was well acquainted with Joshua Lewis and his widow, Catharine Lewis.

On 10 March 1853 Catherine Lewis, age 64, of Windsor Township, Lawrence County, signed an affidavit declaring that she was the widow of Joshua Lewis and that he had died at Norfolk in the line of duty while serving in the 3rd Regiment of the Virginia Militia. She also swore that she had the following children by Joshua: James Lewis (47 years old), Richard Lewis (44), and Samuel Lewis (42), all of them over 16 at the date of the Act (3 February 1853). Also she stated the Military Bounty Land Act of 28 September 1850 had awarded her 40 acres for Joshua's service. She had received Warrant No. 68,990.

On 11 March 1853 Samuel Lewis (55 years old) and Wilson Lewis (sons of Joshua's brother John) made oath that Catherine was the widow of Joshua Lewis and had not remarried and that she had by him sons James, Richard, and Samuel. On 8 July 1853 Catherine gave power of attorney to Lewis Anderson to receive what was due her in this claim. James White and R. B. Lewis witnessed. On 7 February 1859 Lewis Anderson sent a declaration on behalf of Catherine for pension money with the following note: "Mrs. Lewis is almost helpless from age and extreme corpulence." He added that he hoped the document he was enclosing was sufficient and that "Mrs. Lewis was a pensioner under the act of 1853 and drew five years pension." In another letter Lewis Anderson described her as old and in destitute circumstances. A. Griffith, J. P., had Catharine Lewis sign another affidavit (she used an *X*), and at that time, 18 May 1859, she was said to be 70. She was then a resident of Rome Township and her mail was to be sent to Lewis Anderson at Athalia, Ohio. The letter was witnessed by Lewis Anderson and Griffin Sowards. Mark S. Bartram, Clerk, certified that A. Griffith, Esq., was acting Justice of the Peace for Athalia.

Catherine used her Bounty Land Warrant No. 68,990 for 40 acres (resulting from the Act of 1850) to claim land in Lawrence County, Ohio, in the Chillicothe, Ohio, Land District. It was in Windsor Township in the southeast quarter of Section 1, Township 2, Range 16 (recorded in patent vol. 267:108). Her second Bounty Land claim was Warrant No. 63,794, granted her by the Act of 1855 for certain officers and soldiers in the military service of the United States. It was for 120 acres. This grant she sold to Joshua H. Bates of Hamilton County, Ohio. In 1856 he used this warrant to claim land in Section 25, Township 9, Range 3, in the Springfield, Illinois, Land District (recorded in patent vol. 205:296).[1300]

On 4 May 1855 Catherine Lewis sold 44 acres in Section 1, Township 2, Range 16, to John Rapp.[1301]

Joshua and Catherine had the following children:

+ 106   i.   **James J.**[6] **LEWIS** was born 1806 and died 1889.

+ 107   ii.   **John F. LEWIS** was born 1807.

+ 108   iii.   **Richard Burton LEWIS** was born 10 August 1809 and died 15 April 1890.

+ 109   iv.   **Samuel D. LEWIS** was born 1811.

+ 110   v.   **Zebedee B. LEWIS** was born 1813.

The following two were born after Joshua's death:

+ 111   vi.   **Wallace LEWIS** was born 5 October 1819.

+ 112   vii.   **Madison LEWIS** was born about 1823.

Sixth Generation

83.   **Samuel**[6] **LEWIS** (John[5], Samuel[4], Zebulon[3], James[2], James[1]) was born 1797 in Virginia.

The Land Act of 1820 was a federal law that enabled people to more easily buy land in Ohio and other parts of the Northwest Territory and Missouri Territory. Instead of requiring people to buy a minimum of 160 acres, they could buy 80, and the price per acre was reduced from $1.65 to $1.25. Thus only $100 was necessary to buy 80 acres. Three years after the law was passed Samuel Lewis took advantage of it and bought land in Lawrence County. On 4 September 1823 he received a patent for 80 acres in Section 11, Township 2 (Windsor), Range 16.[1302] In 1824 Samuel

Lewis and wife, Mary, of Lawrence County, Ohio, sold 50 acres to James McMahan. Wits: Thomas Singers, John Griffeth.[1303] On 9 July 1824 Samuel Lewis sold 30 acres to John S. Henderson.[1304] John Burcham sold 62 acres to Samuel Lewis on 20 October 1826. Samuel Lewis and wife, Polly, sold the 62 acres on 15 September 1827 to James White. Wits: Simeon Shattrick (Shattuck?), John Lewis.[1305]

On 28 July 1838 Samuel Lewis was awarded a patent for 40 acres. The description was Section 12, Township 2, Range 16.[1306] On 29 August 1838 he sold land to Thomas Henderson.[1307] Samuel sold 35 acres on 23 December 1839 to Horatio Gridley. Wit: Margarette Sowards.[1308]

When the 1850 U.S. census was taken for Mason Township, Lawrence County, Samuel Lewis was described as a physician. His age was 38 (obviously an error), and his wife, Marenda, was 22. Mason Township was home to the Paynes, and living with Samuel and Marenda were Dina Payne, 65, born in Virginia; Malissa Payne, 28, born in Ohio; Austin Payne, 61, born in Virginia; Sarah J. Payne, 6, born in Ohio.[1309] Diana Payne was the mother of Marenda Payne (see the Payne section).

Samuel married (1) **Mary BURCHAM** on 14 October 1819 in Lawrence County, Ohio. Basel Lewis, J. P., officiated at this marriage.[1310] Basil Lewis was a minister for the Baptists who met on Wolf Creek in Windsor Township in 1814.[1311] A Bazel Lewis is found on List A of the Berkeley County, Virginia, Personal Property Taxes for 1787. He was working for himself and John Shirt was working for him.[1312]

Mary Burcham was the daughter of John BURCHAM and wife, Nancy Ann DOWDEN. The Burchams were prominent in Lawrence County right from the beginning. The Justice of the Peace Nathaniel Burcham officiated at the marriages of many of my relatives. Dale Burcham, who served as Clerk of Court of Lawrence County, wrote an article about the Burchams, and it was published in *History of Lawrence County, Ohio, 1990*. The immigrant John Burcham and his family crossed the Ohio River at Fort Gyandotte (now Huntington) in 1808 and lived in a rock cavern near Scottown until their cabin was built.[1313]

Samuel and Mary had the following children and probably others.

    113   i.   **Wilson B.[7] LEWIS**.

                  On 13 June 1846 Wilson B. Lewis bought 41 acres in Lawrence County from Griffin Sowards and wife, Elizabeth. The land was in Section 36, Township 3 (Mason), Range 16. Wits: Nat. Burcham, George N. Sowards.[1314]

                  Wilson married **Elizabeth SOWARDS** on 17 July 1842 in Lawrence County. Justice of the Peace Nathanial Burcham married this couple.[1315]

    114   ii.   **Jesse B. LEWIS** was born 18 November 1827 in Lawrence County.[1316]

Samuel.Lewis married (2) **Mirinda PAYNE** on 15 November 1849 in Lawrence County, Ohio. Sartain McComas, M. G., officiated.[1317] Miranda, born about 1828, was a daughter of William PAYNE and Diana WILSON.

Samuel and Miranda had son John Peter and probably other children.

    115   iii.   **John Peter LEWIS** was born 24 July 1860.[1318]

84.   Jesse[6] LEWIS (John[5], Samuel[4], Zebulon[3], James[2], James[1]) was born about 1800.

The name of Jesse's wife and names of his children were taken from *Pioneer Lewis Familes* by Michael Lewis Cook. Jesse's parents settled in Gallia County, Ohio.[1319]

Jesse married **Hannah DEWITT**.

They had the following children:

	116	i.	**Philena**[7] **LEWIS** was born 18 September 1821.
	117	ii.	**William LEWIS**. William married **Sally CLARK** on 12 April 1838 in Gallia County, Ohio.[1320]
	118	iii.	**Samuel LEWIS**.
	119	iv.	**Jesse LEWIS**.
	120	v.	**John LEWIS**.
	121	vi.	**Richard LEWIS**.
	122	vii.	**Ellen LEWIS**.
	123	viii.	**Melissa LEWIS**.

85. **Wilson**[6] **LEWIS** (John[5], Samuel[4], Zebulon[3], James[2], James[1]) was born 1803 in Virginia. He died 11 December 1883.[1321]

The heirs of George Gibbs sold 160 acres in Lawrence County, Ohio, to Wilson Lewis on 16 July 1832.[1322] Wilson and Sarah Lewis sold 80 acres on 24 July 1836, to David Walls.[1323]

Wilson Lewis was living in Rome Township, Lawrence County, when the 1840 U.S. census was taken. The statistics for his household were one male 40-50, three males under 5, two between 5 and 10, one 10-15; one female 30-40, and one 10-15.[1324]

Names and birth years of children of Wilson and Sarah were taken from *Pioneer LewisFamilies*[1325] and from the 1850 Census for Rome Township. In 1850 Wilson was listed as a farmer, with real estate valued at $1,000. He was 47 years old and wife, Sarah, 44.. In their household were James F., 18; George F., 16; David W., 15; Perry (Alonzo P.), 13; Abel, 10; Mary (Missouri) A., 8; Redman C., 7; Mary (Marietta) A., 3.[1326]

The Rome Township census of 1860 reveals that Wilson and Sarah's household included extended family members. Children of Wilson (b. in Virginia) and Sarah (b. in Kentucky) were Alonzo P., age 23; Abel A., age 20, Missouri A., 18; Redman C., 16; Marietta, 12. Missouri A. Clark (age 14) and Sally K. Clark (age 12) were living with Wilson and Sarah. Also in the household were Wilson M. Lewis, 6; Geo. B. Lewis, 4.[1327] Missouri and Sarah Catherine Clark were children of Wilson and Sara's daughter Rebecca and her first husband, William Clark (1825-1851). Both Rebecca and her husband, William Clark, were said to have died young.[1328] Given that, the six-year-old Wilson M. Lewis and four-year-old Geo. B. Lewis were likely sons of Rebecca by her second husband, Madison Lewis.

Living with Wilson and Sarah Lewis in 1870 was George Brumfield, 21, born in Ohio.[1329]

Wilson married **Sarah BURCHAM**, daughter of John BURCHAM and Nancy Ann DOWDEN, on 3 March 1826 in Lawrence County, Ohio.[1330] Sarah was born 1806 in Kentucky.

They had the following children:

+	124	i.	**Rebecca**[7] **LEWIS** was born about 1827.
+	125	ii.	**John B. LEWIS** was born 1828.
+	126	iii.	**Samuel F. LEWIS** was born 1831 and died about 1900.
	127	iv.	**James F. LEWIS** was born 1832.
+	128	v.	**George S. LEWIS** was born January 1833.
	129	vi.	**David W. LEWIS** was born 1835.
	130	vii.	**Alonzo Perry LEWIS** was born 1837. Alonzo married **Sarah A. PINKERMAN** on 8 November 1860 in Lawrence County, Ohio. Nathaniel Burcham, J.P., married them.[1331]
	131	viii.	**Abel LEWIS** was born 1840.
	132	ix.	**Missouri A. LEWIS** was born 1842. Missouri married **Parkinson NULL**, born about 1849.[1332]

+ 133 x. **Redman C. LEWIS** was born February 1843.

134 xi. **Marietta LEWIS** was born 1847. She married **Thomas Allen NULL**, a brother to Parkinson Null, who married her sister Missouri.[1333]

86. **Joshua**[6] **LEWIS** (John[5], Samuel[4], Zebulon[3], James[2], James[1]) was born in 1808 and died in 1859.

Joshua, a self-taught lawyer, was a Gallia County prosecutor. He and wife, Ann, had 14 children.[1334]

Joshua married **Ann WEATHERHOLT**. Ann, the daughter of John and Rebecca (CLARK) WEATHERHOLT, was 14 years old when she married.[1335]

They had the following children:

135 i. **John**[7] **LEWIS**.

136 ii. **Rebecca LEWIS**.

137 iii. **Robert Allen LEWIS**.

138 iv. **William LEWIS**.

139 v. **Sarah Ann LEWIS**.

140 vi. **Mary LEWIS**.

141 vii. **Virginia LEWIS**.

142 viii. **Missouri LEWIS**.

143 ix. **Joshua LEWIS**.

144 x. **Melissa LEWIS**.

145 xi. **Lydotia LEWIS**.

146 xii. **Samuel LEWIS**.

147 xiii.. **Lavinia LEWIS**.

148 xiv. **Alfonso LEWIS**.

106. **James J.**[6] **LEWIS** (Joshua[5], Samuel[4], Zebulon[3], James[2], James[1]) was born 1806 in Monroe County (West) Virginia.. He died 1889 in Lawrence County, Ohio.

James J. Lewis was still of Monroe County, (West) Virginia, on 6 April 1840, as were Zebedee B. Lewis and wife, Elizabeth, when they and Richard K (B) Lewis and wife, Maryann, of Lawrence County, Ohio, sold 39 acres along Back Creek to George Stephens(on). The land bordered lands of Jacob Halstead, Jacob Maddy, and the said George Stephens(on). The parcel was part of Joshua Lewis's share of the 300-acres granted to Samuel Lewis. The witnesses were Nathaniel Burcham and James White. R. K. [sic] Lewis and wife, Mary Ann, personally appeared before Nathaniel Burcham, an acting Justice of the Peace for Lawrence County, Ohio, and Nathaniel Burcham placed his seal on the deed on 19 August 1840. James J. Lewis and Zebedee B. Lewis and wife, Elizabeth, appeared before Robert Coalter and Joel Stodghill, Justices of the Peace for Monroe County, Virginia. The deed was delivered to Geo. A. Mann for G. Stevenson on 17 June 1850.[1336]

Another deed dated 6 April 1840 was from Zebedee B. Lewis, Elizabeth Lewis, Richard K. [sic] Lewis, and Maryann Lewis, as heirs of Joshua Lewis, to Jacob Halstead for land in Monroe County. This 24 1/2-acre parcel was on the waters of Back Creek and adjoined Halstead's own land and that of Jacob Maddy, George Stephens(on), and others. Again the deed was witnessed by Nathaniel Burcham and James White of Lawrence County, Ohio. Robert Coalter and Joel Stodghill, Justices of the Peace, acknowledged that James J. Lewis and Zebedee B. Lewis and wife, Elizabeth, appeared before them. The deed was delivered 17 June 1850 to Geo. A. Mann for J. Halstead..[1337]

James was living in Windsor Township in 1840 when the federal census was taken. He was in the 40-50 age group. Living with him was a female 16-20 (his wife, Elizabeth Asbury), and a female 60-70, surely his mother, Catherine (Hill) Lewis. Three houses away lived John Griffith; two houses away was John Burcham. James Lewis was listed between James S. Vanwright (?), and George Cheek (?). Isaac Sowards, who also migrated from Monroe County, lived two households away from John Griffith. Also, not far away lived Wilson Manning (oldest male 40-50), and Moses Manning.[1338] There were Mannings living near Zebulon Lewis, James J. Lewis's great-grandfather, in Orange County, but I have not been able to connect them to the Lawrence County group.

Land Patents granted at Chillicothe on 10 April 1843 include two issued to James J. Lewis, each for 40 acres. Certificate No. 11,928 was for land in the southwest quarter of the southeast quarter of Section 13, Township 2 (Windsor), Range 16.[1339] Certificate No. 12,042 was for land in the northwest quarter of the northeast quarter of Section 24, Township 2, Range 16.[1340] Section 13 is on the northern edge of Section 24. On 1 November 1846 Certificate No. 13,193 for 40 acres was issued to James J. Lewis. The parcel was in the southwest quarter of the northeast quarter of Section 24, Township 2, Range 16.[1341] These properties were within walking distance of Scottown.

The 1850 Windsor Township census included James's household. He was 49 [sic], a laborer from Virginia. His assets were worth $1,000. His daughter May (Mary) E. Lewis was 7 and born in Virginia. His mother, Catharine, was 61. Madison Lewis, 27, was a laborer, born in Virginia. James's household was between that of William Brown, born in Ohio, and Richard Lewis, James's brother.[1342]

On 1 July 1852 James J. Lewis was granted 40 acres in the northeast quarter of the northwest quarter of Section 24, Township 2, Range 16.[1343]

James J. Lewis sold 80 acres to Horatio Murphy on 9 September 1851. The parcel was in Windsor Township (in Sections 13 and 24, Township 2, Range 16). S. M. Cown and Robert J. Neely were witnesses.[1344]

On 12 August 1857 James J. Lewis sold 2 1/2 acres to Alexander Pinkerman. This parcel was in the northeast quarter of the northwest quarter of Section 24, Township 2, Range 16. Wits: Nathl. Burcham, James P. Burcham.[1345]

When the census was taken in 1860, James Lewis was entered as 54, a day laborer, born in Virginia. His wife, Rebecca, was 50 (an error). In their household was Lewis E. Burd, 1 year old.[1346]

The 1880 Windsor Township census shows James J. Lewis and his family living between the households of Wm. and Sarah Pinkerman and Griff and Mary Sowards. For this record James J. was 71. Becca 38. Three sons were named: Edward, 21; James, 19; Thomas, 17. There were five daughters: Mary, 10; Sallie, 8; Rose, 6; Stella, 4; Pearl, 2.[1347] The birth years of James and Rebecca's children Sallie, Rose, and Pearl are figured from their ages in 1880.

The pension records for James J. Lewis's mother indicate he was born in 1806. His tombstone says 1800, but no other information supports that date. I can imagine that as people got older they showed some cognitive impairment and forgot their birth years. Or maybe the carver of the tombstone was lazy and found forming two 0s was easier than forming an 0 and a 6.

By the time James and his family arrived in Ohio, Lawrence County was bustling. The first charcoal iron furnace in Lawrence County was constructed in 1826 north of Hanging Rock. Soon the Hanging Rock Iron Region was producing pig iron that was competitive world wide. Iron from the Hecla Furnace was equaled only by a furnace in Spain and one in Asia Minor. Much of the iron was shipped up the Ohio by steamboat to Pittsburg, where it was shaped into pots and pans, tools, and weapons. The Ohio River was considered the highway to the west, and Lawrence County furnished vastly more than its share of riverboat pilots.[1348] The steamboat *Washington* had been launched at Wheeling in 1817, and its builder won a contract to clear snags from the rivers. From then on nearly every port along the Ohio was visited by packet boats carrying mail and passengers.[1349]

James married (1) **Elizabeth ASBURY** on 8 April 1840 in Monroe County, (West) Virginia. Zebadee B. Lewis secured the marriage bond. James COLEY and Polly COLLEY, on April 7th, gave permission for their daughter Elisabeth Asbury to wed James Lewis. Labez Anderson and Zebedee B. Lewis were witnesses.[1350]

I have found no further information on Elizabeth's background, but she was under 21, for her parents had to give her permission to marry. By 1850 she either had died or left James.

James and Elizabeth had the following child:

+ 149 i. **Mary Ellen**[7] **LEWIS** was born December 1841.

James married (2) **Rebecca BURD** on 2 Februrary 1860 in Lawrence County, Ohio. Nathaniel Burcham, J.P., officiated.[1351] Rebecca died in 1903.[1352]

In 1839 Rebecca was born to David BURD and Susannah GREAVER, who married in 1822. Susannah was the daughter of Philip Greaver and wife, Sophia Zimmerman. David and Susannah migrated from Augusta County, Virginia, to Ohio. At that time there was a stagecoach road from Staunton in Augusta County to the Guyandotte River, which joins the Ohio River on the eastern end of Huntington, West Virginia.

Rebecca was born in 1839. Her older brother, George A. Bird (b. 1828), married Elizabeth Scarberry (b. 1832). Other siblings: Philip (b. 1829) married Mary Estes; Sophia (b. 1834) married Daniel Estes; Mary (b. 1837); Andrew (b. 1838) married Cerepter Henderson; Sarah Jane (b. 1842) married George W. Rigney; and Susan (b. 1845) married Albert Henderson.[1353]

David Bird and family were on the 1840 census for Gallia County, Ohio. His household consisted of 1 male in the 30-40 age group and 1 female in same; there was 1 male under 5; 3 males 10-15; 1 male 15-20; there were 2 females under 5, and 2 between 5 and 10.[1354]

It is easy to see how Rebecca met James Lewis. In 1851 James sold 80 acres in Windsor Township to Horatio Murphy. The Rome Township census for 1850 shows George Bird, 23; Betsy Bird, 16; and Mary Bird, 13, living in the home of Horatio Murphy, 27. Elizabeth McBride, 58, born in Virginia, was also part of this household.[1355] The Lewis land in Windsor Township was close to the border with Rome Township.

We wonder why Rebecca would have married someone over 30 years her senior. She was a middle child in a large family, however, and may have felt neglected. James J. Lewis apparently never married until he was 31, and his wife, Elizabeth Asbury, must have died or left him. It looks as if he had not spent much time courting women, and Rebecca may have thrived on the attention he gave her. It is obvious that son Lewis Edward (usually called *Buck*) was born before she and James married. Even this marriage may not have gone well for him, for their age difference surely caused problems.

Rebecca appeared on the 1900 census for Millers Precinct, 58 years old, and living with daughter Stella, 20 years old, and daughter Mary, 15.[1356] If Mary had been Rebecca's daughter, she would have been born when her mother was 45. That is possible, but it seems more likely she was Rebecca's granddaughter

Rebecca died two years after having a cancerous breast removed. She is buried beside her husband at Pleasant (Tick) Ridge.

James and Rebecca had the following children:

+ 150 ii. **Lewis Edward LEWIS** was born February 1858 and died 20 February 1938.

+ 151 iii. **James Albert LEWIS** was born March 1861 and died 1940.

+ 152 iv. **Thomas Jefferson LEWIS** was born April 1863 and died 25 September 1938.

+ 153 v. **Mary LEWIS** was born March 1872 in Lawrence County, Ohio. She died 11 March 1958 in Lawrence County, Ohio.

   Mary's birth month and year were taken from the 1900 census for Millers Precinct.

154 vi. **Sallie LEWIS** was born 1873 (?) in Lawrence County, Ohio.

155 vii. **Rose LEWIS** was born 1874 in Lawrence County, Ohio.

156 viii. **Pearl LEWIS** was born 1878 in Lawrence County, Ohio. She married **Manford PAXTON**.[1357]

157 ix. **Stella LEWIS** was born May 1880 in Lawrence County, Ohio. Stella married **Will KIRKMAN**, brother of May Kirkman, Thomas J. Lewis's wife.[1358]

   Stella's birth month and year were taken from the 1900 Millers Precinct census. At that time she was living with her mother and 15-year-old Mary, probably a niece.

.107. **John F.⁶ LEWIS** (Joshua⁵, Samuel⁴, Zebulon³, James², James¹) was born 1807 in Monroe County, (West) Virginia.

In 1833 John F. Lewis married Mrs. Catharine Spicer of Albemarle County, Virginia. She was a daughter of William Brockman, who had roots in Orange County, Virginia.

It should be noted that when Catherine, widow of Joshua Lewis, was filling out her pension application as a war widow in Lawrence County, Ohio, in 1853, she did not include John F. Lewis as a child by Joshua. She may not have mentioned him because he did not migrate to Ohio with her other sons. Neither did Catherine refer to son Zebedee, likely because he remained in Monroe County, (West) Virginia. The deed below reveals that John F. Lewis was entitled to a small share of the Back Creek tract that his grandfather Samuel Lewis had had surveyed in Monroe County.

On 25 September 1840 John F. Lewis and wife, Catherine, of Albemarle County sold the land they had inherited from John's father, Joshua Lewis, a fifth part of a parcel on Back Creek containing 50 acres. They sold it to John's brother James J. Lewis. The parcel adjoined lands of J. Maddy, George Stevens, and Jo. Halstid. Certificates verifying the private examination of Catherine's willingness to sell, done in Albemarle County before Justices of the Peace John W. Goss and Nimrod Bramham, were received by Jno. Hutchinson, Jr., County Clerk of Monroe, and the deed was recorded.[1359] George *Stephenson* had been conveyed 28 acres of Samuel Lewis's survey by 22 June 1815, and it would have been his land that was the pointer.[1360] This is about the same time that James J. Lewis sold his land on Back/Indian Creeks and moved to Ohio.

John F. Lewis's occupation on the 1850 U.S. census was manager. The approximate birth years of John and Catherine's children were derived from this census, taken in Fredericksville Parish, Albemarle County. Catherine was 48 and John 43; son Morton was 15, son Henry 13. Their household appeared between that of C. F. Walton and Richd. Terrell. Terrell was 65, and living with him was Wm. O. Terrell, 22.[1361] The Terrells and the Mortons had married in neighboring Orange County, Jane, daughter of George and Jane Morton, having married William Terrell.[1362] Henry Morton of Orange County made his will in 1819. His only legatee was his mother Mary Morton. Wits: John Moore, James Nelson, William Morton, Jr., William Terrill, Jr.[1363] Henry Morton's father was John, and his mother, Mary, was a daughter of Henry Tandy.[1364]

There was some connection between the Tandy and Brockman families: Samuel Brockman married Ann (Anestar) Simms, daughter of Capt. William Simms, in 1790, and they lived in Albemarle County. Children: Richard Simms, Tandy, Bluford, Tazewell, Julia A., Agatha, and Simpson.[1365] Perhaps it was the Tandy-Morton tie that led John F. Lewis and wife, Catherine (Brockman) Spicer, to choose the names *Morton* and *Henry* for their sons. Or perhaps it was more John's idea. Zebulon Lewis, John F. Lewis's great grandfather, lived near the Mortons in Orange County. William Morton of Orange County made his will in 1747, naming sons-in-law Andrew Bourne and Henry Bourne.[1366] When the tithables were listed for Orange County in 1766, Zeblon Lewis's name was followed by Mrs. Susannah Davis, and Henry Bourn followed her. Fourteen houses away was Richard Morton.[1367] We saw above that the Mortons intermarried with Zebulon's friends, the Strothers.

Capt. William Simms (d. in 1797) had married Anester Stepp, and their daughter Ann married Samuel Brockman. Capt. Simms' son Richard married Mary Terrill.[1368] William Ballard (b.1732) married Elizabeth Step of Orange County before moving to Monroe County (now West Virginia). Orange County tithables of 176_ show Seblun Lewis 11 households away from James Stapp.[1369]

The question arises as to why John F. Lewis would have gone east to find someone he wanted to marry. It seems likely that his family in Monroe County had corresponded with old friends in Orange and Culpeper Counties. Catherine Brockman's grandfather, William Brockman (m. Betty Embry), had lived in Orange County before moving over to Albemarle. Samuel Lewis and his father, Zebulon, disappeared from Orange-Culpeper County records after 1771, and Samuel surfaced a little over 10 years later by Indian Creek in Monroe County. Samuel and his family may have stopped for a time along the way.

James J. Lewis of 1838:

Five years after John F. Lewis and Catherine married, a James J. Lewis appeared in Orange County records, signing as surety for the marriage of John Hill and Eliza Mildred Herring on 8 September 1838. Eliza was the daughter of Sarah. Wits: Michl. L. Eheart, James J. Lewis, Reynolds Chapman.[1370] Not a lot of people were using middle initials during that time period, and James J. Lewis of Monroe could have been visiting his brother's family in Albemarle and become involved with the Hill-Herring families. Sureties for bonds were usually relatives. John Hill and Aggie Brockman, daughter of Ambrose, married in 1810 in Albemarle County. Jonathan Herring and Susan Hill married in Albemarle in 1809. She was the daughter of Henry Hill; Richard Hill and William Herring were sureties. There were other Herring-Hill marriages in Albemarle.[1371] One branch of the Herring family lived on Swift Run in what today is Greene County, Virginia. Swift Run merges with the Rivanna in Albemarle County. In 1763 William Herring and wife, Mary, of Orange County granted 125 acres on Swift Run to James Stodghill.[1372] The Stodghills moved to Monroe, and James Maddy, whose family also moved to Monroe, had lived on Swift Run.

The Bush-Roach-Madison connections in Orange and Albemarle Counties:

Above we saw that Joseph Bush bought at the estate sale of John F. Lewis's grandfather, Samuel Lewis. And it was mentioned that William Roach was also a buyer and that the Bush, Roach, and Meadows families had intermarried. Ambrose Madison, grandfather of President Madison, in his will of 1732, devised land to James Coleman, Daniel S___ (Stodghill?) and David Roach.[1373] Some think that David's wife, Frances, was a sister of Ambrose. There is also speculation that Ambrose Madison had sisters who married Daniel Stodgill, James Coleman, and Samuel Brockman.[1374] In 1734 Henry Madison of King William County, Virginia, devised to his niece Frances Madison (daughter of his brother Ambrose) 1,000 acres. There was a condition attached: When she turned 21, or died, 150 acres of the land should go to Daniel Stodghill. Wit: Roger Tandy.[1375]

In 1762 Reuben Roach and wife, Easter, of Orange County made a deed of lease and release for 150 acres to James Madison. It was land that Ambrose Madison had devised to David Roach, father of Reuben. James and Reuben Roach had sued Carter Braxton and George, William, and Sarah Brooke, for the recovery of this land. The case had wound up in Chancery.[1376] Reuben Roach died in 1795 in Rockingham County. Samuel Roach was administrator of his estate.[1377]

The Joseph Bush who bought at Samuel Lewis's estate sale in Monroe County was surely part of the family of Philip Bush of Orange County. Philip's son Josiah Bush and his wife, Sarah, were of Albemarle County by 26 December 1773, when they sold 125 acres in Spotsylvania County to Wm. Mastin of same. Wits: Jno. Sanders, Benj. Craig, Geo. Tureman.[1378]

On 31 March 1770 Josiah Bush of Albemarle County had bought 200 acres in Albemarle from John Lewis of Halifax County. The tract was on the sides of the South West Mountain and part of a larger tract that Lewis had bought from Stephen Homes, deceased. It was bordered by Homes Spring Branch and Henry Shelton's corner. Wits: Thomas Walker, John Walker, Danl. Smith, and Thos. Walker, Jr.[1379] On the same day John Lewis, Jr., sold 416 acres to Henry Shelton. The tract was in Albemarle County on both sides of Blue Run and by Wilson's Spring and Homes's Spring Branch. It extended to the Orange-Albemarle County line and land of Richard Wilson was another pointer. Same witnesses.[1380] A few months before, on 27 July 1769, Samuel Brockman and wife, Rebecca, of Orange County sold 350 acres to William Brockman of same. This was land that Samuel Brockman, Sr., had devised to his two sons, Samuel and William. Samuel and Rebecca were selling their share to his brother William. Wits: Mary Willson, Richard Wilson, John Walker, Daniel Fargason.[1381]

The John Lewis who moved to Halifax County was a son of John Lewis, son of Col. Roberrt Lewis and Jane Meriwether. Col. Robert Lewis was a son of Col. John Lewis and Elizabeth Warner. John Lewis, Sr., had married Catherine Fauntleroy of Richmond County, Virginia, and he died in Halifax in 1787. John Lewis, Jr., of Halifax married Lydia Reese.[1382] I have discovered no blood connection between these Lewises and Samuel Lewis of Monroe County (WV).

Philip Bush of Orange County wrote his will in 1771, giving land on the Blue Run to son Josiah Bush and his wife, Sarah. He devised land in Spotsylvania County to son Philip; son William Bush received land on the Blue Run, with reversion to son Francis Bush, provided he give 5 lbs. current money to grandson Lewis Bush. The home plantation went to son John and his wife, Elizabeth. Slaves went to sons Francis and Ambrose Bush and to daughter Sarah Watts and granddaughter Susannah Watts. Granddaughter Frankey Johnson was given a chest of drawers. Sons

Joseph and Joshua were each given 25 lbs. current money, and Joseph was to receive a rifle and Joshua the long shot gun. Daughter Elizabeth Johnson was given 25 lbs. current money. Wits: James Madison, Tho. Barbour, David Thompson.[1383] Capt. William Bush, born 1746 in Orange County, married Frances Tandy Burris, born 1762.[1384] So the Bush family had a tie to the Brockmans through the Tandys. James Madison, father of President Madison, witnessed the 1762 will of Samuel Brockman of Orange County.[1385]

John married **Catharine (BROCKMAN) SPICER** on 25 January 1833 in Albemarle County, Virginia. The minister that officiated at Catherine and John's marriage was John Goss. William O. Harris signed the bond. Wits: N. Burnley and Alexander H. Arthur.[1386] Catharine was born 1802 in Virginia. She was a daughter of William BROCKMAN and Mary SMITH, who married in 1784 in Orange County, Virginia.[1387]

Catharine married Dabney Spicer on 2 April 1817. She was under 21, and William Brockman, her father, gave his consent. Witnesses to the consent were James Brockman and William Spicer. The bond was secured by James Brockman, and William Wertenbaker was witness.[1388]

In 1834 Catherine and her husband, John Lewis, and her sister Frances and her husband James McCallester sold their land along Preddy's Creek. Wits: Mary B. Brockman, James and Jane Brockman, Samuel and Elizabeth Mahanes, Robert and Sarah Brockman, and Thos. and Mary Rodes.[1389] On 13 June 1836 John F. Lewis and wife, Catherine, sold 60 acres in Albemarle County to Horace Pritchett. It was their allotment out of the estate of Catherine's father, William Brockman, deceased. On its borders were lands of Thomas Gilbert, James Pritchett, and Robert Brockman.[1390]

On 3 September 1838 William Brockman's widow, Mary; James Brockman and wife, Jane; Samuel Mahanes and wife, Elizabeth Brockman; Robert Brockman and wife, Sarah Brockman; Thomas Rhodes and wife, Mary Brockman; John Lewis and wife, Catherine Brockman; and James McAlister and wife, Frances Brockman, sold to John D. Salmon land that had been set off from William Brockman's estate for the purpose of paying off debts. It adjoined the widow's dower land and land of James Prichett. The acreage was only 8.1 acres, but it included a mill and water rights involving a canal at the fork of Quarles' and Preddy's Creeks. The canal went through land of Achilles Douglas.[1391]

William O. Harris signed the marriage bond for Catherine (Brockman) Spicer and John Lewis, and on 17 January 1835 William married Sarah Pritchett. William D. Brockman signed the bond with Ira Garrett the witness.[1392]

Catherine Brockman's sister Mary married Thomas Rhodes in 1813. Mary's father, William Brockman, signed the bond. David Rodes was the witness.[1393] Thomas was a son of Epaphroditus Rhodes, who was a grandchild of Hezekiah Rhodes and Ann Hill, who married in Middlesex County in 1720.[1394] Ezechias was baptized in Middlesex in 1696, a son of Ezechias and Elizabeth Nichols.[1395] Hezekiah was of Orange County in 1762 when he made his will, naming grandchild Epaphroditus Rhodes.[1396]

Susannah Rodes of Albemarle County married Thomas Marshall in 1792. Epaphroditus Rodes was surety for the bond.[1397] James Brockman, sister of Catherine (Brockman) Spicer Lewis, married Jane Marshall.[1398]

The Hezekiah Rhodes who was of Orange County when he died had sister Mary, who married John Bradley in 1711 in Middlesex County. He later married Rebecca Hackney. After her first husband, James Jameson, died, she had a child by James Lewis, Jr., of Middlesex, and he was probably the father of Zebulon Lewis of Orange County.

John and Catharine had the following children:

    158   i.   **Morton[7] LEWIS** was born 1835..

    159   ii. **Henry LEWIS** was born 1837.

108. **Richard Burton[6] LEWIS** (Joshua[5], Samuel[4], Zebulon[3], James[2], James[1]) was born 10 August 1809 in Monroe County, (West) Virginia. He died 15 April 1890.

The origin of Richard Lewis's middle name poses a quandary. Teaching for Monroe County schools between 1826 and 1830 was a Richard N. Burton.[1399] Perhaps Burton was admired and the source of Richard Lewis's given names, but I have found no further information on him. May Burton was prominent in Orange County, Virginia, and was named in the accounting of the estate of Robert Medley of Culpeper County in 1761. Charles Brooking and Henry Sparks were also named.[1400] And William Brooking, surely a relative of Charles, was a buyer at the estate sale of Samuel Lewis, Richard's grandfather.

John Griffith and wife, Mary, sold 40 acres in Lawrence County, Ohio, to Richard Burton Lewis on 12 February 1838. The land description: the northwest quarter of the southwest quarter of Section 13, Township 2, Range 16. Wits: Daniel Beller, John Folkner.[1401]

In 1840 Richard Lewis was listed on the federal census for Windsor Township, Lawrence County, Ohio. He appears between John Burcham and John White, Jr. Following White was Isaac(?) Dare. Richard would have been the male in the 30-40 age bracket, and his wife the female in the same bracket. They had a daughter under 5.[1402]

The 1850 census for Windsor Township shows that Richard was a farmer. Both Richard, 43, and his wife, Mary, 33, were born in Virginia. Children in the household were Nancy, age 10; Richard, 7; Harriet, 2; and Lucinda, 10 (an error). Living with the Lewises was Alex Bucklen (?), age 20, born in Ohio.[1403] Richard's brother James Lewis was living in the next house enumerated on the census.

On 17 November 1853 Richard B. Lewis was granted a patent for 40 acres in Lawrence County. The parcel was in the northeast quarter of the southeast quarter of Section 13, Township 2, Range 16.[1404]

On 23 March 1857 Samuel Lewis of Lawrence County conveyed to R. B. Lewis about 30 acres in two parcels, one, 11 acres, and one, 20, in Section 13, Township 2, Range 16. One of the markers was a creek. Wits: Nathaniel Burcham, Madilda Burcham.[1405]

Richard and Mary's household kept growing. When the 1860 U.S. census was taken, there were seven children in their household. Richard was 50, Mary 39; daughter Nancy was 20; Richard, 16; Harriet, 13; Lucinda, 10; Joshua, 7; George, 4; and Mary, 1.[1406] Lucinda must have been 1 when the 1850 census was taken. Also born in 1859 was Fannie, so perhaps Mary's name was Mary Francis.

Lennie Lewis Bundy, a descendant of Richard Burton Lewis, furnished the names of spouses for Richard and Mary Ann's children.

Birth years for Harriet, Lucinda, Joshua, George, and Mary were deduced from the 1860 Windsor Township census. The 1870 census named the following children: Richard, 25; Harriet, 22; Joshua, 17; George, 14; Frances, 11; John, 8; Effie, 4.[1407]

By the time of the 1880 census, Richard was 70 and wife, Mary, 60. Children at home were Joshua, 26; George, 24; Fanny, 21; John, 19; and Effie, 13.[1408]

We recall that Isaac Estill administered the estate of Richard Burton Lewis's grandfather, Samuel Lewis (d.1811) of Monroe County, West Virginia. On 26 September 1814 John Hinton and wife, Eleanor; Even Hinton and wife, Margaret, made a deed of trust to Isaac Estill and Jacob Cook for two tracts of land, one for 156 acres on Indian Draft of Indian Creek and another for 18 acres adjacent the Fishers on Indian Draft. The Hintons were in debt for $183 to Andrew Beirne.[1409] Some say Hinton, West Virginia, now in Summers County, was named for John (Jack) Hinton, who laid out the town in 1831. James H. Miller, in his book, *History of Summers County, West Virginia*, states it was named for Jack's son Evan Hinton. When Evan was a young man he got into a wrestling match with William C. Richmond, and the match ended in a fight that became part of the lore of the county. Technically Evan won the fight, for he persuaded William to yell "enough." But Evan was violently sick afterwards.[1410]

On 30 July 1887 Evan Hinton responded to a letter from Richard B. Lewis of Ohio. Here follows some of the most interesting parts:

> *My Dear Old Friend...I remember you very well and especially on one occasion, & that was you pulled me out of Cook's...dam by the top of the head when I was drowning and a thousand other things...They appointed me Sheriff for two years & they elected me for four more which was the worst thing they could have done for me...I have contended with the most shrewd men in the county & Allen Caperton was one. I will tell you where I live. I live on what we called the white oak Branch, Jerry Meadow used to live at the mouth of the branch about a half a mile west of the licks blocks on Jim's Branch...Richard you have been all over my farm, the ridges and hollows are now filled with people. My father died in the year of 1868, April 14..he had three boys by his last wife..the two are living on the old Henry*

The Scarberrys (Scarboroughs), Doughtys, Lewises, and Paynes of Lawrence County, Ohio

Ballengee place..the greater portion of Hinton is built on it....My father was near seventy years when he died. Polly Miller has been dead about 12 years. David Hinton has been dead nearly a year. Aunt Am[?] died nine years ago, John Maddy died this spring. John Maddy has been married three times. Well Anderson McNeer is dead. ...I married Nancy Milburn, daughter of Isaac Milburn that lived on Greenbrier River we raised nine children the first being a boy he married has four children five of them married...Thurman my youngest son is running the lower ferry at Hinton, he is single all are past 21 years of age, we raised a hearty family, ...my Brother John, he remembers you very well ...Well I am sixty five years old and am a very stout man to my age. I have been hearty all my life. when I was grown, or rather come to myself I weight 168 to 170 pounds and the most I ever weighed was 196 pounds, I was never beat in a scuffle or a fight....I remain your true friend until death, Evan Hinton."

The original of this letter descended to Richard's great-granddaughter, Lennie Lewis Bundy, of Ironton, Ohio.

Evan Hinton referred to Cook's dam. I presume it was somewhere near Cook's fort. Today a plaque stands on the side of State Route 122 just west of Greenville, marking the location of Cook's Fort. This fort enclosed an acre and a half and had a stockade. Indian Creek would have been a water source. In 1778 the Indian threat forced 300 people to enter its gates for safety.[1411]

Evan Hinton, age 58, and wife, Nancy, age 53, appear on the 1880 U. S. census. They were living at Jumping Branch in Summers (County), West Virginia. Living with them were children John David Hinton, age 24; daughter Mary A. Hinton, 16; Evan T. Hinton, 17; Ardelia Hinton, 14, and Thomas L. Hinton, 12.[1412]

Thomas Hinton bought 145 acres on Indian Creek and Indian Draft from William Maddy and his wife in 1795.[1413] In 1806 Jacob Cook and wife, Isabella, sold 36 acres on Indian Creek and Indian Draft to Peter Hinton of Rockingham County, Virginia, adjacent Fisher and Hinton's own land.[1414]

It was about three years after Richard Lewis and Evan Hinton exchanged letters that Richard died. He died from a flu-like illness at the age of 80.[1415]

For many years Richard B. Lewis's farm remained in the hands of his descendants, but eventually it was sold and is thought of today as the Cline Bricker farm.[1416]

Richard married **Mary Ann WHITE** on 9 August 1837 in Lawrence County, Ohio. John Griffeth, J.P., married Richard and Mary Ann.[1417] Mary was born 1817 in Virginia. She died 13 May 1900.[1418]

Richard and Mary had the following children, their spouses furnished by Lennie Lewis Bundy[1419]:

+ 160 i. **Nancy**[7] **LEWIS** was born 1840 and died 1896.
+ 161 ii. **Richard Clark LEWIS** was born 30 November 1843 and died 25 October 1916.
    162 iii. **Harriet LEWIS** was born in 1848. She married **Anderson BROWN.**
    163 iv. **Lucinda LEWIS** was born in 1850.
    164 v. **Joshua LEWIS** was born 1853. He did not marry.
    165 vi. **George LEWIS** was born 1856. He married **Celina SANDERS.**
    166 vii. **Fannie LEWIS** was born 1859. She married **Brunson DILLON.**
    167 viii. **John Calvin LEWIS**.was born 1861.
    168 ix. **Effie LEWIS** was born 1866.

109. **Samuel D.**[6] **LEWIS** (Joshua[5], Samuel[4], Zebulon[3], James[2], James[1]) was born 1811 in Monroe County, (West) Virginia.

On 16 June 1838 Samuel Lewis and wife, Rhoda, of Monroe County sold their interest in Samuel's father's land in Monroe County (WV) to brother Zebidee Lewis. It was noted that the dower land belonging to Samuel's mother had not yet been laid off, and that it could not be sold until she died. They were selling their right to land near the mouth of Back Creek as well as their interest in 200 acres adjoining and abutting the lands of Henry Miller, Sr., being a fifth part of the 200 acres inherited from Samuel's father, Joshua. This deed is indexed as a 57-acre sale.[1420]

On 18 January 1844 Samuel D. Lewis bought 20 acres in Lawrence County, Ohio, from John Burcham and wife, Nancy. The tract was in Section 10, Township 2 (Windsor), Range 16. Wits: Nathaniel Burcham, William Brown.[1421]

In 1857 Samuel D. Lewis sold about 30 acres in Windsor Township to R. B. Lewis, and no wife signed with him.

Samuel D. Lewis married secondly Margaret Johnson, and they appear on the 1860 census for Rome Township, Lawrence County: Saml. 48, Margaret 24. Children Sarah, 17, and Henry, 15, were born to Samuel and his first wife, Rhoda Miller. Samuel and Margaret's child, Alice, was 6 mos, and living with them was Geo. Workman, age 20, born in Virginia.[1422]

Samuel Lewis, 58, and wife, Margaret, 33, were living in Windsor Township in 1870 when the census was taken. Children at home were Alice, 10; Franklin, 8; Georgia, 3.[1423]

By the time of the 1880 U.S. census, Samuel and Margaret had taken their family to Lincoln, West Virginia. Saml. D. Lewis was 69, a farmer, born in Virginia. His wife, Margaret A., was 43 and born in Ohio, and her father was born in New York and her mother in Pennsylvania. All children were listed as "other" under relationship, but we can assume they were all theirs. Alice A. was 21; Franklin was 18; Georgia A. was 12 (these three all born in Ohio). Samuel, 9; Maggie, 9; and Rosa, 4 were all born in West Virginia. The family of Samuel Lewis's step-brother, Wallace Lewis, was living 10 households away.[1424]

Samuel married (1) **Rhoda MILLER**, daughter of Henry MILLER and Rhoda BROOKING, on 3 September 1836 in Monroe County, (West) Virginia. Charles Miller secured Samuel's marriage bond.[1425] Rhoda (Miller) Lewis, born 1819, died in 1849.[1426]

Rhoda's mother, Rhoda (Brooking), was a daughter of Charles and Ann Brooking. Oren Morton, in his book, *A History of Monroe County, West Virginia*, states that Charles and Ann came to Monroe from Albemarle County, Virginia. See Samuel Lewis (d.1811) for more on the Brookings.

Samuel and Rhoda had the following children:

    169   i. **Elizabeth A.⁷ LEWIS** was born 1837.

        Elizabeth A. Lewis, 13, was living with Henry and Rhoda Miller in Monroe County when the 1850 census was taken. Henry was 76 (?) and Rhoda 70.[1427] There is a cemetery along Indian Creek where a Rhoda Lewis is buried, apparently her mother.

+   170   ii. **Barbara Jane LEWIS** was born 8 July 1838, Monroe County, (West) Virginia.

    171   iii. **Sarah LEWIS** was born 1843 in Ohio.

    172   iv. **Henry LEWIS** was born 1845 in Ohio.

Samuel also married (2) **Margaret JOHNSON** on 6 January 1859 in Lawrence County, Ohio.[1428]

They had the following children:

    173   v. **Alice A. LEWIS** was born about 1860 in Ohio.

    174   vi. **Franklin LEWIS** was born about 1862 in Ohio.

    175   vii. **Georgia A. LEWIS** was born about 1868 in Ohio.

    176   viii. **Samuel LEWIS** was born about 1871 in West Virginia

    177   ix. **Maggie LEWIS** was born about 1871 in West Virginia.

178   x.   **Rosa LEWIS** was born about 1876 in West Virginia.

110.   Zebedee B.⁶ LEWIS (Joshua⁵, Samuel⁴, Zebulon³, James², James¹) was born 1813.

Names of children of Zebedee and Elizabeth were taken from the 1850 census for Monroe County. The birth years were deduced from the ages given. Zebidee was a farmer. Zebedee would have had the company of old friends, for George Stephenson, age 70, was still living in Monroe, as was his wife, Mary, 60. In their household were Ruth Stephenson, 26, and Martha Stephenson, 20. Nearby was the home of Samuel Stephenson, 31, and wife, Mary, 30.[1429]

Zebedee married **Elizabeth MANN** on 7 November 1836 in Monroe County (West) Virginia. Zebedee's marriage bond was secured by William Rains, Jr. Jn. Hutchison, Jr. was the witness.[1430]

Zebedee and Elizabeth had the following children:

179   i.   **Caroline⁷ LEWIS** was born 1838.

180   ii.   **James D. LEWIS** was born 1842(?).

181   iii. **John R. LEWIS** was born 1842.

182   iv.   **Rhoda C. LEWIS** was born 1843.

183   v.   **Sarah A. LEWIS** was born 1844.

184   vi.   **Brown B. LEWIS** was born 1846.

185   vii. **Allen G. LEWIS** was born 1848.

186   viii. **Amanda LEWIS** was born 1850.

111.   Wallace⁶ LEWIS (Joshua⁵, Samuel⁴, Zebulon³, James², James¹) was born 5 October 1819 in Monroe County (West) Virginia.

Wallace Lewis was not the son of Joshua, for in 1836 he was young enough that Monroe County Court was trying to get Catherine to turn him over to the overseers of the poor. Joshua had been dead since 1814. This item appears in the Court Orders of 16 May 1836: "Ordered that Catharine Lewis be summoned to shew cause if any she can why her son Waller Lewis shall not be bound by the overseers of the poor...proper person according to law."[1431]

School records for Monroe County show Wallis Lewis as being 12 years old during the 1833-34 school year, with Caty Lewis, his parent or guardian.[1432]

Wallace Lewis and his household appear on the 1860 Rome Township census for Lawrence County, Ohio. He was said to be 40 at the time and born in Virginia. His wife, Elvira, was 36. Children: James M., 16; Robert, 14; William, 13; Harriet, 9; Irvin. 3; and Amelia, 8 mos.[1433] The 1850 census for Rome Township, however, gives Wallace's age as 28 and Elvira's as 25. James M. Lewis was 5; Rachel Lewis 3; son Willem Lewis 2.[1434]

The 1880 U.S. census for District 64, Lincoln, West Virginia, shows Wallace's widow, Elvira, 55, as head of household. Living with her were sons James M. Lewis, age 35; Irving Lewis, 23; Frank Lewis, 17, all born in Ohio. Their father was born in Virginia, and their mother in Ohio. Ten households away lived Wallace's half-brother, Samuel D. Lewis, and his household.[1435]

The birth dates and full names of Wallace and Elvira's children were supplied by Robert and Kathy Lewis of Mentor, Ohio.

Wallace married **Elvira NASH**, daughter of James NASH and Frances GILLETT, on 17 March 1844 in Rome Township, Lawrence County, Ohio. Elvira was born 7 November 1823 in Ohio. She died 15 January 1891 in Lincoln County, West Virginia.[1436]

Robert L. Lewis, Jr., in his article in *History of Lawrence County, Ohio, 1990*, reveals that Frances Gillett was

The Scarberrys (Scarboroughs), Doughtys, Lewises, and Paynes of Lawrence County, Ohio

a sister to Horatio Gillett, who developed the Rome Beauty Apple.[1437]

They had the following children:

	187	i.	**James Madison[7] LEWIS** was born 25 April 1844 in Ohio.
	188	ii.	**Rachel LEWIS** was born about 1845.
	189	iii.	**Robert Allen LEWIS** was born 12 January 1846 in Ohio.
	190	iv.	**William Wallace LEWIS** was born 1847 in Ohio.
	191	v.	**Harriet F. LEWIS** was born 11 May 1851 in Ohio.
	192	vi.	**Lorenzo Dow LEWIS** was born 15 April 1854.

This boy, no doubt, was named for the charismatic preacher, Lorenzo Dow, who died in 1834. Dow drew huge crowds, and many boys were named after him.

	193	vii.	**Ervin Washington LEWIS** was born 21 October 1856 in Ohio.
	194	viii.	**Amelia Belle LEWIS** was born 3 December 1859 in Ohio.
+	195	ix.	**Francis Marion LEWIS** was born 25 February 1863 in Rome Township, Lawrence County, Ohio. He died 25 January 1933 in Lincoln County, West Virginia.

112. **Madison[6] LEWIS** (Joshua[5], Samuel[4], Zebulon[3], James[2], James[1]) was born about 1823 in Monroe County, (West) Virginia.

In 1818 funds were established by the General Assembly of the State of Virginia for free schools, called Literary Schools. Adam Halstead was teaching in Monroe County in 1836, and Mattison Lewis, age 14, was one of his pupils. Katherine Lewis was entered in the records as parent or guardian. William Shanklin taught during the 1838-39 school year, and Madison still was said to be 14. Again Katherine was parent or guardian.[1438] Madison could not have been a son of Joshua Lewis, of course, for Joshua died in 1814.

By the time of the 1860 census for Windsor Township, Madison was married to Martha, age 35, born in Ohio. Madison was also 35, born in Virginia. Son Wilson was 6, and George was 4.[1439]

In 1870 Madison Lewis appears on the Rome Township census as 60 years old, a stave maker, born in Virginia. The only other member of his household was Wilson Lewis, 16, born in Ohio.[1440]

The 1880 U.S. census for Rome Township shows Madison Lewis as 56, born in West Virginia, as were both his parents. His wife, Martha, also 56, was born in Ohio, as were her parents. Son Robt. was 11. Madison's dwelling was numbered 165, and his family was no. 166. (Dwelling and family numbers were not always the same, for sometimes two or more families lived in the same house.) Dwelling 165 included Amanda Short, age 6; James H. Short, age 3; William H. Short, 3 months. A notation to the side says "At House." Also living in dwelling 165 were Wilson M. Lewis, age 26; America, his wife, age 24; Minnie Lewis, age 6; Sarah C. Lewis, age 2; and Matilda Short, a 24-year-old mother. The Short children were part of Family 167, and Wilson's family was No. 168.[1441] James H. Short was a son of John H. Murnahan by Matilda Short. Wilson M. Lewis had married America Murnahan, sister of John H. Murnahan. John H. Murnahan had son James by Matilda Short.[1442]

Madison married (1) **Anna TURNER** on 20 October 1850 in Lawrence County, Ohio.[1443]

Madison married (2) **Rebecca (Lewis) CLARK** on 29 July 1852 in Lawrence County, Ohio.[1444] Rebecca was born in Ohio, the daughter of Wilson Lewis (son of John) and Sarah Burcham. Rebecca and her first husband, William Clark, had two daughters. See below.

Madison and Rebecca had the following children:

+	196	i.	**Wilson M.[7] LEWIS** was born 1854.
	197	ii.	**George LEWIS** was born 1856.

Madison married (3) **Martha CORN** on 26 June 1863.[1445]

They had the following child:

    198   iii. **Robert LEWIS** was born 1869 in Ohio.

Seventh Generation

124.   Rebecca LEWIS (Wilson, John, Samuel, Zebulon, James, James) was born about 1827.

Rebecca married (1) **William CLARK** (1825-1851) in 1845.[1446]

    The 1850 U.S. census for Windsor Township includes William Clarke, 25, and wife, Rebecca, 23. They had two daughters, M. T., 5 years old ; and Salley, 1 year old.[1447]

They had the following children:

    199   i. **Missouri^8 CLARK**, born 1846, married a Mr. **Null**.[1448]

    200   ii. **Sara Catherine CLARK**, born 1848, married a Mr. **Higgins**.[1449]

Rebecca married (2) **Madison LEWIS** on 20 July 1852. Sartin McComas was the minister.[1450]

For children, see Madison and Rebecca (Clark) Lewis.

125.   **John B.**^{7} **LEWIS** (Wilson^6, John^5, Samuel^4, Zebulon^3, James^2, James^1) was born 1828.

    John B. Lewis and wife, Catherine, were on the 1850 U.S. census for Rome Township. John was 23 and Catherine was 22, both born in Ohio. Their only child was 1-year-old Sally E. Lewis. Living next to them was the household of David Walls, 53, and wife, Sally, 47, both born in Virginia. Living with them were Hannah Price, 16, born in Ohio, and David (H?) Lewis, 3.[1451]

    Jno. B. and Catherine Lewis and their children appeared on the 1860 Rome Township census. Jno. was 33 and Catherine, 31. Their children were Salley E., 11; Mary E., 8; Rufus S., 5; Luther P., 3; and Gwinn S., 1 (male). David Wales, 64, and wife, Sally, 57 were five households away.[1452]

    By 1880 the John B. Lewis family had moved to neighboring Gallia County. The census for Guyan Township shows John as 53 years old, a farmer born in Ohio; his father was born in Virginia and his mother in Kentucky. His wife, Catharin, was 52, born in Ohio, and both her parents were born in Ohio. Living with them were sons John B. Lewis, 17; Lewis A. G. J. Lewis, 13; and C. B. B. Lewis, age 8. Daughter Calvania E. Lewis was 11.[1453]

Jonathan married **Catherine L. WALES** on 13 August 1846.[1454]

They had the following children:

    201   i. **Sally E.**^{8} **LEWIS** was born 1849 in Ohio.

    202   ii. **Mary E. LEWIS** was born 1852.

    203   iii. **Rufus S. LEWIS** was born 1855.

    204   iv. **Luther P. LEWIS** was born 1857.

    205   v. **Quincy LEWIS** was born 1859. In *Pioneer Lewis Families*, Michael Lewis Cook lists the child born in 1859 as *Quincy*, not Gwinn S., as above.[1455]

    206   vi. **John B.** LEWIS was born 1863.

    207   vii. **Lewis A. G. J. LEWIS** was born 1867.

    208   viii. **Calvania E. LEWIS** was born 1869.

209 ix. **C. B. B. LEWIS** was born 1872.

126. **Samuel F.⁷ LEWIS** (Wilson⁶, John⁵, Samuel⁴, Zebulon³, James², James¹) was born in 1831 at Scottown, Ohio. He died about 1900 in Marietta, Ohio.[1456]

Names of Samuel's wife and children and birth information are taken from *Pioneer Lewis Families* by Michael Lewis Cook.

The 1860 census for Rome Township includes Samuel F. Lewis, 29; wife, Rachel, 27; Hannah, 6; John W., 4; Sally A., 3; Henrietta, 1.[1457]

In 1880 Samuel and wife, Rachel, and family were living in Athalia, Lawrence County. Children Henrietta, 21; Rebecca, 19; Peter H., 18; Ida E., 15; Rachel, 14; and Jennie, 9, were part of the household. A niece, Sarah Lewis, 18, was living with them.[1458]

Samuel married **Rachel DILLON** on 9 September 1852 in Lawrence County, Ohio.[1459]

They had the following children:

+ 210 i. **Hannah Elizabeth⁸ LEWIS** was born 1854. She died 18 June 1929 in Logan County, West Virginia.[1460] West Virginia death records show Hanna Elizabeth Scarberry, daughter of Rachel Dillon and Samuel Lewis, dying in Logan County, West Virginia. Hannah married **Noah Webster SCARBERRY**.

+ 211 ii. **John Wilson LEWIS** was born 20 January 1856 and died 11 August 1949.

212 iii. **Sally A. LEWIS** was born 1857.

213 iv. **Rebecca LEWIS** was born 1861.

214 v. **Peter H. LEWIS** was born 1862.

215 vi. **Ida E. LEWIS** was born 1865.

216 vii. **Rachel LEWIS** was born 1866.

217 viii. **Jennie LEWIS** was born 1871.

128. **George S.⁷ LEWIS** (Wilson⁶, John⁵, Samuel⁴, Zebulon³, James², James¹) was born January 1833.

In 1860 Geo. S. Lewis, 27, and wife, Mary, 27, and children John W., 6; Sally E., 5; Mahala, J., 3; Griffin C., 2; and George P., 6 months, were living in Rome Township.[1461]

George S. Lewis and his family were living in District 64, Lincoln, West Virginia, when the U.S. census of 1880 was taken. Geo. S. Lewis was a 49-year old farmer, his father having been born in Virginia, his mother in Kentucky. Children were Greffin C., 22; Percy, 20, Wm., 16; Wilson, 14; James, 12; America S., 8, all born in Ohio. Living near them was the family of Isaac and Nancy Sowards.[1462]

George S. Lewis, wife, Mary, and son Wilson were living in Millers Precinct, Lawrence County, Ohio, in 1900. Also living in this household were a granddaughter, Elizabeth Daniels, born in November 1884, a grandson H(?) Daniels, born June 1886.[1463]

George married **Mary "Polly" SOWARDS** on 16 September 1852 in Lawrence County, Ohio.[1464] Mary was born February 1833.

George and Mary had the following children:

218 i. **John W.⁸ LEWIS** was born 1854.

219 ii. **Sally E. LEWIS** was born 1855.

220 iii. **Mahala J. LEWIS** was born 1857.

+ 221 iv. **Griffith C. LEWIS** was born May 1857.

222   v. **George Percy LEWIS** was born 1860.

223   vi. **William LEWIS** was born 1864.

224   vii. **Wilson LEWIS** was born February 1867.

Wilson Lewis, age 44, appears on the U.S. census of 1910 for Rome Township, Lawrence County, Ohio. Living with him was wife, Mamie, and son **Sylvester**, less than a year old. Wilson and his family seem to have been living in the same household as Moses Norman, 77, and wife, Mary A., 63.[1465]

225   viii. **James LEWIS** was born 1868.

226   ix. **America S. LEWIS** was born 1872.

133. **Redman C.^{7} LEWIS** (Wilson^6, John^5, Samuel^4, Zebulon^3, James^2, James^1) was born 11 February 1844 and died 1924.

Redmon Lewis, 26, and wife, America, 16, appeared on the 1870 Rome Township census.[1466]

The names and birth months and years of Redmon C. Lewis's family are taken from the 1900 federal census for Millers Precinct. Redman was 57, born February 1843; wife, Mary M., was 46, born October 1852. Children Blake, Goldie, Nellie, Stanley, and Hazel were named, and their birth months and years given. Also living in the household (Dwelling 118) was a grandson, George Lewis, born in July 1882.[1467]

The 1910 Rome Township census gave middle initials for Goldie, Nellie, Stanley, and Hazel, and another son, apparently named *Richard B.*, was also added. This census shows Redmond C. as 66 and wife, Mary M., 58, born in Virginia. They were in Dwelling 247, and Peter Lewis, 47 (?) was in dwelling 245. This man would have been the son of Samuel F. Lewis, Redmon's brother.[1468]

Redman C. Lewis was 80 when died of cancer of the prostate on 2 June 1924. His death certificate states he was a son of Wilson Lewis and Elizabeth Burcham. The informant was B. C. Lewis. Redman was to be buried at Miller, Ohio.[1469]

Redman married (1) **America S. DOLTON** on 30 October 1869.[1470]

Redman married (2) **Mary Ann WHITE**. According to Jewel M. Callicott, who compiled *Callicott Connections II*, Mary Ann White lived from 1852-1922.[1471]

Redman and Mary were married by the time the census was taken for Rome Township in 1880. Redman was 37 years old and wife, Mary, 34. Both her parents were born in Ohio. They had children Sarah, 4, and Blake, 2.[1472]

They had the following children:

227   i. **Sarah^8 LEWIS** was born 1876.

228   ii. **Blake LEWIS** was born May 1879.

229   iii. **Goldie E. LEWIS** was born May 1885.

230   iv. **Nellie P. LEWIS** was born February 1888.

231   v. **Stanley L. LEWIS** was born December 1890.

232   vi. **Richard (?) B. LEWIS** was born 1893.

233   vii. **Hazel D. LEWIS** was born September 1895.

149. **Mary Ellen^7 LEWIS** (James J.^{6}, Joshua^5, Samuel^4, Zebulon^3, James^2, James^1) was born December 1841.

On 28 November 1857 James Lewis conveyed to Mary Saword, "formerly Mary Lewis," 77 1/2 acres of land described as "The South West quarter of the North East quarter And the North East quarter of the North West quarter of

Section twenty four in Township two in Range Sixteen, All Except two and half acres . . . deeded to Alexander Pinkerman...." Wits: Nathaniel Burcham, Jesse S. Burcham.[1473] The deed to Pinkerman had been made on 12 August 1857. Pinkerman's land was on Peter Cave Run by the Rock Clift. Wits: Nathl. Burcham and James P. Burcham.[1474] Township 2 in Range 16 is Windsor.

Not surprisingly the 1860 census for Windsor Township shows Griffin L. [sic] Sowards, 26, and wife, Mary, 19, living next door to James and Rebecca Lewis. Griffin and Mary had daughters Catherine, 4; Minerva J., 2; and Pheby, less than a year.[1475]

In 1870 the census includes Griffen, 35, and Mary, 29. They had 6 children: Catharine, 14; Minerva, 12; Phoebe, 14; Isaac, 7; Griffen, 5; and Ellene, 2.[1476]

The 1880 U.S. census for Windsor Township, Lawrence County, Ohio, shows Griff Sowards, 47, a farmer, whose parents were born in Virginia. Wife, Mary, was 39, and both her parents born in Ohio (obviously an error). Children: Jane (Pheby?), 20; Isaac, 19; Griff, 17; Lena, 12; Mary, 7; Sallie, 6; and John, 3.[1477]

When the 1900 U.S. census was taken, Mary E. Soward was living in Athalia Village, Millers Precinct. Her year of birth varies from one census to the next, but, if I am interpreting the handwriting correctly, she claimed to have been born in December 1835 in Ohio. Elizabeth Asbury, her mother, and James J. Lewis, her father, were married in April 1840 in Monroe County (now West Virginia), and she was 7 when the 1850 census was taken. The 1835 year of birth has to be wrong. But she wouldn't have forgotten the month in which she was born, and that was correct. Mary E. Soward was head of household, and son John J. Soward, born January 1872, was living with her.[1478]

At the time of the 1920 census Mary C. (?) Sowards, 78, was boarding at the home of Mary Lewis, age 66 (Dwelling 142). Mary Lewis's daughter, Lennie, age 31, and grandson Harry, age 10, were living with her. This household was two houses away from that of James A. Lewis (Dwelling 140).[1479]

Mary married **Griffith S. SOWARDS** on 14 June 1855 in Lawrence County, Ohio. Nathaniel Burcham, J.P., officiated.[1480]

They had the following children:

  234 i. **Catherine**[8] **SOWARDS** was born 1856.

  235 ii. **Minerva J. SOWARDS** was born 12 April 1859 and died 8 November 1912. She married a Mr. **BURCHAM**.

    Jane Burcham was of Rome Township when she died on 8 November 1912. Information on her death certificate: She was born 12 April 1859. Her father was Griffith Sowards, and her mother was Mary Lewis. The informant was Jasper Burcham of Athalia, Ohio. Cause of death was a carcinoma of the uterus, and contributory cause was Bright's Disease. She was to be buried at the Sowards' Cemetery.[1481]

+ 236 iii. **Phoebe SOWARDS** was born 1860. .

  237 iv. **Isaac SOWARDS** was born 1863.

  238 v. **Griffin SOWARDS** was born 1865.

  239 vi. **Ellena SOWARDS** was born 1868.

+ 240 vii. **George SOWARDS** was born 1872.

  241 viii. **Mary SOWARDS** was born 1873.

  242 ix. **Sallie SOWARDS** was born 1874.

  243 x. **John SOWARDS** was born 1877.

+ 244 xi. **Gilbert SOWARDS** was born 1882.

150. **Lewis Edward**[7] **LEWIS**, "Buck," (James J.[6], Joshua[5], Samuel[4], Zebulon[3], James[2], James[1]) was born February 1858 in Lawrence County, Ohio. He died 20 February 1938 in Lawrence County, Ohio.

Lewis Edward Lewis was known as "Buck" and appears in James and Rebecca's household as Lewis E. Bird on the 1860 census for Windsor Township. He was 78 when he died on 20 February 1938, and his name was entered as *Buck Lewis* in the Death Register. He was of Proctorville, Ohio, and a retired farmer. Cause of death was chronic cirrhosis of the liver.[1482] He had a reputation for being a heavy drinker. Relatives tell me that Buck was aware that he was born prior to the marriage of his parents and that he stewed over the matter. But he was known to be kind to animals, threatening to take his horses home when they were borrowed by a man who swore at them.

Some background on Virginia culture would help explain Lawrence County attitudes, for many of its early settlers were from Virginia. A surprisingly large number of women were pregnant when they married in the early days in Virginia, but illegitimate births were less common. It has been figured that between 1749 and 1780 in Kingston Parish, Gloucester County, Virginia, one fourth to one third of brides were already pregnant. People were tolerant of pregnancies before marriage, as long as the couple wed as soon as possible.[1483] One Lawrence County woman with a questionable reputation lived in Scottown. She had her own way of dealing with gossip: She opened her windows wide and played on her phonograph a song with the words, "It's nobody's business but mine."

Buck was known as Buck Lewis, but he occasionally used the name Lewis Burd. Otis Lewis bought land from Lewis E. Burd on 9 August 1916. The tract was in Section 27, Township 2 (Windsor), Range 15.[1484]

According to Arnold Lewis, Buck married Janey Burd, who was born in 1852 and died in 1915. Buck is on the 1900 federal census for Millers Precinct as Lewis E. Burd, born in February 1858, and married to a Louiza J. (Janey?). Son Thos. J., 18, was living with them. Buck's house (Dwelling 229) was listed next to that of Isaac and Elizabeth Susan Scarberry (Dwelling 230).[1485]

Buck E. Lewis appeared on the 1920 census for Union Township. The handwriting is hard to make out, but he appears to have been widowed. He was 55 years old (an error). Also living in his home were Thomas J. Lewis, 29 years old, and wife, Eliza, 21 years old. Their son's name is difficult to read.[1486]

Buck married **Louiza J. BURD**. Louiza was born January 1852 in Ohio. Louiza (?) and her mother were born in Ohio, her father in Virginia.

They had the following child and probably others:

245   i. **Thomas J.**[8] **LEWIS** was born June 1889.

151.   **James Albert**[7] **LEWIS** (James J.[6], Joshua[5], Samuel[4], Zebulon[3], James[2], James[1]) was born March 1861 in Lawrence County, Ohio. He died in 1940 in Lawrence County.

Jim Lewis certainly made his mark on the world. He had a speech defect, but managed to become a justice of the peace. His home was around the bend from where my mother, Faye Lewis, grew up, and she enjoyed walking over to his farm and listening to him hold court under a large tree in his back yard.

Jim's enjoyment of argument extended to religious matters. After he became a member of the Church of Christ, he would attend other denominations and pretend he was considering becoming a member. When he got the attention of the pastor or elders, he would contend with them about Biblical facts, making an effort to convert them to the Church of Christ.

He held strong opinions and did not want to waste time listening to a preacher he didn't like. For a period of time, the Church of Christ on Pleasant Ridge (Tick Ridge), where he was a member, provided two sermons on Sunday mornings, delivered by two preachers. Jim had the habit of showing up for the first sermon but leaving if he did not like the preacher and returning for the second sermon. On one occasion he peeked into the church building to find that the preacher was not one of his favorites. Jim walked the couple of miles to Scottown to bide his time there until the second preacher would take the pulpit. But he returned before the first preacher had finished, and the preacher said, "Well, I see one of our members has missed my sermon. I'll just have to preach it over again."

Relatives tell a tale of Jim's fighting with some man and biting off his ear. This sort of fighting was common in Virginia in the 1800s and probably carried over into Lawrence County, where much of its population had Virginia roots. The man carried his ear around in his pocket for a week or two, but when he asked a doctor to reattach it, it was too late.

Jim, fearing prosecution, fled to West Virginia for a couple of years. It was suspected that Jim had returned with enough money to pay off his victim. Presumably this incident was before he gained enough standing in the community to become a justice of the peace.

The birth months and years of James and Rosella, Ethel, Ezra, Oscar, Otis, and William Berkeley (Bert) were taken from the 1900 census for Millers Precinct.[1487] The 1910 census for Windsor Township included children Ezra, 23; Oscar, 20; Otie, 17; Bert, 1(?); Alva, 10; and Ella, 4.[1488] In 1920 the household of James A. Lewis consisted of him and wife, Rosella; Wm. Berkley, 23; Elva B., 18; and Ella F., 14.[1489] In 1930 James was 69; Rosella was 63. Still at home were Bert, 33; Elva, 29; and Ella 24. The census taker put the James Lewis household in the same dwelling as Daisy Wall, who was head of her household. In the next dwelling was the household of Otis Lewis and wife, Berdie, and family. Listed right after Otis were his brother Ezra and wife, Edna, and their family. William Lewis and wife, Rachel, and family were next.[1490] Rachel was a good friend of Edna (Payne) Lewis, my grandmother, as was Otis's wife, Berdie.

Jim Lewis's farm consisted of five parcels, totaling 94 acres.

James married **Rosella PINKERMAN** on 29 July 1883 in Lawrence County, Ohio.[1491] Rose was a daughter of William Bedford PINKERMAN and Mary Ann JOHNSON.

Rosella died in March 1950. I remember her as extremely thin. She had had tuberculosis at one time. My father said that the Pinkermans were prone to get tuberculosis, but they usually survived it. Rosella was said to have been a beauty when she was young.

Rose's parents, William Pinkerman, 36, and wife, Mary, 24, were living in Rome Township when the 1870 census was taken. Rosalie [sic] was 4 and her sister Arabel was 1 at the time.[1492] William Pinkerman, Jr., had married Mary Ann Johnson on 13 October 1864. William was 21 and Mary, 18. Daniel Beller gave a sworn statement for the marriage license.[1493]

William Pinkerman was a son of William Pinkerman and Margaret Brown, who married 25 January 1827.[1494] The 1860 Windsor Township census shows William Pinkerman as a 54-year-old farmer, born in Virginia. Wife, Margaret, 51, was born in Ohio. Children: William, 25; Sarah A., 23; Andrew, 20; Elias, 17; Francis P., 16; Alexander, 14; Alonzo P., 12; Missouri E., 10.[1495]

According to an article in *History of Lawrence County, Ohio, 1990*, William Pinkerman, Sr., was a son of John Pinkerman and wife, Sarah Holmes, who married in 1802 in Culpeper County, Virginia.[1496] George Holmes's name occurred frequently in Culpeper County records, for he owned a lot of land, but I have not been able to trace this Sarah Holmes.

Randolph Pinkerman has written a paper, seemingly unpublished, stating that William Bidford Pinkerman and wife, Virginia Holmes, were the first to come to America. William's father, William Mathew, owned a fleet of vessels. William Bidford returned to England and died there, but his wife, Jenny, remained in America with her children and grandchildren. A son, William Bidford, married Margaret "Peggy" Brown. Peggy had the finest horses and buggy in their part of the county, and she rode it into Athalia (Lawrence County, Ohio) to buy groceries. She liked to argue politics and became angry if opposed. I have heard people from Lawrence County talk of an opinionated Peggy Pinkerman with a fine horse and buggy.

They had the following children:

+ 246   i.   **Aletha[8] LEWIS** died 1965.

   247   ii.   **Ethel M. LEWIS** was born October 1884 in Lawrence County, Ohio.

+ 248   iii. **Ezra Clare LEWIS** was born 2 December 1886 and died July 1965.

+ 249   iv. **Oscar LEWIS** was born March 1890.

+ 250   v.   **Otis Hartley LEWIS** was born March 1893 and died 1959.

   251   vi. **William Berkeley LEWIS, "Bert,"** was born 28 May 1896 in Lawrence County, Ohio. He died June 1979.[1497]

Bert was living in Chesapeake, Ohio, when his brother Ezra died.

Bert married **Geneva DUNFEE**, born 12 March 1907. She died November 1981.[1498] Geneva Runyan was married previously to Frank Dunfee.

+ 252 vii. **Elva B. LEWIS** was born 31 July 1900 and died November 1969.

+ 253 viii. **Ella G. LEWIS** was born 28 October 1905 and died August 1979.

152. **Thomas Jefferson[7] LEWIS** (James J.[6], Joshua[5], Samuel[4], Zebulon[3], James[2], James[1]) was born April 1863 in Lawrence County, Ohio. He died on 25 Sepember 1938 in Lawrence County.[1499]

Sylvia Fulks, born to Thomas J. Lewis and Maybelle "May" Kirkman, gave background on her family in *History of Lawrence County, Ohio, 1990*. In 1906 Thomas and May Lewis owned a general merchandise store in Scottown. Merchandise was brought to the store by horse and wagon. After World War I, TJ, as he was called, and Mae ran a grocery store in Huntington, West Virginia, but spent their summers on the small farm they bought near Scottown. In 1924 they retired there.[1500]

The 1910 census for Windsor Township includes Thomas J. Lewis's household. He was 47 and wife, May E. was 34. Daughter Aggie A. was 22; son Wilbur R., 19; daughter Ina E.was 16; daughter Mary M., 12; and Sylvia I. was 4. Nicholas G. Kirkman, 75, father-in-law, was living with them.[1501]

By 1920 daughter Mary had married, for this was TJ's household: Thomas J. Lewis, 55; wife, Mable E., 43; daughter Sylvia, 14; and daughter Mary M. Dunfee, 22. Grandson Ray F. Dunfee was 3 1/2.[1502]

The birth and death years of the family of Thomas J. Lewis and the names of spouses are taken from the article by Sylvia Fulks, cited above. TJ died of hypertrophic cirrhosis of the liver.[1503] This condition is now called biliary cirrhosis, and its cause is unknown.

Thomas married (1) **Cora MORRISON**. Cora was born 1870. She died 1894.

They had the following children:

    254 i. **Vivian[8] LEWIS**. She died in infancy.

+ 255 ii. **Aggie A. LEWIS** was born March 1888.

+ 256 iii. **Wilbur R. LEWIS** was born May 1890.

+ 257 iv. **Ina E. LEWIS** was born April 1882.

Thomas married (2) **Maybelle Elizabeth KIRKMAN**, "Mae," daughter of Nicholas G. KIRKMAN and Mary MORRISON. Mae was born December 1875. She died 1976.

They had the following children:

+ 258 v. **Mary M. LEWIS** was born February 1897 and died 1964.

+ 259 vi. **Sylvia I. LEWIS** was born 1905.

153. **Mary[7] LEWIS** (James J.[6], Joshua[5], Samuel[4], Zebulon[3], James[2], James[1]) was born March 1872 in Ohio. She died 1958. Mary's year of death was supplied by Iris (Scarberry) Burd, whose mother was Della Galloway, a niece of John T. M. Galloway.

Mary married **John Thomas Morton GALLOWAY**, son of Henry GALLOWAY and Susannah. John was born May 1856 in Ohio. He died 1946. John Galloway had married first Harriet E. BURD, daughter of George A. BURD and Elizabeth SCARBERRY.[1504] Harriet died of the fits (seizures?) in 1886.

See SCARBERRY (SCARBOROUGH) Section for John and Harriet's children.

The 1900 census for Millers Precinct shows John Galloway as 44, born May 1856; wife, Mary, 28, was born March 1872. The birth month and year of each of their children is given below. Frederick C. was 12; Jackson O. was 8; Oscar E. was 6; Myrtie R. was 4; Evert J. was 9 months. Son Henry H., born September 1879, was 20; Thomas H., born March 1884, was 18.[1505] The last two sons, of course, had been born to John Galloway and Harriet Burd.

The Rome Township census for 1910 includes John and Mary Galloway. Son Thomas H. was 28; Charles F. was 11; Ira was 18; Oscar E., 16; Myrtle R., 14; James E., 10; Jesse M., 9; Franklin E. was 8(?); Norman R., 5; Louis F., 1.[1506]

John and Mary Galloway are on the Rome Township census of 1920. They had children Evert, 20; son Jessie, 18; Frank, 16; Norman H., 14; Myrtle, 23; Forest, 10.[1507]

Mary and John Galloway had the following children:

    260   i.   **Charles Frederick**[8] **GALLOWAY** was born 23 January 1888. He died October 1986 in Lawrence County, Ohio. Charles Galloway's places of residence named on the U.S. Social Security Death Index were Athalia, Proctorville, and Rome, Ohio.[1508] Fred Galloway, 26, son of John Galloway and Mary Lewis, married **Meda CALLICOAT**, daughter of George Washington CALLICOAT and Anna DILLON, on 24 February 1914 (date of marriage license).[1509] Almeda Catherine Callicoat was born 22 October 1893.[1510]

    261   ii.   **Ira Jackson GALLOWAY** was born December 1891.

    262   iii.   **Oscar E. GALLOWAY** was born October 1893.

    263   iv.   **Myrtle Ruth GALLOWAY** was born December 1895. Myrtle married Mr. **JOHNSON**.

    264   v.   **James Everett GALLOWAY** was born August 1899 in Proctorville, Ohio. On 26 March 1919 Everett Galloway married **Willa BAME**. The marriage certificate shows him to have been a farmer, the son of John Galloway and Mary Lewis. Willa was the daughter of John BAME and Mary McCORKLE.[1511]

    265   vi.   **Jesse Morton GALLOWAY** was born 1901.

    266   vii.   **Frank Edwin GALLOWAY** was born 1902.

    267   viii.   **Norman GALLOWAY** was born 1905.

    268   ix.   **Louis F. GALLOWAY** was born 1909. He was called "Forrest."

160. **Nancy**[7] **LEWIS** (Richard Burton[6], Joshua[5], Samuel[4], Zebulon[3], James[2], James[1]) was born 1840 in Lawrence County, Ohio. She died 1896.[1512]

Nancy married **Jacob W. LEMLEY**. Jacob was born 1839.[1513]

They had the following children:

+   269   i.   **Hattie**[8] **LEMLEY** was born 1869 and died 1951.

161. **Richard Clark**[7] **LEWIS** (Richard Burton[6], Joshua[5], Samuel[4], Zebulon[3], James[2], James[1]) was born 30 November 1843. He died 25 October 1916 and was buried in Pleasant Ridge graveyard, Lawrence County.

The birth and death years of Richard C. and Mary A. Lewis are on their tombstones in Pleasant Ridge Cemetery. Buried by them are Myrtie, Lizzie, and George Lewis.

The 1880 U.S. census for Windsor Township includes Richard Lewis, 34, as head of household. Wife, Mary, was 26; daughter Bertha was 8; Myrtie was 6; Lizzie was 3, and Hattie was two months.[1514]

Richard and Mary are on the 1910 census for Windsor Township, Richard 65, born in Ohio, his father born in Virginia and his mother in Ohio. Mary was 57, born in Ohio, her father born in Pennsylvania and her mother in Ohio. Son William H., 20, was living with them.[1515]

Lawrence County death records show Richard Lewis, a 73-year-old farmer, dying of hypertrophic cirrhosis of the liver on 25 October 1916.[1516] Cause of this condition is unknown.

An article in *History of Lawrence County, Ohio, 1990*, written by Lennie Lewis Bundy, has supplied much of the information of Richard and Mary and their children.[1517]

Richard married **Mary Ann BURD**, daughter of George A. BURD and Elizabeth (Betsey) SCARBERRY, on 18 September 1870. Mary was born 15 September 1852. She died 1922 and was buried in Pleasant Ridge graveyard, Lawrence County.[1518]

Mary Ann Burd grew up on Wolfe Creek in Lawrence County, Ohio.[1519]

Richard and Mary had the following children:

- 270   i.   **Ralph⁸ LEWIS**. He died young.
- 271   ii.   **George LEWIS** died 1883 and was buried in Pleasant Ridge graveyard, Lawrence County. He died young.
- 272   iii.   **Ida LEWIS**. She died young.
- 273   iv.   **Bertha LEWIS** was born 1872. She married **Anthony "Crum" FREEMAN** on 24 May 1908. He was a son of Isaac FREEMAN and Vina HAMILTON.[1520]
- 274   v.   **Myrtie M. LEWIS** was born 1874. She died 1910 and was buried at Pleasant Ridge.
- 275   vi.   **Elizabeth LEWIS**, "Lizzie," was born 1877. She died 1908 and is buried in Pleasant Ridge graveyard, Lawrence County.
- 276   vii.   **Hattie LEWIS** was born 1880.
- 277   viii.   **Anna Gertrude LEWIS** was born 1885. She was of Scottown when she married **Edward W. KNIGHT** on 13 February 1907.[1521]
- 278   ix.   **Effie LEWIS** was born 1889. She married **David W. WALL, Jr.**, on 19 April 1908. David was a son of R.F. WALLS and Sarah E. HAYES.[1522]
- + 279   x.   **William Henry Harrison LEWIS** was born 1891 and died 27 May 1940.

170.   **Barbara Jane⁷ LEWIS** (Samuel D.⁶, Joshua⁵, Samuel⁴, Zebulon³, James², James¹) was born 27 February 1838 in Monroe County, (West) Virginia. She died 3 July 1932 in Lincoln County, West Virginia. Her death certificate states she was a daughter of Samuel Lewis and Rhoda Miller.[1523]

Barbara married **John DILLON** on 16 October 1872 in Gallia County, Ohio.

Information on this family was furnished by P. Matthew Sutko.

They had the following children:

- 280   i.   **Nettie DILLON**. She married **John Bunyan VICKERS**.
- 281   ii.   **Allie DILLON**. She married **Albert E. VICKERS**.

195.   **Francis Marion⁷ LEWIS** (Wallace⁶, Joshua⁵, Samuel⁴, Zebulon³, James², James¹) was born 25 February 1863 in Rome Township, Lawrence County, Ohio. He died 25 January 1933 in Lincoln County, West Virginia.

Francis married **Elizabeth Jane HARBOUR**, daughter of George HARBOUR and Emily BURD, on 12 March 1891 in Lincoln County, West Virginia. Elizabeth was born 8 December 1872 in Guyan Township, Gallia County, Ohio. She died 10 January 1949 in Lincoln Co, West Virginia.[1524]

They had the following child:

- 282   i.   **Robert Linuel⁸ LEWIS**, born 8 January 1917 in Lincoln County, West Virginia. He died 6 November 1994 in

Beaver County, Pennsylvania. He married **Barbara GABOR** born in 1921 in Wheeling, West Virginia. She died 31 December 2003.

This information furnished by Robert Linuel Lewis, Jr.

196.   **Wilson M.**[7] **LEWIS** (Madison[6], Joshua[5], Samuel[4], Zebulon[3], James[2], James[1]) was born 1854 in Ohio.

The 1880 U.S. census for Rome Township, shows Wilson M. Lewis, age 26, working for self, and born in Ohio. He worked on a farm. His father was born in West Virginia, his mother in Ohio. His wife, America, was 24, and her father was born in West Virginia, her mother in Ohio. Daughter Minnie was 6, born in Ohio; daughter Sarah C. was 2, born in Ohio. Matilda Short was living with them, and she was born in Ohio, her father in West Virginia, her mother in Ohio. She was said to be a 24-year-old mother.[1525]

Wilson married **America MURNAHAN**. America was born 1856, a daughter of John MURNAHAN and Mary Ann KING.[1526]

They had the following children and others.

    283   i.   **Minnie**[8] **LEWIS** was born 1874 in Ohio.

    284   ii.   **Sarah C. LEWIS** was born 1878 in Ohio.

    285   iii.   **Wilbert LEWIS** was born 1885 at Wilgus, Ohio. He married Sophia **MURNAHAN** on 19 June 1909. The license shows him as 24, a son of Wilson Lewis and America Murnahan. Sophia was 17, a daughter of David MURNAHAN and Rachel HOFFMAN.[1527]

Eighth Generation

210.   **Henrietta (Hattie)**[8] LEWIS (Samuel F.[7], Wilson[6], John[5], Samuel[4], Zebulon[3], James[2], James[1]) was born 1848.

Henrietta married **Noah W. SCARBERRY**, son of Joseph SCARBERRY and Elizabeth SOWARDS. Noah was born 1843.

See the SCARBERRY (SCARBOROUGH) Section for the names of their children.

211.   **John Wilson**[8] **LEWIS** (Samuel F.[7], Wilson[6], John[5], Samuel[4], Zebulon[3], James[2], James[1]) was born 20 January 1856 in Scottown, Ohio. He died 11 August 1949 in Platform, Ohio.[1528]

Birth information on children William, Samuel, Mary, Oscar, and Benjamin comes from the 1900 federal census for Millers Precinct. At that time John, head of household, was said to have been born in January 1852; his wife, Ida, in November 1866.[1529]

When the 1920 Rome Township census was taken, John was 63, head of household, and living with him were some of his children: Maud 16, Hazel 11, and Ben 21, Oscar 28. Ruby Lewis, 26, a daughter-in-law, and grandson Paul, 1 ½, were part of the household.[1530]

John married **Ida Rosalie NULL** in 1881. Ida was born 26 November 1866. She died June 1921 in Platform, Ohio. She was a daughter of William Harrison NULL and Missouri Ann CLARK.[1531]

They had the following children:

+   286   i.   **William Elmer**[9] **LEWIS** was born August 1882 and died 1927.

    287   ii.   **Samuel LEWIS** was born April 1884 and died 1965. He married **Nettie BURCHAM**.[1532]

    288   iii.   **Mae LEWIS** was born May 1887. Mae married **William BULEN** in December 1907. The marriage certificate states that May M. Lewis was a daughter of John Lewis and Ida Null. William M. Bulen, born Franklin County, Ohio, was a son of Wm. BULEN.[1533]

	289	iv.	**John Oscar LEWIS** was born 4 August 1891 and died 14 May 1976.

290   v.   **Benjamin Bryant LEWIS** was born October 1895 and died 1959. He married **Alta DANIELS**.[1534]

291   vi.   **Maude LEWIS**, "Helen," was born 1903. She married **Samuel HOWARD**.[1535]

292   vii.   **Hazel LEWIS** was born 1908. She married **Frank KELLY**.[1536]

221.   **Griffith C.**[8] **LEWIS** (George S.[7], Wilson[6], John[5], Samuel[4], Zebulon[3], James[2], James[1]) was born May 1857 in Ohio.

Birth months and years for Griffith and his family were taken from the 1900 census for Millers Precinct. At that time Griffith was 43; wife, Evaline was 38; Cora M. was 14; William R. was 12; and Owen T. was 8.[1537]

The 1910 census for Rome Township shows Griffith as 52; wife, Evelyn S., 46; William R., 22; Thomas O., 15.[1538] (The handwriting on the census page is faded.)

Griffith married **Evelyn S.** Evelyn was born August 1861 in Ohio.

They had the following children:

293   i.   **Cora M.**[9] **LEWIS** was born December 1883 in Ohio.

294   ii.   **William R. LEWIS** was born February 1889 in West Virginia.

295   iii.   **Thomas O. LEWIS** was born November 1894 in Ohio.

236.   **Phebe**[8] **SOWARDS** (Mary Ellen[7], James J.[6], Joshua[5], Samuel[4], Zebulon[3], James[2], James[1]) was born in 1860.

The U.S. census of 1880 for Windsor Township includes Buck Floyd, 22, and wife, Phebe, 21. They had son Walter Floyd, 1 year old. Also living with them was a girl, Metta Sowards, 1 year old.[1539]

Phebe married **Buck FLOYD**.

They had the following child:

296   i.   **Walter**[9] **FLOYD** was born 1879.

240.   **George**[8] **SOWARDS** (Mary Ellen[7], James J.[6], Joshua[5], Samuel[4], Zebulon[3], James[2], James[1]) was born in 1872.

The 1910 census for Windsor Township includes George W (?). Sowards, 38, and wife, Rose A., 33. In their household were sons Roy E., 15; Griffin S., 5; daughter Willa (?) O., 3; and mother Mary E. Sowards, 73.[1540]

George married **Rose A**. She was born 1877.

They had the following children:

297   i.   **Roy E.**[9] **SOWARDS** was born 1895.

298   ii.   **Griffin S. SOWARDS** was born 1905.

299   iii.   **Willa O. SOWARDS** was born 1907.

244.   **Gilbert**[8] **SOWARDS** (Mary Ellen[7], James J.[6], Joshua[5], Samuel[4], Zebulon[3], James[2], James[1]) was born in 1882.

Gilbert is on the 1910 Windsor Township census as head of family, 28 years old. Living with him were his wife, Ida J., also 28; son Griffin A., 9; a daughter ___il M., 11 months.[1541]

Gilbert married **Ida J**. She was born in 1882.

They had the following children:

    300   i.   **Griffin A.[9] SOWARDS** was born 1901.

    301   ii.   **___il M. SOWARDS** was born about 1909.

246.   **Aletha[8] LEWIS** (James Albert[7], James J.[6], Joshua[5], Samuel[4], Zebulon[3], James[2], James[1]) was born in Lawsrence County, Ohio, and died 1965.

Aletha married **William SYDENSTRICKER**.

They had the following children:

    302   i.   **Edna[9] SYDENSTRICKER**. She was born 24 April 1906 and died 11 April 2000.[1542] She married Mr. **RIGGS**, and they lived in Barboursville, West Virginia.

                    Faye (Lewis) Young remembered fondly the good company of Edna and her sister Pearl.

    303   ii.   **Faye SYDENSTRICKER**.

    304   iii.   **Forest SYDENSTRICKER**.

    305   iv.   **Lee SYDENSTRICKER**.

    306   v.   **Billy SYDENSTRICKER**.

    307   vi.   **Pearl SYDENSTRICKER**. She was born 8 June 1914 and died 13 May 1997.[1543] She married **Martin WALKER**.

    308   vii.   **Betty SYDENSTRICKER**.

248.   **Ezra Clare[8] LEWIS** (James Albert[7], James J.[6], Joshua[5], Samuel[4], Zebulon[3], James[2], James[1]) was born 2 December 1886 in Lawrence County, Ohio. He died July 1965 in Lawrence County, Ohio.

    Ezra C. Lewis, 33, and wife, Edna M., 30, were on the 1920 Windsor Township census. Daughter Fay was 8; son Ray, 5; and son Thurman was a year and three months. Previous to them on the list was the household of John and Sarah Dillon, and following them was the household of David W. and Emma Wall. David and Emma Wall's daughter Mable was 7.[1544] Mable Wall and Faye Lewis, my mother, were good friends. Mable was killed by a lightning strike. She was sleeping on a bed that abutted a wall when the lightning hit. Many houses in that area had neither lightning rods nor indoor plumbing. I grew up in houses with indoor plumbing, but my mother still kept our beds away from the walls of the house, not quite trusting the plumbing to act as a lightning rod.

    By 1930 Ezra and Edna's family had grown. The Windsor census shows Ezra as 43, Edna, 40; Faye, 18; Ray, 14; Thurman, 11; and Erma Ruth, 8. Ezra's brother Otis Lewis and family were next door, their household following that of their parents, James and Rosalie [*sic*]. The household of William Lewis and wife, Rachel, and family followed that of Ezra.[1545]

    Ezra was a caring man. One of his brothers was a heavy drinker, and friends would come in the night to ask him to get his brother home. Ezra never drank, and he felt strongly about the damage done by too much alcohol. Once, a man offered his sons whisky. Ezra picked up his shot gun and paid a visit to the man's home and made it clear he didn't want it to happen again.

    When neighbors became ill, they liked for Ezra to sit with them. I've never heard that he had any special nursing skills, so I presume they just felt secure in his company. His daughter, Betty, said that one night he came home so tired that he fell through the door onto the living room floor and slept there the rest of the night.

    At times Ezra's forthright speech was humorous. When purchasing with credit cards became common, he was still used to paying with cash. He was shopping at a department store in Ironton, and the clerk asked him if he was going to pay for the shirt he had chosen. His response: "You didn't think I was just going to take it, did you?"

Ezra farmed most of his life, but eventually he followed local trends and worked at the chemical plant in South Point, Ohio. He retired from Carolina Lumber Company in Huntington, West Virginia. After Edna died, Ezra learned to drive a car.

He had hardly been sick a day in his life when he came down with pneumonia a few weeks before his death. Son Ray and his wife, Molly, lived just around the bend, and he was invited to stay with them. When it became clear that he was seriously ill, they called for an ambulance. When it arrived, Ezra insisted on walking out to it on his own. And it carried him over little Squirt Creek, up the hill to the road and on to Ironton. He died in Lawrence County General Hospital. His funeral was held at Pleasant Ridge Church of Christ (commonly known as Tick Ridge), and Evangelist C. M. Cleveland officiated. He was buried beside his wife, Edna, and son Donald, at the graveyard of the Fairview Baptist Church at Wilgus.

Ezra married **Edna Mae PAYNE,** 21, daughter of John Shannon PAYNE and Emily HIGGINS, in Lawrence County, Ohio, on 28 February 1911. The marriage license states that Ezra was a 24-year-old farmer from Scottown, a son of James Lewis and Rose Pinkerman. Edna was a daughter of Shannon Payne and Emily Higgins of Wilgus.[1546] Edna was born 19 October 1890 in Lawrence County, Ohio. She died 18 February 1951 in Huntington, West Virginia, and was buried at the Fairview Baptist Church graveyard, Wilgus, Ohio.[1547]

At the time of the 1900 census for Mason Township, Edna M. was 10 years old, born in October 1889. Her parents were John S. Payne, 42, and Emily J., 47. Brothers and sisters were John W., 19; Elizabeth, 17; Bertha O., 15; Sarah B., 12; Charly 8, and Ona, 6.[1548]

Edna was my grandmother, and when my family visited her home, the hugs she gave us children were accompanied by a warm "Love the dear hearts." She was pretty, even at the time of her death. She wore her black hair pulled back into a bun as did most women her age, and it had only a few streaks of gray. She had developed pnuemonia in December and was in and out of the hospital until her death in February. Her doctor suspected there was something else wrong with her that he had never discovered. She died in Guthrie Hospital in Huntington, West Virginia. When she was bedridden at home, Grandpa had kept fixing her favorite food, stewed tomatoes. Cause of death on her death certificate was uremia. Hypertensive C-V Disease, was antecedent cause. Her date of birth was listed as 19 October 1890; her father was Shannon Payne; her mother, Emily Higgins; husband, Ezra Lewis.

At the time of her funeral the road from Scottown to Wilgus was not paved, and I remember the long caravan of cars that traveled the gravel road from her funeral at Tick Ridge (Pleasant Ridge) to the Wilgus graveyard, where baby Donald had been buried many years before. For about 40 years after her burial, my mother and her brothers and sisters and families visited the graveyard there on Memorial Day. And, of course, we also visited the graveyard at Tick Ridge where so many other relatives were buried.

Edna could solve problems with humor. A younger cousin of hers was developing the habit of dropping in on Sunday afternoons with her husband and children for chicken dinner. Grandma tired of having to share meals with them, so one Sunday when they were there, she called people to the table and the lone "dish" was a can of saurkraut. Problem solved.

A few years before Edna died, she finally got the red velveteen sofa she had been wanting, and the living room was papered with a red floral design. All the floors were linoleum, and the kitchen floor and dining room were mopped every day after the evening meal. Thurman, who was still living with his parents, had built a washhouse to the side of the house and back from it, so that a courtyard was created between the house and the old picturous stone well. A glider was placed in front of the washhouse, and I remember sitting on the glider with Thurman and Mom, maybe a summer or two before he killed himself. A man with a good sense of humor, he laughed often, but that night he talked about the deaths of people he knew. It was perfectly dark, except for the stars, for the Petrie cabin was dark, and Berdie Lewis's house around the bend one way and Uncle Ray's house, around the other could not be seen. Thurman was close to his mother and killed himself not long after the 10-year anniversary of her death.

My mother, Faye, once earned some money picking strawberries, and she bought her mother some new dress fabric, and she was delighted with it. A majority of the time she created her dresses from feedsack cloth. Most of the women used feedsack, with its delicate floral patterns, for their house dresses and the bonnets that they wore when they worked in the fields.

After World War II, Thurman and Ray added a kitchen to the house as well as a couple of bedrooms. And they used cinder block to build a sturdy cellar into the side of the bank near the house. Edna stored her many jars of cannned fruit and vegetables in it. She kept a neat row of Snow-on-the Mountain and Zinnias between the house and the cellar. Somehow Morning Glories took hold on the banks of little Squirt Creek, and in the summer the pink, white, and purple flowers proliferated. They spread into the field where Ezra had once planted his cash crops.

They had the following children:

+ 309 i. **Ernestine Faye^9 LEWIS** was born 24 December 1911 and died 10 April 2001.

+ 310 ii. **Ernest Ray LEWIS** was born 15 March 1914 and died 10 February 1993.

   311 iii. **Thurman Orvis LEWIS** was born 12 October 1918 in Lawrence County, Ohio. He died 10 March 1961 in Lawrence County, Ohio, and was buried at Fairview Baptist Church in Wilgus, Ohio.

Thurman was a star athlete. He played on his high-school basketball team and participated in typing contests. He enjoyed going hunting with Lou Calicoat, a neighbor and fellow member of the Church of Christ at Tick Ridge. Lou said Thurman was so quick he could pick a raccoon off the side of a tree.

Both Thurman and his sister Betty could play a guitar, and strumming on the guitar was Thurman's favorite pastime. Aunt Betty, my sister Rachel, and I liked to swing on the grapevines that hung over the rockhouse (a shallow cave) on the hill opposite the farm house, and we would stop to relax on the large boulders and enjoy the mellow tones that drifted up hill from Thurman's guitar.

Thurman was employed for several years as a machinist at the Thomas O'Neal Shop in Huntington, West Virginia. Thurman had never married and was unemployed at the time of his death. During World War II he had attempted to join the army but was rejected because of a heart valve leak, and his self-confidence was hurt. It was not long after he and a woman friend had broken up that he was found dead of self-inflicted knife wounds on Wilson Ridge, across from his home (he lived with his father). The day before Thurman had asked his father to go to Scottown to pick up some cigarettes for him, said he was going to climb the hill behind the house to look for a good spot to plant okra. After his father left, he climbed the the opposite hill, walked back into the woods, and killed himself. When his father returned and couldn't find him, he called his sister Ella Wade, and she reported him missing. Many neighbors gathered at his home to help with the search. Glen Holshuh, owner of the general store in Scottown, provided sandwiches for the search team. Thurman was found the next morning.

Later some of us studied depression and realized how many of the signs of impending suicide had been there. Thurman had visited all his close relatives, making the rounds a few weeks before his death. He would bring up the subject of death now and then. Like his brother, Ray, he was said to be "as good as gold," but the good opinion of others was not enough to sustain him.

+ 312 iv. **Erma Ruth LEWIS** was born 3 February 1922 and died February 1978.

   313 v. **Donald LEWIS** was born in 1925 in Lawrence County, Ohio. He died 26 June 1926 in Lawrence County, and was buried at Fairview Baptist Church Graveyard in Wilgus, Ohio. Donald's death certificate gives his cause of death as scarlet fever. He was one year and 26 days old. The informant was James A. Lewis of Scottown.[1549]

+ 314 vi. **Betty June LEWIS** was born 10 August 1931.

249. **Oscar^8 LEWIS** (James Albert^7, James J.^{6}, Joshua^5, Samuel^4, Zebulon^3, James^2, James^1) was born March 1890 in Lawrence County, Ohio.[1550]

The year and month of Oscar's birth were taken from the 1900 U.S. census for Millers Precinct. Oscar's year of death and Rebecca's maiden name and their children's names were supplied by Arnold Lewis. Oscar and Rebecca lived in Dayton, Ohio.

Oscar married **Rebecca PITTMAN**. Rebecca was born 4 February 1891. She was of Dayton, Ohio, when she died in March 1983.[1551]

They had the following children:

    315   i.   **Charles[9] LEWIS**.

    316   ii.   **Carlos LEWIS**.

250.   **Otis Hartley[8] LEWIS** (James Albert[7], James J.[6], Joshua[5], Samuel[4], Zebulon[3], James[2], James[1]) was born March 1893 in Lawrence County, Ohio. He died in 1959.

The 1930 Windsor Township census includes Otis Lewis and family. He was a 37-year-old farmer, and Berdie was 33. Her mother was born in Ohio and her father in Kentucky. Two of their sons were part of this census: Lyndell, 12 years old, and Arnold 8.[1552]

Otis married **Berdie PETRIE**, daughter of Augustus and Pathenia (RICE) PETRIE, on 26 June 1917.[1553] Berdie was born 24 March 1897. She died April 1983.[1554]

Berdie was a good friend of Faye (Lewis) Young, my mother, who enjoyed her company immensely. Berdie was a happy, carefree person and spent her spare time crocheting, creating flowers from colored stockings and wire, doing other craft work. She taught me how to make the flowers, and I thought she was very kind.

They had the following children:

+   317   i.   **Lyndell[9] LEWIS** was born 3 October 1917 and died October 1986.

+   318   ii.   **Arnold LEWIS** was born 1922 and died June 2008.

+   319   iii.   **Gary LEWIS**.

252.   **Elva B.[8] LEWIS** (James Albert[7], James J.[6], Joshua[5], Samuel[4], Zebulon[3], James[2], James[1]) was born 31 July 1900 in Lawrence County, Ohio. He died November 1969.[1555]

When the 1930 census was taken for Windsor Township, Elva was still living at home with his parents. He was 29 years old, a farm laborer.[1556]

The names of the children of Elva and Fern were supplied supplied by Arnold Lewis.

Elva married **Fern MCCAFFREY**. Fern was born 10 December 1908. She died 29 November 1995.[1557]

Fern McCaffrey was a granddaughter, 1 yr. and 3 (?) mos. in 1910, and living in the household of Jacob and Lucinda Gregory. Meda E. McCaffrey, 24, step-daughter of the Gregorys, was apparently her mother and the mother of May, 4; and Fay S., 6, McCaffrey.[1558]

They had the following children:

    320   i.   **Eugene[9] LEWIS**.

    321   ii.   **Rosemarian LEWIS**.

253.   **Ella G.[8] LEWIS** (James Albert[7], James J.[6], Joshua[5], Samuel[4], Zebulon[3], James[2], James[1]) was born 28 October 1905 in Lawrence County, Ohio. She died August 1979.[1559]

Ella was 4 years old when the 1910 census was taken for Windsor Township. She grew up to be an outspoken, colorful person. She was a school teacher and served as principal. She and her family lived in Scottown, Ohio.

Ella married **Henry WADE**. Henry was born 27 July 1904. He died July 1979.[1560]

They had the following children:

+   322   i.   **Gloria Faye**[9] **WADE**.

+   323   ii.   **Rosemary WADE**.

255.   **Aggie A.**[8] **LEWIS** (Thomas Jefferson[7], James J.[6], Joshua[5], Samuel[4], Zebulon[3], James[2], James[1]) was born March 1888.

Aggie married **Homer NASH**.[1561]

They had the following children:

      324   i.   **Lucille**[9] **NASH**.

      325   ii.   **Fleeta NASH**.

      326   iii.   **Thomas NASH**.

      327   iv.   **Eileen NASH**.

256.   **Wilbur R.**[8] **LEWIS** (Thomas Jefferson[7], James J.[6], Joshua[5], Samuel[4], Zebulon[3], James[2], James[1]) was born May 1890.

      Wilbur was 38 when the census was taken for Windsor Township in 1930. His wife, Nellie, was 35; son Bernard was 18; daughter Helen was 12.[1562]

Wilbur married **Nellie MASSIE** on 16 May 1910. Their marriage certificate shows Wilbur, 20, as the son of T. J. Lewis and Cora Morrison; Nellie, 16, was the daughter of Elza MASSIE and Mary SPEARS.[1563]

They had the following children:

      328   i.   **Bernard LEWIS**[9] was born 1912.

      329   ii.   **Helen LEWIS** was born 1918.

257.   **Ina E.**[8] **LEWIS** (Thomas Jefferson[7], James J.[6], Joshua[5], Samuel[4], Zebulon[3], James[2], James[1]) was born April 1882.

Ina married **Lafe GRAY**.[1564]

They had the following children:

      330   i.   **Hollis**[9] **GRAY**.

      331   ii.   **Harold GRAY**.

258.   **Mary**[8] **LEWIS** (Thomas Jefferson[7], James J.[6], Joshua[5], Samuel[4], Zebulon[3], James[2], James[1]) was born February 1897 and died 1964.[1565]

Mary married (1) **Ova DUNFEE**.

They had the following children:

      332   i.   **Ray**[9] **DUNFEE**.

      333   ii.   **Eloise DUNFEE**.

Mary married (2) **Robert McCOWN**.

They had the following child:

    334   iii. **Lewis Edward McCOWN**.

Mary married (3) **Dillard DUNFEE**.

259.   **Sylvia[8] LEWIS** (Thomas Jefferson[7], James J.[6], Joshua[5], Samuel[4], Zebulon[3], James[2], James[1]) was born 27 October 1905 and died 31 December 2003.[1566]

Sylvia was awarded the title, "Mother of the Year," at the Jeffersonville Missionary Baptist Church in Coal Grove, Ohio, and Louise Sark of *The Ironton Tribune* interviewed her for an article that was published on 14 May 1989. Sark stressed how easy it was for everyone to like Sylvia, for she had a pleasant disposition and took tragedy in good spirit. She and her husband, Dill, had lived in their home at Scottown for over 50 years when it was destroyed by fire. They had run a dairy farm and raised beef cattle. Her husband had taught school for a few years but decided he liked farming better. The fire had taken place four years before the interview, when Dill was already deceased and Sylvia was about 80. She moved to Deering to be near a son and family.

Sylvia liked to work puzzles, read, crochet, and raise flowers.[1567]

Sylvia married **N. D. FULKS,** "Dill."[1568] They married on 11 October 1924.[1569]

Dill graduated from Rio Grande College.

They had the following children:

    335   i. **Charles[9] FULKS** married **Renee KELLER**.

                Charles was an agent for the Federal Bureau of Investigation and lived in Asheville, North Carolina.

    336   ii. **Norma FULKS** married **Charles Ernest JOHNSON**.

                They were living in Crown City, Ohio, in 1989.

    337   iii. **Glenn FULKS** married **Leona SIMPSON**.

                He was a school teacher.

    338   iv. **Claude Vincent FULKS** married **Sue HUNGATE**. Claude was born 26 October 1930.

                Claude earned a bachelor's degree in divinity from The Northern Baptist Theological Seminary. He served as area minister for America Baptist Churches of Pennsylvania and Delaware.[1570]

    339   v. **Jeff FULKS** married (1) **Helen COX**, and (2) **Edith BOLTZ**.

                In 1989 Jeff was a medical technician, living in Clearwater, Florida.

    340   vi. **Dan FULKS** married **Rena WHITE**.

                Dan Fulks wrote an article entitled, "Where the Indian Guyan Flows." It was published in *The Columbus Dispatch Magazine* of 7 August 1966. Dan beautifully described the influence of this wide creek that flows from Gallia County down through Lawrence to the Ohio. He tells of the joys that children experience while playing along its banks and how it has enriched and nourished the people near it.

    341   vii. **Ross FULKS** married **Doris CALDWELL**.

                In 1989 Ross was running a farm at Crown City.

    342   viii. **Leland FULKS** married **Arlene BROUGHTON**.

                Leland settled in Deering, Ohio. He taught school. In 1989 he was employed at Armco.

343 ix. **Joe FULKS** married **Shirley SAUNDERS**. Joe died in 1974.

344 x. **Frank FULKS** married **Beverly MAYNARD**.

Frank farmed and worked as a rural mail carrier.

269. **Hattie[8] LEMLEY** (Nancy[7] LEWIS, Richard Burton[6], Joshua[5], Samuel[4], Zebulon[3], James[2], James[1]) was born 1869 and died 1951.[1571]

Hattie and Sadoc lived on a farm at Kelly's Bridge. They are buried at Sugar Creek.

Hattie married **Sadoc NANCE** in 1884 in Catlettsburg, Kentucky.[1572]

They had the following children:

345 i. **Media[9] NANCE** was born 1886 and died 1965.

346 ii. **Melva NANCE** was born 1889 and died 1914.

347 iii. **Wilbur NANCE** was born 1890 and died 1964.

+ 348 iv. **Lillian NANCE** was born 1892 and died 1976.

349 v. **Lidia NANCE** was born 1895 and died 1986.

350 vi. **Oscar NANCE** was born 1897.

351 vii. **Ode NANCE** was born 1900 and died 1970.

352 viii. **Lottie NANCE** was born 1902 and died 1979.

353 ix. **Ernie NANCE** was born 1904 and died 1976.

354 x. **Daisy NANCE** was born 1906 and died 1987.

355 xi. **Alberta NANCE** was born 1911 and died 1965.

279. **William Henry Harrison[8] LEWIS**, "Willie," (Richard Clark[7], Richard Burton[6], Joshua[5], Samuel[4], Zebulon[3], James[2], James[1]) was born 1891 in Ohio. He died 27 May 1940.[1573]

In 1930 William and Rachel Lewis and family were on the census for Windsor Township. William was 39 and Rachel 37. Son Nelson was 15; son Paul, 13; daughter Mary, 7; Faye, 5, and Lennie was a year and 8 months.[1574]

Willie Lewis served as deputy sheriff for two terms in the 1920s, and was justice of the peace. Some of the information on William and his family was supplied by Lennie (Lewis) Bundy.

Willie married **Rachel Minerva ANDERSON**, daughter of James ANDERSON and Celia Jane DOUGHTY, on 15 November 1913. Rachel died 25 April 1973.[1575]

Rachel's parents lived in Union Ridge, West Virginia. Her father was a minister. Celia was a sister of Elizabeth Susan (Doughty) Scarbery.

They had the following children:

+ 356 i. **Nelson Moody[9] LEWIS** was born 10 September 1914 and died 14 July 2002.

+ 357 ii. **Paul Eugene LEWIS** was born 22 February 1917 and died 22 December 1992.

358 iii. **Arta June LEWIS** was born 14 November 1918 and died 3 September 1923. She is called Arda on her death certificate. One of the causes of her death was muscle spasms—the other cause is difficult to make out. The informant was W. H. Lewis.[1576]

+ 359 iv. **Mary Jane LEWIS** was born about 1923.

	360	v.	**Beatrice Faye LEWIS**, "Faye," was born about 1925.
+	361	vi.	**Lennie Gertrude LEWIS** was born 21 July 1928 and died 24 July 2004.
+	362	vii.	**Virginia Helen LEWIS** was born 20 July 1932 and died 6 June 2002.
	363	viii.	**Richard Anderson LEWIS**, "Dick."

After serving in the U.S. Army during peace time, Dick earned a college degree in Indiana. He and wife, **Judy**, ran a bed and breakfast near Lewisburg, West Virginia. He and his first wife had four children.

Ninth Generation

286. **William Elmer^9 LEWIS** (John Wilson^8, Samuel F.^{7}, Wilson M.^{6}, John^5, Samuel^4, Zebulon^3, James^2, James^1) was born August 1882. He died 1927.[1577]

The 1910 census for Windsor Township includes the family of William W. [*sic*] Lewis, 27. Wife, Minnie, was 24. Son Otha L. was 8.[1578]

William married **Minnie Belle KEARNS** on 29 December 1907. William E., 25, was born at Polkadotte, Ohio. Minnie, 22, was born at Greasy Ridge. She was a daughter of Brady KEARNS and Lucretia HASKINS.[1579]

When the 1930 census was taken for Rome Township, Minnie, age 42, was head of household. In her home were sons Otha, 21; Alvin, 19; and John, 18. Daughter Jesse, 16, was at home; also sons William, 15; Chester, 12; Donald, 10; and daughter Helen, 6.[1580]

They had the following children:

364	i.	**Otha Leland^{10} LEWIS** was born in 1909 and died 1978.
365	ii.	**Alvin Earnest LEWIS** was born in 1910.
366	iii.	**John Denver LEWIS** was born in 1911.
367	iv.	**Jesse Pauline LEWIS** was born in 1913. She died in 1985. Jesse married **Charles Kenneth GALLOWAY**,[1581] son of William Henry GALLOWAY and Pearl PINKERMAN. Kenney was born 14 March 1911 and died 29 October 2000. His death was recorded in West Virginia. Death residence locality was Proctorville, Ohio.[1582]
368	v.	**William Berkley LEWIS** was born in 1915 and died in 1987.
369	vi.	**Chester Woodrow LEWIS.**
370	vii.	**Harry Donald LEWIS** was born in 1920.
371	viii.	**Minnie Helen LEWIS** was born in 1923 and died in 2005.

Minnie supplied the birth and death dates of her brothers and sister in her article in *History of Lawrence County, Ohio, 1990*.[1583] She and her second husband, **Raymond HONAKER**, created a website devoted to her ancestry. She had married first **Randall SPURLOCK**. Regretfully, Minnie died on 29 July 2005. Her husband of 50 years dedicated the homepage of their website to her.[1584]

289.. **John Oscar^9 LEWIS**, "Oscar," (John Wilson^8, Samuel F.^{7}, Wilson M.^{6}, John^5, Samuel^4, Zebulon^3, James^2, James^1) was born 4 August 1891 in Polkadotte, Ohio. He died 14 May 1976 in Huntington, West Virginia.[1585]

Oscar married **Ruby Mae WELLS** on 7 June 1916. Oscar was 24 and Ruby was 23, the daughter of George WELLS and Ellen BRAGG.[1586]

They had the following children:

    372   i. **Paul[10] LEWIS** was born 1918.

    373   ii. **Lillian LEWIS** was born 1921.[1587]

309.   **Ernestine Faye[9] LEWIS** (Ezra Clare[8], James Albert[7], James J.[6], Joshua[5], Samuel[4], Zebulon[3], James[2], James[1]) was born 24 December 1911 in Lawrence County, Ohio. She died 10 April 2001 in Columbus, Ohio.

Faye married **Clarence Hasten YOUNG** on 22 December 1934 in Ironton Ohio. He was the son of Louis YOUNG and Nancy Rachel SCARBERRY. Clarence was born 23 February 1914 in Lawrence County, Ohio. He died 8 December 2005 in Columbus, Ohio.

See the SCARBERRY (SCARBOROUGH) Section for more on Clarence and Faye (Lewis) Young.

310.   **Ernest. Ray[9] LEWIS** (Ezra Clare[8], James Albert[7], James J.[6], Joshua[5], Samuel[4], Zebulon[3], James[2], James[1]) was born 15 March 1914 in Lawrence County, Ohio. He died 10 February 1993 in Lawrence County, Ohio.

    Ray joined the army before the Japanese attacked Pearl Harbor and the U.S. declared war on the Axis powers. Ray sent a postcard from Huntington, West Virginia, to his sister Faye and husband, Clarence, stating that he had passed the exams to get into the army and was headed to Ft. Thomas, Kentucky. It was postmarked 3 July 1941. He knew several of the men in his outfit and was rooming with Kermit Cox. By 13 July 1941, Ray was stationed at Camp Lee, Virginia, near Petersburg. He was trained as a medic in Co.C.4th Med.Inf.Bn. He liked it there. It was hot and rainy and the men were allowed to let their collars remain open and sleeves rolled up. There were several men there from Lawrence County, and he seemed especially to appreciate his friend Ellis. He liked the officers at Camp Lee--they didn't "dog" the men.

    A newspaper clipping shows that Mr. and Mrs. Ezra Lewis of Scottown gave a dinner in honor of their son Ray, who was stationed at Camp Lee, Virginia. People present were daughter Betty, Mr. Thurman Lewis of Scottown, Miss Erma Lewis of Portsmouth, Mr. and Mr. C. H. Young and daughters Mabel and Rachel of Portsmouth, Mr. J. W. Payne and sons Fred and Billy of Greasy Ridge, Mr. and Mrs. Irvin Stephens and children Sandra Jean and Lewis Irvin of Scottown.

    On 26 December 1941 Ray wrote a letter to his sister Faye, pleased with the number of Christmas packages he had received. His address was 56th Gen. Hosp., Ft. Jackson, South Carolina. On 20 January 1942, he sent a postcard from Pennsylvania, stating he was leaving, probably on a boat, destination unknown. The card was postmarked Brooklyn, N.Y. The return address on his next communication was the 4th Gen. Hospital, San Francisco, California, but his letter, dated 5 April 1942, indicated he had been in Australia for about two months. His friend Ellis was still with him and his group. In his letters he mentioned others he was corresponding with and passed along their news. He was a modest man, and his promotions were revealed in the return address on his envelopes. By December 1942 he had made corporal. The return address on a letter written in November 1944 reveals that he had been promoted to T/Sgt. What was absent in his letters was any mention of the work he did. But his duties as a medic took him out to the battlefields.

    He had several furloughs, and my sister Rachel and I were always excited to spot him walking up our street, and we ran to him with open arms. His train would take him to Portsmouth, Ohio, and Dad would drive us all out to Ray's home in Lawrence County.

    Apparently I had decided to write "the war people" to get him sent back home for good. In a letter of 14 June 1943 Ray mentioned that he had told Ellis about my intention, and Ray said he "thought he was going to blow a rib before he quit laughing he said to tell her not to forget about him when she wrote."

    When Ray returned home after he was discharged, he helped his parents on the farm. After he married Molly, he moved around the bend to what had been James and Rosella Lewis's farm. He worked at the Allied Chemical plant along the Ohio River at South Point, farmed, and worked for Lawrence County, administering shots to cattle. While known as "closed mouthed," not telling his parents that he was getting married until the week before, he loved people and kept up with the neighbors around him. He had a ready sense of humor and a hearty laugh.

Ray married **Molly BAILEY** on 2 June 1950. Molly was born 28 May 1924 in Lawrence County. She died 17 October 2006 and was buried in Pleasant Ridge Cemetery. Molly was a daughter of Mr. Lemuel BAILEY of Scottown. Ray and Molly were married at the home of Rev. Calvin Whaley at South Point, Ohio.

Molly enjoyed crafts and gardening.

Ray. and Molly had the following children:

+ 374 i. **Dean**[10] **LEWIS** was born 1951.

+ 375 ii. **Ernest Robert LEWIS** was born 1952.

    376 iii. **Franklin Lee LEWIS** was born 1958 in Lawrence County, Ohio.

> Frank is devoted to the Church of Christ at Pleasant Ridge, helping with services and taking care of the grounds. He has worked as an electrician's helper. After his father's death, Frank cared for his mother, who had disabling arthritis, and he ran the farm. Following his mother's death, he found part-time employment with the local school system. He enjoys keeping up with neighborhood happenings and family history.

312. **Erma Ruth**[9] **LEWIS** (Ezra Clare[8], James Albert[7], James J.[6], Joshua[5], Samuel[4], Zebulon[3], James[2], James[1]) was born 3 February 1922 in Lawrence County, Ohio. She died February 1978 in Portsmouth, Ohio, and was buried at Reynoldsburg, Ohio.

With her black hair, brown eyes, and broad smile, Erma was a pretty woman. She graduated from Windsor High School in Lawrence County and moved in with her sister Faye and her husband, Clarence Young, after they moved to Portsmouth, Ohio. Erma began working at Williams' shoe factory. She met her future husband, Raymond Garner, while in Portsmouth. Raymond was in the army, and after he and Erma married, they lived in Mississippi, where he was stationed. Erma did her housework quickly and efficiently and was especially happy when gardening.

Erma married **Raymond Earl GARNER**. Raymond was born 9 January 1923. He died August 1973.

The son of Kelly GARNER and Bessie Lee HAFER, Raymond grew up in Scioto County, Ohio, and served in the U.S. Army. After being discharged, he worked for a funeral home in Beaver, Ohio, and then took the family to Charleston, West Virginia, where they found a home on the banks of the Kanawha River. North American Aviation recruited him to work as a supervisor in their factory in Columbus, Ohio, and he took his family to Reynoldsburg, on the east side of Columbus. Raymond was a part-time preacher, and after retiring, he and Erma moved to Tennessee, for he found a ministry in the Lenoir area.

They had the following children:

+ 377 i. **Barbara Ann**[10] **GARNER** was born 1945.

+ 378 ii. **Carolyn Jean GARNER** was born 30 August 1946 and died 13 March 2007.

    379 iii. **Thomas Dale GARNER** was born 1951.

> Tom entered Capitol University in Columbus, Ohio, on a football scholarship. He withdrew and later became employed for a title company in Marysville, Tennessee.

314. **Betty June**[9] **LEWIS** (Ezra Clare[8], James Albert[7], James J.[6], Joshua[5], Samuel[4], Zebulon[3], James[2], James[1]) was born 1931 in Lawrence County, Ohio.

Betty was born when her mother was 42. Betty did not seem particularly healthy until she was eight years old. At that time she took a turn for the better and was known thereafter for her good disposition. She laughed easily and was pleasant to be around. She played the guitar, and she, my sister Rachel, and I would sing hymns and folk songs.

Betty was always a good student, and one of her teachers asked her mother if she would allow her to skip a grade. Her mother didn't allow it, for she did not want her to miss any of the courses. Betty attended Charleston School of Business and worked as a bookkeeper for a bank. Since retirement she has worked in sales at a Charleston department store. In her youth she was a strikingly pretty redhead, and she retains her good looks in her 70s. When I was growing up, I admired her good spirit and her willingness to help her mother around the house. She inspired me.

Betty married **William MIDKIFF** "Mac" on 14 September 1950 in Marietta, Georgia. Mac was born 21 May 1927. He died 1 March 2000 in Charleston, West Virginia. He was a son of William R. and Nettie MIDKIFF.

Mac served in the Navy for two years in the South Pacific.

For most of his career, Mac worked for Metropolitan Life Insurance. He became an associate district manager. On 29 September 1964, his photograph appeared in the *Charleston Daily Mail*, along with that of another man. The two were scheduled to teach a six-month course for the Charleston Life Underwriters Association.

After retirement, Mac counseled the grieving at Charleston Area Medical Center. He was lively and joked a lot. There was a very large turn-out for his funeral.

They had the following children:

+ 380 i. **Donald Frederick**[10] **MIDKIFF** was born 1951.

+ 381 ii. **Brenda Joyce MIDKIFF** was born 1954.

+ 382 iii. **Darrell Keith MIDKIFF** was born 1957.

317. **Lyndell**[9] **LEWIS** (Otis Hartley[8], James Albert[7], James J.[6], Joshua[5], Samuel[4], Zebulon[3], James[2], James[1]) was born 3 October 1917 in Lawrence County, Ohio. He died October 1986.[1588]

Lyndell worked as a manager at a plant at South Point. Lyndell's brother Arnold has shared information on this family.

Lyndell married **Maxine WATSON**.

She ran a bakery at South Point, Ohio.

They had the following children:

383 i. **Brenda**[10] **LEWIS**.

384 ii. **Beverly LEWIS** died 1996.

385 iii. **Cathey LEWIS**.

318. **Arnold**[9] **LEWIS** (Otis Hartley[8], James Albert[7], James J.[6], Joshua[5], Samuel[4], Zebulon[3], James[2], James[1]) was born 1922 and died June 2008.

Arnold was interested in family history and provided some of the information on his extended family. He lived with wife, Tommie, in a picturous farmhouse outside Scottown. Arnold worked as an electrician

Arnold married **Tomma THOMPSON**.

They had the following children:

386 i. **Janet** [10]**LEWIS**.

387 ii. **Nelrose LEWIS**.

388 iii. **Keith LEWIS**.

389 iv. **Kimberly LEWIS**.

319. Gary[9] LEWIS (Otis Hartley[8], James Albert[7], James J.[6], Joshua[5], Samuel[4], Zebulon[3], James[2], James[1]).

Gary retired from employment with a railroad. He served as a trustee for Windsor Township, Lawrence County, Ohio.

Gary married **Louise HARDY**.

They had the following child:

    390   i.   **Lisa[10] LEWIS**.

322. Gloria Faye[9] WADE (Ella G.[8] LEWIS, James Albert[7], James J.[6], Joshua[5], Samuel[4], Zebulon[3], James[2], James[1]).

Gloria married **Donald MCCORDER**.

They had the following children:

    391   i.   **Shawn[10] MCCORDER**.

    392   ii.   **D. L. MCCORDER**.

323. Rosemary[9] WADE (Ella G.[8] LEWIS, James Albert[7], James J.[6], Joshua[5], Samuel[4], Zebulon[3], James[2], James[1]).

Rosemary married **Ricard BARTEE**.

They had the following child :

    393   i.   **Tammy[10] BARTEE**.

348. Lillian[9] NANCE (Hattie[8] LEMLEY, Nancy LEWIS[7], Richard Burton[6], Joshua[5], Samuel[4], Zebulon[3], James[2], James[1]) was born 1892 and died 1976.[1589]

In the 1930s Lillian and Carl moved to Butler County, Ohio. Carl was employed by Armco Steel. Lillian worked as a seamstress for a men's clothing store.

Lillian married **Carl G. HAHN** on 2 September 1912 in Ironton, Ohio. He was born 1893 and died 1955.[1590]

They had the following children:

    394   i.   **Carl F.[10] HAHN** was born 1913 and died 1956.

+   395   ii.   **Calvin F. HAHN** was born 1915 and died 1978.

356. Nelson Moody[9] LEWIS (William Henry Harrison[8], Richard Clark[7], Richard Burton[6], Joshua[5], Samuel[4], Zebulon[3], James[2], James[1]) was born 10 September 1914 and died 14 July 2002.

Nelson Lewis enlisted in the U.S. Army and was part of the Normandy invasion. He later served under General Patton in the 79th Division. He was a staff sergeant and received three Battle Stars. Nelson and his wife lived in Huntington, West Virginia.[1591]

According to his obituary in the *Herald-Dispatch* of Huntington, he was retired from Houdaille Industries. His wife had died on 19 May 2002. Son Jerry and his wife, Kun Chain, survived him, as did two granddaughters, Jennifer L. Lewis of Valley Stream, New York, and Kim L. Bowen of Huntington. He was buried in Centenary Cemetery, Chesapeake, Ohio.[1592]

When my parents, Aunt Betty Midkiff and her husband, Mac; Uncle Ray Lewis and wife, Molly, and son Frank; my cousin Iris Burd, and my sisters and their families used to visit Pleasant (Tick) Ridge graveyard on Memorial Day, we often were there at the same time as Nelson and his wife. We enjoyed visiting with them.

Nelson married **Avagene GRAHAM**.

They had the following child:

+ 396 i. **Jerry[10] LEWIS**.

357. **Paul Eugene[9] LEWIS** (William Henry Harrison[8], Richard Clark[7], Richard Burton[6], Joshua[5], Samuel[4], Zebulon[3], James[2], James[1]) was born 22 February 1917 in Lawrence County, Ohio. He died 22 December 1992.[1593]

Paul enlisted on 26 October 1942 in the U.S. Army and fought in the Aleutians and Marshall Islands. Wounded, he was sent to Hawaii. He formed a country and western band and entertained hospitalized soldiers, and his band was broadcast on the radio. The Adjutant General presented him with an award for his volunteer work. He also was awarded with three Battle Stars, and a Purple Heart.[1594] Paul grew up in a family that had a lot of musical talent, and he played the violin.

After the war Paul worked at the South Point chemical plant. Sons Jimmy and Timothy were deceased by 1990. Daughters Linda and Brenda were twins. Some members of this family reside in Athens County, Ohio.

Paul married **Evelyn CARTER**.[1595]

They had the following children:

397	i.	**Tony[10] LEWIS**.	
398	ii.	**Larry LEWIS**.	
399	iii.	**Jimmy LEWIS**.	
400	iv.	**Timothy LEWIS**.	
401	v.	**Nelson Douglas LEWIS**.	
402	vi.	**William LEWIS**.	
403	vii.	**Linda LEWIS**.	
404	viii.	**Brenda LEWIS**.	
405	ix.	**Thelma Michelle LEWIS**.	
406	x.	**Juanita LEWIS**.	

.359. **Mary Jane[9] LEWIS** (William Henry Harrison[8], Richard Clark[7], Richard Burton[6], Joshua[5], Samuel[4], Zebulon[3], James[2], James[1]) was born about 1923.

Mary wrote an article for *History of Lawrence County, Ohio, 1990*, and she furnished information on her family. She graduated from Windsor High School in 1939 and worked for Anchor Hocking for 26 years. She has volunteered for the Republican Party and has served as secretary for the Taft Club.[1596]

Mary married **George NICOLIA** of Lancaster, Ohio.

George and Mary had the following children:

407	i.	**Ruth Ann[10] NICOLIA** married **Darrell NICHOLLS**.
408	ii.	**William NICOLIA** married **Song LEE** of Korea.
409	iii.	**Philip NICOLIA** married **Patricia PINSTOCK**.
410	iv.	**Karen Lee NICOLIA** married **Joseph OSLANZI** of Illinois.

The Scarberrys (Scarboroughs), Doughtys, Lewises, and Paynes of Lawrence County, Ohio

361. Lennie Gertrude[9] **LEWIS** (William Henry Harrison[8], Richard Clark[7], Richard Burton[6], Joshua[5], Samuel[4], Zebulon[3], James[2], James[1]) was born 21 July 1928 in Lawrence County, Ohio, and died July 2004.[1597] She is buried at Pleasant Ridge Cemetery, Lawrence County.

Lennie grew up on what is now referred to as the Cline Bricker farm. Her early schooling was at a one-room school house. She attended Windsor High School and worked as a sales clerk at Leggett's Department Store.

Lennie was a member of the Lawrence County History Book Committee that produced *History of Lawrence County, Ohio, 1990*. Needless to say, she had a strong interest in genealogy. She was a member of the first Families of Lawrence County and the Lawrence County Genealogical Society.[1598] She was a beautiful woman and very caring toward her family.

Lennie married **Wilson BUNDY** on 4 Apr 1945.[1599]

Wilson worked for 40 years as a printer at the Ironton Tribune Publishing Company. Once retired, he worked part-time for Wayne National Forest.[1600]

Wilson and Lennie had the following children:

+ 411   i.   **Janet**[10] **BUNDY** was born 1947.
  412   ii. **Samuel BUNDY** was born 10 December 1948. He died 15 August 1951 in Columbus, Ohio.[1601]

362. Virginia Helen[9] **LEWIS** (William Henry Harrison[8], Richard Clark[7], Richard Burton[6], Joshua[5], Samuel[4], Zebulon[3], James[2], James[1]) was born 20 July 1932 in Lawrence County, Ohio, and died 6 June 2002 at Piketon, Ohio.

Helen and her first husband, Gene, were divorced, and she later married Jim Bates of Ironton. After his death, Virginia worked in nursing homes in Lawrence County and Columbus, Ohio. Her paintings and sketches have been on display in museums in Columbus, Ohio.[1602]

She is buried at Pleasant Ridge Cemetery at Scottown, Ohio. According to her obituary in *The Ironton Tribune*, she was a member of the Millwood Church of Christ at Washington Court House (Ohio). Surviving her were children Mary Ellen Klein of New York; Larry, Stella Jane, and Terry Coldiron of Ironton; and David Coldiron of Burlington (Ohio).[1603]

Virginia married (1) **Gene COLDIRON**.[1604]

They had the following children:

  413   i.   **Gary**[10] **COLDIRON**. Gary was deceased by 1990.
  414   ii.   **Mary Ellen COLDIRON**.
  415   iii. **Stella Jane COLDIRON**.
  416   iv.   **Larry COLDIRON**.
  417   v.   **Terry COLDIRON**.
  418   vi.   **David COLDIRON**.

Virginia married (2) **Jimmy BATES** in 1962.[1605]

Tenth Generation

374. **Dean**[10] **LEWIS** (Ernest Ray[9], Ezra Clare[8], James Albert[7], James J.[6], Joshua[5], Sam el[4], Zebulon[3], James[2], James[1]) uwas born 1951 in Lawrence County, Ohio.

Dean was a good student in school, and after graduating from high school, went to work for the Federal Bureau of Investigation. He later tried his hand at several different occupations and is now a truck driver.

Dean married **Kathy RYAN**.

They had the following children:

    419   i. **Matthew Thomas**[11] **LEWIS** was born 1973.

    420   ii. **Andrea Jerrell LEWIS**.

375. **Ernest Robert**[10] **LEWIS**, "Robert," (Ernest Ray[9], Ezra Clare[8], James Albert[7], James J.[6], Joshua[5], Samuel[4], Zebulon[3], James[2], James[1]) was born 1952 in Lawrence County, Ohio.

Robert was known as a good student, as was his brother Dean. Robert married Della Burd, and they moved to Los Angeles, California, for he had found employment there. After he and Della divorced, he settled in Marietta, Georgia.

Robert married (1) **Della Marie BURD**, daughter of Okey Gene BURD and Iris Mae SCARBERRY, on 17 March 1973. Della was born in 1954 in Columbus, Ohio.

Della worked as a paralegal in Huntington, West Virginia. She enjoys photography and has won awards. She has worked part time for the *Herald-Dispatch* of Huntington as a photographer-reporter. Della publishes electronic novels under a pen name, and she has three in print.

They had the following child:

    421   i. **Evan Robert**[11] **LEWIS** was born in 1978 in Orange County, California.

              Evan majored in education at Marshall University and is now certified to teach in the state of Ohio. He has always enjoyed science, astronomy, and bicycling.

              Evan married (1) **Meridith Brooke DISHMAN** on 27 July 2002 in Athalia, Ohio. They divorced.

              He married (2) **Nicole.Kendall**.

              Nicole majored in sports medicine at Marshall University and is employed as Athletic Director by a Christian college in Circleville, Ohio.

Robert married (2) **Shirley**.

377. **Barbara Ann**[10] **GARNER** (Erma Ruth[9] LEWIS, Ezra Clare[8], James Albert[7], James J.[6], Joshua[5], Samuel[4], Zebulon[3], James[2], James[1]) was born in 1945 in Portsmouth, Ohio.

Barbara graduated from Reynoldsburg High School and worked as a bank teller in Reynoldsburg. She is conscientious and witty and enjoys crocheting, reading, and hiking.

Barbara married **Leslie JEWEL**. Leslie was born in 1943.

Leslie worked in finance for the Defense Construction Supply Center in Columbus, Ohio.

They had the following children:

    422   i. **Stacey**[11] **JEWEL** was born in 1968. Stacey married **Jeffrey AU**.

423 ii. **Karen JEWEL** was born in 1969.

+ 424 iii. **Leanne Ruth JEWEL** was born in 1973.

378. **Carolyn Jean[10] GARNER** (Erma Ruth[9] LEWIS, Ezra Clare[8], James Albert[7], James J.[6], Joshua[5], Samuel[4], Zebulon[3], James[2], James[1]) was born 30 August 1946 in Beaver, Ohio. She died 13 March 2007 in Frostproof, Florida.

Carolyn worked for a photography shop in Portsmouth, Ohio, and as a building inspector. She was a cheer leader in high school and friendly and out-going. She died of congestive heart failure.

Carolyn married (1) **Dean Maurice GAMPP**. Dean was born 27 July 1944 in Ohio. He died June 1985.

Dean graduated from Marshall College in Huntington, West Virginia, and taught social studies at South Webster High School in Scioto County, Ohio. His life was taken in a boating accident on the Ohio River in June 1985. The Scioto Foundation created the Dean Gampp Memorial Scholarship Fund in honor of his tireless efforts to promote academic achievement. The foundation gives financial assistance to students who reside in the Bloom-Vernon Local School District.

They had the following children:

425 i. **Craig[11] GAMPP**.

426 ii. **Beth GAMPP**.

427 iii. **Stephen GAMPP**.

Carolyn married (2) **Lynd JENKINS**. Lynd was born 24 August 1937. He died 7 September 1998 in Frostproof, Florida.

380. **Donald[10] MIDKIFF** (Betty June[9] LEWIS, Ezra Clare[8], James Albert[7], James J.[6], Joshua[5], Samuel[4], Zebulon[3], James[2], James[1]) was born in 1951 in Charleston, West Virginia.

Donald works as a mechanic for DuPont Corporation in Parkersburg, West Virginia. He invented a special wrench to be used on large equipment.

Donald married **Sharon Lou BOOTH** on 23 May 1975. Sharon was born in 1951.

They had the following child:

+ 428 i. **Meredith[11] MIDKIFF** was born in 1978.

381. **Brenda Joyce[10] MIDKIFF** (Betty June[9] LEWIS, Ezra Clare[8], James Albert[7], James J.[6], Joshua[5], Samuel[4], Zebulon[3], James[2], James[1]) was born in 1954 in Charleston, West Virginia.

Brenda graduated from Morris Harvey College in Charleston and is a teacher in the public schools. She and her family have hosted foreign-exchange students.

Brenda married **Paul Eugene CANTRELL** on 14 August 1976. Paul was born in 1953.

Paul, a graduate of Morris-Harvey College, works for General Electric as a sales engineer.

They had the following children:

+ 429 i. **Stacy Renee[11] CANTRELL** was born in 1979.

430 ii. **Carrie Marie CANTRELL** was born in 1982.

Carrie graduated from West Virginia University and is in medical school at Augusta, Georgia, studying to become an ear, nose, and throat specialist.

Carrie married **Stephen BUSH** on 5 January 2008 in Charleston, West Virginia.

Stephen is a pediatrician.

431   iii. **Kasey Beth CANTRELL** was born in 1986.

Kasey graduated from West Virginia University and has entered its dental college.

Kasey married **Andrew GENTILIN**.

Andrew is in medical school at West Virginia University.

432   iv. **Sean Paul CANTRELL** was born in Charleston, West Virginia, in 1990.

Sean is enrolled at Alderson-Broaddus College at Philippi, West Virginia.

382. **Darrell**[10] **MIDKIFF** (Betty June[9] LEWIS, Ezra Clare[8], James Albert[7], James J.[6], Joshua[5], Samuel[4], Zebulon[3], James[2], James[1]) was born in 1957 in Charleston, West Virginia.

Darrell works as a manager at Kroger and Pepperidge Farms stores. He was a big baseball fan, and he and his parents and his aunt Faye Young and husband Clarence drove over to Cincinnati to attend Cincinnati Reds games.

Darrell married **Patricia GATES**. Patricia was born in 1956.

They had the following children:

433   i. **Cameron**[11] **MIDKIFF** was born in 1986.

Cameron has a degree in accounting from West Virginia University and is an employee of United Bank.

434   ii. **Lauren MIDKIFF** was born in 1989.

Lauren attended West Virginia University and then entered nursing school..

395. **Calvin F. HAHN** (Lillian NANCE, Hattie LEMLEY, Nancy LEWIS, Richard Burton, Joshua, **Samuel**, Zebulon, James, James) was born 1915 and died 1978.[1606]

Calvin married **Margaret RIBAR** in 1935.[1607]

They had the following children:

+   435   i. **Jacquetta HAHN** was born 1936.

436   ii. **Jerry HAHN** was born 1940.

437   iii. **Jeffrey HAHN** was born 1941 and died 1941.

438   iv. **Judd HAHN** was born 1943 and died 1943.

439   v. **John HAHN** was born 1946.

440   vi. **Cheryl HAHN** was born 1952.

396. **Jerry**[10] **LEWIS** (Nelson Moody[9] LEWIS, William Henry Harrison[8], Richrd Clark[7], Richard Burton[6,] Joshua[5], Samuel[4], Zebulon[3], James[2], James[1]).

Jerry married **Kun CHAN**.[1608]

They had the following children:

441   i.   **Jennifer L.**[11] **LEWIS**, who lives in Valley Stream, New York.

442   ii.   **Kim L. LEWIS**, who lives in Huntington, West Virginia. She married Mr. **BOWEN**.

411.   **Janet**[10] **BUNDY** (Lennie Gertrude LEWIS[9], William Henry Harrison[8], Richard Clark[7], Richard Burton[6], Joshua[5], Samuel[4], Zebulon[3], James[2], James[1]) was born in 1947.

Janet attended Ashland Community College and worked in the Title Department of the Clerk of Courts office. She has taken a course in art and sold paintings. Information on her and her children comes from her article in *History of Lawrence County, Ohio, 1990*.[1609]

Janet married **Paul BOWMAN**.

They had the following children:

443   i.   **Jody Lynn**[11] **BOWMAN**.

Jody and her sister, Lori, were in the Ironton High School band, and Jody is a talented pianist.

444   ii.   **Lori Jane BOWMAN**.

Eleventh Generation

424.   **Leanne Ruth**[11] **JEWEL** (Barbara Ann[10] GARNER, Erma Ruth[9] LEWIS, Ezra Clare[8], James Albert[7], James J.[6], Joshua[5], Samuel[4], Zebulon[3], James[2], James[1]) was born in 1973.

Leanne married **Eric MATHER**.

They had the following child:

445   i.   **Braeden**[12] **MATHER** was born October 2005.

428.   **Meredith**[11] **MIDKIFF** (Donald Frederick[10] MIDKIFF, Betty June[9] LEWIS, Ezra Clare[8], James Albert[7], James J.[6], Joshua[5], Samuel[4], Zebulon[3], James[2], James[1]) was born in 1978.

Meredith graduated from West Virginia University with a degree in physical therapy.

Meredith married **Jason WILLIAMSON**.

He is a physical therapist.

They had the following child:

446   i.   **Hayden**[12] **WILLIAMSON** was born 2006.

429.   **Stacy Renee**[11] **CANTRELL** (Brenda Joyce[10] MIDKIFF, Betty June[9] LEWIS, Ezra Clare[8], James Albert[7], James J.[6], Joshua[5], Samuel[4], Zebulon[3], James[2], James[1]) was born 1979.

Stacy holds a doctor of philosophy degree in microbiology from the University of Minnesota and is currently doing post-graduate work. She graduated from the University of Texas Medical School.

Stacy married **Ryan HAGEMEIER** on 5 August 2006.

He is a manager at General Electric.

They had the following child:

    447   i.   **Cooper[12] HAGEMEIER** was born in 2010.

435.   **Jacquetta[11] HAHN** (Calvin F.[10] HAHN, Lillian[9] NANCE, Hattie[8] LEMLEY, Nancy[7] LEWIS, Richard Burton[6], Joshua[5], Samuel[4], Zebulon[3], James[2], James[1]) was born 1936.

Jackie enjoys quilting and genealogy. After living many years in Lima, Ohio, Jackie and her husband, Jim, retired to The Villages in Florida.

I am indeed grateful to Jackie Lynch for so generously giving me copies of the pension papers of our common ancestor, Joshua Lewis, who died in 1814 during the War of 1812. I have met her and found her gracious and intelligent. I am sure all her ancestors would be proud of her.

Jacquetta married **James LYNCH** in 1955.

He made a career of service in the Marines.

They had the following children:

    448   i.   **Catherine[12] LYNCH** was born 1956.

    449   ii.   **Jim LYNCH** was born 1958.

    450   iii.   **Bob LYNCH** was born 1959.

    451   iv.   **Pat LYNCH** was born 1960

328

1 Wool'd bag — 42
3 Geese — 1
3 Hogs — 4

The foregoing statement of the valuation of the property of Samuel Lewis dec'd is correct as far comes within our knowledge from an under our hand this 27th of July 1811.

Jacob Cook
Wm Franklin
Michael Miller

At a court held for the county of Monroe the 18th day of December 1815

This appraisement of the Estate of Samuel Lewis dec'd was returned into court and ordered to be Recorded

A copy
Test
Isaac Hutchison CMC

A list of the property sold at the sail of the Estate of Samuel Lewis deceased on the 16 of August 1811

	$	Cts		$	Cts
Isaac Fisher 2 Books		42	Adam Man Jur Cald cask		48
Do 1 book		18	John Man Odd hinges		30
Thos Buckett paid		15	James Maddy Spools		75
Barnabas Dugan 2 book		30	John Maddy 1 prow		57
Abraham Mars 2 books		23	Barnabas Dugan bag handles		
Isaac Fisher 2 books		6	& hinges		57
Abraham Mars 2 book		8	John Maddy sundry		18
Barnabas Dugan 2 books		12½	Do Do basket & cels		15½
Samuel Lewis One large bible	3		Do Do Sanghoe		57
Do one Suit		33	James Chambers & tether		18
Do tinpan & candlestick		26	Stephan Buckland Shovel	1	11
Henry Miller 5 Spoons		36	Barnabas Dugan Stilyards	2	50
Abraham Mars 1 dish	1	26	John Maddy 1 shot gun	5	1
Samuel Lewis 1 log chain	3		Saml Lewis Chains & harnes		
John Larence 1 sheod plow	1	57	to 2 Mars		50
Saml Lewis 2 augers	1	1	Adam Man Jun chairs &		
William Brothers target	1	25	traings		62
			Do D Do	2	66

Estate sale of Samuel Lewis (d. 1811), Will Book 1-A: 328-329, Monroe County (WV)

Erma, Ray, Betty, Thurman, and Faye Lewis, children of Ezra Lewis and Edna Payne

Ezra and Edna (Payne) Lewis

Ray Lewis and sister Betty

Sarah Payne (b. 1882) in front of her cabin

Jim Lewis (1861-1940) with his horses

Faye Lewis (1911-2001) on right with friends

Sources

[482] Darrett B. and Anita H. Rutman, *A Place in Time, Middlesex County, Virginia 1650-1750* (New York: W. W. Norton & Company, 1984), 46, 153.

[483] Nell Marion Nugent, *Cavaliers and Pioneers, Abstracts of Virginia Land Patents and Grants 1623-1666*, (Baltimore: Genealogical Pub. Co., Inc., 1979), 1:99.

[484] Nugent, *Cavaliers and Pioneers*, 1:181.

[485] Rutman, *A Place in Time*, 258n.18.

[486] Ruth & Sam Sparacio, *Deed & Will Abstracts of Lancaster County, Virginia, 1652-1657*, Virginia County Court Records series (McLean, Va.: Antient Press, 1991), 58.

[487] Nugent, *Cavaliers and Pioneers*, 1:384-385.

[488] Ruth & Sam Sparacio, *Order Book Abstracts of Lancaster County, Virginia, 1662-1666*, Virginia County Court records series (McLean, Va.: Antient Press, 1993), 96.

[489] Ruth & Sam Sparacio, *Deed & Will Abstracts of Lancaster County, Virginia, 1652-1657*, 66.

[490] Ruth & Sam Sparacio, *Order Book Abstracts of Lancaster County, Virginia, 1662-1666*, 30.

[491] John Nicholls and Nicholas George jointly owned 700 acres on the Corotoman River in Lancaster County, Virginia, and John Nicholls sold his part in 1652. Nicholas George was living in Isle of Wight County. John Nicholls' deed and Nicholas George's bond are found in *Deed & Will Abstracts of Lancaster County, Virginia, 1652-1657*, compiled by Ruth & Sam Sparacio, page 43. On page 13 is the letter from Nicholas George of Isle of Wight County [Virginia] to John Nickliss, in which Nicholas George told John he could have the lower part of the tract. Nicholas George asked that his kind love be remembered to him and his sister and children. Isaac George of Isle of Wight County moved to Middlesex County not long before he died. In 1663 his son David was given a red cow and a bull calf by his "kinsman" Henry Nichols, planter. This deed is found on page 27 in Ruth & Sam Sparacio's *Deed & Will Abstracts of Lancaster County, Virginia, 1661-1702*, Virginia County Court Records, series (McLean, Va.: Antient Press, 1991).

[492] John Otto Yurechko, *Christ Church Parish Register, Middlesex County, Virginia, 1653-1812* (1996; reprint, Westminster, MD: Willow Bend Books, 2000), 13.

[493] Michael L. Cook, C.G., *Pioneer Lewis Families*, 5 vols. (Evansville, Ind.: Cook Publications, 1978-1986), 4:649.

[494] Yurechko, *Christ Church Parish Register*, 11.

[495] Ibid., 26.

[496] Ruth Sparacio, *Order Book Abstracts of Middlesex County, Virginia, 1697-1700* (McLean, Va.: Antient Press, 1995), 33.

[497] Ruth & Sam Sparacion, *Will Abstracts of Lancaster County, Virginia, 1690-1709*, Virginia County Court Records series (McLean, Va.: Antient Press), 23.

[498] William Lindsay Hopkins, *Middlesex County, Virginia, Wills and Inventories, 1673-1812 and Other Court Papers* (Richmond, Va.: GEN-N-DEX, 1989), 179.

[499] Ibid., 177.

[500] Nugent, *Cavaliers and Pioneers*, 1:257.

[501] John Sprunt Hill, "Dudley Families of Virginia, North Carolina, and Other Southern States," in *Genealogies of Virginia Families: From Tyler's Quarterly Historical and Genealogical Magazine* (Baltimore: Genealogical Pub., Inc., 1981), vol. 1 (Albridgton-Genlock):625-626.

[502] Nugent, *Cavaliers and Pioneers*, 1:300.

[503] Robert J.C.K. Lewis, *Lewis Patriarchs of Early Virginia and Maryland, With Some Arms and Origins* (Bowie, Md: Heritage Books, Inc., 1991), 99, 109.

[504] Hopkins, *Middlesex County, Virginia, Wills and Inventories, 1673-1812*, 75.

[505] John B. Boddie, *Southside Virginia Families*, 1: 315; Robert J.C.K. Lewis, *Lewis Patriarchs of Early Virginia and Maryland with Some Arms and Origins*, 153-154.

[506] William Waller Hening, *The Statutes at Large. Being a Collection of all the Laws of Virginia, from the First Session of the Legislature in the year 1619*, vol. I (1823; reprinted for Jamestown Foundation of the Commonwealth of Virginia by the University Press of Virginia, Charlottesville, 1969), 91.

[507] Sparacio, *Order Book Abstracts of Lancaster County, Virginia, 1662-1666*, 5. Richard Lewis inherited items from the estate of Abraham Appleton, who made his will in 1659. Appleton asked that a hogshead be delivered to Will. Nusham for his coffin. Others mentioned in the will, Mrs. Obirt, Mr. Corbyn, Tho. Williams, and John Welsh, were all neighbors of Richard Lewis. See Ruth &

Sam Sparacio, *Deed & Will Abstracts of Lancaster County, Virginia 1654-1661*, Virginia County Court Records series (McLean, Va.: Antient Press), 33.

[508] Ruth & Sam Sparacio, *Deed and Will Abstracts of Lancaster County, Virginia, 1652-1657*, Virginia County Court Record series (McLean, Va.: Antient Press, 1991), 44.

[509] Ibid., 55.

[510] Lindsay O. Duvall, *Lancaster County, Virginia, Court Orders and Deeds, 1656-1680*, Virginia Colonial Abstracts, Series 2, v. 2 (reprint Easley, S.C.: Southern Historical Press, 1979), 63.

[511] Ida J. Lee, *Abstracts Lancaster County, Virginia, Wills, 1653-1800* (Richmond, Va.: Dietz Press, inc., 1959), 4.

[512] Sparacio, *Order Book Abstracts of Lancaster County, Virginia, 1662-1666*, 7.

[513] Ruth & Sam Sparacio, *Deed & Will Abstracts of Lancaster County, Virginia, 1661-1702*, Virginia County Court Records series (McLean, Va.: Antient Press, 1991), 7.

[514] Duvall, *Lancaster County, Virginia, Court Orders and Deeds, 1656-1680*, 45.

[515] Ibid., 75.

[516] Lee, *Abstracts Lancaster County, Virginia, Wills, 1653-1800*, 110.

[517] Ibid., 143.

[518] Ibid., 110.

[519] Lewis, *Lewis Patriarchs of Early Virginia and Maryland*, 120, 123-4, 126.

[520] Lee, *Abstracts Lancaster County, Virginia, Wills, 1653-1800*, 205.

[521] Duvall, *Lancaster County, Virginia, Court Orders and Deeds, 1656-1680*, 8.

[522] Ibid., 65.

[523] Lee, *Abstracts Lancaster County, Virginia, Wills, 1653-1680*, 221.

[524] Ibid., 137.

[525] Hopkins, *Middlesex County, Virginia, Wills and Inventories 1673-1812*, 244.

[526] Yurechko, *Christ Church Parish Records*, 11; Hopkins, *Middlesex County, Virginia, Wills and Inventories 1673-1812*, 253.

[527] Duvall, *Lancaster County, Virginia, Court Orders and Deeds, 1656-1680*, 56.

[528] Ibid., 40.

[529] Caroline Kemper Bulkley, "Notes on Immigrant Lawsons of Tidewater," in *Genealogies of Virginia Families: From the William and Mary College Quarterly Historical Magazine* (Baltimore: Genealogical Pub. Co., 1982), vol. III (Heale-Muscoe), 338.

[530] Rutman, *A Place in Time*, 49-50.

[531] Ibid.; Matthew Kemp and William Barbee took John Degge and wife, Johanna, to court on August 7, 1713. The will of Francis Hooper was probated July 8, 1713. His heirs were Katherine and William Killbee, children of William Killbee. See Hopkins, *Middlesex County, Virginia, Wills and Inventories 1673-1812*, 227, 70.

[532] Duvall, *Lancaster County, Virginia, Court Orders and Deeds, 1656-1680*, 12, 44-45.

[533] "Major Edward Dale. Lancaster County, Virginia, 1655-1694," in *Genealogies of Virginia Families: From the William and Mary College Quarterly Historical Magazine* (Baltimore: Genealogical Pub. Co., Inc., 1982), vol. II (Dobb-Hay), 112.

[534] Ibid., 36.

[535] Sparacio, *Deed & Will Abstracts Lancaster County, Virginia, 1661-1702*, 20-21.

[536] Hopkins, *Middlesex County, Virginia, Wills and Inventories*, 183; Yurechko, *Christ Church Parish Register*, 14.

[537] Yurechko, *Christ Church Parish Register*, 2.

[538] Ruth & Sam Sparacio, *Deed Abstracts of Middlesex County, Virginia, 1694-1703*, 89.

[539] Rutman, *A Place in Time*, 49-50.

[540] Nugent, *Cavaliers and Pioneers*, 2:274.

[541] Rutman, *A Place in Time*, 74, 76, 208.

[542] Ruth & Sam Sparacio, *Deed Abstracts of Middlesex County, Virginia, 1694-1703*, Deed Book 2, Part III, 13 November 1694 – 6 September 1703, Virginia County Court Records series (McLean, Va.: Ruth & Sam Sparacio, 1989), 71.

[543] Ibid., 41.

[544] "Edmundson Family," in *Genealogies of Virginia Families* (Baltimore: Genealogical Pub. Co., Inc. 1981), vol. I (Albridgton-Gerlach), 661.

[545] Essex County, Virginia, Will Book 5:126-127.

[546] Ruth & Sam Sparacion, *Order Book Abstracts of Middlesex County, Virginia, 1686-1690*, Virginia County Court Records, series (McLean, Va.: Antient Press, 1994), 88.

[547] Ruth & Sam Sparacio, *Deed Abstracts of Middlesex County, Virginia, 1694-1703*, 28-29.

[548] Ruth & Sam Sparacio, *Order Book Abstracts of Middlesex County, Virginia, 1694-1697*, Virginia County Court Records (McLean, Va.: Antient Press, 1995), 102.
[549] Ruth & Sam Sparacio, *Order Book Abstracts of Middlesex County, Virginia, 1694-1705*, Virginia County Court Record series (McLean, Va.: Antient Press, 1995), 21.
[550] Hopkins, *Middlesex County, Virginia, Wills and Inventories*, 87.
[551] Ibid., 77.
[552] Ibid., 53.
[553] Ibid., 83, 178.
[554] Ruth & Sam Sparacio, *Order Book Abstracts of Middlesex County, Virginia, 1697-1700*, 10-11.
[555] Ruth & Sam Sparacio, *Deed Abstracts of Middlesex County, Virginia, 1694-1703*, 42.
[556] Hopkins, *Middlesex County, Virginia, Wills and Inventories*, 58.
[557] Yurechko, *Christ Church Parish Records*, 10.
[558] Ruth & Sam Sparacio, *Deed Abstracts of Middlesex County, Virginia, 1688-1694*, Deed Book 2, 3 Dec 1688 – 14 Nov 1694, Virginia County Court Records, series (McLean, Va.: Antient Press, 1989), 42.
[559] Ruth & Sam Sparacio, *Deed Abstracts of Middlesex County, Virginia, 1679-1688*, Deed Book 2, Part I, 16 January 1679/80 to 27 August 1688, Virginia County Court Records, series (McLean, Va.: Ruth & Sam Sparacio, 1989), 15-17.
[560] Ruth & Sam Sparacio, *Order Book Abstracts of Middlesex County, Virginia, 1673-1678*, Part I, Order Book No. 1, 1673-1680, Virginia County Court Records series (McLean, Va.: Ruth & Sam Sparacio, 1989), 39-40; John Sprunt Hill, "Dudley Families of Virginia, North Carolina, and Other Southern States," *Genealogies of Virginia Families: From Tyler's Quarterly Historical and Genealogical Magazine* (Baltimore: Genealogical Pub. Co., 1981), vol. I (Albridgton-Gerlach), 632.
[561] Ruth & Sam Sparacio, *Deed Abstracts of Middlesex County, Virginia, 1694-1703*, 66-67.
[562] Rutman, *A Place in Time*, 62.
[563] Ibid., 88.
[564] Hopkins, *Middlesex County, Virginia, Wills and Inventories*, 50.
[565] Rutman, *A Place in Time*, 110.
[566] Ibid., 109.
[567] "The Robinson Family of Middlesex, &c, Virginia," *Genealogies of Virginia Families: From The Virginia Magazine of History and Biography* (Baltimore: Genealogical Pub. Co., 1981), vol. V (Randolph-Zouch), 145.
[568] Hopkins, *Middlesex County, Virginia, Wills and Inventories*, 56.
[569] Yurechko, *Christ Church Parish Register*, 24.
[570] Hopkins, *Middlesex County, Virginia, Wills and Inventories*, 218.
[571] Ruth & Sam Sparacio, *Deed Abstracts of Middlesex County, Virginia, 1694-1703*, 69-70.
[572] Yurechko, *Christ Church Parish Register*, v.
[573] C. G. Chamberlayne, *The Vestry Book of Christ Church Parish, Middlesex County, Virginia, 1663-1767* (1927; reprint Bowie, Md: Heritage Books, Inc., 1997), 53-55.
[574] Hopkins, *Middlesex County, Virginia, Wills and Inventories*, 54.
[575] Yurechko, *Christ Church Parish Register*, 12.
[576] Ruth & Sam Sparacio, *Order Book Abstracts of Middlesex County, Virginia, 1690-1694*, Virginia County Court Records series (McLean, Va.: Antient Press, 1994), 76.
[577] Ruth & Sam Sparacio, *Order Book Abstracts of Middlesex County, Virginia, 1694-1705*, 21.
[578] Ibid., 32.
[579] Ibid., 101.
[580] Nugent, *Cavaliers and Pioneers 1666-1695*, 2:190.
[581] Ruth & Sam Sparacio, *Middlesex County, Virginia, Orders, 1716-1719*, Virginia County Court Records series (McLean, Va.: Antient Press, 1999), 2.
[582] Ruth & Sam Sparacio, *Deed Abstracts of Middlesex County, Virginia, 1703-1709*, Deed Book 3, Part I, 4 October 1703 to 6 December 1709, Virginia County Court Records series (McLean, Va.: Ruth & Sam Sparacio, 1989), 46-47.
[583] Ruth & Sam Sparacio, *Deed Abstracts of Middlesex County, Virginia, 1679 – 1680*, Deed Book 2, Part I, 16 January 1679/80 to 27 August 1688 (McLean, Va.: Ruth & Sam Sparacio, 1989), 39. William and Elizabeth Hackney lived about a mile below the lower chapel. Rutman, *A Place in Time*, 121.
[584] Duvall, *Lancaster County, Virginia, Court Orders and Deeds, 1656 – 1680*, 22.

585 Ibid., 7.
586 Ruth & Sam Sparacio, *Deed Abstracts of Middlesex County, Virginia, 1709 – 1720*, Deed Book 3, Part II, 6 March 1709 – 7 June 1720, Virginia County Court Records series (McLean, Va.: Ruth & Sam Sparacio, 1989), 32.
587 "Watts Family, Middlesex County Records," in *The Edward Pleasants Valentine Papers* (Baltimore: Genealogical Pub. Co., Inc., 1979), 2:1593.
588 Ruth & Sam Sparacio, *Deed Abstracts of Middlesex County, Virginia, 1679-1680*, 54.
589 Ruth & Sam Sparacio, *Middlesex County, Virginia, Order Book 1705-1707*, Virginia County Court Records series (McLean, Va.: Antient Press, 1998), 3, 50.
590 Rutman, *A Place in Time*, 208.
591 Ruth & Sam Sparacio, *Middlesex County Order Book, 1708-1710*, Virginia County Court Records series (McLean, Va.: Antient Press, 1998), 30.
592 Chamberlayne, *The Vestry Book of Christ Church Parish Middlesex County, Virginia, 1663-1767*, 164.
593 Sparacio, *Deed Abstracts of Middlesex County, Virginia, 1694-1703*, 31.
594 Sparacio, *Deed Abstracts of Middlesex County, Virginia, 1688-1694*, 42.
595 Sparacio, *Deed Abstracts of Middlesex County, Virginia, 1709-1720*, 88.
596 Hopkins, *Middlesex County, Virginia, Wills and Inventories*, 253.
597 Ibid., 77.
598 Cook, *Pioneer Lewis Families*, 4:655.
599 Yurechko, *Christ Church Parish Register*, 56.
600 Ibid., 54, 64, 65, 72.
601 Sparacio, *Deed Abstracts of Middlesex County, Virginia, 1703-1709*, 96.
602 Nugent, *Cavaliers and Pioneers*, 2:189.
603 Ibid., 2:261.
604 Ruth & Sam Sparacio, *Middlesex County, Virginia, Orders 1712-1714*, Virginia County Court Records series (McLean, Va.: Antient Press, 1998), 69.
605 Hopkins, *Middlesex County, Virginia, Wills and Inventories*, 70.
606 Sparacio, *Middlesex County, Virginia, Order Book 1705-1707*, 70.
607 Hopkins, *Middlesex County, Virginia, Wills and Inventories*, 70, 227.
608 Ibid., 227.
609 Yurechko, *Christ Church Parish Register*, 30.
610 Hopkins, *Middlesex County, Virginia, Wills and Inventories*, 85.
611 Tripodfamilytree122104 – pafg40 – Generated by Personal Ancestral File, online http://beejay1.tripod.com/pafg40.htm, downloaded 30 July 2010.
612 Sparacio, *Deed Abstracts of Middlesex County, Virginia, 1709-1720*, 23-27.
613 Rutman, *A Place in Time*, 265, n27.
614 Rutman, *A Place in Time*, 139.
615 Ibid., 150.
616 Yurechko, *Christ Church Parish Records*, 25; Sparacio, *Deed Abstracts of Middlesex County, Virginia, 1688-1694*, 1.
617 Hopkins, *Middlesex County, Virginia, Wills and Inventories*, 54.
618 Ibid., 204.
619 Ruth & Sam Sparacio, *Middlesex County, Virginia, Orders, 1712-1714*, Virginia County Court Records series (McLean, Va.: Antient Press, 1998), 5.
620 Yurechko, *Christ Church Parish Register*, 73.
621 Sparacio, *Order Book Abstracts of Middlesex County, Virginia, 1694-1705*, 87.
622 Sparacio, *Deed & Will Abstracts, Lancaster County, Virginia, 1661-1702*, 38-39.
623 Hopkins, *Middlesex County, Virginia, Wills and Inventories*, 58.
624 Yurechko, *Christ Church Parish Register*, 2, 4.
625 Lee, *Abstracts Lancaster County, Virginia, Wills 1653-1800*, 137.
626 William Armstrong Crozier, *Early Virginia Marriages*, Virginia County Records series (Berryville, Va.: Virginia Book Company, 1982), 4:49.
627 Yurechko, *Christ Church Parish Register*, 15.

[628] Ruth & Sam Sparacio, *Order Book Abstracts of Middlesex County, Virginia 1700-1702*, Virginia County Court Records series (McLean, Va.: Antient Press, 1996), 48.
[629] Caroline Kemper Bulkley, "Notes on Immigrant Lawsons of Tidewater," 340.
[630] Duvall, *Lancaster County, Virginia, Court Orders and Deeds, 1656-1680*, 23.
[631] Caroline Kemper Bulkley, "Notes on Immigrant Lawsons of Tidewater," 341.
[632] Ibid., 340-341.
[633] Ibid., 334-335.
[634] Yurechko, *Christ Church Parish Register*, 31.
[635] Ibid., 32.
[636] Ibid., 11.
[637] Hopkins, *Middlesex County, Virginia, Wills and Inventories 1673-1812*, 213.
[638] Nugent, *Cavaliers and Pioneers*, 1:319.
[639] Hopkins, *Middlesex County, Virginia, Wills and Inventories*, 244, 78.
[640] Nugent, *Cavaliers and Pioneers*, 2:333.
[641] Duvall, *Lancaster County, Virginia, Court Orders and Deeds, 1656-1680*, 16.
[642] "Tithables of Lancaster County,VA., 1654," *Virginia Tax Records: From The Virginia Magazine of History and Biography, the William and Mary College Quarterly, and Tyler's Quarterly* (Baltimore: Genealogical Pub. Co., 1983), 251
[643] Yurechko, *Christ Church Parish Register*, 13.
[644] Lewis, *Lewis Patriarchs of Early Virginia and Maryland*, 137.
[645] Yurechko, *Christ Church Parish Register*, 13.
[646] Hopkins, *Middlesex County, Virginia, Wills and Inventories*, 64.
[647] Nugent, *Cavaliers and Pioneers*, 2:381.
[648] Ibid., 1:337.
[649] Ibid., 3:25.
[650] Yurechko, *Christ Church Parish Register*, 44.
[651] Hopkins, *Middlesex County, Virginia, Wills and Inventories*, 119-120.
[652] Ibid., 78.
[653] Ruth & Sam Sparacio, *Will Abstracts of Essex County, Virginia (1730-1735)*, Virginia County Court Records series (McLean, Va.: Ruth & Sam Sparacio, 1988), 65-66.
[654] Nugent, *Cavaliers and Pioneers*, 1:335-336.
[655] Ruth & Sam Sparacio, *Middlesex County, Virginia, Orders 1714-1716*, Virginia County Court Records series (McLean, Va.: Antient Press, 1999), 5.
[656] Ruth & Sam Sparacio, *Middlesex County, Virginia, Orders 1716-1719*, Virginia County Court Records series (McLean, Va.: Antient Press, 1999), 8.
[657] Ruth & Sam Sparacio, *Middlesex County, Virginia, Orders, 1719-1721*, Virginia County Court Records series (McLean, Va.: Antient Press, 2000), 38.
[658] Yurechko, *Christ Church Parish Register*, 117.
[659] Sparacio, *Middlesex County, Virginia, Orders, 1719-1721*, 43.
[660] Ibid., 99.
[661] Ruth & Sam Sparacio, *Middlesex County, Virginia, Orders 1721-1724*, Virginia County Court Records series (McLean, Va.: Antient Press, 2000), 87.
[662] Essex County, Virginia, Will Book 5:126-127.
[663] Yurechko, *Christ Church Parish Register*, 122.
[664] Ibid., 140.
[665] Ruth & Sam Sparacio, *Will Abstracts of Essex County, Virginia (1735-1743)*, Virginia County Court Records series (McLean, Va.: Ruth & Sam Sparacio, 1989), 125.
[666] Yurechko, *Christ Church Parish Register*, 28.
[667] Ibid., 27.
[668] Ruth & Sam Sparacio, *Middlesex County, Virginia, Orders 1710-1712*, Virginia County Court Records series (McLean, Va.: Antient Press, 1998), 94.
[669] Sparacio, *Middlesex County, Virginia, Orders 1712-1714*, 5-6.

[670] Sparacio, *Middlesex County, Virginia, Orders 1710-1712*, 79-81.
[671] Sparacio, *Middlesex County, Virginia, Orders 1712-1714*, 5.
[672] Yurechko, *Christ Church Parish Register*, 60.
[673] Sparacio, *Middlesex County, Virginia, Orders 1716-1719*, 106.
[674] Sparacio, *Middlesex County, Virginia, Orders 1719-1721*, 3.
[675] Sparacio, *Middlesex County, Virginia, Orders 1721-1724*, 13.
[676] George Harrison Sandford King, *King George County, Virginia, Will Book A-1, 1721-1752* (Fredericksburg, Va.: King, 1978), 239-240.
[677] Ruth & Sam Sparacio, *Order Book Abstracts of King George County, Virginia, 1721-1723*, Virginia County Court Records series (McLean, Va.: Antient Press, 1992), 26.
[678] Yurechko, *Christ Church Parish Register*, 59.
[679] Ibid., 270.
[680] Ibid., 41, 119.
[681] Ibid., 121, 95.
[682] Hopkins, *Middlesex County, Virginia, Wills and Inventories*, 116.
[683] Ruth & Sam Sparacio, *Order Book Abstracts of Essex County, Virginia, 1716-1723*, Virginia County Court Records series, 3:58.
[684] T. E. Campbell, *Colonial Caroline, A History of Caroline County, Virginia* (Richmond: Dietz Press, 1954), 477.
[685] John Frederick Dorman, *Caroline County, Virginia, Order Book 1746-1754*, Part One, 1746-1748, four volumes bound as one (Washington, D.C.: John Frederick Dorman, 1968-1971), 11.
[686] William Armstrong Crozier, *Spotsylvania County 1721-1800, Being Transcriptions, from the Original Files at the County Court House, of Wills, Deeds, Administrators' and Guardians' Bonds, Marriage Licenses, and Lists of Revolutionary Pensioners*, Virginia County Records, series, v. 1(1905; reprint, Baltimore: Genealogical Pub. Co., Inc., 1978), 21.
[687] Ibid., 27.
[688] Ibid., 73.
[689] Ibid., 72.
[690] Hopkins, *Middlesex County, Virginia, Wills and Inventories*, 85.
[691] Spotsylvania County, Virginia, Order Book 1749-1755:15.
[692] Spotsylvania County, Virginia, Will Book B:23.
[693] Crozier, *Spotsylvania County 1721-1800*, 328.
[694] Dorothy Ford Wulfeck, *Marriages of Some Virginia Residents 1607-1800* (reprint 1995; Baltimore: Genealogical Pub. Co., 1986), originally published in seven volumes, 1961-1967, vol. 1 (surnames A-H), vol. 2 (surnames I-Z), surnames I-Me, 153.
[695] John W. Herndon, "A Genealogy of the Herndon Family," in *Genealogies of Virginia Families*, vol. IV (Healy-Pryor), 9.
[696] John Vogt & T. William Kethley, Jr., *Albemarle County Marriages, 1780-1853* (Athens, Ga.: Iberian Pub. Co., 1991), 2:196.
[697] Hugh Mercer – Wikipedia, the free encyclopedia, http://en.wikipedia.org/wiki/Hugh_Mercer, downloaded 8/14/2010.
[698] Cook, *Pioneer Lewis Families*, 5:496. Cook came to believe that James Lewis (d.1720) of Middlesex County was a brother to Henry Lewis, whose son Henry lived in Spotsylvania and Culpeper (later Madison) County. See vol. 4:654-655. And he speculates that Henry Lewis was related to William Lewis of Spotsylvania County. See vol. 5:449. He believed that the James Lewis who married Elizabeth Long was part of the John Warner family (Group 9). See vol. 4:62, 64 (the last page identifying Group 9 as the Warner Lewis group).
[699] Ruth & Sam Sparacio, *Record Book abstracts of Middlesex County, Virginia, 1721-1813*, Virginia County Court Records series (McLean, Va.: Antient Press, 1996), 64-65.
[700] Yurechko, *Christ Church Parish Register*, 32.
[701] Hopkins, *Middlesex County, Virginia, Wills and Inventories*, 74.
[702] Yurechko, *Christ Church Parish Register*, 29.
[703] Ibid., 69.
[704] Ibid., 115, 134.
[705] Ibid., 120, 91, 95.
[706] Ruth & Sam Sparacio, *Deed Abstracts of Middlesex County, Virginia, 1709-1720*, Virginia County Court Record series (McLean, Va.: Ruth & Sam Sparacio, 1989), 40.
[707] Sparacio, *Middlesex County, Virginia, Orders 1721-1724*, 9.
[708] Lewis, *Lewis Patriarchs of Early Virginia and Maryland*, 138.
[709] Campbell, *Colonial Caroline, A History of Caroline County, Virginia*, 487.

[710] Ibid., 400-401.
[711] Robert K. Headley, Jr., *Wills of Richmond County, Virginia, 1699-1800* (Baltimore: Genealogical Pub. Co., 1983), 33.
[712] John Frederick Dorman, *Caroline County, Virginia, Order Book 1746-1754*, Part Three 1750-1752, 4 vols. bound as one, 3.
[713] John Frederick Dorman, *Caroline County, Virginia, Order Book 1746-1754*, Part One 1746-1748, 67.
[714] Barbara Vines Little, *Orange County, Virginia, Tithables 1734-1782*, Part One (Dominion Market Research Corp., 1988), 22, 65.
[715] Yurechko, *Christ Church Parish Register*, 59.
[716] Ibid., 54, 67, 73, 79, 84.
[717] Ibid., 141.
[718] Hopkins, *Middlesex County, Virginia, Wills and Inventories*, 64.
[719] Yurechko, *Christ Church Parish Register*, 117.
[720] John Frederick Dorman, *Orange County, Virginia, Will Book Two, 1744-1778* (Washington, D. C.: John Frederick Dorman, 1961), 67-68.
[721] Yurechko, *Christ Church Parish Register*, 31.
[722] Sparacio, *Middlesex County, Virginia, Orders 1721-1724*, 97.
[723] Isle of Wight County, Virginia, Deed Book 4:197-199.
[724] Blanche Adams Chapman, *Wills and Administrations of Isle of Wight County, Virginia, 1647-1800*, three volumes in one (Smithfield, Va.: Blanche Adams Chapman, 1938), 2:91, 93.
[725] Ibid., 2:108.
[726] Blanche Adams Chapman, *Wills and Administrations of Southampton, Virginia, 1749-1775*, Book I (Smithfield? Va.: Blanche Adams Chapman, 1947), 47.
[727] William Lindsay Hopkins, *Surry County, Virginia, Deeds and Estate Accounts 1734-1755* (Richmond, Va.: W. L. Hopkins, 1991), 111.
[728] William Lindsay Hopkins, *Surry County, Virginia, Deeds, 1684-1733, and Other Court Papers* (Richmond, Va.: W. L. Hopkins, 1991), 105.
[729] John Bennett Boddie, *Births, Deaths and Sponsors, 1717-1778, from the Albemarle Parish Register of Surry and Sussex Counties*, Virginia (Baltimore: Genealogical Pub. Co., 1974), 111.
[730] Ibid., 149.
[731] Murtie June Clark, *Colonial Soldiers of the South, 1732-1774* (Baltimore: Genealogical Pub. Co., 1983), 592.
[732] Ibid., 287.
[733] Ibid., 290.
[734] Ibid., 363.
[735] Netti Schreiner-Yantis and Florene Speakman Love, *The 1787 Census of Virginia: An Accounting of the Name of Every White Male Tithable Over 21 Years....* 3 vols. (Springfield, Va.: Genealogical Books in Print, 1987), 2:951.
[736] Ibid., 2:923.
[737] Yurechko, *Christ Church Parish Register*, 41.
[738] Cook, *Pioneer Lewis Families*, 4:656.
[739] William Lindsay Hopkins, *Isle of Wight County, Virginia, Deeds 1720-1736 and Deeds 1741-1749* (Richmond: Southside Virginia Pub. Co., 1994), 54.
[740] Hopkins, *Isle of Wight County, Virginia, Deeds 1720-1736 and Deeds 1741-1749*, 81.
[741] Ibid., 124.
[742] Cook, *Pioneer Lewis Families*, 4:655. Boddie, *Southside Virginia Families* (Redwood City, Va.: Pacific Coast Publishers, 1955-56), 1:315.
[743] Samuel Kercheval, *A History of the Valley of Virginia*, 4th edition (1925; reprint, Harrisonburg, Va.: C.J. Carrier, 1986), 72; Hu Maxwell and H. L. Swisher, *History of Hampshire County, West Virginia, From its Earliest Settlement to the Present* (1897; reprint, Parsons, WV: McClain Print. Co., 1972), 38-39.
[744] Hu Maxwell and H. L. Swisher, *History of Hampshire County, West Virginia*, 36-37.
[745] Clark, *Colonial Soldiers of the South*, 314.
[746] Charles Hughes Hamlin, *They Went Thataway* (1964-1966; reprint, Baltimore: Genealogical Pub. Co., 1975), 3 vol. in one, 13-14.
[747] Oren F. Morton, *A History of Monroe County, West Virginia* (1916; reprint, Baltimore: Regional Pub. Co., 1988), 38.

[748] Francis B. Heitman, *Historical Register of Officers of the Continental Army during The War of the Revolution* (1914; reprint Baltimore: Genealogical Pub. Co., 1982), 348.

[749] Louis K. Koontz, *The Virginia Frontier 1754-1763* (Baltimore: Johns Hopkins Press, 1925), 162.

[750] Clark, *Colonial Soldiers of the South*, 434.

[751] *Virginia Military Records: From the Virginia Magazine of History and Biography, The William and Mary College Quarterly, and Tyler's Quarterly* (Baltimore: Genealogical Pub. Co., 1983), 356.

[752] June Whitehurst Johnson, *Fairfax County, Virginia, Will Book A, 1742-1752, Will Book B, 1752-1767* (Fairfrax, Va.: J. W. Johnson, 1982), 74.

[753] William Lindsay Hopkins, *Isle of Wight County, Virginia, Deeds 1750-1782* (Athens, Ga.: Iberian Pub. Co., 1995), 59.

[754] Blanche Adams Chapman, *Wills and Administrations of Southampton County, Virginia* (Smithfield? Va., 1947-1958), Book I, 1749-1775, 32, 33.

[755] Yurechko, *Christ Church Parish Register*, 119.

[756] Ibid., 41.

[757] Stephen E. Bradley, Jr., *The Deeds of Northampton County, North Carolina, 1774-1787* (Keysville, Va..: S. E. Bradley, 1993), 31.

[758] David B. Gammon, *Records of Estates, Northampton County, North Carolina, Vol. I, Accounts, Sales, Divisions, 1781-1801* (Raleigh, N.C.: David B. Gammon, 1987), 70.

[759] Ibid., 70.

[760] Yurechko, *Christ Church Parish Register*, 87, 141.

[761] Ibid., 89.

[762] Margaret M. Hofmann, *Abstracts of Deeds 1741-1759, Northampton County, North Carolina, Public Registry Deed Book One and Deed Book Two* (Weldon, N.C.: Roanoke News Co., 1983), 93.

[763] Ibid., 132.

[764] Ibid., 138.

[765] Yurechko, *Christ Church Parish Register*, 116, 30.

[766] Sparacio, *Deed Abstracts of Middlesex County, Virginia, 1709-1720*, 32.

[767] Yurechko, *Christ Church Parish Register*, 58.

[768] Ibid., 59.

[769] Ibid., 58.

[770] Ibid., 31, 41.

[771] Ibid., 45.

[772] Ruth & Sam Sparacio, *Deed Abstracts of Richmond County, Virginia, 1721-1725*, Virginia County Court Records series (McLean, Va.: Antient Press, 1993), 93-94.

[773] George Harrison Sanford King, *Marriages of Richmond County, Virginia, 1668-1853* (Fredericksburg, Va.: George H.S. King, 1964), 10.

[774] John Frederick Dorman, *Essex County, Virginia, Wills, Bonds, Inventories, etc., 1722-1730* (Washington, D.C.: John Frederick Dorman, 1961), 28.

[775] Ruth & Sam Sparacio, *Deed Abstracts of Richmond County, Virginia, 1720-1733*, Virginia County Court Records series (McLean, Va.: Antient Press, 1995), 12.

[776] King, *Marriages of Richmond County, Virginia*, 244.

[777] William C. Kozee, *Early Families of Eastern and Southeastern Kentucky and Their Descendants* (Baltimore: Genealogical Pub. Co., 1979), 694.

[778] Robert K. Headley, Jr., *Wills of Richmond County, Virginia, 1699-1800* (Baltimore: Genealogical Pub. Co., 1983), 74.

[779] Wulfeck, *Marriages of Some Virginia Residents, 1607-1800*, vol. II,(surnames Mi-Q), 60-61.

[780] John Bailey Calvert Nicklin, "The Strother Family," in *Genealogies of Virginia Families*, vol. III (Pinkethen – Tyler), 378-379. Nicklin states that Jane Strother (1731-1830) married Thomas Lewis (1718-1790), *son* of Col. Andrew Lewis and wife, Margaret Lynn. Jane's husband was a *brother* of Andrew Lewis. Dr. William Lynn of Spotsylvania County, Virginia, made his will in 1757, naming sister Lewis and nephews Thomas, Andrew, William, and Charles Lewis of Augusta County [Virginia]. See Crozier's *Virginia County Records, Spotsylvania County, 1721-1800*, 16-17.

[781] Morton, *A History of Monroe County, West Virginia*, 343. Morton enters Elizabeth's name as Elizabeth C. Frogg, but *Botetourt County History Before 1800*, by J. William Austin (Botetourt County, Va.: American Bicentennial Pub. Commission, 1977), page 30, shows Elizabeth's middle name to have been *Strother*.

[782] Hopkins, *Middlesex County, Virginia, Wills and Inventories*, 258.
[783] Ruth and Sam Sparacio, *Deed Abstracts of King George County, Virginia, 1735-1752*, Virginia County Court Records series (McLean, Va.: Antient Press, 1987), 118-119.
[784] William Lindsay Hopkins, *Suffolk Parish Vestry Book, 1749-1784, Nansemond County, Virginia, and Newport Parish Vestry Book, 1742-1772, Isle of Wight County, Virginia* (Richmond, Va.: W.L. Hopkins, 1988), 78.
[785] Ibid., 77.
[786] Isle of Wight County, Virginia, Deed Book 4:197-199.
[787] William Lindsay Hopkins, *Isle of Wight County, Virginia, Deeds 1720-1749* (Richmond, Va.: Southside Virginia Pub. Co., 1994), 81.
[788] Hofman, *Abstracts of Deeds 1741-1759, Northampton County, North Carolina*, 82.
[789] Cook, *Pioneer Lewis Families*, 4:655-656.
[790] Yurechko, *Christ Church Parish Register*, 75.
[791] Ibid., 78.
[792] Ibid., 81.
[793] Cook, *Pioneer Lewis Families*, 4:660.
[794] David H. Pannill, "The Genealogy of Gen. J. E. B. Stuart and of his Collateral Relations on his Mother's Side—Pannill, Strother, Banks, Bruce, Etc.," *Genealogies of Virginia Families, from The William and Mary College Quarterly Historical Magazine* (Baltimore: Genealogical Pub. Co., 1982), vol. IV (Neville-Terrill), 635.
[795] Barbara Vines Little, *Orange County, Virginia, Tithables, 1734-1782* (Dominion Market Research Corp., 1988),1:22.
[796] *Virginia Vital Records from the Virginia Magazine of History and Biography, the William and Mary College Quarterly and Tyler's Quarterly* (Baltimore: Genealogical Pub. Co., 1982), 330-331.
[797] Little, *Orange County, Virginia, Tithables*, 1:65.
[798] Culpeper County, Virginia, Will Book A:158-160.
[799] John Frederick Dorman, *Culpeper County, Virginia, Deeds*, (Washington, D.C., 1976), 2:32.
[800] John Frederick Dorman, *Culpeper County, Virginia, Will Book A, 1749-1770* (Washington, D. C.: J. F. Dorman, 1956), 21.
[801] John Frederick Dorman, *Orange County, Virginia, Deed Books* (Washington, D.C.: Dorman, 1966), 2:19.
[802] Raleigh Travers Green, *Genealogical and Historical Notes on Culpeper County, Virginia, Embracing a Revised and Enlarged Edition of Dr. Philip Slaughter's History of St.Mark's Parish* (1900; reprint Bowie, Md.: Heritage Books, Inc., 1995), part I, 4-5.
[803] John Frederick Dorman, *Orange County, Virginia, Will Book 2, 1744-1778* (Washington, D. C.: 1961), 29.
[804] Nugent, *Cavaliers and Pioneers*, 3:310.
[805] Ruth and Sam Sparacio, *Deed Abstracts of Orange County, Virginia (1759-1778)* (Sparacio, 1986),158.
[806] John Frederick Dorman, *Orange County, Virginia, Deed Books 3 and 4, 1738-1741*, part II (Washington, D.C.: 1966), 59.
[807] Dorman, *Culpeper County, Virginia, Will Book A, 1749-1770*, 10-11.
[808] John Frederick Dorman, *Orange County, Virginia, Deed Books* (Washington, D.C.: 1961), 1:27.
[809] Dorman, *Culpeper County, Virginia, Will Book A*, 21-22.
[810] Ruth and Sam Sparacio, *Will Abstracts of Culpeper County, Virginia (1749-1770)*, 35.
[811] John Frederick Dorman, *Culpeper County, Virginia, Deeds* (Washington, D. C.: Dorman, 1975-), 2:6-7.
[812] Sparacio, *Will Abstracts of Culpeper County, Virginia (1749-1770)*, 6.
[813] Little, *Orange County, Virginia, Tithables*, 1:65.
[814] Ruth and Sam Sparacio, *Deed Abstracts of Orange County, Virginia (1759-1778)*, 38.
[815] Yurechko, *Christ Church Parish Register*, 121.
[816] Ruth and Sam Sparacio, *Deed Abstracts of Orange County, Virginia (1778-1786)*, Virginia County Court Records series (McLean, Va.: Ruth and Sam Sparacio, 1986), 50.
[817] Crozier, *Spotsylvania County, 1721-1800*, 139-140.
[818] Middlesex County, Virginia, Deed Book 7 (1740-1754), 41(?), Library of Virginia Land Records, Reel 5.
[819] Ibid., Deed Book 7:268.
[820] Yurechko, *Christ Church Parish Register*, 58.
[821] John Otto Yurechko, *Virginia Genealogies Along and Near the Lower Rappahannock River, 1607-1799* (Westminster, Md.: Willow Bend Books, 1999), 58, 41, 42.
[822] Sparacio, *Deed Abstracts of Orange County, Virginia (1759-1778)*, 173-174.
[823] Little, *Orange County, Virginia, Tithables*, 1:77.

[824] Orange County, Virginia, Order Book 7:42.
[825] Ruth and Sam Sparacio, *Orange County, Virginia, Orders 1757-1759*, Virginia County Court Records series (McLean, Va.: Antient Press, 1998), 56.
[826] Ibid., 80.
[827] Crozier, *Spotsylvania County, 1721-1800*, 18-19.
[828] Ibid., 466.
[829] Ibid., 72.
[830] Ibid., 6.
[831] Morton, *History of Monroe County, West Virginia*, 57.
[832] Larry G. Shuck, *Greenbrier County (West) Virginia Records* (Athens, Ga.: Iberian Pub. Co., 1988-c1995), 5:139.
[833] Little, *Orange County, Virginia, Tithables*, 1:88.
[834] Ruth and Sam Sparacio, *Order Book Abstracts of Spotsylvania County, Virginia, 1738-1740*, Virginia County Court Records series (McLean, Va.: Antient Press, 1992), 83.
[835] Cook, *Pioneer Lewis Families*, 4:654.
[836] Captain Maracus Bainbridge Buford, *History and Genealogy of the Buford Family in America, With Records of a Number of Allied Families*, revised and enlarged edition by George Washington Buford and Mildred Buford Minter, (1903; reprint, LaBelle, Mo.: Mildred Buford Minter, 1924), 74.
[837] Orange County, Virginia, Order Book 7:201.
[838] Sparacio, *Deed Abstracts of Orange County, Virginia (1759-1778)*, 20.
[839] Green, *Genealogical and Historical Notes on Culpeper County, Virginia*, part II, 58.
[840] Hopkins, *Middlesex County, Virginia, Wills and Inventories*, 117.
[841] Yurechko, *Christ Church Parish Register*, 120.
[842] Ruth Sparacio, *Deed Abstracts of Culpeper County, Virginia, 1781-1783*, Virginia County Court Records series (McLean, Va.: R. & S. Sparacio, 1990), 37.
[843] Ruth and Sam Sparacio, *Will Abstracts of Madison County, Virginia (1793-1813): Madison County Will Book 1 (1793-1804), Madison County Will Book 2 (1804-1813) and Abstracts of Marriage Bonds (1793-1800)* (McLean, Va.: R. Sparacio, 1986), 11.
[844] Morton, *A History of Monroe County, West Virginia*, 315.
[845] Ruth and Sam Sparacio, *Will Abstracts of Madison County, Virginia (1793-1813)*, 111-112.
[846] John Vogt & T. William Kethley, Jr., *Culpeper County, Virginia, Marriages, 1780-1853*, Virginia Historic Marriage Register series (Athens, Ga.: Iberian Press, 1986), 171.
[847] John Vogt and T. William Kethley, Jr., *Madison County Marriages, 1792-1850*, Virginia Historic Marriage Register series (Athens, Ga.: Iberian Press, 1983), 48.
[848] Yurechko, *Christ Church Parish Register*, 118, 87.
[849] Kozee, *Early Families of Eastern and Southeastern Kentucky*, 699-700.
[850] Vogt & Kethley, *Madison County Marriages, 1792-1850*, 142.
[851] Orange County, Virginia, Deed Book 14:91.
[852] Orange County, Virginia, Order Book 7:400.
[853] Crozier, *Spotsylvania County, 1721-1800*, 7, 26.
[854] Kozee, *Early Families of Eastern and Southeastern Kentucky*, 692.
[855] Dorman, *Culpeper County, Virginia, Deeds*, 1:3.
[856] King, *Marriages of Richmond County, Virginia*, 249; George Harrison Sanford King, *King George County, Virginia, Will Book A-1, 1721-1752, and Miscellaneous Notes* (Fredericksburg, Va.: King, 1978), 127.
[857] King, *Marriages of Richmond County, Virginia*, 249.
[858] Little, *Orange County, Virginia, Tithables*, 1:77.
[859] Ruth L. and Sam Sparacio, *Will Abstracts of Orange County, Virginia (1778-1821)*, (McLean, Va.: R. L. Sparacio, 1985), 37.
[860] Sparacio, *Will Abstracts of Culpeper County, Virginia (1749-1770)*, 6.
[861] Ruth L. and Sam Sparacio, *Deed Abstracts of Orange County, Virginia (1743-1759* (McLean, Va.: R. L. and S. Sparacio, 1985), 84.
[862] King, *Marriages of Richmond County, Virginia, 1668-1853*, 248.
[863] Crozier, *Spotsylvania County, 1721-1800*, 85.
[864] Ibid., 7.

[865] Ruth and Sam Sparacio, *Order Book Abstracts of Spotsylvania County, Virginia, 1744-1746*, Virginia County Court Records series (McLean, Va.: Antient Press, 1996), 93-94.

[866] John Frederick Dorman, *Orange County, Virginia, Deed Books* (Washington, D.C.: 1971), vol. 3, Deed Books 5, 6, 7, and 8 (1741-1743), 48.

[867] Dorman, *Orange County, Virginia, Will Book 2, 1744-1778*, 63-64.

[868] Lela C. Adams, *Abstracts of Pittsylvania County, Virginia, Wills, 1767-1820* (Easley, S.C.: Southern Historical Press, Inc., 1986), 7.

[869] Larry G. Shuck, *Monroe County [W] Virginia Abstracts, Deeds (1799-1817), Wills (1799-1829), Sim's Land Grant Index (1780-1862)* (Apollo, Pa.: Closson Press, 1996), 89.

[870] Wayne B. Ingles, *Symmes Creek, Historical Events and Stories of "The Symmes Valley," including Jackson, Gallia, and Lawrence Counties, Ohio* (Zanesville, Ohio: Franklin Printing., 1976), 30-31.

[871] Morton, *History of Monroe County, West Virginia*, 59.

[872] Agnes B. Pearlman's 1985 letter included in Larry G. Shuck's *Monroe County [W] Virginia Abstracts*.

[873] Schreiner-Yantis, *The 1787 Census of Virginia*, 1:594.

[874] Amelia C. Gilreath, *Frederick County, Virginia, Deed Books 5, 6, 7, 8, 1757-1763*, Deed Book series, vol. 2 (Nokesville, Va.: A. C. Gilreath, 1990), 92.

[875] Lewis-McDaniel marriage, Monroe County, West Virginia, marriage returns, Jacket 1522.

[876] John Vogt & T. William Kethley, Jr., *Botetourt County Marriages, 1770-1853* (Athens, Ga.: Iberian Pub. Co., 1987), 1:186; Monroe County Deed Book H:19 shows Wilson Lewis, son of Wilson Lewis, deceased, of Knox County, Kentucky, declaring insolvency in 1822. Wilson referred to his sister Mary Basham and brother Abner. One tract of land Wilson was giving up was on the New River and had belonged to Henry McDaniel.

[877] F. B. Kegley, *Kegley's Virginia Frontier: the Beginning of the Southwest; the Roanoke of Colonial Days, 1740-1783*, 1st edition (Roanoke, Va.: Southwest Virginia Historical Society, 1938), 604-605.

[878] Lewis-Kearns-Burcham-Dillon-Seward/Sowards-Null-Daily-Clark-Haskins-Scarbrough/Scarberry and related families, FamilyTreeMaker Online. http://familytreemaker.genealogy.com/users/h/o/n/Raymond-H-Honaker...

[879] Nugent, *Cavaliers and Pioneers*, 3:397.

[880] Dorman, *Culpeper County, Virginia, Deeds*, 1:47.

[881] Sarah Travers Lewis (Scott) Anderson, *Lewises, Meriwethers and Their Kin* (Richmond, Va.: Dietz Press, 1938), 358, 357, 61, 38.

[882] Crozier, *Spotsylvania County, 1721-1800*, 34.

[883] Little, *Orange County, Virginia, Tithables*, 1:157.

[884] Yurechko, *Christ Church Parish Register*, 48.

[885] Ibid., 50.

[886] Sparacio, *Middlesex County, Virginia, Order Book, 1708-1710*, 95.

[887] Ruth and Sam Sparacio, *Deed Abstracts of Middlesex County, Virginia, 1709-1720*, Virginia County Court Records series (McLean, Va.: R. & S. Sparacio, 1989), 84-85.

[888] Orange County, Virginia, Order Book 4:162.

[889] Sparacio, *Deed Abstracts of Orange County, Virginia (1743-1759)*, 115.

[890] Ruth and Sam Sparacio, *Orange County, Virginia, Orders, 1748-1749*, Virginia County Court Records series (McLean, Va.: Antient Press, 1997), 2.

[891] Culpeper County, Virginia, Deed Book F:177-178.

[892] Yurechko, *Christ Church Parish Register*, 119.

[893] Goare-Tuggle marriage, Yurechko, *Christ Church Parish Register*, 58.

[894] Ruth and Sam Sparacio, *Deed and Will Abstracts, Lancaster County, Virginia, 1661-1702*, Virginia County Court Records series (McLean, Va.: Antient Press, 1991), 13.

[895] Ruth and Sam Sparacio, *Spotsylvania County, Virginia, Orders, 1749-1751*, Virginia County Court Records series (McLean, Va.: Antient Press, 2000), 97.

[896] Ruth and Sam Sparacio, *Order Book Abstracts of Spotsylvania County, Virginia, 1744-1746*, Virginia County Court Records series (Mclean, Va.: Antient Press, 1996), 76.

[897] Sparacio, *Will Abstracts of Culpeper County, Virginia, 1749-1770*, 125.

[898] Dorman, *Culpeper County, Virginia, Deeds*, 4:26.

[899] Ruth and Sam Sparacio, *Deed Abstracts of Culpeper County, Virginia (1769-1773)*, Virginia County Court Records series (McLean, Va.: R. & S. Sparacio, 1988), 2.
[900] Sparacio, *Deed Abstracts of Orange County, Virginia (1759-1778)*, 173-174.
[901] U. P. Joyner, Jr., *The First Settlers of Orange County, Virginia* (Baltimore: Gateway Press, 1987), 181-182.
[902] Robert Baylor Semple, *History of the Baptists in Virginia* (Berryville, Va.: Virginia Book Co., 1972, 154.
[903] Dorman, *Culpeper County, Virginia, Will Book A (1749-1770)*, 34-35.
[904] Sparacio, *Will Abstracts of Culpeper County, Virginia (1749-1770)*, 127.
[905] Dorman, *Orange County, Virginia, Will Book 2, 1744-1778*, 79.
[906] Mrs. P. W. Hiden, "Adam Banks of Stafford County," *Genealogies of Virginia Families, From Tyler's Quarterly Historical and Genealogical Magazine* (Baltimore: Genealogical Pub. Co., 1981), vol. 1 (Albridgton-Gerlach), 90.
[907] Ruth and Sam Sparacio, *Orange County, Virginia, Order Book 1752-1753*, Virginia County Court Records series (McLean, Va.: Antient Press, 1998), 58, 94.
[908] Sparacio, *Will Abstracts of Culpeper County, Virginia (1749-1770)*, 43.
[909] Ruth and Sam Sparacio, *Orange County, Virginia, Orders, 1759-1762*, Virginia County Court Records series (McLean, Va.: Antient Press, 2000), 83.
[910] Ruth and Sam Sparacio, *A Digest of Orange County, Virginia, Will Books 1734-1838* (R. and S. Sparacio, 1987), 31.
[911] Little, *Orange County, Virginia, Tithables*, 1:77.
[912] Ibid., 83.
[913] Ruth and Sam Sparacio, *Deed Abstracts of Orange County, Virginia, (1743-1759)*, 76.
[914] David H. Pannill, *The Genealogy of Gen. J. E. B. Stuart and of his Collateral Relations*, 636.
[915] Sparacio, *A Digest of Orange County, Virginia, Will Books 1734-1838*, 31.
[916] Ann Brush Miller, *Orange County Road Orders, 1750-1800*, Historic Roads of Virginia series (Charlottesville, Va.: Virginia Transportation Research Council, 1989), 129, 147.
[917] Orange County, Virginia, Will Book 2:431.
[918] Orange County, Virginia, Will Book 2:440.
[919] Dorman, *Culpeper County, Virginia, Will Book A, 1749-1770*, 88.
[920] Dorman, *Orange County, Virginia, Will Book 2, 1744-1778*, 100.
[921] Sparacio, *Deed Abstracts of Orange County, Virginia (1743-1759)*, 166.
[922] Ruth and Sam Sparacio, *Spotsylvania County, Virginia, Orders, 1749-1751*, Virginia County Court Records series (McLean, Va.: Antient Press), 44.
[923] Wulfeck, *Marriages of Some Virginia Residents, 1607-1800*, vol. II (surnames R-S), 221.
[924] John Frederick Dorman, *Caroline County, Virginia, Order Book, 1746-1754* (Washington, D.C.: the author, 1968), 2:17.
[925] John Frederick Dorman, *Essex County, Virginia, Wills, Bonds, Inventories, Etc., 1722-1730* (Washington, D.C.: the author, 1961), 67-68.
[926] Nicklin, "The Strother Family," 450.
[927] Ibid., 73.
[928] Elizabeth Petty Bentley, *Virginia Marriage Records, From The Virginia Magazine of History and Biography, the William and Mary College Quarterly, and Tyler's Quarterly* (Baltimore: Genealogical Pub. Co., 1982), 463.
[929] Dorman, *Orange County, Virginia, Will Book 2, 1744-1778*, 63.
[930] Wulfeck, *Marriages of Some Virginia Residents, 1607-1800*, vol. I (surnames F-H), 238.
[931] Kozee, *Early Families of Eastern and Southeastern Kentucky*, 693-695.
[932] Sparacio, *Deed Abstracts of Orange County, Virginia, 1743-1759*, 166-167.
[933] Sparacio, *Will Abstracts of Orange County, Virginia (1778-1821)*, 7; John Vogt & T. William Kethley, Jr., *Orange County Marriages, 1747-1850*, Virginia Historic Marriage Register series (Athens, Ga.: Iberian Press, 1984), 54.
[934] Sparcio, *Deed Abstracts of Orange County, Virginia (1759-1778)*, 72.
[935] Ibid., 174.
[936] Yurechko, *Christ Church Parish Register*, 21, 115.
[937] Cook, *Pioneer Lewis Families*, 4:653.
[938] John Vogt & Wm. Kethley, Jr., *Orange County Marriages, 1747-1850*, Virginia Historic Marriage Register series (Athens, Ga.: Iberian Press, 1984), 169.
[939] Lloyd DeWitt Bockstruck, *Virginia's Colonial Soldiers* (Baltimore: Genealogical Pub. Co., 1988), 100.
[940] Clark, *Colonial Soldiers of the South*, 439-440.

[941] Ruth and Sam Sparacio, *Deed Abstracts of Culpeper County, Virginia, 1785-1786*, Virginia County Court Records series (McLean, Va.: R. & S. Sparacio, 1992), 22-23.
[942] Ruth and Sam Sparacio, *Deed Abstracts of Culpeper County, Virginia, 1789-1790*, Virginia County Court Records series (McLean, Va.: Antient Press, 1992), 47-48.
[943] Ruth and Sam Sparacio, *Deed Abstracts of Culpeper County, Virginia, 1783-1785*, Virginia County Court Records series (McLean, Va.: R. & S. Sparacio, 1990), 87.
[944] Ruth and Sam Sparacio, *Deed Abstracts of Culpeper County, Virginia (1775-1778)*, Virginia County Court records series (McLean, Va.: Antient Press, 1988), 97.
[945] Ruth and Sam Sparacio, *Deed Abstracts of Culpeper County, Virginia, 1781-1783*, Virginia County Court Records series (McLean, Va.: R. & S. Sparacio, 1990), 85.
[946] Morton, *A History of Monroe County, West Virginia*, 304.
[947] King, *Marriages of Richmond County, Virginia, 1668-1853*, 154.
[948] Green, *Genealogical and Historical Notes on Culpeper County, Virginia*, part 1, 98.
[949] Yurechko, *Christ Church Parish Register*, 150.
[950] Green, *Genealogical and Historical Notes on Culpeper County, Virginia*, part 2, 49-50.
[951] Ruth and Sam Sparacio, *Deed Abstracts of Culpeper County, Virginia (1770-1779)*, Virginia County Court Records series (McLean, Va.: R. & S. Sparacio, 1988), 11-12.
[952] Morton, *A History of Monroe County, West Virginia*, 367.
[953] Sparacio, *Deed Abstracts of Orange County, Virginia (1759-1778)*, 130.
[954] Wulfeck, *Marriages of Some Virginia Residents*, vol. II (surnames R-S), 108.
[955] Ibid., vol. I (surnames C-E), 173.
[956] Ibid.
[957] Dorman, *Orange County, Virginia, Will Book 2, 1744-1778*, 112.
[958] Little, *Orange County, Virginia, Tithables*, 1:197.
[959] William Lindsay Hopkins, *Isle of Wight County, Virginia, Deeds 1720-1736 and Deeds 1741-1749*, 96.
[960] Ibid., 123.
[961] Blanche Adams Chapman, *Wills and Administrations of Southampton County, Virginia* (Smithfield? Va.: 1947-1958), 1:25.
[962] Cook, *Pioneer Lewis Families*, 4:660.
[963] Chapman, *Wills and Administrations of Southampton County, Virginia*, 1:50.
[964] Ibid., 1:62.
[965] Ibid., 1:66.
[966] Ibid., 1:96.
[967] Cook, *Pioneer Lewis Families*, 4:659
[968] Chapman, *Wills and Administrations of Southampton County, Virginia*, 2:5.
[969] Ibid., 2:35.
[970] Ibid., 2:97-98.
[971] Ibid.; Wulfeck, *Marriages of Some Virginia Residents*, vol. II (surnames T-Z), 67.
[972] Chapman, *Wills and Administrations of Southampton County*, 2:32.
[973] L. H. Hart, "Unrecorded Southampton County Deeds," *The Southside Virginian* 7(4) (July 1984), 2:170.
[974] Cook, *Pioneer Lewis Families*, 4:661.
[975] Ibid.
[976] Ibid., 4:662.
[977] Ibid.
[978] Ibid.
[979] Ibid., 4:661.
[980] Gay Neale, *Brunswick County, Virginia, 1720-1975* (Lawrenceville? Va.: Brunswick County Bicentennial Committee, 1975), 74.
[981] Dennis Hudgins, "Saint Andrews Parish Parishoners of 1762-1773," *The Southside Virginian*, 10(3) (September 1992), 108.
[982] William Lindsay Hopkins, *Bath Parish Register (Births, Deaths & Marriages), 1827-1897, of Dinwiddie County, Virginia, and St. Andrews Parish Vestry Book, 1732-1797, of Brunswick County, Virginia* (Richmond, Va.: 1989), 81.
[983] Ibid., 103.

[984] Dennis Ray Hudgins, *Cavaliers and Pioneers, Abstracts of Virginia Land Patents and Grants* (Virginia Genealogical Society, 1998-) 6:423; 7:162.
[985] Dr. Stephen E. Bradley, Jr., *Brunswick County, Virginia, Will Books* (Lawrenceville, Va.: 1997), 2:63.
[986] Ibid., 1: 35.
[987] Emimae Pritchard Langly, *The DuPre Trail: Abstracts of Documents and Miscellaneous Information Relating to the DuPre, DuPree, Dupres, DeuPree French Huguenot Families* of the *United States of America* (Greensborn, N.C.: 1965-), 7:20.
[988] Bradley, Jr., *Brunswick County, Virginia, Will Books*, 3:64.
[989] Ibid., 66.
[990] Ibid., 60-61, 77-78.
[991] Blanche Adams Chapman, *Wills and Administrations of Isle of Wight County, Virginia, 1647-1800*, 3 vols. bound as 1 (Smithfield, Va.: 1938), 3:6.
[992] Ibid., 2:132.
[993] William Lindsay Hopkins, *Isle of Wight County, Virginia, Deeds, 1750-1762* (Athens, Ga.: Iberian Pub. Co., 1995), 65.
[994] Lunenburg County, Virginia, Deed Book 18:40-42, courthouse, Lunenburg.
[995] Cook, *Pioneer Lewis Families*, 4:660-661.
[996] Ibid.
[997] Bradley, *Brunswick County, Virginia, Will Books*, 3:89.
[998] Boddie, *Births, Deaths and Sponsors, 1717-1718, from the Albemarle Parish Register*, 58.
[999] Ibid., 111.
[1000] Cook, *Pioneer Lewis Families*, 4:650. This is also the source of the names of the children of Patience (Lewis) and John Harris (other than those found in Albemarle Parish registry).
[1001] Yurechko, *Christ Church Parish Register*, 86.
[1002] Hofman, *Abstracts of Deeds, 1741-1759, Northampton County, North Carolina*, 54.
[1003] Stephen E. Bradley, The *Deeds of Northampton County, North Carolina, 1759-1774* (Keysville, Va.: E. Bradley, 1990), 22.
[1004] Stephen E. Bradley, *The Deeds of Northampton County, North Carolina, 1774-1787*, 31.
[1005] David B. Gammon, *Records of Estates, Northampton County, North Carolina, Volume II. Estates Found in Court Records 1792-1816* (Raleigh, N.C.: David B. Gammon, 1988), 13.
[1006] Ibid., 75.
[1007] Hofman, *Abstracts of Deeds, 1741-1759, Northampton County, North Carolina*, 138.
[1008] *Genealogies of Virginia Families from Tyler's Quarterly Historical Magazine* (Baltimore: Genealogical Pub. Co., 1981), 30. Google Books, by permission of Genealogical Publishing Company.
[1009] "Armistead Family," in *Genealogies of Virginia Families From the William and Mary College Quarterly Historical Magazine* (Baltimore: Genealogical Pub. Co., 1982), vol. I (Adams-Clopton), 140.
[1010] Schreiner-Yantis and Love, *1787 Census of Virginia*, 1:155-159.
[1011] Morton, *A History of Monroe County, West Virginia*, 474-479.
[1012] Greenbrier County, West Virginia, Survey Book 2:197-198.
[1013] Greenbrier County West Virginia, Survey Book 3:335.
[1014] Monroe County, West Virginia, Deed Book 1:224-225.
[1015] Anne Lowry Worrell, *Early Marriages, Wills, and Some Revolutionary War Records, Botetourt County, Virginia* (Baltimore: Genealogical Pub. Co., 1976), 38.
[1016] Larry G. Shuck, *Monroe County (W) Virginia Abstracts, Deeds (1799-1817), Wills (1799-1829), Sim's Land Grant Index (1780-1862)* (Apollo, Pa.: Closson Press, 1996), 12.
[1017] Ibid., 87.
[1018] Ibid., 36.
[1019] Ibid., 21.
[1020] Sparacio, *Deed Abstracts of Orange County, Virginia (1759-1778)*, 38-39.
[1021] Helen S. Stinson, *Land Entry Book, Greenbrier Co. W.Va.* (Dallas: Helen S. Stinson, 1984), 192.
[1022] John Vogt & T. William Kethley, Jr., *Rockingham County Marriages, 1778-1850*, Virginia Historic Marriage Register series (Athens, Ga.: Iberian Pub. Co., 1984), 98.
[1023] Morton, *A History of Monroe County, West Virginia*, 57.
[1024] Stinson, *Land Entry Book, Greenbrier Co. W. Va.*, 191.
[1025] Garten-Durgon marriage, Monroe County, West Virginia, Ministers' Returns 1, Jacket 63.

[1026] Monroe County, West Virginia, Deed Book F:162.
[1027] Worrell, *Early Marriages, Wills, and Some Revolutionary War Records, Botetourt County, Virginia*, 15.
[1028] Botetourt County, Virginia, Deed Book 7:776-778.
[1029] Robert Douthat Stoner, *A Seed-Bed of the Republic: A Study of thePioneers in the Upper (Southern) Valley of Virginia* (Roanoke Historical Society, 1962), 300, 303.
[1030] Augusta County (Va.), *Chronicles of the Scotch-Irish Settlement in Virginia, Extracted from the Original Court Records of Augusta County, 1745-1800* (Rosslyn, Va.: The Commonwealth Print. Co., 1912-1913), 534.
[1031] Kozee, *Early Families of Eastern and Southeastern Kentucky*, 696.
[1032] Nicklin, "The Strother Family," 381.
[1033] Randolph S. Hancock, "The Man Buried 'Sitting Up,'" Newspaper Article: Colonel George Hancock – The Man Buried Sitting Up. http://richmondthenandnow.com/Newspaper-Articles/George-Hancock, downloaded 9/24/2010.
[1034] Green, *Genealogical and Historical Notes on Culpeper County, Virginia*, part II, 51.
[1035] Vogt & Kethley, *Rockingham County Marriages, 1778-1850*, 190.
[1036] Shuck, *Monroe County [W] Virginia Abstracts*, 84.
[1037] Vogt & Kethley, *Rockingham County Marriages, 1778-1850*, 262.
[1038] Morton, *A History of Monroe County, West Virginia*, 374.
[1039] James H. Miller, *History of Summers County, West Virginia* (Hinton, W.V.: the author, 1908), 535.
[1040] Larry G. Shuck, *Greenbrier County (West) Virginia, Records* (Athens, Ga.: Iberian Pub. Co., 1988-1995), 5:34.
[1041] Ibid., 139.
[1042] John Walter Wayland, *Virginia Valley Records: Genealogical and Historical Materials of Rockingham County, Virginia, and Related Regions (With Map)* (1930; reprint, Baltimore: Genealogical Pub. Co., 1965),159.
[1043] Morton, *A History of Monroe County, West Virginia*, 381.
[1044] Shuck, *Monroe County [W] Virginia Abstracts*, 107.
[1045] Monroe County, West Virginia, Fiduciary File 110.
[1046] Shuck, *Monroe County [W] Virginia Abstracts*, 85.
[1047] Monroe County, West Virginia, Will Book 2:40.
[1048] Morton, *A History of Monroe County, West Virginia*, 462.
[1049] Ibid., 343.
[1050] Ibid., 342.
[1051] Stinson, *Land Entry Book, Greenbrier Co. W.Va.*, 156.
[1052] Shuck, *Monroe County [W] Virginia Abstracts*, 75.
[1053] Morton, *A History of Monroe County, West Virginia*, 84, 343.
[1054] Ibid., 90.
[1055] John Frederick Dorman, *Culpeper County, Virginia, Deeds* (Falmouth, Va.: 1992), 6:37.
[1056] Shuck, *Monroe County [W] Virginia Abstracts*, 3, 9.
[1057] Yurechko, *Christ Church Parish Register*, 125, 74, 58.
[1058] Monroe County Will Book 1-A:327-329.
[1059] Shucks, *Monroe County [W] Virginia Abstracts*, 16.
[1060] Sparacio, *Deed Abstracts of Albemarle County, Virginia, 1768-1772*, 88.
[1061] Morton, *A History of Monroe County, West Virginia*, 315.
[1062] Evans, *Monroe County (West) Virginia Marriages*, 7.
[1063] Morton, *A History of Monroe County, West Virginia*, 315.
[1064] Ruth and Sam Sparacio, *Deed Abstracts of Madison County, Virginia, 1793-1804; Madison County Deed Book 1 (1793-1794), Madison County Deed Book 2 (1796-1801), Madison County Deed Book 3 (1801-1804)* (McLean, Va.: R. &. S. Sparacio, 1986), 39.
[1065] Sparacio, *Will Abstracts of Madison County, Virginia (1793-1813)*, 98.
[1066] Sparacio, *Deed Abstracts of Madison County, Virginia*, 3-4.
[1067] Culpeper County, Virginia, Deed Book B:262-263.
[1068] Little, *Orange County, Virginia, Tithables*, 32, 35, 40.
[1069] Sparacio, *Deed Abstracts of Orange County, Virginia (1743-1759)*, 170.
[1070] Ruth and Sam Sparacio, *Deed Abstracts of Albemarle County, Virginia, 1768-1770*, Virginia County Court Records, series (McLean, Va.: Antient Press, 1990), 50-51.

[1071] Ruth and Sam Sparacio, *A Digest of Orange County, Virginia, Will Books 1734-1838* (R. and S. Sparacio, 1987), 37.

[1072] Lenora Higginbotham Sweeny, "The Upshaw Family of Essex," *Genealogies of Virginia Families, From the William and Mary College Quarterly Historical Magazine* (Baltimore: Genealogical Pub. Co., 1982), vol. V (Thompson-Yates), 253, 255, 257.

[1073] Rutman, *A Place in Time*, 113.

[1074] Schreiner-Yantis and Love, *1787 Census of Virginia*, 2:839.

[1075] Sparacio, *Will Abstracts of Culpeper County, Virginia (1749-1770)*, 95.

[1076] Yurechko, *Christ Church Parish Register*, 121, 123.

[1077] Crozier, *Spotsylvania County, 1721-1800*, 40-41.

[1078] Wulfeck, *Marriages of Some Virginia Residents*, vol. II (surnames I-Me), 154, 151.

[1079] Sparacio, *Middlesex County, Virginia, Orders 1712-1714*, 4.

[1080] Shuck, *Monroe County [W] Virginia Abstracts*, 85.

[1081] Evans, *Monroe County (West) Virginia Marriages*, 10, 16.

[1082] Ibid., 13.

[1083] Ibid., 3, 6, 7, 24.

[1084] Vogt & Kethley, *Rockingham County Marriages, 1778-1850*, 60, 154.

[1085] Morton, *A History of Monroe County, West Virginia*, 319.

[1086] Shuck, *Monroe County (West) Virginia Abstracts*, 82.

[1087] Shuck, *Greenbrier County (West) Virginia Records*, 5:20.

[1088] Evans, *Monroe County (West) Virginia Marriages*, 10.

[1089] Morton, *A History of Monroe County, West Virginia*, 351.

[1090] Ibid., 327.

[1091] Evans, *Monroe County (West) Virginia Marriages*, 8.

[1092] Shuck, *Monroe County [W] Virginia Abstracts*, 9.

[1093] Morton, *A History of Monroe County, West Virginia*, 404.

[1094] Shuck, *Greenbrier County (West) Virginia Records*, 5:44.

[1095] Wayland, *Virginia Valley Records*, 158, 157.

[1096] Shuck, *Monroe County [W] Virginia Abstracts*, 31.

[1097] Morton, *A History of Monroe County, West Virginia*, 366.

[1098] Ibid., 375.

[1099] Shuck, *Monroe County [W] Virginia Abstracts*, 44.

[1100] Morton, *A History of Monroe County, West Virginia*, 374.

[1101] Ibid., 380.

[1102] Evans, *Monroe County (West) Virginia Marriages*, 1.

[1103] Morton, *A History of Monroe County, West Virginia*, 381.

[1104] Ibid.

[1105] Ibid., 59.

[1106] Sparacio, *Deed Abstracts of Orange County, Virginia (1759-1778)*, 28.

[1107] John Frederick Dorman, *Orange County Deed Books 5, 6, 7 and 8, 1741-1743* (Washington, D.C.: the author, 1971), part 2, 62.

[1108] Sparacio, *Deed Abstracts of Orange County, Virginia (1759-1778)*, 64.

[1109] Ibid., 125.

[1110] Marguerite B. Priode, *Abstracts of Executor, Administrator, and Guardian Bonds of Rockingham County, Virginia, 1778-1864* (Harrisonburg, Va.: Harrisonburg-Rockingham Historical Society, 1978), 22.

[1111] Shuck, *Monroe County [W] Virginia Abstracts*, 103.

[1112] Ibid., 37.

[1113] Sparacio, *Deed Abstracts of Orange County, Virginia (1759-1778)*, 14.

[1114] Ibid., 66.

[1115] Shuck, *Monroe County [W] Virginia Abstracts*, 79.

[1116] Yurechko, *Christ Church Parish Register*, 58.

[1117] Ibid., 65, 123.

[1118] Ibid., 125.

[1119] Wulfeck, *Marriages of Some Virginia Residents*, vol. I (surnames C-E), 132-133; William Everett Brockman, *Orange County, Virginia, Families Volume IV, Brockman, Brown, Embree, Harvey, Robertson, Rothwell, and Allied Families* (Minneapolis: the author, 1965), 17-19.
[1120] Kimberly Curtis Campbell, *Caroline County, Virginia, Court Records, Will Book 1793-1897, Will & Plat Book 1742-1840, Will Book 19, 1814-1818* (Athens, Ga.: Iberian Pub. Co., 1998), 14.
[1121] Wulfeck, *Marriages of Some Virginia Residents*, vol. I (surnames F-H), 93.
[1122] Ibid., 93.
[1123] Greenbrier County, West Virginia, Deed Book 1:214-216.
[1124] Shuck, *Monroe County [W] Virginia Abstracts*, 21.
[1125] Ibid.
[1126] Morton, *A History of Monroe County, West Virginia*, 96.
[1127] Ibid., 367-368.
[1128] Cook, *Pioneer Lewis Families*, 5:496.
[1129] Ibid., 5:449-450.
[1130] Shuck, *Greenbrier County (West) Virginia Records*, 5:154.
[1131] Ibid., 5:138.
[1132] Cook, *Pioneer Lewis Families*, 4:1128.
[1133] Ruth and Sam Sparacio, *Albemarle County, Virginia, Deeds, 1780-1783*, Virginia County Court Records series (McLean, Va.: Antient Press, 1997), 17, 18-19.
[1134] Shuck, *Greenbrier County (West) Virginia Records*, 5:41.
[1135] Wulfeck, *Marriages of Some Virginia Residents*, vol. I (surnames F-H), 49. This reference gives the name of Mosias Jones as *Josias* Jones.
[1136] Rosalie Edith Davis, *Louisa County, Virginia, Deed Books A and B, 1742-1759* (Bellevue, Washington: the author, 1976), 80-81.
[1137] Ruth and Sam Sparacio, *Deed & Will Abstracts of Albemarle County, Virginia, 1748-1752*, Virginia County Court Records series (McLean, Va.: Antient Press, 1990), 63, 57.
[1138] Sparacio, *A Digest of Orange County, Virginia, Will Books*, 60.
[1139] Sparacio, *Deed Abstracts of Orange County, Virginia (1759-1778)*, 142.
[1140] Sparacio, *Deed Abstracts of Orange County, Virginia (1759-1778)*, 114.
[1141] Sparacio, *Will Abstracts of Orange County, Virginia (1778-1821)*, 34.
[1142] Crozier, *Spotsylvania County, 1721-1800*, 20.
[1143] Ibid., 73.
[1144] William B. Newman, "Towles and Clark Families," in *Genealogies of Virginia Families: From Tyler's Quarterly Historical and Genealogical Magazine* (Baltimore: Genealogical Pub. Co., 1981), vol. III (Pinkethman-Tyler), 584-585.
[1145] Crozier, *Spotsylvania County, 1721-1800*, 477.
[1146] Ibid., 476.
[1147] Shucks, *Greenbrier County (West) Virginia Records*, 5:17.
[1148] Ruth and Sam Sparacio, *Deed Abstracts of Orange County, Virginia, 20 September 1786 – 25 April 1791*, Virginia County Court Records series (McLean, Va.: the authors, 1988), 84.
[1149] Little, *Orange County, Virginia, Tithables*, 1:83.
[1150] Shuck, *Greenbrier County (West) Virginia Records*, 5:45.
[1151] Shuck, *Monroe County [W] Virginia Abstracts*, 27.
[1152] Morton, *A History of Monroe County, West Virginia*, 285.
[1153] Ibid., 223-224.
[1154] Norvel P. Mann, *History of Indian Creek Primitive Baptist Church, Greenville, West Virginia*, 150, 152.
[1155] Monroe County, West Virginia, Deed Book D:410-411.
[1156] Monroe County, West Virginia, Will Book 2:40.
[1157] Morton, *A History of Monroe County, West Virginia*, 320.
[1158] Yurechko, *Christ Church Parish Register*, 102, 124.
[1159] Newman, "Towles and Clark Families," in *Genealogies of Virginia Families: From Tyler's Quarterly Historical and Genealogical Magazine*, 585.

[1160] Crozier, *Spotsylvania County, 1721-1800*, 484-485.
[1161] Morton, *A History of Monroe County, West Virginia*, 206.
[1162] Sparacio, *Deed Abstracts of Madison County, Virginia*, 152.
[1163] Morton, *A History of Monroe County, West Virginia*, 343.
[1164] Wulfeck, *Marriagaes of Some Virginia Residents*, vol. II (surnames R-S), 215.
[1165] Sparacio, *Will Abstracts of Madison County, Virginia (1793-1813)*, 154.
[1166] Morton, *A History of Monroe County, West Virginia*, 92.
[1167] Ibid., 407.
[1168] Shuck, *Monroe County [W] Virginia Abstracts*, 84.
[1169] Monroe County, West Virginia, Deed Book M:446-447.
[1170] Monroe County, West Virginia, Deed Book D:402-403.
[1171] Monroe County, West Virginia, Deed Book M:447-448.
[1172] Sparacio, *Deed Abstracts of Madison County, Virginia*, 114.
[1173] Dorman, *Orange County, Virginia, Will Book 2, 1744-1778*, 21.
[1174] Sparacio, *Will Abstracts of Madison County, Virginia (1793-1813)*, 11.
[1175] The 1810 Census, Monroe County, Virginia (St. Louis Genealogical Society, St. Louis, Missouri), Microfilm Reel No. M252-70.
[1176] Kelly-Tillett marriage, Giles County, Virginia, Marriage Bonds, vol. I.
[1177] Shuck, *Monroe County [W] Virginia Abstracts*, 101.
[1178] Monroe County, West Virginia, Deed Book H:177-178.
[1179] Evans, *Monroe County (West) Virginia Marriages*, 1; Lewis-Ellison marriage, Ministers' Returns 1, Jacket No. 4.
[1180] Wayland, *Virginia Valley Records*, 157.
[1181] Ibid., 159.
[1182] Shuck, *Greenbrier County (West) Virginia Records*, 5:161.
[1183] Morton, *A History of Monroe County, West Virginia*, 341.
[1184] Thomas Marshall Green, *Historic Families of Kentucky. With Special Reference to Stocks Immediately from the Valley of Virginia* (1889; reprint, Baltimore: Regional Pub. Co., 1889), 88.
[1185] Lewis-Stephenson marriage, File No. 1, Jacket No. 68, county clerk's office, Monroe County, West Virginia.
[1186] Hill-Lewis marriage, Ministers' Returns 1, Jacket No. 1011.
[1187] Monroe County, West Virginia, Deed Book D:402-403.
[1188] Monroe County, West Virginia, Deed Book C:504-505.
[1189] Monroe County, West Virginia, Deed Book D:410-411; Deed Book F:11-12.
[1190] Chapman, *Wills and Administrations of Southampton County*, 2:161.
[1191] Cook, *Pioneer Lewis Families*, 4:661.
[1192] Ibid., 4:662.
[1193] Hopkins, *Bath Parish Register of Dinwiddie County, Virginia, and St. Andrews Parish Vestry Book of Brunswick County, Virginia*, 106.
[1194] Bradley, *Brunswick County, Virginia, Will Books, Volume 3*, 60-61.
[1195] Cook, *Pioneer Lewis Families*, 4:662.
[1196] Ibid.
[1197] Ibid., 2:1761.
[1198] Ibid., 4:663.
[1199] Boddie, *Southside Virginia Families*, 1:317.
[1200] Ibid.
[1201] Neale, *Brunswick County, Virginia, 1720-1975*, 141.
[1202] Boddie, *Southside Virginia Families*, 1:317.
[1203] Ibid.
[1204] Ibid.
[1205] Ibid.
[1206] Ibid.
[1207] Ibid.

[1208] The birth and death dates of the children of Benjamin Lewis, Sr., and wife, Elizabeth, were taken from "A Copy from the Register of Benjamin Lewis, Sr.," *The Southside Virginian* 1 (2) (January 1983), 92.
[1209] Dorman, *Culpeper County, Virginia, Will Book A*, 101.
[1210] Sparacio, *Deed Abstracts of Culpeper County, Virginia (1775-1778)*, 73.
[1211] Newman, "Towles and Clark Families," 587-588.
[1212] Ibid.
[1213] Green, *Genealogical and Historical Notes on Culpeper County, Virginia*, part 2, 66.
[1214] Ibid.
[1215] Ibid.
[1216] Vogt & Kethley, *Culpeper County, Virginia, Marriages, 1780-1853*, 159.
[1217] Green, *Genealogical and Historical Notes on Culpeper County, Virginia*, part 2, 61.
[1218] Ibid., part 2, 66.
[1219] Cook, *Pioneer Lewis Families*, 4:1376.
[1220] Monroe County, West Virginia, Survey Book 1:221.
[1221] Monroe County, West Virginia, Deed Book D:58.
[1222] Monroe County, West Virginia, Deed Book D:402-403.
[1223] Ingles, *Symmes Creek*, 33.
[1224] Wulfeck, *Marriages of Some Virginia Residents*, vol. 2 (surnames I-Me), 154.
[1225] Monroe County, West Virginia, Will Book A:35.
[1226] Gallia County, Ohio, Marriages, vol. 1, p. 78, FHL film no. 317652, roll no. 299.
[1227] Haskins – Lewis marriage, International Genealogical Index, v.5.0 (no sources given). FHL, Salt Lake City, Utah.
[1228] Gallia County, Ohio, Marriages, vol. 1, p. 207, FHL film no. 317652, roll no. 299.
[1229] Cook, *Pioneer Lewis Families*, 4:663, 668.
[1230] Monroe County, West Virginia, Old Surveys 3:335.
[1231] Anne Burgstaller Snodgrass, *Clark County, Ohio, Newspaper Abstracts, 1829-1832, Obituaries, Marriages, and Selected General Notices*, (1977-78), 1. (pub. 1984).
[1232] Lewis-Best marriage, Monroe County courthouse, File no. 1, Jacket No. 48.
[1233] Monroe County, West Virginia, Deed Book D:410-411.
[1234] Skaggs – Lewis marriage, Index to Marriages, Greenbrier County courthouse, 1-A:136.
[1235] Shuck, *Monroe County [W] Virginia Abstracts*, 10-11.
[1236] Morton, *A History of Monroe County, West Virginia*, 82.
[1237] Ibid., 87, 90.
[1238] Ibid., 408.
[1239] Charles B. Motley, *Gleanings of Monroe County, West Virginia, History* (Danville, Va.: Charles B. Motley, 1973), 194-195.
[1240] Monroe County, West Virginia, Deed Book F:103-104.
[1241] War of 1812 Pension Application, The National Archives "Old War" Widow File No. 12110.
[1242] Lewis-Hand marriage, Monroe County, West Virginia, File No. 1, Jacket No. 240.
[1243] Shires-Hand marriage, Monroe County, West Virginia, File No. 2, Jacket No. 631.
[1244] Morton, *A History of Monroe County, West Virginia*, 350.
[1245] Lewis-Hill marriage, Monroe County, West Virginia, File No. 1, Jacket No. 431.
[1246] Pensioner, Catharine, Widow; Veteran, Joshua Lewis, War of 1812, Pension Application, The National Archives "Old War" Widow File No. 12110.
[1247] 1810 Census, Monroe County, Virginia, page 15 (St. Louis Genealogical Society, St. Louis, Missouri) Microfilm Reel No. M252-70.
[1248] Morton, *A History of Monroe County, West Virginia*, 108.
[1249] Shucks, *Greenbrier County (West) Virginia Records*, 5:161.
[1250] Margaret Ballard, *William Ballard: A Genealogical Record of his Descendants in Monroe County* (Baltimore, 1957), 9-10.
[1251] Evans, *Monroe County (West) Virginia Marriages*, 1.
[1252] Crozier, *Spotsylvania County, 1721-1800*, 217.
[1253] Ruth and Sam Sparacio, *Albemarle County, Virginia, Deeds, 1790-1791*, Virginia County Court Records series (McLean, Va.: Antient Press, 1997), 96.

[1254] Morton, *A History of Monroe County, West Virginia*, 304.
[1255] Evans, *Monroe County (West) Virginia Marriages*, 13.
[1256] Dare-Harvey marriage, Monroe County, West Virginia, Ministers' Returns 1, Jacket No.1031.
[1257] Morton, *A History of Monroe County, West Virginia*, 350-351.
[1258] Sparacio, *Deed Abstracts of Orange County, Virginia (1759-1778)*, 42.
[1259] Sparacio, *A Digest of Orange County, Virginia, Will Books 1734-1838*, 121.
[1260] Wulfeck, *Marriages of Some Virginia Residents*, vol. II (surnames R-S), 241.
[1261] Ibid., vol 2 (R-S), 241, 167. That Ambrose Brockman was an uncle of the wife of John F. Lewis, see William Everett Brockman, *Virginia Wills and Abstracts, Brockman, Bell, Bledsoe, Burris, Collins, Durrett, Graves, Henderson, and Tatum Families* (Minneapolis: W. E. Brockman, 1948).
[1262] Dorman, *Orange County, Virginia, Deed Books*, 3:48.
[1263] Wayland, *Virginia Valley Records*, 315.
[1264] John W. Wayland, *A History of Rockingham County, Virginia* (1912; reprint, Bowie, MD.: Heritage Books, Inc., 1990), 36.
[1265] Shuck, *Greenbrier (West) Virginia Records*, 18.
[1266] Pensioner, Catherine, Widow, Joshua Lewis, Veteran, War of 1812 Pension Application, Widow's File No. 12110.
[1267] Morton, *A History of Monroe County, West Virginia*, 422.
[1268] Virgil A. Lewis, *Soldiers of West Virginia* (Baltimore: Genealogical Pub. Co., 1978), 176-177.
[1269] The Library of Virginia Soldiers of the War of 1812 (Research Notes Number 19), http://www.lva.virginia.gov/public/guides/rn19_sold.htm.
[1270] Wayland, *Virginia Valley Records*, 55.
[1271] Lewis Peyton Little, *Imprisoned Preachers and Religious Liberty in Virginia* (Lynchburg, Va.: J. P. Bell Co., 1938), 85; unidentified newspaper clipping states that the New Valley Church was in the Lucketts area.
[1272] Loudoun County, Virginia, Will Book A:310.
[1273] King, *Marriages of Richmond County, Virginia, 1668-1853*, 268; for children of Thomas and Catherine Thatcher, see his will in King, *King George County, Virginia, Will Book A-1, 1721-1752*, 196-197.
[1274] Lee, *Abstracts of Lancaster County, Virginia, Wills, 1653-1800*, 53.
[1275] Ruth and Sam Sparacio, *Tithables: Loudoun County, Virginia, 1770-1774*, Virginia County Court Records series (McLean, Va.: Antient Press, 1992), 12.
[1276] Lewis-Hill marriage, Monroe County, West Virginia, File No. 1, Jacket No. 431.
[1277] Morton, *A History of Monroe County, West Virginia*, 354.
[1278] Records of Literary Schools, 1826-1855, Monroe County (West Virginia), FHL microfilm no. 1,017,649, item 7, Salt Lake City, Utah.
[1279] Shuck, *Greenbrier County (West) Virginia Records*, 1:176.
[1280] In 1789 John and Mary Dyer sold land on Sinking Creek/Greenbrier River to Edward Tomlinson. The tract was adjacent Lewis, Hugh Miller, John Harris, and Richards. In 1797 Thomas and Susanah Tinsley sold land that had been granted to Wm. Frogg and T. Tinsley in 1786. This parcel was on the head branch of Muddy Creek and a branch of Sinking Creek. See Shuck, *Greenbrier County (West) Virginia Records*, 5:13, 44.
[1281] Amherst County, Virginia, Marriage Register, 59.
[1282] Ibid., 70.
[1283] Amherst County, Virginia, Deed Book L:263.
[1284] W. Mac. Jones, *The Douglas Register, being a detailed record of Births, Marriages and Deaths together with other interesting notes, as kept by the Rev. William Douglas, from 1750-1797* (1928; reprint Baltimore: Genealogical Pub. Co., 1977), 36.
[1285] Bailey Fulton Davis, *An Abstract of all items in Deed Book O with cross-index*, Amherst County, Virginia, Courthouse Miniatures series (Amherst: B. F. Davis, 1966), 55.
[1286] Bailey Fulton Davis, *Abstracts of All Will Book Data, 1761-1919, Pertaining to Persons With Last Names Beginning with E, F, G, and I-full index for each Alphabetical Section*, Amherst County, Virginia, Courthouse Miniatures (Amherst: B. F. Davis, 1964), 22.
[1287] Amherst County, Virginia, Marriage Register, 31.
[1288] W. Mac. Jones, *The Douglas Register*, 32.
[1289] Bailey Fulton Davis, *Abstract of Deed Book P, Cross-index for grantors and grantees and Genealogical and geographical data*, Amherst County Courthouse Miniatures series (Amherst: B. F. Davis, 1966), 23.

[1290] Bailey Fulton Davis, *Abstract of Deed Book R*, Amherst County Courthouse Miniatures series (Amherst: B. F. Davis, 1967), 13.
[1291] Bailey Fulton Davis, *Abstract of Deed Book U*, Amherst County Courthouse Miniatures series (Amherst: B. F. Davis, 1968), 33.
[1292] Sparacio, *Deed and Will Abstracts of Albemarle County, Virginia, 1748-1752*, 17.
[1293] Morton, *A History of Monroe County, West Virginia*, 371-372.
[1294] Ibid., 374-375.
[1295] John Vogt & T. William Kethley, Jr., *Albemarle County Marriages, 1780-1853*, in three volumes (Athens, George: Iberian Pub. Co., 1991), 2:364.
[1296] Shuck, *Monroe County [W] Virginia Abstracts*, 63.
[1297] Ibid., 99-100.
[1298] Billy Joe Peyton, "James River & Kanawha Turnpike," *The West Virginia Encyclopedia*. http://www.wvencyclopedia.org/articles/978, downloaded 7/26/2011.
[1299] Carrie Eldridge, An Atlas of Appalachian Trails to the Ohio River (Chesapeake, Ohio: Carrie Eldridge, 1998), 29.
[1300] Pensioner, Catherine, Widow; Joshua Lewis, Veteran, War of 1812, Pension Application, Widow's File No. 12110.
[1301] Lawrence County, Ohio, Deed Book 17:239.
[1302] Certificate No. 185; Acc./Ser.Nr.: OH0150__.184; Patentee: Samuel Lewis; Issue Date: 9/4/1823. http://www.glorecords.blm.gov/PatentSearch/Image_Conversion.asp?P...
[1303] Lawrence County, Ohio, Deed Book 4:141.
[1304] Lawrence County, Ohio, Deed Book 4:158.
[1305] Lawrence County, Ohio, Deed Book 5:69, 107.
[1306] Certificate No. 7038; Acc./Ser.Nr.: OH1210__409; Patentee: Samuel Lewis; Issue Date: 7/28/1838. http://www.glorecords.blm.gov/PatentSearch/Image_Conversion.asp?P...
[1307] Lawrence County, Ohio, Deed Book 7:613.
[1308] Lawrence County, Ohio, Deed Book 8:263.
[1309] 1850 U.S. census, pop. sch., Lawrence County, Ohio, Mason Township, p.733, dwelling/family 159/162.
[1310] Billee Hammond Schlaudt, *Marriage Records of Lawrence County, Ohio* (Houston: B. H. Schlaudt, 1987), Books 1-6, p. 99.
[1311] "Windsor Township," in *History of Lawrence County, Ohio, 1990*, Lawrence County Historical Book Committee, eds. (Walsworth Publishing, 1990), 5.
[1312] Schreiner-Yantis and Love, *1787 Census of Virginia*, 2:1408.
[1313] Dale Burcham, "John S. Burcham," in *History of Lawrence County, Ohio, 1990*, 57.
[1314] Lawrence County, Ohio, Deed Book 10:299.
[1315] Schlaudt, *Marriage Records of Lawrence County, Ohio*, Books 1-6, p. 99.
[1316] "Personal History Department—Gallia County," *History of Gallia County, Ohio* (1882; reprint, 1976, Chicago and Toledo: H.H. Hardesty & Co., Publishers), 40.
[1317] Schlaudt, *Marriage Records of Lawrence County, Ohio*, Books 1-6, p. 99.
[1318] Cook, *Pioneer Lewis Families*, 4:1376.
[1319] Ibid., 5:496.
[1320] Clark-Lewis marriage, 12 April 1838 in Marriage Registry, Gallia County Courthouse, LDS Film No. 317652, Roll No. 299, Ohio, No. 1, p. 302.
[1321] Jewel M. Callicott, *Callicott Connections II* (St. Petersburg, Fla.: Genealogical Computer Services, 1986), 632.
[1322] Lawrence County, Ohio, Deed Book 7:22.
[1323] Lawrence County, Ohio, Deed Book 7:398.
[1324] 1840 U.S. Census., Lawrence County, Ohio, p.49.
[1325] Cook, *Pioneer Lewis Families*, 5:496-497.
[1326] 1850 U. S. Census, pop. sch., Lawrence County, Ohio, Rome Township, p. 835, dwelling/family 169/150.
[1327] 1860 U.S. Census, pop. sch., Lawrence County, Ohio, Rome Township, p.164, dwelling/family 1108/1098.
[1328] Callicott, *Callicott Connections II*, 632.
[1329] 1870 U.S. Census, pop. sch., Lawrence County, Ohio, Rome Township, p. 479, dwelling/family 36/35.
[1330] Schlaudt, *Marriage Records of Lawrence County, Ohio*, Books 1-6, p. 99.
[1331] Ibid.

[1332] Callicott, *Callicott Connections II*, 633.
[1333] Ibid.
[1334] R. Lewis Sakal, "Lewis Family of Harrison Twp.," in *Gallia County, Ohio, People in History to 1980* (Gallia County Historical Society, 1980), 211-212.//
[1335] Ibid.
[1336] Monroe County, West Virginia, Deed Book M:447-448.
[1337] Monroe County, West Virginia, Deed Book M:446-447.
[1338] 1840 U.S. Census, Lawrence County, Ohio, Windsor Township, p. 36
[1339] Certificate No. 11,928;Acc./Ser. Nr.: OH1310__.380; Patentee: James J. Lewis; Issue Date: 4/10/1843. http://www.glorecords.blm.gov/PatentSearch/Image_Conversion.asp?P...
[1340] Certificate No. 12,042; Acc./Ser. Nr.: OH1310__.493; Patentee: James J. Lewis; Issue Date: 4/10/1843. http://www.glorecords.blm.gov/PatentSearch/Image_Conversion.asp?P...
[1341] Certificate No. 13,193; Acc./Ser.Nr.: OH1340__.139; Patentee: James J. Lewis; Issue Date: 11/1/1846.http://www.glorecords.blm.gov/PatentSearch/Image_Conversion.asp?P...
[1342] 1850 U.S. Census, pop. sch., Lawrence County, Ohio, Windsor Township, p. 793, dwelling/family 18/19.
[1343] Certificate No. 17,021; Acc./Ser.Nr.: OH1420__.455; Patentee: James J. Lewis; Issue Date: 7/1/1852. http://www.glorecords.blm.gov/PatentSearch/Image_Conversion.asp?P...
[1344] Lawrence County, Ohio, Deed Book 18:265.
[1345] Lawrence County, Ohio, Deed Book 18:260.
[1346] 1860 U.S. Census, pop. sch., Lawrence County, Ohio, Windsor Township, p. 40-41, dwelling/family 254/254.
[1347] 1880 U.S. Census, pop. sch., Lawrence County, Ohio, Windsor Township, p.399B, FHL film no. 1,255,039; National Archives film no. T9-1039.
[1348] *History of Lawrence County, Ohio, 1990*, ii.
[1349] George W. Knepper, *Ohio and Its People* (Kent, Ohio: Kent State University Press, 1989), 148.
[1350] Lewis-Asbury marriage, Monroe County courthouse, File No. 6, Jacket No.4015.
[1351] Schlaudt, *Marriage Records of Lawrence County, Ohio*, Books 1-6, 99.
[1352] Sylvia Fulks, "Thomas Jefferson Lewis," in *History of Lawrence County, Ohio, 1990*, 217-218.
[1353] Patricia Lewis Joyce, "David and Susannah Bird," in *History of Lawrence County, Ohio, 1990*, 80.
[1354] 1840 U. S. Census, Lawrence County, Ohio, Perry Township, p. 107.
[1355] 1850 U.S. Census, pop. sch., Lawrence County, Ohio, Rome Township, p.837, dwelling/family 162/164.
[1356] 1900 U. S. Census, pop. sch., Lawrence County, Ohio, Millers Precinct, p.133, dwelling/family 246/247.
[1357] Sylvia Fulks, "Thomas Jefferson Lewis," in *History of Lawrence County, Ohio, 1990*, 217-218.
[1358] Ibid.
[1359] Monroe County, West Virginia, Deed Book N:52-53.
[1360] Monroe County, West Virginia, Deed Book F:11-12.
[1361] 1850 U.S. Census, pop. sch., Albemarle County, Virginia, Fredericksville Parish, p.349, dwelling/family 271/271.
[1362] Sparacio, *A Digest of Orange County, Virginia, Will Books 1734-1838*, 76.
[1363] Ibid.
[1364] Wulfeck, *Marriages of Some Virginia Residents*, vol. II (surnames Mi-Q), 61.
[1365] Brockman, *Orange County Virginia Families Volume IV*, 83-84.
[1366] Sparacio, *A Digest of Orange County, Virginia, Will Books 1734-1838*, 77.
[1367] Little, *Orange County, Virginia, Tithables, 1734-1782*, 1:83.
[1368] Wulfeck, *Marriages of Some Virginia Residents*, vol. II (surnames R-S), 170,171.
[1369] Little, *Orange County, Virginia, Tithables, 1734-1782*, 1:110.
[1370] Vogt & Kethley, *Orange County Marriages, 1747-1850*, 67.
[1371] Vogt & Kethley, *Albemarle County Marriages, 1780-1853*, 1:161, 163.
[1372] Sparacio, *Deed Abstracts of Orange County, Virginia (1759-1778)*, 31.
[1373] Crozier, *Spotsylvania County, 1721-1800*, 3.
[1374] William Everett Brockman, *Orange County (Va.) Families and Their Marriages, A Supplement to and Including Virginia wills and Abstracts, A Genealogy of Colonial Virginia Families, With a Thousand Marriage Bonds to 1800* (Minneapolis: Burgess Pub. Co., 1949), 9d.
[1375] Crozier, *Spotsylvania County, 1721-1800*, 135-136.

[1376] Sparacio, *Deed Abstracts of Orange County, Virginia (1759-1778),* 28.
[1377] Priode, *Abstracts of Executor, Administrator, and Guardian Bonds of Rockingham County, Virginia, 1778-1864,* 23.
[1378] Crozier, *Spotsylvania County, 1721-1800,* 313.
[1379] Sparacio, *Deed Abstracts of Albemarle County, Virginia, 1771-1772,* Virginia County Court Records series (McLean, Va.: Antient Press, 1990), 16-17.
[1380] Sparacio, *Deed Abstracts of Albemarle County, Virginia, 1768-1770,* 97.
[1381] Ibid., 62-63.
[1382] Wulfeck, *Marriages of Some Virginia Residents,* vol. 2 (surnames I-Me), 155.
[1383] Dorman, *Orange County, Virginia, Will Book 2,* 94-95.
[1384] Wulfeck, *Marriages of Some Virginia Residents,* vol. I (surnames A-B), 236.
[1385] Brockman, *Virginia Wills and Abstracts, Brockman, Bell, Bledsoe, Burris, Collins, Durrett, Graves, Henderson, and Tatum Families,* 16.
[1386] Vogt & Kethley, *Albemarle County Marriages, 1780-1853,* 2:636.
[1387] Bentley, *Virginia Marriage Records,* 473.
[1388] Vogt & Kethley, *Albemarle County Marriages, 1780-1853,* 1:296.
[1389] Brockman, *Virginia Wills and Abstracts,* 40-41.
[1390] Albemarle County, Virginia, Deed Book 34:91-92.
[1391] Brockman, *Virginia Wills and Abstracts,* 153-155.
[1392] Vogt & Kethley, *Albemarle County Marriages, 1780-1853,* 1:154.
[1393] Ibid., 1:263.
[1394] Yurechko, *Christ Church Parish Register,* 117.
[1395] Ibid., 13, 30.
[1396] Dorman, *Orange County Will Book 2,* 67-68.
[1397] Wulfeck, *Marriages of Some Virginia Residents,* vol. II (surnames I-Me), 258.
[1398] Brockman, *Virginia Wills and Abstracts,* 41.
[1399] Records of Literary Schools, Monroe County (West Virginia), item 7.
[1400] Sparacio, *Will Abstracts of Culpeper County, Virginia (1749-1770),* 60-61.
[1401] Lawrence County, Ohio, Deed Book 7:614-615.
[1402] 1840 U.S. Census, Lawrence County, Ohio, Windsor Township, p. 33.
[1403] 1850 U.S. Census, pop. sch., Lawrence County, Ohio, Windsor Township, p.793, dwelling/family 19/20.
[1404] Certificate No. 11,753; Acc./Ser.Nr.: OH1430__.155; Patentee: Richard B. Lewis; Issue Date: 11/17/1853. http://www.glorecords.blm.gov/PatentSearch/Image.asp?PatentDocCla...
[1405] Lawrence County, Ohio, Deed Book 18: 251-252.
[1406] 1860 U.S. Census, pop. sch., Lawrence County, Ohio, Windsor Township, p. 40, dwelling/family 250/250.
[1407] 1870 U.S. Census, pop. sch., Lawrence County, Ohio, Windsor Township, p. indecipherable, dwelling/family 217/209.
[1408] 1880 U.S. Census, pop. sch., Lawrence County, Ohio, Windsor Township, p. 410D, FHL film no. 1,255,039; National Archives film no. T9-1039.
[1409] Shuck, *Monroe County [W] Virginia Abstracts,* 61.
[1410] James H. Miller, *History of Summers County (West Virginia), From the Earliest Settlement to the Present Time* (Hinton, WV: James H. Miller, 1908), 535-536.
[1411] Morton, *A History of Monroe County, West Virginia,* 45.
[1412] 1880 U.S. Census, pop. sch., Summers County, West Virginia, Jumping Branch, p.195C, FHL film no. 1,255,413; National Archives film no. T9-1413.
[1413] Morton, *A History of Monroe County, West Virginia,* 95.
[1414] Shuck, *Monroe County [W] Virginia Agstracts,* 26.
[1415] Record of Deaths, No. 2, Probate Court, Lawrence County, Ohio.
[1416] Janet Bowman, "Janet Bundy Bowman," in *History of Lawrence County, Ohio, 1990,* 88.
[1417] Schlaudt, *Marriage Records, Lawrence County, Ohio,* Books 1-6, 99.
[1418] Lennie Lewis Bundy, "Richard Burton Lewis," in *History of Lawrence County, Ohio, 1990,* 61-62.
[1419] Ibid.
[1420] Monroe County, West Virginia, Deed Book L:694-695.

[1421] Lawrence County, Ohio, Deed Book 9:396.

[1422] 1860 U.S. Census, pop. sch., Lawrence County, Ohio, Rome Township, dwelling/family 1059/1049.

[1423] 1870 U.S. Census, pop. sch., Lawrence County, Ohio, Windsor Township, p. 6, dwelling/family 42/41.

[1424] 1880 U.S. Census, pop. sch., Lincoln, West Virginia, District 64, p. 148B (family of Samuel Lewis), p. 149C (family of Elvira Lewis), FHL film no. 1,255,406; National Archives film no. T9-1406.

[1425] Lewis-Miller marriage 3 September 1836, Monroe County, West Virginia, File No. 5, Jacket No. 3615.

[1426] Everett W. Miller, *Genealogy of Jacob Miller and His Descendants, With Some Brief History Thereto* (Huntington, WV: Cook Printing Co., 1952), 21.

[1427] 1850 U.S. Census, pop. sch., Monroe County, West Virginia, FHL film no. M432, roll no. 961.

[1428] Schlaudt, *Marriage Records, Lawrence County, Ohio*, Books 1-6, 99.

[1429] 1850 U.S. Census, pop. sch., Monroe County, West Virginia, FHL film no. M432, roll no. 961.

[1430] Lewis-Mann marriage, Monroe County courthouse, File No. 5, Jacket No. 3681.

[1431] Monroe County, West Virginia Court Orders, J:120.

[1432] Records of Literary Schools, 1826-1855, Monroe County (West Virginia), FHL microfilm no. 1,017, 649, item 7.

[1433] 1860 U.S. Census, pop. sch., Lawrence County, Ohio, Rome Township, p.145, dwelling/family 973/963.

[1434] 1850 U.S. Census, pop. sch., Lawrence County, Ohio, Rome Township, p. 840, dwelling/family 183/185.

[1435] 1880 U.S. Census, pop. sch., Lincoln, West Virginia, District 64, p.149C, FHL film no.1,255,406; National Archives film no. T9-1406.

[1436] Andrew Francis Lewis, "Nash-Lewis," in *History of Lawrence County, Ohio, 1990*, 267.

[1437] Robert L. Lewis, Jr., "Gillett," in *History of Lawrence County, Ohio, 1990*, 171.

[1438] Records of Literary Schools, 1826-1855, Monroe County (West Virginia), item 7.

[1439] 1860 U.S. Census, pop. sch., Lawrence County, Ohio, Windsor Township, p.37, dwelling/family 229/229.

[1440] 1870 U.S. Census, pop. sch., Lawrence County, Ohio, Rome Township, p.479, dwelling/family 37/36.

[1441] 1880 U.S. Census, pop. sch., Lawrence County, Ohio, Rome Township, p.16, dwelling/family 165/166 (Madison Lewis); dwelling/family 165/167 (Amanda, James H., and William H. Short); dwelling/family 165/168 (Wilson M. Lewis family and Matilda Short).

[1442] Mrs. Carl Murnahan, "John H. Murnahan," in *History of Lawrence County, Ohio, 1990*, 257; Carl Edward Murnahan, "Murnahan-Clark," in *History of Lawrence County, Ohio, 1990*, 62.

[1443] Schlaudt, *Marriage Records, Lawrence County, Ohio*, Books 1-6, 99.

[1444] Ibid.

[1445] Lewis-Corn marriage, Lawrence County, Ohio, FHL Batch No. M514522; Source Call No. 0317717 V. 6-8. http://www.familysearch.org/eng/search/frameset_search.asp.

[1446] Callicott, *Callicott Connections II*, 632.

[1447] 1850 U.S. Census, pop. sch., Lawrence County, Ohio, Windsor Township, p.795, dwelling/family 32/34.

[1448] Callicott, *Callicott Connections II*, 632.

[1449] Ibid.

[1450] Schlaudt, *Marriage Records of Lawrence County, Ohio*, Books 1-6, p. 99.

[1451] 1850 U.S. Census, pop. sch., Lawrence County, Ohio, Rome Township, p. 836, dwelling/family 151/152 (John B. Lewis household); dwelling/family 150/151 (David Walls household).

[1452] 1860 U.S. Census, pop. sch., Lawrence County, Ohio, Rome Township, pp.164-165, dwelling/family 1109/1099 (Jno. B. Lewis household); dwelling/family 1114/1104 (David Wales household).

[1453] 1880 U.S. Census, pop. sch., Gallia County, Ohio, Guyan Township, p. 383C, FHL film no. 1,255,018; National Archives film no. T9-1018.

[1454] Schlaudt, *Marriage Records, Lawrence County, Ohio*, Books 1-6, 99.

[1455] Cook, *Pioneer Lewis Families*, 5:497.

[1456] Ibid., 5: 497.

[1457] 1860 U.S. Census, pop. sch., Lawrence County, Ohio, Rome Township, p. 165, dwelling/family 1110/1100.

[1458] 1880 U.S. Census, pop. sch., Lawrence County, Ohio, Athalia, p.293B, FHL film no. 1,255,039; National Archives film no. T9-1039.

[1459] Schlaudt, *Marriage Records, Lawrence County, Ohio*, Books 1-6, 99.

[1460] Harriet E. Scarberry, death, June 18, 1929, Logan County, West Virginia. West Virginia Death Register. http://www.wvculture.org/vr/va.

[1461] 1860 U.S. Census, pop. sch., Lawrence County, Ohio, Rome Township, p. 165, dwelling/family 1112/1102.

[1462] 1880 U.S. Census, pop. sch., Lincoln, West Virginia, District 64, p.151C, FHL film no. 1,255,406; National Archives film no. T9-1406.

[1463] 1900 U.S. Census, pop. sch., Lawrence County, Ohio, Millers Precinct, p. 23A, dwelling/family 420/422.

[1464] Schlaudt, *Marriage Records, Lawrence County, Ohio*, Books 1-6, 99.

[1465] 1910 U.S. Census, pop. sch., Lawrence County, Ohio, Rome Township, p.14B, dwelling/family 258/259.

[1466] 1870 U.S. Census, pop. sch., Lawrence County, Ohio, Rome Township, p.479, dwelling/family 31/30.

[1467] 1900 U.S. Census, pop. sch., Lawrence County, Ohio, Millers Precinct, p. 6B, dwelling/family 118/119.

[1468] 1910 U.S. Census, pop. sch., Lawrence County, Ohio, Rome Township, p.15(?)B, dwelling/family 147/148.

[1469] Redman C. Lewis, death certificate no. 35040 (1924), West Virginia State Department of Health.

[1470] Lewis-Dolton marriage, Lawrence County Marriage Records 1817-1953 and Index 1895-1914, Lawrence County, Ohio, Probate Records, Batch 1866-1874, FHL film no. 0317718.

[1471] Callicott, *Callicott Connections II*, 633.

[1472] 1880 U.S. Census, pop. sch., Lawrence County, Ohio, Rome Township, p.297B, FHL film no. 1,255,039; National Archives film no. T9-1039.

[1473] Lawrence County, Ohio, Deed Book 18:242-243.

[1474] Lawrence County, Ohio, Deed Book 18:260.

[1475] 1860 U.S. Census, pop. sch., Lawrence County, Ohio, Windsor Township, p.41, dwelling/family 255/255 (the Sowards household); pp. 40-41, dwelling/family 254/254 (the Lewis household).

[1476] 1870 U.S. Census, pop. sch., Lawrence County, Ohio, Windsor Township, p. 6, dwelling/family 40/39.

[1477] 1880 U.S. Census, pop. sch., Lawrence County, Ohio, Windsor Township, p.399B, FHL film no. 1,255,039; National Archives film no. T9-1039.

[1478] 1900 U.S. Census, pop. sch., Lawrence County, Ohio, Millers Precinct, p.2B, dwelling/family 40/40.

[1479] 1920 U.S. Census, pop. sch., Lawrence County, Ohio, Windsor Township, p.7B, dwelling/family 142/144.

[1480] Schlaudt, *Marriage Records, Lawrence County, Ohio*, Books 1-6, 157.

[1481] Jane Burcham, death certificate no. 60686 (1912), Ohio Bureau of Vital Statistics.

[1482] Record of Deaths, No. 2, Probate Court, Lawrence County, Ohio, 1868-1938, Ledger 29, Register 3:25.

[1483] Donna Rachal Mills, *Some Southern Balls, from Valentine to Ferdinand, and Beyond* (Orlando, Fla.: Mills Historical Press, 1993), 74-75. Ms. Mills was quoting Daniel Blake Smith, *Inside the Great House: Planter Family Life in Eighteenth-Century Chesapeake Society* (Ithaca: Cornell University Press, 1980), 120-121.

[1484] Lawrence County, Ohio, Deed Book 101:508-509.

[1485] 1900 U.S. Census, pop. sch., Lawrence County, Ohio, Millers Precinct, p. 12B, dwelling/family 229/230 (Lewis E. Burd household).

[1486] 1920 U.S. Census, pop. sch., Lawrence County, Ohio, Union Township, p.10A, dwelling/family 189/195.

[1487] 1900 U.S. Census, pop. sch., Lawrence County, Ohio, Millers Precinct, p.13A, dwelling/family 237/238.

[1488] 1910 U.S. Census, pop. sch., Lawrence County, Ohio, Windsor Township, p.7A, dwelling/family 128/128.

[1489] 1920 U.S. Census, pop. sch., Lawrence County, Ohio, Windsor Township, p.7B, dwelling/family 149/142,

[1490] 1930 U.S. Census, pop. sch., Lawrence County, Ohio, Windsor Township, p.2B, dwelling/family 34/35 (James Lewis household); dwelling/family 35/36 (Otis Lewis household); dwelling/family 36/37 (Ezra Lewis household); dwelling/family 37/38 (William Lewis household).

[1491] Lawrence County, Ohio, Marriagaes, vol. 23-25 (p. 1-300), 1910-1916, certificate no. 6570. FHL film no. 1,574,145.(Ezra Lewis was a son of James Lewis and Rose Pinkerman.)

[1492] 1870 U.S. Census, pop. sch., Lawrence County, Ohio, Rome Township, p.6, dwelling/family 39/38.

[1493] Billee Hammond Schlaudt, *Marriage Records, Lawrence County, Ohio*, Books 7-11 (Houston: the author, 1989), p. 62.

[1494] Schlaudt, *Marriage Records, Lawrence County, Ohio*, Books 1-6, p. 134.

[1495] 1860 U.S. Census, pop. sch., Lawrence County, Ohio, Windsor Township, p.41, dwelling/family 258/258.

[1496] Kay (Pinkerman) Skogland, "William H. Pinkerman," in *History of Lawrence County, Ohio, 1990*, 277.

[1497] Berkley Lewis, no. 289-18-2565, Social Security Death Index, *FamilySearch* (Salt Lake City: Family History Library, 2010). The SSDI component of FamilySearch is drawn from the *Social Security Death Benefits Index* of the U.S. Social Security Administration.

[1498] Geneva Lewis, no. 273-62-0823, Social Security Death Index, *FamilySearch* (Salt Lake City: Family History Library, 2010).

[1499] Record of Deaths, No. 2, Probate Court, Lawrence County, Ohio, 1868-1938, ledger 30, page 68, register 12.
[1500] Fulks, "Thomas Jefferson Lewis," in *History of Lawrence County, Ohio, 1990*, 217-218.
[1501] 1910 U.S. Census, pop. sch., Lawrence County, Ohio, Windsor Township, p.11B, dwelling/family 222/222.
[1502] 1920 U.S. Census, pop. sch., Lawrence County, Ohio, Windsor Township, p.7A, dwelling/family 129/130.
[1503] Record of Deaths, No. 2, Probate Court, Lawrence County, Ohio, 1868-1938, ledger 30, page 68, register 12.
[1504] Joyce, "David and Susannah Bird," in *History of Lawrence County, Ohio, 1990*, 80-81.
[1505] 1900 U.S. Census, pop. sch., Lawrence County, Ohio, Millers Precinct, p.12B, dwelling/family 226/227.
[1506] 1910 U.S. Census, pop. sch., Lawrence County, Ohio, Rome Township, p. 8B, dwelling/family 138/138.
[1507] 1920 U.S. Census, pop. sch., Lawrence County, Ohio, Rome Township, p.2B, dwelling/family 36/36.
[1508] Charles Galloway, no. 275-34-6209, Social Security Death Index, *FamilySearch* (Salt Lake City: Family History Library, 2010).
[1509] Lawrence County, Ohio, Marriages, vol. 23-25 (p. 1-300), 1910-1916, certificate no. 8236. FHL film no. 1,574,145.
[1510] Mary Georgiana Stumbo Montrose, "Fred, Meda Galloway," in *History of Lawrence County, Ohio, 1990*, 169.
[1511] Lawrence County, Ohio, Marriages, vol. 25 (p. 299-end)-27, 1914-1919, certificate no. 11616. FHL film no. 1,574,146.
[1512] Jacquetta L. Lynch, "Jordan and Elizabeth Nance," in *History of Lawrence County, Ohio, 1990*, 266.
[1513] Ibid.
[1514] 1880 U.S. Census, pop. sch., Lawrence County, Ohio, Windsor Township, p.410D, FHL film no. 1,255,039; National Archives film no. T9-1039.
[1515] 1910 U.S. Census, pop. sch., Lawrence County, Ohio, Windsor Township, p. 7B, dwelling/family 135/135.
[1516] Record of Deaths, No. 2, Probate Court, Lawrence County, Ohio, 1868-1938, Register 3.
[1517] Lennie Lewis Bundy, "Richard Clark Lewis," in *History of Lawrence County, Ohio, 1990*, 217.
[1518] Ibid.
[1519] Ibid.
[1520] Lawrence County, Ohio, Marriages, vol. 21-22, 1905-1910, certificate no. 5072. FHL film no. 317,724.
[1521] Lawrence County, Ohio, Marriages, vol. 21-22, 1905-1910, certificate no. 4380. FHL film no. 317,724.
[1522] Lawrence County, Ohio, Marriages, vol. 21-22, 1905-1910, certificate no. 5011. FHL film no. 317,724.
[1523] Barbara Jane Dillon, death certificate no. 9210 (1932), West Virginia State Department of Health.
[1524] Patricia Lewis Joyce, "David and Susannah Bird," in *History of Lawrence County, Ohio, 1990*, 80-81.
[1525] 1880 U.S. Census, pop. sch., Lawrence County, Ohio, Rome Township, p. 290D, FHL film no. 1,255,039; National Archives film no. T9-1039.
[1526] Carl Edward Murnahan, "Murnahan-Clark," in *History of Lawrence County, Ohio*, 62.
[1527] Lawrence County, Ohio, Marriages, vol. 21-22, 1905-1910, certificate no. 5616. FHL film no. 317,724.
[1528] Cook, *Pioneer Lewis Families*, 5:497.
[1529] 1900 U.S. Census, pop. sch., Lawrence County, Ohio, Millers Precinct, p. 16A, dwelling/family 293/294.
[1530] 1920 U.S. Census, pop. sch., Lawrence County, Ohio, Rome Township, p. 11-12A, dwelling/family 225/225.
[1531] Cook, *Pioneer Lewis Families*, 5:497.
[1532] Minnie Helen Honaker, "Lewis-Kearns," in *History of Lawrence County, Ohio, 1990*, 216.
[1533] Lawrence County, Ohio, Marriages, vol. 21-22, 1905-1910, certificate no. 4875. FHL film no. 317,724.
[1534] Honaker, "Lewis-Kearns," in *History of Lawrence County, Ohio, 1990*, 216.
[1535] Ibid.
[1536] Ibid.
[1537] 1900 U.S. Census, pop. sch., Lawrence County, Ohio, Millers Precinct, p.17B, dwelling/family 322/323.
[1538] 1910 U.S. Census, pop. sch., Lawrence County, Ohio, Rome Township, p.13B(?), dwelling/family 141/143.
[1539] 1880 U.S. Census, pop. sch., Lawrence County, Ohio, Windsor Township, p.400C, FHL film no. 1,255,039; National Archives film. No. T9-1039.
[1540] 1910 U.S. Census, pop. sch., Lawrence County, Ohio, Windsor Township, p. 8B, dwelling/family 163/164.
[1541] 1910 U.S. Census, pop. sch., Lawrence County, Ohio, Windsor Township, p. 8B, dwelling/family 162/163.
[1542] Edna Riggs, no. 234-16-1557, Social Security Death Index, *FamilySearch* (Salt Lake City: Family History Library, 2010).
[1543] Pearl Walker, no. 234-12-3984, Social Security Death Index, *FamilySearch* (Salt Lake City: Family History Library, 2010).
[1544] 1920 U.S. Census, pop. sch., Lawrence County, Ohio, Windsor Township, p.6B, dwelling/family 120/121 (Ezra C. Lewis household); dwelling/family 118/129 (John Dillon); dwelling/family 121/122 (David W. Wall).

[1545] 1930 U.S. Census, pop. sch., Lawrence County, Ohio, Windsor Township, p.2B, dwelling/family 36/37 (Ezra Lewis household); dwelling/family 35/36 (Otis Lewis household); dwelling/family 34/35 (Daisy Wall and James Lewis household); dwelling/family 37/38 William Lewis household).

[1546] Lawrence County, Ohio, Marriages, vol. 23-25 (p. 1-300), 1910-1916, certificate no. 6570. FHL film no. 1,574,145.

[1547] Edna May Lewis, death certificate no.1243(1951), West Virginia State Department of Health, Division of Vital Statistics.

[1548] 1900 U.S. Census, pop. sch., Lawrence County, Ohio, Mason Township, pp. 6A-6B, dwelling/family 111/112.

[1549] Donald Lewis, death certificate no. 1:39495, dist. No. 5057, Ohio Department of Health, Division of Vital Statistics.

[1550] 1900 U.S. Census, pop. sch., Lawrence County, Ohio, Millers Precinct, p. 13A, dwelling/family 237/238.

[1551] Rebecca Lewis, no. 293-22-0487, Social Security Death Index, *FamilySearch* (Salt Lake City: Family History Library, 2010).

[1552] 1930 U.S. Census, pop. sch., Lawrence County, Ohio, Windsor Township, p. 2B, dwelling/family 35/36.

[1553] Lawrence County, Ohio, Marriages, vol. 25 (p.299-end)-27, 1914-1919, certificate no. 10375. FHL film no. 1,574,146.

[1554] Berdie Lewis, no. 295-22-7915, Social Security Death Index, *FamilySearch* (Salt Lake City: Family History Library, 2010).

[1555] Elva Lewis, no. 290-07-4515, Social Security Death Index, *FamilySearch* (Salt Lake City: Family History Library, 2010).

[1556] 1930 U.S. Census, pop. sch., Lawrence County, Ohio, Windsor Township, p. 2B, dwelling/family 35/36.

[1557] Fern Lewis, no. 284-62-2649, Social Security Death Index, *FamilySearch* (Salt Lake City: Family History Library, 2010).

[1558] 1910 U.S. Census, pop. sch., Lawrence County, Ohio, Windsor Township, p. 7B, dwelling/family 132/132.

[1559] Ella Wade, no. 283-34-8083, Social Security Death Index, *FamilySearch* (Salt Lake City: Family History Library, 2010).

[1560] Henry Wade, no. 234-05-1163, Social Security Death Index, *FamilySearch* (Salt Lake City: Family History Library, 2010).

[1561] Fulks, "Thomas Jefferson Lewis," in *History of Lawrence County, Ohio, 1990*, 217-218.

[1562] 1930 U.S. Census, pop. sch., Lawrence County, Ohio, Windsor Township, p. 1A, dwelling/family 6/6.

[1563] Lawrence County, Ohio, Marriages, vol. 23-25 (p. 1-300), 1910-1916, certificate no. 6444. FHL film no. 1,574,145.

[1564] Fulks, "Thomas Jefferson Lewis," in *History of Lawrence County, Ohio, 1990*, 217-218.

[1565] Ibid. (This reference also gives names of Mary's spouses and children.)

[1566] Sylvia Fulks, no. 285-48-0256, Social Security Death Index, *FamilySearch* (Salt Lake City: Family History Library, 2010).

[1567] Louise Sark, "Who's Who in Lawrence County," *The Ironton Tribune*, May 14, 1989, page 6.

[1568] Fulks, "Thomas Jefferson Lewis," 217-218. (This reference also gives the names of Sylvia and N.D.'s children and their spouses.)

[1569] Sark, "Who's Who in Lawrence County." (This reference supplies information on the careers of the Fulks' children.)

[1570] Claude Vincent Fulks, "Claude Vincent Fulks," in *History of Lawrence County, Ohio, 1990*, 164.

[1571] Lynch, "Jordan and Elizabeth Nance," in *History of Lawrence County, Ohio, 1990*, 266.

[1572] Ibid.

[1573] Bundy, "Richard Clark Lewis," in *History of Lawrence County, Ohio, 1990*, 217.

[1574] 1930 U.S. Census, pop. sch., Lawrence County, Ohio, Windsor Township, p. 2B, dwelling/family 37/38.

[1575] Bundy, "Richard Clark Lewis," in *History of Lawrence County, Ohio, 1990*, 217.

[1576] Arda Lewis, death certificate no. 55319, Registration District No. 5057, File No. 39, State of Ohio Bureau of Vital Statistics.

[1577] Honaker, "Lewis-Kearns," in *History of Lawrence County, Ohio, 1990*, 216.

[1578] 1910 U.S. Census, pop. sch., Lawrence County, Ohio, Windsor Township, p. 8A, dwelling/family 141/141.

[1579] Lawrence County, Ohio, Marriages, vol. 21-22, 1905-1910, certificate no. 4878. FHL film no. 317,724.

[1580] 1930 U.S. Census, pop. sch., Lawrence County, Ohio, Rome Township, p. 7B, dwelling/family 149/146.

[1581] Honaker, "Lewis-Kearns," in *History of Lawrence County, Ohio, 1990*, 216-217.

[1582] Charles Galloway, no. 234-18-9667, Social Security Death Index, *FamilySearch* (Salt Lake City: Family History Library, 2010).

[1583] Honaker, "Lewis-Kearns," *History of Lawrence County, Ohio, 1990*, 216-217.

[1584] FamilyTreeMaker Online. http://familytreemaker.genealogy.com/users/h/o/n/Raymond-H-Honaker....

[1585] Cook, *Pioneer Lewis Families*, 5:498.

[1586] Lawrence County, Ohio, Marriages, vol. 25 (p. 299-end)-27, 1914-1919, certificate no. 9660. FHL film no. 1,574,146.

[1587] Cook, *Pioneer Lewis Families*, 5:498.

[1588] Lyndell Lewis, no. 284-20-0576, Social Security Death Index, *FamilySearch* (Salt Lake City: Family History Library, 2010).

[1589] Lynch, "Jordan and Elizabeth Nance," in *History of Lawrence County, Ohio, 1990*, 266.

[1590] Ibid.

[1591] Lennie Lewis Bundy, "Paul Eugene Lewis," in *History of Lawrence County, Ohio, 1990*, 217.

[1592] "Nelson M. Lewis," *The Herald-Dispatch*, December 2, 2009, obituaries. http://news.herald-dispatch.com/obituaries/index.php?id=41634.
[1593] Paul Lewis, no. 273-18-9876, Social Security Death Index, *FamilySearch* (Salt Lake City: Family History Library, 2010).
[1594] Lennie Lewis Bundy, "Paul Eugene Lewis," in *History of Lawrence County, Ohio, 1990*, 217.
[1595] Ibid.
[1596] Mary Lewis Nicolia, "Mary Jane Lewis Nicolia," in *History of Lawrence County, Ohio, 1990*, 269.
[1597] Lennie Bundy, no. 297-24-5020, Social Security Death Index, *FamilySearch* (Salt Lake City: Family History Library, 2010).
[1598] Lennie Lewis Bundy, "Lennie Lewis Bundy," in *History of Lawrence County, Ohio, 1990*, 104.
[1599] Ibid.
[1600] Ibid.
[1601] Ibid.
[1602] Lennie Lewis Bundy, "Virginia Helen Lewis," in *History of Lawrence County, Ohio, 1990*, 218.
[1603] "Virginia Bates," *The Ironton Tribune*, June 10, 2002, obituaries. http://www.irontontribune.com/news/2002/jun/10/virginia-bates/
[1604] Bundy, "Virginia Helen Lewis," in *History of Lawrence County, Ohio, 1990*, 218.
[1605] Ibid.
[1606] Lynch, "Jordan and Elizabeth Nance," in *History of Lawrence County, Ohio, 1990*, 266.
[1607] Ibid.
[1608] "Nelson M. Lewis," *The Herald-Dispatch*, December 2, 2009, obituaries.
[1609] Janet Bowman, "Janet Bundy Bowman," in *History of Lawrence County, Ohio, 1990*, 88.

The PAYNES

Speculation on the ancestry of John Payne (b. abt. 1760) of Bedford County, Virginia.

Sorting out the Paynes who lived in Bedford County, Virginia, in the late 1700s is a daunting task. There were several families of Paynes living there at that time. Family tradition says that John and Sarah Payne, the progenitors of the Lawrence County, Ohio, Paynes, had owned land in Bedford and Franklin Counties in Virginia and moved to Jackson County, Tennessee, before settling in Lawrence County early in the 1800s. Evidence supports this chain of events.

It is tempting, however, to try to discover the county John Payne or his parents were living in before moving to Bedford. And the first step is to ferret out relatives of John's who were living in the Bedford area at the same time. The task is complex, for we must consider the Flayl Payne family of Goose Creek, who came from Maryland;[1610] Josias and James Payne of Beaverdam Creek; the Joseph Payne family along the Staunton River (that separates Bedford and Franklin Counties); and Colonel John Payne, who owned land around New London (part of Bedford County before 1781 when Campbell County was formed). Colonel John Payne's will was proved in 1784 in Goochland County, Virginia. He devised to son Philip all his plantation in Campbell County and part of a tract, called the Forest, in Bedford County. Son Smith was given the Flat Creek Quarter in Campbell County and a house and lot in New London. (Other children were named.) Colonel John Payne was a son of George Payne of Goochland, as was Josias Payne, whose will was probated in Pittsylvania County, Virginia, in 1785. And he had son Josias.[1611]

A Josias Payne owned land along Beaverdam Creek in Bedford County, as did the John Payne who moved to Ohio, and land owned by both Josias and John shared a pointer: the flat rock in Beaverdam Creek.[1612] Josias does not seem to have been close to the Flayl Payne group, but he probably was related to both the John Payne who moved to Ohio and the Joseph Payne family. (Or this Josias and Joseph may have been one and the same.)

When people migrated to an area in early Virginia, they usually were joining people they already knew. So it pays to take a close look at the people who were surety and/or witnesses for marriage bonds, who sold land to whom, who witnessed their deeds and wills, and who had land adjoining. I have found no evidence that John and Sarah were involved with the Flayl Payne group, nor the John Payne family of New London, so it is the others that are discussed.

Josiah Payne of Bedford County:

On 19 January 1764 Josiah Payne had a survey made for 336 acres on Mulberry Creek in Bedford County. The point of beginning was Phair's corner line.[1613] Mulberry Creek is a north branch of Falling River, which flows through present-day Campbell County, and Mulberry Creek is now in Appomattox County, Virginia.

In 1767 Benjamin Greer sold to Matthew Talbot 163 acres on the north side of Blackwater River. Wits: Peter Holland, Josias Payne, Benj. Holland, Mary Sinkler.[1614] This deed was recorded in Bedford County, but Blackwater River is now in Franklin County, Virginia, formed in 1785 from parts of Bedford and Henry Counties. The *Slinkers* intermarried with the Joseph Payne family, so *Josias* may have been substituted for *Joseph*.

On 15 April 1774 Josiah Payne had surveyed 790 acres on Beaverdam Creek, bounded by lands of Mead, Board, and Walton.[1615]

In 1778 Josiah Payne deeded to Nimrod Newman 142 acres on south side of the Little Otter River, adjacent Walton, Jacob Eccles corner, Pate's line, Haynes' corner. Josiah had bought this land from Merry Carter in 1769.[1616]

In 1784 Josiah Payne sold 200 acres adjacent Craddock to Stephen Goggin.[1617] Stephen Goggin wrote his will in 1802 and devised to his son Pleasant M. Goggin the mill tract on Beaverdam Creek. It included the surveys bought by Stephen Goggin, deceased, from Josiah Payne and Joseph Wright.[1618]

An interesting aside: Stephen Goggin was an ancestor of Samuel Clemens (Mark Twain). Stephen Goggin's daughter Pamela married Samuel Clemens, and their son John Marshall Clemens, born 1798, married Jane Lampkin and had son Samuel Lampkin Clemens (Mark Twain), born 1835 in Missouri.

Bedford County Court Orders of 1784-1786 include a notation regarding Josiah Payne. He was being declared exempt from paying county levy.[1619] Old age was a common reason for exemption.

In 1787 Josiah Payne of Bedford County sold to Wm. McCormack of same 300 acres on Beaverdam Creek, adjacent Walton and Board and extending to John Pane's upon a corner by the flat rock on Beaverdam. Wits: R. Nimmo, James Board, Jr., James Board, Sr.[1620] The 1788 personal property tax list for Bedford County shows James Payne, son of Josiah, being visited by the tax collector on June 21st; and James Payne and John Payne being visited on June 24th. In 1789 we find Joseph Payne, William Payne, and James Payne, son of Josias, being visited on June 16th and another James Payne being visited the same day. Josias (?) Payne was visited on April 26th. In 1791 John Payne (BD) was visited on March 24th and James Payne (Turk) was visited on March 31st. James, Joseph, and Barnard Payne were visited on April 9th. In 1794 James Payne (Turk) was visited on March 18th and John Payne on March 20th. Reul Shrewsbury was visited on March 22nd.[1621] The handwriting for these records is not always easy to decipher, but I did not find a Josiah Payne named, with the possible exception of the 1789 list. Josiah had been declared exempt from taxation, and it seems only one Josiah Payne owned land in Bedford at that time. "BD," of course, stood for Beaverdam Creek. The importance of the Shrewsburys will be seen below.

The will of Josias Payne of Pittsylvania County, Virginia, son of George Payne of Goochland County, was probated in December 1785,[1622] so the Josias of Beaverdam Creek was not the Josias of Pittsylvania.

James Payne of Beaverdam Creek:

James Payne sold land to James Wheeler. John and Sarah Payne moved from Franklin County to Flynn's Creek in Jackson County, Tennessee, following the migration of the William Wheeler family. The Wheelers, Wrights, McCormacks, and Mays intermarried, so we can assume that the James Payne who was involved with these families was related to John and Sarah Payne.

Burr Barton sold James Payne 150 acres on the waters of Beaverdam Creek on 25 January 1774. The land was adjacent John Wright's land, Brown's line, and John Wright's corner. Other pointers were lines of Tommy Wright and James Mays. Wits: Tommy Wright, John Wright, Wm McCormack.[1623] James Payne would have been of legal age by the time he bought land, so he must have been born by 1753. As we saw above, there were at least two James Paynes in the area at that time. Joseph Payne had son James, thought to have born between 1760 and 1770 (see below). When John and Sarah Payne sold land to John Jeter in 1804, an *R* was placed in parentheses beside the name of witness James Payne, probably to distinguish him from another James Payne. People of the same name were sometimes identified by words that indicated where they lived, such as *river* or *mountain* (or abbreviations for same).

Some background on the Bartons and Wrights: David Barton and Elizabeth McCormack married on 22 December 1792. Elisha Barton was surety. Thomas and Sarah Barton and Mecager and ____McCormack gave their consent.[1624] According to a note posted on the internet, Burr Barton and wife, Elizabeth, moved to Bedford County, Virginia, by 1742. Their son Jacob was called *Burton*, and he and wife, Edith, moved to Jackson County, Tennessee.[1625] Anthony Wright and Elizabeth Mays married on 18 December 1789. James Mays was surety, and John Wright, father of Anthony, gave consent.[1626] William Wheeler and Sarah Wright married on 10 December 1785. Rowland Wheeler was surety.[1627] William McCormack and Judith Wright married on 3 January 1791, Micajah McCormack serving as surety. Joseph Wright, Judith's father, gave consent.[1628]

On 20 May 1788 John Dollard of Bedford County sold James Pane 15 acres bordering his (Dollard's) own property on a branch near Beaverdam Creek. Wits: R. Nimmo, Anderson McCormack, Micager McCormack.[1629]

In 1789 James Payne of Bedford County sold to James Wheeler of same 30 acres on a branch of Beaverdam Creek in Dollard's line. Signed *IP* (JP). (*I*, with a horizontal line through it, was a common way of signing with a *J* in those days.) Wits: Wm. Nimmo, John Dollard, Robert Nimmo.[1630]

On 21 August 1798 James Payne and wife, Anny, and William Brown and wife, Elizabeth, sold 150 acres to Charles Anthony. The land was in Bedford County and abutted land of Burr Barten's, Benson (?), and Tommy Wright, John Wright, Pates' road, James Seal's, to the land James Payne bought from William Brown. Wits: Robert Nimmo, Joseph Johnson, Jesse Johnson, James Johnson. James Payne signed his name *IP*.[1631] James Payne, William Brown, and Jesse Brown were witnesses to the 1791 will of Elizabeth Anderson. She named son John Anderson and she gave to him, among other things, her part of a still which she had bought from John Payne. John Anderson became administrator of the will, and Benjamin and Joseph Stith were securities for the bond.[1632]

John and Sarah Payne who settled in Ohio, with attention to their close friends, the McCormacks, Wheelers, and Wrights:

On 2 September 1799 John and Sary Pane signed permission for their daughter Elizabeth Pane to marry James Moorman. Anderson McCormack secured the bond. The witness was Anthony Wright. Elizabeth's last name was spelled *Payne* in the body of the license, but when John and Sary signed, their last name was spelled *Pane*, and they each signed with an *X*.[1633] In early Virginia the county clerks sometimes spelled a name more than one way within a document, as if to demonstrate there was variation in the spelling of the names.

On 21 February 1801 John and Sarah Payne sold 100 acres on Beaverdam Creek in Bedford County to Anthony Wright. Pointers were lands of Anthony Wright, John Payne, John Hook, William Anderson, John Wright, Matthew Pate. In the body of this deed John and Sarah's last name was written *Payne*, but when written out for the signatures (*X*s), the name was *Pain*. There were no witnesses.[1634]

In 1790 Roland and Ann Wheeler sold 300 acres on the middle fork of Beaverdam Creek to Mathew Pate. Pointers: lands of John Wright, Anderson Wheeler, Wm. Wheeler. Wits: Nathaniel Shrewsbury, John Shrewsbury, John Buckhannon.[1635] Theodore Buckhannon had married Elizabeth Nimmo in 1789. Nathaniel Shrewsbury was surety for the bond. Robert Nimmo, father of Elizabeth, signed.[1636]

On 23 July 1793 Micajah McCormack sold 60 acres to John Payne. The parcel was on the north side of Beaverdam Creek. Some pointers: lands of Wm. Anderson, John Tomas(?) Wheller, and Talbot's old line. Wits: Robert Nimmo, John Melton, John Dollard.[1637] Micajah McCormack had sold 60 acres on the waters of Beaverdam Creek to John Howell on 29 August 1791. The point of beginning was the line of John Pane, and the parcel extended to Anthony Wright's corner. Wits: Robert Nimmo, Abner Howell, James Wheeler.[1638] The 1793 Bedford County personal property tax lists show John Howell and James Payne being interviewed on March 30th. John Payne (BD), Jeremiah Pate, and Benjamin A. Pate were visited on March 20th.[1639]

Beaverdam Creek references can be confusing. The West Fork of Beaverdam Creek begins up in the Blue Ridge near the Botetourt County, Virginia, line and flows southeasterly toward the Staunton River. The Middle Fork, east of the main branch, is the shortest branch, and it flows southward, and it and the East Fork join the main branch near Virginia State Route 24. The West Fork joins the main branch not long before Kate's Creek joins. The combined waters empty into the Staunton River. Jumping Run joins the Staunton at about the same place, the two creeks forming a small peninsula near Goodview. On downstream the Staunton River (also called the Roanoke) combines with Blackwater River to form Smith Mountain Lake, created by a dam in 1963.

On 26 September 1795 John Payne and John Howell and wife, Nancy, of Bedford County sold 100 acres on a branch of Beaverdam Creek to Anthony Wright of same. Point of beginning was Holland's old corner (Pate's by then), and the land extended to John Talbot's line, John Payne's corner, to the head of Paynes' Spring Branch, and on to the Meador Branch. All three grantors signed with an *X*.[1640]

On 3 September 1801 Benjamin Allen Pate sold to John Payne 100 acres bordering his (Pate's) own land. The tract was on both sides of the Staunton River. The point of beginning was Pate's line on the north side of the river. Wits: Anderson McCormick, Thomas Pearson, James Brambill.[1641] The Bedford County personal property taxes for 1803 show Matthew Pate, Jr., being visited on June 18th; James Payne on June 19th; and John Payne and Thomas Pearson on the 20th.[1642]

On 18 July 1802 William McCormick of Franklin County and John Pain of Bedford County jointly sold 150 acres on Beaverdam Creek to John Carner of Bedford County. Wits: Joseph Stith, Wm. Carner, Wm. Dollard. John Pain signed with an *X*.[1643]

On 24 July 1802 John Pain of Bedford County sold 60 acres to William McCormick of Franklin County. The point of beginning was the flat rock on Beaverdam Creek. Other pointers were McCormack's line, Samuel Morgan's line, John Carner's line. Wits: Joseph Stith, Wm. Carmer, John Carner. John Pain signed with an *X*.[1644]

George Quesenbery had surveyed 90 acres on Beaverdam Run on 12 April 1774. Pointers were lands of William Anderson, Holland, and Talbot. The tract was transferred to Micajah McCormack.[1645]

On 21 January 1804 John Payne and wife, Sarah, of Franklin County sold to John Jeter of Bedford County 100 acres on the north side of Staunton River in Bedford County. Wits: Matthew Pate, James Payne (R), Charles Anderson,

John Wheeler. John and Sarah's last name was spelled *Payne*, and John signed with an X.[1646]

After leaving Franklin County, John and Sarah Payne and their son Ellis lived for a few years on Flynn's Creek in Jackson County, Tennessee. Living there also was James Ragland, who married Nancy Wheeler. William Wheeler and wife, Sarah, were of Jackson County, Tennessee, in 1810 when they sold 159 acres on the south side of Beaver Dam Creek to Anthony Wright. The tract was adjacent James Johnson's Mill Pond.[1647] William Wheeler and Sarah Wright had married in 1785. Roland Wheeler was surety.[1648] Bedford County Court Orders of 1808-1811 included an order for Anderson McCormack to take Joseph Payne's place in completing the opening of the road from Johnson's Mill to the Staunton.[1649]

An incident of historical interest: We saw above that when John and Sarah Payne sold land on Beaverdam Creek to Anthony Wright, John Hook owned adjacent land. John Hook was a wealthy man and a Scotch Tory and thus not sympathetic to the Americans during the Revolution. An army commissary, John Venerable, confiscated two of Hook's steers for the use of the American army. Mr. Cowan, a prominent lawyer, persuaded Hook to get compensation by taking the case to court. Patrick Henry appeared in New London Courthouse to defend Mr. Venerable. Henry's famous "Beef" speech resulted. Henry painted a picture of a destitute American army in dire need of food, with the implication that anyone opposed to aiding them would be un-American and heartless. Henry's attack on Hook was so effective that Hook fled temporarily in fear of being tarred and feathered. Actually, the verdict was in favor of Hook, in the amount of one penny damages.[1650]

John Payne, son of Joseph Payne, and the Barnett Paynes:

In 1788 John Pane of Bedford County sold to Samuel Morgan 130 acres on the north side of Beaverdam Creek, adjacent James Board, Wm. McCormack, Steven Goggin. Wits: R. Nimmo, James Pane, Wm. Nimmo.[1651] The 1802 deeds of John and Sarah Payne show that they were close to the McCormacks of Bedford. Yet the John Pane who sold to Morgan signed with an O instead of an X, the mark of John Payne who was married to Sarah. And no wife signed away her dower, so this John Payne apparently was not married or perhaps was widowed. (Sometimes the wife signed away her dower at a later date.) There is the possibility that the John (O) Payne was a brother to Josiah (or Joseph) Payne. When Samuel Morgan of Bedford County made his will in 1814, witnesses were Barnett Payne, John (X) Payne, and John Jeter.[1652] Barnett Payne was a son of Joseph Payne, who died in 1803.[1653] The John Payne who married Sarah had left the area around 1804. Joseph Payne's son John might have signed with an X or Joseph could have had a grandson named *John* by this time. Or the John Pane who shared a common border with Josiah may have been his brother and perhaps the father of the John Payne who married Sarah.

Joseph Payne had 340 acres surveyed in Bedford County on 10 March 1775. This acreage was added to 75 acres of his that was adjoining. The land was on the north side of the Staunton River, including a cliff by the river. It was bounded by land of Mead.[1654] When Joseph first entered this survey, it was said to be on Jumping Run.[1655] Joseph and Phebe's son Thomas Payne had 750 acres surveyed on 8 March 1775. His survey was on Linville Creek, on the south side of the Staunton River, in what is now Franklin County.[1656] Joseph's son James (born ca 1760-1770) married Sarah Anderson in 1802, signing the bond with an X, George Payne as surety; son Joseph married Elizabeth Slinker; son Obediah married Jemima Oney; Barnett married Jane Martin; daughter Lucy married a Mr. Stanley; daughter Betsey married a Mr. Crabtree; Susannah married Frederick Slinker; Nancy married Aaron Brown, and Dicey married Jesse Brown. Joseph and Phebe's son John Payne, born 27 March 1754, married Elizabeth Litt, and John and Elizabeth are buried in Sumner County, Tennessee. He died in 1839, and she in 1847.[1657]

On 1 February 1777 Joseph and Phebe Payne sold 238 acres to Joseph Brown. This tract was on the east branch of Beaverdam Creek and on the headwaters of Stony Fork of Goose Creek. Weaver's line was a pointer. Wits: John Dent, Robert Nimmo, William Asberry. John Wright of Bedford County made his will in 1803 naming wife, Elizabeth; sons Anthony, Tommy, John, Joseph; daughters Sarah, Betsy, Polley, Rhoda, Ruth, and Nancy Asbury. Wits: Joel Shrewberry, James Johnson, Nancy Lancaster.[1658] Anthony Wright witnessed the marriage bond of James Moorman and Elizabeth Payne, daughter of John and Sarah. Robert Nimmo was involved with the Shrewsburys, as were the Wrights and the Asberrys, so Joseph and Phebe Payne had several associates in common with John and Sarah Payne.

Another Barnett Payne lived in Virginia during this time period. He was named in the 1764 will of John Pain of Spotsylvania County, Virginia. John's executor's bond was signed in 1770. John had wife, Frances, sons John,

Thomas, Barnett, William, Robert, and George (children probably listed in order of birth). John referred to his daughters, but did not name them.[1659] In 1745 John Pain and wife, Frances, of Spotsylvania County sold 100 acres to John Talburt of same. It was part of a tract devised Wm. Samms by his father. Wits: Jos. Brock, James Lea, John Graves.[1660] In 1748 Robert Coleman of Spotsylvania County, and wife, Elizabeth, sold 140 acres to John Pain of same. Robert Coleman was living on the land, and he had bought 50 acres of the tract from Phebe Hobson. Wits: Edmund Waller, Richd. Phillips, Jr.[1661] In 1764 John Payn and wife, Frances, of Spotsylvania County deeded 100 acres to son John Payn.[1662] In 1773 Thomas Payne and wife, Elizabeth, of Spotsylvania County sold 100 acres to Thomas Coleman, Jr., of Caroline County, Virginia.[1663] In 1786 Joseph Hewell and wife, Frances, of Halifax County sold land in Spotsylvania County to Spilsby Coleman. Wits: Jno. Poole, Jos. Hewell, Jr., Barnet Payne.[1664]

A John Pain who had wife, Sarah, appeared in Culpeper County, Virginia, deeds. On 19 November 1770 Joseph James and wife, Mary, and John Pain and wife, Sarah, of Culpeper County conveyed to John James of same 54 acres, part of a larger tract granted William Lobb and part belonging to a deed to John Dillard that included a mill on the Hazel River.[1665] When James Samms of Spotsylvania County made his will on 22 February 1726, he devised land to sons William and James, and Daniel Brown's land was a pointer. The testator's wife was Katherine. Wits: John Corbet, John Nalle, and James ____.[1666] John Nalle married Mary, daughter of Daniel Brown and Elizabeth Coleman. Daniel's will was proved in St. Mark's Parish (later Culpeper County) in 1747, and he named daughter Mary Nall. William Lobb was a witness.[1667] In 1754 Mary (Wheeler) James, widow of George James, released her dower in 900 acres in Prince William County, Virginia, to her oldest son, Thomas. But she also mentioned children Mary, Dianah, Joseph, Daniel, and Henry James. The deed was recorded in Spotsylvania County in 1755.[1668] As soon as this deed was recorded, on 3 June 1755, Thomas James of Prince William County (heir of George James) leased lots in Fredericksburg that included the Long Ordinary. He and wife, Jenny, were of the first part; Henry Field of Culpeper County, Gent., and wife, Esther, were of the second part; Mary James, widow, of George James, was of the third part; and Mary, Dianah, Joseph, Daniel, and Henry James, the youngest children of George and Mary, were of the fourth part. Wits: Joseph Steward, George James, Ann Kenny.[1669] Obviously John Pain and wife, Sarah, and Joseph James and wife, Mary, were related. This John Pain may have belonged to the Spotsylvania Paynes discussed above, for both families were involved with the Samms. If Joseph Payne (wife Phoebe) of Bedford County was part of the Spotsylvania Paynes, then there is a greater degree of likelihood that this John and Sarah Payne are the ones who lived on Beaverdam Creek in Bedford County, for John and Sarah Payne and the Joseph Payne families were involved with many of the same people.

The John Payne of Spotsylvania County who died in 1770 was surely descended from the Barnett Paine of King and Queen County who sold 350 acres in Spotsylvania County in 1741 to John Farish.[1670] Ann Payne, wife of Barnett Payne, Jr., was a granddaughter of Edward Pigg, whose will was probated in Spotsylvania County in 1741.[1671] In 1717 Edward Pigg, Henry Pigg, John Yorke, John Rogers, Peter Rogers, and John Madison had patented a large tract that included territory in both Spotsylvania and Caroline Counties.[1672] In 1740 Barnett Pain became administrator of the estate of Barnett Pain, Jr., deceased. Wm. Johnston was surety.[1673]

On 15 October 1796 John Pane of Bedford County deeded to Samuel Morgan 50 acres on the south side of Beaverdam Creek. Pointers: lines of John Wright, Wm. McCormack, Joseph Wright, Goggin, and Mead. Wits: Robert Nimmo, William Nimmo, Theodore Buckhannon, and (?). This John Pane 's mark resembled an *S*.[1674] We saw above that when John Pain sold land to William McCormick in 1802, the flat rock on Beaverdam Creek was a pointer, as was land of Samuel Morgan. And that John signed with an *X*. Josias Payne had sold land to Goggin, so one of these John Paynes may have been a son of Josias; or the John Payne who married Sarah may have been John Payne, Jr., his father still living in the area, but if the father was still alive, "Junior" was usually indicated. The *S* may have stood for Staunton River.

William Payne of Hanover County, Virginia, and the Shrewsburys:

The Shrewsburys owned land along the middle fork of Beaverdam Creek in Bedford County, and Roland and Ann Wheeler sold land in 1790 on the middle fork to Matthew Pate, and Nathaniel and John Shrewsbury were two of the witnesses. When John and Sarah Payne sold land in 1801 to Anthony Wright, Mathew Pate's land was a pointer. George Walton of Prince Edward County sold Saml. Shrewsberry 192 acres on the middle fork of Beaverdam Creek.

The deed was recorded 29 May 1769.[1675] (Josias Payne's survey for 790 acres bordered Walton's line.) Ruel Shrewsbury married Sarah Sinkler of Bedford County on 19 December 1788. Nathl. Shrewsbury was surety. Isaac Sinkler, father of Sarah, consented.[1676]

On 27 October 1783 Samuel Shrewsbury of Bedford County sold to George Scott of same 131 acres on the northeast fork of Beaverdam Creek. Pointers: lands of Valentine Mattock, Benjamin Wheeler.[1677]

Rule Shrewsbury and Elizabeth Shrewsbury were administrators of the estate of William Payne of Hanover County, Virginia, who died in 1735. Sureties were John Snead and Anthony Pouncy. The appraisal of the estate of William Payne was made by John Glinn, John Raglin, and George Daivis. The inventory was returned on 2 October 1735, and included were "1 Negro woman 25; 1 Negro child 8; 2 cows 2; 1 old bed and furniture 2.08; a percil of old puter 1; old tin pan .0.0; 2 Erthen pots and 1 Erthen strainer .03.6; 2 old pails .03; 1 iron pot and some old iron .15; 1 percil of old iron .01; 1 old spining wheal and wool cards .07; 1 old fluke hoe .0.6; 1 old side saddle .07; 1 sow .05; 1 old chist of drawers .08; 1 old chear .01; 3 hed of sheep .13; 1 old horse 1.10." [1678] William Payne's widow had been an Elizabeth (see the power of attorney below), and she seems to have married Ruel Shrewsbury.

In March 1753 Sarah Brechin of Louisa County, Virginia, wrote her will. She named her nine children, Thomas and John Poindexter, William and James Brechin, Susanna Snead, Elizabeth Shresberry, Sarah Rice, Ann Rutherford, and Jean Ireland. Executors were son Thomas Poindexter and son-in-law John Snead. The testator, Sarah, daughter of David Crafford, had married first Thomas Poindexter and secondly James Brechin.[1679]

Over in Tidewater Virginia, in Westmoreland County, in 1722, James Breechin died. His will was written on 19 October 1721. He referred to his late wife, Ann, and named his current wife, Sarah. Also included were sons William and James, daughters Anna and Jane; Dennis Lynsey, Thomas Poindexter, James and Anna Sorrell, kinsman Thomas Sorrell. Execs: wife and Capt. George Turberville.[1680]

A 1759 Louisa County deed from Samuel Ragland, heir and executor of John Ragland, late of Hanover Co., deceased, to Richard Anderson of Fredericksville Parish, refers to James Bricken's line. The tract was "on both sides Cauthorn's Run...John Price's corner on the south side the River...James Bricken's line....Wit: Thomas Johnson, Jr., Tarlton Brown, John Poindexter." [1681] Louisa County deeds of 1753 include one from James Brickin (Breeckin) and wife, Elizabeth, of Fredericksville Parish to John Dasper of same. Land was at the head of Cawthorn's Run in John Ragland's line.[1682] So John Ragland owned land next to James Brickin. See below for more on the Raglands.

On 8 August 1723 Elizabeth Payn, wife of William Payn of Hanover County, formerly of Westmoreland County, Virginia, gave power of attorney to Mr. William Sturman and Mr. John Aubrey to relinquish her dower in the 100 acres her husband had sold to Mr. Francis Aubrey. John Poindexter and Sarah Brechin witnessed.[1683] Elizabeth Payne apparently was the daughter of James and Sarah Brechin.

The Brickeys of Westmoreland County were seemingly the same people as the Brechins, for both were close to the Sorrells and Paynes. On 23 March 1729 Sarah Byard, spinster, of Cople Parish, sold 22 acres to Amy Brickey. John Owen had been a previous owner of the tract, and it bordered land of Daniel Occany, George Turberville, and the line of the late Mr. Thomas Sorrell, land of John Payne. Wits: Wharton Ransdell, Richd: Sutton.[1684] *The Historical Atlas of Westmoreland County, Va. Patents* shows many land grants belonging to John Payne and several to Richard Searle. Whether these patents involved more than one John Payne is not clear. The patent most pertinent to our story is the one for 400 acres made to John Payne on 1 June 1664, for abutting it was a 112-acre patent to Jas Byard, made on 26 May 1712.[1685] When John Owen sold 20 acres to James Byard in 1714, witnesses were John Awbrey, John Erwin, and Orlando Payne.[1686]

John Awbrey was residing at the home of Jane Martin when she made her will in 1677. She was living by the Machotoc River in Cople Parish in Westmoreland County, and she stated that John Awbrey was to be allowed to remain on her land as manager of the estate she was leaving to her daughter Jane Johnstone. If she died without heirs, her inheritance was to revert to John Awbrey and James Gaylor. She gave daughter Elizabeth Pain the equivalent of 40 shillings sterling. Wits: Thomas and Jane Davis and John Awbrey.[1687] John Payne of Westmoreland County, in his will of 1698, named wife, Elizabeth, and sons John and William. Elizabeth was a daughter of Cornelius Murphy, and after the death of John Payne, she married John Atwell, who died in 1713. John and Elizabeth Payne's son William is the one who moved to Hanover County.[1688] John Howell of Westmoreland County died in 1738, naming wife, Winifred; son John, and daughter Martha Atwell. Major George Turbeville was executor.[1689] Capt. George Turbeville and Mr. William Sturman were executors of the January 1725 will of Thomas Sorrell of Cople Parish.[1690]

The records following the 1735 death of William Payne of Hanover County left no evidence of his having children. Yet a Pondexter Payne was remembered in the 1771 will of his father, William Payne, of Halifax County, Virginia. Pondexter was William's oldest son; Daniel Payne, the youngest. William gave his wife, Ruth, the home plantation for her lifetime, with reversion to son Daniel. William Coughlin was devised the land whereon he was living, plus 48 acres. William Payne, son of John Payne, was given 101 acres whereon he was living. Other lands went to oldest son Pondexter Payne. Movable estate went to wife, Ruth, and she was to give it as she saw fit to daughters Anne, Mary, and Milly Payne. Execs: Thomas Payne and Pondexter Payne. Wits: Thomas Hill, Moses Ayers, Regimalick Baker Ayers, William Collie. Nathaniel Terry, Gent., was security for the executors' bond.[1691] The appraisement of William Payne's estate was returned in August 1772, and it included blacksmith's tools and carpenter's tools. Appraisers were Thos. Hill, Richard Kearby, John Hall.[1692] Note that William Payne (d.1735) of Hanover County was also a blacksmith and that Thomas Poindexter had married into the Brickey (Brechin) family and would have been an in-law of William Payne of Hanover.

William Payne and wife, Ruth, were Quakers, for records of 1758 show William Payne and wife, Ruth, being received into Quaker fellowship by request. The South River Meeting records show that William died in 1771 and Ruth in 1774.[1693]

Halifax County is on the eastern border of Pittsylvania County. Moses Ayers, who witnessed the will of William Payne of Halifax County, also witnessed the will of John Payne of Pittsylvania County, who died in 1781. John's wife, Elizabeth, was his second wife. At her death, his estate was to be divided among John and Charles Payne and the children of his last wife. John also had sons William, Samuel, Josiah, and daughter Rhoda Payne. He devised land to sons Charles and Reuben Payne. Son John would receive cattle when he married. The testator wanted his land in Wilkes County, North Carolina, to be sold. Execs: William Durrett and John Payne. Wits: Moses Ayers, Gabriel Richards, and Charles Payne.[1694]

We saw that in 1735 John Glenn was an appraiser of the estate of William Payne of Hanover County. William Austin(e), who died in 1801 a resident of Bedford County, married Hannah Glin on 10 March 1758 in Goochland County.[1695] In 1781 he married Esther Alexander of Bedford County.[1696] In his will of 1798 he named wife, Esther, and referred to money sent to Chapman Austin of Hanover County. He provided for children by both marriages but did not name them all. Execs: sons James and Robert Austin and William Alexander. Wits: Austin D. Leake, James Campbell, Robert Austin, Ja. Steptoe, Samuel Crockett, and Willm. Thorp.[1697]

The Austins and Poindexters had shared interests over in Louisa County, Virginia. John Austin and wife, Margaret, of Hanover County owned land jointly with William Poindexter and wife, Elizabeth, of Trinity Parish, Louisa County, for in 1767 the couples sold 130 acres to Thomas Peers of Trinity Parish. Pointers were lands of Nathl. Pope, Marks, Wm. Baker, Wm. Thompson of Hanover, Gent., and Nathan Luck.[1698]

John and Sarah (Ellis?) Payne, known to have sons William and Ellis, also appeared to have son Austin. Austin Payne was 61 when the 1850 U.S. Census was taken for Mason Township, Lawrence County, Ohio. He was living in the same household as Deana (Wilson) Payne, widow of William Payne, son of John and Sarah. See below.

An Austin Payne owned land in Goochland County, Virginia, in 1760, when John Martin patented 36 acres on the east side of Great Byrd Creek. Pointers: the Byrd Road, William Britt, Bryant Connerley, William Pearce, Austin Payne, and John Britt's old line.[1699] George Payne of St.James Parish, Goochland County, made his will on 3 December 1744. He named wife, Mary; sons Josias, George, John; granddaughter Agnes Payne; grandson Jesse Payne. Sons Josias and George and grandson Augustine were devised 800 acres on a branch of Little Bird to be divided equally among them. Son George could also have the 400-acre tract on Lickinghole Creek on which he was already living.[1700] The George Payne family, we can see, is associated with the Byrd Creeks in Goochland County, so we have to wonder whether the Austin Payne on Great Byrd Creek was really Augustine Payne, grandson of George. We saw above, however, that John and Margaret Austin and William and Elizabeth Poindexter were associated with Louisa and Hanover Counties, both of which are found on the northeast border of Goochland County, Louisa being close to Lickinghole and the Byrd Creeks.

A source of relationships among the Poindexters, Shrewsburys, and the William Payne family was revealed above. The Shrewsburys owned land on the middle fork of Beaverdam Creek and John and Sarah (Ellis?) Payne lived nearby. Samuel Shursbery, Nathaniel Shewsbery, and Elizabeth Shrewsbery were witnesses to the 1767 will of Edward Pate of Bedford County. Edward devised to son Matthew 274 acres; to son Anthony 100 acres; son Thomas, 100 acres; son Jeremiah, 100 acres. Daughter Judith Pate would receive the home plantation with 200 acres adjoining. A grandson, son of John and Judeth Pate, would receive 10 lbs. cash if he lived to be 10 years old, and the money was to be used for his education. Edward gave slaves to his wife and each of his children. Execs: wife and son Jeremiah.[1701] Edward Pate had Ragland connections: Frances Ragland married Jeremiah Pate in 1755.[1702] (See below for more on the Raglands.) When John and Sarah Payne sold 100 acres on Beaverdam Creek in 1801, the tract bordered on land of Matthew Pate.

Jarret Brickey of Bedford County made his will on 7 October 1790. He named as executors Thomas and Matthew Pate. Tommy Wright and John Board were securities for the executors' bond. Jarret named wife, Elizabeth, and referred to her four children, Patsy, Christopher, Nancy, and Milly. Jarret made bequests to his sons John, Jarret, and Peter; to daughters Molley Slinker, Winey Thompson, and Temprence Thompson. Wits: George Rusher, Anney Rusher, Federick Slinker.[1703] According to the International Genealogical Index (v.5), Jarret Brickey was born in Westmoreland County.[1704] Joseph Payne, son of Joseph Payne (d.1803), married Elizabeth Slinker.

In St. Paul's Parish, Hanover County, Virginia, in 1731/2 we find the Raglands, Moormans, Sneads, and Geo. Davis families living near each other. (Remember that George Davis and John Raglin appraised the estate of William Payne.) Boundaries of the following owners were examined, and we can see who had lands that abutted: "Stephen Ragland, John Ragland, John Guess, Edwd Davis, John Smithin, Chas. Moorman Widd: Cole, John Snead, John Pulliam, Chile's Orphans, Michael Holland, Francis Clarke, John Gilchrist, Geo Davis...."[1705] Processioning in 1755 includes other names associated with the Paynes and Raglands: "The Land that was John Johnsons now John Winns, Thos. Johnson's now Rule Shrewsburys, & John Anthony... Benjamin Allin, Luke Anthony, John Winn, John Andrew, Richard Anderson, Thos. Prosser's, John Ragland's Estate, Cornelius Tinsleys."[1706]

Payne- McCormack-Wheeler associations:

We saw that John Pain of Bedford County joined with Wm McCormack of Franklin County, Virginia, on 18 July 1802, to sell 150 acres to John Carner. This tract was on Beaverdam Creek and abutted land of Wm Carner.

In 1748 Carners were in the section of Albemarle County that became Buckingham County. In August of that year, John Harris, Gent., of Goochland County sold John Daniel Carner and William Carner of Albemarle County 200 acres in Albemarle County on the Great Buffaloe Creek of Willises River (now in Buckingham County). Anthony Shareon had land abutting. John Daniel Carner received the lower half the parcel, and William the upper. Wits: James Meredith, G. Marr, John Hunter.[1707]

On 14 March 1740 John Pain, blacksmith, of Goochland County sold 380 acres to Henry Cary, Gent., of Henrico County. This tract was in St. James Parish on the north side of the Willis River, on Pain's Creek, and included all houses. John signed his name *IP*.[1708] On 1 June 1750, Archibald Cary was granted 440 acres on the Barren Lick of Willis's Creek in Goochland County. The land was adjacent Alexander Trent, Gent., John Hardiman, James Wilkins, John Payne, John Wheeler, and Henry Beard.[1709] On 10 July 1745 John Wheeler had patented 400 acres on Barren Lick Creek of Willis's River. The tract was adjacent lands of Henry Cary, Gent., John Payne, and Samuel Ridgway.[1710]

Besides their both having owned land on Bedford County's Beaverdam Creek that included the flat rock pointer, the strongest connection between Josias and John Payne (married Sarah) may have been their common association with William McCormack and his family. (Josiah sold land to William McCormack in 1787.) A William McCormick, presumably the father of this one, owned land in Goochland County in 1748, as he was named in the processioning records of that year. The line between John Wright and John Mullins, was being affirmed, and McCormick owned abutting land, as did John Mims and Charles Tony.[1711] In Bedford County the McCormacks and Wheelers intermarried with the Wrights. (See above.)

William McCormack made his will on 31 July 1775. Legatees included wife, Agness, and children John, David, William, Lucy, Jesse, and Nancy. He asked that 100 acres of land on Willises Creek be sold to pay his debts. Execs: wife, Agness, and William Adams. Wits: Michael Gash, Moses Pullen, Absalom Adams. William Adams became the executor, and James Mitchell and John Otty were securities. A notation was made by William McCormack's name, "late of Buckingham now of Bedford County...."[1712] Willis Creek runs through Buckingham

County and into Cumberland County, flowing into the James River opposite Goochland County. Not many early records of Buckingham County have survived a fire in 1869. Buckingham County was cut out of Albemarle County in 1761, and Albemarle from Goochland in 1744.

The will of William McCormick of Fredericksville Parish, Louisa County, Virginia, was recorded on 25 September 1753. It was dated 9 December 1748, and Rebecca, his wife, was executor. Children were Wm., Thos., David, Micajah, Chas., Mary, Lucy, Sarah, and Elizabeth. Son Wm. was to receive the home plantation after Rebecca died, and 150 additional acres. Son Thomas received 100 acres in Goochland County, purchased of Layne. Wits: John McGeorge, Rich'd Richardson.[1713]

First Generation

1.   John[1] PAYNE was born about 1760.

As early as 1784 John Payne was living in Bedford County, Virginia. In 1784 the Bedford County personal property taxes show John Payne, with 11 cattle, followed by James Payne, with 10 cattle. Another John Payne followed, and he had 6 cattle. This list was alphabetized, but people of the same surname who lived near each other appeared in clusters on the list.[1714] The John Payne with only 6 cattle may have been the youngest of the three. A likely scenario is that the John Payne who married Sarah was living next to his father and an uncle or brother. He was living on land agreeable to farming, the gently rolling land of the Piedmont. To the northwest rose the Blue Ridge. Today the Beaverdam Creek watershed is a mixture of grazing and crop land and forests. It is sparsely populated. The spectacular Peaks of Otter, about 4,000 feet high, dominate the landscape.

By early 1804 John and Sarah Payne had moved to the south side of the Staunton River, for they were of Franklin County on 21 January 1804 when they sold land in Bedford County. See above for Bedford County deeds relating to this John Payne. John Payne and his family are next discovered living in Jackson County, Tennessee. According to Vivian Pyles Coleman, who wrote an article for *History of Lawrence County, Ohio 1990*, John had bought land in Lawrence County by 1812, and sons William and Ellis left Tennessee for Ohio soon after John's move.[1715]

A 10-acre deed was recorded for John Payne in Jackson County, Tennessee, on 13 April 1813. The tract was at the "head of Horse Hollow of dry fork of Flynn's Cr.. near said Payne's house...to include said Payne's improvement."[1716] (John may have bought land in Ohio before he moved there.) On 12 October 1816 Nathan Haggard's claim on 20 acres was entered in the records. His tract was at the "head of Horse Branch of Flynn's Cr...to include improvement where the widow Dudley now lives where John Paine formerly lived."[1717] Martin and Flynn's Creeks were on the Smith County line. The Wheelers from Bedford County also lived on Flynn's Creek. On 15 August 1816, Elijah Wheeler claimed 15 acres on the Dry Fork of Flynn's Creek, abutting lands of Wm. Wheeler and James Ragland.[1718]

The Lawrence County, Ohio, tax records for 1822 include John Pain. He was living in Range 16, Township 3 (Mason), Section 20.[1719] Section 20 is northwest of Rappsburg. A map of early settlers (dated 1887 and found in the Lawrence County Courthouse) shows John B. Payne, Thompson Payne; Elliott Payne (b. 1821) and sons Alonzo and Howard Payne (b. 1857), all descendants of Ellis Payne, living in Section 29, just south of Section 20 and directly west of Rappsburg. In 1823 John Payne owned 160 acres.[1720] In 1824 Wm. Paine was also living in Range 16, Township 3, Section 20.[1721] In 1826 John Payne had 1 horse and 2 neat cattle.[1722]

When the 1830 U. S. census was taken for Mason Township, Lawrence County, Ohio, John Pain's household consisted of one male in the 60-70 age group, one 10-15, and one 5-10. There was one female 30-40 and one under 5.[1723] A John Payne married Nancy Carpenter on 12 July 1829 in Lawrence County.[1724] Sarah may have died and John could have married a younger woman.

Background on Mason Township is given in *History of Lawrence County, Ohio 1990*, and it names William Payne and Elias Payne among the first settlers and states that Elliott Payne and John Payne came soon after. *Elias* was sometimes confused with *Ellis*, but Elliott, son of Ellis, was 33 in 1860 and would have been born about 1827, so John may also have had son Elliott. The first school in Mason Township was conducted in 1822 on Buck Creek. It was made of logs and had paper pasted over window openings.[1725]

245

When Lawrence County was first settled, there still were buffalo, panther, bear, elk, and minks in the wild. Turkeys were abundant and sometimes so fat they had trouble flying onto a tree branch. Dogs could not roam alone because of the wolves. Sheep had to be penned at night. Ten wolves calling to others to gather for a sheep kill would sound like a thousand. And the hills would echo with their howling.[1726]

John married **Sarah ELLIS (?)**.

More than one student of this family has concluded that John Payne's wife, Sarah, was born an *Ellis*. The notion is supported by their naming a son *Ellis*. When tracing family history, it also helps to consider the given names of relatives of relatives. John and Sarah Payne's son William named a son Uriah. John and Sarah's daughter Elizabeth married James Moorman. In 1794 Uriah Ellis married Susannah Moorman of Bedford County. William Ellis was surety.[1727] Uriah Anderson, as an assignee of Roddom Home, claimed 75 acres on the Dry Fork of Flynn's Creek in 1808. James Raglan was then living on this land. This deed was recorded in Jackson County, Tennessee, in 1815.[1728]

On 25 April 1794 William Ellis conveyed to Benjamin Ellis 80 acres in Bedford County, Virginia. The tract was on the north branches of the Staunton River, adjacent John Bozwell's and Mitchell's lines.[1729] William and Maryann Ellis, on 25 July 1796, sold John Boyer 79 acres in Bedford County, bounded by the lines of Benjamin Ellis, Murphy, and said Boyer.[1730] In 1766 James Wheeler had sold 53 acres on the north side of the Staunton River to John Murphy.[1731]

Quaker records reveal that Samuel Ellis, son of Mordecai and Mary, deceased, moved from the Hopewell Friends group to the South River Meeting House in 1788. They had a daughter named Mary.[1732] So there were Ellises living in Bedford County at the same time as the John Payne who had sons William and Ellis.

The Quaker meeting place in Lynchburg, Virginia, near the border of Bedford County, was referred to as the South River Meeting House, because it was south of the James River. The South River Meeting House has been restored and is only a few yards away from Quaker Memorial Presbyterian Church. The old Quaker graveyard is on the property, and it contains many old and weather-worn stones, several unreadable, marking the graves of the early Quakers of the area. John Lynch, the namesake for Lynchburg, is buried there and some Paynes, as well. A husband and wife were not buried next to each other, making it difficult to identify the deceased with certainty. And it is only rumored that my Payne ancestors were Quakers. It has been said that, like the Quakers, they did not believe in slavery.

John and Sarah Payne had the children following children and possibly others:

+   2   i.   **Elizabeth² PAYNE** was born about 1784.

+   3   ii. **William PAYNE** was born about 1785.

     4   iii. **Austin PAYNE** was born 1789 in Virginia. See Diana (Wilson) Payne below.

+   5   iv. **Ellis PAYNE** was born about 1789.

     6   v.   **Nancy PAYNE** was born about 1795.

Nancy is said to have married a Vitito,[1733] and Nancy Vitito appears on the 1830 Mason Township census, Lawrence County, Ohio. William Pain is on the same page; John Pain and Elias [*sic*] Pain appear on the previous page. Nancy Vitito was head of household and in the 30-40 age group. There were two males under 5, one 5-10, one 10-15; one female under 5, one 5-10, one 10-15.[1734]

Nancy married **James VITITO**.

A James Vitito lived near the Paynes when they were in Tennessee, so it is assumed that Nancy married James.

On 19 December 1814 James Vettito claimed 6 acres on the ridge between Martin's and Flynn's Creeks in Jackson County, Tennessee. The parcel was adjacent John Petty and included improvements on the land whereon Ellis Payne formerly lived.[1735]

Second Generation

2.	**Elizabeth² PAYNE** (John¹) was born in 1784 in Virginia. The bond for the marriage of Elizabeth Payne and James Moorman was signed on 2 September 1799. Anderson McCormack was surety, Anthony Wright and Anderson McCormack witnesses. On the same day John and Sary Pane gave permission for their daughter to marry. All signatures, except that of Wright, were made with an X. [1736]

Elizabeth's birth year is figured from her age on the 1850 U. S. census for Decatur Township, Lawrence County, Ohio. Decatur is on the western border of Symmes Township, which sits directly north of Aid. Decatur's western boundary is Scioto County, while Mason Township, on the eastern border of Aid, borders Gallia County. In 1850 Elizabeth was 66, born in Virginia, and living next to son James Moorman and his family. James was in Dwelling 68 and his household was Family 69. Elizabeth Moorman was in Dwelling 69, and her Family was number 51.[1737] John Payne, born in Tennessee, was in Dwelling 71 and his was Family 73. John, age 35, had wife, Elizabeth, age 21, born in Indiana. In their household at that time were Elliott Payne, 24, Burrel Payne, 21, and Banister Nance, 26.[1738] Elliott and Burrell were children of Ellis and Mary Payne, 61 and 60, who were on the 1850 federal census for Mason Township. When their family members were listed, they included Elliot, Jane, Burrel Payne, and Thomas Payne (age 4), probably a grandchild (Dwelling 162).[1739] The John Payne who was living in Decatur Township would have been the son of Ellis and Mary Payne. John Payne, born in 1815, married Elizabeth Fallowell, born in Indiana.

Anderson McCormack and Anthony Wright were witnesses to the marriage bond of Elizabeth Payne and James Moorman. By the time of Elizabeth's marriage, the McCormacks and Wrights were in-laws. On 3 January 1791 William McCormack married Judith Wright, Micajah McCormack, giving security. Joseph Wright, father of Judith, consented.[1740]

Bedford County Court Orders of 1795-1799 note that Anderson McCormick had registered a complaint against James Payne, and that James had appeared in court on his own recognizance.[1741] Court Orders of 1799-1803 show John Payne, James Moorman, and Anderson McCormick appearing in court because of a breach-of-the-peace complaint by Chas. McCormack.[1742]

During the same period (1795-1799) John Payne, a child of Mary Payne (unplaced), became indentured to James Johnson. John's sister Nancy was slated to become indentured to Micajah McCormick, but the indenture was quashed.[1743] There were three men by the name of James Johnson who married in Bedford County between the years 1779 and 1785: James Johnson, who married Milly Mooreman on 1 September 1779; James Johnson who married Ann Cotterill on 26 September 1780; and James Johnson who married Elizabeth Scarborough on 22 October 1785. (Of course, one of these men may have married twice.) Micajah McCormick married Sarah Barker on 29 May 1798 in Bedford County, Edward Barker, surety.[1744] James, Joseph, and Jesse Johnson, Edward B____ , and David Anderson were witnesses to the will of Joseph Payne (d.1803). A court case followed Joseph's death, for he had had dementia when he made his will. Milly Slinker, who had taken care of him for seven or eight years, testified that Joseph's son James and old James Johnson had urged him to make a will.[1745] This child of Mary Payne seems more closely associated with the Joseph Payne family than that of John and Sarah Payne.

Elizabeth married **James MOORMAN,** son of Charles MOORMAN and Judith MOON, on 2 September 1799 in Bedford County, Virginia.

James and Elizabeth Moorman's son James was born in Virginia, and James and Elizabeth followed her parents westward to Ohio.

The Moorman family is well known in the Lynchburg, Virginia, area, for they were active in the Society of Friends (Quaker) community. Thomas Moorman (b. 1705) married Rachel Clark, and moved from Louisa County, Virginia, to Bedford County. His will was dated 22 July 1765. Thomas Moorman had a sister, Judith, who married John Douglas. Their son, Achilles Douglas, born 1752, was a leader in the South River Meeting of Friends. In 1779 Achilles married Elizabeth Terrell, daughter of Micajah and Sarah Lynch Terrell.[1746] The Clarks, Lynches, Terrells, and Moormans were among Quakers who moved from the Sugar Loaf Mountain Meeting in Albemarle County, Virginia, to the Lynchburg neighborhood in 1754.[1747]

The will of Charles Moorman of Louisa County, Virginia, grandfather of James Moorman, was dated 2

September 1778. Children named were Robt., Thos., Jas., Chas., Elizabeth Johnson, Lucy Johnson, Agnes Venable, Mary Taylor. Son Robert received all the land in Albemarle Co., on the branches of Totier Creek; son Thomas, the rest of the Totear tract, and 100 aces in Louisa County, bought from David Bunch, joining land of son James. James received 360 acres on Camp Creek and Sycamore Fork. Charles's three daughters and children of his daughter Judith Anthony, deceased, received equal parts of the home plantation of 367 acres. His wife, Mary, received for life one third of the profits from the mill. Daughter Mary Taylor inherited the land he had bought for her. The executors were John Pain and son Thomas. Wit: James Bunch, Pouncy Bunch, David Bunch. Robert Moorman became the executor, and his sureties were James Moorman, Saml. Richardson, and Wm. Ragland. Thos. & Chas. Moorman, about a month later, signed an administration bond, with Nathl. Anderson and Js. Barnett as sureties. Their son Charles (Towhead) Moorman was born 28 June 1746, and married Judith Moon in 1766. He died in 1803 in Bedford County.[1748]

Louisa County shares a boundary with Goochland County, where George Payne had settled. Exactly which John Pain was named as an executor of the will of Charles Moorman is not certain, but Samuel Richardson married Ann Thompson, daughter of George.[1749] Her sister Mary married William Payne in 1768.[1750] Isaac Ragland married Elizabeth, daughter of Samuel Thompson in 1757.[1751] And Robert Payne and Sam'l Richardson were living next to each other on 6 March 1740, when Obediah Woodson and John Woodson of Goochland County sold 690 acres in St. James Parish to William Miller. Pointers were Dover Mill Creek, lands of Phillip Webber, Joseph Johnson, Robert Payne, Sam'l Richardson, and Robert Adams. Wits: J. Terry, Joseph Terry, Gideon Glen. Elizabeth Woodson and Constant Woodson also signed the deed.[1752]

John Payne, father of Dolley, who married James Madison (president of the United States from 1809-1817), was born in 1736 in Goochland County, Virginia. His wife, Mary Coles, was a Quaker, and they joined some other Quakers in North Carolina in 1766, but returned to Virginia in 1769. It was not until 1783 that this family moved to Philadelphia.[1753] So he could possibly have been the John Pain who was asked to become an executor of the will of Charles Moorman, a fellow Quaker.

James and Elizabeth had the following child:

+   7   i. **James³ MOORMAN** was born 1820.

3.   **William² PAYNE** (John¹) was born about 1785 in Virginia.

Lawrence County, Ohio, tax records for 1823 include Wm. Paine. He owned 83 acres in Range 16, Township 3 (Mason), Section 20. In 1826 he owned 2 horses and 7 neat (*neat* referred to common domestic cattle) calves.[1754]

William appeared on the 1830 Mason Township census. He was in the 40-50 age bracket, as was his wife. In their household were one male 5-10, one 10-15, one 15-20, one female under 5, one 5-10, one 10-15, one 15-20, one 20-30. His household was listed between John Higgins and Daneal Nance.[1755]

William married **Diana WILSON** daughter of John Culpeper WILSON and Sarah MARTIN of Henry County, Virginia, on 28 April 1806. William Payne was said to be of Franklin County, Virginia. John Martin was surety for the marriage bond.[1756] Diana was born about 1785 in Virginia.

Diana's birth year is figured from the 1850 U.S. census for Mason Township, Lawrence County, Ohio. At that time, Dina, 65, was living with Samuel and Miranda (Payne) Lewis. Other Paynes in the household (Dwelling 159, Family 162) were Malissa, 28, Austin, 61, Sarah J., 6. Next door (Dwelling 160, Family 162) was the family of Moses Payne, 38. Next door to Moses was Marstie Payne, 28, and wife, Elizabeth; and next to him was Ellis Payne, 61, wife, Mary, 60, and their family.[1757]

The 1860 Mason Township census shows Deana Payne as 74, born in Virginia. She was living in Dwelling 1203, and was head of Family 1193. Living with her were Joel Payne, 50, also born in Virginia, and Wm. M. Payne, 26, born in Ohio. Milton Payne, age 40, and wife, Sarah, 49, and their family were in Dwelling 1204.[1758]

William and Diana had the following children and possibly others:

	8	i. **Joel³ PAYNE** was born 1810 in Virginia (his birth year deduced from the 1860 census).
+	9	ii. **Moses Marion PAYNE** was born about 1812.
+	10	iii. **Marstie (Mathew?) PAYNE** was born about 1822.
	11	iv. **Malissa PAYNE** was born about 1822.
+	12	v. **William Uriah PAYNE** was born about 1825.
	13	vi. **Miranda PAYNE** was born about 1828. She married Dr. **Samuel LEWIS**, son of John Lewis and Rebecca Sowards. *See Lewis Section.*

5. **Ellis² PAYNE** (John¹) was born 1789 in Virginia. He died in Lawrence County, Ohio.[1759]

The Lawrence County, Ohio, tax duplicates for 1826 reveal that Ellis Payne owned 1 horse, 1 neat calf.[1760]

Ellis left his residence on Martin's and Flynn's Creek in Jackson County, Tennessee, by 19 December 1814, when James Vittio acquired 6 acres that included improvements on land that had once belonged to Ellis Payne.[1761]

The 1830 U. S. census for Mason Township includes Elias [*sic*] Pain. He was in the 30-40 age bracket; there were three males in the under 5 category, one in the 10-15, one in the 15-20. Females included two in the 5-10 group, one in the 20-30, one in the 30-40.[1762]

The 1850 Mason Township census shows Ellis as 61, born in Virginia, and his wife, Mary, as 60, born in Ohio (obviously an error). Son Elliot was 26, Jane 26, Burrel 21, and Thomas was 4. Ellis was in Dwelling 162.[1763]

Ellis married **Mary RAGLAND**. Mary was born about 1790 in Virginia. She died 1860 in Lawrence County, Ohio.[1764] Hardesty's *History of Lawrence County, Ohio, 1882*, states that Ellis Payne married Mary Raglandt. When this atlas was compiled, relevant information was still fresh in the minds of contributors, giving support for the traditional belief that Mary's last name was *Ragland*.[1765]

In 1776 Peter Holland sold 400 acres on Goose Creek in Bedford County, Virginia, to Jacob Ragland of Goochland County, Virginia.[1766] Jacob and Martha (Loftus) Ragland had sons Reuben and William who migrated to Tennessee, Reuben to Macon County and William to Smith County.[1767] Yet it is the Raglands who lived near John and Sarah Payne in Jackson County, Tennessee, who likely intermarried with them. Sarah Ragland of Goochland County married William Ellis in 1770.[1768] Sarah's brother John Ragland, born about 1761, in Goochland County, moved to Jackson County, Tennessee. He had sons James, Jacob, and John, who also resided in Jackson County.[1769]

On 13 April 1813 a 14-acre parcel was recorded for John Ragland on the "head waters of dry fork of Flynn's Cr...to include the improvement where said Ragland now lives...."[1770] On 10 January 1814 an additional 4 acres were recorded for him, described as on Flynn's & Martin's Creeks.[1771] John Martin, assignee of Sampson Williams, acquired "50 acs...the ridge that divides the Dry fork of Martin's Creek & dry fork of Flynn's Creek... to include place where John Ragland now lives...14 Apr. 1813."[1772] William Ragland's property, 30 acres, was located on "Pigeon Roost Cr...Thomas Ridge's Corner on the Military line...." This deed was recorded 22 December 1813.[1773]

James Ragland and Nancy Wheeler married in 1803 in Bedford County, Virginia, John Wheeler surety.[1774] On 30 June 1808 James Raglan was living by Uriah Anderson in Jackson County, Tennessee. Anderson claimed 75 acres on the Dry Fork of Flynn's Creek. His deed included his own improvements, and James Ragland was mentioned.[1775] Elijah Wheeler's claim for 15 acres on the Dry Fork of Flynn's Creek was recorded on 15 August 1816. The parcel was adjacent Wm. Wheeler and James Ragland.[1776]

Ellis Payne's mother, Sarah, is thought to have been an Ellis. The Ragland-Ellis connection went back several years. The Sarah Ragland who married William Ellis was a daughter of Isaac Ragland (1713-1796) of Goochland County and wife, Elizabeth Thomson (d. 1808). Sarah had brothers Nathan, Joel, Isaac, James, and John Ragland, and sister Mary (m. William Utley in 1766). Sarah's brother John Ragland resided in Jackson County, Tennessee, for about 16 years, beginning in about 1800. He had sons James (ca 1779-1839), Jacob (ca 1780-1828), and John (ca 1785-1848).[1777]

Jacob Ragland (m. Martha Loftus) was a son of Jacob Ragland, born 1715, in New Kent County, Virginia.[1778]

He was brother to Isaac Ragland, born 1713, of Goochland County, Virginia. They had sister, Elizabeth, born 1718. Jacob, Isaac, and Elizabeth were children of Thomas Ragland (1685-1719). Thomas was a son of Evan Ragland (1656-1717), of New Kent County, Virginia. Evan had been born in St. Decuman's Parish, Somerset, England. He married Susanna Pettus, daughter of Stephen. Evan and Susanna's son John was born in 1690 and died 1751 in Hanover County, Virginia. John married Anne Beaufort and had children, Samuel, John, William, Edward, Evan, James, Pettus, Martha, Mary, Anne, Frances, Susanna, and Sarah. John's son Samuel, born 1719, lived in Louisa County, Virginia.[1779]

The line of descent of the Raglands who lived by the Wheelers and Andersons in Tennessee: John Ragland (b. 1761), who lived on Flynn's Creek in Jackson County, Tennessee, was a son of Isaac Ragland (b. 1713) and Elizabeth Thomson of Goochland County. Isaac was a son of Thomas Ragland (1685-1719), who was a son of Evan Ragland (1656-1717) and Susanna Pettus of New Kent County.

The Rocky Creek group of Louisa County, Virginia:

A woman who had married a Ragland intermarried with the Tisdales, who owned land on Rocky Creek in Louisa County, Virginia. Charles Moorman, Andrew Hunter, and John Wheeler also had land on Rocky Creek. Members of all these families moved on to Bedford County.

John Tisdale's will was recorded in Louisa County in 1785. He named sons John and Shirley Tisdale; daughters Elizabeth Moss, Mary Wheeler, Susannah Aleegre, and children of daughter Sally Morris. Execs: son John Tisdale and son-in-law Daniel Alegrea.[1780] Ursula (Terrell), widow of John Ragland, married Shirley Tisdale in 1770. This John Ragland was a son of Samuel Ragland, son of John Ragland of Rippon Hall, Hanover County, Virginia.[1781]

Above we saw that the Jacob Ragland who moved from Goochland County to Bedford County had married Martha Loftus. Charity Loftus married William Hunter in 1760 in Goochland County, and George Hunter married Mildred Austine in 1763.[1782]

Andrew Hunter of St. Martin's Parish, Louisa County, Virginia, made his will in 1764. He named children Peter, Andrew, Stephen, Wm., Geo., Mary, and Jane. Execs: wife and son George. Wife, Jane, and son George signed the executors' bond in 1767.[1783] On 8 July 1752 Andrew Hunter had given son Andrew 400 acres on Rocky Creek in Fredericksville Parish, and pointers were lands of John Price and Charles Moorman. When Andrew gave 400 acres to son Peter on 28 July 1752, the land was described as being on Rocky Creek near a small branch of Bird Creek.[1784] On 12 January 1773 Andrew Hunter, Sr., of Bedford County, sold to Stephen Hunter of Louisa County land on the south fork of Rocky Creek. Pointers: Charles Moreman's corner and John Price's line. Wits: Peter Shelton, Peter Hunter, George Hunter.[1785] Francis Hunter married Jane Wright in Bedford County in 1787. John Wright was surety.[1786]

The Wheelers owned land on Rocky Creek. In 1765 John Wheeler and wife, Mary, of Louisa County, sold 157 acres to John Ross. Pointers were Ross's line, the mountain road, Clasbey's (Clasby's) line, Tisdale's line, and the north side of Rocky Creek. Wits: Wm. Pettit, Geo. Bell.[1787] (The name *Claspy* was also spelled *Galasby* and may have been another way of writing *Gillespie*.) On 11 January 1761 Benjamin Brown, Jr., and wife, Susannah, of St. Martin's Parish, Hanover County, had sold to John Wheeler of Louisa County 600 acres in Fredericksville Parish. The tract was adjacent lands of John Tisdale, George Bell, Alexander Galasby, the estate of John Ross, deceased, and land of Thomas Ballard on the south side of the South Anna River.[1788]

When the accounting of the estate sale of John Tisdale (d. 1785) was reported, among people named were Daniel Alligree, Shirley Tisdale and Shirley Tisdale, Sr., Geo. Holland, Rbt. Anderson, Wm. Ragland, Turner Anderson, Forrester Green, Stephen Hunter, Saml. Morris, and Jessee Payne.[1789] This Jessee Payne was probably the grandson that George Payne of Goochland named in his will of 1744. On 26 February 1739 Benjamin Wheeler of Goochland County conveyed 190 acres to Giles Allegre. The tract was on both sides of Machunk Creek, on the north side of the Rivanna River. Wits: Howard Cash, Wm. Cornish.[1790]

A deed was recorded in 1767 in Bedford County from Benj. Arnold of Buckingham County to Andrew Hunter. It was for 185 acres on both sides of Welchman's Ordinary Branch. Wits: Wm. Arnold, Micajah MacCormick, Edward Arnold.[1791]

The McCormack-Anderson-Payne-Pate-Ragland circle:

Micajah McCormack was surety when Richard Anderson and Hannah Payne married on 11 January 1793 in Bedford County. Sarah Payne, mother of Hannah, gave consent.[1792] The absence of permission from a father promotes doubt as to whether Hannah was a daughter of John and Sarah (Ellis?) Payne. The estate of a Richard Anderson was appraised in Bedford County by Mathew Pate, Benjamin Wheeler, and John Wright. They reported their results in 1783. Reference was made to cash in the possession of William Anderson, Charles Anderson, and Widow Anderson.[1793] Charles Anderson of Franklin County, Virginia, gave a deposition regarding the will of Joseph Payne, who died by 24 September 1803.[1794] Joseph Payne's son James Payne, born around 1760, married Sarah Anderson in 1802. She was a daughter of David Anderson, and George Payne was surety for the marriage bond, signed 20 November 1802.[1795]

In 1759 Samuel Ragland of Louisa County, heir of John Ragland, sold to Richard Anderson 140 acres in Fredericksville Parish, adjacent land of John Price.[1796] The Pates were also in Fredericksville Parish. In 1748 Anthony Pate and wife, Sarah, of Fredericksville Parish sold 96 ½ acres to James Power. Wits: Barttelot Anderson, James Littlepage, Chs. Barret.[1797] William Anderson and Sarah, daughter of Matthew and Anne (Reade) Pate, married on 18 February 1737.[1798]

Frances Ragland married Jeremiah Pate, and members of both the Pate and the Ragland families migrated to Bedford County. We saw above that when land was processioned in 1755 in Hanover County, land of Richard Anderson was separated from John Ragland's estate by only one dwelling.[1799] In 1783 Richard Anderson and wife, Elizabeth, of Bedford County made a deed to Elizabeth Priddy. The deed, recorded in Hanover County, was witnessed by Wm. Anderson, Bartlett Anderson, Charles Anderson, and John Priddy.[1800] In 1738 Robert Anderson sold 200 acres in Louisa County to Charles Anderson. The tract was part of a 400-acre patent made to Robert Anderson in 1733. In 1746 Charles Anderson and wife, Jennet, of St. Paul's Parish, Hanover County, sold the 200 acres to John Thomson.[1801] In 1749 John Thomson of St. Paul's Parish conveyed the 200 acres to kinsman John McGeorge of Fredericksville Parish, Louisa County. Pointers were lands of John Thomson, Dansie (formerly Mitchell), Wm. McCormick (formerly King's), and the county line.[1802]

The Raglands, Tisdales, and Pates intermarried, and John Pain, John Wheeler, and David McCormack had once owned land on Willis Creek in what is now Buckingham County. The Andersons, Raglands, Wheelers, and Hunters were associated with each other back in Louisa County. The Wheelers and McCormacks were close to John and Sarah (Ellis?) Payne. Anderson McCormack was surety for the marriage bond of John and Sarah's daughter Elizabeth

The possibility is strong that the John Payne who married Sarah (Ellis?) was related to the Joseph Payne who married Phoebe. Both were close to Anderson McCormick, and Buckingham County, Virginia, surveyor's records show David McCormick claiming 282 acres on the head branch of Willis' River in 1767. The tract abutted lands of Epaphroditus Guilliam and Lambeth T. Blackbourn.[1803] When Thomas Boaz's deed for 72 acres on the north fork of Holladay River in Buckingham County was recorded in 1771, it was noted that the land was transferred to Joseph Payne.[1804] (This may not be the same Joseph Payne who moved to Bedford County, however.) Holladay Creek flows directly into the Appomattox River, but the headwaters of the Willis River are nearby. A John Payne and John Wheeler were living side by side on the Barren Lick of the Willis River in 1750.[1805]

You get the feeling that if some of the Andersons, McCormacks, Wheelers, Moormans, and the Raglands had known each other before moving to southern Bedford County, then the Paynes who were part of their Bedford County network had already known them, too.

Raglan Castle and the Ragland immigrants:

Raglan Castle, in southern Wales near the River Usk, was once the home of ancestors of the Ragland family of New Kent County, Virginia. Sir William Herbert lived at Raglan Castle. It was at about that time that families were required to have surnames. William's brother Evan died, and one of his children, Robert, took on the name Ragland. Robert married Joan Clerk (Clark) and had five sons. Some of them left Wales before 1600, going across the Bristol Channel to Somersetshire. Beauforts lived there, and John Ragland, son of the immigrant Evan Ragland, married Anne Beaufort, a kinswoman, so it is assumed he descended from one of the Somerset lines.[1806] In 1492 Elizabeth Herbert had married Sir Charles Somerset, an illegitimate son of Henry Beaufort (third duke of Somerset). The Somersets were responsible for the final architectural work on the castle.[1807]

Construction of Raglan Castle was begun in 1435 by Sir William ap Thomas, father of Sir William Herbert.

William ap Thomas had bought the manor Raglan in 1432. During the War of the Roses, Henry Tudor (later King Henry VII) lived in the castle under the care of William Herbert. The English Civil Wars (1642-1651) developed when the Parliamentarians under the leadership of Oliver Cromwell, rebelled against the King. Raglan Castle came under siege, for Henry Somerset, first marquis of Worcester, was sympathetic to King Charles I. In August 1646 it became obvious to the marquis that he had to surrender, but he was able to negotiate a document that would allow his garrison to march away with dignity. Soon Oliver Cromwell's men began tearing down the castle.[1808] The ruins still stand today and they are open to tourists.

The first Ragland immigrant to Virginia was Evan Ragland (1656-1717), who lived in St. Peter's Parish, New Kent County.[1809] His son John Ragland married Anne Beaufort and lived in Hanover County, Virginia. He owned the large plantation called Rippon (sometimes written *Ripping*) Hall. John also owned land in Louisa County, buying 1,800 acres from John Smithson in 1747. Tax receipts from the 1750s show John Ragland owning about 5,000 acres. John's daughter Frances married Jeremiah Pate.[1810] The Edward Pate family settled on Beaverdam Creek in Bedford County.

Other Raglands of interest: Reuben F. Ragland was prominent in Petersburg, Virginia, during the American Civil War and afterwards. Bed & Breakfast listings for the city of Petersburg, Virginia, include the mansion built by him in the 1850s. It is located in the historic district. The listing describes Reuben as a descendent of Welsh aristocracy.[1811] The raglan sleeve originated with 1st Baron FitzRoy James Henry Somerset Ragland (1788-1855). Ragland served as the Duke of Wellington's military secretary during the Napoleonic Wars. He lost an arm during the Battle of Waterloo, and a special sleeve with a diagonal cut was designed for his benefit.[1812]

Ellis and Mary Payne are thought to have had at least nine children.[1813]

+ 14 i. **John B.^{3} PAYNE** was born 30 June 1815.
+ 15 ii. **Milton PAYNE** was born 1819.
   16 iii. **Rhoda PAYNE**.
+ 17 iv. **Jane PAYNE** was born 1824.
+ 18 v. **Elliott PAYNE** was born 1827.
+ 19 vi. **Burrell PAYNE** was born May 1829.
   20 vii. **Oty PAYNE** was born by 1813. His parents are assumed. Oty married **Cynthia PAYNE** on 21 February 1838 in Lawrence County, Ohio.[1814]

Third Generation

7. **James^3 MOORMAN** (Elizabeth^2 PAYNE, John^1) was born about 1819 in Virginia.

When the U.S. census was taken for 1850, James and Jane Moorman were living in Decatur Township, Lawrence County, Ohio, in Dwelling 68 (Family 69). James was 31, born in Virginia; and Jane, 30, was born in Ohio. In their household were Wm. H. Moorman, 10; James P. Moorman, 9; John V. Moorman, 7; Hiram Moorman, 6; Zach Moorman, 2. Next door, in Dwelling 69 (Family 51) was Elizabeth Moorman, 66.[1815]

James married **Jane**. Jane was born about 1820 in Ohio.

They had the following children (birth years figured from the 1850 census):

21 i. **William H.^{4} MOORMAN** was born 1840 in Ohio.
22 ii. **James P. MOORMAN** was born 1841 in Ohio.
23 iii. **John V. MOORMAN** was born 1843 in Ohio.

24   iv.   **Hiram MOORMAN** was born 1844 in Ohio.

25   v.   **Zach MOORMAN** was born 1848 in Ohio.

9.   **Moses Marion³ PAYNE** (William², John¹) was born 1815 in Tennessee. He died 9 October 1884.[1816]

When the U.S. census was taken in 1850 for Mason Township, Lawrence County, Ohio, it included Moses Payne, 35, born in Ohio. His wife, Malinda, was 28, also born in Ohio. Children were James W., 8; Uriah L., 4. Moses was living in Dwelling 160 (Family 163). His mother, Dina Payne, 65, was living as part of Family 162. She was living with her daughter Marinda and her husband, Samuel Lewis. Living with them also were Malissa Payne, 25; Austin Payne, 61, born in Virginia, and Sarah J. Payne, 6.[1817]

The 1860 census for Mason Township shows Moses Payne as 45 and born in Virginia. The rest of his family was born in Ohio. It included Melinda, 34; James W., 17; Uriah L., 13; John C., 8; Merinda, 7; Moses M., 2; and Melinda L., a month old.[1818]

The 1870 Mason Township census shows Moses as 58 and born in Tennessee. He was in Dwelling 116; his wife, Malinda, was 44. The ages of the children are difficult to decipher. The names of the children were Uriah, John C., Marinda, Moses M., Melinda L., and Melissa. Dwelling 117 was the household of Elliot Payne.[1819]

The 1880 U.S. census of Mason Township includes the household of Moses Payne, age 64, born in Tennessee. He was a farmer and both his parents were born in Virginia. Wife, Malinda, was 56 and born in Ohio, and her parents were born in Virginia. Children were John C., 28; Marinda M., 26; Marion, 21; Louisa, 20; Sarah M., 16. A granddaughter, Rosa G. Payne, age 4, was in the household, and Moses's brother, Joel Payne, age 70, lived with them.[1820]

Moses married **Melinda (JUSTICE) TALLEY** on 27 Sep 1843 in Lawrence County, Ohio.[1821] Melinda was born about 1816 in Ohio. She had been married previously to George Talley.[1822]

Moses and Melinda had the following children (birth years figured from census records):

       26   i.   **James W.⁴ PAYNE** was born 1843.

+   27   ii.   **Uriah L. PAYNE** was born 1847.

       28   iii.   **John C. PAYNE** was born 1851.

       29   iv.   **Marinda PAYNE** was born 1853

+   30   v.   **Moses Marion PAYNE** was born 11 November 1858.

       31   vi.   **Melinda Louise PAYNE** was born 1860.

       32   vii.   **Sarah Melissa PAYNE** was born 1864.

10.   **Marstie³ (?) PAYNE** (William², John¹) was born about 1822 in Virginia.

The 1850 U.S. census for Mason Township, Lawrence County, Ohio, shows Marstie (?) Payne, 28, born in Ohio, living in Dwelling 161 (Family 164). His wife, Elisabeth, was 23 and born in Virginia. They had daughter Dina, 6 (?) years old, and daughter Milly, 2 months. Uriah Payne, 28, was living with them. Family 163 was that of Moses Payne, and Family 165 was that of Ellis Payne, 61 years old.[1823]

Mathew [*sic*] married **Elizabeth McNICHOLS (?)** on 11 November 1847. Jesse Corn, the elder, officiated.[1824]

They had the following children (birth years deduced from the 1850 census):

       33   i.   **Dina⁴ PAYNE** was born about 1844 in Ohio.

       34   ii.   **Milly PAYNE** was born 1850 in Ohio.

12. **William Uriah[3] PAYNE** (William[2], John[1]) was born about 1825 in Ohio.

The 1880 U.S. census for Mason Township, Lawrence County, Ohio, shows Uriah Payne, 55, born in Ohio, and having both parents born in Virginia. His wife, Margaret, was 53, also born in Ohio, with both parents Virginians. Children at home were Wm. U., 28; Levi, 22; Elizabeth, 21; Lincoln, 18. Also in their home was Serena Allen, 22, a servant.[1825]

Uriah married **Margaret CLARK** on 16 January 1851 in Lawrence County, Ohio.[1826]

They had the following children (the birth years of Elizabeth and Lincoln are deduced from the 1880 census):.

+ 35 i. **William U.[4] PAYNE** was born January 1852.

+ 36 ii. **John Alva PAYNE** was born 9 November 1855.

+ 37 iii. **Levi PAYNE** was born about 1858.

    38 iv. **Elizabeth PAYNE** was born about 1859.

    39 v. **Lincoln PAYNE** was born about 1862.

14. **John B.[3] PAYNE** (Ellis[2], John[1]) was born 30 June 1815 in Jackson County, Tennessee.[1827]

The 1850 U.S. census for Decatur Township, Lawrence County, Ohio, includes the family of John and Elizabeth Payne. He was 35, born in Tennessee; she was 21, born in Indiana. They were in Dwelling 71 (Family 73). Included in their household were Catharen Payne, 4; Elliott Payne, 24; Burrel Payne, 21; and Banister Nance, 20, a laborer. Dwelling 69 was the household of John's aunt Elizabeth Moorman, 66, born in Virginia.[1828] Burrel and Elliott Payne, John's brothers, were also on the Mason Township census, living with their parents.[1829]

John Payne, 42, born in Tennessee, was on the 1860 census for Mason Township, living in Dwelling 1213. Wife, Elizabeth, 28, was born in Indiana. Children were Katherine J., 12; Ellis J., 10; Rhoda 9; George W. 5; Columbus 4; and John C. 2. John's sister, Jane Payne, 35, was living in Dwelling 1212.[1830]

The 1870 Mason Township census shows John Payne as 59, his wife, Elizabeth, 41. They were in Dwelling 6. The list of children includes Catherine J., 22; Ellis J., 21; Roda, 19; George, 15; Columbus, 13; John S., 12; Anna M., 10; Martha E.,5; Sarah E., 2. Next door, in Dwelling 7, lived Jane Fallowell, 45, and family. Next to her, in Dwelling 8, lived Milton Payne and family.[1831]

In 1880 the census for Mason Township includes John Payne and family. He was 65; wife, Elizabeth, 52. At home at this time were the following children: Catherine, 34, a teacher; Ellis, 30; Columbus, 24; Anna, 18; Martha E., 16; Sarah 10.[1832]

Hardesty, in his *History of Lawrence County, Ohio*, included a paragraph on John B. Payne. The article supplied his birth date and that of his wife, Elizabeth Fallowell, and their children. It noted the names of her parents. It states that John, born in Jackson County, Tennessee, came with his parents to Mason Township in 1815. It tells us John was the son of Ellis and Mary (Raglandt) Payne.[1833]

On 6 August 1862 John became a private in Company D, 91st Ohio Volunteer Infantry. He was discharged in October 1863 due to disability and received a pension of $4 a month.[1834]

John married **Elizabeth FALLOWELL**, daughter of Marcus FALLOWELL and Arramancie ALCORN, on 11 November 1845 in Lawrence County, Ohio. Elizabeth was born 13 December 1828 in Columbus County, Indiana.[1835]

They had the following children (birth dates and death dates supplied by the Hardesty article.):

    40 i. **Mary A.[4] PAYNE** was born 28 April 1847 and died June 1847.

    41 ii. **Catherine J. PAYNE** was born 13 June 1848 in Lawrence County, Ohio. She married **Vincent MASSIE**.[1836]

+ 42 iii. **Ellis J. PAYNE** was born 21 March 1850.

43	iv.	**Rhoda PAYNE** was born 9 March 1852 in Lawrence County, Ohio. She married **Benjamin ROUNDS**.[1837]
44	v.	**George W. PAYNE** was born 13 February 1854 in Lawrence County, Ohio. He died 21 November 1878.
+ 45	vi.	**Columbus PAYNE** was born 10 January 1856.
+ 46	vii.	**John Shannon PAYNE** was born 10 February 1858 and died 11 August 1914.
47	viii.	**Anna M. PAYNE** was born 21 August 1860 in Lawrence County, Ohio.
48	ix.	**Martha E. PAYNE** was born 2 January 1863 in Lawrence County, Ohio.
49	x.	**Milton S. PAYNE** was born 1865 in Lawrence County, Ohio, and deceased by the compiling of *Hardesty's Atlas* for Lawrence County, Ohio.
50	xi.	**Sarah E. PAYNE** was born 21 October 1869 in Lawrence County, Ohio.
51	xii.	**Marcus F. PAYNE** was born in 1871. He was deceased by the writing of *Hardesty's Atlas* for Lawrence County, Ohio.

15. **Milton³ PAYNE** (Ellis², John¹) was born 1819 in Lawrence County, Ohio. He was a farmer and died at age 52 on 15 May 1871 of consumption.[1838]

Year of birth of Milton Payne's wife, Sarah, and children Mary, Jackson, and Lee Roy were derived from the 1870 Mason Township census. The names of the other children were taken from the 1850 census, and their birth years were figured from the ages given. Polly and Mary were obviously the same person.

When 1850 census for Mason Township, Lawrence County, Ohio, was taken, Milton and his family were included. He was 30, born in Ohio; wife, Sally, was 33, also born in Ohio. Children were Amanda, 15; Nancy A., 11; Ellen, 8; Polly, 6; Ellis, 6; Jackson, 2; Mahala, less than a year.[1839]

The 1860 Mason Township census has Milton Payne in Dwelling 1204. He was 40 years old; wife, Sarah, was 49, born in Kentucky. Children at home were Sarah E. (Ellen?), 17; Mary, 14; Allia? J., 14; Jackson, 12; Mahala, 10; and Leroy, 7. Deanna Payne, 74, was in Dwelling 1203.[1840]

In 1870 Mason Township census shows Milton as 51. His wife, Sarah, was 59. Living with them were Mary, 24; Jackson U., 23; Lee Roy Payne, 17.[1841]

Milton married **Sarah JUSTICE** on 4 October 1843 in Lawrence County, Ohio.[1842] Sarah was born about 1811 in Kentucky.

They had the following children:

52	i.	**Amanda⁴ PAYNE** was born 1835 in Ohio.
53	ii.	**Nancy A. PAYNE** was born 1839.
54	iii.	**Ellen PAYNE** was born 1842.
55	iv.	**Mary (Polly) PAYNE** was born 1844.
56	v.	**Ellis PAYNE** was born 1844.
+ 57	vi.	**Jackson PAYNE** was born Jan 1847.
58	vii.	**Mahala PAYNE** was born 1850.
59	viii.	**Lee Roy PAYNE** was born May 1853.

The 1900 U.S. census for Mason Township includes LeRoy C.(?) Payne. He was 47 years old, and his wife, **Carrie**, was 35.[1843]

17. **Jane³ PAYNE** (Ellis², John¹) was born in 1824 in Lawrence County, Ohio, and died in 1900.

Jane Payne was living in Dwelling 1212 in Mason Township, Lawrence County, Ohio, when the U.S. census was taken in 1860. She was a farmer. Living with her was Thompson Payne, 13; Mary Payne, 4; America Payne, 1. She was living next to John and Elizabeth Payne (Dwelling 1213) and Elliot and Charlotte Payne (Dwelling 1211).[1844]

When the 1870 census was taken for Mason Township, Jane Followell was head of Dwelling 7. She was 45 and keeping house. Living with her was Thompson Payne, 28; Mary E. Payne, 14; America Payne, 11; and Ellis J. Followell, 7.[1845]

The 1880 census for Mason Township shows Jane Followell, 55, both parents born in Virginia. Son Ellis J. Followell, 17, and daughter America Payne, 21, were living with her.[1846]

Jane married **Marcus B. FALLOWELL** on 24 December 1860 in Lawrence County, Ohio. The International Genealogical Index gives the marriage date and also states that Jane died 12 March 1900.[1847]

They had the following children:

+   60   i.   **Thompson F.**[4] **PAYNE** was born in 1847 in Ohio.

      61   ii.   **America FALLOWELL** was born about 1859.

+   62   iii.   **Ellis J. FALLOWELL** was born 1863 in Ohio.

18.   **Elliott**[3]**PAYNE** (Ellis[2], John[1]) was born 1826 in Lawrence County, Ohio. He died 1898.[1848]

The 1860 U.S. census for Mason Township, Lawrence County, Ohio, gives Elliot's age as 33, born in Ohio; his wife, Charlotte N., as 21, born in New York. Children: Alonzo, 4; Howard, 2; and Benj. F., 7 mos.[1849]

The 1870 census for Mason Township shows Elliot Payne, 42, and his family in Dwelling 117. Elliot's wife, Charlotte A., was 31. Children named were Alonzo, 13; Howard, 11; Rebecca, 5; Willis,1; and Elmer E., a month old. (Rebecca and Willis had indecipherable middle initials.) Moses Payne and family were in Dwelling 116.[1850]

Elliott was 54 and wife, Charlotte, 41, when the 1880 census was taken for Mason Township. At home were children Alonzo, 23; James Me., 18; Ruby, 15; William, 12; Elmer, 10, Amy J., 8. Also in their household were son Howard Payne, 22, and his wife, Diantha Payne, 23.[1851]

Elliott married **Charlotte Ann PERRY** on 23 August 1855 in Lawrence County, Ohio.[1852] Charlotte was born 1839 in New York. She died 1909.[1853]

The 1900 U.S. census for Mason Township shows Charlotte Payne, 61, living in Dwelling 16 as head of household. A granddaughter, Clona (?), 15, was living with her. Charlotte's son Elmer Payne and his family were in Dwelling 17.[1854]

They had the following children:

+   63   i.   **Alonzo**[4] **PAYNE** was born 1857.

+   64   ii.   **Howard PAYNE** was born November 1857.

      65   iii.   **Benjamin PAYNE** was born about 1860.

      66   iv.   **James PAYNE** was born 1862.

      67   v.   **Rebecca (Ruby?) PAYNE** was born 1865.

+   68   vi.   **William Willis PAYNE** was born 1868. He died 18 July 1897.

+   69   vii.   **Elmer E. PAYNE** was born May 1870.

      70   viii.   **Amy J. PAYNE** was born 1872.

19.   **Burrell**[3] **PAYNE** (Ellis[2], John[1]) was born May 1829 in Lawrence County, Ohio.

The Scarberrys (Scarboroughs), Doughtys, Lewises, and Paynes of Lawrence County, Ohio

The 1860 U.S. census for Mason Township, Lawrence County, Ohio, has Burel Payne, 29, and wife, Myra J., 26, living in Dwelling 1210. Daughter Myra J. was 3; daughter Victoria was less than a year old. Dwelling 1211 belonged to Burrell's brother Elliot and his wife, Charlotte.[1855]

Burrel, 41, and Myra J., 38, were in Dwelling 4 when the 1870 census was taken for Mason Township. Children: Isadora M., 13; Victoria, 10; Viola C., 8; Ellesworth S., 5; and Charity L., 3.[1856]

The 1880 U.S. census for Mason Township showed Burrell as 51; wife, Myra J., was 47; Isadora M., 23; Victoria, 20; Viola, 18; Sherridan, 15, Charity, 13.[1857]

Burrell and Myra J. were still living when the 1900 U.S. census was taken for Mason Township. He was 71, born May 1829, and she was 66, born August 1833. Living with them was daughter Dora M., 43, born April 1857.[1858]

Burrell married **Mary (Myra?) J. PERRY** on 9 September 1855 in Lawrence County, Ohio. Myra was born August 1833 in New York.[1859]

They had the following children:

    71   i.   **Myra J.⁴ PAYNE** was born 1857.

    72   ii.   **Isadora M. PAYNE** was born 1857.

                  The 1920 census for Mason Township shows Dora M. Payne, 62, as head of household. She was a teacher, living alone.[1860]

    73   iii.   **Victoria L. PAYNE** was born 1860.

    74   iv.   **Viola C. PAYNE** was born 1862.

+   75   v.   **Ellesworth S. PAYNE** was born May 1865.

    76   vi.   **Charity L. PAYNE** was born 1867.

Fourth Generation

27.   **Uriah L.⁴ PAYNE** (Moses Marion³, William², John¹) was born 1847 in Ohio.

Places of residence for Uriah L. Payne's children are revealed in the article "Clay - Payne," by Verla Payne Watrons Switzer, printed in *History of Lawrence County, Ohio, 1990*.[1861]

The 1880 U. S. census for Mason Township, Lawrence County, Ohio, shows Uriah L. and Celestia A., Payne, ages 32 and 31 respectively, as having children John W., 8 years old; Amos M., 6; Lewis W., 4; Oscar E., 2. Uriah was a lawyer and his wife a housekeeper.[1862]

Uriah married **Celesta A. DARLING**.[1863] Celesta was born about 1849 in Virginia.

They had the following children:

+   77   i.   **John W.⁵ PAYNE** was born 1872.

    78   ii.   **Amos M. PAYNE** was born 1874. He resided in Gallipolis.

    79   iii.   **Lewis W. PAYNE** was born 1876. He lived in Fort Wayne.

+   80   iv.   **Oscar Enoch PAYNE** was born 1878.

    81   v.   **James PAYNE** (Reverend) lived at Kitts Hill in Lawrence County, Ohio.

    82   vi.   **A. T. PAYNE** owned a shoe shop across from the Lawrence County Court House and was called "Doc."

    83   vii.   **Charles E. PAYNE** was born 1883 in Wilgus, Ohio.

                  He was Judge Charles Payne of Ironton. On 1 September 1918 Charles E. Payne was inducted into the army at Camp Gordon, Georgia. He was 35 1/2 years of age and a lawyer. He was 5 feet 11 1/2 inches tall, had brown eyes, black hair, and a fair complexion. He received an honorable discharge from the service on 21 November 1918 because his services were no longer required (the war had ended on November 11). He was said to have been of excellent character.[1864]

84 viii. **Anna PAYNE** was born 1889 in Aid Township, Lawrence County, Ohio. Anna married **Evert BUNN** on 31 December 1908 in Lawrence County, Ohio. Evert was 22 and Anna was 19 and born at Aid. Strangely, the marriage record shows Anna as the daughter of *James* Payne and Celesta Darling.[1865]

30. **Moses Marion[4] PAYNE** (Moses Marion[3], William[2], John[1]) was born 11 November 1858. He died 25 March 1946.

Drusilla Payne Mogavero's article in *History of Lawrence County, Ohio 1990* provides the death date for Moses, the name of his wife and date of marriage, as well as Curt Payne's first name.[1866]

Moses and Almira were on the 1900 U.S. census for Mason Township, living in Dwelling 191. He was 41, and she, 40. Children were James R., 18; Curtis, 16; Calvin, 14; Marinda, 12; and Minnie, 9. They were neighbors to Howard Payne's household (Dwelling 190).[1867]

Moses married **Sarah Almira ROBERTS** on 2 October 1880. Sarah was born March 1860.[1868]

They had the following children:

85 i. **James R.[5] PAYNE** was born October 1881. James married **Virgie DANIELS** on 27 March 1907 in Lawrence County, Ohio. Virgie was 18, born in Kentucky. He was 25, the son of Moses M. Payne and Elmira Roberts.[1869]

86 ii. **Louis Curtis PAYNE**. Curtis was born January 1884. Curtis married **Minnie NANCE** on 12 October 1913 in Lawrence County, Ohio. He was 29 and she, 27. The certificate states that he was the son of Moses Payne and Almira Roberts.[1870]

87 iii. **Calvin PAYNE** was born April 1886.

88 iv. **Marinda L PAYNE** was born February 1888.

89 v. **Minnie J. PAYNE** was born May 1891. Minnie married **Isaac SPENCE** on 5 June 1909. He was 22 and she, 18. The marriage certificate stated she was born in Lawrence County, Ohio, to Moses Payne and wife, Sarah Roberts.[1871]

35. **William Uriah[4] PAYNE** (William U.[3], William[2], John[1]) was born January 1852.

The 1900 U.S. census for Mason Township includes William U. Payne, born January 1852. He had wife, Rebecca, and children Margaret E., born April 1842; and Clara B., born April 1845. William R. Brown, 74, William's father-in-law, was also in the dwelling.[1872]

William married **Rebecca BROWN**.

They had the following children:

90 i. **Margaret E.[5] PAYNE** was born April 1882.

91 ii. **Clara B. PAYNE** was born April 1885.

36. **John Alva[4] PAYNE** (William U.[3], William[2], John[1]) was born March 1855 in Ohio.

Alva A. Payne, 44, was on the 1900 U.S. census for Mason Township. His wife, Blanch, was 29; daughter Nellie M. was 1. Living with them were Uriah Payne, 75, father; Margret Payne, 72, mother; and Elizabeth Payne, 38, sister.[1873] When the 1910 U.S. census was taken, Alva A. Payne was shown as *John A. Payne*. He was 54 years old; his wife, Blanch, was 32. Children were Nettie, 11; Cornelius, 10; Hobert, 8; Emmet, 4; Justin, 2. A sister, Elizabeth Payne, 47, was living with them.[1874]

John Alva married **Blanch PAYNE** who was born 19 May 1878 and died 29 July 1964.[1875]

Blanch is revealed to have been a two-year-old daughter of Jackson PAYNE when the 1880 census was taken. See below for more on the Jackson Payne family.

They had the following children:

    92   i.   **Nellie M.**[5] **PAYNE** was born January 1899.

    93   ii.   **Cornelius PAYNE** was born about 1900.

    94   iii.   **Hobert PAYNE** was born about 1902.

    95   iv.   **Emmit PAYNE** was born about 1906.

+   96   v.   **Alva Justin PAYNE** was born 21March 1908.

    97   vi.   **Leslie PAYNE** married a Mr. **ROBINSON**.[1876]

37.   **Levi PAYNE**[4] (William U.[3], William[2], John[1]) was born April 1857 in Ohio.

The Mason Township census for 1900 shows Levi Payne as 43 years old. Wife, Carrie E., was 30. Daughter Leslie L. was 10.[1877]

Levi married **Carrie E.** She was born June 1869.

They had the following child:

    98   i.   **Leslie L.**[5] **PAYNE** was born January 1890.

42.   **Ellis J.**[4] **PAYNE** (John B.[3], Ellis[2], John[1]) was born September 1845 in Lawrence County, Ohio.

The 1880 U.S. census for Mason Township includes the household of Ellis. J. Payne, age 34. His wife, Mary M., was 26. Children at home were Elwood, 10; Fenton B., 8; Edith L., 6; Lenna M., 4; and Charles F., 8 months.[1878]

The 1900 U.S. census for Mason Township shows Ellis, 54, born September 1845, and wife, Mary, 46, born December 1853. Children were Charles F., 20; Sarah A., 15; Verdie E., 13; and Ethel G., 11. Ellis J. Payne was the census enumerator.[1879]

Ellis married **Mary Melvina DILLON**. Melvina was born about 1853. See marriages of daughters Sarah and Ethel for proof of this marriage.

They had the following children:

    99   i.   **Elwood**[5] **PAYNE** was born about 1870.

    100   ii.   **Fenton B. PAYNE** was born about 1872.

    101   iii.   **Edith L. PAYNE** was born about 1874.

    102   iv.   **Lenna M. PAYNE** was born about 1876.

    103   v.   **Charles F. PAYNE** was born 1879.

    104   vi.   **Sarah A. PAYNE** was born 1884 in Mason Township, Lawrence County, Ohio. Sarah married **Nathan O. ROACH**, son of William ROACH and Elizabeth MILLER, on 2 March 1909 in Lawrence County, Ohio. Nathan was 22 and born in Mason Township. Sarah was 24, the daughter of Ellis Payne and Melvina Dillon.[1880]

    105   vii.   **Verla E. PAYNE** was born 1887. On 15 January 1916 Verla, age 28, married **J. Ancil BROWN**, 27,

of Wilgus.. She was a daughter of Ellis Payne and Melvina Dillon.[1881]

106   viii.   **Ethel PAYNE** was born 1889. Ethel married **Charles SNYDER**, age 27, on 13 August 1910. He was born in Rappsburg, the son of B. F. SNYDER and Effie DELLON. Ethel, 22, was the daughter of Ellis Payne and Melvina Dillon.[1882]

45.   **Columbus[4] PAYNE** (John B.[3], Ellis[2], John[1]) was born 10 January 1856 in Lawrence County, Ohio.

The 1900 U.S. census for Mason Township includes Columbus Payne, 44, and family. His wife, Amanda, was 25, and they had sons Otto, 8; and Archie, 2.[1883]

Columbus married **Amanda SHORT**. Amanda was born January 1875 in Ohio. For proof of marriage, see daughter Sylvia below.

They had the following children:

107   i.   **Otto[5] PAYNE** was born April 1892.

108   ii.   **Archie PAYNE** was born February 1898.

109   iii.   **Sylvia PAYNE** was born 1901 at Wilgus. Sylvia married **Virgil VITITOE** on 15 May 1919. She was 18, a daughter of Columbus Payne and Amanda Short/ Virgil was 21 and born at Rappsburg, a son of Perry VITITOE and Jane MART.[1884]

46.   **John Shannon[4] PAYNE** (John B.[3], Ellis[2], John[1]) was born 10 February 1858 in Lawrence County, Ohio. He died 11 August 1914 in Lawrence County, Ohio. Daughter Edna's marriage certificate reveals that he was called *Shannon*.

The 1880 U.S. census for Mason Township, Lawrence County, Ohio, includes the household of John S. Payne, 22, a farmer, born in Ohio. His wife, Emma [sic], was also 22 and born in Ohio. They were living between the households of Jane Followell and Elliott Payne.[1885]

When the 1900 U.S. census was taken for Mason Township, John S. Payne was shown to have been born in February 1858. He was living in Dwelling 111. He was a 42-year-old farmer. His wife, Emily J., was also 42, born March 1858. Children were John W., 19; Elizabeth, 17; Bertha O., 15; Sarah B., 13; Edna M., 10; Charley, 8; and Ona, 6. Thompson F. Payne's family was in Dwelling 112; Jackson Payne was in Dwelling 115; Columbus Payne lived in Dwelling 110; Burrell Payne was in Dwelling 106.[1886] The John S. Payne family did not want for the support and friendship of relatives.

John and Emily were living next to Howard Payne when people were enumerated in Mason Township in 1910. At home were children Sarah, Edna, Charles, and Ona. An 11-year-old nephew, Robert B____, was also part of their household. (The handwriting on this record is barely readable.)[1887]

John married **Emily J HIGGINS**, daughter of Thomas HIGGINS and Hannah CORN, in Lawrence County, Ohio.[1888] Emily was born 28 March 1858 in Lawrence County, Ohio. Judging by the age of their first child, John and Emily were married in 1880.

Betty (Lewis) Midkiff remembers her grandmother Emily Payne. Until Betty spent the night in her home, Betty thought Emily was overweight. But then she saw her in her nightgown. As was the custom among some of the women in those days, Emily had been wearing several dresses at a time and she only appeared to be heavy.

The 1880 U.S. census for Mason Township includes Thomas Higgins, 66, born in West Virginia,. He had in his home a large family that included his wife, Hannah, 67, born in North Carolina, and several children: Reuben Higgins, 33, a teacher; Sarah Higgins, 29; Clarke Higgins, 31; Emily Swords, 25; and son Kelley Higgins, 21. There were also 4 grandchildren in the home. Albert Franklin, 18; Alonzo Higgins, 4; Della J. Swords, 2; and Callie A. Swords, 9 months. Children and grandchildren alike were said to have had a father born in West Virginia and a mother born in North Carolina, a reporting that is surely in error.[1889] By the time the enumeration was done in Mason Township for the 1900 U.S. census, Thomas Higgins, 85, had married a second time, for wife, Mary, 73, was living with him. She had been born in Ohio. Also in the household were grandsons Alonzo Higgins, 24; and William Swords, 13.[1890]

Emily Higgins' father, Thomas Higgins, married Hannah Corn, daughter of George Corn and Elizabeth

Snodgrass, on 20 March 1834 in Lawrence County, Ohio. George Corn's second wife, Dolly Litteral, is said to have had noble lineage, having King John, Alfred the Great, Edward the First of England, and other nobility in her background.[1891] The Briggs Lawrence County Public Library has a copy of this lineage in its files.

Jesse Corn, a brother of Hannah Corn, married Louisa Doddrige in 1867. Louisa was a daughter of Enoch Doddrige and Susan Dewitt. Enoch was a son of Josiah Doddridge, son of John Doddrige (b.1745) and Elizabeth Schrimplin. The Reverend Joseph Doddridge was a half brother of Josiah. This Doddridge family is related to Philip Doddridge (1702-1751), of England, who composed many hymns.[1892] The Rev. Dr. Joseph Doddridge (1769-1826) wrote *Notes on the Settlement and Indian wars of the western part of Virginia and Pennsylvania, from 1763-1783, inclusive: together with a view of the state of society and manners of the first settlers of the western country.*

John Higgins, father of Thomas, married Margaret Dennison in Greenbrier County (WV). James Corn (1808-1900) married Margaret, daughter of John and Margaret Higgins.[1893] When the 1860 census was taken for Mason Township, Margaret Higgins, 90 years old, was living with James Corn (b. in Pennsylvania) and wife, Margaret. The household consisted of the parents and children James, 18; George, 17; Jesse, 15; Martha, 13; Sarah, 11; Elisabeth, 9; Harrison, 7. Also in their household was Hannah Zimmerman, 20, a maid; Theodore Carnes, 5; Alice Carnes, 3; and Wm. Zimmerman, one month..[1894] James Corn and Margaret Higgins had married in 1829. In addition to the children named in the 1860 census, they had John, Charlotte, Nancy, William, Margaret, Frances M., and Richard. Incidentally, John A. Higgins (1804-1884) married Sarah Payne in 1829, and his brother James Higgins married Deloras De(O)dridge. James and Sarah Higgins' sister Elizabeth married Sinkler Pettry; sister Nancy married Valentine Sampson.[1895]

Samuel Kerchival, in his *A History of the Valley of Virginia*, tells how John Higgins traveled to the Shawnee Village at the mouth of the Scioto to rescue a woman and her son from the Shawnees. Mrs. Sarah Erskine, who at that time was married to John Pauly, was moving to Kentucky with their two-year-old son. On 23 September 1779, while on the east branch of the New River, they were attacked by five Shawnees and a white man named Morgan. Pauly and the boy were killed. While in captivity, Sarah gave birth to another son. Sarah remained a captive for three years before John Higgins redeemed her.[1896] This same story is related by Mary B. Jones in her article, "John Higgins," that appears in *History of Lawrence County, Ohio 1990*. Mary B. Jones included a photograph of Thomas Higgins and Hannah Corn. Hannah has passed on several features to her great-granddaughter, Faye Lewis, who was born about 100 years later than she. Both had large wide-set eyes and prominent cheekbones. Faye's brother, Ray Lewis, had smaller eyes and a wide mouth, as did Thomas Higgins.[1897]

During the Civil War Thomas Higgins unfortunately met up with a group of Confederate soldiers trying to find their way through Lawrence County to the Ohio River. Brigadier-General John Hunt Morgan and about 2,000 Confederate soldiers had crossed the Ohio, landing in Indiana on 8 July 1863. Most of their efforts were spent in plundering and trying to put a scare into the hearts of citizens of Indiana and Ohio. When the Confederates arrived in Jackson County, Ohio, a splinter group of 41 soldiers traveled south into Lawrence County, winding up on Greasy Ridge in Mason Township. They stole horses from a Corn family. They captured Thomas Higgins and Thomas Tagg, in order to use them as guides to the Ohio River. The group traveled toward Scottown, planning to reach Athalia on the Ohio River. Dr. Clarke, who lived on Greasy Ridge, followed behind, but not with enough care, for he was shot and killed. His was the only death of a resident of Lawrence County at the hands of these Confederates. Units of the 91st Ohio and the 9th Virginia were on their way and captured 33 of the Confederates. The others tried to swim the Ohio River, and two drowned.[1898]

The wedding of Lucy Corn, sister of Hannah, is well told in an article in Wayne B. Ingles' *Symmes Creek*. The article, "An Old-Time Wedding," was written by Davis Mackley in 1873, and, as Mackley tells it, Lucy's wedding to Big Jep Massie was certainly a lively celebration involving horse racing and dancing, with the old folks telling tales of Indian wars. The author also mentioned that George Corn, Lucy's father, bragged about having 20 children.[1899] I have in my records 15 children by Elizabeth Snodgrass and 6 by Dolly Litteral.

George Corn received a pension for his Revolutionary War service. He enlisted first in 1777 for three years and served as a lieutenant in Capt. Van Swearingen's Company. He was stationed at Redstone Fort near present-day Pittsburgh and fought in the battles of Pickaway, Floyd's Defeat, Estill's Defeat, and Blue Licks. He suffered a wound to the jaw during this last one.[1900] The latter two battles were fought in 1782, after the British had surrendered at

Yorktown, Virginia. At the Battle of Blue Licks, in Robertson County, Kentucky, 300 Indians and 50 Canadian and American Loyalists attacked 182 Americans.[1901] Estill's Defeat took place around Boonesborough, Kentucky. Captain James Estill lost his life in the battle. He was trying to fight with a broken arm and the Kentuckians were outnumbered by the Indians. Estill County, southeast of Lexington, is named for the captain.[1902] The *Symmes Creek* article notes that George Corn was a small man but had stout, healthy sons. George must have been heartier than he appeared.[1903]

John Shannon and Emily Payne had the following children:

+ 110 i. **John William**[5] **PAYNE** was born 2 November 1880 and died 1948.
  111 ii. **Elizabeth PAYNE** was born August 1882 in Lawrence County, Ohio.
+ 112 iii. **Bertha O. PAYNE** was born 18 September 1884 and died 3 July 1956.
+ 113 iv. **Sarah B. PAYNE** was born August 1886.
+ 114 v. **Edna Mae PAYNE** was born 19 October 1890 and died 18 February 1951.
+ 115 vi. **Ona PAYNE** was born March 1894 and died 15 September 1966.
  116 vii. **Charles O. PAYNE** was born 4 May 1898 in Wilgus, Ohio. He died 1 March 1919 in France and was buried in 1921 in the Fairview Baptist Church graveyard at Wilgus, Ohio.

  Charley Payne enlisted in the army on 2 August 1917, during World War I, and was ranked private first class. He died of bronchial pneumonia after the war ended. Next of kin listed on his graves registration card was Sarah Payne of Wilgus, Ohio. Although he died on 1 March 1919, it was not until 1921 that he was buried at Wilgus.[1904]

57. **Jackson**[4] **PAYNE** (Milton[3], Ellis[2], John[1]) was born January 1847.

The 1880 U.S. census for Mason Township shows Jackson, a farmer, working for himself. He was 33 years old; his wife, Samantha, was 30, and born in Kentucky. Daughter Blanche M. was 2. Living with them was his mother, Sarah Payne, 70 years old, and Polly Payne, his sister, 35 years old.[1905]

Jackson Payne is found on the 1900 Mason Township census. He was 53, born January 1847. His wife, Samantha, 50, was born in October 1849. Children were Jonas B., 16 (born December 1883); and Ella L., 12 (born May 1887).[1906]

Jackson married **Samantha**. Samantha was born October 1849 in Kentucky.

They had the following children:

+ 117 i. **Blanche M.**[5] **PAYNE** was born 19 May 1878 and died 1964.
+ 118 ii. **Jonas B. PAYNE** was born December 1883.
  119 iii. **Ella L. PAYNE** was born May 1887.

60. **Thompson F.**[4] **PAYNE** (Jane[3], Ellis[2], John[1]) was born November 1846.

The 1880 U.S. census for Mason Township, Lawrence County, Ohio, shows Thompson F. Payne, 33, a farmer, born in Ohio. His father was born in Maine, his mother in Ohio. Wife, Ella E., was 28. She was born in Ohio, her father in Pennsylvania, her mother in Ohio. Children: Mary J., 8; Armina, 6; Albert, 4; and Maud, 2.[1907]

Thompson married (1) **Ella E.** Ella E. was born 1852.

They had the following children:

  120 i. **Mary J.**[5] **PAYNE** was born 1872.
  121 ii. **Armina PAYNE** was born 1874.

122　iii.　**Albert PAYNE** was born 1876.

123　iv.　**Maud PAYNE** was born 1878.

Thompson (2) **Nina A.** Nina A. was born November 1860.

The 1900 Mason Township census reveals that Thompson F. Payne was born November 1846. His wife was Nina A., and she was born November 1860. Living with them were daughters Lona C., born September 1881; Gussie O., born November 1885; Eva R., born August 1888.[1908]

They had the following children:

124　v.　**Lona C. PAYNE** was born September 1881.

125　vi.　**Gussie O. PAYNE** was born November 1885.

126　vii.　**Eva R. PAYNE** was born August 1888.

62.　**Ellis J.^{4} FOLLOWELL** (Jane^3, Ellis^2, John^1) was born March 1863.

The 1900 U.S. census for Mason Township includes Ells J. Followell and family. Ellis was 37; wife, Emma E., was 29. Children were Evan E., 10; Manby (?), 6; Eva N. J., 3; and Bessie E., 9 months.[1909]

Ellis married **Emma E**. Emma was born July 1870.

They had the following children:

127　i.　**Evan E.^{5} FALLOWELL** was born January 1890.

128　ii.　**Manby(?) FALLOWELL** was born July 1893.

129　iii.　**Eva N. J. FALLOWELL** was born May 1897.

130　iv.　**Bessie E. FALLOWELL** was born August 1899.

63.　**Alonzo^4 PAYNE** (Elliott^3, Ellis^2, John^1) was born 1857.

Alonzo married **Minerva THORNTON**. She was born July 1854.

When the 1900 U.S. census was taken for Mason Township, Minerva Payne was head of household (Dwelling 18, Family 18). Living with her were children Bertha E., 17; Earnest A., 12; Clarence S., 10; Orin M., 8, and Eva A., 4.[1910]

They had the following children:

131　i.　**Bertha E.^{5} PAYNE** was born October 1882.

132　ii.　**Earnest A. PAYNE** was born July 1887.

133　iii.　**Clarence S. PAYNE** was born July 1889.

+　134　iv.　**Orin M. PAYNE** was born October 1891.

135　v.　**Eva A. PAYNE** was born May 1896. Eva married **Oliver MASSIE** on 19 January 1918. She was 21 and he 25 and both were born at Wilgus. He was a son of James MASSIE and Lena STEWART and she the daughter of Alonzo Payne and Minerva Thornton.[1911]

64.　**Howard^4 PAYNE** (Elliott^3, Ellis^2, John^1) was born November 1857 in Ohio.

Howard Payne and wife, Diantha, were living in the home of his parents, Elliott and Charlotte Payne, when the Mason Township census was taken in 1880. The 1900 U.S. census for Mason Township, Lawrence County, Ohio, shows Howard Payne, 42, and wife, Diantha J., 43. At home were Adolphus, 18; Eliza. J., 13; Lenard H., 10; Thomas S., 4; and Amy A., less than a year.[1912]

Howard married **Diantha J. THORNTON**. Diantha was born March 1857 in Ohio.

Howard and Diantha had the following children:

+ 136   i.   **Adolphus[5] PAYNE** was born November 1882.

    137   ii.   **Eliza. J. PAYNE** was born April 1883 at Wilgus. Eliza married **Columbus C. MANNON**, 36, son of Vint MANNON and Jane FULLER, on 28 July 1907. The marriage certificate indicates she was 21 and the daughter of Howard Payne and Dina Thornton.[1913]

    138   iii.   **Lenard H. PAYNE** was born June 1890.

    139   iv.   **Thomas S. PAYNE** was born November 1895.

    140   v.   **Amy A. PAYNE** was born August 1899.

68.   **William Willis[4] PAYNE** (Elliot[3], Ellis[2], John[1]) was born 1868 and died 1897.

Much of the information on this family comes from an article entitled "Payne," in *History of Lawrence County, Ohio, 1990*.[1914]

William married **Mary Emmer CLARK** (1868-1946) on 3 October 1891.

They had the following children:

    141   i.   **Amel[5] PAYNE** was born 1891 and died 1966.

    142   ii.   **Estelle PAYNE** was born 1894 and died 1988. Estelle, 18 years old, married **John E. WILSON**, 32, on 28 August 1912. He was born on Greasy Ridge, a son of John A. WILSON and Sarah LANE. Estelle was 18, the daughter of Wm. Payne and wife, Mary E. Clark, of Wilgus.[1915]

    143   iii.   **Zelda PAYNE** was born 1896 and died 1983. Zelda married **Henry Roscoe PYLES** on 23 December 1914.

    144   iv.   **Willa PAYNE** was born 1898, after her father's death.

Mary Emmer (Clark) Payne married **John WILSON** on 6 January 1906.

69.   **Elmer E.[4] PAYNE** (Elliott[3], Ellis[2], John[1]) was born May 1870.

The 1900 census for Mason Township includes the household of Elmer Payne. Elmer was 30 and his wife, Arminia, was 29. Children were son Lasco (?), 5; son Elliott, 4; son Wilson, 1; and daughter Ethelinda, less than a year.[1916]

Elmer married **Arminia**. Arminia was born April 1876 in Ohio.

They had the following children:

    145   i.   **Lasco (?)[5] PAYNE** was born December 1894 in Ohio.

    146   ii.   **Elliott PAYNE** was born March 1896.

    147   iii.   **Wilson PAYNE** was born November 1898.

    148   iv.   **Ethelinda PAYNE** was born March 1900.

75.   **Ellesworth S.[4] PAYNE** (Burrell[3], Ellis[2], John[1]) was born May 1855.

Ellesworth S. Payne appears on the 1900 census for Mason Township. He was 35 years old, his wife, Della, 49. At home were a daughter, Eva G., 6, and a son, Cecil H., 5.[1917]

Ellsworth married **Della LAWLER,** who was born 1860.

They had the following children:

149   i.   **Eva G.**[5] **PAYNE** was born June 1893.

150   ii.   **Cecil H. PAYNE** was born 1895. Cecil, 22, of Wilgus married **Grace McMAHAN,** 20, on 15 September 1917. Cecil was the son of E. S. Payne and Della Lawler. Grace was a daughter of G. J. McMAHAN and Florence VERMILLION.[1918]

Fifth Generation

77.   **John W.**[5] **PAYNE,** "Will" (Uriah L.[4], Moses Marion[3], William[2], John[1]) was born 1872.

Dr. Payne lived at Willow Wood, in Windsor Township, and went by "Will."[1919]

The 1910 U.S. census for Windsor Township calls John W. Payne *William J. Payne*. He was 38, and no wife was named. At home were children Thomas O., 15; Fred W., 14; Pauline, 12; and Willanelle 11. They had a boarder living with them, Sarah O'Neill, 72, born in Ohio, both parents born in Virginia.[1920]

Will married (1) **Daisy WEAVER**.

They had the following children:

151   i.   **Thomas O.**[6] **PAYNE** was born about 1895.

152   ii.   **Fred W. PAYNE** was born 1896.

153   iii.   **Pauline PAYNE** was born about 1897 at Willow Wood. Pauline, 19, married **Jacob METZ,** 24, of Andis, Ohio, on 6 December 1916. The marriage record shows that Pauline was a daughter of J. W. Payne and Daisy Weaver.[1921]

154   iv.   **Willanelle PAYNE** was born about 1899. Willanette Payne, 20, married **John HOLDERBY**, 23, on 28 June 1919. She was born at Willow Wood, the daughter of J. W. Payne and Daisy Weaver. John was a son of O. P. HOLDERBY and Mahala McCOMAS.[1922]

Will married (2) **Minnie SLOAN** on 1 November 1911 in Lawrence County, Ohio. J. Will Payne was a 39-year-old widower from Willow Wood when he married Minnie SLOANE, daughter of Marion VERMILLION and Sarah GRIFFITH. Will Payne was a farmer and physician, a son of Uriah L. Payne and Celesta Darling.[1923]

When the 1920 census was taken for Windsor Township, it shows John to have been the head of an extended family: Son Fred W. Payne, 23, and daughter-in-law Beatrice Payne, 20, were living with him. John was 47 and wife, Minnie G., was 43.[1924]

80.   **Oscar Enoch**[5] **PAYNE** (Uriah L.[4], Moses Marion[3], William[2], John[1]) was born 1878.

The approximate birth years of Oscar and Lillian's children were deduced from the 1930 census for Lawrence Township.. Information on marriages of the children was taken from the article by Verla Payne Watrous Switzer, included in *History of Lawrence County, Ohio, 1990*.[1925]

Oscar E. Payne and family were on the 1930 U.S. census for Lawrence Township, Lawrence County, Ohio. He was 52 and wife, Lillian L., was 44. Children were Ralph E., 21; Lola M., 17; Verla L., 14; Stanley E., 8, and Lesta L., 5.[1926]

Oscar married **Lillian CLAY** on 10 April 1907 in Andis, Ohio. The marriage certificate shows Oscar E. Payne, 27, marrying Gillian Clay, 21, daughter of John CLAY and Lucretia HALL. Lillian was born at Andis. Oscar was a son of U. L. Payne and Celesta Darling. Marriage certificate was recorded 27 April 1907.[1927]

Oscar and Lillian had the following children:

    155   i.   **Ralph E.[6] PAYNE** was born 1909. Ralph married **Thelma GOODALL.**

    156   ii.   **Lola M. PAYNE** was born 1913. Lola married **Hayes McCOY.**

+   157   iii.   **Verla L. PAYNE** was born 10 May 1915 in Andis, Ohio. She died 5 May 2010 at the Masonic Home in Springfield, Ohio.

    158   iv.   **Stanley E. PAYNE** was born 1922. Stanley married **Helen JOHNSON.**

    159   v.   **Lesta F. PAYNE,** "Betty," was born 1925. Betty married **Robert MORGAN.**

96.   **Alva Justin[5] PAYNE** (John A.[4], William Uriah[3], William[2], John[1]) was born 21 March 1908. He died 18 January 1973.

The 1930 census for Mason Township shows Justin A. Payne as 21 years old. His wife, Pearl G., was 22. Alva B., was 2 months. Justin and Pearl were living in the home of Henry B. Vermillion, and Alva B. was listed as the Vermillion's grandson. Henry B. Vermillion, 51, had wife, Kate E., 48; daughter Blanche M., 10, and Charles F., 8.[1928]

Alva Justin married **Pearl Grey VERMILLION.** Pearl was born 17 August 1907.[1929]

They had the following children:

    160   i.   **Alva Burton[6] PAYNE** was born 1 February 1930 at Arabia, Ohio, north of Wilgus. Dr. Payne married **Leona DARLING**, born 31 August 1933, the daughter of Jess Herbert DARLING and Mollie ELLCESSOR.[1930]

    161   ii.   **William Paul PAYNE** was a physician.

    162   iii.   **Justine Genieth PAYN** married a Mr. **HAAS.**

    163   iv.   **Blanche Elizabeth PAYNE** married a Mr. **MAYER.**

    164   v.   **Charles David PAYNE**

110.   **John William[5] PAYNE** (John Shannon[4], John B.[3], Ellis[2], John[1]) was born 2 November 1880 at Long Creek in Wilgus, Lawrence County, Ohio. He died in 1948.

William Payne, 38, and wife, Eva, 31, appear on the 1920 U.S. census for Mason Township. William was born in Ohio and Eva in Kentucky. Son F. Raymond was 8; daughter Pauline, 6; son Fredrick, 2.[1931]

An article by Sharon Conner in *History of Lawrence County, Ohio, 1990*, supplies the name of another child, William Earl, born 1924. The full names of their children and birth dates were taken from this article.[1932]

John married **Eva ROACH**, daughter of Ephraim ROACH and Abbie WATTS, on 28 January 1909 in Ironton, Ohio. Eva was born 18 January 1888. She died in 1940. The marriage certificate describes John as a 26-year-old farmer, the son of J. S. Payne and Emily Higgins. Eva, 24, was said to have been born in Rappsburg, the daughter of Ephraim Roach and Ebbie Watts.[1933]

John and Eva had the following children:

+   165   i.   **Raymond Forest[6] PAYNE** was born 25 July 1911.

+   166   ii/   **Pauline Olive PAYNE** was born 18 September 1913 and died 4 November 1977.

+   167   iii.   **Charles Frederick PAYNE** was born 30 December 1917 and died 25 November 1983.

+   168   iv.   **William Earl PAYNE** was born 5 January 1924.

112.   Bertha Olive^5 PAYNE (John Shannon^4, John B.^{3}, Ellis^2, John^1) was born 18 September 1884 in Wilgus, Ohio. She died 3 July 1956 in Latham, Ohio.

An obituary of Olive Payne Corn, clipped from an unidentified newspaper, says she was born in Lawrence County near Wilgus and was married to George Corn on 25 December 1907. They had one daughter, Gladys Lyon, of Wilmington, Ohio. The obituary states "She was a friend to every one, never speaking an unkind word to anyone."

Olive married **George C. CORN** on 25 December 1907 in Lawrence County, Ohio. George was born 1871 in Ohio. George C. Corn, 36, born in Lawrence County, and living at Byington, Ohio, a farmer, married Ollie Payne, 23, born at Wilgus, Ohio. George was a son of Amos CORN and Sarah ALLEN; Ollie was a daughter of John S. Payne and Emily Higgins.^{1934}

I remember George and Ollie. They came to our home in Sciotoville, Ohio, to visit. George was a thin man, who was always in good spirits and kept candy in his pockets.

George C. and Berthie O. Corn are found on the Pike County, Ohio, U.S. census for 1930. They were in Dwelling 183 (Family 190) in Mifflin Township. George was a farmer. Con Lyons, 23, and wife, Gladys, 21, were also in Dwelling 183 (Family 191).^{1935}

George and Olive had the following child:

169   i.   **Gladys^6 CORN** married **Con LYONS**

113.   Sarah B.^{5} PAYNE (John Shannon^4, John B.^{3}, Ellis^2, John^1) was born August 1886 in Lawrence County, Ohio.

The 1920 U.S. census for Mason Township includes Adolphus Payne, 37, and wife, Sarah, 33. They had two daughters, Florence, 13, and Thelma, 1 and 1/2.^{1936} The 1930 U.S. census for Mason Township shows Sarah as 43 years old; husband Adolphus G. Payne was 47; children Thelma A. was 11; Alma G., 8; Hazel F., 4; and Howard L., 2 and 3 months.^{1937}

Aunt "Sary" Payne was the sister of Edna Payne, my grandmother. For about 50 years after Edna died, some of her children and their families made a visit on Memorial Day to her grave and the graves of others at Fairview Baptist Church at Wilgus. On the way back from the graveyard, several of us would often stop to visit Sary. She lived in a log cabin by a stream near Wilgus. The cabin appeared well made, but it most decidedly was leaning. It was neat inside and had a country look, with rocking chairs and braided rugs. Sarah always greeted us with a friendly gusto. She was a jolly, happy person. I doubt that she ever knew that a castle in Wales is named for her Ragland ancestors. Were its occupants as content with life as she?

Sarah's cabin has been moved across the road and is now an historic landmark.

Sarah married **Adolphus G. PAYNE** son of Howard PAYNE and Diantha J. THORNTON. Howard was a son of Elliott Payne, son of Ellis, son of John. Adolphus was born November 1882.

Adolphus and Sarah are buried, with many other members of the Mason Township Paynes, at the Fairview Baptist Church graveyard. The church is on a hill at Wilgus, and when we visited on Memorial Day, we were surrounded by the green of forested hills patched with meadows. Many pink, white, and red flowers decorated the graves. As the years passed by, the flowers more often were made of plastic, but, still, the scene remained lovely.

They had the following children:

170   i.   **Florence^6 PAYNE** was born 1907.

171   ii. **Thelma PAYNE** was born about 1918.

172	iii.	**Alma G. PAYNE** was born 1922.
173	iv.	**Hazel F. PAYNE** was born 1926.
174	v.	**Howard L. PAYNE** was born 1928.

114. **Edna Mae[5] PAYNE** (John Shannon[4], John B.[3], Ellis[2], John[1]) was born 19 October 1890 in Lawrence County, Ohio. She died 18 February 1951 in Huntington, West Virginia, and was buried in Fairview Baptist Church graveyard at Wilgus, Ohio.[1938]

Edna married **Ezra Clare LEWIS** on 28 February 1911 in Lawrence County, Ohio. The marriage license states Edna was 21, the daughter of Shannon Payne and Emily Higgins. Ezra was a 24-year-old farmer, the son of James LEWIS and Rose PINKERMAN. Edna was born at Wilgus and Ezra at Scottown.[1939] Ezra was born 2 December 1886. He died July 1965 in Ironton, Ohio.

See the LEWIS Section for more information on Edna and Ezra Lewis and their descendants.

115. **Ona[5] PAYNE** (John Shannon[4], John B.[3], Ellis[2], John[1]) was born March 1894 in Lawrence County, Ohio. She died 15 September 1966 in Huntington, West Virginia. Ona was 71 years and 6 months old at the time of her death of a vascular accident.[1940]

Ona married **Herbert SCARBERRY**, son of Joseph SCARBERRY and Susan A. RIGNEY. Herbert was born 1901.

See the SCARBERRY (SCARBOROUGH) Section for more information on Ona and Herbert Scarberry.

117. **Blanche M.[5] PAYNE** (Jackson[4], Milton[3], Ellis[2], John[1]) was born 19 May 1878 in Lawrence County, Ohio. She died 1964.

The birth and death dates of Blanche and her husband and the names of her children and their spouses came from an article by Leona D. Payne that appears in *History of Lawrence County, Ohio, 1990*.[1941]

Blanche married **John Alva PAYNE**. John was born 9 November 1855 in Mason Township, Lawrence County, Ohio. He died 1924. John was a son of William Uriah PAYNE, son of William and Diana Payne.

They had the following children:

	175	i.	**Nettie[6] PAYNE** married a Mr. **DRUMMOND.**
	176	ii.	**Cornelius PAYNE.**
	177	iii.	**Hobert PAYNE.**
	178	iv.	**Emmit PAYNE.**
+	179	v.	**Alva Justin PAYNE** was born 21 March 1908 and died 18 January 1973.
	180	vi.	**Leslie PAYNE** married a Mr. **ROBINSON.**

118. **Jonas B.[5] PAYNE** (Jackson[4], Milton[3], Ellis[2], John[1]) was born 12 December 1883, and died September 1978. His residence at the time of his death was Willow Wood, Lawrence County, Ohio.[1942]

The 1910 U.S. census for Mason Township includes Jonas B. Payne. He was 26; his wife, Emma, was 20. Son Merril was named (age indecipherable). Jonas's parents, Jackson W. and Samantha, were living with him.[1943]

The 1920 U.S. census for Mason Township shows Jonas B. Payne living in Dwelling 34 (Family 34). He was 36; his wife, Emma C., was 30. Children were Merrill O., 11; Carl B., 8; Dorothy M., 1 ½ (?). Living with them were Jonas's parents, Jackson Payne, 72, and Samantha J., 70.[1944]

Jonas married **Emma C.** She was born about 1890 in Ohio.

They had the following children:

181	i.	**Merrill O.[6] PAYNE** was born about 1909.
182	ii.	**Carl B. PAYNE** was born about 1912.

183   iii.   **Dorothy M. PAYNE** was born about 1918.

134.   **Orin⁵ PAYNE** (Alonzo⁴, Elliott³, Ellis², John¹) was born about 1891.

The 1920 U.S. census for Mason Township, Lawrence County, Ohio, shows Orin Payne, 28, and wife, Verga, 24. They had son Forrest O, 2 years old and 1 month. Orin's mother, Minerva, 60, was also living with him.[1945]

Orin married **Verga BROWN** on December 22, 1916. Verga was 20, and Oren 24. The license reveals that she was a daughter of Elmer BROWN and wife, Martha. He lived in Wilgus and was a son of Alonzo Payne and Minerva Thornton.[1946]

They had the following child:

184   i.   **Forrest O.⁶ PAYNE** was born about 1918.

136.   **Adolphus⁵ PAYNE** (Howard⁴, Elliott³, Ellis², John¹) was born Nov 1882.

Adolphus married **Sarah B. PAYNE**, daughter of John Shannon PAYNE and Emily J. HIGGINS. Sarah was born August 1886 in Lawrence County, Ohio. *See above.*

Sixth Generation

157.   **Verla L.⁶ PAYNE** (Oscar Enoch⁵, Uriah L.⁴, Moses Marion³, William², John¹) was born 10 May 1915. She died 5 May 2010 at the Masonic Home in Springfield, Ohio.

I have a copy of a letter Verla sent to my uncle Ernest "Ray" Lewis, in which she gave some background on the Payne family. She wrote that when the Paynes originally came to Lawrence County, they were "something like Quakers," not believing in slavery.

Some of the Paynes of Bedford County were part of the Quaker community that attended South River Meeting House in Lynchburg. At this point I have been unable to determine if our Payne ancestors attended. It is obvious, however, that many of our Payne relatives became Baptists after moving to Ohio, for the graveyard at Fairview Baptist Church at Wilgus (Mason Township) contains many Paynes. In fact, Captain Uriah Payne was a charter member of the Fairview church. The first church building was erected in 1871, and the present brick building replaced it in 1966.[1947]

Verla died at the age of 94. She had lived a highly productive life. She was a charter member of St. Mark's United Methodist Church; a member of the Lawrence County Genealogical Society; First Families of Lawrence County, Ohio; the Virginia Genealogical Society; and the Orchid Society. Verla's obituary states that she was a former president of the Ohio Cosmetology Association. Her husbands, Melvin L. Watrous and Frank Switzer, preceded her in death, as did her son Melvin Watrous, brothers Ralph and Stanley Payne, and sister Lola McCoy. Her son Daniel Watrous; step-son Jack (Pat) Switzer, sister Betty Payne, half-sister Doris Gillette, and step-brother Jim Payne survived her.[1948]

Verla married (1) **Melvin L. WATROUS**.

They had the following children:

185   i.   **Melvin⁷ WATROUS**.

186   ii.   **Daniel WATROUS**.

She married (2) **Frank X. SWITZER**. Frank had a child from a previous marriage, Jack "Pat" SWITZER.

165.   **Raymond Forest⁶ PAYNE** (John William⁵, John Shannon⁴, John B.³, Ellis², John¹) was born 25 July 1911.

Raymond worked at various jobs in Springfield, Ohio, and retired from Mercy Medical Center in 1976.

Information on Raymond and his family is taken from the article by Sharon Conner in *History of Lawrence County, Ohio 1990*.[1949]

Raymond married **Clara Fern SAUNDERS,** daughter of Henry A. SAUNDERS and Nancy MYERS, on 2 July 1938 in Ironton, Ohio.

They had the following children:

    187   i.   **Leland**[7] **PAYNE** was born 26 February 1939.

    188   ii.   **Lowell PAYNE** was born 24 February 1941.

    189   iii.   **Marlene PAYNE** was born 3 October 1942.

166.   **Pauline Olive**[6] **PAYNE** (John William[5], John Shannon[4], John B.[3], Ellis[2], John[1]) was born 18 September 1913. She died 4 November 1977.[1950]

Pauline and her family lived at South Point, Ohio. She was a pretty woman with a lot of charm.

A clipping from an unidentified newspaper tells of a birthday dinner given by Mrs. Irwin Stephens of Scottown in honor of her father, J. W. Payne, and her aunt Mrs. Ezra Lewis. Pauline's husband and children Sandra Jean and Lewis Irvin were there. Guests included Mr. and Mrs. Raymond Payne and sons Lowell and Leland of Arabia; Mr. and Mrs. Herbert Scarberry and children Homer and Mary of Huntington; Mr. Fred and Billy Payne of Greasy Ridge; Norman Galloway; Mr. and Mrs. C. H. Young and daughters Rachel and Mabel of Portsmouth; Mr. Ezra Lewis; Mr. Paul Lewis; Thurman Lewis; Miss Betty Lewis; Carlas Lewis, all of Scottown; Miss Erma Lewis of Portsmouth.

J. W. Payne, Mrs. Ezra Lewis, and Mrs. Herbert Scarberry were brother and sisters. Edna (Payne) Lewis was born in October and J. W. Payne in November. Mrs. C. H. Young (Faye) was Pauline's niece. The clipping has no date, but the dinner would have occurred between 1938 and 1943.

Pauline married **Irvin STEPHENS**.

They had the following children:

+   190   i.   **Louis Irvin**[7] **STEPHENS.**

    191   ii.   **Sandra Jean STEPHENS** married and had five children

    192   iii.   **Peggy STEPHENS.**

167.   **Charles Frederick**[6] **PAYNE** (John William[5], John Shannon[4], John B.[3], Ellis[2], John[1]) was born 30 December 1917. He died 25 November 1983.

Charles served in World War II. After returning home, he moved to Evansville, Indiana.[1951]

Charles married **Kathryn**.

They had the following child:

    193   i.   **Bobby**[7] **PAYNE.**

168.   **William Earl**[6] **PAYNE**, "Billy," (John William[5], John Shannon[4], John B.[3], Ellis[2], John[1]) was born 5 January 1924.

Billy was ordained as a United Baptist minister and was a chaplain for the Veterans of Foreign Wars. During World War II he fought in the South Pacific. He enjoyed singing and was part of the "Payne Family," a group who performed on WIRO radio. He was a truck driver, self-employed.

Information on Billy Payne and his family is taken from an article by Larry and Sharon Conner in *History of Lawrence County, Ohio 1990*.[1952]

William married **Mimia Juanita CARROL,** the daughter of Thomas H. CARROL and Nancy Rose Ann BROWN, on 11 April

1942.

They had the following children:

+ 194 i. **Ronald Lee[7] PAYNE** was born 21 December 1942.
+ 195 ii. **Sharon Kay PAYNE** was born 20 May 1949.
+ 196 iii. **Brenda Sue PAYNE** was born 4 February 1956.
    197 iv. **Jimmy PAYNE** was born 16 January 1960.
    198 v. **Timmy PAYNE** was born 16 January 1960.
+ 199 vi. **Terry Von PAYNE** was born 24 April 1961.
+ 200 vii. **Teddy Don PAYNE** was born 24 April 1961.

179.   **Alva Justin[6] PAYNE** (Blanche M.[5] PAYNE, Jackson[4], Milton[3], Ellis[2], John[1]) was born 21 March 1908. He died 18 January 1973.

Alva married **Pearl Grey VERMILLION**, daughter of Henry Burton VERMILLION and Katherine Elizabeth DAVISSON. Pearl was born 17 August 1907.[1953]

> See above, the Fifth Generation, for Alva and Pearl's children. Blanche M. Payne, descended from Ellis Payne, was over 20 years younger than her husband, John A. Payne, descended from Ellis Payne's brother, William.

Seventh Generation

190.   **Louis Irvin[7] STEPHENS**, "Louie,"(Pauline Olive[6] PAYNE, John William[5], John Shannon[4], John B.[3], Ellis[2], John[1]) was born 1936.

Louie attended Harding College, Searcy, Arkansas, majoring in business. Religion was his minor. He worked for a religious publication company and at one time raced boats.

Louis married **Violet SPURLOCK** on 12 June 1965.

Violet runs her own business in her home. She does monogramming for sporting goods store.

They had the following children:

    201 i. **Tanya[8] STEPHENS** was born 1969.
    202 ii. **Anita STEPHENS** was born 1973.

194.   **Ronald Lee[7] PAYNE** (William Earl[6], John William[5], John Shannon[4], John B.[3], Ellis[2], John[1]) was born 1942.

Ronald worked at Ashland Oil Company.

Ronald married **Betty Lou SWINDLER**

They had the following children:

    203 i. **Dwayne Lee[8] PAYNE**.
    204 ii. **Kara Denise PAYNE**.

195.   **Sharon Kay[7] PAYNE** (William Earl[6], John William[5], John Shannon[4], John B.[3], Ellis[2], John[1]) was born 1949.

A certified teacher, Sharon is employed by the Lawrence County Head Start Program.

Sharon married **Larry Franklin CONNER.**

They had the following children:

    205   i. **Angela Denise^8 CONNER**.

    206   ii. **Spring Dawn CONNER**.

196.   **Brenda Sue^7 PAYNE** (William Earl^6, John William^5, John Shannon^4, John B.^{3}, Ellis^2, John^1) was born 1956. She is associated with a privately owned carpet business.

Brenda married **Darrell FOWLER.**

They had the following children:

    207   i. **Bryan Keith^8 FOWLER**.

    208   ii. **Tiffany Nicole FOWLER**.

199.   **Terry Von^7 PAYNE** (William Earl^6, John William^5, John Shannon^4, John B^3., Ellis^2, John^1) was born 1961. Terry is employed by Auto Works as a manager.

Terry married **Angie KINCAID.**

They had the following children:

    209   i. **Andrew Marshall^8 PAYNE**.

    210   ii **Dustin Mitchell PAYNE**.

200.   **Teddy Don^7 PAYNE** (William Earl^6, John William^5, John Shannon^4, John B.^{3}, Ellis^2, John^1) was born 1961. Teddy uses his skills as a certified welder at Ashland Asphalt.

Teddy married **Becky GORBY.**

They had the following child:

    211   i. **Hazel Irene^8 PAYNE**.

Sources

[1610] John Payne of Maryland from the executors of Richard Randolph, Gent., 112 acres on the Middle and North Forks of Rock Castle Creek [a branch of Goose Creek], 1774, Bedford Co. Deed Book 5:209; Mary and John Payne to George Nichols 120 acres on both sides of Goose Creek, adjacent Greer, 1789. Wits: Wm. Payne, Flayl Payne, Archibald Nichols, Bedford Co. Deed Book 6:142.

[1611] "The Payne Family of Goochland &c." in *Genealogies of Virginia Families from Tyler's Quarterly and Historical and Genealogical Magazine*, 4 vols. (Baltimore: Genealogical Pub. Co., 1981), vol. 4, Healy-Pryor, 630-631, 635.

[1612] Bedford County, Virginia, Deed Books 8:232; 11:588.

[1613] Bedford County, Virginia, Survey Book 1:63.

[1614] Ann Chilton, *Bedford County, Virginia Deed Book, C-3* (Mountain Press, 1992), 14.

[1615] Bedford County, Virginia, Survey Book 2:329.

[1616] Bedford County, Virginia, Deed Books 6:65, 3:318.

[1617] Bedford County, Virginia, Deed Book 7:319.

[1618] Joida Whitten, *Abstracts of Bedford County, Virginia, Will Book 2 With Inventories and Accounts 1788-1803* (Dallas: Joida Whitten, 1980), 93.

[1619] Bedford County, Virginia, Court Orders 1784-1786, 8:279.

[1620] Bedford County, Virginia, Deed Book 8:232.

[1621] Bedford County Personal Property Taxes 1782-1805, Library of Virginia, microfilm reel 34.

[1622] "The Payne Family of Goochland &c." 635.

[1623] Bedford County, Virginia, Deed Book 9:267.

[1624] Earle S. Dennis and Jane E. Smith, *Marriage Bonds of Bedford County, Virginia 1755-1800* (Baltimore: Genealogical Pub. Co., Inc., 1975), 5.

[1625] Janice Lewis, http://genforum.genealogy.com/va/Bedford/messages/773.html.

[1626] Dennis and Smith, *Marriage Bonds of Bedford County, Virginia 1755-1800*, 72

[1627] Ibid.,.72.

[1628] Ibid.,.47.

[1629] Bedford County, Virginia, Deed Book 8:112-113.

[1630] Bedford County, Virginia, Deed Book, 8:400-402.

[1631] Bedford County, Virginia, Deed Book, 11:181.

[1632] Whitten, *Abstracts of Bedford County, Virginia, Will Book 2*, 66-67.

[1633] Loose records, Bedford County, Virginia, courthouse.

[1634] Bedford County, Virginia, Deed Book 11:321-322.

[1635] Bedford County, Virginia, Deed Book 8:421

[1636] Bedford County marriages, index (husbands), Bedford County, Virginia, courthouse, 7.

[1637] Bedford County, Virginia, Deed Book 9:208-209.

[1638] Bedford County, Virginia, Deed Book 9:21.

[1639] Bedford County Personal Property Taxes 1782-1805, Library of Virginia, microfilm reel 34.

[1640] Bedford County, Virginia, Deed Book 10:26.

[1641] Bedford County, Virginia, Deed Book 11:912-913.

[1642] Bedford County Personal Property Taxes 1782-1805, Library of Virginia, microfilm reel 34.

[1643] Bedford County, Virginia, Deed Book 11:588-589.

[1644] Bedford County, Virginia, Deed Book 11:588.

[1645] Bedford County, Virginia, Survey Book 2:283.

[1646] Bedford County, Virginia, Deed Book 11:961-962.

[1647] Bedford County, Virginia, Deed Book 13:589.

[1648] Dennis and Smith, *Marriage Bonds of Bedford County, Virginia 1755-1800*, 72.

[1649] Bedford County, Virginia, Court Orders 1808-1811, 15:72.

[1650] W. Christian, *Lynchburg and Its People* (Lynchburg: J. P. Bell, Co., 1900), 20; http://Familytreemaker.genealogy.com/users/m/a/r/Thomas-A-Markham and

[1651] Bedford County, Virginia, Deed Book 8:113-114.

[1652] Bedford County, Virginia, Loose Wills.
[1653] "Family XXIII Joseph Payne and Phebe of Bedford or Franklin Co Va," from the Payne Family files of Dorothy PayneMcClure, P.O. Box 2889 Evergreen, CO 80439 updated 22 Apr 1985 (Bedford City/County Museum).1.
[1654] Bedford County, Virginia, Survey Book 2:269.
[1655] "Family XXIII Joseph Payne and Phebe," 2.
[1656] Bedford County, Virginia, Survey Book 2:269.
[1657] "Family XXIII Joseph Payne and Phebe," 1. James Payne's signature from Bedford Co. loose records, Bedford Co. courthouse.. Among the loose records there is also a bond signed by Wm. Payne when he was going to marry Peggy Anderson in 1813, and William signed with an X. James Payne secured the bond, and he, too, signed with an X, both these men making the Xs look more like crosses.
[1658] Bedford County, Virginia, Deed Book 5:496; Bedford County, Will Book 3:13.
[1659] William Armstrong Crozier, *Virginia County Records Spotsylvania County 1721-1800* (Baltimore: Genealogical Publishing Co., 1978), 25.
[1660] Ibid., 170.
[1661] Ibid., 177.
[1662] Ibid., 239.
[1663] Ibid., 307.
[1664] Ibid., 401.
[1665] John Frederick Dorman, *Culpeper County, Virginia, Deeds, Volume Five 1769-1772* (Falmouth, Va., 1991), 47-48.
[1666] Crozier, *Virginia County Records Spotsylvania County 1721-1800*, 1.
[1667] John Frederick Dorman, *Orange County, Virginia, Will Book 2, 1744-1778* (Washington D. C., 1961), 20-21.
[1668] Crozier, *Virginia County Records Spotsylvania County 1721-1800*,199.
[1669] Ibid., 199-200.
[1670] Crozier, *Virginia County Records Spotsylvania County 1721-1800*, 158.
[1671] Ibid..6.
[1672] Ibid., 143.
[1673] Ibid., 56.
[1674] Bedford County, Virginia, Deed Book 11:84.
[1675] Chilton, *Bedford County Virginia Deed Book C-3*, 27.
[1676] Dennis and Smith, *Marriage Bonds of Bedford County, Virginia 1755-1800*, 65.
[1677] Bedford County,Virginia, Deed Book 7:252-253.
[1678] Rosalie Edith Davis, *Hanover County, Virginia Court Records, 1733-1735: Deeds, Wills, and Inventories* (Manchester, Mo: Davis, 1979), 78, 74.
[1679] John Poindexter Landers and Robert Downs, *Poindexter, Poingdestre-Poindexter A Norman Family Through the Ages 1250-1977* (Austin: Robert Downs Poindexter, 1977), 95.
[1680] William Armstrong Crozier, *Virginia County Records*, new series, v. 1 (1913; reprinted Baltimore: Genealogical Publishing Company, 1962), 31.
[1681] Rosalie Edith Davis, *Louisa County, Virginia, Deed Books A and B 1742-1759* (Bellevue, Washington, 1976), 145.
[1682] Ibid., 98.
[1683] *Virginia Land Records: from the Virginia Magazine of History and Biography, the William and Mary College Quarterly, and Tyler's Quarterly*, indexed by Gary Parks (Baltimore: Genealogical Pub. Co., 1982), 440.
[1684] Ruth & Sam Sparacio, *Westmoreland County, Virginia, Deed & Will Abstracts 1732-1734* (McLean, Va: The Antient Press, 1995), 19.
[1685] Eaton, David Wolfe, *Historical Atlas of Westmoreland County, Virginia, Patents, Showing How Lands Were Patented From the Crown & Proprietors of the Northern Neck of Virginia, Including Some History of the Patentees, Indians, Church & State, Parishes, Ministers, Prominent Men, Surveys, Portraits, Maps, Airplane Views & Other Data* (Richmond: The Dietz Press, 1942), 70.
[1686] John Frederick Dorman, *Westmoreland County, Virginia, Deeds and Wills No. 5 1712-1716* (Washington, D.C., 1989), 63.
[1687] John Frederick Dorman, *Westmoreland County, Virginia, Deeds, Patents, Etc., 1665-167*, pt.III (Washington, D.C., 1974), 65.
[1688] Brooks Payne, *The Paynes of Virginia*, 2nd ed., (Harrisonburg, Va: C. J. Carrier Co, 1977), 3.
[1689] Augusta Bridgland Middleton Fothergill, *Wills of Westmoreland County, Virginia, 1654-1800* (Richmond, Virginia: Appeals Press, 1925), 105.

[1690] Ibid., 85.
[1691] Marian Dodson Chiarito, *Will Book O, 1752-1773, Halifax County, Virginia* (Nathalie, Va: Clarkton Press, 1982), 52-53.
[1692] Ibid., 56.
[1693] William Wade Hinshaw, *Encyclopedia of American Quaker Genealogy* (Ann Arbor, Mich.: Edwards Brothers, Inc., 1936-1950), 6:335.
[1694] Lela C. Adams, *Abstracts of Pittsylvania County, Virginia, Wills, 1767-1820* (Easley, S.C.: Southern Historical Press, Inc., 1986), 43-44.
[1695] William Douglas, *The Douglas Register: Being a Detailed Record of Births, Marriages, and Deaths Together with Other Interesting Notes, as Kept by the Rev. William Douglas from 1750 to 1797; an Index of Goochland Wills, Notes on the French-Huguenot Refugees who Lived in Manakin-town* (Baltimore: Genealogical Pub.Co., 1977, c1966), 98.
[1696] Dennis and Smith, *Marriage Bonds of Bedford County*, 1.
[1697] Whitten, *Abstracts of Bedford County, Virginia, Will Book 2*, 80-81.
[1698] Rosalie Edith Davis, *Louisa County, Virginia, Deed Books A & B* (Bellevue, Wash.: Davis, 1976-c1983), 84.
[1699] Dennis Ray Hudgins, *Cavaliers and Pioneers: Abstracts of Virginia Land Patents and Grants: Volume Six, 1749-1762* (Virginia Genealogical Society, 1998), 284. (Patent Book 33:898.)
[1700] Benjamin B. Weisiger III, *Goochland County, Virginia, Wills and Deeds 1742-1749* (Richmond: Rocky Road Press, 1984), 12.
[1701] Joida Whitten, *Abstracts of Bedford County, Virginia, Wills, Inventories and Accounts 1754-1787* (Dallas: Joida Whitten), 17-18.
[1702] Malcolm Harris, *A History of Louisa County, Virginia* (Richmond: Dietz Press, 1936), 408A; Charles James Ragland, Jr., *The Raglands: The History of a British-American Family* (Winston-Salem, N.C.: Charles James Ragland, Jr., 1987), 2:102.
[1703] Whitten, *Abstracts of Bedford County, Virginia, Will Book 2*, 11.
[1704] Jarret or Jarred or Garrad Brickey entry, *International Genealogical Index (IGI)* (Salt Lake City: Family History Library, printed June 22, 2010), citing source call no.: 1553483, batch 5009960, sheet 10.
[1705] C. G. Chamberlayne, *The Vestry Book of St. Paul's Parish, Hanover County, Virginia, 1706-1786*, reprint ed. (Richmond: Virginia State Library and Archives, 1989), 277.
[1706] Ibid., 342-343.
[1707] Ruth & Sam Sparacio, *Virginia County Court Records, Deed & Will Abstracts of Albemarle County, Virginia, 1748-1752* (McLean, Va: The Antient Press, 1990), 55.
[1708] Benjamin B. Weisiger, III, *Goochland County, Virginia, Wills and Deeds, 1736-1742* (Richmond: Weisiger, c1984), 55.
[1709] Dennis Ray Hudgins, *Cavaliers and Pioneers: Abstracts of Virginia Land Patents and Grants: Volume Six, 1749-1762*, p.7. [Patent Book 29:113].
[1710] Dennis Ray Hudgins, *Cavaliers and Pioneers: Abstracts of Virginia Land Patents and Grants: Volume Five, 1741-1749* (Richmond: Virginia Genealogical Society, 1994), 87 [Patent Book 22:296].
[1711] William Lindsay Hopkins, *St. James Northam Parish Vestry Book 1744-1850, Goochland County, Virginia* (Richmond: William Lindsay Hopkins, 1987), 6.
[1712] Whitten, *Abstracts of Bedford County, Virginia, Wills, Inventories and Accounts 1754-1787*, 61.
[1713] Nancy Chappelear and Kate Binford Hatch, *Abstracts of Louisa County, Virginia, Will Books 1743-1801* (Nancy Chappelear and Kate Binford Hatch, 1964), 7.
[1714] Bedford County Personal Property Taxes 1782-1805, Library of Virginia Microfilm reel 34.
[1715] Vivian Pyles Coleman, "Payne," in *History of Lawrence County, Ohio, 1990*, Lawrence County Historical Book Committee, eds. (Walsworth Publishing, 1990), 271.
[1716] Betty Huff Bryant, *Building Neighborhoods: Jackson County, Tennessee, Prior to 1820: Abstractions from Record Group 50, Early Land Records, Tennessee State Library and Archives* (Austin, Texas: B. H. Bryant, c1992), 28-325-10583, FHL microfiche no. 6101877-3.
[1717] Ibid., 30-471-17741.
[1718] Ibid.,, 30-433-17448.
[1719] Early Tax Returns, Ohio, Auditor of State Tax Duplicates, Lawrence County, 1820-1829, Archives Library Division, Ohio Historical Society, Franklin County, Ohio, GR2533, v. 738 (Utah no. 2095).
[1720] Ibid., v. 739.
[1721] Ibid., v. 740.
[1722] Ibid., v. 742.

[1723] 1830 U. S. census, Lawrence County, Ohio, Mason Township, p. 331.

[1724] Lawrence County, Ohio, Marriage Records Vol. 1-5, 1817-1857, p. 123, FHL film no. 317,716.

[1725] Lawrence County Historical Book Committee, eds. *History of Lawrence County, Ohio, 1990*, 4.

[1726] T. A. Walton, *Ironton Register (Ironton, Ohio) Lawrence County, Continuation of History of Early Times*, entry of 10 March, 1904, 53-53.

[1727] Hinshaw, *Encyclopedia of American Quaker Genealogical History*, 6: 911.

[1728] Bryant, *Jackson County, Tennessee, Building Neighborhoods*, 24-27-1981.

[1729] Bedford County, Virginia, Deed Book 9:371-372.

[1730] Bedford County, Virginia, Deed Book 10:161-162.

[1731] Bedford County, Virginia, Deed Book 3:19.

[1732] Hinshaw, *Encyclopedia of American Quaker Genealogical History*, 6:384.

[1733] Drusilla Payne Mogavero, "Payne and Wilson," in *History of Lawrence County, Ohio, 1990*, 63.

[1734] 1830 U.S. census, Lawrence County, Ohio, Mason Township, 331-332.

[1735] Bryant, *Jackson County, Tennessee, Building Neighborhoods*, Book 29-482-14083.

[1736] Bedford Co., Va., loose records, Bedford Courthouse.

[1737] 1850 U.S. census, pop. sch., Lawrence Co., Decatur Township, p. 652, dwelling/family 69/51 (Elizabeth Moorman household); dwelling/family 68/69 (James Moorman household).

[1738] Ibid., p. 653, dwelling 71, family no. indecipherable.

[1739] 1850 U.S. census, pop. sch., Lawrence Co., Mason Township, p. 734, dwelling/family 162/165.

[1740] Dennis and Smith, *Marriage Bonds of Bedford County*, 47.

[1741] Bedford County, Virginia, Court Orders 11:349.

[1742] Bedford County, Virginia, Court Orders 12:139.

[1743] Bedford County, Virginia, Court Orders 11:343, 351.

[1744] Dennis and Smith, *Marriage Bonds of Bedford County*, 37, 46.

[1745] Norman L. Payne of Louisville, Ky., "Joseph Payne of Bedford County, Virginia" (research found in Bedford County Museum, Bedford, Va.), 6.

[1746] Douglas Summers Brown, *A History of Lynchburg's Pioneer Quakers and Their Meeting House*, bicentennial ed. (Session of Quaker Memorial Presbyterian Church, c1986), 60-61.

[1747] Jay Worrall, Jr., *The Friendly Virginians, America's First Quakers* (Athens, Ga: Iberian Pub. Co., 1994), 272-273.

[1748] Will of Charles Moorman, Louisa Co. Will Book 2:432-434, http://www.stanford.edu/~jamila/Moorman_Will.html; the source for the parents of the James Moorman who married Elizabeth Payne is found in Dorothy Ford Wulfeck, *Marriages of Some Virginia Residents 1607-1800* (1966; reprinted, Baltimore: Genealogical Pub. Co., 1986), vol. II (surnames Mi-Q), 48.

[1749] Nancy Chappelear and Kate Binford Hatch, *Abstracts of Louisa County, Virginia, Will Books 1743-1801* (Delaplane, Va:, 1964), 86.

[1750] Douglas, *The Douglas Register*, 145.

[1751] Ibid.

[1752] Weisiger, *Goochland County, Virginia, Wills and Deeds, 1736-1742*, 57.

[1753] Dolley Madison Biography – National First Ladies' Library (http://www.firstladies.org/biographies/firstladies.aspx?biography=4).

[1754] Early Tax Returns, Lawrence County 1820-1829, v. 738.

[1755] 1830 U.S. census, Lawrence County, Ohio, Mason Township, p.332.

[1756] Hinshaw, *Encyclopedia of American Quaker Genealogical History*, 6:976; Drusilla Payne Mogavero, "Curtis Payne," in *History of Lawrence County, Ohio, 1990*, 271-272.

[1757] 1850 U. S. census, pop. sch.,, Lawrence County, Mason Township, p. 733, dwelling/family 159/162 (Samuel Lewis household); dwelling/family 160/163 (Moses Payne household); pp. 733-734, dwelling/family 161/164 (Marstie Payne household); p. 734, dwelling/family 162/165, Ellis Payne household.

[1758] 1860 U.S. census, pop. sch., Lawrence County, Mason Township, p. 177, dwelling/family 1203/1193.

[1759] Coleman, "Payne," 271.

[1760] Early Tax Returns, Lawrence County 1820-1829, v. 738.

[1761] Bryant, *Jackson County, Tennessee, Building Neighborhoods*, Book 29-482-14083.

[1762] 1830 U.S. census, Lawrence County, Ohio, Mason Township, p.331.

[1763] 1850 U.S. census, pop. sch., Lawrence County, Ohio, Mason Township, p.734, dwelling/family 162/165.

[1764] Vivian Pyles Coleman, "Payne," 271.
[1765] *Atlas of Lawrence County, Ohio; Hardesty – 1882, Lake -1887* (Chicago and Toledo: H. H. Hardesty & Co.,1882), 23.
[1766] Bedford County, Virginia, Deed Book 5:386.
[1767] Charles James Ragland, Jr., *The Raglands: The History of a British-American Family* (Charles James Ragland, Jr.,1987), 2:220.
[1768] Douglas, *The Douglas Register*, 84.
[1769] Ragland, *The Raglands: The History of a British-American Family*, 2:205.
[1770] Bryant, *Jackson County, Tennessee, Building Neighborhoods*, 28-326-10586.
[1771] Ibid., 29-133-11992.
[1772] Ibid., 28-338-10627.
[1773] Ibid., 29-114-11889.
[1774] Hinshaw, *Encyclopedia of American Quaker Genealogical History*, 6:981.
[1775] Bryant, *Jackson County, Tennessee, Building Neighborhoods*, 24-27-1981.
[1776] Ibid., 30-433-17448.
[1777] Ragland, *The Raglands: The History of a British-American Family*, 2 205.
[1778] Ibid., 2: 220.
[1779] Ibid., 2:100-101.
[1780] Chappelear and Hatch, *Abstracts of Louisa County, Virginia, Will Books 1742-1801*, 80.
[1781] Harris, *A History of Louisa County, Virginia*, 408.
[1782] Douglas, *The Douglas Register*, 109.
[1783] Chappelear and Hatch, *Abstracts of Louisa County, Virginia, Will Books 1742-1801*, 16.
[1784] Davis, *Louisa County, Virginia, Deed Books A & B*, 75-76.
[1785] Louisa Deed Book D ½: 435, http:// www.whitakergiftfoundation.com/deeds/deed9.htm.
[1786] Dennis and Smith, *Marriage Bonds of Bedford County*, 30.
[1787] Rosalie Edith Davis, *Louisa County, Virginia, Deed Books C, C ½, D, and D ½, 1759-1774* (Manchester, Mo., Rosalie Edith Davis, 1977), 45.
[1788] Louisa Co. Deed Book C:77, www.whitakergiftfoundation.com/deeds/deed6.htm.
[1789] Chappelear and Hatch, *Abstracts of Louisa County, Virginia, Will Books 1742-1801*, 111.
[1790] Weisiger, *Goochland County, Virginia, Wills & Deeds, 1736-1742*, 52.
[1791] T. L. C. Genealogy, *Bedford County, Virginia, Deeds, 1761-1766* (Miami Beach, Fla: T.L.C. Genealogy,1991), 4.
[1792] Dennis and Smith, *Marriage Bonds of Bedford County*, 2.
[1793] Whitten, *Abstracts of Bedford County, Virginia, Wills, Inventories and Accounts 1754-1787*, 141-142.
[1794] Norman L. Payne of Louisville, Ky., "Joseph Payne of Bedford County, Virginia" (research found in Bedford County Museum), 4-5.
[1795] Bedford County, Virginia, loose records, found at Bedford County Courthouse.
[1796] Davis, *Louisa County, Virginia, Deed Books A & B*, 145.
[1797] Ibid., 39.
[1798] Dorothy Ford Wulfeck. *Marriages of Some Virginia Residents 1607-1800* (Baltimore: Genealogical Publishing Co., 1986), vol. I (surnames A-B), 26.
[1799] Chamberlayne, *The Vestry Book of St. Paul's Parish, Hanover County, Virginia, 1706-1786*, 342-343.
[1800] Ancestors of Richard Anderson, http://mccormack.cherrytreewv.com/mccormackandalliedfamiliesofvaa..,, Downloaded June 8, 2010.
[1801] Davis, *Louisa County, Virginia, Deed Books A & B*, 28.
[1802] Ibid., 49.
[1803] Eric G. Grundset, *Buckingham County, Virginia, Surveyor's Plat Book 1762-1858* (Burk, Va.: E. G. Grundset, 1983), 5.
[1804] Ibid., 7.
[1805] Dennis Ray Hudgins, *Cavaliers & Pioneers: Abstracts* and *of Virginia Land Patents Grants: Volume Six, 1749-1762*, p. 7. [Patent Book 29:113]
[1806] Mrs. Stacy, "Ragland: Gwillam ap Jenkin ap Adam, Master Sergeant of Abergavenny," in *Genealogies of Virginia Families: from Tyler's Quarterly Historical and Genealogical Magazine,* 4 vols. (Baltimore: Genealogical Pub. Co., 1981), v.III (Pinkethman-Tyler): 111-114.

[1807] John R. Kenyon, *Raglan Castle* (1988, Cardiff: Cadw: Welsh Historic Monuments, Brunel House, revised edition 1994), 14.
[1808] Ibid., 6-9, 18-21.
[1809] Ragland, *The Raglands: The History of a British-American Family*, 2:100-101.
[1810] Malcolm Harris, *A History of Louisa County, Virginia*, 408A, 407-408.
[1811] Petersburg Area Regional Tourism: Bed & Breakfast, http:www.petersburgarea.org/Index.aspx?page=205.
[1812] *The New Encyclopaedia Britannica in 30 Volumes*, Micropaedia, 15th ed. s.v. "Raglan, FitzRoy James Henry Somerset, 1st Baron"; Raglan sleeve – Wikipedia, the free encyclopedia, http://en.wikipedia.org/wiki/Raglan_sleeve.
[1813] Coleman, *Lawrence County, Ohio, 1990*, 271.
[1814] Lawrence County, Ohio, Marriage Records, Vol. 1-5, 1817-1857, p. 176, FHL film no. 317, 716, Salt Lake City, Utah.
[1815] 1850 U.S. census, pop. sch., Lawrence County, Ohio, Decatur Township, p. 652, dwelling/family 68/ 69 (James Moorman household), and dwelling/family 69/ 51 (Elizabeth Moorman household).
[1816] Drusilla Payne Mogavero, "Curtis Payne," in *History of Lawrence County, Ohio, 1990*, Lawrence County Historical Book Committee, eds. (Walsworth Publishing Co., 199), 271-272.
[1817] 1850 U.S. census, pop. sch., Lawrence County, Ohio, Mason Township, p. 733, dwelling/family 160/163 (Moses Payne household); dwelling/family 159/ 162, (Samuel Lewis household).
[1818] 1860 U.S. census, pop. sch., Lawrence County, Ohio, Mason Township, p. 178, dwelling/family 1208/1197.
[1819] 1870 U.S. census, pop. sch., Lawrence County, Ohio, Mason Township, dwelling/family 116/110 (Moses Payne household); dwelling/family 117/111 (Elliot Payne household).
[1820] 1880 U.S. census, pop. sch.,, Lawrence County, Ohio, Mason Township, p. 240A, FHL film no. 1,255,039, National Archives film no.T9-1039.
[1821] Billee Hammond Schlaudt, *Marriage Records of Lawrence County, Ohio*, (Houston: B.H. Schlaudt, 1987), Books 1-6, p. 130.
[1822] Mogavero, "Curtis Payne," 272.
[1823] 1850 U.S. census, pop. sch., Lawrence County, Ohio, Mason Township, pp. 733-734, dwelling/family 161/164 (Marstie Payne household); dwelling/family 160/163 (Moses Payne household); dwelling/family 162/ 165 (Ellis Payne household).
[1824] Schlaudt, *Marriage Records of Lawrence County, Ohio*, Books 1-6, p. 130.
[1825] 1880 U.S. census, pop. sch., Lawrence County, Ohio, Mason Township, p. 242A, FHL film no. 1,255,039; National Archives film no.T9-1039.
[1826] Schlaudt, *Marriage Records of Lawrence County, Ohio*, Books 1-6, p. 130.
[1827] *Atlas of Lawrence County, Ohio: Hardesty- 1882; Lake - 1887*, 23.
[1828] 1850 U.S. census, pop. sch., Lawrence County, Ohio, Decatur Township, pp. 652-653, dwelling/family 69/ 73 (John B. Payne household); dwelling/family 69/ 51 (Elizabeth Moorman household).
[1829] 1850 U.S. census, pop. sch., Lawrence County, Ohio, Mason Township, p. 734, dwelling/family 162/165.
[1830] 1860 U.S. census, pop. sch., Lawrence County, Ohio, Mason Township, p.178, dwelling/family 1213/ 1203 (John Payne household); dwelling/family 1212/ 1202 (Jane Payne household).
[1831] 1870 U.S. census, pop. sch., Lawrence County, Ohio, Mason Township, pp. 1-2, dwelling/family 6/6 (John Payne household); dwelling/family 7/7 (Jane Fallowell household); dwelling/family 8/8 (Milton Payne household).
[1832] 1880 U.S. census, pop. sch., Lawrence County, Ohio, Mason Township, p. 252B, FHL film no. 1,255,039; National Archives film no.T9-1039.
[1833] *Atlas of Lawrence County, Ohio: Hardesty – 1882; Lake – 1887*, 23.
[1834] Ibid.
[1835] Ibid.
[1836] Ibid.
[1837] Ibid.
[1838] Ohio Probate Court (Lawrence County), *Death Records, 1867-1938*, Vol. 1, 1867-1888, FHL film no. 317,746, Salt Lake City, Utah.
[1839] 1850 U.S. census, pop. sch., Lawrence County, Ohio, Mason Township, p. 712, dwelling/family 23/23.
[1840] 1860 U.S. census, pop. sch., Lawrence County, Ohio, Mason Township, pp. 177-178, dwelling/family 1204/1194 (Milton Payne household); dwelling/family 1203/1193 (Deana Payne household).
[1841] 1870 U.S. census, pop. sch., Lawrence County, Ohio, Mason Township, p. 2, dwelling/family 8/8.
[1842] Schlaudt, *Marriage Records of Lawrence County, Ohio*, Books 1-6, p. 130.
[1843] 1900 U.S. census, pop. sch., Lawrence County, Ohio, Mason Township, sheet 8A, dwelling/family 144/145.

[1844] 1860 U.S. census, pop. sch., Lawrence County, Ohio, Mason Township, pp. 178-179, dwelling/family 1212/1202 (Jane Payne household); dwelling/family 1211/1201 (Elliot Payne household); dwelling/family 1213/1203 (John Payne household).
[1845] 1870 U.S. census, pop. sch., Lawrence County, Ohio, Mason Township, p. 2, dwelling/family 7/7.
[1846] 1880 U.S. census, pop. sch., Lawrence County, Ohio, Mason Township, p. 252B, FHL film no. 1,255,039; National Archives film no.T9-1039.
[1847] Payne – Followell marriage, International Genealogical Index, v5.0. (No sources given). FHL, Salt Lake City, Utah.
[1848] Coleman, "Payne," 271.
[1849] 1860 U.S. census, pop. sch., Lawrence County, Ohio, Mason Township, p. 178, dwelling/family 1211/1201.
[1850] 1870 U.S. census, pop. sch., Lawrence County, Ohio, Mason Township, p. (indecipherable), dwelling/family 117/111 (Elliot Payne household); 116/110 (Moses Payne household).
[1851] 1880 U.S. census, pop. sch., Lawrence County, Ohio, Mason Township, p. 252B, FHL film no. 1,255,039; National Archives film no. T9-1039.
[1852] Schlaudt, *Marriage Records of Lawrence County, Ohio*, Books 1-6, p. 130.
[1853] Coleman, "Payne," 271.
[1854] 1900 U.S. census, pop. sch., Lawrence County, Ohio, Mason Township, p. 360, dwelling/family 16/16 (Charlotte Payne household); dwelling/family 17/17 (Elmer Payne household).
[1855] 1860 U.S. census, pop. sch., Lawrence County, Ohio, Mason Township, p. 178, dwelling/family 1210/1200 (Burrell Payne household); dwelling/family 1211/1201 (Elliot Payne household).
[1856] 1870 U.S. census, pop. sch., Lawrence County, Ohio, Mason Township, p.1, dwelling/family 4/4.
[1857] 1880 U.S. census, pop. sch., Lawrence County, Ohio, Mason Township, p. 253C, FHL film no.1,255,039; National Archives film no. T9-1039.
[1858] 1900 U.S. census, pop. sch., Lawrence County, Ohio, Mason Township, p. 6A, dwelling/family 106/107.
[1859] Schlaudt, *Marriage Records of Lawrence County, Ohio*, Books 1-6, p. 130.
[1860] 1920 U.S. census, pop. sch., Lawrence County, Ohio, Mason Township, p. 3A, dwelling/family 41.
[1861] Verla Payne Watrons Switzer, "Clay – Payne," *History of Lawrence County, Ohio, 1990*, 117.
[1862] 1880 U.S. census, pop. sch., Lawrence County, Ohio, Mason Township, p. 240A, FHL film no.1,255,039; National Archives film no.T9-1039.
[1863] Switzer, "Clay-Payne," in *History of Lawrence County, Ohio, 1990*, 117.
[1864] Charles E. Payne, "Honorable Discharge from the United States Army," World War I Record File No. C4954. Charles' identification: #4570297, PVT. C. D. 4th Regt. Casuals White. Record found at Lawrence County Court House, Ironton, Ohio.
[1865] Lawrence County, Ohio, Marriages 1905-1910, vol. 22, 1908-1909, certificate no. 5411; Roll No. VDS 360, Ohio. FHL film no. 317,724.
[1866] Mogavero, "Curtis Payne," 272.
[1867] 1900 U.S. census, pop. sch., Lawrence County, Ohio, Mason Township, p. 10A, dwelling/family 191/192 (Moses . Payne household); dwelling/family 190/191 (Howard Payne household).
[1868] Mogavero, "Curtis Payne," 272.
[1869] Lawrence County, Ohio, Marriages 1905-1910, vol. 21, 1905-1908, certificate no. 4441; Roll No. VDS 360, Ohio. FHL film no.317,724.
[1870] Lawrence County, Ohio, Marriages vol. 23-25, 1910-1916, vol. 24, certificate no. 8013. FHL film no.1,574,145.
[1871] Lawrence County, Ohio, Marriages vol. 21-22, 1905-1910, vol. 22, 1908-1909, certificate no. 5586. FHL film no. 317,724.
[1872] 1900 U.S. census, pop. sch., Lawrence County, Ohio, Mason Township, p. 2B, dwelling/family 33/33.
[1873] 1900 U.S. census, pop. sch., Lawrence County, Ohio, Mason Township, p. 7B, dwelling/family 133/134.
[1874] 1910 U.S. census, pop. sch., Lawrence County, Ohio, Mason Township, p. 14, dwelling/family 143/145.
[1875] Leona D. Payne, "Alva Burton and Leona Payne," in *History of Lawrence County, Ohio, 1990*, 271.
[1876] Ibid.
[1877] 1900 U.S. census, pop. sch., Lawrence County, Ohio, Mason Township, p. 7B, dwelling/family 134/135.
[1878] 1880 U.S. census, pop. sch., Lawrence County, Ohio, Mason Township, p. 253C, FHL film no. 1,255,039; National Archives film no. T9-1039.
[1879] 1900 U.S. census, pop. sch., Lawrence County, Ohio, Mason Township, p. 1, dwelling/family 1/1.
[1880] Lawrence County, Ohio, Marriages, vol. 21-22, 1905-1910, certificate no. 5474. FHL film no. 317,724.
[1881] Lawrence County, Ohio, Marriages, vol. 25 (p. 299-end)-27, 1914-1919, certificate no. 9378, FHL film no. 1,574,146.

[1882] Lawrence County, Ohio, Marriages, vol. 23-25 (p. 1-300), 1910-1916, certificate no. 6412, FHL film no. 1,574,145.
[1883] 1900 U.S. census, pop. sch., Lawrence County, Ohio, Mason Township, p. 6A, dwelling/family 110/111.
[1884] Lawrence County, Ohio, Marriages, vol. 25 (p.299-end)-27, 1914-1919, certificate no. 11724, FHL film no. 1,574,146.
[1885] 1800 U.S. census, pop. sch., Lawrence County, Ohio, Mason Township, p.252B. FHL film no. 1,255,039, National Archives film no. T9-1039.
[1886] 1900 U.S. census, pop. sch., Lawrence County, Ohio, Mason Township, p. 6A-6B, dwelling/family 111/112 (John S. Payne household); dwelling/family 112/113 (Thompson F. Payne household); dwelling/family 115/116 (Jackson Payne household); dwelling/family 110/111 (Columbus Payne household); dwelling/family 106/107 (Burrell Payne household).
[1887] 1910 U.S. census, pop. sch., Lawrence County, Ohio, Mason Township, p. 2, dwelling/family 19/19 (John S .Payne household; dwelling/family 18/18 (Howard Payne household).
[1888] Mary B. Jones, "John Higgins," in *History of Lawrence County, Ohio, 1990*, 60.
[1889] 1880 U.S. census, pop. sch., Lawrence County, Ohio, Mason Township, p. 251D. FHL film no. 1,255,039; National Archives film no.T9-1039.
[1890] 1900 U.S. census, pop. sch., Lawrence County, Ohio, Mason Township, p. 14B, dwelling/family263/263.
[1891] Archie H. Jones, "Jacob Saunders," in *History of Lawrence County, Ohio, 1990*, p. 294.
[1892] Mary Brammer Jones, "Josiah Doddridge," in *History of Lawrence County, Ohio, 1990*, p. 58.
[1893] Mary B. Jones, "John Higgins," in *History of Lawrence County, Ohio, 1990*, 60,
[1894] 1860 U.S. census, pop. sch., Lawrence County, Ohio, Mason Township, p. 182-183, dwelling/family 1239/1229.
[1895] Jones, "John Higgins," in *History of Lawrence County, Ohio, 1990*, 60.
[1896] Samuel Kerchival, *A History of the Valley of Virginia*, 4th edition (Strasburg, Va: Shenandoah publ. house, 1925), 370.
[1897] Mary B. Jones, "John Higgins," 60.
[1898] John L.E. Jones, "Morgan's Raid," in *History of Lawrence County, Ohio, 1990*, 45; "Morgan's Raid," Ohio History Central, An Online Encyclopedia of Ohio History, online http://www.ohiohistorycentralorg/entry.php?rec=519.
[1899] Wayne B. Ingles, writer and compiler, *Symmes Creek* (Zanesville, Ohio: Franklin Printing Co., 1976), 24-25.
[1900] George Corn Revolutionary War pension claim S. 2143 shows he served as private and lieutenant in Captain Van Swearingin's Company, Colonels Brodhead and Bayard's Eighth Pennsylvania Regiment and discharged after three years' service. He enlisted again in June 1780 and served in the Virginia Troops. He was born October 1758, and his first enlistment was at Red Stone Fort, Pennsylvania. Certificate No. 421 was issued on September 3, 1832, allowing $80 per annum. This summary of his pension claim is found in a letter dated June 24, 1927, from Winfield Scott, Commissioner, to the Honorable Thomas A. Jenkins, Ironton, Ohio.
[1901] "Battle of Blue Licks," from Wikipedia, the free encyclopedia, online http://en.wikipedia.org/wiki/Battle_of_Blue_Licks, downloaded July9, 2010.
[1902] Ralph Barnes, "Battle of Estill's Defeat," online http://www.fewpb.net/~ralphbarnes/defeat.htm, downloaded April 24, 2010.
[1903] Ingles, p. 24.
[1904] Charles O. Payne, Graves Registration Card, WWI Serial No. 2389245, filed in Lawrence County Court House, Ironton, Ohio.
[1905] 1800 U.S. census, pop. sch., Lawrence County, Ohio, Mason Township, p. 240A, FHL film no. 1,255,039; National Archives film no. T9-1039.
[1906] 1900 U.S. census, pop. sch., Lawrence County, Ohio, Mason Township, p. 6B, dwelling/family 115/116.
[1907] 1880 U.S. census, pop. sch., Lawrence County, Ohio, Mason Township, p. 252A. FHL film no. 1,255,039; National Archives Film T9-1039.
[1908] 1900 U.S. census, pop. sch., Lawrence County, Ohio, Mason Township, p. 6B, dwelling/family 112/113.
[1909] 1900 U.S. census, pop. sch., Lawrence County, Ohio, Mason Township, p. 1A, dwelling/family 5/5.
[1910] 1900 U.S. census, pop. sch., Lawrence County, Ohio, Mason Township, p. 1B, dwelling/family 18/18.
[1911] Lawrence County, Ohio, Marriages, vol. 25 (p.299-end)-27, 1914-1919, certificate no. 10879. FHL film no. 1,574,146.
[1912] 1900 U.S. census, pop. sch., Lawrence County, Ohio, Mason Township, p. 10A, dwelling/family 190/191.
[1913] Lawrence County, Ohio, Marriages, vol. 21-22, 1905-1910, certificate no. 4620. FHL film no. 317, 724.
[1914] Vivian Pyles Coleman, "Payne," 271.
[1915] Lawrence County, Ohio, Marriages, vol. 23-25, (p. 1-300), 1910-1916, certificate no. 7303. FHL film no. 1,574,145.
[1916] 1900 U.S. census, pop. sch., Lawrence County, Ohio, Mason Township, p. 1B, dwelling/family 17/17.
[1917] 1900 U.S. census, pop. sch., Lawrence County, Ohio, Mason Township, p. 1A, dwelling/family 2/2.
[1918] Lawrence County, Ohio, Marriages, vol. 25, (p.299-end)-27, 1914-1919, certificate no. 10638. FHL film no. 1,574,146.
[1919] Verla Payne Watrons Switzer, "Clay-Payne," in *History of Lawrence County, Ohio, 1990*, 117.
[1920] 1910 U.S. census, pop. sch., Lawrence County, Ohio, Windsor Township, p. 2B, dwelling/family 32/32.

[1921] Lawrence County, Ohio, Marriages, vol. 25 (p.299-end)-27, 1914-1919, certificate no. 10053. FHL film no. 1,574,146.
[1922] Lawrence County, Ohio, Marriages, vol. 25 (p. 290-end)-27, 1914-1919, certificate no. 11830. FHL film no. 1,574,146.
[1923] Lawrence County, Ohio, Marriages, vol. 23-25 (p. 1-300), 1910-1916, certificate no. 6876. FHL film no. 1,574,145.
[1924] 1920 U.S. census, pop. sch., Lawrence County, Ohio, Windsor Township, p. 2A, dwelling/family 34/34.
[1925] Verla Payne Watrons Switzer, "Clay-Payne," 117.
[1926] 1930 U.S. census, pop. sch., Lawrence County, Ohio, Lawrence Township, p. 3A, dwelling/family 47/47.
[1927] Lawrence County, Ohio, Marriages, vol. 21-22, 1905-1910, certificate no. 4480. FHL film no. 317,724.
[1928] 1930 U.S. census, pop. sch., Lawrence County, Ohio, Mason Township, p.5B, dwelling/family 112/115 (Justin A. Payne household); dwelling/family 112/114 (Henry B. Vermillion household).
[1929] Leona D. Payne, "Alva Burton and Leona Payne," in *History of Lawrence County, Ohio, 1990*, 271.
[1930] Ibid.
[1931] 1920 U.S. census, pop. sch., Lawrence County, Ohio, Mason Township, p. 2B, dwelling/family 36/36.
[1932] Sharon Conner, "John William Payne," in *History of Lawrence County, Ohio, 1990*, 272.
[1933] Lawrence County, Ohio, Marriages, vol. 21-22, 1905-1910, certificate no. 5437. FHL film no. 317,724.
[1934] Lawrence County, Ohio, Marriages, vol. 21-22, 1905-1910, certificate no. 4851. FHL film no. 317,724.
[1935] 1930 U.S. census, pop. sch., Pike County, Ohio, Mifflin Township, p. 9A, dwelling/family 183/190, 191.
[1936] 1920 U.S. census, pop. sch., Lawrence County, Ohio, Mason Township, p. 2B, dwelling/family 39/38.
[1937] 1930 U.S. census, pop. sch., Lawrence County, Ohio, Mason Township, p. 2A, dwelling/family 25/24.
[1938] Edna May Lewis, death certificate no. 1243 (1951), West Virginia State Department of Health. http://www.wvculture.org/vrr/va.
[1939] Lawrence County, Ohio, Marriages, vol. 23-25 (p. 1-300), 1910-1916, certificate no. 6570. FHL film no. 1,574,145.
[1940] Ona Scarberry death, September 15, 1966, in Death Registry, West Virginia Vital Records. http://www.wvculture.org/vrr/va.
[1941] Leona D. Payne, "Alva Burton and Leona Payne," 271.
[1942] Jonas B. Payne, no. 283-14-2676, Social Security Death Index, *FamilySearch*.
[1943] 1910 U.S. census, pop. sch., Lawrence County, Ohio, Mason Township, p. 7B, dwelling/family 149/151.
[1944] 1920 U.S. census, pop. sch., Lawrence County, Ohio, Mason Township, p. 2B, dwelling/family 34/34.
[1945] 1920 U.S. census, pop. sch., Lawrence County, Ohio, Mason Township, p. 1B, dwelling/family 15/15.
[1946] Lawrence County, Ohio, Marriages, vol. 23-25 (p. 1-300), 1910-1916, certificate no. 9341. FHL film no. 1,574,145.
[1947] "Fairview Baptist," in *History of Lawrence County, Ohio, 1990*, 15.
[1948] Verla L. Payne Watrous Switzer obituary, *The Columbus Dispatch*, Columbus, Ohio, May 7-8, 2010. http://www.legacy.com/obituaries/dispatch/obituary-print.aspx?n=verla-l-payne-watrous-switzer.
[1949] Sharon Conner, "John William Payne," 272.
[1950] Ibid.
[1951] Ibid.
[1952] Larry and Sharon Conner, "William and Juanita Payne," in *History of Lawrence County, Ohio, 1990*, 272-273.
[1953] Leona D. Payne, "Alva Burton and Leona Payne," 271.

INDEX

Both given names and surnamces are indexed with what seems to have been their most common spellings. In other words, *Phillip* is indexed as *Philip*. The surname *Barwick* is indexed as *Barrick*. Middlesex County, Virginia, clerks recorded this name in a variety of ways. The name *Shelton* is indexed as *Chelton*. The name *Riston* was also spelled *Wriston*, and so forth. Name entries in the body of this work, however, reflect the spellings in the documents that are sourced.

Abbott, Wilson, 18
Abell
   Hannah, 11
   Jeremiah, 11
Achenbach
   Amalie, 50
   Edward, 50
   Elizabeth, 50
Adams
   Absalom, 244
   Emmer, Mrs., 42
   Mary Ada, 42
   Robert, 248
   Samuel, 14
   Thos., 133
   William, 244
Adcock, Simon, 106, 107
Adkinson, Jane, 135
Alcorn, Arramancie, 254
Alderson
   Ja., 119
   John, 141, 153, 154
   John, Jr., 145, 153, 156
   Mary, 153
   Thomas, 153
Alexander
   Esther, 243
   H., 151
   Henry, 18
   James, 14
   William, 243
Alfred the Great of England, 261
Alfred, Thomas, 153
Aliff, Sarah, 22
Allaman
   Contiten, 106
   Judith, 106
   Sarah, 106
   Thomas, 106
Allegre
   Daniel, 250
   Giles, 250
   Susannah (Tisdale), 250

Allen
   Andrew, 15, 141
   Benjamin, 244
   Samuel, 138
   Sarah, 267
   Serena, 254
Allison
   Ann, 107, 109
   Catherine, 109
   David, 107, 110
   Elizabeth, 109
   Joan, 110
   Mary, 107, 127
Amos, Agness Setty, 48
Anderson
   Bartlett, 251
   Celia Jane (Doughty), 190
   Charles, 239, 251
   David, 247, 251
   Elizabeth, 16, 238, 251
   George, 108
   James, 40, 190
   Jennet, 251
   John, 112, 238
   Labez, 163
   Lewis, 158
   Nathl., 248
   Rachel Minerva, 40, 48, 190
   Rbt., 250
   Richard, 242, 244, 251
   Robert, 251
   Sarah, 130, 240, 251
   Turner, 250
   Uriah, 246, 249
   Widow, 251
   William, 109, 130, 239, 251
   Wm., 239
Anderton, Eliza, 134
Andrew, John, 244
Angil, John, 123
Anthony
   Charles, 238
   John, 244

Judith (Moorman), 248
Luke, 244
Applewhite
   Ann, 134
   Ann (Harris), 133
   Arthur, 134
Arbuckle, Charles, 16
Armentrout, Henry, 142
Armistead
   Anthony, 136
   Anthony, Jr., 136
   Anthony, Sr., 136
   Capt., 108
   Elizabeth, 136
   Henr., 115
   Jno., 106
   Mary, 136
   Mary (Tucker) Curle, 136
   Robert, 136
Armstrong
   Alexr., 10
   Isaac, 21
   William, 16
   Wm., 10
Arnold
   Benj., 250
   Edward, 250
   Wm., 250
Arthur
   Alexander H., 167
   Isaac, 32
   James, 32
   Louie, 38
   Rebecca, 32
Artis, Abraham, 118
Asbury
   Elizabeth, 158, 163, 176
   Francis, Bishop, 12
   Nancy (Wright), 240
   William, 240
Ash, Evelyn, 22
Ashburn, John, 106
Asher
   Charles, 126
   Diana, 127
   John, 125, 126, 127
   John, Jr., 126
   John, Sr., 125
   Moley, 126
   Sarah, 127
   Susanna, 127
   William, 127
Ashley, Sarah, 3
Ashton, Sarah Blair, 150
Askew, Charles, 127
Atkins, John, 130
Atkinson, Joseph, 120

Attley, Willm., 106
Atwell
   John, 242
   Martha (Howell), 242
Au, Jeffrey, 198
Aubrey
   Francis, 242
   John, 242
Austin
   Chapman, 243
   David, 158
   Eli, 158
   Elizabeth, 158
   Fanny, 158
   Garrett, 158
   James, 243
   John, 243
   Margaret, 243
   Mildred, 250
   Nancy, 158
   Robert, 243
   William, 243
Averell, William Woods, 34, 35
Axome, Richard, 111
Ayers
   Moses, 243
   Regimalick Baker, 243
Aylor
   Ann Magdalena, 147
   Henry, 147
   Jacob, 150
Babcock, Joel, 20
Bailey
   Clinton, 61
   George, 13, 15
   Henry, 135
   James, 8, 10
   Joseph, 104
   Lemuel, 193
   Miss, 8
   Molly, 193
   Robert, 134
   Sarah, 123, 125, 128, 131, 156
   William, 8, 10, 117
Baker
   Blake, 119
   Frederick, 12
   Joseph, 18
   Ralph, 110
   Wm., 120, 243
Ball
   Hannah (Heale), 105
   Jos., 105
   Joseph, 141
   Samuel, 122
   William, 105, 128
   Wm., 131

Ballard
  Ann, 154
  David O., 158
  Elijah, 152
  James, 154
  Jeremiah, 154
  Johnston, 154
  Js., 144
  Lucy, 154
  Margaret, 154
  Millie, 142, 154
  Mollie, 154
  Nancy, 154
  Philip, 152, 154
  Susan, 141, 154
  Thomas, 144, 250
  William, 131, 141, 154, 155, 165
  William, Jr., 154
  Willis, 154
  Wilson, 158
Ballengee, Henry, 169
Balynger, Sarah, 122
Bame
  John, 180
  Willa, 180
Bane, Susanna, 117
Banks, Lynn, 127, 130
Baptist, Frances, 151
Barbee
  Jone, 112
  William, 109, 111, 123
  William, Jr., 111
Barbour, Tho., 167
Barker
  Edward, 247
  Othniell, 106
  Sarah, 247
Barnard, Walter, 16
Barnes
  Eleanor, 120
  Leo'd, 125
  Leonard, 131
  Nancy, 158
  Richard, 119
  Thomas, 120
Barnett
  James, 142
  Js., 248
Barrett
  Chs., 251
  Thos., Jr., 118
Barrick
  David, 108
  Geo., 108
  George, 116
Barrow, Aunt, 131

Bartee
  Ricard, 195
  Tammy, 195
Bartlett
  Anthony, 144
  Edmund, 144
  Mary, 144
  Thomas, 144
Barton
  Burr, 238
  David, 238
  Edith, 238
  Elisha, 238
  Elizabeth, 238
  Jacob "Burton", 238
  Sarah, 238
  Thomas, 238
Bartram, Mark S., 159
Bates
  Jim, 197
  Jimmy, 197
  John, 16
  Joshua H., 159
Battaley, Jno., 126
Baugh, Littleberry, 149
Bawdes
  Mary, 106
  Wm., 111
Beard
  Adam, 10
  David, 10
  Henry, 244
  Sam'l, 10
  Wm., 108
Beaufort
  Anne, 250, 251
  Henry, 251
Beaumont
  Hope, 111
  William, 111
Beckham
  Henry, 129, 145
  James, 129, 145
  William, 128, 155
  Wm., 129
Beeson, Rachel, 6
Beirne
  Andrew, 17, 137, 168
  George, 18, 137
Bell
  Bertha, 45
  David, 118
  Geo., 250
  Joseph, 117
  William, 125
  Wm., 123

Beller, Daniel, 168, 178
Benger, Elliott, 123
Benner, Mary, 27, 95
Bennett, William, 135
Benson, Priscilla, 119
Berkeley, Edmund, 115
Berridge, Christopher C., 26
Berry
    Bradley, 139
    John, 123
Bess, a slave, 107
Best
    Frances, 152
    Francis, 136
    Jane, 136
    Jean, 152
Beverley, Ursula, 143
Bias, Terrie, 68
Bibb
    Thomas, 158
    Thos., 155
Bickett
    Michael, 15, 21
    Thomas, 141
Bingamin, Mrs., 14
Birchett, Edward, 134
Birchill, Edward, 134
Birthright, Peter, 149
Black
    Mary, 141
    Samuel, 141
Blackburn
    Blackburn, 111
    Edward, 111
    Lambeth T., 251
    William, 111
Blagg, Wm., 92
Blair, Thomas, 32
Blake
    Bertha Ann, 58
    Emma, 26
Bland
    Hope, 111
    Perregrine, 111
Blanton, William, 141
Blick, Benjamin, 134
Bloodworth, Joseph, 155
Blossingham, Thomas, 114
Blow, Michael, 132
Blow, Mich'l, 135
Board
    James, 240
    James, Jr., 238
    James, Sr., 238
    John, 244
Boaz, Thomas, 251
Bobo
    Jude, 144
    Spencer, 144
Boddie, John Bennett, 104
Bohannan
    Benjamin, 124
    John, 124
    Thomas, 124
    William, 127
Bolter, William, 120
Boltz, Edith, 189
Bonner, James, 111
Boodle, Robert, 108
Booth
    Harriet, 150
    John, 149
    Sharon Lou, 199
Booton
    Hannah, 140
    Lewis, 139, 155
    Travis, 139, 155
    William, 139, 155
    Wm., 142, 155
Boseley, Hannah, 143
Bostick, Sarah, 157
Boswell, Edward, 103, 104
Boulden
    Richard, 134
    William, 134
Bourn
    Andrew, 128, 165
    Francis, 122
    Henry, 129, 145, 165
    John, 128
Bowen
    George W., 24
    Kim L., 195
    Mr., 201
    Susan, 24
Bowman
    Jody Lynn, 201
    Lori Jane, 201
    Myrtle Marie, 61
    Paul, 201
Boyd
    Barbara, 137
    Margaret, 156
    Robert, 139
    William, 7
    Wm., 137
Boyer, John, 246
Boykin, Francis, 119
Bozwell, John, 246
Braddock, General, 118
Bradley
    Absalem, 131
    Ann, 116
    Chester, Mrs., 50

The Scarberrys (Scarboroughs), Doughtys, Lewises, and Paynes of Lawrence County, Ohio

Eliz., 135
Elizabeth, 116
Hen., 105
Hezekiah, 116
James, 115
John, 115, 116, 117, 120, 121, 131, 135, 139, 167
Mary, 115
Rebecca, 115
Rebecca (Hackney) Jameson, 115
Rebecca (Hackney) Jamison, 121, 123
Robert, 116
Robt., 50
W., 131
William, 116
Bragg, Ellen, 191
Brambill, James, 239
Branham
  Daniel, 130
  Gaydon, 130
  James Webb, 130
  John, 124, 130
  Mary (Marks), 128
  Milly, 130
  Nelly, 129, 130
  Rachel, 130
  Richard, 130
  Taverner, 130
Brassell
  Jane (Lewis), 116
  John, 116, 120, 136
Braxton, Carter, 166
Bray, Robt., 105
Brechin
  Ann, 242
  Anna, 242
  Elizabeth, 242
  James, 242
  James, Jr., 242
  Jane, 242
  Sarah, 242
  William, 242
Brecht
  Catharine, 50
  Charles, 50, 53
  David, 50
  George, 50
  Mary, 50
Breedlove, Mary, 127
Bricker
  Benjamin F., 46
  Cline, 169
  John, 46
  Nannie, 50
Brickey
  Amy, 242
  Christopher, 244

Elizabeth, 244
Jarret, 244
Jarret, Jr., 244
John, 244
Milly, 244
Nancy, 244
Patsy, 244
Peter, 244
Bridger, Col., 117, 118
Bristow
  Elizabeth, 119
  John, 111
  Thomas, 111
  William, 111
Britt
  John, 243
  William, 243
Brock
  Jos., 241
  Joseph, 114
  Richard, 5
Brockenbrough, Winifred, 120
Brockman
  Agatha, 165
  Aggie, 166
  Ambrose, 155, 166
  Bluford, 165
  Catherine, 116, 137, 140, 155
  James, 167
  Jane, 167
  John, 140, 143
  Julia A., 165
  Mary, 116, 167
  Mary B., 167
  Rebecca, 166
  Richard Simms, 165
  Robert, 167
  Saml., 137
  Samuel, 165, 166, 167
  Samuel, Sr., 140, 166
  Sarah, 167
  Simpson, 165
  Tandy, 165
  Tazewell, 165
  William, 165, 166, 167
  William D., 167
Brodnax, Wm. Edwards, 135
Bromwell, Diana, 112
Bronaugh, William, 118
Bronte
  Anne, 1
  Charlotte, 1
  Emily, 1
Brook
  George, 166
  Sarah, 166

William, 166
Brooking
  Ann, 139, 170
  Charles, 124, 139, 140, 147, 168, 170
  John, 124, 140
  Mary, 109, 139
  Nancy, 139
  Rhoda, 109, 124, 139, 140, 142, 170
  Robert, 124, 140
  Samuel, 124, 140
  Susanna, 139, 141
  William, 109, 124, 139, 140, 168
Brooks
  Elisha, 14
  Lewis, 29, 30
  Lewis C., 29
  Mary Susan, 48
  Nancy, 28
  Nancy (Scarberry), 45
Broughton, Arlene, 189
Brown
  Aaron, 240
  Alred, 96
  Anderson, 169
  Ann, 96
  Arminta, 96
  Benjamin E., 149
  Benjamin, Jr., 250
  Clay Vaughn, 65, 71
  Daniel, 241
  Dolly, 117
  Edna (Beardmore), 65
  Elizabeth, 238
  Elmer, 269
  Eltie T., 96
  Henry, 129
  Henry, Jr., 12, 14
  Henry, Sr., 14
  J. Ancil, 259
  Jared Eldon, 71
  Jennifer, 71
  Jesse, 240
  John, 14
  Joseph, 240
  Joshua Thomas, 71
  Kathryn Lorena, 71
  Lizetta, 96
  Lloyd, 65
  Margaret, 178
  Mary, 7
  Nervella, 96
  Olie, 96
  Philena, 96
  Rebecca, 258
  Rebecca Faye, 65, 72
  S., 157
  Susannah, 250
  Tarlton, 242
  Thomas, 131
  Thomas Garfield, 65
  Tom, 59
  Verga, 269
  William, 152, 156, 163, 170, 238
  William R., 258
Broyles
  Jacob, 131
  Tobias, 146
Bruce
  Charles, 128, 129
  Charles, Sr., 128
  Chs., 129
Brumfield, George, 161
Brunson
  Harriet, 19
  Seymore, 19
Buckett, Thos., 139
Buckhannon
  John, 239
  Theodore, 239, 241
Buckland
  Stephen, 139, 141
  Stephenson, 141
  Thomas, 141, 142
Bucklen, Alex, 168
Buckner
  George, 123
  John, 114
  Richard, 125
Buffoon
  Ann, 118, 136
  Mathew, 118, 119, 136
Buford
  Agatha, 125
  Anna, 124
  Capt., 11
  James, 10
  John, 107, 124
  John Thomas, 124
  Judith (Early), 124
  Simeon, 124
  Thomas, 11, 124
Bulen
  William, 182
  Wm., Sr., 182
Bullard
  Bill, 64
  Glorida Darlene (Coston), 64
Bullis, Samuel, 155
Bunch
  David, 248
  Henry, 144
  James, 248
  Pouncy, 248
Bundy

Janet, 197, 201
Lennie (Lewis), 168, 169, 181
Samuel, 197
Wilson, 197
Bunn, Evert, 258
Bunyan, John, 2
Burbage, Col., 104
Burbridge
　Ben., 132
　Benja., 131
　Benjamin, 131
Burcham
　Dale, 160
　Elizabet, 175
　James P., 163, 176
　Jane, 176
　Jasper, 176
　Jesse S., 176
　John, 160, 161, 163, 168, 170
　John, Jr., 19
　Mary, 160
　Matilda, 168
　Mr., 176
　Nancy, 170
　Nathaniel, 24, 25, 158, 160, 162, 164, 168, 170, 176
　Nathl., 163
　Nettie, 182
　Sarah, 161, 172
Burd
　Andrew, 164
　Becky, 61
　Betsy, 164
　Brandie Nickole, 68
　Charles, 46
　Charles Oliver, 61
　David, 32, 164
　Delia, 46
　Della Marie, 62, 67, 198
　Emily, 181
　Emily Catherine, 46
　Emily R., 32
　George, 32, 43
　George A., 164, 179, 181
　Harriet, 43, 180
　Harriet E., 32, 47, 179
　Iris, 53, 195
　Iris (Scarberry), 41, 48, 179
　James Francis, 32
　Janey, 177
　Lewis E., 163, 177
　Martha, 46
　Mary, 32, 164
　Mary Ann, 32, 46, 49, 181
　Okey Gene, 61, 198
　Oliver Perry, 32, 46
　Otis, 46

　Perry, 61
　Philip, 164
　Raymond, 46
　Rebecca, 43, 47, 164
　Rickey Ryan, 62, 68
　Sarah Jane, 164
　Sophia, 164
　Susan, 164
　Susan A., 32
　Thos. J., 177
　Tiffany Renae, 68
　William, 46
Burden, Robert, 95
Burgess
　Frederick, 134
　J., 92
Burke, Jno., 104
Burks, Francis, 9
Burnley
　N., 167
　Zachy., 140
Burris
　Frances Tandy, 167
　Henry, 157
　Martha, 157
Burt, Moses, 129
Burton
　May, 167
　Richard N., 167
Bush
　Ambrose, 166
　Archibald, 141
　Elizabeth, 166
　Frances, 141
　Francis, 166
　Jerry, 138
　John, 166
　Joseph, 139, 141, 166, 167
　Joshua, 167
　Josiah, 166
　Lewis, 166
　Philip, 166
　Sarah, 166
　Stephen, 200
　William, 166
Buster, Claudius, 14
Butler, John, 122
Butts
　Benjamin, 133, 148, 149
　Elizabeth (Lewis), 133
　Fanny (Lewis), 133
　James, 133
　Jenny, 149
　Peter, 132
　Polly, 149
　Robert, 148, 149

Byard
   Jas., 242
   Sarah, 242
Bye
   Albert, 69
   John, 70
   Kevin, 70
   Tony, 70
Byrnside
   Benjamin, 141
   James, 141
   James, Jr., 141
   John, 14, 139, 141, 148
   Joseph, 141
   Joshua, 141
   Katherine, 141
   Martha, 141
   Mary, 141
   Peggy, 138
   Rachel, 141
   Sarah, 141
   Wm., 138
Cahoon, Johanna, 10
Caldwell, Doris, 189
Callanone, William, 110
Callicoat
   Almeda Catherine "Meda", 180
   Billy, 49
   George Washington, 180
   Lew, Mr. and Mrs., 49
   Lou, 186
Campbell
   Archd., 117
   James, 243
   Robt., 117
   William, 16, 17
Canaday
   Leroy, 140
   Sally, 140
   Wharton, 140
Canby, Thomas, 4
Candler, William, 13
Canter, Jim, 15
Canterbury
   John, 17
   Mary, 146
   Nancy, 17
Cantley, Florence Belle, 22
Cantrell
   Carrie Marie, 199
   Kasey Beth, 200
   Paul Eugene, 199
   Sean Paul, 200
   Stacy Renee, 199
Caperton
   Allen, 168
   Elizabeth (Miller), 143
   Hugh, 18, 141
   Hugh, Jr., 15
   Jane, 15
Caragan, John, 113
Caraway, Thomas, 144
Cargin, John, 112
Carlyle, John, 118
Carner
   John, 239, 244
   John Daniel, 244
   Wm., 239, 244
Carnes
   Alice, 261
   Michael, 8
   Theodore, 261
Carpenter
   Mary Cordelia, 39
   Nancy, 245
   R. H., 53
Carr
   Agnes Brooks, 145
   Charles Brooks, 144
   Phebe, 145
   Susannah, 144
   Thomas, 145
   Walter Chiles, 145
   Wm., 144
Carrol, Juanita, 270
Carson, David, 156
Carter
   Betty, 120
   Charles, 120
   Chs., 122
   Daniel, 123
   Edward, 106
   Evelyn, 196
   Jno., 104
   Merry, 237
Cartwright, Polly, 141
Carver
   Jane (Moor), 117
   William, 117
Cary
   Archibald, 244
   Henry, 244
Cash, Howard, 250
Casto
   J. C., Dr., 27
   Louis, 39
Catlett
   John, 125
   Rebecca, 125
Cavendish, W. H., 144
Cawthorn, Thomas, 157
Chambers
   Abraham, 123
   James, 139, 141

Thomas, 128, 129
Chan, Kun, 195, 201
Chancelor, William, 115
Chapman
    Erasmus, 125
    Isaac, 20
    Marilyn Kay, 58
    Reynolds, 166
    Thomas, 139, 141
Charles I of England, 252
Charles the Second of England, 3
Charles, Elisha, 149
Cheek, George, 163
Chelton
    Abigail, 110
    Mary, 119
    Peter, 110
    Zebulon, 112
    Zebulun, 110
Chew, Mary, 146
Chicheley, Henry, 115
Chisam, Wm., 129
Chiswell, John, 139
Chowning
    George, 112
    Robert, 108
Christopher, John, 125
Christy
    Catherine, 15
    Elizabeth, 15
    Isabel, 15
    James, 11, 15
    James, Sr., 15
    Robert, 15
Churchill
    Armistead, 120, 150
    Madm., 115
    William, 106, 120
    Wm., 111
Claiborn, Martha Ann, 149
Clapham
    J., 156
    William, Jr., 106, 156
    William, Sr., 156
Clark
    Bill, 28
    Debby, 29
    Dr., 261
    Edward, 107, 109
    Elizabeth, 119
    Ellie, 29
    Francis, 244
    Joan, 251
    John, 18
    Lucy, 129
    Margaret, 254
    Mary, 114
    Mary Emmer, 264
    Missouri, 173
    Missouri A., 161
    Missouri Ann, 182
    Rachel, 247
    Ralph, 16
    Rebecca (Lewis), 161, 172
    Sally, 161
    Sally K., 161
    Samuel, 14, 141
    Sara Catherine, 173
    Thomas, 28, 129, 152
    William, 28, 138, 161, 172, 173
    Wm., 134, 141
Clarkson, John, 149
Claxton, Manoah, 144
Clay, John, 266
Clemens
    John Marshall, 237
    Samuel, 237
    Samuel Lampkin, 237
Clements
    Benjamin, 132
    Benjamin, Jr., 132
    Richard P., 148
Clendinen
    George, 145
    Isaac, 139
Clerk
    Henry, 105
    Samuel, 15
Cleveland, C. M., 41, 185
Coalter
    Isabella, 152
    Jane, 157
    Robert, 162
Coats, Michael, 16
Cobler, Frederick, 122
Cocke
    John, 117
    John H., 117
Coghill, Zachariah, 123, 128
Coldiron
    David, 197
    Gary, 197
    Gene, 197
    Larry, 197
    Mary Ellen, 197
    Stella Jane, 197
    Terry, 197
Cole
    Isaac, 154
    Widdow, 244
Coleman
    Elizabeth, 241

James, 124, 140, 166
Robert, 241
Spilsby, 241
Thomas, Jr., 241
Vivian Pyles, 245
Coles, Mary, 248
Colley
   James, 163
   Polly, 163
   William, 243
Collier
   Catherine, 95
   Mr., 38
Collins
   John, 114
   Joseph, 143
   Joseph, Jr., 143
   Linda, 67
   Mary, 143
   William, 143
   Wm., 129
Comer
   Augustine, 139, 141
   Augustus, 141
   Barbara, 141
   Catharine, 141
   Elizabeth, 141
   Frederick, 141
   Jacob, 141
   John, 127, 141
   Mary, 141
   Michael, 141
   Sarah, 141
Compton, Phoebe, 21, 92
Connell, Andrew, 67
Connelly, Edmond, 112
Conner
   Angela Denise, 272
   James, 122
   Larry, 270
   Larry Franklin, 272
   Lewis, 128, 129
   Margaret, 122, 127
   Sharon, 266, 270
   Spring Dawn, 272
   William, 122
Connerley, Bryant, 243
Conners, Dennis, 104
Connocoe, William, 130
Conway
   Catlett, 125
   Fran., 130
   Francis, 125
   Francis, Jr., 125
Cook
   Barbara, 146
   Daniel, 146
   Elizabeth, 146
   Isabella, 169
   Jacob, 12, 138, 142, 146, 148, 168, 169
   John, 147, 148
   Michael, 160
   Michael Lewis, 115, 121, 124, 143, 145, 151, 152, 173
   Valentine, 141
Coon, Mary, 152
Cooper
   Benjamin, 116
   Demsey, 116
   Edmund, 135
   James, 116
   Jesse, 116
   John, 116
   Mary, 116
   Philip R., 91
   William, 116
Corbet, John, 241
Corbin
   Francis, 115
   Richard, 115
Corbly, John, 127, 128
Corn
   Amos, 267
   Charlotte, 261
   Elizabeth, 261
   Frances M., 261
   George, 260, 261, 267
   George C., 267
   Hannah, 260, 261
   Harrison, 261
   James, 261
   Jesse, 94, 261
   Jesse, Sr., 253
   John, 261
   Lucy, 261
   Margaret, 261
   Martha, 173, 261
   Nancy, 261
   Olive (Payne), 267
   Richard, 261
   Sarah, 261
   William, 261
Cornelius, William, 122
Cornstalk, Chief, 11
Coston
   Chester, 64
   J. R., 64
   Juanita, 64
   Lesterine, 64
Cotterill, Ann, 247
Cottle
   Diana (Conner), 71
   Jennifer, 71
   Joe, Jr., 71
   Joe, Sr., 71

John, 154
Marc Elliott, 71
Tamara, 71
Cottrell, Malissa J., 44
Coughlin, William, 243
Coulter, Adam, 92
Coursey, William, 126
Cowan
  Mr., 240
  Robert, 8
Cown, S. M., 24, 163
Cowper, Thos., 124
Cox
  Helen, 189
  Kermit, 192
  Tho., 104
Crabtree, Mr., 240
Crafford
  David, 242
  Sarah, 242
Craig
  Benj., 166
  Elijah, 128
  Jane, 132
  Jno., 132
  John, 131, 132, 142, 154, 155
  Joseph, 128
  Taliaferro, 131
  Taliaferro, Jr., 128, 132
  Toliver (Taliaferro), 132
Crawford, Thomas, 147
Creed
  Margaret, 142
  Mathew, 137, 142
Creel, John, 151
Crews, Archibald, 157
Crocker
  Benjamin, 132
  Elizabeth, 132
  Sarah, 132
Crockett, Samuel, 243
Cromwell, Oliver, 252
Crook. George, 35
Crozier
  Andrew, 15
  Margaret, 15
Crutcher
  Anthony, 144
  Martha, 144
  Thomas, 144
Crutchfield, William, 111, 123
Cumming, Robert, 147, 152
Cunningham, Jean, 13
Curle
  Joshua, 136
  Judith, 136
  Mary, 136
Curry, James, 139, 156
Curtis
  Ann, 110
  Ann (Moone), 110
  George, 108
  Jno., 108
  Jo., 110
  Savanah, 114
Cyavanne, Peter, 110
Dabney, Susannah, 138
Daingerfield
  Elizabeth, 113
  Wm., 113
Dale
  Edward, 104, 106, 112, 123
  Mary, 105, 106, 112
Daley, Samuel, 141
Dalton
  Bradley, 9, 16, 18
  John, 118
  Thos., 41
Daniel
  Charles, 130
  Constance, 107
  Elizabeth, 134
  Henry, 156
  James, 130, 140
  Jane, 130
  John, 156
  Margaret, 146
  Overton, 115
  Reuben, 125
  Sarah, 123
  Tho., 105
  Vivian, 140
  Vivion, 130, 140
  William, 110
  William, Jr., 107
  William, Sr., 107
Daniels
  Alta, 183
  Ira, 57
  Mr., 57
  Myrtle, 57
  Virgie, 258
Dare
  Isaac, 168
  John, 124
  Parks, 154, 155, 158
Darling
  Celesta, 265, 266
  Celesta A., 257
  Leona, 266
Darnett, Isaac, 144
Darrow

A. E. P., Mrs., 4
Mrs., 4
Dasper, John, 242
Davidson
   Alexander, 114
   Alexander, Jr., 114
Davis
   Benjamin, 109, 114, 124, 140
   Berryman, 123, 128, 129
   Berryman (Benjamin?), 123
   Edwd., 244
   Eliz., 104
   Ella, 20
   Evan, 103, 104
   Frances E., 11
   Geo., 244
   George, 242
   Jane, 242
   John, 111
   John, Sr., 108
   M., 149
   Mary, 128
   Mrs., 129, 145
   Mrs. Susannah, 145
   Nicholas Edmunds, 150
   Sarah, 128
   Susannah, 128, 129, 165
   Thomas, 242
   Widow, 128
   William, 112
   Williamson, 115
Davisson
   Katherine Elizabeth, 271
   R., 92
Dawson
   John, 125, 129, 130
   Joseph, 145
   Mary, 129, 155
   Mary (Waugh), 125, 129
   Millie M., 93
   Musgrove, 125, 129
   Nelson C., 157
   R., 125
   Robert, 116, 121, 123, 125, 129, 155
   Robert, Jr., 129
   Robert, Sr., 123, 125, 128
   Robt., 129, 130, 131, 132, 145
   Robt., Jr., 129, 145
Day
   Jane, 132
   Mary Ann, 157
   Polly, 157
   Samuel, 157
   Thomas, 132
   Thos., 157
Deagle, James, 111
DeBoy (DuBois), Katey, 15

Defoe, Daniel, 2
Degge
   Anthony, 109
   Capt., 109
   James, 109
   Johanna, 109
   John, 106, 109, 110, 121
Delaney
   Leeza, 130
   Mary, 130
Deloach, Francis, 136
Dennison, Margaret, 261
Dent, John, 240
DeOrto, Louis, 56
Derr
   Diane, 63, 69
   Erica, 69
   Katelyn, 70
   Marge, 69
   Mark, 63
   Mark R., 63, 70
   Raymond A., 63
   Timmy, 69
   Timothy, 63, 69
Deupree, Lewis, 134
Dewitt
   Hannah, 160
   Susan, 261
Diaz, Porfirio, 55
Dick
   Archibald, 146
   Mary (Towles), 146
Dicken
   Frances, 124
   Martha (Lewis), 125
Dickens, Lucrezia "Lucy", 22
Dickenson
   Lucy, 143
   Thos. Cooper, 119
Dickson, William, 154
Dillard
   Edward, 140
   Jas., 157
   John, 241
   Thos., 124
Dillon
   Allie, 181
   Anna, 180
   Brunson, 169
   Effie, 260
   John, 181, 184
   Maggie, 26
   Mary Melvina, 259
   Nettie, 181
   Rachel, 37
   Sarah, 184
Dinwiddie, Robert, 117, 118

Dishman, Meridith Brooke, 68, 198
Dismukes, Elisha, 124
Dixon, Geo., 8
Dixon, Roger, 126
Dodd, Josias, 139
Doddridge
    Deloras, 261
    Enoch, 261
    John, 261
    Joseph, 261
    Josiah, 261
    Louisa, 261
    Philip, 261
Dodson, John Hackney, 117
Dollard
    John, 238, 239
    Wm., 239
Dolton
    America S., 175
    Dorothy, 16
    George W., 93
Donley, Beulah, 60
Donnel, Jonathan, 151
Doran, Mr., 11
Doty, John, 91
Dougherty, John, 11
Doughty
    Albert L., 39
    Alvira, 94
    Arminta S., 38
    Arstella B., 39
    Bertha, 95
    Catharine, 95
    Celia J., 26
    Celia Jane, 28, 40
    Charles M., 92, 93, 95
    Clarissa, 94
    Eliza Jane, 38
    Elizabeth, 93
    Elizabeth S., 26
    Elizabeth Susan, 27, 40, 44, 47, 91
    Ennis L., 39
    Francis, 94
    Franklin, 95
    George, 95
    Henry, 95
    Henry C., 39
    Hester, 31
    Hester A., 26, 27, 31, 38, 94
    Hester M., 92, 93
    Ina, 38
    Isaac W., 31, 92
    Isaac Wesley, 26, 31, 44, 91, 93
    Isaac Wesley "Wesley", 95
    Ivy M., 39
    J. M., 94
    James, 92
    James L., 92, 93
    James M., 93, 94
    James W., 39
    Jesse D., 93
    Jessy D., 92
    John, 21, 91, 92, 94
    John A., 39, 92, 93
    John W., 27
    John Wesley, 27, 38
    Laura Susan, 93, 94
    Lewis, 91
    Lewis M., 92, 93
    Manda E., 38
    Marion Lafayette, 94
    Mary, 91, 93
    Mary C., 39
    Mary J., 21, 92, 94
    Mary Jane, 91
    Milford, 40
    Milford O., 39
    Missouri A., 38
    Nancy, 94
    Nora N., 39
    Obra C., 39
    Orville Fleet, 38
    Percy, 95
    Phebe E., 94, 96
    Phoebe, 91, 94
    Phoebe A., 26, 28, 44
    Rachel, 39
    Rachel (Scarberry), 26, 40, 44
    Rachel C., 39
    Robert, 92, 93
    Robert E., 93
    Sarah E., 93, 94
    Thomas, 95
    William, 27, 95
    William A., 39
    Zachariah, 27, 38
Douglas
    Achilles, 167, 247
    John, 247
Dowden, Nancy Ann, 160, 161
Dowdy
    Adonna, 138
    Arnold, 138
    John, 121
Downing
    Ruth, 107
    William, 107, 109, 110
    William, Jr., 110
    William, Sr., 110
Drake
    Ann, 132
    Mr., 143

Philip, 132
Drummond
  Berl, 92
  Mr., 268
Dubois
  Conrad, 138
  John, 138
Dudley
  Col., 108
  Edward, 104
  Elizabeth, 108
  James, 108, 109, 121
  John, 108, 111, 112, 123, 143
  Mary (Bawd), 107
  Robert, 107, 108, 114
  Thomas, 112
  Ursula, 143
  Widow, 245
  William, 106, 107
Dunbar, Robert, 154
Duncan
  Clifton, 60
  Mary Lou, 60
  Opal, 60
Dunfee
  Dillard, 189
  Eloise, 188
  Frank, 179
  Mary M. (Lewis), 179
  Ova, 188
  Ray, 188
  Ray F., 179
Dunkinton, Ann, 107
Dunlap, Alexander, 141
Dunmore, Lord, 11
Dunn
  Agrippa, 115
  Edmund, 134
  Ishmael, 134, 149
  Lewis, 134
  Thomas, 158
Durgan
  Barnabas, 137, 139, 141, 146, 147, 148, 151, 153
  John, 137
  Nancy, 137
  Peggy, 137, 141
Durrett, William, 243
Dyer
  Jno., 133
  John, 157
Early
  Jubal, 26
  Paschal, 147
Eaves, Wm., 118
Eccles, Jacob, 237
Edgar, Thomas, 145
Edison, Thomas, 59

Edmondson
  James, 106
  James, Jr., 106
Edmunds
  Charles, 134
  Elizabeth Gray, 149
  James, 149
  John Flood, 149
  S., 134
  Sterling, 134
  Thomas, 134
Edward I of England, 261
Edwards
  Chester, 60
  Dillie, Mr. and Mrs., 50
  Earl, Mr. and Mrs., 50
  Ernestine, 60
  John, 104
  Loretta Kay, 68
  Sarah, 68
  Thos., 109
  W. H., 149
Eheart, Michl. L., 166
Eley, John, 120
Ellcessor, Mollie, 266
Ellinger, Clair Elizabeth, 69
Elliott
  John, 134
  Myrtle, 53
  Thomas, 112
  William, 106, 109
  Wm., 108
Ellis
  Anne, 114
  Benjamin, 246
  Elizabeth, 114
  Hezekiah, 114
  John, 114
  Mary, 114, 246
  Maryann, 246
  Mordecai, 246
  Robert, 114
  Samuel, 246
  Sarah, 114
  Uriah, 246
  William, 114, 246, 249
Ellison
  Ann, 148
  Asa, 148
  Elizabeth, 155
  Elizabeth "Betsy", 148
  James, 139, 148
  James, Jr., 137
  James, Sr., 137
  John, 148
  Jos., 138
  Joseph, 137

Mary, 148
Embry
    Betty, 165
    John, 140
    John, Sr., 130
    Richard, 140
English
    Thomas, Jr., 117
    Thomas, Sr., 117
Erskin
    Michael, 12
    Sarah, 261
Ervin, Sam'l, 10
Erwin
    George, 91
    John, 242
Estes
    Daniel, 164
    Mary, 164
    Thomas, 114
Estill
    Boud, 137, 143
    Elizabeth, 150
    Elizabeth H., 124, 138
    Isaac, 14, 120, 121, 123, 124, 137, 138, 141, 143, 145, 148, 168
    James, 262
    Jane, 143
    John, 132, 137, 143
    Miss, 143
    Priscilla, 137
    Ruth, 139, 155
    Susanna, 143
    Wallace, 136, 138, 139
    Wallace, Jr., 138
Eubank, John, 144
Evenden, James W., 50
Ewing
    Chas., 8
    Jno., 10
    John, 10
    Martha, 10
    Ro., 10
    Robt., 8, 10
    William, 10
    Wm., 10
Faldoe, Robert, 113
Fallowell
    America, 256
    Bessie E., 263
    Elizabeth, 247, 254
    Ellis J., 256, 263
    Emma E., 263
    Eva N. J., 263
    Evan E., 263
    Jane, 254, 260
    Manby, 263

Marcus, 254
Marcus B., 256
Fargason
    Daniel, 166
    Henry, 10
Farish, John, 241
Farley
    Ester, 141
    Francis, 14
    Matt, 141
Farrell
    John O., 152
    Richard, 106
    William, 154
Faulconer, John, 132
Faulkener, Georgia, 54
Faulkner
    Ellis, 114
    John, 168
    Thomas, 114
Fauntleroy, Catherine, 166
Feamster, William, 154
Fearn, John, 114
Feil
    Charles, Mrs., 45
    Clarence, 45
Fell
    Benjamin, 5, 7
    Charles, 5
    Judge, 5
    Margaret Askew, 5
Felts
    Kinchen, 133
    Philip, 133
Ferneyhough, John, 145
Ferrell, John, 158
Field
    Anne, 135
    Esther, 241
    Henry, 131, 241
    Jean, 131
    Richard, 135
Fisher
    Elizabeth, 8
    Elizth., 4
    Isaac, 139, 141, 147
    John, 5, 8
    John, Jr., 8
    John, Sr., 5
    Polly, 147
    Rachel, 147
    William, 147
Fitch
    John, Mr., 42
    Virginia, 42
Fleshman

Hannah, 146
John, 150
Michael, 142, 146
Peter, 131, 142, 146, 147
Fletcher, William, 16
Flinn, Polly, 142
Flower, Geo., 106
Floyd
    Buck, 176, 183
    Phebe, 183
    Walter, 183
Foldin
    James, 10, 13, 14, 19
    Mary "Polly", 19, 22
Fore, Sarah, 141
Fort
    Arthur, 132
    John, 116, 120
    Joseph, 133
    Joshua, 118, 132
    Lewis, 133
Fortner, Miss, 54
Foster
    Anthony, 144
    Anthony, Jr., 144
    Anthony, Sr., 144
    Christopher, 116
    Edmund, 144
    Frances (Jones), 144
    George, 154
    Henry, 144
    John, 144
    John, Mrs., 45
    Lucy, 144
    Mary, 144
    Moses, 133
    Robert, 144
    Sarah, 144
    Thomas, 144
    Thos., 145
Fowler
    Bryan Keith, 272
    Darrell, 272
    Tiffany Nicole, 272
Fox
    George, 2, 5
    John, 129
    Thomas, 129
Fraizier
    Alexander, 116, 121, 124, 128, 129, 130, 131, 140
    John, 128, 129, 130
    William, 129
    Wm., 119
Franklin, Albert, 260
Frazer
    James, 144
    Jas., 145
    Robert, 144
    Thomas, 144
Freeman, Anthony "Crum", 181
Freidenberg, Hannah, 50
French, David, 147
Frissell
    William, 106
    Wm., 111
Frogg
    Elizabeth, 123, 145
    Elizabeth (Strother), 130
    Elizabeth Strother, 120, 138
    John, 120, 123, 126
    John, Jr., 120
Fulgham
    Joseph, 134
    Michael, 119
Fulks
    Charles, 189
    Claude Vincent, 189
    Dan, 189
    Dill, 189
    Frank, 190
    Glenn, 189
    Jeff, 189
    Joe, 190
    Leland, 189
    N. D. "Dill", 189
    Norma, 189
    Ross, 189
    Sylvia, 179
    Sylvia (Lewis), 179, 189
Fuller
    David, 44
    Girard R., 42
    Henry, 44
    Jane, 264
    Jennette, 44
    Laura, 33
    Tina, 44
Fulton
    Claire Elaine, 72
    Marcus, 72
    Mary, 72
    Michael, 72
    Nathaniel Thomas, 72
    Rebecca "Becky", 72
Gaar
    Andrew, 147
    Benjamin, 147
Gabor, Barbara, 182
Gaines
    Martha, 130
    Richard, 131
    Richd., 131
    Thomas, 150
    William, 130

Gallaspie
  Andrew, 250
  Hugh, 16
Galloway
  Augustus, 25
  Charles Frederick, 180
  Charles Kenneth, 191
  Chloe, 58, 62
  Chloe (Scarberry), 43, 51
  Delia Clara, 47, 57
  Della, 179
  Della Mae, 56
  Evert J., 180
  Frank Edwin, 180
  Frederick C., 180
  Henry, 47, 179
  Henry H., 180
  Ira Jackson, 180
  Jackson O., 180
  James Everett, 180
  James Nicholas, 56
  Jesse Morton, 180
  John, 41, 43, 47, 179, 180
  John Thomas Morton, 47, 179
  Louis F., 180
  Mary, 41, 50
  Mary (Lewis), 180
  Myrtie R., 180
  Myrtle Ruth, 180
  Norman, 180, 270
  Oscar E., 180
  Susannah, 47, 179
  T. H., Mrs., 42
  Thomas H., 180
  Thomas Hastings, 43, 47
  Tom, 43, 52, 58
  Walter, 56
  William H., 47
  William Henry, 191
Gampp
  Beth, 199
  Craig, 199
  Dean Maurice, 199
  Stephen, 199
Gardner
  Ann, 115
  Martha, 115
  William, 140
Garlick, James M., 27
Garner
  Barbara Ann, 193, 198
  Carolyn Jean, 193, 199
  Kelly, 193
  Mary, 6
  Raymond Earl, 193
  Thomas Dale, 193
Garnett
  Edmund, 131, 155
  James, 131
Garrett
  Ira, 167
  William, 128
Garrison
  Charles, 70
  Christy Dyan, 70
Garton
  Anne, 141
  Charles, 138, 147
  Elijah, 124, 137, 138
  Eliza, 138
  Elizabeth, 15
  Griffith, 138
  Griffy, 137
  Isaac, 138
  Mary, 137
  Milly, 141
  Nathaniel, 124, 137, 138, 141
  Richard, 137, 141, 152
  Sarah, 124, 138
  Thompson, 138
  Uriah, 124, 137
  William, 15, 137
  Zachariah, 138
  Zachary, 124
Gash, Michael, 244
Gates, Patricia, 200
Gatewood, Peter, 154
Gatliff
  Charles, 139
  Martha, 139
  Widow, 139
Gay, William, 118
Gaylor, James, 242
Gee, John, 149
Gentilin, Andrew, 200
George
  Bird, 143
  Catherine, 143
  Catherine (Spencer), 130
  Edward, 130
  Elizabeth, 143
  Isaac, 124, 128, 129, 130, 145
  John, 115, 143
  John Dudley, 143
  Joseph, 122, 130
  Reuben, 143
  Reuben, Jr., 143
  Reuben, Sr., 143
  Richard Dudley, 143
  Robert, 143
  Sarah, 128, 143
  Sarah (Marks), 128

Thomas, 156
William, 115, 130, 143
William Francis, 143
Winiford, 130
Gibbons, Garrison, 142
Gibbs
    Charles R., 125
    Churchill, 140
    Elizabeth, 113
    George, 161
    James, 123
    John, 108
Gilbert, Thomas, 167
Gilchrist, John, 244
Gilfilen
    Dessie, 41
    Dessie (Galloway), 56
    Louis, 56
Gill, John, 147
Gillette
    Doris, 269
    Frances, 171
    Horatio, 172
Gilliland, Susannah, 157
Gilpin, Henry, 116
Gimbo, Jas., 124
Glassell, Andrew, 146
Glinn
    Gideon, 248
    Hannah, 243
    John, 242, 243
Goath, Hugh, 111
Goggin
    Pamela, 237
    Pleasant M., 237
    Stephen, 7, 237
    Steven, 240
Gold, Priscilla, 137, 143
Golding, John, 142
Goodall
    Charles, 142
    Elizabeth, 138
    John, 142, 144, 154, 155
    Parks, 158
    Thelma, 266
Goodwin, Thomas, 111
Gorby
    Becky, 272
Gordon, John, 126
Gore
    Henry, 109, 126, 127, 139
    James, 138
    John, 107, 121, 127
    John, Jr., 123, 127
    Joseph, 104, 107, 108, 109, 112, 121, 126, 127, 138, 139, 156
    Margaret, 107
    Mary, 112, 127, 138

    Reuben, 127
    Sarah, 107, 121, 126, 127, 143
Goss, John, 167
Goulding, Wm., 111
Graham
    Avagene, 196
    James, 138
    Lanty, 157
    Wm., 157
Grant, Will, 142
Graves
    John, 241
    William, 144
Gray
    Ann, 109
    Benjamin, 109
    Harold, 188
    Hollis, 188
    John, 128
    Joseph, 120
    Lafe, 188
    Lucy, 149
    Samuel, 109
    William, 108, 119
    William, Jr., 117
Greaver
    Philip, 164
    Susannah, 32, 164
Greecion
    James, 114
    Mary, 114
Green
    Forrester, 250
    Nan, 67
    Thomas, 138
Greer, Benjamin, 237
Gregory
    Charles, 118
    Charles, Jr., 119
    Christian, 113
    Jacob, 187
    Lucinda, 187
Gregson, Tho., 107
Gresham
    Amy, 115
    Charles, 115
    Frances, 114, 115
    John, 115
    Mary, 115
    Thomas, 115
Gressum, Ann, 114
Gridley, Horatio, 160
Griffen, Eli, 129
Griffith
    Cynthia A., 92
    Edgar, 92
    John, 156, 160, 163, 168, 169

The Scarberrys (Scarboroughs), Doughtys, Lewises, and Paynes of Lawrence County, Ohio

Mary, 168
Mary (Jones), 156
Patterson, 11, 12
Rachel, 126
Sarah, 156, 265
Griggs
   Patience, 119
   Robert, 105
Grills, John, 144
Grimes
   John, 109, 110, 127
   Patrick, 126
   Thos., 157
Grimm, Melissa, 73
Grove
   Helen, 37
   Henry, 10
Guess, John, 244
Guilliam, Epaphroditus, 251
Gulley, John, 120
Guthry
   James, Jr., 13
   James, Sr., 13
Gutrich, John, 130
Gwinn, Eliza, 157
Haas, Mr., 266
Hackley
   Elizabeth, 131
   Jas., 131
   John, 131
   Lucy, 131
   Richard, 131
   Sarah, 131
   William, 139
Hackney
   Mary, 115
   Rebecca, 115, 167
   Wid., 108
   William, 111, 115, 120
Hadley
   John, 110
   Sarah, 112
Hafer, Bessie Lee, 193
Hagemeier
   Cooper, 202
   Ryan, 201
Haggard, Nathan, 245
Hagood, Gresham, 149
Hahn
   Calvin F., 195, 200
   Carl F., 195
   Carl G., 195
   Cheryl, 200
   Jacquetta, 200
   Jacuetta "Jackie", 202
   Jeffrey, 200

Jerry, 200
   John, 200
   Judd, 200
Haighe, William, 110
Hail, Jonas, 118
Haines, Charles, 108
Hairston, Saml., 7
Hale
   George, 105
   Mary, 105
   Nich., 105
Hall
   John, 69, 153, 243
   Jonas, 119
   Lucretia, 266
   Mathew, 7
Halstead
   Adam, 172
   Amos, 148, 155
   Elizabeth, 147
   Enos, 154
   J., 163
   Jacob, 142, 147, 162
   James, 155
   Jo., 165
   John, 139, 142, 147, 154, 155
   William, 147
Hamilton
   Albert, 36
   G. W., 36
Hancock
   George, 138
   Julia, 138
Hand
   Christopher, 154
   George, 154
   Margaret, 154
Handley
   James, 9, 11
   John, 11, 15
Hanes, Noah, 27
Hanly
   John, Sr., 15
   John, Jr., 15
Hannah, Joseph, 144
Harbour
   Elizabeth Jane, 46, 181
   George, 46, 181
Harden, George, 111
Hardiman, John, 244
Hardiway, Thomas, 135
Hardy, Louise, 195
Harper
   Celia, 20, 91, 95
   Eleanor, 13, 18, 24
   Elizabeth, 18

Henry Harrison, 20
John, 18, 20
Joseph, 18, 20, 91
Nancy, 20
Harris
   Amos, 133
   Edward, 133, 135
   Frances, 135
   Hardy, 133, 148
   Jesse, 135
   Jno., 144
   John, 116, 135, 142, 244
   John, Jr., 135
   Joseph, 133
   Lewis, 133, 135
   Lydia, 135
   Mary, 133, 135
   Mial, 133
   Mollie, 135
   Moses, 142
   Nancy, 135
   Olive, 133
   Patience, 117, 135
   Priscilla, 133
   Rebecca, 135
   Robert, 134, 144
   Sarah, 142
   William O., 167
Harrison
   Frances (Lewis), 125
   Henry, 118
   Nathaniel, 120
   Nich., 157
   Thelma, 61
Hart, Hardy, 119
Hartford, Wilma R., 62
Hartwell, William, 114
Harvey
   Ankey, 141
   Benjamin, 141, 154
   Elizabeth, 154
   James, 154
   John, 130, 143, 154
   John, Jr., 154
   Joseph, 154
   Margaret, 154
   Mary, 130
   Millie, 142
   Nancy, 142
   Nicholas, 154
   Sarah, 154
   Susannah, 154
   Thomas, 147
Harwick, Robert, 53
Haselwood
   Ann, 108
   Anne, 113
   Geo., 110
   George, 108, 113
   John, 108
Haskew, John, 144
Haskins
   Joseph, 8, 152
   Julia, 20
   Lucretia, 191
   Nancy, 30
   William, 30
Hassler, Mr., 11
Hatcher
   Jessee, 31
   Mary F., 31
   Minerva M., 31
   Uriah, 31
Hatfield, John, 116
Hawkins
   Benja., 126
   John, 130
   Mary, 132
   Matilda, 151
   Sarah, 151
   William, 145
   Wm., 129
Hayde, Arthur, 50
Haydon, Thomas, 114
Hayes
   Elijah, 119
   Elisha, 118, 119
   Mark, 40, 41
   Mary, 40, 41
   Rutherford B., 35
   Sarah E., 181
Hayworth
   Absalom, 6
   George, 4, 6, 7
   James, 6
   John, 6
   Mary, 7
   Rachel, 6
   Sarah, 4
   Stephanus, 6
Head
   Alexr. Spence, 154
   Anthony, 114
Heale
   Ellen, 105
   George, 105
Healy, Jno., 115
Heapps, Virginia, 57
Heastand, Henry. *See* Halstead
Heid, Willis, 50
Henderson
   Albert, 164
   Cerepter, 164
   James, 8, 11, 24, 36, 136, 139, 145

The Scarberrys (Scarboroughs), Doughtys, Lewises, and Paynes of Lawrence County, Ohio

John, 8, 136
John S., 160
John T., 19
Mary, 36
Thomas, 160
William, 139
Henry III of England, 1
Henry VII of England, 252
Henry, Patrick, 240
Hensley, Cora Mae, 37
Herbert
   Elizabeth, 251
   Evan, 251
   John, 136
   William, 251
Herndon
   David, 114
   Edward, 114, 144
   Wm., 145
Herring
   Eliza Mildred, 166
   Jonathan, 166
   Mary, 166
   Sarah, 166
   William, 145, 166
Hesson
   Charles, 50
   Willie, Mr. and Mrs., 50
Hester, Dovie, 39
Hewell
   Frances, 241
   Jos., Jr., 241
   Joseph, 241
Hewit
   Elizabeth, 137
   Mary, 137
   Patrick, 137
Hicks
   Ann E., 149
   Edwin, 149
   Harriet, 149
   Louisa, 149
   Malinda, 37
   Reuben, 149, 150
   Sally E., 149
   Thomas, 150
Higgins
   Alonzo, 260
   Clark, 260
   Elizabeth, 261
   Emily, 185, 266, 267, 268
   Emily J., 57, 260, 269
   Hannah (Corn), 260
   James, 261
   John, 248, 261
   John A., 261
   Kelly, 260
   Margaret, 261
   Mary, 260
   Nancy, 261
   Reuben, 260
   Sarah, 260
   Thomas, 260, 261
Hill
   Ambrose P., 151
   Ann, 129, 157, 167
   Anne, 116
   Armistead, 151
   Audrey (Barrick?), 108
   Betty, 132
   Catherine, 106, 110, 141, 145, 154, 156, 157, 158
   Charles, 108, 111, 139
   Dorothy, 111
   Eliz., 157
   Elizabeth, 130
   Frances, 157
   Francis, 157
   Green, Jr., 136
   Harmon, 136
   Henry, 118, 119, 129, 136, 150, 151, 155, 166
   Hermon, 118, 119, 136
   James, 157
   Jas., Jr., 157
   Jas., Sr., 157
   John, 132, 157, 166
   Jos. R., 157
   Judith, 139, 155, 157
   Letitia (Morgan), 111
   Madison, 157, 158
   Malvina, 156
   Martin, 156
   Mary, 153, 157
   Nancy, 156, 157
   Needles, 111, 139, 151
   Polly (Day), 157
   Reuben, 137, 139, 141, 146, 147, 148, 151, 153, 157
   Reuben D., 157
   Richard, 129, 166
   Richd., 129
   Russell, 151
   Sarah, 151
   Spencer, 156
   Susan, 166
   Susannah, 157
   Swinfield, 16
   Thomas, 106, 130, 151, 243
   William, 112, 120, 139, 151, 156
   Wm., 157
   Wm. D., 157
Hilliard
   Martha, 115
   Thomas, 115

Hillman, Joseph, 145
Hinchman
   Jno., 157
   Joseph, 8
   William, Sr., 8
Hinton
   Ardelia, 169
   David, 169
   Eleanor, 168
   Evan, 138, 156, 168
   Evan T., 169
   John, 138, 142, 168, 169
   John "Jack", 168
   John David, 169
   Margaret, 168
   Mary, 156
   Mary A., 169
   Nancy (Milburn), 169
   Peter, 169
   Thomas, 8, 141, 148
   Thomas L., 169
   Thurman, 169
Hipkins
   John, 140
   Thomas, 106, 140
Hix, Malinda, 25
Hobson, Phebe, 241
Hoffman
   George H., 29
   Rachel, 182
Holcombe, Jacob, 4
Holden, Joseph, 118
Holder
   Caleb, 123
   Joane, 2
Holderby
   John, 265
   O. P., 265
Holland
   Benj., 237
   Geo., 250
   Michael, 244
   Peter, 237, 249
Hollingworth, George, 66
Holloday, John, 144
Holmes
   George, 178
   Sarah, 178
   Virginia, 178
Holshuh, Glen, 186
Holt, Jesse, 132
Home, Roddom, 246
Homes, Stephen, 166
Honaker
   Ralph, 23
   Raymond, 191
Hook, John, 239

Hook, John, 240
Hooper, Francis, 109
Hoover
   David F., 27
   George, 16
   Herbert Clark, President, 6
   Jesse Clark, 6
   President, 4
   President Herbert, 1
Horne
   Eldon, 71
   Jennifer Lynn, 71
Horner, Mrs., 118
House, Alexander, 11
Howard
   Agnes (Lewis), 143
   Charles, 143
   Mordecai, 134
   Samuel, 183
   William, 130
Howell
   Abner, 239
   John, 239, 242
   Nancy, 239
   Thomas, 111
   Winifred, 242
Hubbard
   Ephraim, 127
   Mary, 127
   Mathew, 134
Hucklescot, Thomas, 107
Hudnall, William, 14
Huffman
   Elizabeth, 50
   John, 50
Hughes
   Ann, 130
   Anthony, 130, 131, 155
   Daniel, 113, 114, 115
   Elizabeth, 130, 131
   Francis, 129, 130, 131
   John, 123, 125, 128, 130
   Mathew, 130
   Mrs., 123, 128, 129, 145
   Rebecca, 115
   Thomas, 130, 131
   Thomas, Jr., 130
   Thomas, Sr., 130
   William, 130
Hume
   G., 126
   John, 131
Humphreys
   John, 144
   Robert, 110, 111
Hungate, Sue, 189
Hunt, Ann, 134

Hunter
    Andrew, 250
    Andrew, Jr., 250
    Francis, 250
    George, 250
    Jane, 250
    John, 244
    Mary, 250
    Peter, 250
    Stephen, 250
    William, 122, 125, 126, 250
Huston, Jas., 144
Hutchinson
    John, 158
    Sarah, 8
    Wm., 154
Hutchison
    Isaac, 14, 146, 151, 154, 158
    J., 138
    Jn., Jr., 171
    John, 15, 136, 137, 143, 151, 154
Ingles
    Mary Draper, 14
    Wayne, 92
    Wayne B., 91, 261
Inglish
    Nathan, 118
    Thomas, 118, 120
    Thomas, Jr., 118
    Thomas, Sr., 118
Ingo
    Frances, 119, 120
    James, 119
    Mary, 120
Ingram
    Elizabeth, 123
    Hannah, 123
    Jemima, 134
    John, 111, 123, 134
    John, Jr., 123
    Samuel, 111, 123
Ireland, Jean, 242
Irvine
    Christopher, 7
    William, 8
Irwin
    Geprge, 92
    John T., 91
Jack, a slave, 107
Jackson
    Ann, 135
    David, 135
    Henry, 135
    Mark, 135
    Rebecca, 135
    Robert, 149
    Sandal, 135
    Stephen, 135
    Tabitha, 134
James
    Agnes, 119
    Ann, 114, 125
    Daniel, 241
    Dianah, 241
    George, 241
    Henry, 241
    Jenny, 241
    John, 241
    Joseph, 241
    Mary, 241
    Mary (Wheeler), 241
    Sherwood, 114
    Thomas, 241
    Wm., 119
Jameson
    James, 115, 129, 167
    Rebecca, 113
    Rebecca (Hackney), 115
    Thos., 131
Jammal
    Ayah Samih, 68
    Issa Samih, 68
    Muhammad Samih, 68
    Samih, 68
    Yousef Fadel, 68
    Zackariya Samih, 68
Jarboe, Lucille (Malan), 64
Jarrell
    Lemuel, 18
    Thomas, 120
Jarvis, Lindsay, 111
Jenkins
    Albert, 35
    Celia, 151
    Lynd, 199
Jeter, John, 238, 239, 240
Jewel
    Karen, 199
    Leanne Ruth, 199, 201
    Leslie, 198
    Stacey, 198
John, King of England, 261
Johnson
    Barnabas, 143
    Charles Ernest, 189
    Elizabeth (Bush), 167
    Elizabeth (Moorman), 248
    Esther Ann Bates, 28
    Frances, 166
    Helen, 266
    Isaac, 129
    Jacob, 108

James, 9, 238, 240, 247
Jane, 143
Jesse, 238, 247
John, 115, 244
Joseph, 238, 247, 248
Laural, 67
Lucy (Moorman), 248
Margaret, 130, 170
Mary, 12
Mary Ann, 178
May, 50
Mr., 180
Peter, 126
Richard, 137
Robert, 143
Thomas, 12
Thomas, Jr., 242
Thos., 157, 244
William, 18, 107, 122

Johnston
    Andrew, 14, 128
    Anne, 128
    Elizabeth, 128, 131, 132
    James, 9
    Jane, 242
    John, 127, 128, 131
    Larkin, 114
    Margaret, 128, 132
    Peter, 126, 128, 130, 131, 132
    Peter, Jr., 128
    Priscilla, 128
    Sarah, 128
    Thomas, 10
    William, 128
    Wm., 241

Jones
    Benjamin, 144
    Bob, 42
    Catey, 144
    Catlett, 144
    Elizabeth, 125, 144
    Foster, 144
    Gabriel, 130
    George, 144, 145
    George Webb, 144
    H. C., 64
    Hugh, 144
    Hugh, Jr., 144
    Humphrey, 107
    Humphrey, Jr., 106
    Humphrey, Sr., 106
    Humphry, 106
    James, 125, 156
    John, 109, 144
    Joseph, 125, 126, 127, 144
    Joseph, Jr., 125
    Joshua, 156
    Lola, 67
    Margaret (Strother), 130
    Margaret Morton, 130
    Mary, 156
    Mary B., 261
    Morton, 144
    Mosias, 144, 145
    Mosias, Jr., 144
    Phebe, 145
    Robert, 119
    Robt., 144
    Rose (Morgan), 111
    Strother, 130
    Thomas, 144
    William, 95, 144, 156
    Wm., 144

Jopling, Thomas, 157

Jordan
    Batt, 119
    George, 119
    John Morton, 120
    Mary, 143

Joyner, John, 134
Justice, Sarah, 255
Kafer, Michael, 147
Kaiser, The, 54
Kavanaugh, William, 139
Kearns, Minnie Belle, 191

Keaton
    Jennie, 154
    Lucy, 142

Keenan, Edward, 11

Keeny
    Catherine (Lewis), 143
    David, 144
    Moses, 144

Keller
    Adam, 148
    Anna Catherine, 126, 139
    Conrad, 126
    Renee, 189

Kello, Richard, 133, 148

Kelly
    Ann, 122
    Frank, 183
    James, 123, 139
    Jesse, 147
    John, 129

Kemp
    Ann, 115
    Dorothy, 105
    Edmund, 106, 111
    Elizabeth, 111
    Mathew, 107, 109, 111, 115
    Mathew, Jr., 105, 115
    Matthew, 106, 111
    Matthew, Sr., 105

Robert, 103, 106
Kendall, Nicole, 68
Kennedy
    James, 9
    Rachel, 9, 16
Kennerly
    James, 138
    James, Jr., 144
    Mary, 138
    Samuel, 138
Kenny, Ann, 241
Kentish, Richard, 106
Kentsler, John, 50
Kerchival, Samuel, 261
Kessinger
    Anne, 141
    Mary, 142
    Mathew, 137
    Mathias, 137, 154
Kidd, Thomas, 109
Kilby
    Agatha, 150
    Armistead, 150, 151
    Catharine, 136
    Catherine, 105, 110, 117, 120, 121
    Catherine (Hill), 108
    Catherine (Lewis), 120
    Chris., 136
    Christopher, 106, 108, 109, 110, 111, 116, 117, 119, 120, 121, 139, 150
    Elizabeth, 119, 120, 121
    Epaphroditus, 120, 121, 136, 150
    Epar., 136
    Fanny, 151
    Frances, 120, 121
    Henry, 151
    James, 136, 150
    Joanna, 110, 121
    Johanna, 109, 119
    Joseph, 151
    Katherine, 109, 119
    Katherine (Lewis), 116
    Kathi., 109
    LeRoy, 151
    Lucy (Sparks), 150
    Mary, 105, 110, 119
    Sarah, 120, 121
    Thomas, 150, 151
    Will., 109
    William, 105, 106, 108, 109, 110, 111, 116, 119, 121, 150
Kilpatrick
    Ann, 148
    Elizabeth, 148
    James, 143
    Roger, 143, 148
    Thomas, 143, 148

Kincaid
    Angie, 272
    Betsey, 23
    James, 18, 144
    Jane, 20
    John, 10, 18
    Thomas, 10
Kinchen, William, 116, 120
King
    Agnes, 2
    John, 134, 141
    Joseph, 150
    Mary, 136
    Mary Ann, 182
    Nathaniel, 134
    Wm., 136
    Zebulon, 134, 149
Kippers, John, 153
Kirby
    John, 132
    Richard, 243
    Richard, Jr., 132
    Richard, Sr., 132
Kirk, Margaret, 9
Kirkman
    Mary, 164
    Maybelle "May", 179
    Maybelle Elizabeth, 179
    Nicholas G., 179
    Will, 164
Kirtley
    Francis, 140
    Thomas, 125
    William, 140
Kitterman, Elizabeth Jane, 37
Kizer, Martin, 144
Klein, Mary Ellen, 197
Knight
    Edward W., 181
    Lucy, 128
    Orson, 157
    Patrick, 123
Knox
    Elisha, Sr., 137
    Nancy, 137, 141
    Owen "Nubby", 92
    Wm., 114
Lacy, Daniel, 18
LaFayette, Marquis de, 133
Laffoon, Mathew, 134
Lafore, Rose May, 60
Lain, Thomas M., 92
Lamburt, Daniel, 129, 130, 132
Lampkin, Jane, 237
Lancaster, Nancy, 240
Landale, And., 123

Lane, Sarah, 264
Lanning, James, 37
Lanson (Lawson), John, 110
Larney, Hannah, 123
Larue
    Abraham, 132, 143
    Ann, 132, 143
    Anna, 143
    Elizabeth, 143
    Jacob, 143, 147
    John M., 143
    Margaret, 143
    Martha J., 143
    Nancy, 143
    Peter, 132, 137, 143
    Polly F., 143
    Rebecca, 143
    Reuben, 132
    Sarah, 143
    Wilson, 143
Laurie, D. J., 64
Lawler
    Della, 265
Lawrence
    John, 114, 139, 141
    William, 139
Lawson
    Epa., 104
    Epaphraditus, 110
    Epaphroditus, 105, 110, 120, 156
    Jane, 109, 110
    Joanna, 110
    Johannah, 110
    John, 105
    Rowland, 110
Lawyers
    Elizabeth, 155
    Joseph, 155
Lea, James, 241
Leak
    Austin D., 243
    Elizabeth, 130, 140
    William, 130, 140
Leaps, Henry, 16
Lee
    Hen., 105
    James, 115
    Joan, 105
    Johannah (Morgan), 111
    Song, 196
Lemley
    Hattie, 180, 190
    Jacob W., 180
Leonard
    Adam, 8
    Agnes, 17
    David, 17
    Edy, 17
    Elizabeth, 17
    Jacob, 17
    John, 17
    William, 17
Lewis
    Abel, 161
    Abraham, 125
    Agatha, 120, 146
    Aggie A., 179, 188
    Aletha, 178, 184
    Alfonso, 162
    Alice, 170
    Alice A., 170
    Allen G., 171
    Alonzo Perry, 161
    Alva, 178
    Alvin Earnest, 191
    Amanda, 149, 171
    Amanda Melvina, 150
    Amelia Belle, 172
    America, 172
    America (Dolton), 175
    America (Murnahan), 182
    America S., 174
    Andrea Jerrell, 198
    Andrew, 11, 118, 120, 124, 145, 146, 148
    Ann, 127, 146
    Anna, 148, 152, 153
    Anna Gertrude, 181
    Anne, 119, 125
    Arnold, 177, 186, 187, 194
    Arta June, 190
    B. C., 175
    Barbara Jane, 170, 181
    Basel, 160
    Beatrice Faye, 191
    Becky, 133
    Benjamin, 116, 117, 132, 133, 134, 135, 136, 143, 148, 149, 150, 182
    Benjamin Bryant, 183
    Benjamin, Jr., 133, 149
    Berdie, 178, 185
    Berdie (Petrie), 187
    Bernard, 188
    Berry, 124
    Bertha, 180, 181
    Betty, 184, 186, 192, 270
    Betty June, 186, 193
    Beverly, 194
    Blake, 175
    Bob, 28
    Brenda, 194, 196
    Brown B., 171
    C. B. B., 173, 174
    Calvania E., 173
    Carlas, 270

Carlos, 187
Caroline, 171
Catharine, 146
Catherine, 118, 119, 121, 139, 150, 153, 156, 159, 163, 165, 167, 171, 172
Catherine (Brockman), 167
Catherine (Brockman) Spicer, 165
Catherine (Hill), 126, 155, 158, 163
Catherine (Wales), 173
Cathey, 194
Caty, 125
Charles, 105, 118, 125, 127, 187
Chester Woodrow, 191
Cora M., 183
David, 140, 144, 173
David W., 161
David, Jr., 140
Dean, 193, 198
Donald, 185, 186
Dorcas, 119
Dr., 149
Edmund, 104, 105, 106, 109, 112, 113, 117, 118, 119
Edna (Payne), 178, 185, 270
Edna M., 184
Edward, 120, 163
Edwin G., 149
Edwin Gray, 149
Effie, 168, 169
Eleanor, 134, 152
Eliza, 177
Eliza Ann, 152
Elizabeth, 104, 114, 133, 140, 147, 148, 149, 152, 162
Elizabeth (Mann), 171
Elizabeth A., 170
Elizabeth Sandal, 150
Ella, 178
Ella G., 179, 187
Ellen, 161
Elva B., 179, 187
Elvira, 171
Erma, 192, 270
Erma Ruth, 184, 186, 193
Ernest "Ray", 192, 269
Ernest Ray, 59, 186, 192
Ernest Robert, 68, 193
Ernestine Faye, 59, 186, 192
Ervin Washington, 172
Ethel, 178
Ethel M., 178
Eugene, 187
Evan Robert, 68, 198
Evelyn S., 183
Ezra, 178, 184, 185, 192
Ezra C., 184
Ezra Clare, 178, 268
Fannie, 169

Faye, 58, 177, 184, 190, 261
Fielding, 127, 130
Fran., 127
Frances, 133, 168
Francis, 152
Francis Marion, 46, 172, 181
Frank, 171, 195
Franklin, 170
Franklin Lee, 193
Gary, 187, 195
Geo. B., 161
George, 114, 143, 145, 168, 169, 172, 175, 180, 181
George F., 161
George P., 174
George S., 161, 174
Georgia, 170
Georgia A., 170
Goldie, 175
Goldie E., 175
Grace, 130
Griffin C., 174
Griffith C., 183
Gwinn S., 173
Hannah, 174
Harriet, 168, 169, 171
Harriet F., 172
Harry, 176
Harry Donald, 191
Hattie, 180, 181
Hazel, 175, 182, 183
Hazel D., 175
Helen, 188
Henrietta, 174
Henrietta "Hattie", 182
Henrietta (Hattie), 37
Henry, 118, 124, 125, 131, 136, 139, 149, 165, 167, 170
Henry, Jr., 124
Ida, 181
Ida (Null), 182
Ida E., 174
Ina E., 179, 188
Irvin, 171
Isabella, 152
J., 126, 130, 140
James, 103, 104, 105, 106, 107, 108, 109, 110, 112, 114, 115, 117, 118, 119, 121, 123, 125, 127, 131, 132, 136, 140, 149, 155, 158, 163, 164, 168, 174, 175, 176, 184, 185
James A., 176, 186, 192
James Albert, 164, 177
James D., 171
James Edmunds, 150
James F., 161
James G., 152
James J., 43, 47, 147, 154, 156, 158, 159, 162, 163, 165, 176, 177
James M., 171

James Madison, 172
James W., 149
James William, 150
James, Jr., 110, 113, 115, 121, 167
James, Sr., 112, 114
Jane, 104, 116, 152
Jane (Jean), 136
Jane (Jenny), 133
Janet, 194
Jas., Jr., 145
Jean (Best), 152
Jennie, 174
Jennifer L., 195, 201
Jenny, 133
Jenny (Butts), 148
Jerry, 195, 196, 200
Jesse, 152, 160, 161
Jesse B., 160
Jesse Pauline, 191
Jimmy, 196
Joanna, 110, 114, 117, 118, 119
Joel, 140, 144
Johanna, 108, 109, 112, 123
John, 103, 104, 107, 114, 115, 124, 125, 126, 127, 130, 131, 140, 143, 144, 145, 146, 147, 148, 151, 152, 153, 154, 159, 160, 161, 162, 166, 167, 168, 172
John B., 161, 173
John Calvin, 169
John Denver, 191
John F., 116, 137, 140, 149, 155, 159, 165, 166, 167
John F. E., 149
John Flood Edmunds, 150
John H., 149
John Oscar, 183, 191
John Peter, 160
John R., 171
John W., 174
John Wilson, 174, 182
John, Jr., 143, 166
John, Sr., 166
Jone, 121
Joseph, 153
Joseph Warner, 150
Joshua, 26, 106, 109, 112, 113, 114, 117, 118, 119, 120, 126, 136, 138, 142, 145, 146, 147, 148, 151, 152, 153, 154, 155, 156, 157, 158, 162, 165, 168, 169, 170, 171, 172, 202
Joshua, Capt., 118
Josua, 141
Juanita, 196
Judith (Long), 114
Katharine, 119
Katherine, 107, 109, 110, 113, 140, 143
Kathy, 28, 171
Keith, 194
Kim L., 201
Kimberly, 194
Larry, 196

Lavinia, 162
Lennie, 176, 190
Lennie Gertrude, 191, 197
Lewis A. G. J., 173
Lewis Edward, 164
Lewis Edward "Buck", 177
Lillian, 192
Linda, 196
Lisa, 195
Lizzie, 180
Lorenzo Dow, 172
Lucinda, 168, 169
Lucy, 146, 147, 153
Lucy Gray, 150
Luther P., 173
Lydotia, 162
Lyndell, 187, 194
Madison, 126, 156, 159, 161, 163, 172, 173
Mae M., 182
Maggie, 170
Mahala J., 174
Margaret A. (Johnson), 170
Marietta, 161, 162
Marinda (Payne), 253
Martha, 118, 119, 172
Martha (Marston), 117
Mary, 43, 47, 103, 111, 115, 133, 137, 141, 143, 146, 152, 162, 163, 164, 168, 176, 179, 182, 188, 190
Mary "Polly", 137, 148, 157
Mary (Burcham), 160
Mary (Harris), 133
Mary (Sowards), 174
Mary A., 180
Mary Ann, 145, 147, 162
Mary E., 163, 173
Mary Ellen, 164, 175
Mary Jane, 190, 196
Mary M., 175, 179
Matthew Thomas, 198
Maud, 182
Maude "Helen", 183
Melissa, 161, 162
Mille, 118, 119
Minnie, 172, 182
Minnie (Kearns), 191
Minnie Helen, 191
Miranda (Payne), 248
Mirinda, 160
Missouri, 162
Missouri A., 161
Molly, 185, 195
Molly (Bailey), 192
Morton, 165, 167
Myrtie, 180
Myrtie M., 181
Nancy, 125, 133, 168, 169, 180
Nancy Best, 153

Nathan, 116, 117, 135
Nathaniel, 117, 135
Nellie, 175
Nellie (Massie), 188
Nellie P., 175
Nelrose, 194
Nelson, 190
Nelson Douglas, 196
Nelson Moody, 190, 195
Nicholas E., 149
Nicholas Edmunds, 149
Norborne, 149
Norborne W., 149
Norborne Wesley, 150
Oscar, 178, 182, 186
Otha Leland, 191
Otis, 177, 178, 184
Otis Hartley, 178, 187
Patience, 116, 117, 135
Paul, 182, 190, 192, 270
Paul Eugene, 190, 196
Pearl, 163, 164
Percy, 174
Perry, 161
Peter, 134, 175
Peter H., 174
Phebe, 143
Philena, 161
Quincy, 173
R. B., 170
R.J.C.K., 104
Rachel, 171, 172, 174, 178, 184
Rachel (Anderson), 190
Rachel (Dillon), 174
Ralph, 181
Ray, 184, 185, 186, 192, 195, 261
Rebecca, 133, 161, 162, 163, 173, 174, 176
Rebecca (Burd), 177
Rebecca (Sowards), 151
Redman C., 161, 162, 175
Rhoda (Miller), 169
Rhoda C., 171
Richard, 103, 104, 106, 107, 111, 112, 113, 115, 124, 127, 130, 140, 143, 161, 163, 168
Richard Anderson, 191
Richard B., 147, 158, 162, 168, 175
Richard Burton, 46, 138, 154, 159, 167
Richard Clark, 46, 49, 169, 180
Richard, Jr., 104
Robert, 127, 143, 166, 171, 173
Robert Allen, 162, 172
Robert J.C.K., 111
Robert L., Jr., 171
Robert Linuel, 181
Robt., 172
Rosa, 170, 171

Rose, 163, 164
Rosella, 184, 192
Rosella (Pinkerman), 178
Rosemarian, 187
Ruby, 182
Rufus S., 173
Sally, 149, 163, 164
Sally A., 174
Sally E., 173, 174
Sally Edmunds, 150
Saml. D., 170
Samuel, 14, 107, 109, 115, 116, 120, 121, 123, 124, 126, 127, 128, 129, 131, 132, 136, 137, 138, 139, 140, 141, 142, 143, 144, 145, 146, 147, 151, 152, 153, 154, 155, 156, 159, 160, 161, 162, 165, 166, 168, 170, 181, 182, 248, 253
Samuel D., 109, 124, 139, 159, 169, 171
Samuel F., 37, 161, 174, 175
Samuel, Jr., 138, 141, 142, 146, 147, 148, 151, 153, 170
Samuel, Sr., 146, 147, 148, 151, 153, 155
Sandal (Jackson), 134
Sarah, 114, 115, 118, 119, 131, 133, 143, 145, 161, 170, 174, 175
Sarah (Burcham), 161
Sarah A., 171
Sarah Ann, 162
Sarah C., 172, 182
Shirley, 198
Simeon, 125
Sophia, 134
Stanley, 175
Stanley L., 175
Stella, 163, 164
Susanna, 143
Sylvester, 175
Sylvia, 189
Sylvia I., 179
Sylvia L., 179
T., 125
T. J., 188
Tene, 119
Thelma Michelle, 196
Thomas, 113, 120, 121, 125, 163
Thomas Jefferson, 164, 179
Thomas O., 183
Thurman, 184, 185, 192, 270
Thurman Orvis, 186
Timothy, 196
Tony, 196
Tureman, 140
Virginia, 162
Virginia Helen, 191, 197
Vivian, 179
W. H., 190
Wallace, 46, 159, 170, 171
Warner, 125, 149
Wilbur R., 179, 188

Wilburt, 182
William, 104, 105, 106, 114, 115, 119, 123, 124, 125, 127, 128, 129, 131, 134, 143, 144, 145, 146, 156, 161, 162, 171, 174, 178, 182, 184, 196
William Berkeley "Bert", 178
William Berkeley (Bert), 178
William Berkley, 191
William Elmer, 182, 191
William H., 180
William Henry Harrison, 181, 190
William Henry Harrison "Willie", 49
William R., 183
William Terrell, 144
William Wallace, 172
William, Jr., 114, 124, 143
Wilson, 126, 144, 152, 159, 161, 172, 174, 175
Wilson B., 160
Wilson M., 161, 172, 182
Wilson, Jr., 126
Winifred, 145
Wm., 143
Zachary, 115, 143
Zachary, Jr., 126
Zebedee, 165
Zebedee B., 147, 159, 162, 163, 171
Zebidee, 170
Zebulon, 103, 104, 107, 109, 110, 112, 113, 115, 116, 117, 120, 121, 122, 123, 124, 125, 127, 128, 129, 131, 132, 133, 134, 136, 137, 138, 140, 142, 143, 145, 146, 147, 148, 149, 150, 151, 152, 153, 155, 163, 165, 167
Zebulon, Jr., 116, 121
Lewises of Warner Hall, 104
Lewis-Jameson
    Child, 113
Lightfoot
    Gutridge, 122
    John, 123, 126
    W., 131
Lincoln, President, 27
Lines, Robert, 126
Litt, Elizabeth, 240
Litteral, Dolly, 261
Littlepage, James, 251
Lively
    Benj., 157
    Benjamin, 157
    Bethel, 157
    Cottrell, 157, 158
    Cottrell, Jr., 157
    Cottrell, Sr., 157
    Elizabeth, 157
    Jane, 157
    John, 157
    Joseph, 157, 158
    Joseph, Jr., 157
    Judith, 157
    Madison, 157
    Mark, 157
    Martha, 157
    Mary, 157
    Philip, 157
    Sarah, 157
    Thomas, 157
    William, 157
    Wilson, 157
Livisay, Delaney, 142
Lobb
    Catherine, 140
    Elizabeth, 140
    William, 140, 241
Lockhart, Patrick, 137
Loftus
    Charity, 250
    Martha, 249, 250
Logan, Robert, 108
London, Jno., 157
Long
    Ann, 114
    Elizabeth, 114
    Fanny Ball, 131
    Gabriel, 131
    Isabella, 130
    Jeremiah, 114
    John, 122, 130
    Judith, 114
    Lawrence, 157
    Paul, 137, 141, 155
    Philip, 155
    Richard, 114
    Samuel, 114
Longest, Richard, 108
Longshore, Alice, 5
Loving
    George, 157
    Sukey, 157
    Will, Jr., 157
    Wm., 157
Low
    Samuel, 108, 112
    Thomas, 119, 154
Lowen
    John, 123, 128, 130
    Rachel, 130
    Thomas, 128
Lowry
    Elizabeth, 142
    Robert, 114
Lucas
    Elizabeth, 155
    Fredk., 134
    Nathl., 134
Luck, Nathan, 243
Lumpkin
    Tho., 12

Thomas, 14
Lunsford, Edward, 106
Lupton
    Ann (Hall), 5
    Joseph, 5
    Joseph, Jr., 5
Lykins, Nancy, 48
Lynch
    Bob, 202
    Catherine, 202
    Elizabeth, 122
    James, 202
    Jim, 202
    John, 246
    Pat, 202
Lynn
    Jane, 148
    Margaret, 148
Lynsey, Dennis, 242
Lyon
    Alex., 157
    Judith, 157
    Peter, 157
    Susanna, 157
    Wm., 157
Lyons
    Con, 267
    Gladys (Corn), 267
MacDaniell
    Joan, 109
    Randolph, 109
Machen, Thomas, 119
Machin
    Francis, 19
    Thos., 19
Mackay, Roan, 63
Mackley, Davis, 261
Macrory, Frances, 107
Maddox, John, 16
Maddy
    Ann, 142
    Anne, 141
    Anny, 141
    Barbara (Miller), 143
    Eleanor, 138, 142
    Elizabeth, 138, 141, 142, 145
    Henry, 13, 158
    J., 165
    Jacob, 147, 162
    James, 138, 139, 141, 142, 145, 158, 166
    James C., 142
    John, 17, 139, 141, 142, 158, 169
    John C., 142
    Mary, 141
    Mary "Polly", 142
    Polly, 154
    Sarah, 157, 158
    William, 137, 141, 145, 169
    Wm., 138, 147
Madestard
    Elizabeth, 105, 156
    Thomas, 105
Madison
    Ambrose, 142, 166
    Frances, 166
    Henry, 166
    James, 125, 142, 166, 167
    James, President, 248
    John, 126, 241
    President, 166, 167
    Rowland, 126
Madras, Mary, 121, 127
Maggart, Samuel, 138
Magot
    Saml., 117
    Wm., 117
Mahanes
    Elizabeth, 167
    Elizabeth (Brockman), 167
    Samuel, 167
Mahon. Jno., 11
Malan
    Bill, 64
    Eileen, 64
    Eric Paul, 65
    Geraldine (Coston), 64
    Gregory Franklin, 64
    Paul, 64
    Tamara Michelle, 65, 71
Mallory
    John, 123
    Mary, 124
    Roger, 124
    Sarah, 129
    Uriah, 122
    Urial, 144
    Uriel, 124, 128, 129, 130, 132
    William, 144
Manly, Penelope, 120
Mann
    Adam, 137, 141, 142, 154
    Adam, Jr., 139
    Elizabeth, 141, 154, 171
    Geo. A., 147, 162
    Isaac, 142
    Jacob, 137, 139, 142, 147, 153, 154
    Jacob, Jr., 142
    James, 142
    John, 139, 142, 153
    Lewis, 145
    Michael, 142
    Moses, 142

Norvel P., 145
Parthena, 142
Susan, 142
Manning
   Moses, 163
   Wilson, 163
Mannon
   Columbus C., 264
   Samuel, 20
   Vint, 264
Margerum, Jane, 5
Marks
   Elizabeth, 128
   John, 122, 128
   Marvell, 38
   Sarah, 128
Marlin, Julia, 149
Marr
   G., 244
   Js., 157
Mars, Abraham, 139, 142
Marsh, Benjamin, 109
Marshall
   Jane, 167
   Tho., 105
   Thomas, 167
Marston
   Ann, 114
   Elizabeth, 123
   John, 108, 114, 123
   Martha, 114, 118
   Mrs., 111
   Thomas, 108, 114
   William, 114
Martin
   Benjamin, 129
   Henry, 145
   Jane, 240, 242
   John, 243, 248, 249
   Joseph, 144
   Sarah, 248
Mary, Eleanor, 151
Massey
   Martha, 22
Massie
   Big Jep, 261
   Elza, 188
   James, 263
   Nellie, 188
   Oliver, 263
   Vincent, 254
Massinghall, James, 136
Mastin, Wm., 166
Mather
   Braeden, 201
   Eric, 201
Matthews, William, 109

Mattock, Valentine, 242
Mauldin, Richard, 130
Maury, Elizabeth, 114
Maxwell, Elizabeth, 15
Mayberry
   Frederick, 10
   Henry, 10
Mayer, Mr., 266
Maynard, Beverly, 190
Mays
   Elizabeth, 238
   James, 238
McAlister
   Frances (Brockman), 167
   James, 167
McBride, Elizabeth, 32, 164
McCaffrey
   Fay S., 187
   Fern, 187
   May, 187
   Meda E., 187
McCallester
   Frances (Brockman), 167
   James, 167
McCausland, John, 35
McClamary
   Bathsheba, 137
   Lydia, 137
   Mathew, 137
   Sarah, 137
McClenahan, Absalom, 10
McClung, Wm., 145
McComas
   Mahala, 265
   Sartain, 160
   Sartin, 173
McCorder
   D. L., 195
   Donald, 195
   Shawn, 195
McCorkle, Mary, 180
McCormack
   Agnes, 244
   Anderson, 238, 239, 240, 247, 251
   Chas., 245, 247
   David, 244, 245, 251
   Elizabeth, 238, 245
   Jesse, 244
   John, 244
   Lucy, 244, 245
   Mary, 245
   Micajah, 238, 239, 245, 247, 250
   Nancy, 244
   Rebecca, 245
   Sarah, 245
   Thos., 245
   William, 238, 244, 247

William, Jr., 244
Wm., 238, 240, 241, 244, 245, 251
McCormick
  Micajah, 247
  William, 239
McCown
  Lewis Edward, 189
  Robert, 188
  S., 158
McCoy
  Hayes, 266
  Lola, 269
McCreery
  John, 137, 143
  Mary, 143
  Susanna, 143
McDaniel
  Alexander, 151
  Henry, 126, 139, 151
  Henry, Jr., 126
  Henry, Sr., 126
  James, 112, 148
  Peggy, 126
McDonald, Mary, 138
McGeorge, John, 245, 251
McGhee
  Holdin, 20
  Peter, 157
  Sallie, 20
McGuire
  Joseph, 9
  Lawrence, 9, 16
  Mary, 16
McKenny, Betsy, 149
McKenzie, Capt., 118
McKinley
  Harrison, 33
  Maggie, 33
  William, 35
McKinsey, Mary "Polly", 24
McMahan
  Curtis, 92
  G. J., 265
  Grace, 265
  J., 92
  James, 160
  Marion, 92
  Sadie, 60
McMakhan, James, 19
McMullen, Daniel, 11
McNeally, John, 158
McNeer
  Anderson, 169
  Richard, 138, 139, 142
McNeill, John, 118
McNichols, Elizabeth, 253

McNiel, James, 133
McNutt
  James, 9, 13, 15, 137
  John, 16
McQueen
  Alexr., 122
  John, 123
McTyre
  Elizabeth, 143
  Hugh, 143
  James, 143
  Jane, 143
Meacham, Thomas, 114
Mead, W., 8
Meadows
  Anna, 141
  Elijah, 138, 141
  Francis, 141
  Jeremiah, 141
  Jerry, 138, 168
  Mary, 141
  Milly, 141
  Susanna, 141
  William, 141
Medley
  Ambrose, 140
  Robert, 168
Melton, John, 239
Mercer
  Capt., 118
  George, 118
  Hugh, 114, 115
  Hugh Weedon, 115
  John, 118
  Johnny, 115
Meredith
  Bradley, 18
  James, 244
Meriwether, Jane, 127, 166
Merriman, Jno., 104
Metz, Jacob, 265
Michener, John, 7
Mickelborough
  Jane, 130
  Tobias, 104
Midkiff
  Betty, 195
  Betty (Lewis), 260
  Brenda Joyce, 194, 199
  Cameron, 200
  Darrell, 194, 200
  Darrell Keith, 194
  Donald, 199
  Donald Frederick, 194
  Lauren, 200
  Mac, 195

Meredith, 199, 201
William "Mac", 194
Milburn
   Isaac, 138, 169
   Nancy, 169
Milkin, Francis, 130
Miller
   Adam, 148, 155
   Anna B., 142
   Barbara, 141, 142
   Charles, 170
   Daniel, 141
   Elizabeth, 142, 259
   Geo., 148
   George, 143
   Hanna, 138
   Henry, 109, 124, 139, 140, 142, 154, 170
   Henry, Sr., 170
   Hugh, 157
   Jacob, 137, 138
   Jacob, Jr., 143
   Jacob, Sr., 142, 143
   James, 137, 145, 152
   James H., 168
   John, 139, 143
   Joseph, 29, 143
   Margaret, 143
   Michael, 138
   Patrick, 106
   Peter, 143
   Polly, 169
   Rhoda, 109, 124, 139, 142, 143, 170, 181
   Sally, 143
   William, 114, 248
Millet, Paul, 69
Mills, David, 144
Mims, John, 244
Minor
   Elizabeth, 114
   Jno., 145
   John, 114
   Sarah (Carr), 114
   William, 144
Minson, Minor, 103
Minter, Jesse, 158
Minthorn
   Huldah, 6
   Theodore, 6
Mitchell
   Capt., 149
   David, 126
   Diana, 134
   James, 244
   Jane, 107
   John, 134
   Mary J., 141
   Polly, 141
   Will., 106
   William, 134, 149
Mogavero, Drusilla Payne, 258
Monroe
   James, President, 125
   Spence, 125
Montague
   Thomas, 130
   Thomas, Jr., 130
   William, 107
Montgomery, Ann, 146
Moon
   Judith, 247, 248
   Will, 12
Moore
   Ann (Marks), 128
   Deborah, 69
   Francis, 125, 128
   Frans., 126
   Harbin, 128, 130
   Joel, 134
   John, 165
   John R., 136
   Lucinda, 38
   Sarah, 134
   William, 133, 134
   Wilson, 134
   Wm., 123
Moorman
   Charles, 247, 248, 250
   Charles (Towhead), 248
   Chas., 244, 248
   Elizabeth, 247, 252, 254
   Elizabeth (Payne), 247
   Hiram, 252
   James, 239, 240, 246, 247, 248, 252
   James P., 252
   James, Jr., 247
   James, Sr., 247
   Jane, 252
   Jas., 248
   John V., 252
   Judith, 247
   Mary, 248
   Milly, 247
   Robt., 248
   Susanna, 246
   Thomas, 247
   Thos., 248
   William H., 252
   Zach, 252
Morgan
   Ann, 111
   Ann (Barbee), 111
   Barbee, 111
   Edward, 111
   James, 111

John, 111, 113, 133
John Hunt, 261
Joseph, 111
Josiah, 111, 123
Mark, 111
Nathan, 111
Robert, 266
Rosamond, 111
Samuel, 239, 240, 241
William, 111, 123
Morris
   Elizabeth, 124
   Findlay, 123
   Margaret, 124
   Mary, 124
   Robert, 134
   Saml., 250
   Sarah, 124
   Thomas, 124
   Thomas, Jr., 124
   William, 124
   Wm., 155
Morrison
   Catherine, 128
   Catherine (Johnston), 128
   Cora, 179, 188
   Findley, 128
   Hannah, 123
   Hugh, 128
   John, 123, 128
   Lucy, 128
   Margaret, 128
   Mary, 179
   Sarah, 128
   Thomas, 123, 129, 130
   William, 128
Morton
   Ann, 120, 129
   Elijah, 120, 129
   Elizabeth, 120
   George, 120, 129, 130, 165
   Henry, 165
   Jane, 120, 165
   Jere., 144
   Jeremiah, 120, 122, 129
   John, 120, 122, 128, 129, 130, 165
   John, Jr., 122
   Joseph, 120
   Margaret Beckwith, 120
   Mary, 165
   Mary Beckwith, 120
   Oren, 8, 13, 132, 139, 142, 145, 146, 170
   Oren F., 154
   Richard, 122, 165
   Robert B., 144
   Sarah, 120, 122

   William, 122, 129, 144, 165
   William, Jr., 165
   Wm., 123, 129
Moseley
   Eaton J., 149
   Maxwell, 104
   Sarah T., 149
Moser, W. B., Mrs., 49
Moss
   Elizabeth (Tisdale), 250
   Frances, 119
   William, 119
Mothershead
   Alvin, 120, 129
   Nathl., 123, 128, 129
Muhlenburg, Peter, 133
Mullins, John, 244
Mulvern, Conrad, 8
Munday, John, 114
Murnahan
   America, 172, 182
   David, 182
   James, 172
   John, 182
   John H., 172
   Sophia, 182
Murphy
   Cornelius, 242
   Horatio, 32, 163, 164
   James, 137
   John, 246
   Sylvester, 142
Muscoe, Capt., 119
Music, William, 38
Myrick
   Mary, 133, 134
   Owen, 133
Nalle
   John, 241
   Mary, 241
   Mary (Brown), 241
Nance
   Alberta, 190
   Banister, 247, 254
   Daisy, 190
   Daniel, 19, 248
   Ernie, 190
   Lidia, 190
   Lillian, 190, 195
   Lottie, 190
   Media, 190
   Melva, 190
   Minnie, 258
   Ode, 190
   Oscar, 190
   Sadoc, 190

Wilbur, 190
Nash
   Arthur, 104
   Eileen, 188
   Elvira, 46, 171
   Fleeta, 188
   Homer, 188
   James, 171
   John, 104
   Lucille, 188
   Thomas, 188
Neal
   Charles, Sr., 92
   John, 12
   Walter, Jr., 94
Needham, Prudence, 110
Needles, Frances, 139
Neel
   Richard, 14, 18
   Walter, 15
   Wineford, 15
Neely
   Hannah (Gatliff), 139
   Robert J., 163
Neesham, Will., 104
Nelson, James, 165
Nettles, Robert, Sr., 109
Newberry, Agnes, 124
Newman, Nimrod, 237
Newport
   Betsy, 129
   John, 155
Newsom, Thomas, 120
Newton, Thomas, 111
Nicholas
   John, 15, 129
   Margaret, 15
   Wilson Cary, 19
Nicholls, Darrell, 196
Nichols
   Elizabeth, 111, 116, 167
   Hen., 103
   Henry, 104, 107
   John, 103, 111, 116
   Sarah, 103, 115, 140
   Sheila, 67
Nicholson
   Grace, 130
   Joshua, 133
   Mary, 133
   Polly (Butts), 148
   Rebecca, 134
   Robert, 116
   Robt., 134
   William, 130
Nicholson, Robert, 120
Nickell
   Barbara, 156
   William, 156
Nicolia
   George, 196
   Katen Lee, 196
   Philip, 196
   Ruth Ann, 196
   William, 196
Nimmo
   Elizabeth, 239
   R., 238, 240
   Robert, 238, 240, 241
   William, 241
   Wm., 238, 240
Nipton, Jno., 156
Nixon, Henry, 123, 127
Noel, John, 140
Norman
   Mary A., 175
   Moses, 175
Norris, Jno., 105
Norsworthy, Charles, 118
Norvel
   Betty, 157
   Reuben, 157
   Spencer, 157
Null
   Ida Rosalie, 182
   Janet Diana, 62
   Nicholas, 155
   Parkinson, 161
   Thomas Allen, 162
   William Harrison, 182
   Wm., 142
Nunely, Elizabeth, 11
Obert
   Bartram, 104
   Michael, 61
O'Brissell
   Elizabeth, 104
   Eusebias, 104
   Thomas, 104
Occany, Daniel, 242
Odom, Bethany, 135
Ogg, John, 144, 155
Ohler, Lea Ann, 70
Oliver, Thomas, 148
O'Neal
   John, 107, 115, 121, 126, 127, 131, 143
   Mary (Gore), 115
   Robert, 126
   Sarah, 127, 131
Oney, Jemima, 240
Orgain
   John, 134
   Littleberry, 149
   William D., 134

Oslanzi, Joseph, 196
Otty, John, 244
Overstreet, Thomas, 16
Owen
    Gronow, 134
    John, 242
Pace
    Mary, 140
    Thos., 136
    William, 140
Pack
    Bartlett, 138
    Bartly, 138
    Loammi, 157
    William, 138
Padget, Abner, 157
Page, William, 117
Pannell, 123
    Catherine, 156
    David, 122, 123
    Elizabeth, 123, 128
    Frances, 123
    J., 123
    John, 122, 123
    Joseph, 123
    Priscilla, 115
    Sam'l, 131
    Samuel, 122, 123
    Sarah, 123
    Sarah (Bailey), 121, 129, 138
    William, 115, 120, 121, 122, 123, 125, 128, 129, 130, 131, 132, 145, 156
    William, Jr., 123, 129
    Wm., 126, 128, 129, 145
Parham, Ephraim, 134
Parish, Joseph, 129
Parker
    Archibald, 133
    Ephraim, 149
    Gabriel, 136
    George, 141
    Grissell, 131
    Polly, 157
    Richard, 131
    Richard, Jr., 132
    Rob., 119
    Thomas, 119
Parks
    James, 114
    Jechonias, 118
    Rachel, 127
Parr
    Judith, 106
    Mary, 106
    Philip, 106
Pate
    Ann (Reade), 251
    Anthony, 244, 251
    Benjamin A., 239
    Benjamin Allen, 239
    Edward, 244, 252
    Jeremiah, 239, 244, 251, 252
    John, 244
    Judith, 244
    Mathew, 239, 241, 244, 251
    Mathew, Jr., 239
    Sarah, 251
    Thomas, 244
Patterson
    James, 10
    Joseph, 119
Patton
    General, 195
    George S., Jr., 115
    Homer, 54
    Margaret, 156
Paul
    Frances, 148
    Hugh, 148
    Isaac, 147, 148
    John, 148
Pauly, John, 261
Paxon, Henry, 4
Paxton, Manford, 164
Payne
    A. T., 257
    Adolphus, 264, 267, 269
    Adolphus G., 267
    Agnes, 243
    Albert, 263
    Alma G., 267, 268
    Alonzo, 245, 256, 263, 269
    Alva Burton, 266
    Alva Justin, 259, 266, 268, 271
    Amanda, 255
    Amanda (Short), 260
    Amel, 264
    America, 256
    Amos M., 257
    Amy A., 264
    Amy J., 256
    Andrew Marshall, 272
    Ann, 241
    Anna, 258
    Anna M., 254, 255
    Anne, 243
    Anny, 238
    Archie, 260
    Armina, 262
    Arminia, 264
    Augustine, 243
    Austin, 160, 243, 246, 248, 253

Barnett, 240, 241
Barnett, Jr., 241
Beatrice, 265
Benj. F., 256
Benjamin, 256
Bernard, 238
Bertha E., 263
Bertha O., 185, 260, 262
Bertha Olive "Ollie", 267
Betsy, 240
Betty, 269
Billy, 192, 270
Blanch (Payne), 258
Blanche Elizabeth, 266
Blanche M., 262, 268
Bobby, 270
Brenda Sue, 271, 272
Burrel, 247, 249, 254
Burrell, 252, 257, 260
Calvin, 258
Carl B., 268
Carrie, 255
Catherine, 254
Catherine J., 254
Cecil H., 265
Celesta A., 257
Charity L., 257
Charles, 243
Charles David, 266
Charles E., 257
Charles F., 259
Charles Frederick, 266, 270
Charles O., 262
Charley, 185, 260
Charlotte, 256, 257, 263
Clara B., 258
Clarence S., 263
Columbus, 254, 255, 260
Cornelius, 259, 268
Curt, 258
Cynthia, 252
Daniel, 243
Deana (Wilson), 243
Diana, 253, 268
Diana (Wilson), 248
Dianna, 255
Diantha, 256
Diantha (Thornton), 263
Dicey, 240
Dina, 160, 253
Dolly, 248
Dora M., 257
Dorothy M., 268
Dustin Mitchell, 272
Dwayne Lee, 271
Earnest A., 263
Edith L., 259

Edna M., 260
Edna Mae, 185, 262, 268
Elias, 245
Eliza J., 264
Elizabeth, 185, 239, 240, 241, 242, 243, 246, 247, 248, 253, 254, 256, 258, 260, 262
Elizabeth (Murphy), 242
Elizabeth F., 6
Ella E., 262
Ella L., 262
Ellen, 255
Ellesworth S., 265
Elliot, 249, 253, 256, 257
Elliott, 245, 247, 252, 254, 256, 260, 263, 264, 267
Ellis, 240, 243, 245, 246, 247, 248, 249, 253, 254, 255, 259, 267
Ellis J., 254, 259
Ellsworth A., 257
Ellsworth S., 257
Elmer E., 256, 264
Elwood, 259
Emily, 260
Emily (Higgins), 260
Emma C., 268
Emmit, 259, 268
Estelle, 264
Ethel, 260
Ethelinda, 264
Eva (Roach), 266
Eva A., 263
Eva G., 265
Eva R., 263
Fenton B., 259
Flayl, 237
Florence, 267
Forrest O., 269
Frances, 240
Fred, 192, 270
Fred W., 265
George, 237, 238, 240, 241, 243, 248, 250, 251
George W., 254, 255
George, Jr., 243
Gussie O., 263
Hannah, 251
Hazel F., 267, 268
Hazel Irene, 272
Henry N., 18
Hobert, 259, 268
Howard, 245, 256, 258, 260, 263, 267
Howard L., 267, 268
Isadora M., 257
Isadora M. "Dora", 257
J. S., 266
J. W., 192, 270
J. Will, 265
Jackson, 255, 259, 260, 262, 268
James, 237, 238, 239, 240, 245, 247, 251, 256, 257
James R., 258

The Scarberrys (Scarboroughs), Doughtys, Lewises, and Paynes of Lawrence County, Ohio

James W., 253
Jane, 247, 249, 252, 254, 256
Jesse, 243, 250
Jim, 269
Jimmy, 271
Joel, 248, 249, 253
John, 237, 238, 239, 240, 241, 242, 243, 244, 245, 246, 247, 248, 249, 251, 256, 267
John "Shannon", 268
John Alva, 254, 258, 268
John B., 245, 252, 254
John C., 253, 254
John S., 185, 267
John Shannon, 57, 185, 255, 260, 269
John W., 185, 257, 260, 265
John William, 262, 266
John, Jr., 241, 242, 243
Jonas B., 262, 268
Joseph, 237, 238, 240, 241, 247, 251
Joseph, Jr., 244
Joseph, Sr., 244
Josiah, 6, 237, 240, 243
Josias, 237, 238, 241, 242, 243, 244
Kara Denise, 271
Kathryn, 270
Lasco, 264
Lee Roy, 255
Leland, 270
Lenard H., 264
Lenna M., 259
Leona D., 268
LeRoy, 255
Leslie, 259, 268
Lesta F., 266
Lesta L., 266
Levi, 254, 259
Lewis W., 257
Lillian (Clay), 265
Lincoln, 254
Lola M., 266
Lona C., 263
Louis Curtis, 258
Lowell, 270
Lucy, 240
Mahala, 255
Malinda, 253
Malissa, 160, 248, 249, 253
Marcus F., 255
Margaret, 258
Margaret (Clark), 254
Margaret E., 258
Marinda, 253
Marinda L., 258
Marlene, 270
Marstie, 248
Marstie (Mathew?), 249, 253

Martha (Sheppard), 6
Martha E., 254, 255
Mary, 243, 247, 248, 255, 256
Mary "Polly", 255
Mary (Ragland), 254
Mary A., 254
Mary J., 262
Mary M., 259
Maud, 263
Melinda L., 253
Melinda Louise, 253
Melissa, 253
Merinda, 253
Merrill O., 268
Milly, 243, 253
Milton, 248, 252, 254, 255
Milton S., 255
Minerva, 263, 269
Minnie J., 258
Miranda, 249
Moses, 253, 256
Moses M., 253
Moses Marion, 249, 253, 258
Myra J., 257
Nancy, 240, 246, 247
Nancy A., 255
Nellie M., 258, 259
Nettie, 268
Nina A., 263
Obediah, 240
Ona, 185, 260, 262, 268
Orin, 269
Orin M., 263
Orlando, 242
Oscar Enoch, 257, 265
Otto, 260
Oty, 252
Pauline, 265
Pauline Olive, 266, 270
Phebe, 240, 241
Philip, 237
Phoebe, 251
Poindexter, 243
Polly, 262
Ralph, 269
Ralph E., 266
Raymond, 270
Raymond Forest, 266, 270
Rebecca, 256
Rebecca (Brown), 258
Rebecca (Ruby?), 256
Reuben, 243
Rhoda, 243, 252, 254, 255
Robert, 241, 248
Ronald, 271
Ronald Lee, 271

Rosa G., 253
Ruby, 256
Ruth, 243
Samantha, 262
Samantha J., 268
Samuel, 243
Sarah, 237, 238, 239, 240, 241, 244, 245, 247, 248, 249, 251, 255, 261, 262
Sarah (Ellis?), 243, 246, 251
Sarah (Justice), 255
Sarah A., 259
Sarah B., 185, 260, 262, 267, 269
Sarah E., 254, 255
Sarah J., 160, 248, 253
Sarah M., 253
Sarah Melissa, 253
Shannon, 185
Sharon Kay, 271
Sherridan, 257
Smith, 237
Stanley, 269
Stanley E., 266
Susannah, 240
Sylvia, 260
Teddy Don, 271, 272
Terry Von, 271, 272
Thelma, 267
Thomas, 240, 241, 243, 247, 249
Thomas O., 265
Thomas S., 264
Thompson, 245, 256
Thompson F., 256, 260, 262
Timmy, 271
U. L., 266
Uriah, 246, 253, 258, 269
Uriah L., 253, 257, 265
Verga (Brown), 269
Verla, 269
Verla E., 259
Verla L., 266, 269
Victoria, 257
Victoria L., 257
Viola C., 257
Willa, 264
Willanelle, 265
William, 238, 241, 242, 243, 244, 245, 246, 248, 268
William "Willis", 256
William Earl, 267, 270
William Paul, 266
William U., 254
William Uriah, 249, 254, 258, 268
William Willis, 264
Willis, 256
Wilson, 264
Wm., 245
Wm. M., 248
Wm. U., 254

Zelda, 264
Paynter, John, 117
Pearce, William, 243
Pearson
    Amy, 16
    Wilson, 4
Pearson, Thomas, 239
Pease, Nathan, 119
Pedro, Jno., 104
Peebles, Sterling, 135
Peers, Thomas, 243
Peete, Will, 119
Pendleton
    Henry, 124
    Jemima, 131
Penn
    John, 154
    William, 3, 4, 5
Penny, Reuben, 157
Peredo, Lizzie, 50
Perkins, Mr., 152
Perry
    Charlotte, 256
    Charlotte Ann, 256
    Lewis, 130
    Myra J., 257
    Obadiah, 13
Pershing, John J., 54, 55
Peters
    Christian, 148
    Conrad, 138
    John, 141, 147
    Tobias, 12, 17
Peterson, Jno., 119
Petrie
    Augustus, 187
    Berdie, 187
    Pathenia (Rice), 187
Petteway
    Hannah, 117, 135
    Jno., 117
    Joseph, 117, 135
    Lucy, 135
    Sterling, 117, 135
Pettit, Wm., 250
Pettry
    Rebecca, 46
    Sinkler, 261
Pettus
    Stephen, 250
    Susanna, 250
Petty, John, 246
Peyroune, Wm., 118
Phelps, John, 8, 13
Phillips
    Josephus, 124
    Josiah, 15

The Scarberrys (Scarboroughs), Doughtys, Lewises, and Paynes of Lawrence County, Ohio

Richd., Jr., 241
Phinny
    Betty (Ward), 14
    Joshua, 14
Pickering
    Mary (Scarborough), 4
    Samuel, 4, 5
Pierson, Mary, 4
Pigg
    Edward, 241
    Henry, 241
Pine
    George, 91
    Mary (Gatliff), 139
    W. D., Mr. and Mrs., 49
Pinion, Wm., 128
Pinkerman
    Alexander, 163, 176, 178
    Alonzo P., 178
    Andrew, 178
    Arabel, 178
    Elias, 178
    Francis P., 178
    John, 25, 178
    Margaret, 60
    Missouri E., 178
    Pearl, 191
    Randolph, 178
    Rose, 185
    Rosella, 178
    Sarah, 163
    Sarah A., 161, 178
    William Bedford, 178
    William Mathew, 178
    William, Jr., 178
    William, Sr., 178
    Wm., 163
Pinstock, Patricia, 196
Pitcher, Wm., 155
Pittman
    John, 116, 120
    Rebecca, 187
Pleasant, Beuford, 135
Plymale
    Anthony, 137
    John, 137
Plyman, John, 137
Poe, Edwd., 140
Poindexter
    Elizabeth, 243
    John, 242
    Thomas, 242
    William, 243
Poleton, Isaac, 141
Pollard
    Lt., 55

Pollard, Robert, 105, 131
Pollock, William, 130, 140
Ponsonby
    Ann, 134
    Mary, 134
    William, 134
    William, Jr., 134
Poole
    Jno., 241
    Warren Rowan, 153
Pope
    Elizabeth, 16
    Henry, 16
    Jacob, 16
    Nathl., 243
Porter
    Abner, 126
    Alvira, 94
    Ambrose, 126
    Ann, 126
    Benjamin, 125, 126
    Betty, 126
    Charles, 126
    Frances, 126
    Jane, 126
    Joseph, 126
    Mary, 126, 135
    Mary Ann, 126, 139
    Nicholas, 126
    Thomas, 126, 128
Posey, Thos., 145
Potter, Cuth., 103
Pouncy, Anthony, 242
Pound, Wm., 123
Powell
    Ann, 151
    Joab, 92
    Lucinda, 92
    Permelia Ann, 92
    Prosser, 157
Power, James, 251
Presledge, William, 124
Price
    Hannah, 173
    John, 242, 250, 251
    Mary (Miller), 143
    Robert, 107
    Samjuel, 157
Prichard, Swan, 118, 119
Priddy
    Elizabeth, 251
    John, 251
Pritchard
    Bessie, 44
    George, 44
Pritchett

The Scarberrys (Scarboroughs), Doughtys, Lewises, and Paynes of Lawrence County, Ohio

Dorothy, 109
Horace, 167
James, 167
Sarah, 167
Prosser, Thos., 244
Pullen, Moses, 244
Pulliam, John, 244
Pye, Joseph, 106
Pyles, Henry Roscoe, 264
Quesenbery, George, 239
Rader, Michael, 16
Ragland
  Anne, 250
  Edward, 250
  Elizabeth, 250
  Evan, 250, 251
  Frances, 244, 250, 251, 252
  Isaac, 248, 249, 250
  Jacob, 249, 250
  Jacob, Jr., 249
  James, 240, 245, 246, 249, 250
  James Henry Somerset, 252
  Joel, 249
  John, 242, 244, 249, 250, 251
  Martha, 250
  Martha (Loftus), 249
  Mary, 249, 250
  Nathan, 249
  Pettus, 250
  Reuben, 249
  Reuben F., 252
  Robert Herbert, 251
  Samuel, 242, 250
  Sarah, 249, 250
  Stephen, 244
  Susanna, 250
  Susanna (Pettus), 250
  Thomas, 250
  Ursula (Terell), 250
  William, 249, 250
  Wm., 248, 250
Raiford, William, 118
Rains, William, Jr., 171
Ramsey
  Andrew, 149
  Barttholemew, 139
  Richard, 152
Ransdell, Wharton, 242
Ransom
  Elizabeth, 107
  George, 107
Ransted, Richard, 111
Rapp, John, 159
Rawlings
  Hartwell, 149
  John B., 149
Ray

Gabriel, 113
Gabriell, 110
John, 137
Priscilla, 143
Thomas, 143
Reaburn, John, 148
Read
  John, 126
  Thomas, 109
Reckard, Wilbur, 43
Redman
  Jacob, 140
  Joseph, 140
Reed, Sam'l, 131
Reese
  Betsy, 157
  D., 24
  David, 144
  Lydia, 166
  Pasey, 157
  Stephen, 157
Reinhard
  Charles, 63
  Charles McCormick, 70
  Christy, 70
  Dorothy Maureen, 70
  Lilly (Hakes), 63
  Rachel, 2
  Rawn Howard, 64, 70
  Robert, 52
  Robert Garrison, 70
  Robert Vernon "Bob", 63
Reins, James, 145
Revell, Humphrey, 119
Reynolds
  John, 14, 122
  Joseph, 129
  Richard, 129
Rhodes
  David, 167
  Epaphroditus, 116, 167
  Ezechias (Hezekiah), 111
  George, 113
  Hezekiah, 116, 167
  John, 111, 120
  Mary, 116, 167
  Mary (Brockman), 167
  Robert, 130
  Susannah, 167
  Thomas, 116, 167
  Thos., 167
Ribar, Margaret, 200
Rice
  Jacob, 117
  Sarah, 242
Richards
  Elizabeth, 114

Gabriel, 243
Robert, 129
Sarah, 114, 145
William, 114, 124
Winifred, 114
Wm., 145
Richardson
  Rich'd, 245
  Saml., 248
Richmond, William C., 168
Ricketts
  Polly, 157
  Sally, 157
Ridgway, Samuel, 244
Ridley, James, 116
Riggin, Thomas, 21
Riggs, Mr., 184
Rigney
  Arch, 57
  George R., 47
  George W., 164
  John, 57
  Sarah J., 57
  Susan, 47, 57
  Susan A., 268
Riner, Polly, 157
Riston
  Amanda, 30
  Anderson, 30
  Elisha, 15
  Elizabeth, 21
  Floyd, 30
  Isaac, 21, 30
  James, 30
  John, 18
  Keziah, 30
  Malinda, 30
  Mary, 30
  Nancy, 30
  Rachel, 21, 30
  Reason, 21
  Reason, Sr., 21
  Rebecca, 21, 22
  Robert, 21, 30
  Virginia, 30
  William A., 30
  Zachariah, 21, 30
Roach
  David, 142, 166
  Easter, 166
  Elizabeth, 94, 114
  Ephraim, 266
  Esther, 141
  Eva, 266
  Frances, 166
  Isaac, 142

James, 129, 145, 166
John, 142
Jonathan, 142
Lanty, 138
Mickleberry, 141
Nancy, 141
Nathan O., 259
Reuben, 142, 166
Samuel, 166
William, 139, 141, 142, 166, 259
Roane, Wm., 110
Robards, John, 13
Robb, James, 145
Roberts
  George, 123
  Orlyn, 92
  Sarah Almira, 258
  Wyman, 92
Robertson
  David, 24
  Hudson Brice, 24
  Rebecca, 24
Robin, a slave, 113
Robinson
  Ann, 107, 108
  Anne, 113
  Catherine, 143
  Christopher, 107, 108, 114
  Frances, 107
  Giles, 112
  John, 15, 104, 120
  Margaret, 108
  Mr., 259, 268
  Richard, 104, 107, 108, 110, 112, 113
  William G., 91
Rochelle
  Levi, 133
  Sally, 133
Rodgers
  John, 144
  Thomas, 144
Rogers
  John, 241
  Peter, 241
Roles, M., 138
Roosevelt, Franklin D., 6
Rosebrough, John, 142
Ross, John, 250
Rounds, Benjamin, 255
Row
  William, 114
  Wm., 114
Ruble
  John, 11
  Peter, 6
  Sarah, 139

Rucker
    Anthony, 157
    Ephraim, 144
    John, 142
    Rebecca, 157
Ruddell
    George, 138
    George, Jr., 138
    Margaret (Kennerly), 138
Ruffin
    Joseph, 133
    William, 117
Runyan
    Geneva, 179
    J. C., 55
    Nell (Littlejohn), 55
    Thelma, 55
Ruppenburg, George, 50
Rusher
    Anny, 244
    George, 244
Russell, Robert, 7
Rutherford, Ann, 242
Ryan
    Edmond, 112
    Kathy, 198
Rynard, Adam, 8
Sailor
    Janet (Scarberry), 55
    John, 61
    Nichole Lynn, 67
    Rhea Lynette, 61
    Robert Lewis, 61, 67
    Sarah Rae, 67
Salmon
    Antherd, 131, 155
    Eve, 131, 155
    John D., 167
Sammons
    Don, 73
    Julia, 72
    Justin Mark, 73
    Susan, 73
    Troy, 73
Samms
    James, 241
    Katherine, 241
    William, 241
    Wm., 241
Sampson, Valentine, 261
Samuel, Thomas, 114
Sanders
    Celina, 169
    Edmund, 110
    Elizabeth, 110
    George, 114
    H. H., 27
    Jno., 166
    John, 109, 110, 113, 132
Sandiford
    Frances, 115
    John, 106
    Willliam, 115
Sands, Mr., 122
Sark, Louise, 189
Sarten, Joel Salem, 20
Sauls, Benjamin, 119
Saunders
    Clara Fern, 270
    Shirley, 190
Scarberry
    Ada, 35
    Adam, 47
    Albert, 25, 36
    Albert E., 28
    Alexander, 25
    Alexander (Elemender), 24
    Alva, 42, 54
    Alva E., 42, 53
    Alve E., 41
    Amanda, 34
    Andrew Jackson, 30
    Archie, 26
    Arminta, 44
    Arthur, 42
    Arthur William, 44, 56
    Austella, 37
    Averiel (Orval), 42
    Averill, 36
    Banks, 34, 47
    Benjamin Harrison, 36
    Betsy, 38, 43
    Bill, 28
    California, 25
    Catherine, 24, 28, 54
    Cecil Judson, 37
    Celia, 20, 24, 30
    Celia (Harper), 19
    Charles, 24, 36
    Charles E., 48
    Charles Owen, 28
    Charlie, 35
    Chas., 24
    Chloe, 55
    Chloe M., 41, 43, 47
    Christopher Ashly, 62
    Christopher Columbus, 26
    Clifford, 54
    Cloie Irene, 48
    Columbus, 25
    Dan, 25
    Danny Douglas, 56, 62
    David Merle, 58
    Della (Galloway), 41

The Scarberrys (Scarboroughs), Doughtys, Lewises, and Paynes of Lawrence County, Ohio

Dwayne, 8, 12, 14, 22
Dwayne J., 24, 30, 37, 48, 58
Easter, 25
Edward Maxium, 30
Elemender, 25, 37, 48
Elijah, 8
Eliza, 37
Eliza Jane, 28
Elizabeth, 20, 24, 25, 26, 164, 179
Elizabeth "Betsy", 24, 32, 181
Elizabeth "Mary", 24
Elizabeth (Sowards), 25, 26
Elizabeth Susan, 41, 177
Elizabeth Susan (Doughty), 190
Ellen, 26
Elmer C., 48
Ernest E., 48
Eve, 34
Fidelia, 36
Floyd, 53
Floyd Garland, 61, 67
Forrest, 53
Forrest B., 53, 61
Francis "Marion", 33
Francis M., 24
Francis Marion, 24
Galen Forrest, 61, 67
George, 19, 24, 25, 27, 33
George Fred, 35
George V., 25
Georgia (Faulkener), 54
Gilbert "Bert", 48
Goldie, 33
Goldie Marie, 48
Gordon, 24, 25
Gretchen Elizabeth, 62, 68
Grover, 42, 43, 49, 51
Grover C., 41, 54
Hannah, 25
Hannah Elizabeth (Lewis), 174
Hannah Renee, 73
Hazel, 53, 60
Henrietta, 33, 37
Herbert, 47, 57, 268, 270
Herman, 34
Hollie, 48
Homer, 57, 270
Homer E., 57
Icy Harriet "Hattie", 48
Ira, 48, 58
Irene, 48
Iris Mae, 56, 61, 198
Isaac, 7, 19, 20, 24, 25, 26, 27, 28, 32, 33, 34, 36, 37, 39, 40, 42, 177
Isaac Edward, 29, 34, 41, 44, 47, 91
James, 19, 24, 28, 35

James F., 25
James Preston, 35
Janet Marian, 56, 61
Jasper, 42, 49, 58
Jasper L., 41, 55
Jasper Lewis, 43, 54
Jean Emily, 56
John, 19, 20, 24, 25, 28, 37
John J., 25, 26
John R., 25
Joseph, 19, 20, 24, 25, 33, 34, 47, 182, 268
Joseph Lee, 48
Joseph M., 25, 26
Judson, 37
Julia (Hamlin), 36
Kimberly Paige, 67
Lana Leona, 37
Laura, 34
Laura Elizabeth, 48
Lawrence H., 47
Lennie, 53
Leo, 54
Lewis, 41
Lewis Brille, 37
Lewis Edward, 48
Logan Alexander, 73
Louis G., 36
Lucinda, 20
Lucy, 35, 47, 57
Luis, 28
M. E., 27
Maggie, 48
Maggie Virginia, 48
Malinda, 24, 25
Malinda (Hix), 24
Manuel, 40, 42
Manuel N., 41
Manuel Newton, 42
Margaret, 26, 33
Margaret J. (Watts), 33
Marian Eileen, 57, 63
Marie, 53, 60
Marion, 33, 36
Marriah, 67
Martha E., 36
Martha Jane, 37
Mary, 28, 33, 34, 36, 41, 48, 50, 58, 91, 270
Mary "Polly", 44
Mary (Adams), 40
Mary Ada (Adams), 42
Mary Elizabeth, 37, 38
Mary F., 25
McKinley, 33
Melissa, 29, 30, 41
Melissa (Milly), 45
Michael, 67

Milley, 28
Misouri, 33
Mona Eve, 34
Nancy, 20, 28, 40, 50, 51
Nancy Rachel, 7, 19, 42, 49
Nellie R., 38
Noah, 19, 24, 25
Noah Harper, 20, 28
Noah J., 28
Noah W., 25, 26, 37, 182
Noah Webster, 174
Ona (Payne), 57
Orval, 41, 58
Orval Franklin, 44, 56
Orville (Orval) F., 41
Oscar, 24, 25
Paul Arthur, 57
Pauline, 57
Pearlie, 36
Perry, 35
Phoebe "Eva", 47
Polly, 32
Rachel, 19, 20, 26, 28, 31, 41, 44, 91, 95
Rachel A., 25, 26
Rachel N., 41
Richard, 36
Rosanna, 24, 25
Roy Dallas, 38
Roy Odell, 48
Russell, 54
Ruth, 25
Ruth Lucille, 57, 62
Sally, 20
Sarah C., 25, 26
Sayres, 34
Shane Anthony, 67, 73
Sherman, 35
Sophronia, 33
Stacie Danielle, 62
Susan, 7, 40, 42, 57, 58, 62
Susan (Doughty), 19, 39
Susan E., 42
Sylvester, 26
Sylvia Banks, 48
Thelma "Marylene", 66
Thelma Marylene, 61
Thomas Jefferson, 30
Thomas W., 48
Thomas William, 48
Tom, 28
Trevor Anthony, 73
Virginia C., 28
Wilbert, 37
William, 24, 25, 33, 41, 42, 48
William A. (Arthur), 41
William Gilbert, 36
William P., 28

William Preston, 26
William Sherman, 35
Zachariah, 15, 19, 20, 24, 25, 28, 38, 95
Zilda, 24
Scarberry (Scarborough)
  Zachariah, 19
Scarborough
  Abigail, 2
  Agnes, 11, 12
  Ann, 3
  Appa, 19, 23
  Asa, 17
  Avie Basil, 45
  Baldwin, 3
  Bertha (Bell), 45
  Catherine, 11
  Charity, 10
  Charles, 17
  Crispin, 16
  Cynthia, 17
  Darris D., 31
  David, 9, 15, 136
  Dellis M., 31, 45
  Deresa, 23
  Doras, 22
  E.E., 23
  Edy, 11, 17
  Elam, 22
  Eleanor, 18
  Elender (Eleanor), 17
  Elijah, 12
  Elijah Wilson, 17
  Eliza, 12
  Elizabeth, 3, 5, 7, 8, 9, 10, 15, 22, 247
  Ellen, 22
  Emezella, 22
  Emikly (Wood), 8
  Euclides, 5, 6
  George L., 31
  George W., 31
  Gilbert, 22, 31
  Hannah, 4, 5
  Hester A. (Doughty), 31
  Isaac, 1, 3, 7, 9, 10, 12, 14, 17, 19, 22
  Isaac Pearson, 4
  Isabinda, 23
  James, 7, 8, 9, 10, 11, 15, 17, 19, 23, 136
  James D., 23, 31
  Jane, 7, 22
  Jane (Ball), 23
  John, 1, 2, 3, 4, 5, 7, 8, 9, 11, 13, 16, 17, 21, 91
  John Bryant, 18, 22
  John M., 22
  John W., 18, 23
  John Ward, 14, 17, 23
  John Wesley, 19
  John Winfred, 45

The Scarberrys (Scarboroughs), Doughtys, Lewises, and Paynes of Lawrence County, Ohio

Jonathan, 2
Jonathan Lupton, 11
Joseph, 10
Keziah, 9
Kiziah, 7
Leah J., 31
Lucinda, 31
Lucy, 23
MacEnda, 19
Mahala, 10
Malinda, 23
Margaret, 2
Martha, 2, 22
Mary, 2, 3, 4, 5, 9, 19, 22, 23, 38
Mary "Polly", 15, 20, 94
Mary (Ward), 12, 13, 18
Mary F., 31
Mary J., 31
Mildred May, 45
Minerva M. (Hatcher), 31
Miram, 23
Morrison S., 22, 31, 38
Nancy, 22
Noah, 22
Pearson, 17
Prudence, 11
Rachel, 7, 9, 10, 11, 12, 15, 17, 21, 22
Raymond Ray, 46
Rebecca, 22
Rhoda, 22
Richard, 2, 3
Robert, 1, 4, 5, 6, 7, 8, 9, 12, 13, 14, 15, 16, 136
Robert "Robin", 15, 18, 22
Robert C., 31
Robert Webb, 18, 22, 23, 38
Robert, Jr., 18
Robin, 18
Roger, 2
Salina, 19
Samuel, 16
Samuel F., 31
Sarah, 1, 2, 3, 4, 6, 9, 11, 15
Seth, 8
Silas, 22
Susanna, 3
Susannah, 5, 9
Teddy Roosevelt, 46
William, 1, 2, 3, 4, 5, 7, 8, 9, 10, 11, 12, 14, 17, 107, 136
William L., 31
Zachariah, 21, 91
Scarbro
   Elam, 22
   Ronnie, 22
   Speed, 22
   Thomas Byron, 22
Schaub
   Barbara, 57
   Hazel, 57
   William, 57
Schrimplin, Elizabeth, 261
Scott
   Daniel, 67
   George, 242
   Joseph, 134
Seager, Randolph, 107
Seal, James, 238
Searle, Richard, 242
Seleger, Irving, 50
Seward, Benjamin, 149
Shackleford
   Ambrose, 124
   Francis, 115
   John, 155
   Roger, 110, 115
Shanklin
   Absolam, 147
   R., 151
   Richard, 148
   Roberrt, 158
   William, 138, 148, 172
   Wm., 146
Shannon
   Jane, 11
   Susannah, 11
Shareon, Anthony, 244
Sharp
   Adam, 10
   Richd., 130
Shaton, Edward, 117
Shattrick, Simeon, 160
Sheilds, Ann, 143
Shelford, Richard, 107
Shelton
   Henry, 166
   Peter, 250
Shepherd
   Andrew, 130, 144
   Cloe, 141
   Daniel, 141
Sheppard
   Alexander, 107
   Clara, 107
   Frances, 107
   John, 107, 153
Sheridan, General, 26
Sherman, General, 35
Shires, John, 154
Shirley
   James, 137
   Jas., 124
   Jno., Jr., 124
   John, Jr., 124

Shoemaker, John, 144
Shoenley, Ella, 33
Short
   Amanda, 172, 260
   Anderson, 134
   David, 119
   James H., 172
   John C., 134
   John, Sr., 134
   Matilda, 172, 182
   William, 134
   William H., 172
   William, Jr., 134
Shrewsbury
   Elizabeth, 242, 244
   Joel, 240
   John, 239, 241
   Nathaniel, 239, 241, 244
   Reul, 238
   Ruel, 242, 244
   Saml., 241
   Samuel, 242, 244
Shropshire, Walter, 128
Shull, Ruby, 64
Shumate, David, 21
Sickel, Horatio G., 35
Simmons
   Benjamin, 117, 120, 132
   Charles, 132
   J., 116
   James, 148
   John, 132
   John, Sr., 133
   Spratley, 133
   Susannah, 133
   William, 133
Simms
   Anestar "Ann", 165
   Elijah, 131
   Nancy, 155
   Richard, 165
   William, 155, 165
Simpson, Leona, 189
Singers, Thomas, 160
Sinkler
   Isaac, 242
   Mary, 237
   Sarah, 242
Sirket, Samuel, 122
Sisson
   Caleb, 129, 130
   Wm., 129
Sites, William, 26
Skaggs
   Ann, 148
   Anne (Lewis), 153
   Catherine, 153
   Icy, 153
   James, 146, 153
   John, 146, 153
   Joseph, 146, 148, 153
   Levi, 157
   Lucy, 153
   Mary, 146, 153
   Mary "Polly", 153
   Richard, 153
   Samuel, 146, 153
   Thomas, 153
   Zebulon, 146, 153
Skipwith
   Diana, 106
   Gray, 115
   William, 111, 115
Slaughter
   Robt., Jr., 131
   Thos., 123
Slinker
   Elizabeth, 240, 244
   Frederick, 240, 244
   Milly, 247
   Molly, 244
Sloan, Minnie, 265
Smith
   Alexander, 107
   Anderson, 157
   Bruten, 142
   Danl., 166
   Elizabeth (Miller), 143
   Flood, 119
   Isham, 135
   J. A., 45
   James, 108, 151
   Jno., 137
   John, 9, 106, 108, 130, 131, 146, 157
   John H., 45
   John W., 45
   John, Mrs., 42
   Joseph, 106
   Lawrence, 119
   Lewis, 45
   Mary, 167
   Mary (Lively), 157
   Michael, 147
   Millie, 45
   Preston, 45
   Rebecca Ella, 45
   Samuel, 138
   Thomas, 108
   William, 147
Smithin, John, 244
Smithson, John, 252
Snead
   John, 242, 244
   Susanna, 242

Snelling
  Acquilla, 109
  Alexander, 109
Snodgrass, Elizabeth, 261
Snow, Mollie, 154
Snyder
  Adam, 146, 150
  B. F., 260
  Charles, 260
  Dorothea, 147
  Henry, 147
  Samuel, 146
Sockwell, Lancelot, 110
Somerset
  Charles, 251
  Henry, 252
Sorrell
  Anna, 242
  James, 242
  Thomas, 242, 243
Southall, Edward, 125
Southern
  John, 107
  William, 107
Souvene, Charles, 50
Sowards
  Callie A., 260
  Catherine, 176
  Della J., 260
  Elizabeth, 25, 28, 160, 182
  Ellena, 176
  Ellene, 176
  Emily, 260
  George, 176, 183
  George N., 160
  Gilbert, 176, 183
  Griff, 163
  Griffin, 152, 159, 160, 176
  Griffin A., 183
  Griffin L., 176
  Griffin S., 183
  Griffith S., 176
  Ida J., 183
  Isaac, 19, 141, 151, 163, 176
  Isaac, Jr., 152
  Isaac, Sr., 136
  John, 176
  John J., 176
  Lena, 176
  Margaret, 160
  Mary, 163, 175, 176
  Mary "Polly", 174
  Mary E., 176
  Metta, 183
  Mileston, 152
  Mileston, Jr., 152

  Minerva J., 176
  Nelly, 152
  Phebe, 176, 183
  Phoebe, 176
  Rebecca, 151, 152
  Rose A., 183
  Roy E., 183
  Ruth, 152
  Sallie, 176
  Sally, 176
  Solomon, 141, 142
  Sophia, 141
  Thomas, 136, 152
  Willa O., 183
  William, 260
Sparks
  Ann, 150
  Frances, 150
  Henry, 150, 168
  Humphry, 150
  John, 150
  Lucy, 150
  Mary, 150
  Mildred, 151
  Sarah, 144
  Thomas, 150
  Thomas, Jr., 150
  Zachary, 145
Speaker, Mr., 118
Spearman, John, 129
Spears, Mary, 188
Spence, Isaac, 258
Spencer
  Edward, 123, 125
  Joseph, 129, 130
  Sarah, 130
  Seth, 145
Sperry, Lorene, 71
Spicer
  Catherine, 165
  Catherine (Brockman), 167
  Dabney, 167
  William, 167
Spickard (Shepheard), George, 16
Spivey
  Aaron, 118
  Aron, 117
  William, 117
Spotswood
  Alexander, 114, 123, 126, 131, 132
  Capt., 118
  Col., 121
  Governor, 122
  John, 127
Spurlock
  Randall, 191

Silas, 91
Violet, 271
Stamper
  Cary, 107
  John, 107
  Powell, 107
Stamps, Widow, 122
Stanard
  Anne, 113
  Wil., 108, 119
  William, 113
Stanford, Vincent, 105, 112
Stanley, Mr., 240
Stanton, Frederick, 119
Stapleton, Charles, 8
Steele, Robert, 148
Steidl
  Evie Marie, 72
  Mathew Hunsaker, 72
  Peter, 72
  Susan, 72
Stencer
  Karen Renee, 67
  Mervil, 66
Stephens
  Adam, 118
  Anita, 271
  Ervin, 270
  Irvin, 192
  Lewis Irvin, 192, 270
  Louis Irvin, 270, 271
  Peggy, 270
  Sandra Jean, 192, 270
  Tanya, 271
Stephenson
  George, 146, 148, 151, 165, 171
  Lucy, 142, 148
  Martha, 171
  Mary, 171
  Ruth, 171
  Samuel, 153, 171
Stepp
  Anester, 165
  Elizabeth, 131, 154, 165
  James, 124, 155, 165
  Joshua, 131, 155
Steptoe
  Ja., 243
  John, Jr., 110
Stern, 121
  David, 115
  Frances, 115, 128, 130, 131
  Peyton, 115
Stevens
  Mary (Morgan), 111
  Mumford, 129
  Richard, 115

Stevenson
  G., 162
  George, 146
  Samuel, 146
Steward, Joseph, 241
Stewart
  A. N., 91
  Calvin, 93
  Capt., 118
  Cynthia, 93
  George, 93
  George W., 92
  James, 122
  James E., 158
  John, 93, 128
  John C., 91, 92
  Lena, 263
  Sarah, 93
  Sarah Lavisa (McCartney), 92
Stiff, Jacob, 119
Stith
  Benjamin, 238
  Buckner, Jr., 134
  Joseph, 238, 239
  Thomas, 134
Stobo, Capt., 117
Stodghill
  Daniel, 166
  James, 142, 166
  Jesse, 147
  Joel, 162
  John, 154, 155
  Wm., 142
Stover
  Charles, 95
  Clarinda C., 95
  Cynthia, 95
  Elijah, 20, 91, 94, 95
  Elza, 95
  Fanny, 20, 91
  Jacob, 20, 21, 91, 155
  John, 18, 20
  Jubel, 21, 91, 94
  Jubel M., 95
  Lewis M., 95
  Malinda A., 95
  Marinda, 95
  Mary M., 95
  Paulina, 21
  Phebe J., 95
  Rachel E., 95
  Sarilda C., 95
Street
  John, 113
  Sarah, 120, 129
Strigler, Abraham, 155
Stringfellow, Horace, 125

Strother
    Agatha, 126
    Anthony, 131
    Elizabeth, 120, 123, 126
    Francis, 122, 130, 138
    Frans., 130, 131
    French, 131
    George, 138
    Harriet, 125
    James, 122
    Jane, 120
    Jeremiah, 125
    John, 131
    John Dabney, 125
    Joseph, 125
    Louisa G., 125
    Margaret, 120, 138
    Mildred, 125
    Sarah, 124, 128
    Sarah (Bailey) Pannell, 122
    William, 120, 121, 122, 123, 125, 126, 127, 128, 130, 131, 132, 138, 155
    Wm., 122, 123, 124, 128, 130, 131, 132
Stuart
    Alex, 139
    Alexander, 139
    Frances Gibbons, 150
    Thomas, 141
Stuart, Charles Edward, 150
Sturman, William, 242, 243
Summers
    John, 107
    Margaret, 107
Suthards, Lucy, 35
Sutko, P. Matthew, 181
Sutton
    Ann (Morgan), 111
    Christopher, 111, 123
    Hope, 111
    Richd., 242
    Rowland, 111
Swan, Robert, 105, 106
Swindler, Betty Lou, 271
Swinney
    Rebecca, 157
    Sarah, 142
Switzer
    Frank, 269
    Frank X., 269
    Jack (Pat), 269
    Verla Payne Watrous, 265
Switzer, Verla Payne Watrons, 257
Swope
    Jane, 153
    Margaret, 153
Sydenstricker
    Betty, 184
    Billy, 184
    Edna, 184
    Faye, 184
    Forest, 184
    Lee, 184
    Pearl, 184
    William, 184
Taft, President, 55
Tagg, Thomas, 261
Talbot
    Isham, 7
    J., 8
    John, 239, 241
    Mathew, 237
Taliaferro
    Ann, 131
    Charles, 125
    Francis, 123, 128
    Henry, 131
    John, 123, 125, 128, 130, 157
    Lawrence, 125, 144
    Lucy, 126, 127
    Martha, 126
    Mary, 125
    Mary "Molly", 126
    Mildred, 125
    Robt., 114
    Samuel, 157
    Sarah, 125
    William, 126
    Wm., 125
Talley
    George, 253
    Melinda (Justice), 253
Tandy
    Henry, 165
    Mary, 165
    Roger, 166
Tanner
    Abraham, 147
    Elizabeth, 147
    Frederick, 146
    John, Jr., 147
    John, Sr., 147
    Wm., 121
Taylor
    Charles, 132
    Ethelred, 133
    George, 142
    Isaac, 137
    John, 122
    Mary (Moorman), 248
    Selby, 118
    William, 8, 118
Terrell

Elizabeth, 247
Joel, 144
Mary, 165
Micajah, 247
Miss, 140
Richd., 165
Sarah, 146
Sarah (Lynch), 247
William, 165
William, Jr., 165
Wm. O., 165
Terry
  J., 248
  Joseph, 248
  Nathaniel, 243
Tews
  Arthur, 66
  Erin Patricia, 66, 72
  Julia Marie, 66, 72
  Margaret Norma (Doerr), 66
  Paul Arthur, 66
  Zachary Paul, 66
Thacker
  Edwin, 107, 108
  H., 109
  John, 108
Thatcher
  Elizabeth, 156
  Frances, 156
  James, 156
  John, 156
  Joshua, 156
  Mary, 156
  Samuel, 156
  Sylvester, 156
  Thomas, 156
  William, 156
Therriot
  Dme., 106
  Dnc., 104
  Dne., 105
  Dominie, 105
  William, 104
  Wm., 105
Thilman, Paul, 110
Thomas
  Carrie Scarborough, 2
  Edw. Ball, 131
  Edward, 108, 128
  Elizabeth (Waugh), 125
  Fanny Ball, 131
  John, 158
  Joseph, 125, 129, 156
  Joseph, Jr., 144
  Mary, 125
  Richard, 125
  Robert, 125, 146

  Robt., 130
  T. R., 41
  William ap, 251
Thompson
  Ann, 248
  Charles, 119
  David, 167
  Elizabeth, 248
  Isabel, 154
  Jaley, 154
  John, 12
  Mary, 248
  Samuel, 248
  Temperance (Brickey), 244
  Tomma, 194
  Winny (Brickey), 244
  Wm., 243
Thomson
  Elizabeth, 249, 250
  John, 251
  William, 7
Thornhill, William, 9
Thornton, 108
  Daniel, 129
  Diantha J., 264, 267
  James, 128
  Luke, 123
  Minerva, 263, 269
  Timothy, 105
Thorp
  Joshua, 133
  Mary, 133
  Timothy, 116
  Willm., 243
Threlkeld
  Ann (Johnston), 128
  Christopher, 130
  John, 128, 130
  William, 128
Thurmond
  Eliz., 157
  Ricd., 157
Tignor, William, Jr., 111
Tillett
  Hannah, 147
  Lucy, 147
  William, 147
  Wm., 147
Tilly
  Henry, 140
  Margt., 140
Tinsley, Cornelius, 244
Tipton, A., 94
Tisdale
  John, 250
  John, Jr., 250
  Shirley, 250

Shirley, Jr., 250
Shirley, Sr., 250
Tombs
    Ann Dawson, 129
    Gabriel, 116, 121, 123, 130
Tomlin, William., 113
Tomlinson, Edward, 119
Tony
    Charles, 244
    Leah, 139
Toole
    Aaron, 6
    Ann, 6
Toon, Lewis, 122, 123, 129, 130
Torbert, James L., 152
Torrey, Philip, 4
Towles
    Ann, 146, 151
    Beverley, 146
    Henry, 146
    John, 146
    Joseph, 146
    Mary, 150
    O., 144
    Oliver, 146
    Oliver, Sr., 146
Trainer, Mary Ann, 36
Tram, John, 134
Travers, Charles, 118
Tremble, Abby, 139
Trener, James, 137
Trent, Alexander, 244
Tucker
    Anthony, 136
    Rosea, 136
Tuggle
    Henry, 107
    Lucretia, 127
    Thomas, 127
Tull, Ruhama, 46
Turberville, George, 242
Tureman
    Ann, 140
    Geo., 166
    George, 140
    Ignatius, 140
    John, 154
    Mary, 140
Turk, Thomas, 144
Turner
    Anna, 172
    Arthur, 133
    Benjamin, 133
    Catherine, 115
    Edwin, 133
    Elizabeth, 133
    John, 134
    Littleton, 133
    Nanny (Lewis), 133
    Thomas, 115, 133
Twain, Mark, 237
Tweley, Jane, 137
Twisdill, William, 145
Twyman
    George, 125
    Katie, 125
    William, Jr., 124
    Wm., 125
Tyler, Francis, 122
Tynes, Robert, 134
Upshaw
    Cordelia, 140
    John, 140
    Susanna, 140
    William, 140
Upshur, John, 106
Utley
    Mary (Ragland), 249
    William, 249
Utz, George, 147
Vallot
    William, 107
Vallot, William, 107
Van Swearingen, Capt., 261
Vanwright, James S., 163
Varner, Wm., 16
Vaughan, Martin, 118
Vause, John, 108
Vawter
    John H., 138, 147, 158
    Richard, 150
    Russell, 151
    William, Jr., 143
Venable, Agnes, 248
Venerable, John, 240
Vermillion
    Blanche M., 266
    Charles F., 266
    Florence, 265
    Henry B., 266
    Henry Burton, 271
    Kate E., 266
    Marion, 265
    Pearl Grey, 266, 271
Vicaris
    Mary, 109
    Mr., 109
    Parson, 109
    Thomas, 109
Vickers
    Albert E., 181
    John Bunyan, 181

Villa, Pancho, 55
Vitito
   James, 246, 249
   Nancy (Payne), 246
   Virgil, 260
Vivion
   John, 107, 108
   John, Sr., 108
Vols, Wm., 18
Wadding, George, 111
Wade
   Ella, 186
   Gloria Faye, 188, 195
   Henry, 188
   Rosemary, 188, 195
Waggener, Capt., 118
Waggener, Thomas, 118
Wales
   Catherine L., 173
   David, 173
   Sally, 173
Walker
   Catherine (Miller), 143
   Cynthia, 142
   Edward, 149
   Freeman, 149
   George, 138, 146, 147, 148
   Harper, 147
   James, 144
   Joel, 151
   John, 144, 166
   Martin, 184
   Thomas, 166
   Thos., Jr., 166
   William, 149
Wall
   Arthur, 119
   Daisy, 178
   David W., 184
   David W., Jr., 181
   Emma, 184
   Joseph, Jr., 117
   Mabel, 60
   Mable, 184
   Mary, 117
   Maureen, 70
   Sampson, 119
Wallace
   Dr., 123
   Michael, 123
Waller
   Benjamin, 124
   Berryman, 124
   Edmjund, 124
   Edmund, 241
   Mary, 126
   William, 124, 127

Walls
   Amanda, 34
   David, 161, 173
   Margaret J., 33
   R. F., 181
   Sally, 173
Walton
   C. F., 165
   George, 241
   John, 145
   Nancy, 145
Ward
   Catherine, 14
   Elizabeth, 14
   John, 12, 14
   Mary, 14
   Zachariah, 14
Ware
   Edward, 115
   James, 114
   Nicholas, 114
Warner, Elizabeth, 127, 166
Warr, James, 118, 119
Warwick, Jeremiah, 136
Washington
   Catherine, 130
   Col., 117
   George, 118
   George, President, 146
Washington, George, 14
Wasley
   Ann, 6
   Henry, 6
   Mary, 6
Waters, John, 108
Watkins
   John, 111, 118
   William, 118
Watrous
   Daniel, 269
   Melvin, 269
   Melvin L., 269
Watson
   E. P., 49
   Maxine, 194
   Paul, 49
   Wm., 140
Watts
   Abbie, 266
   Eliza, 108
   Isaac, 2
   John, 108
   Margaret, 120
   Sarah, 166
   Susannah, 166
Waugh
   Abner, 125

Alexander, 125, 126, 129
Alexander, Jr., 125
Edward, 125
George, 125
John, 125
Mary, 125
Richard, 125, 128, 131
Richd., 129
Sarah, 125
Wayt
   Elizabeth, 140
   George, 140
   James, 140
   John, 140
   Keziah, 140
Weatherholt
   Ann, 162
   John, 162
   Rebecca (Clark), 162
Weaver, Daisy, 265
Webb
   George, 144
   Hill, 118, 119
   J. Cr., 155
   James, 106
   Jesse, 118, 119
Webber, Philip, 248
Weeks, Mark, 111
Welch
   John, 144
   Thomas, 123, 129
Wellford, R., 145
Wells
   George, 191
   Ruby Mae, 191
Welsh, Daniel, 127
Wertenbaker, William, 158, 167
Wesley
   John, 2
   Susanna, 2
West
   Ignatius, 128
   Mary, 138
   Nicholas, 107
Westbrook
   Henry, 133
   Thomas, 118, 120, 133
   Thomas, Jr., 118
Wetherall, John, 122
Whaley, Calvin, 193
Wharton
   Jas., 105
   John, 128
   Michael, 112
   Thomas, 107
Whatley, Michael, 126

Wheeler
   Anderson, 239
   Ann, 239, 241
   Benjamin, 242, 250, 251
   Elijah, 245, 249
   James, 238, 239, 246
   John, 240, 244, 249, 250, 251
   John Thomas, 239
   Jos. C., 33
   Mary, 250
   Mary (Tisdale), 250
   Nancy, 240, 249
   Rowland, 238, 239, 240, 241
   Sarah, 240
   William, 238, 240
   Wm., 239, 245, 249
Whitaker, Walter, 104
White
   Benjamin, 117
   Carr B., 35
   James, 159, 160, 162
   John, 117
   John, Jr., 168
   Lucy, 117
   Maggie, 44
   Mary Ann, 46, 169, 175
   Rena, 189
Whitehead, John, 108
Whittaker, Walter, 108, 110
Wiatt, Thos., 13
Wickline
   Margaret, 141
   R. M., 92
Wiglesworth
   John, 124
   Mary, 124
Wiley
   Allan, 128
   Allen, 131, 132
   Robert, 141
Wilkins, James, 244
Wilks, Burl, 45
Will, Mrs. Wm., 51
Willey
   Happy (Gatliff), 139
   James, 139
Williams
   Amy, 149
   Ann, 20
   Annie G., 44
   Benjamin, 115
   Charles, 108
   Edward, 155
   Elihu, 44
   Elijah, 19, 26, 44
   Elijah G., 44

Elizabeth, 20, 155
Ellen, 20
Francis, 155
Francis, Jr., 155
Icy B., 44
Isaac, 23
Jacob, 124, 129, 130, 140, 145
James, 20
John, 19, 122, 123, 124, 128, 129, 130, 145
John L., 20
John R., 149
John, Jr., 124
Letha, 20, 23
Lewis, 18
Loyd, 23
Lucinda, 19
Mallory, 140
Mary J., 44
P., 23
Phebe, 19
Phebe (Doughty), 26
Richard, 17
Sampson, 249
Sarah, 20
Tho., 103
William, 20, 134, 149

Williamson
   Andrew, 107, 108
   Augustine, 107
   Benjamin, 107
   Hayden, 201
   James, 107
   Jason, 201
   Robert, 107, 140
   Robert, Jr., 143
   Robert, Sr., 143
   Sarah, 140
   Tho., 107

Willis
   Lucy, 141
   Tho., 103

Wills
   Francis, 116
   Mathew, 116
   William, 136

Wilson
   Andrew, 107
   Diana, 248
   Edward, 111, 123
   John, 264
   John A., 264
   John Culpeper, 248
   John E., 264
   Mary, 166
   President, 55
   Richard, 166

Wimpey, Robert, 111

Winburne, John, 119

Winn
   John, 244
   Margaret, 122

Wiseman
   Agnes (Neel(, 15
   J., 12
   John, 15, 21
   Joseph, 16
   Stewart, 92

Wolf
   Edward, 50
   Henry, 51, 53
   Henry W., 52
   John H., 51, 53
   John P., 51, 53
   Lorelene, 51
   Margaret, 53
   Margaret M., 51
   Mary E., 51
   Rozellia, 51
   Tressa, 51

Wood
   Ann, 153
   Bailey, 153
   David Lynn, 63, 69
   Elizabeth, 69
   Elza "Woody", 62
   Emily (Milley), 10
   George, 62
   Hannah, 122
   James, 153
   James P., 93
   James, Lee, Jr., 20
   Jesse, 157
   Jim, 14, 18
   John, 139
   Marietta, 62
   Mary, 26, 93
   Megan Amanda, 69
   Miss, 151
   Rachel, 12
   Ressie (Snuffer), 20
   Sarah, 6
   William Francis, 63, 69
   Wilma, 69
   Wm., 122
   Wm., Jr., 139
   Zachary Norman, 69
   Zea Renee, 69

Wood, Fred E., 62
Woods, Francis, 157
Woodson
   Constant, 248
   Elizabeth, 248
   John, 248
   Obediah, 248

William, 157
Woodward, Capt., 118
Woolfolk, Thomas, 140
Wooten, Thomas, 126
Workman
    Clara, 32
    David, 53
    Geo., 170
    Lennie, 53
Wormeley
    Christopher, 103
    Elizabeth, 109
    Esquire, 107
    Mr., 110
    Ralph, 103, 108, 113
Wortham
    Charles, 140
    Elizabeth, 110
    George, 107, 109, 110, 115, 140
    Jane, 110
    John, 110, 115
    Mary, 110
    Oswald, 110
    Prudence, 110
    Samuel, 114
Wray
    J. W., Mrs., 42
    John, 137
    Thomas, 137
Wright
    Anthony, 238, 239, 240, 241, 247
    Betsy, 240
    Bonnie, 69
    David, 10
    Elizabeth, 240
    Jane, 250
    John, 122, 140, 238, 240, 241, 244, 250, 251
    Joseph, 237, 238, 240, 241, 247
    Judith, 238, 247
    Mrs., 52
    Nancy April, 69
    Polly, 240
    Rhoda, 240
    Ruth, 240
    Sarah, 238, 240
    Tommy, 238, 240, 244
Wroughton, William, 105, 106
Wyatt, Edward, 15
Wykle
    George, 16, 17
    Phillip, 16
Wylie, James, 143
Wythe, George, 125, 127
Yager, Samuel, 124
Yates
    Charles, 114
    Harry B., 115
York, a slave, 10
Yorke, John, 241
Young
    C. H., 192, 270
    Clarence, 32, 38, 40, 41, 42, 43, 44, 52, 53, 54, 55, 192, 193, 200
    Clarence H., 26
    Clarence Hasten, 53, 58, 192
    Edith Marie, 60, 66
    Eleanor, 52
    Elizabeth, 50, 142
    Faye, 200, 270
    Faye (Lewis), 184, 187, 192, 193
    Frank, 50
    Louis, 49, 50, 51, 53, 192
    Mabel, 192, 270
    Mabel June, 60, 64
    Marie E., 50
    Nancy, 42, 49, 52
    Nancy (Scarberry), 40, 43, 51, 54, 55
    Nannie, 49, 54
    Nanny, 58
    Rachel, 52, 56, 61, 192, 193, 270
    Rachel May, 60, 63
    Rena, 41
    Rena Sue, 60, 65
    William, 137, 143
Young (Jung), Maria Elizabeth, 50
Yowell
    Christopher, 150
    James, 131
Zachary, William, 147
Ziglar
    Ann, 121
    Barbara, 122
    Chr., 129
    Chris'r, 131
    Christopher, 121
    Elizabeth, 121
    Leonard, 121, 122, 127, 129, 132, 155
    Leonard, Jr., 121
    Susanna, 121
Zimmerman
    Barbara, 122, 147, 155
    Christopher, 122, 147, 155
    Christopher, Jr., 122
    Elizabeth, 122
    Frederick, 121, 122, 129
    Hannah, 261
    John, 122, 147, 150
    Katherine, 122
    Mary, 147
    Pauline, 60
    Sophia, 164
    William, 261